ALSO BY ROBERT H. WIEBE

Businessmen and Reform

The Search for Order, 1877–1920

The Segmented Society

THE
OPENING
OF
AMERICAN
SOCIETY

THE
OPENING
OF
AMERICAN
SOCIETY

*From the
Adoption
of the
Constitution
to the
Eve of
Disunion*

ROBERT H. WIEBE

ALFRED A. KNOPF

NEW YORK
1984

THIS IS A BORZOI BOOK
PUBLISHED BY ALFRED A. KNOPF, INC.

COPYRIGHT © 1984 BY ROBERT H. WIEBE
ALL RIGHTS RESERVED UNDER INTERNATIONAL AND PAN-AMERICAN COPYRIGHT
CONVENTIONS. PUBLISHED IN THE UNITED STATES BY ALFRED A. KNOPF, INC.,
NEW YORK, AND SIMULTANEOUSLY IN CANADA BY RANDOM HOUSE OF CANADA
LIMITED, TORONTO. DISTRIBUTED BY RANDOM HOUSE, INC., NEW YORK.

LIBRARY OF CONGRESS CATALOGING IN PUBLICATION DATA

WIEBE, ROBERT H.
THE OPENING OF AMERICAN SOCIETY.

BIBLIOGRAPHY: P.
INCLUDES INDEX.
1. SOCIAL CLASSES—UNITED STATES—HISTORY.
2. ELITE (SOCIAL SCIENCES)—HISTORY. 3. UNITED STATES
—SOCIAL CONDITIONS—TO 1895. I. TITLE.
HN90.S6W53 1984 306'.0973 84-47678
ISBN 0-394-53583-9

MANUFACTURED IN THE UNITED STATES OF AMERICA
FIRST EDITION

For
my mentor, Norman Johnston,
and
my sustaining friends

Contents

Acknowledgments   ix

Preface   xi

Part One

THE REVOLUTIONARY REPUBLIC   *1*

1   Leadership   7
2   The Politics of Form   *21*
3   The Politics of Character   *35*
4   The Politics of Independence   67
5   The Edges of Violence   90
6   The Jeffersonian Resolution   *110*

Part Two

BEGINNINGS AND ENDINGS   12*7*

7   Space   *131*
8   Revolution in Choices   *143*
9   The Last Tournament   *168*
10   The Era of State Power   *194*

11   Comprehensive Programs   *209*

12   The Jacksonian Resolution   *234*

Part Three

DEMOCRATIC SOCIETY   *253*

13   Economy   *257*

14   Democratic Culture   *265*

15   The Institutional Web   *291*

16   A Society in Halves   *321*

17   A Crisis in Parallelism   *353*

Epilogue   *376*

Notes   *385*

Selected Bibliography   *403*

Index   *415*

Acknowledgments

Beyond my incalculable debt to those historians whose work underlies this study, I have accumulated particular ones to a number of generous people. Douglas, Eric, and Patrick grew up during the project's evolution and still wished me well at the end. I thank each of them. Lonnie's humane understanding of the present deepened my understanding of the past. The wise counsel of James J. Sheehan, John L. Thomas, Sam Bass Warner, and Harry L. Watson greatly improved a draft of the manuscript, and their warm encouragement worked miracles with my spirits. Ashbel Green, Peter Hayes, and Thomas Johnson saved me from many an embarrassing quirk in style. It does seem reasonable to me that these people share a bit of the responsibility for the final version. Joyce Appleby and David Roediger challenged portions of my interpretation in very helpful ways, and several people supplied useful suggestions or information: Josef Barton, T. H. Breen, Karen Halttunen, T. W. Heyck, Keith Hopkins, J. R. T. Hughes, William E. Parrish, George Roeder, Clarence L. Ver Steeg, and Garry Wills. Kenneth Greenberg kindly allowed me to read his unpublished essay on dueling in the south. Among the librarians who facilitated my research, Marjorie L. Carpenter and James McMahon were especially cooperative. Finally, financial support from the National Endowment for the Humanities, the John Simon Guggenheim Memorial Foundation, and Northwestern University allowed me the time to complete this study.

ROBERT H. WIEBE

Preface

My subject is the process of creating a national society in the United States where none existed. It unfolded during the first seventy years of independence in two distinct stages, one a self-conscious venture that originated with the Constitution, proceeded through the administrations of George Washington and John Adams, and peaked with the election of Thomas Jefferson, the other an unplanned accumulation of activities that gained momentum in the 1820s, spread rapidly during the 1830s, and acquired form by the 1840s. Behind my subject lies a preoccupation with the great transformation in American life that occurred during these same seven decades. Nothing came out its far end unchanged, as we are reminded by a variety of familiar phrases: from a republic to a democracy, from Enlightenment to Romanticism, from an Atlantic civilization to a continental empire, and others of a similar sweep. While at a superficial level something called the United States ran a continuous history from the 1780s to the 1850s, fundamental changes were reshaping life within it.

Because the first half of my subject coincides with the final years of an 18th-century world and the second half parallels the emergence of a new 19th-century world, the process of creating a national society traces one path through this great transformation. Like any route, it limits what we see. The primary cast of characters in the first venture was a tiny elite of revolutionary leaders whose influence spread well beyond their own small circle but who neither spoke nor acted for a comprehensive national constituency. Even in the early 19th century as the process of constructing a national society came to engage more and more Americans until they numbered in the millions, these people did not mirror the views and aspirations of other millions. In fact, nothing plays a more crucial role in my account than the various gaps and divisions between society builders and other Americans. Moreover, this particular angle of vision shades my treatment of every person and event throughout the long transforming process. Anyone seeking a complete discussion of the Constitutional Convention or the Alien and Sedition Acts or the Jacksonian Bank War will not find it here, for I look at all of them through the special lens of my subject: what can they tell us about the creation of a national society?

At the same time, I have tried to broaden our understanding of this great transformation by according equal weight to its two sides. Almost all studies in American history from the 1780s to the 1850s root themselves in either the 18th-century or the 19th-century end of the transformation, and hence remarkably few treat the massive changes in between as much more than an epilogue or a prelude. As a result, they tend to picture Americans either thrown helter-skelter from the security of the 18th century into the chaos of the 19th or else drawn ineluctably from the old into the new ways of life. To appreciate such a fundamental transformation we must neither push nor pull Americans through it. They should be allowed to walk it at a human pace, experiencing a full complement of apathy, insight, and uncertainty as they go. To maintain this perspective requires an equal immersion in the very different worlds of the late 18th and early 19th centuries, an acceptance of each as a legitimate frame of life in its own right, and an evenhanded respect for what passes, what rises, and what transpires between them.

With these objectives in mind, I have divided my study into three sections. Part I examines the first venture in creating a national society from the vantage point of the gentry minority who made it their cause. Beginning with the movement for a new constitution, it follows them through the 1790s against a backdrop of explosive conflict in Europe and erratic popular behavior at home, changes that none of them, including Washington, Hamilton, Jefferson, Madison, and Adams, could either predict or control. It ends at the turn of the century with Jefferson securing his power as president and holding precariously to his perch of national authority. Part II opens with the new century and traces an interaction between thrusts of innovation and adaptations of tradition that continued for about four decades. Although such prominent men as Henry Clay, John C. Calhoun, John Marshall, and Andrew Jackson made substantial contributions to this clashing and mingling of new and old, the range of actors now broadened and their aggressiveness mounted with each decade as the exciting possibilities of a popular self-determination encouraged more and more Americans to participate in the molding of their society.

The pivot of my study appears early in Part II under the title "Revolution in Choices," an attempt to give specificity to that indispensable catchword for early-19th-century America—democracy. In Part II democracy serves primarily as the destroyer, leaving by the 1840s almost nothing of the revolutionary gentry's venture except the shell of their Constitution. Part III, on the other hand, explains democracy's constructive role, and hence "Revolution in Choices" also underlies this section's examination of the many, extensive activities that moved once again toward the creation of a national society. Circling back to the 1820s when the new democracy flowered, Part III traces its consequences from family life, individual values, and social institutions to the consolidation of a nationwide class division. Here, in other words, I address more precisely who was affected in what ways by the democratizing process. Although the proper climax of my study comes around midcentury, with the formation of a democratic society, it seemed important to summarize how naturally secession and civil war developed out of the new society and to suggest how well it survived the upheaval. Hence a study that begins neatly with the Constitution drifts toward a conclusion.

My understanding of American society between the 1780s and the 1850s emerges from a dialogue with the finest body of scholarship I have encountered as an American historian. Because these exchanges almost always lie hidden beneath the text, a few results of general significance to my study may deserve mention here. I find no basic ideological conflict separating Hamilton and his Federalist associates from Jefferson and his Republican colleagues: no aristocracy versus democracy, no mercantilism versus laissez-faire, no Court versus Country value systems. Their differences certainly mattered—enough, in fact, to threaten America with a civil war. Nevertheless, their agreement on the broad requirements of an independent republic, their commitment to a common brand of gentry governance, and their more or less interchangeable condemnations of one another compressed those differences into a struggle over the interior design of the same ideological house. In addition, I resist the familiar images of clear-eyed statesmen at the helm, guiding the young republic past the shoals of foreign danger and domestic disintegration. On the contrary, I am far more impressed by the distance between this gentry elite and the people they purported to lead. My emphasis, therefore, falls much more on the revolutionary gentry's helplessness than on their mastery.

I am equally unconvinced that during the heart of the great transformation Americans in the mass responded pathologically to the changes they were experiencing. We might all take pause from the accumulation of studies, now awaiting their synthesizer, that employ some variant of an equation between social change and acute anxiety to explain human behavior in almost every decade from the middle of the 17th to the late 20th century. The history of a paranoid society? I believe that adjective and its near relations have lost their analytical value. To say of the early 19th century that Americans were participating in patterns of change that they did not understand simply consigns them to the human condition. To say that they tried to salvage values from the past implies that they might otherwise have cut loose from history and floated freely in the present, or perhaps selected values through a foreknowledge of the future. To say that with only fragments of information they envisaged groups of people scheming to aggrandize wealth and power suggests, on balance, that they understood their world reasonably well. Guessing the wrong group does not create a twisted conspiratorial mentality. As a corollary, I reject those historical interpretations that, taken together, ask us to see one great social crisis piling atop another during these years. There are many evidences of personal stress and social confusion during the early 19th century. In the end, however, I am much more impressed by how effectively countless Americans functioned during the long transformation, often making their provincialism a source of livability and usually keeping their mistaken visions of the future in line with a manageable present.

Teleology is as much my enemy as pathology. So much of early-19th-century American history has been written with an eye toward an emerging industrial revolution that it has become exceedingly hard to disentangle what was there from what was still to come. The standard attributes of an industrial revolution—large-scale factory production, a rationalized urban work force, strategic centers of investment capital, the extensive marketing of standardized products, and the like—did not come to characterize the United States until the last decades of the 19th century. Although manufacturing increased enormously during the early part of the century, neither the United States nor any appreciable part of it developed an industrial society in the usual sense of this term. All the world was not Lowell, Massachusetts. For the same reasons, I find the popular term of anticipation "preindustrial" just as misleading as "industrial" itself. During the early 19th century a strikingly new commercial economy formed throughout the nation, and its common dependence on America's extraordinary scattering of farms and towns gave that economy—and the social institutions entwined with it—common qualities everywhere. Despite the profound significance of American slavery, then, I differ sharply with those interpretations of a growing sectional conflict that pit an industrial north against an agrarian south.

North and south, east and west, city and country, from the 1780s to the 1850s the most powerful influence in the shaping of American society was space. The ideas about space, the uses of space, the projects across space, and the accommodations to space, above all else, charted the basic changes that occurred between these years. In the broadest terms each part of my study is a chapter in the unfolding story of an interplay between space and authority. As Americans stretched out the elastic in their federal union, spurred the continental growth of their commercial capitalism, and turned the revolutionary generation's hierarchical republic into the class-riven democracy of the mid-19th-century, space was setting the essential preconditions, and successive groups of leaders either rode with its effects or fell into futility. Even if every detail in Frederick Jackson Turner's speculations has failed the test, his vision, turned to our understanding of historical processes, remains central to the meaning of this great transformation and the societies at the two ends of it.

But does either of them qualify as a national society? One of the fascinations of these years, when by later standards we can take so little about political union and social organization for granted, is that they allow no clear, self-confident answer. If an authentic society requires consistent penetration into the everyday lives of its members, the first venture fell far short. At the same time, it channeled very intense popular feelings, attached the states to a national government, and surmounted the differences between its northern and southern branches. If an authentic society requires private and public institutions to mesh in a sturdy political whole, the second effort just as obviously failed. Nevertheless, it reached into the daily lives of millions, connected the east with an enlarging west, and continued to thrive after the Civil War substituted a mandatory for a voluntary political union. In all, this second enterprise has the greater claim as a national society.

Keeping these qualifications in mind, I offer a title that carries three messages with several possible meanings. The opening of American society connotes its initial appearance, its democratization, and its physical expansion: an opening occasion, an opening up, an opening out. At the same time, an American society arrived in deep dependence on Europe, then spread rapidly westward because it could glide there on British credit. The democratization of American society coincided with the strengthening of the slave system, the drive to exterminate native Americans, and the establishment of a class line. An opening for some meant a cruel closing to many others. The same society that encouraged its members to disperse throughout a vast domain made the issue of expansion a justification for division and war. Yet a distinctive American society did appear, however ambiguously; a democracy did develop, however brutally; and a national expansion did occur, however costly in lives. These things happened, and this study addresses them not as triumphs but as challenges to our understanding.

Part One

THE REVOLUTIONARY REPUBLIC

AMONG THE AMERICAN REVOLUTIONS of the 1770s one was national. It emerged out of the continental congresses that were convened in 1774 and 1775, evolved through the military, economic, and diplomatic activities that these bodies and their successors sponsored, and reached a momentary climax between the victory at Yorktown in 1781 and the Treaty of Paris in 1783, which sealed independence for the confederation's thirteen states. For those gentry leaders who became immersed in continental affairs, this sequence would always be the true revolution. Lives that had once been rooted in a colony, often no more than a fragment of a colony, were transformed forever by a flow of events that swept through North America and ran back and forth across the Atlantic. Although some of them still referred to their states as "countries," they now pictured a nation spanning those states. The highest service to his "country" of Virginia, Richard Henry Lee concluded, came from "the original friends to the just rights of America, whose wise and firm perseverance" had won independence for the entire United States.[1] "It is my first wish," declared John Jay of New York in 1785, "to see the United States assume and merit the character of one great nation, whose territory is divided into countries and townships for the like purposes."[2]

Jay could express no more than a wish because the immediate effects of the war were decentralization and diffusion. A multitude of small political units, governmental and quasi-governmental, rushed to fill the vacuum of British authority, resisted the pulls from patriot capitals almost as stubbornly as they resisted the British, and conducted affairs more or less as they chose. Although the fighting lasted long enough and shifted among the states in sufficiently threatening ways to win ratification for the Articles of Confederation in 1781, liberty for most Americans remained a local matter. State constitutions acknowledged these centrifugal forces by curbing executive privileges, strengthening legislative rights, and formalizing the importance of their many local subdivisions. After the war the state governments provided the backbone of the new nation. However well they managed their own affairs, they showed little inclination to delegate power beyond their boundaries, and as a result restricted government under the Articles largely to a caretaker's role. The federal Congress took steps to organize the western wilderness, and went through the motions of representing the United States in Europe, but commanded little attention or respect anywhere.

Nationally minded gentlemen responded to this state of affairs with a stabbing sense of loss. "From the high ground we stood upon," George Washington lamented in 1786, "from the plain path which invited our footsteps, to be so fallen! so lost! it is really mortifying. . . ."[3] John Adams in England and Thomas Jefferson in France longed for a revival of "the spirit of 1776." In a profoundly personal fashion they identified the meaning of their own lives with a revolution that for them could only succeed as a national venture. Simply and honestly, Jefferson equated "my own existence" with republican America's.[4] In their grandest visions they saw it as a revolution that would never die, offering those whose lives merged with it a prospect of immortality that far transcended the usual 18th-century aspirations for honor. Perforce it became their continuing revolution, with the war itself "nothing but the first act" of a great unfolding drama.[5] To this deeply personal quest they brought the Enlightenment's powerful feeling of a universal incipience. A new age was dawning, and in its wonderful morning glow stood this new nation. "The Revolution of America," wrote one veteran of the war, ". . . Seems to have broken off all those devious Tramels of Ignorance, prejudice and Superstition which have long depressed the Human Mind. Every door is now Open to the Sons of genius and Science to enquire after Truth. Hence we may expect the darkening clouds of error will vanish fast before the light of reason; and that the period is fast arriving when Truth will enlighten the whole world."[6]

Set against such glorious dreams, the threat of failure was terrible indeed. Depression at home and rejection abroad, disorder in the states and bickering in the federal Congress, sharpened fears that the curtain was about to fall abruptly on their magnificent drama. Stirring a sense of crisis among themselves, the keepers of a national revolution supported the Annapolis Convention of 1786 to discuss broader commercial powers for the federal Congress, then the Philadelphia Convention of 1787 to consider revisions of the Articles as a whole. Because the gentry had already aired the basic issues of national sovereignty during the war years and because they shared so many common assumptions about the structure of a proper republic, they moved quite efficiently through the debates over a new constitution and the steps to implement it. Yet the Constitution only rephrased the stubborn problems that lay behind its creation. How could any leaders maintain a national authority over America's huge, thinly populated territory? And how could they preserve the independence of this sprawling, disjointed union against the great powers of Europe?

An initial set of answers, provided largely by Washington and Hamilton, placed the leaders of the new government on a high prominence and relied on the sharpness of authority at the nation's peak to command allegiance below. Jefferson and Madison, fearing the return of monarchy and aristocracy, mounted an opposition that sought to bridge this ominous distance between rulers and people, but not many Americans cared enough early in the 1790s to fight over the right relationships in a national republic. Only when the effects of the French Revolution shook the foundations of American life in the mid-nineties did those issues of national authority stir a fierce general conflict. Now the Constitution made a critical difference, as it channeled a swirl of local, state, and regional impulses into a national struggle over freedom, and encouraged the belief that in this battle the winner would take all. Big stakes in an experimental republic. On the one hand, such widespread passions had the potential to bind America's loosely united states into a cohesive nation. On the other hand, those same passions might as easily tear the nation apart in the name of freedom. If Americans did care enough to fight for a proper republic, could the nation survive their commitment?

Leadership

By the 1780s America's gentry shared a common agenda for public affairs. They demanded republican governments in the United States, claimed the right to lead those governments, and committed themselves to maintaining their independence. Before the gentry could proceed, however, they needed to know what each step meant both to their republic and to their own careers as its leaders. Thought first, then action. To behave otherwise invited the most damning of all labels—a man without "principles." Such self-conscious procedure inextricably wove their particular way of thinking into the substance of their three guiding precepts.

The gentry reasoned by formulating broad categories, sorting information into them, then explaining the information through the rules governing their categories. It was a scheme for encasing knowledge rather than redrawing its boundaries. Nothing better exemplified their ideal than the magnificently arching branches of biological classification: phylum down to genus to species to subspecies, ordering all of life in one grand pattern. Inside such an encompassing architecture of knowledge the gentry concentrated on careful compilations and differentiations. They found their excitement in illuminating the dark corners of an otherwise finished structure and sought creativity in the imaginative rearrangement of its parts.

Each scrap of information had its use. Whether it originated in observation or rumor, whether it came singly or in a bunch, everything found a place along one of the stalks of a classifying system. In such a neat, contained scheme a detail substantiated a principle as readily as a principle explained a detail. Appropriately, "facts" ranged indiscriminately from the minutiae of a financial report to the "fact in human nature" that the closer an object of affection, the stronger an individual's attachment to it would be.[1] As the gentry slid effortlessly between facts-specific and facts-general, they felt free to make the same kinds of "deductions" from all of them.

Accustomed to managing bits of information, they tended to become disoriented in the face of a sudden abundance. They reasoned most effectively from a trickle of incoming data that they could assimilate at their own pace. When the Whiskey Rebellion inflamed western Pennsylvania in 1794, the enthusiastic republican Alexander Dallas immediately classified it as a popular resistance to the government's tyranny. Riding from Philadelphia into the interior, however, Dallas found that as he actually encountered the hurly-burly of a backcountry uprising, his sympathies grew confused, and only after returning home could he eliminate the contradictory evidence, set his responses in order again, and reaffirm his original faith. Jefferson issued his clearest and most confident judgments on American violence when he was in France, and on French violence when he was in America. In March 1799, with the United States on the brink of war and the government in turmoil, President Adams retained his equilibrium by leaving the capital for seven months, contemplating matters in isolation, and in his own time determining to seek peace.

If the gentry had relied on a time-bound sequence of events for their understanding, they might have benefited from occasional floods of information. Where categories controlled their evidence, however, they broke up the flow of time as they sorted events one by one into the appropriate containers. They reasoned causatively rather than chronologically. Hence in the Declaration of Independence, Jefferson listed America's grievances to reveal a logical progression of British tyranny that depended neither on the spacing of incidents nor on their temporal sequence. News of important happenings was always relevant, whatever the order of its arrival. The gentry mined history with the same indifference to chronology. Caesar and Solon, the Hanseatic League and the Roman Republic, the decline of Holland and the fall of Athens, all formed a huge mount of evidence in which to rummage for suitable pieces of an argument.

A favorite adage explained to what end: "History is philosophy teaching by example." Here was the perfect repository of wisdom, a fixed record that they could study and sort at their leisure for its proofs on an immutable human nature. The present might befuddle even a thoughtful man, but the past would never lie. It "is the oracle of truth," James Madison declared; "and where its responses are unequivocal, they ought to be conclusive and sacred."[2] It was a matter of pride among the gentry not to "be blinded by enthusiasm or prejudice in favor of any modern system."[3] Even in a revolution—for many of them, especially then—every move required a test against all the historical evidence that by their lights belonged in the same category of human experience. As Madison was reported as saying, a sound revolutionary "government ought to secure the permanent interest of the country against innovation."[4]

A second vast reservoir of proofs accumulated through principles of comparability that bound all areas of their knowledge into a comprehensive whole. Axioms explaining an individual's behavior applied equally to families, communities, states, and nations. Whatever rules governed the natural sciences covered politics and the arts as well. Appropriate to the symmetry of this vision, the common element uniting their universe of knowledge was the standard of balanced relationships, a gauge that measured everything from agriculture and government to beauty and happiness. Selecting any one issue, they could draw on their total fund of knowledge to analyze it. When Jefferson and Hamilton employed medical language to describe the state of America, specifying its diseases and prescribing its cures, they meant to be taken literally. So did William Plumer of New Hampshire when he deplored the size of the new nation: "An extension of the body politic will enfeeble the circulation of its powers & energies in the extreme parts."[5] Society suffered from excesses exactly as a sick body with ill-proportioned humors, and purging society would make it well again exactly as a healthy body in equilibrium. By the same logic, Jay confidently assured Washington in 1795 that the slightest entry into the trade of the British West Indies would bring more because "the least stream from a mass of water passing through a bank will enlarge its passage."[6]

Simple maxims and endless analogies gave an almost limitless scope to a gentleman's competence. If science enticed him, he made himself a scientist—observing, collecting, sorting, speculating. In an era of wars and war threats, many qualified themselves as military experts. Hamilton's interests ranged from the army's table of organization to its hemispheric strategy, Jefferson's from the navy's battle logistics to its docking specifications. Washington and Gouverneur Morris were attracted to canal engineering. One gentleman who volunteered to direct the building of a new capital city offered as his credentials "a good deal of leisure, some little taste and a talent for contrivance."[7] Nobody scoffed because nobody had a more exacting standard. When Thomas Paine and David Rittenhouse proposed an attack of red-hot iron arrows on the British or Edward Rutledge concluded that the Creek nation had descended from the ancient Carthaginians, they simply set their logic against anyone else's who cared to challenge them.

In an age of revolution every member of the gentry became a judge of good government. Like any broad subject, government had its own place in their architecture of knowledge and hence its own scheme of classification, in this case one that derived from the three major headings from ancient philosophy: monarchy, aristocracy, and democracy. Even the gentry's unprecedented reliance on a sovereign people to justify their revolution did not shake the dependence on these categories as an invariable frame of reference for analyzing and evaluating the nature of American government. As persistent a champion of the people's sovereignty as James Wilson of Pennsylvania still used the standard concepts to explain the Constitution: "In its principle, it is purely democratical"—that is, it represented the people exclusively: "but that principle is applied in different forms, in order to obtain the advantages . . . of the simple modes of government"—monarchy, aristocracy, democracy.[8] Republics in this scheme of things had the characteristics of "mixed governments," the very embodiment of balance and the only form of government, Madison wrote in behalf of them all, that "would be reconcilable with the genius of the people of America [and] with the fundamental principles of the Revolution."[9] It was the gentry's charge to apportion the qualities of monarchy, aristocracy, and democracy in precisely the way to ensure a true republic and not a disguised version of one of those "simple modes."

Part of the solution lay in coordinating the frame of government with the "genius" or "manners"—the essential characteristics—of the American people. The more local the scope of government and the perspective of these gentlemen, the more likely they were to consider the government's structure a reflection of the people's spirit. Under all circumstances, as Madison's statement implied, the form of government should not clash with its citizens' predispositions. Because Jefferson considered the French people too deeply mired in oppression for a sudden jump to freedom in 1789, he counseled his Parisian friends to adjust the government's structure in very cautious stages. As jurisdictions and visions broadened, however, the gentry assigned more and more shaping power to the forms of government. Asking his locally oriented associates to think in national terms, the antifederalist * Melancton Smith of New York warned: "Government operates upon the spirit of the people, as well as the spirit of the people operates on it—and if they are not conformable to each other, the one or the other will prevail. . . ."[10] Under the Constitution, Smith made it very clear, the people, not the government, would yield. "We accordingly find," James Winthrop of Massachusetts declared with the same formative influences from the Constitution

---

* In order to distinguish the combatants over the Constitution from those later antagonists the Federalists and the Republicans, I use lowercase for federalists and antifederalists.

in mind, "that in absolute governments, the people . . . are [in] general lazy, cowardly, turbulent, and vicious to an extreme. On the other hand, in free countries are found in general, activity, industry, arts, courage, generosity, and all the manly virtues."[11] Early in 1776 Adams identified government structure as "the most difficult and dangerous Part of the Business Americans have to do in this mighty Contest," for "It is the Form of Government which gives the decisive Colour to the Manners of the People. . . . Under a Monarchy . . . [the people] cannot but be vicious and foolish."[12] In May of that year Jefferson was straining to return from Philadelphia and help establish Virginia's "form of government": "In truth it is the whole object of the present controversy. . . ."[13] Just as categories of knowledge molded their data, so in the end structures of government would mold their people.

The gentry's next basic precept—that their characters qualified them to lead these republican governments—derived from their view of all civilized societies as hierarchies. At root the concept of a social hierarchy rested on the model of the patriarchal family, and in this sense Washington did indeed become the father of his country early in the Revolutionary War. Satisfying the complexities of a social order, however, required many more tiers than a family's structure. Blackstone listed forty-odd gradations in Britain, for example. In an infant republic that lacked a tradition of estates, banned aristocratic titles, and contained so much local and regional diversity, no one could match Blackstone's precision. Nevertheless, every member of the gentry presupposed both the existence and the necessity of a scheme that layered Americans according to their talents and society's needs. Hierarchies produced order only if they were essentially stable. Describing "that tacit compact which all classes reciprocally enter into," an ardent republican emphasized that "when they have partitioned and distributed among them the different occupations conducive to general prosperity, they will pursue these occupations to contribute to the general happiness. . . ."[14] When Jefferson made his novel proposal that each year twenty bright boys "be raked from the rubbish" at the bottom of Virginia society and educated for higher stations at state expense, he meant to improve, not challenge, a tiered order. Humans came with a variety of fixed qualities, hierarchies contained a range of levels, and healthy societies matched the two.

The ultimate purpose of Jefferson's plan was to enlarge the small pool of leaders at the top of the pyramid where gentlemen of breeding, wealth, and talent made their contribution "to the general happiness" by forming and directing the revolutionary republics. Even the notoriously radical Pennsylvania Constitution of 1776 specified that only "persons most noted for wisdom and virtue" would hold the important offices. Within their own ranks the gentry assumed that they also were divided by degrees of talent, and their political gatherings always began with the participants arranging themselves into a rough order of leaders and followers. At no level could serious business proceed without a rule-of-thumb hierarchy. Hence, as Madison entered a new political setting he naturally sought out "the general sentiments of leading characters," and just as naturally he omitted from his notes on the Philadelphia Convention the contributions of those delegates he considered inferior.[15] Some of those same delegates, in turn, explained their acceptance of the Constitution as an expression of deference to Madison and other "Gentlemen of the first consideration."

The gentry winnowed and sorted according to their concept of character, a structure that shaped the individual's interior much as a government form shaped society's substance. Five qualities framed its meaning at the top of the hierarchy: courage, resolution, moderation, dedication, and control. Courage might show itself in the risk of exposure when others hung back—Patrick Henry challenging British rule in the Virginia assembly. Or in fortitude—Washington at Valley Forge. Or in actual physical encounter. Resolution enabled leaders to move steadily, persistently forward: convene a continental congress, declare independence, mobilize an army, pursue the war. Moderation meant a Golden Mean in judgment, and in the republican version especially that capacity to avoid a monarchic tyranny at one end and a democratic despotism at the other. Because moderation implied neither accommodation nor caution, it suited a tenacious, driving commitment to the right cause, and dedication connoted just such single-mindedness. Among the gentry, "republican zeal" was a common term of flattery. A man otherwise as wild as John Randolph of Roanoke, who stalked the halls of Congress with hunting dogs, sprayed his contemporaries with dueling challenges, and condemned almost every primary leader of his time for corruption, evoked in some circles a kind of adulation for the "purity" of his republicanism.

Randolph's weakness lay in the keystone of character's structure, control. If the sources of character came from a pure heart, its proof derived from a cool head. Through a pervasive, unwavering self-management, a gentleman harnessed the other attributes of character to their appropriate purposes. Control was the generator of resolution and the governor of moderation. Without it courage became mere recklessness and dedication mere passion. It played the reins of the personality like a ceaselessly alert driver. Internally, control maintained a sense of proportion and enabled the mind to reason. James Monroe's very slowness of thought enhanced his reputation for grave, balanced judgment. Externally, control presented a face of perfect composure—an erect, easy bearing, an unflinching eye, a flawless decorum. No matter what else Aaron

Burr did, he maintained standing among many of his peers by public composure alone. Control also assured a "simple" or "candid" course of behavior. The devious path of "complicated" individuals revealed that they could command neither their passions nor their ambitions.

In the gentry's symmetrical world a gentleman's private and public lives joined to complete the architecture of his character. Although he might move, he required a home. Rootless people by definition were unstable and unscrupulous. Whether these gentlemen identified themselves with the city or the countryside, they required an appropriately distinctive, detached estate to validate their status as gentry, and leaders as different as Hamilton and Jefferson drained their resources to maintain a proper one. Moreover, a secure attachment to a home provided the gentry's standard surety of public virtue. After the model of their heroes from the Roman Republic, they assured one another that public glory held no charms and that their deepest longings always drew them from office to quiet retirement: Washington to Mount Vernon, Adams to Braintree, Jefferson to Monticello. Like Cincinnatus and Cato, they served from duty and farmed from love. No doubt many of them did treasure their estates, and certainly all of them felt at one time or another that public service meant only thankless burdens. Nevertheless, what mattered was not the subtle issue of how sincerely they believed in these priorities but how ritualistically they repeated the same self-abnegating, power-denying sentiments.

A felicitous household provided the final element of gentlemanly symmetry. Madison's long search for a wife involved his credentials for public leadership as well as his desires for private happiness, and his marriage in 1794 to Dolly Payne Todd, therefore, marked a political as much as a personal victory. Yet marriage alone was not enough. Each gentleman carried the obligation of maintaining an orderly household—a governance at home that mirrored his capacity to govern at large—and after a period of public service each of them announced as his first charge the need to resume command over the people and property under his care. Troubled families brought sympathy from the gentleman's friends but vicious gossip from his enemies, as rumors about his wife's virtue and his stepson's wild ways soon taught Madison. At the same time, gentlemen remained relatively free to roam. The pleasures of companionable tomcatting cemented some fast friendships of the era, including the rare one across party lines between Caesar A. Rodney and James Bayard of Delaware. The pursuit of women, like the pursuit of wealth, never by itself disqualified a public leader. Even Hamilton's sleazy affair with Maria Reynolds and Jefferson's reputed liaison with the slave Sally Hemings did not significantly affect their standing as premier national leaders.

The interpretation of a gentleman's character fell along a spectrum from honor to shame. Try as he might, he could never rest comfortably with an inner sense of righteousness or a private satisfaction over a job well done. Accomplishments required public ratification, criticisms public vindication. Gentry leaders had no alternative to accepting this perpetual peer review and at least claiming to live by its standards. With only a touch of extra pomposity the stiff-backed Jay declared that "I love . . . my honour better than my friends, and even my family, and am ready to part with them all whenever it would be improper to retain them." [16] Both the stakes and the demands of these ceaseless judgments made them extraordinarily sensitive to every prick of attack, and their pretense to a thick hide invariably dissolved in the telling. "My Commission for Peace was envied by one Man. . . ," Adams recalled just after the war, "and this dirty Passion, put him upon a series of falsehood, of insidious underhand Maneuvre and other base practices. . . . These Proceedings distressed me, not for myself for I never cared a farthing for any consequence they Could have upon me, but for the Publick. . . ." [17] "I am not afraid of the priests," Jefferson wrote late in life of his clerical enemies. "They have tried upon me all their various batteries, of pious whining, hypocritical canting, lying and slandering, without being able to give me one moment of pain." [18] A specter of public humiliation mercilessly haunted Adams. During stretches of his career Monroe devoted as many hours to the defense of his public record as to the making of it. Jefferson sank into depression over a public inquiry on his wartime governorship of Virginia; feared "the disgrace of a recall" as minister to France; mourned the fact that "the pain of a little censure, even when it is unfounded, is more acute than the pleasure of much praise"; and decided after a triumphant term as president that the feeble voices of criticism forced him to seek vindication in reelection. [19]

Every detail in a career mattered. In an election gentlemen sought "a Majority that, under all circumstances, will be deemed honorable." [20] When it did not materialize, friends pretended it had, as Washington did in congratulating Madison for his hairbreadth victory "by a respectable majority." [21] Political appointments had to reflect their reputations at a minimum, and preferably improve them. In a characteristic gentleman's idiom the indigent, office-seeking Thomas Rodney of Delaware assured his son Caesar that if he took a position "it would not be any Petty office," and the prickly Monroe rejected one suspect post after another as beneath his stature. [22] As Jefferson anticipated becoming secretary of state under Washington, he felt the same goad of honor and inflated the position in his imagination to combine "the Secretaryship of foreign affairs, and . . . the whole domestic administration (war and finance excepted) into one principal department." [23]

Moreover, everything mattered all the time. If a leader's attention ever flagged, an occasional object lesson helped him concentrate. The Virginian Edmund Randolph, wellborn and well bred, took his first important government post at 22, became a delegate to the Continental Congress at 25, served as governor of Virginia, opened the Philadelphia Convention of 1787 with a major new plan of government, and at 36 entered Washington's administration as attorney general. His ability to find a moderate ground in the midst of fierce cabinet debates made him a valued adviser, strengthened his claims to a high character, and elevated him to secretary of state in 1794. Then in 1795 his enemies presented Washington with evidence that Randolph was secretly conniving with the French to distribute bribes. The president confronted him abruptly and Randolph cracked. Fumbling, begging, and blustering, he dropped instantly and shamefully from national prominence. The plotters, lacking solid evidence, played the game by gentry rules and shrewdly calculated that "Mr. Randolph's conduct at the time an explanation was required would probably furnish the best means of discovering his true situation. . . ."[24] Quite apart from the accuracy of the charges, Randolph at the moment of crisis revealed flaws of character so devastating that no record past or future could possibly redeem him.

The pressures of an incessant control exacted their price from all gentry leaders. Washington's icy exterior shattered in sudden eruptions of monumental wrath, "those passions," Jefferson called them, "when he cannot command himself."[25] Apoplectic explosions shot so often from Adams that he was rumored to be insane. Jefferson again described one outburst when Adams flung his wig to the floor and stamped on it like a boy in a tantrum. At the most solemn moments of public ceremony, another contemporary noted, "an unmeaning kind of vacant laugh" popped from Adams' mouth.[26] On his part Jefferson suffered from periodic headaches so severe that they incapacitated him for weeks at a time, seizures that disappeared only when he retired from public life. Madison adapted to what his biographer called "epileptoid hysteria" with a reticent, mumbling public style that became his buffer against his gentry judges. Beneath Monroe's surface dignity lay fits of childish pique and streaks of paranoia that, among other examples, led him in 1800 to identify a group of cabbage farmers outside Richmond as the advance guard for Federalist subversion. Elbridge Gerry stammered, and the accomplished orator Rufus King froze before a suspicious audience. From time to time Patrick Henry's impressively smooth manner dissolved in geysers of rage as formidable as Washington's.

Their schematic process of reasoning, in combination with the stress from a relentless judgment, spread a quality of rigidity through the gentry's public style. As orators or writers they walled in their subject with granite blocks of deduction, then dispatched the issue in thunderclaps of truth. Gentlemen who considered their conclusions "as demonstrable as any proposition in Euclid" left little margin for adjustment.[27] Although most members of the gentry did, in fact, change their minds over the years, they invested extraordinary energies in denying it, for the truth never varied and a shift in opinion only revealed a gentleman's weakness. "When men are uniform in their opinions," one writer offered as a commonplace, "it affords evidence that they are sincere."[28] Madison referred to a change of mind as "the mortification of acknowledging" a mistake.[29] Fashioning the exact balance in an experimental republic while they protected their own reputations from the abyss of shame gave their exchanges on every detail the tone of brittle absolutes clashing over the fate of freedom.

The same standards of honor and shame applied to the United States as a nation in the world. "The man or the nation without attachment to reputation or honor, is undone," Adams declared. "What is animal life, or national existence, without them?"[30] After Britain's defeat in the war for independence, Jay feared its "mortified ambition," and Richard Henry Lee pictured it as "a strong, proud, & sullen Man angry from unexpected defeat."[31] ". . . [P]unish the first insult," Jefferson advised on the protection of America's maritime rights: "because an insult unpunished is the parent of many others."[32] "A nation, despicable by its weakness, forfeits even the privilege of being neutral," Hamilton warned.[33] Madison sponsored a new constitution in 1787 to "redeem the honor of the Republican name" and opposed the Jay Treaty eight years later because it violated "the most sacred dictates of National honour."[34] A gathering of Kentucky Republicans called that treaty "shameful to the American name; Because, the American character is disgraced by its very language, it being on the part of Great Britain couched in terms haughty and imperious, and on the part of America in Language submissive and humiliating."[35] "Haughty" was also a favorite condemnation of French policy in the late 1790s.

For years after the treaty of independence, America's prospects of preserving its honor could scarcely have been worse. Although its trade ranked well in European calculations, the United States as a nation did not. Europe's rulers judged its venture in self-government somewhere between a curiosity and an absurdity. Most of them expected it to fail, and if they had not been so preoccupied with European matters, they would have pondered more carefully various strategies for reclaiming pieces of this errant colony. Even the small nations of Europe refused to take the United States seriously, as an exasperated John Adams discovered during his service abroad. Better than the American gentry, Europe's leaders recognized the impossibility of mobilizing the United States in response to anything short of a wholesale invasion. Hence, Britain and France imposed rules on American commerce and demanded concessions from its government in an exaggerated version of major powers dealing with a minor one: usually by declaration, occasionally with the semblance of negotiation. Almost all European envoys who were assigned to the American backwash viewed it contemptuously and treated it as a client of some great power. Every weak nation searched out a sponsor, they assumed, and this ragtag collection of former colonies appeared to need one more than most.

To these insults the American gentry responded with belligerent, self-consciously American pride, and foreign observers of any astuteness reported this fact. Again and again, America's leaders emphasized the chasmic differences between the old world and the new, to the obvious advantage of the latter, and one after another of them warned against entangling America in Europe's affairs. Nothing drove home those feelings like a tour of foreign service. For Adams in England and Jefferson in France during the 1780s, for Rufus King in England and Charles Cotesworth Pinckney in France during the 1790s, European society and European hauteur sharpened their American exclusiveness to a keen edge. "My God!" Jefferson exclaimed to Monroe in 1785. "How little do my countrymen know what precious blessings they are in possession of, and which no other people on earth enjoy."[36] From its own strength, the gentry insisted, America must command the respect and the concessions that did not come graciously, and beginning in the 1780s the ways of reaching that end became a gentry obsession. "Let Americans disdain to be the instruments of European greatness!" Hamilton thundered. "Let [the United States] . . . dictate the terms of the connection between the old and the new world."[37]

Brave words from a dependent people. In one sense they simply echoed the bravado of countless weak nations summoning courage against the strong. In the American version, however, these boasts revealed a deeper meaning, a distinctive mentality of such importance that it shaped the gentry's final commandment, the commitment to national independence. The leaders of the Revolution had been born colonials, and they had come of age as colonials. Few of them anticipated rebellion until it was almost upon them, and when it arrived, they had justified it as aggrieved Englishmen. Revolution, in effect, made them independent colonials and their nation an independent colony inside a European universe, and they could no more break this cast of mind than they could break the international framework reinforcing it. As long as they lived, the revolutionary gentry would only understand independence as it came refracted through these neocolonial lenses.*

In their yearnings to generate what they called a "national character," the gentry relied on republicanism as the codeword to distinguish both America from Europe and true Americans from false. Yet they could only explain what they were by what they were not. Initially a republican was not a Tory and a republic not a monarchy. To Hamilton it became not something else: "the prohibition of titles of nobility may truly be denominated the corner-stone of republican government. . . ."[38] Some did search industriously for the sources of a unique America. Adams thought he found an indigenous spirit of liberty, Jefferson an indigenous agrarian virtue. But in the end they translated their findings into the same old terminology of negation. "If you have no attachments or exclusive friendships for any foreign nation," Adams informed one group of citizens, "you possess the genuine character of true Americans."[39] Only Europe could define America.

That defining process insinuated itself throughout gentry life, for the trappings of their colonial past lay everywhere. Hard money was largely European coin with an American authorization, law was largely British dictum with an American gloss, and news was largely London copy with an American filler. "We think in English . . . ," a perceptive Hamilton was quoted as saying.[40] When the gentry did step beyond the shadow of England, they moved into the shade of France by borrowing its styles, admiring its culture, or reckoning with its opinion of the new nation. In one exemplary neocolonial exchange, the French scientist the Comte de Buffon, applying his own principle of comparability to America, concluded that its zoology had an inferiority appropriate to an inferior country, and Jefferson, mustering every fact and conjecture in rebuttal, argued that animals in America actually grew larger, stronger, sturdier than the European varieties. As always, it mattered so much more to the sensitive American than to the casual European. Buffon soon lost interest; but Jefferson was badgering the Frenchman with new evidence until Buffon died—and still claiming victory on the eve of his own death almost forty years later.

Most important, neocolonialism fixed America's place in a world of wars and diplomacy. As rebels they had entered the Revolution with Thomas Paine's confident assurances of European help ringing in their ears, and they had won it only with French assistance. In the immediate

---

* I use "neocolonial" to cover a broad reciprocal process that includes both an imperial nation's arrogation of superior rights in dealing with a former colony and a former colony's acute sensitivity in protecting its independence. Because the former colony is my subject, I emphasize one side of the interaction, but I always assume that the other side is churning away.

aftermath Robert R. Livingston expressed their consensus: ". . . independence and the alliance with France, connect themselves so closely together, that we never speak of them separately."[41] Foreign policy continued to be calculated in degrees of European danger and American dependence. In Richard Henry Lee's terse summary, ". . . Great Britain is upon our Northern quarter and Spain upon the Southern. We are therefore compelled to mix with their Councils in order to be guarded against their ill designs."[42] France remained the informal guarantor of independence. The gentry were not, however, the wily leaders of a weak nation maneuvering like Brer Rabbit among the bears and foxes of Europe. No American tradition taught them the cunning and the temperament for this kind of survival, and as raw neocolonials, they veered between the courtship of a champion and the longing for a total separation from all of Europe. When Europe went to war in the 1790s, it generated almost unbearable tensions among the gentry. The specter of recolonization relentlessly haunted them. With characteristic distortion they assumed that European eyes scrutinized every twitch in American behavior and European power perched to deliver instant rewards and punishments. Shift a mite toward France, Hamilton predicted, and "there would be in less than six months *an open war between the U States & Great Britain.*"[43] Shift a mite toward Britain, Monroe warned, and it would "separate us from France & ultimately unite us with England."[44] Although every arrogant twist in European policy infuriated Americans, it also accentuated their sense of weakness. Such important envoys as Jay in London and Monroe in Paris proved so susceptible to a little attention from a great power that they came to act as its apologist and spokesman. Fierce in their independence and instinctive in their dependence, proud of their accomplishments and humiliated by their marginality, the revolutionary gentry moved with the tide of these neocolonial facts and feelings because they alone made sense of America's prospects in a world of titans.

Occasionally someone caught a glimpse beyond these mental boundaries. "It takes Time to make Sovereigns of Subjects," Jay presciently remarked.[45] "A national spirit is the natural result of national existence," Gouverneur Morris wrote in 1784; "and although some of the present generation may feel colonial oppositions of opinion, that generation will die away, and give place to a race of Americans."[46] In a similar vein, Jefferson commented in 1789, "the rising race are all republicans. We were educated in royalism: no wonder if some of us retain that idolatry still."[47] Yet neither Jay, who took whatever the British offered him in 1794, nor Morris, who probably drew some of his pay from the British government, nor Jefferson, who glorified the first wave of French revolutionaries as world saviors, doubted for a minute that his own pure Americanism was untainted by attitudes from the past or biases in the present. His brand of neocolonialism was always true patriotism. To the either-or categories of their deductive logic and the demanding calculus of honor and shame, the gentry added the incessant pressures of preserving an independence that exceeded their nation's powers to secure. Although the meaning of independence defied a precise definition, it either existed or it did not. It never came in hues. Either the United States stood honorably before the world or it lay in a shambles of disgrace. The uncertainty of it all wound them that much nearer to the snapping point.

From the interaction among these three convictions—the commitment to republican government, leadership through character, and the preservation of independence—came an attempt to build a national society that began with the movement for a new constitution and culminated with Jefferson's first years as president. Into it went a full array of selfish, parochial, and mercenary motives. There was not a saint in the lot of these gentlemen. Nevertheless, all of them had only this common framework of gentry values to express their needs and be heard. When they lined up for battle, they divided over what they shared: the same deductive approaches to government, the same prickly defenses of honor, the same hypersensitivities to European power. Whatever their many difficulties, they never had trouble understanding one another during this distinctive era of creative combat.

The Politics
of Form

"The State of the Union is yet as loose as ever," an associate wrote to James Wilson in the summer of 1786.[1] Where looseness in the character of an individual or a nation denoted the loss of an indispensable control, it placed the United States on the brink of chaos, and there, the keepers of a national revolution warned one another, the entire republican experiment teetered on the eve of the Philadelphia Convention. Without respectability abroad or at home, Rufus King informed his close friend Elbridge Gerry, "dissolve our Government will, unless the several States immediately exert themselves in its favor," then adding an ominous intimation of the wild days to come: ". . . it behooves every one to withdraw in season, to Effect, if possible, some sort of personal Security."[2]

King's vision of total disintegration reflected the standard gentry assumption that influences flowed from superior to inferior levels of a social hierarchy like the invisible pulls of gravity in the solar system. A feeble government at the top, nationally minded leaders were convinced, left the rest of society to spin out its worst passions toward anarchy. Establish a legitimate national government, on the other hand, and its authority would radiate throughout the states, contain those destructive impulses, and tighten the republican system everywhere. "If no effectual [national] check be devised for restraining the instability & encroachments of the [state legislatures]," Madison argued in behalf of a new constitution, "a revolution of some kind or other would be inevitable."[3] Without a hitch in his reasoning, Richard Henry Lee predicted that the mere presence of an authentic national government would counteract "the injustice, folly and wickedness of the State Legislatures," and in France, Jefferson anticipated the same kind of rein on the state legislatures from an improved national structure. None of these gentlemen pictured the national government forcing changes below it, and of the three only Madison foresaw the need even for much legal coercion. The crucial power was an authority emanating from the peak of their symmetrical social order to its base.

In designing a form of government appropriate to their broad American vision, the national gentry began with the commonplaces of western political thought. A proper government required the separation of its functions into distinct agencies: executive, legislative, judicial. A proper republic required a balance among the qualities of government: monarchic, aristocratic, democratic. In this instance, however, balance meant the correction of a specific imbalance, an excess of democratic powers. During the 1770s the resistance to Britain and then revolution had unleashed a great range of popular assertions, triggering protests among hitherto passive farmers and townspeople and elevating a number of their spokesmen to office. Occasionally their wartime committees resembled direct government by the people, and a rough-edged rhetoric of liberty cheered them on. Although only Pennsylvania's unicameral government came at all close to embodying this spirit in a constitution, the ferment of popular politics continued to bubble in public gatherings and state legislatures after the war. Just this kind of raucous democracy, many of the national gentry believed, spawned the debtor uprising of 1786 in western Massachusetts called Shays' Rebellion and generally threatened the "national Character" with ruin.

The standard counter to an overweening democratic force was an enlarged monarchic component in government, and the leaders of the movement for a new constitution relied above all on a strong executive to tip the scales toward stability. As Madison summarized their case, a powerful national executive would check these "pernicious" tendencies in the state legislatures, then check them again in the national legislature if "it might be infected with a similar propensity."[4] Pure monarchy all of them rejected. "I am told that even respectable characters speak of a monarchical form of Government without horror," wrote a disconsolate Washington, one of the proponents of a strong executive. ". . . [W]hat a triumph for the advocates of despotism to find that we are incapable of governing ourselves . . . !"[5] Either devise a sensible republic, echoed Jay, or "the more sober part of the people may even think of a king."[6] Like everything in the world, it was a matter of balance.

The apportionment of greater power to the executive involved questions of balance across the top of the national government, and as gentry leaders worked this familiar terrain, they had relatively little trouble formulating their issues and finding general grounds for agreement. A second set of considerations descended a vertical line running from the national government to the people. On these matters existing theory gave the gentry scant guidance. Since the early 1770s the great revolutionary surge of creativity had been pushing up that axis, establishing ultimate sovereignty in the people, enabling the people to divide their sovereignty at different levels of government, and glorifying the close connection between the people and their representatives. The din of angry debates over impending tyranny and imminent chaos within the states demonstrated that Americans had not assimilated these revolutionary changes even there, and disagreement at the state level became downright confusion from a national perspective. What channels could possibly gather the wishes of a widely dispersed American people and carry them all the way to the top of a single, national republic?

To compound the confusion, state government had one meaning when it was seen from the vantage point of the state and an entirely different meaning when it was viewed nationally. On the one hand, each state had monarchic, aristocratic, and democratic elements to balance within its own government. Considered this way, the states were distinctive republican sovereignties. In comparison with a national government, on the other hand, every part of a state government seemed strikingly popular: close to the people, intimate with their concerns, ready to voice their wishes. Considered from this perspective, the republican complexity of the state government collapsed into an undifferentiated unit of democracy, and its actions expressed, in a common phrase, "the will of the community." If the delegates to Philadelphia were selected by their state governments, Jay argued, any changes in the national structure would be "deducible from the only source of just authority—*the People!*"[7] After all, the very legitimacy of the Articles of Confederation as an expression of the people's will rested on its ratification by the state governments. Under the Articles only states conducted elections, and their governments then appointed representatives to the national Congress. Quite reasonably by gentry logic, Richard Henry Lee called the end product of this sequence from people to states to Congress "Simple Democracy."[8]

Construing each state as a republican sovereignty at home and a democratic unit in national affairs left the kind of theoretical ambiguity that the gentry, with their categorizing habits of thought, normally found intolerable. Only the sharpest minds never lost track of these separate meanings for state government as they wove themselves into the complicated debates over a new national structure. Appropriately, the deepest conflicts over the Constitution occurred in this soft area of the states' dual roles. At the same time, the confusion sometimes had its uses, especially to the small band of centralizers, led by Madison and Wilson, who seized the initiative at Philadelphia, won broad approval among the delegates for designing an entirely new national government, and showed a way to accomplish it.

By committing the Philadelphia Convention at the outset to a new form of government, the centralizers drove a handful of dissenters outside the boundaries of discussion and consolidated a wide area of likemindedness among the remaining delegates. Issues involving only the top level of government never seriously jeopardized the enterprise as a whole. A large working majority always favored a strong executive, an independent judiciary, and a bicameral legislature with an expanded jurisdiction over commerce, taxation, and warfare and with the flexibility to pass those laws "necessary and proper" to implement the government's powers. Despite some sharp exchanges over the place of slavery in the new constitution, a substantial body of northern delegates made it quite clear that they stood ready to grant the important concessions: the right to count three male slaves the equivalent of five free men in the apportionment of representatives, and the untouchable twenty-year moratorium on national laws regulating the importation of slaves. The gentry's dogmatic declarations poured over every subject, of course. Yet on these matters, a sizable majority preferred a common constitution to the pure truth.

The one issue with the potential to explode the convention was the role of the states in the new government. Hostility toward the states permeated everything that the centralizers proposed. Madison's Virginia Plan, which based the legislature exclusively on distribution of population, threatened all the states, not just the small ones. Wilson's many efforts to ground elections directly in the people had a single objective: to undermine the states. Although the centralizers doubted "the practicability of annihilating the States," in Rufus King's phrase, they did want to paralyze them in national affairs, consign them to the routines of local governance, and in an ideal future watch them wither away.[9] Meanwhile, they railed at those "imaginary beings called States" with their "phantom" sovereignty, contrasted a truly national government with the fragmenting provincialism of the states, and identified them with the forces of anarchy and subversion.[10]

These attacks pushed to the nub of the states' survival, and the primary battle at Philadelphia, therefore, concentrated on their rights as authentic sovereignties. In those terms the centralizers found themselves overwhelmed by more moderate gentlemen who, with Gerry, believed that the American states "were neither the same Nation nor different Nations," secured the existence of the states in a revamped Senate, and defeated Wilson's schemes for a new nationwide grillwork of districts to elect national officials.[11] None of the leading centralizers facilitated the basic compromise that made the Senate equally representative of each state. Unrepentant, they simply lost the vote, and in the process they became federalists in spite of themselves. Nor did the centralizers quit the fight. Chipping away at every opportunity, they managed to win an impressive string of lesser victories. Special conventions, where the states' "first characters" were expected to prevail over the defenders of local rights, would pass on the document. Along the top of the government, only the Senate had ties to the state legislatures, and these remained as weak as possible. By empowering senators to vote as individuals rather than as pairs of ambassadors from their home sovereignties, by avoiding any mention of recall during their terms, and by paying them with national rather than state funds, the delegates established a Senate "to represent & manage the affairs of the whole, and not to be the advocates of State interests."[12] Nevertheless, the unyielding James Wilson undoubtedly glowered at his own words as he sketched the only accurate preamble for the new document: "We The People of the States of New Hampshire &C do . . ." Despite his best efforts, and Madison's, the people were still trapped inside these enemy camps.[13]

On September 17, after almost four months of labor, the signers of this document hurried home to argue their cause in the language of likemindedness that they had grown accustomed to using among themselves. There they met a very different kind of opposition, one that rejected the comfortable premises of consensus at Philadelphia and, in sum, challenged almost every clause in their work. Matters of hard bargaining and great moment at Philadelphia—the impeachment power, the states' share in the authority over their militia, a shortened term for the president, and the like—these critics-at-large dismissed as mere sops to the innocent. The president was a monarch in mufti and the Senate his aristocratic cabal, the judiciary neither independent enough nor weak enough to tolerate, and the House of Representatives helpless to counter the rest. The pardoning power would make the government safe for corruption, the taxing power would impoverish the people, and the military power would hold them in bondage. Passing any law it considered "necessary and proper," the government would do whatever it chose, and, enacting the supreme law of the land, it would throttle all state alternatives. The list continued endlessly and ominously, for by most accounts it was rallying a majority in such crucial states as Massachusetts, New York, and Virginia.

Ominous, yet artificial. As these opponents bombarded the plan from all sides, they were also hitting one another with enough contradictory arguments to mark a rough but critical division in their ranks. On one side stood the irreconcilables: guardians of local rights, wartime patriots with a firm state attachment, enemies of those speculators and commercial adventurers who clustered in the federalist camp. New York's most powerful leader, George Clinton, and his allies spoke for these antifederalists. So did Patrick Henry in Virginia and James Winthrop in Massachusetts. By residence, occupation, or inclination they tended to lie outside the main lines of America's mercantile bustle. On the other side gathered gentlemen with a strong commitment to the Revolution's national legacy who found this particular form of government too flawed to accept. Gerry represented them in Massachusetts, and an especially impressive group, including Richard Henry Lee, George Mason, Monroe, and the anonymous "Federal Farmer," stated their case in Virginia. No characteristics clearly distinguished them from their federalist opponents other than their judgment of the document. In the dynamics of the constitutional debate a number of gentlemen, including Melancton Smith in New York and Samuel Adams in Boston, vacillated or drifted along this antifederalist spectrum. Nevertheless, at its two ends the responses to the Philadelphia challenge were strikingly different.

The semblance of unity among the antifederalists came from their common preoccupation with the issue of a republic's acceptable size. "Federal Farmer" called it "the great question." Clinton, citing the standard authority of Montesquieu, used it to open his attack, and Winthrop set it at the foundation of his long analysis.* Both theory and history told them that no large or heterogeneous republic could succeed. By contrast to the thirteen sovereign republics operating under the Articles, the new constitution established a "consolidated government" that laid an imperial power across the entire nation. Distant government, all of them agreed, meant corrupt government. "So extensive a territory as that of the U. States, including such a variety of climates, productions, interests; and so great difference of manners, habits, and customs; cannot be governed in freedom . . . ," Lee wrote. In small republics, "*opinion*, founded in the knowledge of those who govern, procures obedience without *force*. But remove *opinion*, which must fall with a knowledge of characters in so widely extended a country, and *force* then becomes necessary to se-

---

* With Herbert J. Storing I am inclined to identify "Cato" with George Clinton—or more precisely Clinton and a coach.

cure the purposes of Civil society."[14] In order to avoid anarchy, "Federal Farmer" predicted, these detached rulers would impose despotism through "a multitude of officers and military force . . . continually kept in view . . . to make the government feared and respected."[15]

For the committed defenders of local and state liberties, that settled the matter. Everything else in their arguments elaborated on this basic conflict between freedom and the scope of the national government. They simply spelled out the details of an inevitable despotism. Where the Constitution lifted powers from the states, these antifederalists demanded their return. Their conflict with the federalists had a clear, hard ring to it, and their long list of defects in the new plan translated into sections of a barricade to protect an existing state sovereignty against a usurping tyrant—one that sounded dangerously like the old colonial master. No mere doctoring of the document would do. America's leaders needed to start again and this time actually amend the Articles.

For the national antifederalists, however, size led to a problem rather than a solution. Acknowledging weaknesses in the Articles, they showed no desire to preserve it, and they held no preconceptions against a distinct national government for the whole republic. Gerry and Mason negotiated for one to the very end at Philadelphia, and on the sidelines Lee welcomed the prospect of "a ballanced government where the powers shall be placed independently as in England," one with "Tone enough for the unruly passions of men."[16] Instead of calling the Philadelphia delegates plotters against the Revolution, as did the angry Abraham Yates of New York, "Federal Farmer" wrote respectfully of their eminence. Gentlemen who sought "Tone" along the horizontal axis could not condemn the monarchic president and the aristocratic Senate out of hand, and the Senate in particular attracted several appreciative comments. As always, the issue devolved into a question of balance. To correct an excess of democracy, the national antifederalists believed, the Philadelphia Convention had thrown everything on the other side of the scale and threatened America with a monster of monarchy and aristocracy. Hence as they compiled their own long list of tyrannical dangers in the Constitution, almost all of them were looking for ways not to scrap the new structure but to modify it, to redress the critical imbalance.

Theoretically their answer lay in the new government's democratic component, the House of Representatives. Antifederalists of all types ridiculed the House as a travesty on the democratic principle. How could one representative for 30,000 scattered citizens offer "a true picture of the people; possess the knowledge of their circumstances and wants; . . . [and] seek their true interests"?[17] "Under the pretence of different branches of government," Winthrop charged, "the members [of the House] will in fact be chosen from the same general description of citizens"—"the natural aristocracy," "Brutus" in New York and "Federal Farmer" in Virginia called them. But where an immovable Clinton used the deficient House merely to prove the inevitability of despotism, national antifederalists wrestled with it as a monumental frustration in its own right. Was there any way to refurbish it into an authentic democratic component? Reluctantly they concluded not. Although several of them toyed with a lower ratio, they were working with a democratic standard of about 2,000 representatives for the nation, and anything close to that total, they agreed, would be "so numerous and unwieldy . . . as to be incapable of transacting public business."[18]

So they turned to the alternative source of democracy in national affairs, the state governments, where—in Mason's emphatic phrase—the people had "real, actual, substantial representation."[19] There, claimed "Federal Farmer," "will be nineteen-twentieths of the representatives of the people; they will have a near connection, and their members an immediate intercourse with the people . . . possess the confidence of the people, and be considered generally as their immediate guardians." Waxing a bit hyperbolic, he termed state officials "so numerous as almost to be the people themselves . . . in some degree a periodical assemblage of the people, frequently formed." From these antifederalist premises the conclusion was "undeniable, that the federal government will be principally in the hands of the natural aristocracy, and the state governments principally in the hands of the democracy, the representatives of the body of the people."[20] But where to go from there? Irreconcilable antifederalists, arraying their sovereign states against a national government, wanted to take as much as possible from a limited pool of powers and pile it on their side of the barricade. National antifederalists, construing the states as democratic units rather than sovereign republics, had glimmerings of a very different vision. Somehow they needed to bring those states-as-democracies into the national governing process and incorporate them as the missing element in an otherwise unbalanced national structure. Tentatively, inconclusively, they were playing with the pieces of an innovative vertical pole—people, states, House—that if they could ever assemble offered an ingenious solution to their whole tangle of problems about size and liberty and stability, a peculiarly American democratic pillar to sustain a national republican government.

As national antifederalists fumbled with these pieces, the centralizing federalists sharpened their hatchets. They would tolerate no democratic pole that enhanced the importance of the states. The standard equation between states and people, of course, they knew well. Not only did it lie behind their use of state ratifying conventions—one of the few matters of principle on which federalists and antifederalists generally agreed—

but it occasionally worked to the centralizers' benefit. They could oppose a national bill of rights, for example, on the grounds that state governments already protected the people's basic freedoms. Nevertheless, the centralizers were flattering the states into impotence. When Hamilton grandiloquently declared that under the new constitution the states would not only "be the VOICE, but, if necessary, the ARM" of the people, he actually offered them nothing more than a gentry's cliché, the residual right of revolution in case the national government became a military tyranny.[21] Otherwise the centralizers' government would rest directly on the people and hold a monopoly on all national dealings with them. By "raising the federal pyramid to a considerable altitude," in Wilson's phrase, they scattered the people far below at its base and, in effect, turned the principle of democracy into a check on its practices—a diffuse, neutralized people-at-large to counter a mobilized, assertive people in their states.[22] This autonomous national pyramid stood boldly at odds with the antifederalist model, where state governments served as "the body or props, on which the federal head rests, and . . . cannot remain a moment after they cease."[23]

What the centralizers did offer the states was the guarantee of a sovereign existence, the upshot of their failure at Philadelphia and now the proof of their federalist faith. How absurd to cry consolidation, they emphasized, when the Constitution's electoral mechanisms could function only through the states. For national purposes, however, the centralizers wanted to seal the states apart as inert sovereignties, housing some of the machinery of government but producing nothing of their own with it. There the devils of localism could fight it out among themselves. Commenting on the proper realm of the states, Hamilton barely suppressed a sneer: "I confess I am at a loss to discover what temptation the persons intrusted with the administration of the general government could ever feel to divest the States [of their authority under the Constitution]. . . . The regulation of the mere domestic police of a State appears to me to hold out slender allurements to ambition."[24] Precisely, replied the antifederalists. What respect would citizens give to officials "who shall meet once in a year to make laws for regulating the heighth of your fences and the repairing of your roads?" asked Melancton Smith. ". . . The state governments, without object or authority, will soon dwindle into insignificance, and be despised by the people themselves."[25] Precisely, thought the centralizers.

Ever the brilliant lawyers, the leading centralizers chose to concede nothing. Did a republic require a homogeneous population? By fiat, Jay created one out of America's diversity—"a people descended from the same ancestors, speaking the same language, professing the same religion."[26] Did citizens worry about imperial tendencies in the new government? Wilson asked them to welcome a scheme that would bring "the vigour and decision of a wide spreading monarchy."[27] Madison opened his defense of the Constitution in the same tone. *Federalist* 10 confidently took on the giant itself, the problem of size. Confronting Montesquieu directly, Madison argued that a large republic was actually healthier than a small one because the very multiplicity of local, self-serving interests made it more difficult for them to combine in national affairs. Moreover, by placing representatives at a sufficient remove from the people, the best among them would break their parochial ties and act for the entire nation. It was a chillingly comprehensive summary of the antifederalists' worst fears. The phantom states, tainted with faction, barely qualified as inferior republics. The distance between the representatives and their constituents, so appalling to every antifederalist, now appeared as an asset, a way of extracting the aristocratic benefits of virtual representation from the revolutionary tradition of direct representation. All the essay lacked was blunt Roger Sherman's boast of a consolidating constitution.

Madison, however, proved the exception. No agent of compromise at Philadelphia, he had clung as tenaciously as anyone to the extreme centralizers' end of the spectrum while others made the necessary accommodations. Moreover, he had remained stubbornly deaf to popular sentiment, choosing instead to decide on principle and counting on the delegates' public authority to win an eventual adoption. As Madison later summarized it, only "their ignorance of the opinions & confidence in the liberality of their respective constituents" had enabled the delegates to frame a constitution at all.[28] Now this blessed ignorance was dissolving in one grim lesson after another on the power of the opposition. By January 1788, pessimistic appraisals had reached him on the Constitution's prospects in Massachusetts and New York. In his own state the composition even more than the number of dissenters sobered Madison. From abroad Jefferson criticized the Constitution in a gentle antifederalist idiom. At home the venerable Edmund Pendleton, whom Madison deeply admired, could scarcely tolerate it. Unlike Hamilton in New York and Wilson in Pennsylvania, who gazed at their enemies across a divide of hatred, Madison could never dismiss these Virginia gentlemen as mere democratic knaves. Above all, Madison, who had no other credentials for national greatness than this constitution, invested his very character as a leader in its adoption and, beyond that, in a sufficiently broad base to implement it.

How to win that support? Sensibly he abandoned the irreconcilables and concentrated on the national antifederalists, whose views blended so imperceptibly with those of moderate federalists that only the need to choose sides divided them. Who could have guessed to the very end at

Philadelphia that Madison's sometime ally Edmund Randolph would not sign but that the vacillating Caleb Strong of Massachusetts would? John Dickinson of Delaware and Oliver Ellsworth of Connecticut, who endorsed the document, shared more common constitutional ground with George Mason and Elbridge Gerry, who did not, than any of them shared with the likes of Alexander Hamilton and Gouverneur Morris. In advocating the Constitution, Dickinson, for example, acknowledged that "a territory of such extent as that of United America, could not be safely and advantageously governed, but by a combination of republics," and identified the people with "the sovereign wills of the several confederated states."[29] No national antifederalist could have phrased it better. Madison, who had studied those middle ranges of opinion as he opposed them at the convention, knew exactly what they contained. While his centralizing colleagues were widening the chasm in debate, Madison set out to build a bridge for the national antifederalists.

He used persuasion. Shelving the nationalist logic of *Federalist* 10, Madison proceeded to treat the states with a respectful seriousness in number 39. In particular he made the crucial concession—clear enough at the Philadelphia Convention but since obscured by the centralizers— that the people acted through their states, not "as individuals composing one entire nation," and that the very "foundation" of the Constitution, its ratification, would express this segmentation of the republic's sovereign power.[30] In number 45, instead of describing the ideal representative as a detached aristocrat, he likened the members of the House to state legislators, those stereotypical spokesmen for local interests. Then in sharp contrast to Hamilton's picture, Madison sketched a national government concentrating "principally on external objects" and leaving the "most extensive and important" functions of government to the states "in times of peace and security."[31] When he identified the natural loyalties of the people with their state governments in number 46 and associated these governments with "the popular bias," he had rhetorically corralled the people back into their states and offered encouragement to each element in a democratic linkage of people, states, and House. Madison certainly did not abandon all the old beliefs. But in number 51 when he returned to the central theme of number 10—self-canceling little factions as the security of a large republic—he now subordinated this social argument to a structural one that made a multiplicity of federated states the final guarantor of the nation's republicanism.

A plan of action was even more important. Here Madison benefited immeasurably from the living proof of his theory about conflicting little factions. Scattered antifederalist voices around the country changed their tunes and contradicted one another with demands for another convention, for ratification only after amendments, for ratification with recommended amendments, and for myriad modifications, conditional or advisory, that clashed in both spirit and substance. Centralizers fought them all. To win a tight struggle in Massachusetts, however, moderate federalists did accept an advisory list of amendments. They were a "blemish," Madison admitted to Washington in February, then noted in explanation: "The minority also is very disagreeably large. . . ."[32] The more he thought about those amendments, the more attractive they became, and by early April he settled on the course that he would follow doggedly for the next year and a half. Without some concessions, he reasoned, the Constitution would fail. A new convention he considered "fatal." If the state conventions themselves inserted amendments as they ratified the document, they would pick it to death. Advisory amendments, on the other hand, delayed the actual decisions to a calmer time and a safer place—the first new Congress—where Madison expected to be a leader. There he could make the choices from a surplus of alternatives. Certain that he had found the one workable formula for an essential compromise, Madison wrote to that exemplar of the indecisive center, Edmund Randolph: "I shall be extremely happy to see a coalition among all the real federalists. Recommendatory alterations are the only ground. . . ."[33]

With amendments in the air, close victories in Virginia and New York assured the adoption of the Constitution, highlighted the strength of its opposition, and sent Madison along a tightrope toward the first ten amendments. As he threaded his private way, he deceived everybody except himself, but he made no friends in the process. To his centralizing colleagues who remembered Madison's help in dismissing a bill of rights at Philadelphia, he masked his commitment in bland, belittling phrases. To Jefferson he disingenuously claimed that he had "always been in favor of a bill of rights" and only doubted its expediency.[34] To those Virginians who expected the states to receive more power over taxation, armies, and the like, he posed as a champion of amendments without ever specifying their nature. Madison's determination to press for amendments during the first session of the new Congress caught the centralizers by surprise. Just as suspicious antifederalists had predicted, they sought to bury the issue, and only Madison's unique stature among them kept it alive in 1789. They must act immediately, Madison insisted, "in order to quiet the anxiety which prevails in the public mind . . . , stifle the voice of complaint, and make friends of many who doubted [the Constitution's] merits."[35] Popularity-seeking, a centralizer whispered. While antifederalists on their part waited for substantial changes in the balance of power, Madison—unreconstructed centralizer to the end—carefully discarded every proposal "abridging the sum of power transferred from the States to the general Government" and even tried to insert one—

"the most valuable amendment on the whole list"—empowering the national government to police state actions.³⁶ Richard Henry Lee, who came into the Senate to fashion a proper set of amendments, angrily protested their lack of substance, and Massachusetts, the originator of advisory amendments, refused to ratify the final set.

Nevertheless, Lee remained in the Senate, and Massachusetts remained in the union. A critical delay and a timely concession calmed enough doubts to secure the Constitution. Madison watched one after another of the national antifederalists march across his bridge into the new government, fill its offices with pride, and protect it by their very presence. His claim as architect of the Constitution rested as much on what he did at the very end of the building process as on what he did at the very beginning. If the Constitution succeeded through compromises, his one crucial contribution was the Bill of Rights. Madison wanted to be father of an enduring constitution badly enough to bargain for it, and he had the wit to seek out the minimum price he would have to pay.

But what did this last great compromise mean? The centralizers knew. Referring to such lists of basic liberties as the "personal rights of individuals," they divorced the collective people from state government and construed the Bill of Rights as a direct relationship between the national government and its atomized citizenry. The Tenth Amendment, reserving all unstated powers "to the States respectively, or to the people," was merely a bit of redundance: the powers that they still held they still held. Anything more assertive from the states would be a first step toward treason. The moderates at the borderline between federalism and antifederalism also knew. As even the inveterate centralizers admitted, the states were the natural "guardians of the people's liberties." What the original document had lacked, as "Federal Farmer" complained, was any means "by which the state governments can constitutionally and regularly check the arbitrary measures of congress."³⁷ Now, according to another partisan of amendments, Jefferson, the states had "the text whereby they will try all the acts of the federal government."³⁸ By this interpretation states and people in the Tenth Amendment stood essentially in apposition, the former serving as the latter's constitutional protector against national abuse. Anything less assertive from the states would be an acquiescence in tyranny. The Bill of Rights, in other words, provided the indispensable ambiguity for an acceptable constitution.

Grudging accommodations among categorizing minds reinforced each gentleman's tendency to construe compromise as some other gentleman's capitulation and foreshadowed the bitter battles to come over these conflicting interpretations. The struggle over the Constitution flushed out the primary combatants: a body of centralizers with their greatest strength in New York and Massachusetts and a looser cluster of moderate nationalists with their firmest support in Virginia. The former focused on the national executive. The latter inherited the components of an original right-angled structure that coupled the top of the government with its vertical, democratic line at the House of Representatives, integrated the states into national governance, and thereby offered the prospect of a functioning rather than just a schematic federalism. To complete the structure required some means of joining House, states, and people into a democratic column and then learning how to use this novel creation in national government. For the next dozen years these experiments and the centralizers' implacable opposition to them dominated the national gentry's politics of form.

3

The Politics of Character

Shaping a nation was heady business, and the triumphant federalists approached it as men of destiny. Even during the mid-1780s when America's drift prompted a string of glum predictions about slippage and decline, some of the national gentry tempted fate by invoking it. "Such a variety of circumstances," Jay had assured Washington, "would not, almost miraculously, have combined to liberate and make us a nation for transient and unimportant purposes."[1] Now a new constitution raised the prospect of a fresh miracle, this one under their own control. Likening themselves to the fabled "lawgivers" of ancient times whose work required "the strongest efforts of human genius," the leading delegates at Philadelphia shared Madison's solemn conviction that they would "decide forever the fate of Republican Govt."[2] Appropriately, Madison's thinking about the Constitution drew part of its inspiration from David Hume's essay "Idea of a Perfect Commonwealth." If, as Jefferson later wrote, history "only informs us what bad government is," federalists dared to believe that the United States could show the world what good government was, and for the first time since early in the war they dreamed of achieving that rarefied state of tranquil stability called "happiness."[3]

Happiness defined a social goal, with government an indispensable means but no more than a means. In the gentry's logical progression, society always came first: no society, no government. What made the Constitution such a startling departure was its attempt to reverse the natural sequence of things. Because no national society existed in the American league of states, the federalists had no choice except to begin with government. But because a national government without a national society was unthinkable, they needed simultaneously to create an American society as well.

Creating a society meant fashioning a proper hierarchy—no hierarchy, no society—and the federalists set about this task with the only mechanism at their disposal, the Constitution. At its base, of course, rested the people. Those who saw state governments as the people's guardians in national affairs placed them at the next level. Others moved immediately to the House of Representatives. Indirect election then marked the higher tiers of the hierarchy. "I have ever observed that a choice by the people themselves is not generally distinguished for it's wisdom," Jefferson had written some years before to Edmund Pendleton. "This first secretion from them is usually crude and heterogeneous. But give to those so chosen by the people a second choice themselves, and they generally will chuse wise men."[4] The more elaborate and honorable the procedures of selection, the more exalted the social ranking became. To illustrate this rule, Madison used the Maryland senate, chosen by an electoral college and empowered to fill its own vacancies. As a consequence, Madison concluded, that august body gave the government in Maryland "a reputation in which it will probably not be rivalled by that of any state in the Union."[5] Hence the United States Senate, which the state governments filled, stood well above the directly elected representatives. The Supreme Court the federalists located between the Senate and the House. Although selected by other gentlemen, the justices would only qualify as a superior class of appointed officials. The Senate rather than the Supreme Court should judge the president in an impeachment trial, Hamilton argued, because the justices probably would not "be endowed with so eminent a portion of fortitude, as would be called for in the execution of so difficult a task; and it is still more to be doubted, whether they would possess the [necessary] degree of credit and authority. . . ."[6] Finally, the most elevating procedures of all set the president at the peak of the new hierarchy. Here was at least the scaffolding for a national society.

All participants in the debate over the Constitution recognized it as self-conscious social construction. A central theme in antifederalism attacked it for creating orders that could not otherwise exist in America— "a *permanent* ARISTOCRACY," in Samuel Bryan's cry of alarm.[7] Federalists on their part praised a structure that would mold a "natural aristocracy" in the service of the nation. Promoting the new framework was simultaneously a way of recruiting for it. Among themselves federalists worried that their government would not attract enough of America's "first characters"; to the public they emphasized the dignity and stability of its important offices, especially in contrast to their state counterparts. Entwined in the battle over the states' role in the new government lay issues of social structure as well as power. State-oriented leaders feared that a nationally superimposed hierarchy would declass them. If the state governments shrank to mere housekeepers, however, centralizing federalists expected to entice those gentry who resented the nouveaux politicians in their states and would welcome an escape to a higher, safer national plane. Whatever their persuasions, gentlemen anticipated a profound reordering from the Constitution. In the nature of things it would give the nation a new social symmetry.

To succeed, the national hierarchy had to master Montesquieu's stubborn problem of size and define a republican relationship between America's new leaders at the top and a dispersed, diverse population at its base. The national gentry accomplished this in three steps. First, like gentlemen everywhere, they restricted entry into the sovereign people. Women disappeared in subordinance to whichever men held authority over their interests. Relying on a common 18th-century distinction between an authentic *Volk* and the *Pöbel* or *canaille* or rabble, gentlemen excluded the rootless and impoverished, those whom Blackstone described as "in so mean a situation as to be esteemed to have no will of their own." Through that test and additional assumptions of barbarism, they cast all but a bare scattering of native Americans and free blacks beyond the pale into dependent, inferior societies of their own. Slaves, as Edmund Pendleton argued in 1776, simply fell outside of society altogether. By an assortment of private standards, gentlemen then refined the people still further. James Winthrop eliminated the Scotch-Irish. Uriah Tracy, a centralizer from Connecticut, banned the Pennsylvania Germans, whom he called slavish, "stupid, ignorant, and ugly."[8] Others barred Catholics. Finally, to contain the scope of American society, most of the gentry set a vague boundary somewhere to the west. In that spirit, Thomas McKean of Pennsylvania banished an indeterminate number of upcountry "clodpoles," and John Randolph swept away all the "Yahoos" on the frontier. The interchangeable uses of "people" and "community" indicated that only those who in some subtle sense belonged would be counted. More bluntly, the gentry's people were who the gentry said they were.

Second, the gentry gave the people form. To function as republican sovereigns they became a category in the gentry's scheme of understanding, a construct that stood apart from its individual elements, as the

Virginian Wilson Cary Nicholas illustrated when he spoke about "the persons of the people."[9] Persons came of age, aspired, suffered, and died; the people lived on in abstract perpetuity. On the loose, the mass of individual citizens diffused their energies in dangerously erratic ways— now rushing after a demagogue, now falling back into an inert provincialism. Madison's picture of a violent "majority trampling on the rights of the minority" and producing "factions and commotions" implied something like a raging state of nature in the ill-structured state governments of 1788, and almost every federalist treated Shays' Rebellion as the logical extension of such formlessness.[10] Gentlemen responded to the unpredictable eruptions of city dwellers in a similar fashion. John Adams condemned them as mobs. "Of this be certain," warned Oliver Wolcott of Connecticut, "that when the country becomes possessed of the same spirit and character which is prominent in most of our great towns, the happiness and liberty of our country will be terminated."[11] By the same logic, partisans of a vertical axis in the national government praised an assertive people only because constitutional mechanisms set the people firmly within a republican structure. Adrift as individuals, the people would never preserve their rights. Acting through the House or through the states or even through public conventions with a cadre of gentlemen on the rostrum, their assertions infused life into the meaning of liberty. Both Madison and "Federal Farmer" likened the true people to a "properly formed" militia, conjuring an image of elected gentlemen-officers directing a determined and disciplined body of citizens.

Third, the gentry assigned attributes to the sovereign people appropriate to the solemnity and difficulty of national governance. At the highest level of theory, of course, the people were everything. Their ultimate sovereignty provided the revolutionary base for American republicanism, their inalienable rights required written constitutions with specific delegations of power, and their indispensable endorsement enabled government to function at all. As governments actually operated, however, the sovereigns were asked to assume their proper place, and the more distant and esoteric the affairs of state, the more subdued their voice was expected to become. Only an elite who stood well above the ordinary farmers and mechanics could grasp the essentials of national policy. The people at this remove, in Hamilton's phrase, were "rather reasoning than reasonable."[12] They could follow an argument but not construct one. "I am *sure* the mass of Citizens in the United States *mean well*," Washington decided, "—and I firmly believe they will always *act well* whenever they can obtain a right understanding of matters. . . ."[13] Or in Rufus King's version: "If the people are truly informed of their situation, they will eventually accede to such measures as will best secure their freedom and honor."[14] Hence the delegates working *in camera* at Philadelphia felt quite confident that they could teach the people the merits of their private creation in government.

Not every gentleman treated the people as imperiously as King. Nevertheless, even the people's warmest advocates among the antifederalists based much of their opposition to the Constitution on comparable premises. By its very nature, they argued, government at such a distance would fall beyond the ken of the people and into the lap of the aristocracy. In describing an effective national government, Melancton Smith spoke not about the people's active role but about their "confidence" in the system or their "good opinion" of it, consequences that followed directly from the way their leaders talked about the government. It was to escape this trap of passivity that James Winthrop flatly rejected an overarching national policy: "It is only by protecting local concerns that the interest of the whole is protected."[15] Those antifederalists who could not follow Winthrop more or less followed the federalists. Were the people ill equipped to reckon with the large questions of governance? Then school them in "a correct knowledge of the principles of government," the antifederalist Monroe recommended, so that they would "never fall into the excesses" that destroyed republics.[16] In a well-ordered republic, leaders instructed, the people learned, leaders acted, the people responded, and so the cycle endlessly repeated itself.

For those gentry with some kind of commitment to a national government, Madison offered an approximate summary of the consensus: ". . . it is the reason, alone, of the public, that ought to control and regulate the government. The passions ought to be controlled and regulated by the government."[17] In this fashion they freed themselves from the constraints of their sovereigns. Each of them became a seer of the public mind, divining its true character and delivering oracular pronouncements on its future state. Just as the people were who the gentry said they were, so the people thought what the gentry said they thought. Cautious gentlemen such as Jay and Washington tended to find a cautious people, not yet "ripe" for a new government in 1786 and just "gradually coming right" after the Constitution had been ratified.[18] An impatient leader such as Hamilton, on the other hand, concluded that the people would learn as he acted.

Everything the national gentry said about government and politics accentuated this independence from their sovereigns. No claim rang more often than a gentleman's detachment from popular favor. A virtuous official represented the people by attending to republican truth, not to them. To sacrifice popularity in the name of his own integrity brought him honor, just as to seek it meant instant shame. In 1788, Madison illustrated one of the most common slurs on an opponent in his dismissal of John Hancock as "a courtier of popularity."[19] A year later the disgusted Fisher Ames of Massachusetts flung the same charge at Madison for sponsoring a bill of rights. Jefferson's enthusiasm for the people's liberties elicited Oliver Wolcott's sneering remark that he wanted "popularity in ale houses."[20] Yet even Jefferson's relatively friendly ear heard little authority in the faint, dissonant voice of the people. On learning of the people's discontent from one of their ardent local champions, he responded with a gentleman's cool grace: ". . . where a measure not agreeable to them has been adopted, it is desirable to know it, because it is an admonition to a review of that measure to see if it has been really right. . . ."[21]

Gentlemen calculated majorities and minorities by counting their own heads, not the people's. Although the antifederalist Aedanus Burke of South Carolina claimed "⅘ of the people" behind his cause, he continued to call it the minority position because a majority of the state's gentry favored the Constitution.[22] In Virginia the antifederalist Spencer Roane offered the same analysis: "great Numbers" against the Constitution but still a "minority" of the men who mattered.[23] Such a vision could cause acute frustration, as Jefferson expressed in his quick, despairing account of a defeat in North Carolina: "The lawyers all tories, the people substantially republican, but uninformed & deceived by the lawyers who are elected of necessity. . . ."[24] Appropriately the gentry addressed their speeches and pamphlets, rich with learned allusions and first principles, to one another, not to the people, who would have to receive their instruction from others closer to them in the hierarchy. The art of persuasion centered around the conversion of a secondary tier of gentlemen who, it was hoped, would respond as one of them did to the endorsers of a national bill of rights: ". . . some of the greatest men I ever knew . . . men whose experience and wisdom are sufficient to give authority and support to almost any opinion they may choose."[25] Once elected by the people, representatives became fair game for their superiors. Much of the gentry gossip surrounding any legislative session reported the efforts of a few leaders to "infuse good opinions" into these secondary figures—or, at the bias of the observer, to "corrupt" them.[26] Lesser men responded accordingly. As New York's delegates gathered to pass on the Constitution, one preliminary estimate indicated 46 against and 19 for it. When enough delegates changed their minds to ratify the Constitution, leading antifederalists expressed considerable anger but no special shock.

Distancing themselves from the people and presiding over a vast territory, national leaders assumed a particularly wide latitude as their right and America's necessity. No hierarchy maintained itself. Even the most libertarian among their antifederalist opponents accepted the common wisdom that too little power at the top of society invited a deadly sequence of chaos to despotism. Precisely because they also expected leaders to exercise such leeway, antifederalists attacked the Constitution's "necessary and proper" clause so vehemently. The moderates among them signified their compliance most openly by accepting the Philadelphia delegates' right not only to frame an entirely new government but even to set the terms for their illegal document's ratification. After recounting the facts in this "usurpation," "An Old Whig" of Philadelphia concluded, "I will not say that in doing so they have exceeded their authority. . . ."[27] "Federal Farmer" climaxed his account by bemoaning the absence of "eight or nine" delegates who would have demanded a better document. The wrong gentlemen had exceeded the law. Little wonder that the constraints of the law hung quite loosely around the new government's leaders. "A strict observance of the written laws is doubtless *one* of the highest duties of a good citizen, but it is not *the highest* . . . ," Jefferson wrote later in life. "To lose our country by a scrupulous adherence to written law, would be to lose the law itself . . . thus absurdly sacrificing the end to the means. . . ."[28] To the same point, Hamilton declared more concisely: "It is easy to sacrifice the substantial interests of Society by a strict adherence to ordinary rules."[29]

What emerged from these common assumptions was a sharply personalized manner of governance. The 18th-century platitude that the "success of governments depended on the selection of the men who administer them" expressed far more than a timeless preference for talent and honesty over incompetence and corruption. Just as surely as the wrong forms of government would render the wisest leaders helpless, so the wrong leaders would destroy the wisest forms. Vice, like virtue, flowed irresistibly from the top of the hierarchy. "There is scarce such a thing under the sun as a corrupt people where the government is uncorrupt," their British mentor James Burgh had written; "it is that and that alone which makes them so. . . ."[30] By the same logic, Jefferson predicted early in the eighties that when evil came to America, it "will have seized the heads of government, and be spread by them through the body of the people. . . ."[31] With a monopoly of reason's highest powers and everything in the balance, no national leader would willingly imprison himself in a box of his own making. If none of them quite claimed that the end justified the means, they did come close to believing that the right official justified his own actions. Once the basic constitutional form was in place, they had neither a way nor a desire to distinguish the government from the governors.

Personal government meant government through character. There the focus rested in 1789, for in the gentry's merger of society-government-character, the fate of the first two now hinged on the third. At the outset the enterprise depended fundamentally on a single man—Washington, the hero of the national revolution, the automatic first character in any gentry gathering he joined, and now the uncontested choice as first character of the nation. Far more than Benjamin Franklin, his nearest competitor in fame, men elevated the general above mere mortals simply by the way they uttered or printed his name: "WASHINGTON." In an act as reflexive as buckling a shoe, the delegates at Philadelphia made him president of the convention, and when he issued a lone, late request of them, he won instant and unanimous approval on a heated subject, even though it required their scribe to mark over the official copy. No single factor had a greater influence in the Constitution's adoption than the inevitability of this man as president. Without him, how many of the waverers would have risked the dangers of centralized power? Under him, how many could really fear tyranny? With Washington in mind, John Marshall later concluded that "had the influence of character been removed, the intrinsic merits of the instrument would not have secured its adoption."[32]

Considerably more was at stake than just adulation. In an 18th-century political hierarchy there could be only one first character. Everything in history from Solon to George III told the gentry that the critical man made the critical difference. Confusion at the peak triggered the rise of factions, the struggle for power, then the loss of liberty. Hence Washington's presence anchored the entire hierarchy. As he secured the structure, the gentry believed, the first character also conditioned life throughout its ranks. In his character resided "The dignity of the commonwealth," John Adams declared. All aspects of his behavior "are made the daily contemplation and conversation of the whole people."[33] A great man in office would "refine and enlarge the public views," Madison wrote; a "sinister" one would degrade them.[34] "Let the first magistrate be a professed infidel," a New York minister threatened during a later election, ". . . and to frequent public worship will become unfashionable." Elect an infidel, and "you will declare, by a *solemn national act*" that you have no religion "in your collective character."[35] Through a majestic power of this kind, gentry leaders expected that Washington quite literally would embody the precious national spirit, and in a decentralized land with so few visible symbols of national power, it was a necessary dream. As Jefferson joined the new government, he summarized these hopes to Lafayette: "If the President can be preserved a few years till habits of authority and obedience can be established, generally, we have nothing to fear."[36]

Around the peak of the hierarchy gathered a small group of gentlemen who vied for the right to serve as the president's counselor, set the tone and direction of the new government, and consequently participate in shaping an American society. They too rested their claims to leadership on character. Although each of them entered office in the belief that he deserved power, none of them minimized its risks. As the principals in a personal government, they understood its rules. Every action a leader took once again placed his character in the balance. At a critical turn in the national experiment, his reputation might soar or sink. And to a gentleman they were the proud, ceaseless guardians of that "sacred honour."

As their first task they had to map the human environment. In his home territory a gentleman could rely against almost any contingency on an inner core of family, neighbors, and longtime associates. In a setting filled with acquaintances and strangers, however, these natural sources of allegiances no longer sufficed. Then whom could a person trust? Among the keepers of the national revolution, the favored touchstone was the revolutionary experience itself. For those gentry leaders who had gambled on a confrontation with Britain in 1776, the Revolutionary War molded their lives, and by standards as idiosyncratic as the decisions to revolt, each of them drew from that experience a circle of comrades who stood apart from all other human relations. This revolutionary fraternity might exclude a lifelong neighbor in favor of a temporary colleague at a peak moment in that man's revolution. By an equally private calculus, individuals selected some of the war's outstanding leaders and rejected others as their true compatriots in revolution. Once formed, these personal circles transformed the ordinary rules governing gentry associations. A revolutionary bond, for example, joined John Adams to Mercy Warren and Thomas Jefferson to Abigail Adams in ways that violated the customary male banishment of women from public affairs. It enabled Elbridge Gerry to retain the confidence of both Adams and Jefferson at the point of greatest hostility between the two, despite his own substantial differences with each one, and eventually it allowed Adams and Jefferson themselves to renew their friendship through the mediation of another fraternity member, Benjamin Rush. Although qualities of temperament, style, and judgment seemed to make Washington and Patrick Henry polar opposites, a revolutionary connection somehow maintained their strange, strained relationship. Through these fraternities, the revolutionary gentry defined themselves, in Jefferson's simple language, as a distinctive "generation" whose "mutual labors & perils begat mutual confidence and influence."[37]

The same criterion also worked marvelously as a source of national authority. Year after year the talisman of revolutionary leadership continued to work its magic in American politics. The perennial governors —John Hancock in Massachusetts, George Clinton in New York, Thomas Mifflin in Pennsylvania, and Patrick Henry in Virginia—merely presented themselves to the people as first characters of their states' revolutions, and the voters made them first characters of their states' political hierarchies. Before 1789 the one national analogue was the Society of the Cincinnati, an organization of officers from the Continental Army and Navy. Inevitably its influence in national affairs ranked among the most controversial topics of debate in the 1780s. Such sober gentlemen as Elbridge Gerry, Rufus King, and George Mason thought that as the sole organized expression of the national revolution, the Cincinnati would automatically dominate a national government. Once again, only Washington could ease those fears. In 1787, by avoiding a meeting of the society in Philadelphia and attending the Constitutional Convention instead, he located his prestige with the emerging government, and wherever he stood, the greatest revolutionary authority came to rest.

Next, the government's diverse officials, like any gentry gathering, had to order themselves in ranks of leaders and followers. Only Washington knew in advance where he belonged, and even he relied heavily on individuals whose support and trust he had already tested. As secretary of war he selected his quintessential field officer, the loyal and obedient Henry Knox. Washington's first choice for secretary of the treasury was Robert Morris, the general's bulwark in Philadelphia late in the war. Then for a series of critical appointments at difficult times during his presidency, Washington called the roll of his wartime aides-de-camp: Gouverneur Morris as minister to France, Hamilton as secretary of the treasury after Robert and Gouverneur Morris rejected the post, Edmund Randolph as attorney general and then Jefferson's successor as secretary of state, Monroe as Gouverneur Morris's successor in France, and finally James McHenry as Knox's replacement.

Below the president the rest of the gentlemen studied one another's behavior and probed one another's intentions to the mutual ends of gauging their colleagues' characters and preserving their own. As they sorted themselves in an unfamiliar environment, they developed an American variant of 18th-century court politics. It was a recognizably republican court: austere by European standards, thinned through the absence of church and military establishments, improvisational in its procedures, and short on sex. Yet the jealous competition for Washington's favor, the shifting patterns of personal alliance, and the dark hints of treason wove a Shakespearean web of intrigue over its affairs. Rumor and slander were the everyday weapons of political advantage. A gentleman's conversational asides, his dinner companions, his presence or absence from the seat of government—certainly his trip to another fiefdom such as the famous "botanical" journey of Jefferson and Madison into the northern states—all carried electric meanings in a personalized government of plot and counterplot. Friends wrote in code and hushed one another with cautions of silence. In fact, the interception of private letters and the suppression of unwanted information occurred so often that at times the fortunes of politics seemed to turn on the merits of its couriers. If a gentleman had no taste or talent for these endless games of parry and thrust, he soon slipped into the shadows of the new government. In the unfolding court drama Hamilton, Jefferson, and Madison emerged to join Washington as protagonists, and it was the interaction among these four that dominated the first round of government under the Constitution.

Washington knew that he mattered most. In an exemplary demonstration of gentry leadership, he fused his character to his office and lived the role of the hero president with the intense self-consciousness of a gentleman who was watching his every action as closely as he assumed others were. Because Washington set his own terms for executive leadership, its style reflected his special qualities of personality. A stiff public protocol suited his dignity, so it was followed. Lacking both the agility and fertility of mind to formulate policy himself, Washington commanded proposals from his counselors, sat on the throne of judgment, and expected absolute compliance with his decisions. His temperament followed the laws of inertia. Slow to get underway, he held doggedly to the course he eventually chose. He could appreciate a similar caution in others, but he despised vacillation. Advisers came and went according to their willingness to abide by these standards.

When Hamilton later referred to Washington as *"an aegis very essential to me,"* he merely noted the obvious with characteristic Hamiltonian brashness. By choice Washington responded to other people's initiatives, then selectively issued his indispensable stamp of approval. As he legitimized the new government itself, in other words, he also legitimized each of its major decisions. Yet if Washington was everybody's aegis, he was nobody's fool. He recognized that no significant step could be taken without his authority, and he husbanded his power so that it would last throughout a difficult presidency. Although increasingly criticized during his second term, he was never effectively challenged as America's guarantor of virtuous government. Opponents could only bark at the heels of the hero's decisions. Moreover, with the important exception of the Jay Treaty, the president endorsed just those policies that expressed his own convictions. As committed a centralizer as Rufus King or James Wilson, he expected the national government to stand paramount over the states, resist the pulls of local opinion, and quash disorders with whatever force they required. "I do not conceive we can exist long as a nation," he had written to Jay in 1786, "without having lodged some where a power, which will pervade the whole Union in as energetic a manner, as the authority of the different State Governments extends over the several States."[38] At the top of the new government the executive should dominate. Between the national government and the people no vertical axis should intrude. Hence, as Hamilton's domestic policies prevailed during Washington's tenure, so did Washington's sentiments.

By merging his honor with the government's, Washington did make the government vulnerable to one man's sensibilities. Among the revolutionary gentry, differences over policy always entailed character judgments, and debates over the major issues of government inevitably affected personal relations. Washington applied this general rule with unusual force. Benjamin Rush, no model of charity himself, tellingly called Washington "deficient in that mark of true greatness . . . *the talent to forgive.*"[39] In response to the antifederalism of his old neighbor and associate George Mason, Washington abruptly severed ties. When Oliver Wolcott and Timothy Pickering arranged the dramatic confrontation between Washington and Edmund Randolph in 1795, the conspirators calculated both principals exceedingly well. With no hesitation, the president thrust off one of his most trusted associates. Intimations of personal criticism raised Washington's sensitivities to their icy heights. Mason's great sin in 1787 may well have been his harsh statements about an "elective monarchy" when everybody knew who America's first elected monarch would be. Both Madison's fall from grace and the president's grim drive against the Whiskey Rebellion in 1794 stemmed from their common linkage in Washington's mind to those democratic-republican clubs that were noisily attacking his reputation. The same web of pride bound Washington to the Jay Treaty, the crucial event of his second term. The gentlemen he suspected as his enemies were also the treaty's enemies; its loudest critics were also his critics. When his animus toward its opponents outweighed his own distaste for the treaty, he signed it.

Always the most effective route to Washington's mind lay through his honor. No one traced the path more daringly than Hamilton, who risked the president's terrible ire by striking so hard but who reached his goal so often by thrusting straight at it. Might the president decline a second term in 1792? Hamilton's phrases jabbed at the general's tender core: ". . . your declining would be deplored as . . . critically hazardous to your own reputation . . . indeed it would have been better, as it regards your own character, that you had never consented to come forward, than now to leave the business unfinished and in danger of being undone . . . an imputation either of want to foresight or want of firmness. . . ."[40] To soothe the pain, Hamilton assured the president that once again the electoral vote would be unanimous. Even in 1796, as Washington longed to retire, Hamilton held him ready for an emergency. The weary president, caught in a hero's calling, echoed Hamilton's latest appeal to him and acknowledged that "imperious circumstances . . . might render a retreat dishonorable."[41]

Washington's stolidity provided a tableau of strength for the new government, and a relatively uncomplicated mind freed him to make the most of his appointed role. It was Hamilton, the master mechanic of Washington's tough, simple machinery, who supplied the internal dynamics for the first presidency, and in Hamilton's case, it was the private complexities behind the public mask that accounted for his unexpected success. A less original thinker than Madison and a less far-ranging one than Jefferson, Hamilton used other people's ideas more effectively than either of them. He made no important contribution in 1787 to the shaping of a novel constitution, but he grasped its possible applications more quickly than its creators. He rode to power on the borrowed prestige of Robert Morris' financial and political network, wielded the borrowed authority of Washington, and accomplished more in an exceptionally short time than either of them could have achieved. Hamilton's mind concentrated marvelously on its purposes. As a tactician and logician, he had no American peer. While his contemporaries were pondering principles and piling allusions, Hamilton moved briskly to his task and dispatched it with crisp phrases. When he garbled an argument, as in a statement to Washington on America's neutrality in 1790, he did it in order to scramble the issue. Nevertheless, his was a supple rather than a subtle intelligence. To attain such clarity of vision, Hamilton had to hold the focus narrow. He saw a long way, but he excluded a great deal in the process.

With little taste for legislative bargaining, Hamilton willingly entered Washington's cabinet as secretary of the treasury and assumed command of the centralizing federalists by giving substance to their impulses. The heart of his economic program—the comprehensive funding of war debts, the creation of a national bank, the generation of income from a tariff and an excise tax—he adapted from British precedents by way of Robert Morris. Never the blind imitator, however, Hamilton knew exactly how these particular means should achieve his particular end: molding a new core of central power. First, these policies would establish the national government's economic independence: credit abroad, the resources at home to conduct its affairs proudly, and the funds to arm itself against its enemies. Correlatively, his program would attract loyalty to the national government by demonstrating its capacity to manage its own affairs, disperse benefits, and maintain order. Hamilton envisaged ambitious Americans gravitating to the national government much as a transatlantic constellation of interests had once revolved around America's royal governments. For the lost imperial level in a colonial society, he would substitute a new national level for an American society. Where the British had faltered in applying force against colonial unrest and allowed a revolution, Hamilton's government would eliminate domestic trouble swiftly and secure the whole society.

There was a wealth of genius in the scheme as Hamilton implemented it. By expressing a pure version of the Philadelphia Convention's centralism, it commanded enthusiastic support from the most powerful bloc of gentlemen who had sponsored the Constitution. The British origins of the program meant that both its outlines and the habits to sustain it were already familiar to a scattered American gentry who would have had great difficulty agreeing on a fresh set of premises. Moreover, it fell within the broad bounds of republicanism as almost all national gentry defined it in 1789. To later attacks on his republican credentials, Hamilton simply pointed to *The Federalist,* which Jefferson himself extolled as a pinnacle of republican wisdom. If his co-author Madison qualified as a republican, so did Hamilton, who throughout his career hewed more closely to the reasoning in *The Federalist* than his Virginia collaborator. Indeed, Hamilton remained strikingly persistent and clear in his objectives. An unreconstructed Philadelphia centralizer to the end, he stuck with the principle of executive supremacy even after Jefferson's victory in 1800. He never wavered in his conviction that state power posed the primary danger to an American nation. After 1794, when most Federalists were using "Jacobin" and "French" to identify the treasonous Republicans, Hamilton continued to prefer "anti's," and by that term he meant the same old state-based opposition from the 1780s who wanted to dilute the power of an executive-dominated national government. Every major tactic Hamilton adopted, from the federal funding of state debts and the national suppression of tax evaders in the early nineties to the recruitment of a national army and the punishment of recalcitrant states in the late nineties, reflected this single-minded pursuit of a precisely defined goal. Those who followed him would always know their enemies.

Hamilton's enemies, in turn, might have been less shocked if they had known him as the Publius of *Federalist* 37: "I acknowledge my aversion to every project that is calculated to disarm the government of a single weapon, which in any possible contingency might be usefully employed for the general defense and security."[42] He chose to seize objectives, not negotiate for them, and in his boldness he spread his plans across the table for a horrified opposition to see: the primacy of executive leadership, the elevation of national authority, the detachment of both senators and representatives from their constituents, the desire for a national army. Hamilton did not await the emergence of a new national society; he set out to build one. Fittingly, he had no use for Madison's theory of self-canceling factions in a large republic. Nothing happened, he re-

minded himself at the Philadelphia Convention, unless someone made
it happen. Hence he constructed the economic magnets to attract a commercial elite. When most moderate federalists and antifederalists pas-
sively assumed that the representatives from each state would vote as a
unit, Hamilton thrust his power into the House, recruited individuals to
his cause, and formed his own personal coalition. In fact, during his early
years in office he drew as much strength from Congress as from the
president himself. Here lay the secret to his leadership among so many
status-conscious gentlemen who were his seniors in age and social prestige. They wanted what he wanted, but he, not they, went out to get it.
While Washington and Jay stood pat, Hamilton acted. While George
Cabot of Boston and Ralph Izard of Charleston never transcended their
local circles, Hamilton did battle for a new nation. Acknowledging the
difference, they deferred to a young leader whom almost no one had
expected to figure prominently in Washington's administration.

A second source of Hamilton's leadership came from an efficiency
peculiarly his own. Never wasting motion, he set a whirlwind pace next
to the measured movements of his contemporaries, and, as Napoleon
would demonstrate in Europe, speed itself was a potent tactic in battle.
In each successful engagement—the ratification of the Constitution in
New York, the incorporation of Vermont into the union, the enactment
of an economic program—Hamilton pushed his opponents on the defensive by mastering the issues, coordinating his forces, and driving them
to victory. While Madison and Jefferson were still wrestling with complexities, Hamilton, the man who visualized each issue as a fight to win,
had already struck. That aura of action was particularly attractive to such
younger gentlemen as Oliver Wolcott and William Loughton Smith.
Hamilton's letters had none of Jefferson's courtliness and indirection. To
his lieutenants he used quick, intimate phrasing that suggested the dash
of a Dumas hero. Yet he wrote not as a comrade but as a commander,
often an imperious one at that. Hamilton's leadership best suited those
young gentlemen with a strong sense of hierarchy whose heads naturally
cocked upward for their orders.

Action did not mean passion. The reverse side of Hamilton's method-
ical command was a distinctive freedom from the emotional snarls of his
colleagues, a coolness that derived much more from a psychological detachment than from an even temperament. The French Revolution did
not rattle and frighten Hamilton as it did other Federalists. Without their
thirst for revenge, he read them lessons in the tactical use of force when
they simply wanted to punish. In public life Hamilton gave no evidence
of loving his friends or hating his enemies—including Aaron Burr. He
surveyed the gentlemen around him like a student of the breed. About
an able and industrious lieutenant, William Loughton Smith, Hamilton

wrote matter-of-factly to Washington: "He is popular with no description of men, from a certain *hardness* of character. . . ."[43] Hamilton would never let Smith's or any other man's ambition interfere with his. In the midst of deadly partisan warfare, Hamilton said a good word for Madison and tried to calm the worst fears about Jefferson, his two most powerful antagonists in national affairs. Characteristically, he neither enjoyed nor sought a personally close relation with Washington. This peculiar style of a chess master playing with the pieces on an American board led Talleyrand to single him out as the one gentry leader who "would understand Europe."

Born a bastard in the West Indies, raised to prominence in New York by an advantageous marriage, and drawn to the top of the national hierarchy by Washington's patronage, he could never completely shake the reputation of a marginal man, a rootless adventurer, as Jefferson insinuated to Washington and John Adams blurted in fury to Abigail. His enemies touched an essential truth about him that at one level Hamilton himself recognized. Significantly, the only time in public battle that he lost his temper, ignored his own rules, and squandered his authority came in response to President Adams' charge that the foreign-born Hamilton was leading a foreign faction within the United States.* At another level, however, Hamilton clearly did not understand the Hamilton difference. By operating a step removed from the involvements of his contemporaries, he saw what they missed, and hence he could maneuver with a remarkable precision. Yet by escaping their turmoils, Hamilton missed what they saw, and hence he could lose contact with the wellsprings of American political life. In 1790 his singular vision led him to the pinnacle of power; by 1800 his singular blindness had toppled him. Even as he approached the peak Hamilton revealed this ambiguous mixture of strength and weakness. In the simultaneous struggles to win congressional votes for debt assumption and to fix the future site of the national capital, Hamilton shrewdly encouraged his opponents on debt assumption to expend their political energies on locating the capital between Maryland and Virginia. Without the usual gentry sensibilities, Hamilton failed to recognize the price of his concentration: isolating the capital from the centers of economic power, placing it in a mediating position between suspicious southerners and northerners alike, and preparing the

---

* Hamilton's precarious movements between safety and jeopardy approximate the dangerous boundary-hopping between orthodoxy and deviance that Erik Erikson considers typical of the marginal stepson/bastard: the impeccable New York conservative *and* the flamboyant revolutionary, the detached theoretician of force *and* the soldier courting death, the steely tactician *and* the rash pamphleteer, the designer of rational state policies *and* the dreamer of romantic imperial ventures, the cool calculator of a social marriage *and* the hot pursuer of a foolish affair, and so on down an impressively long list.

way for Jeffersonian nationalism even before Jefferson took office. Where the peak of the hierarchy rested geographically had a profound symbolic importance, but Hamilton so readily discarded symbol for substance because he did not perceive how much substance other gentlemen invested in the symbol.

Unlike Hamilton, Jefferson brought the credentials of a leader with him to Washington's administration. As principal author of the Declaration of Independence, he ranked among the most visible revolutionary patriots, and as minister to France from 1785 to 1789, he represented the new nation at the critical center of its European support. The grace of his prose, the range of his mind, and the breadth of his interests had already established his reputation at home as one of America's outstanding intellects and even made him a minor celebrity abroad. In some New England circles, Jefferson was considered too susceptible to the radical currents of continental philosophy to be wholly reliable. No one, however, took him lightly. His assignment as secretary of state placed him, along with Vice-President John Adams, in the tier of leaders just below Washington.

Although these sources of prestige satisfied his fellow gentry, they did not speak precisely to Jefferson's capacity for leadership in the new government. To the special challenges of its first administration, he also brought with him certain gentry weaknesses that placed him at a signal disadvantage to the more detached Hamilton. If Hamilton eventually died for his honor, Jefferson devoted many more waking hours to the preservation of his. The need to check his actions and measure his words for their effect on his reputation not only drained Jefferson's attention; it slowed his reflexes in court battle. Like other gentry, Jefferson felt adrift without an anchoring group of associates who would reinforce his self-esteem and supplement his own understanding of public policy. Where Hamilton quickly created his network through command, Jefferson wove his gradually through gentlemanly exchange. Conversations and letters were the kinetics of Jefferson's leadership, merely the instruments of Hamilton's. Hence, in a strange setting Jefferson required a good deal of time to construct a comfortable network. Even more than most of his peers, he assumed that he would have the time. His suggestion to Madison that "a twelvemonth" elapse between the passing and the implementing of a law under the Constitution revealed a sense of government pace that could not reckon with Hamilton's style. Add to these characteristics Jefferson's considerably lesser skills in close court maneuver— "I do not understand bargaining nor possess the dexterity requisite to make them," he acknowledged to Madison—and his weaknesses became the backdrop to highlight Hamilton's strengths.[44]

In one other way Jefferson's gentry heritage complicated his emergence as a government leader. Jefferson the reputed democrat had a more deeply ingrained sense of hierarchy than Hamilton the reputed aristocrat. Hamilton used it; Jefferson lived it. That sensitivity to hierarchical propriety helped to account for his persistent deference to such a conservative gentleman as Edmund Pendleton and his ability in 1796 to consider granting John Adams the presidency in case of a tie between them, despite his suspicions about the vice-president's republicanism. He was Adams' "junior," he explained. Jefferson regarded Burr's hankering to take advantage of their tie four years later as an unforgivable sin against rank. When a contest for the presidency brewed in 1808 between his close friends Madison and Monroe, Jefferson applied all his persuasive charm to ensure that the two men would take office in proper sequence: first Madison, who was senior in service, then Monroe.

Hamilton, by contrast, manipulated presidential possibilities like tokens in a game. In the long run that practice hurt him badly, but in the early nineties his keen-eyed appraisal of the first president gave him an additional advantage over Jefferson. Where Hamilton already thought of Washington as his aegis, Jefferson viewed him on one side of a great divide with "the residue of mankind, on the other."[45] Although adamantly opposed to the constitutional provision for presidential reelection, Jefferson happily waived his principles "during the life of our great leader."[46] When Washington followed Hamilton's path, Jefferson responded with a deep sadness, and in his most notorious letter of criticism, he likened the president not to Caesar but to Samson, the pure, deluded giant who was being "shorn by the harlot England."[47] That posture seriously hampered Jefferson early in the 1790s. Not only did Washington's approval of Hamilton's policies muffle Jefferson's criticism, but Jefferson's forlorn pursuit of that same approval also blunted his counterpolicies. For personal as much as public reasons, Jefferson continued to seek Washington's benediction even as he was leaving the administration, and in his notes he carefully preserved Washington's flattering plea that he could not "find another character" suitable for Jefferson's high office.[48]

Obtuseness as well as awe contributed to Jefferson's confusion over Washington's course. Unlike Hamilton, Jefferson was a mediocre judge of his associates. He distributed his trust with a disconcertingly lavish hand, confiding private letters to couriers who delivered them to his enemies, recommending officials who abused their offices, and revealing his ardent republicanism to conservatives who agreed with his opponents. Although that openness made him a warm and generous friend, it left him vulnerable to numerous mistakes, especially his failure to gauge the wide gap between his version of federalism and Washington's. They had served in different settings during the Revolution, often differed in

Virginia politics, and remained in touch only out of mutual respect. Because it was inconceivable to Jefferson that a leader he revered could actually disagree with him on basic issues, he characteristically let faith triumph over the evidence.

As Jefferson was feeling his way around the new government, he faced policy questions in his field of lowest competence, economics. Issues of finance alternately obsessed, angered, and depressed him, no doubt in part because of his long, doleful slide into personal debt. His own ventures into public economic planning withered under scrutiny. When he outlined a program for abolishing debts every nineteen years, for example, Madison gently, systematically, exposed its impracticality, and in later years, Jefferson repeated the general goal without the embarrassing details. The longer he lived with Hamilton's economic policies, the more bitter he grew and the more obscure they grew until in 1802 he simply abandoned all hope of understanding their legacy. An otherwise comprehending intelligence should not have faltered over a program that relied on the customary economic wisdom of the day, but the fact that it did set immediate limits on Jefferson's leadership in 1790.

Jefferson's confusion over economic matters was doubly important because he also considered them basic to America's experiment in national republicanism. After a revolution spent mostly in Virginia, he left for Europe still a provincial, and the American vision that other gentry sharpened in their own national politics came to Jefferson from his European experience. In its mass poverty he saw the most horrible danger his own nation could face. If the American people ever sank to a similar level, American liberties would sink irretrievably with them. That fear sent Jefferson on an urgent quest for first causes. The immediate blame for such mass destitution he assigned to taxation, and those taxes, in turn, flowed from the terrible burdens of public debt. What generated the debt? Wars above all else. And who precipitated the wars? Monarchs above all others. The people, given a voice in their own behalf, would never have buried themselves beneath this mountain of oppression. Jefferson had completed an iron circle of logic: monarchy to war to debt to poverty to tyranny and hence back to monarchy again. Although he condemned the churches, hereditary privileges, and illiteracy as auxiliary agents in this awful sequence, Jefferson focused on the circle itself as his primary guide to public policy.

The ramifications of this crucial European lesson spread in every direction. Jefferson's abhorrence of excise taxes, his conception of a sound military policy, his search for alternatives to war, his dream of territorial expansion, all flowed in large measure from his central insight of the late 1780s. Immediately, however, Jefferson turned it to two particular purposes. First, he wanted to eliminate all traces of "the Paper System."

Government finances, he wrote in 1788, should rely exclusively on bullion, for paper was "only the ghost of money, and not money itself."[49] The real ghost, of course, was the specter of European war finance that floated on a dark sea of interest-bearing, tax-inducing paper. Bullion alone would not purchase much of an American war around 1790. When Jefferson used the ominous term "an interest," he invariably meant those who held debt certificates. To Washington he defined "a pure legislature" as one "cleansed of all persons interested in the bank or public stocks."[50]

Second, Jefferson applied his European lesson to America's new structure of government. Before he arrived in France, Jefferson stood firmly with other keepers of the national revolution in deploring legislative excesses, with his own tribulations as a wartime governor the painfully vivid example. He never abandoned that concern, nor, as Hamilton noted, did he ever lose his regard for executive authority. Jefferson too welcomed greater "tone in the governing powers."[51] Nevertheless, his European experience cast these issues in a very different perspective. There centralized power extinguished liberties and released its beasts of prey to "devour" the poor. The Indians of America, with no government at all, enjoyed an "infinitely greater degree of happiness" than the citizens of Europe, Jefferson concluded.[52] In that mood Jefferson responded initially to the Constitution as a moderate antifederalist. "Indeed I think all the good of the new constitution," Jefferson decided in Paris, "might have been couched in three or four new articles to be added to the good, old, and venerable fabrick" of the Articles of Confederation.[53] In Virginia, Richard Henry Lee was arriving at the same judgment.

The support of so many other gentlemen whom Jefferson admired, the prospect of Washington as the first president, and the addition of a bill of rights changed that initial reaction into quite an optimistic acceptance by 1790. Yet Jefferson's personal route to this conclusion left him with a distinctive point of view toward America's problems. Aristocracy, one of the angriest issues in the recent constitutional debate, scarcely crossed his mind. Instead, he isolated monarchy as the sole republican enemy and lumped all other elements of government into a common countervailing force. Appropriately, he reserved his deepest satisfaction for the Constitution's "effectual check to the Dog of war by transferring the power of letting him loose from the Executive to the Legislative body, from those who are to spend to those who are to pay." In the neatest summary of his attitudes he wrote Madison: "I own I am not a friend to a very energetic government. It is always oppressive."[54] "Energetic," one of Hamilton's favorite words, denoted an independent executive leadership with the will and the power to impose its authority across the nation. In a word, Jefferson saw a circle: monarchy-war-debts-tyranny. Unlike the rest of Washington's court, he retained considerable confidence in the states as the people's guardians in national affairs. Hence, without recognizing the constitutional confusions and implications, Jefferson brought to office a reflexive sympathy for the components of a vertical axis in the new government, a sense that legislature, states, and people would naturally league in resistance against a dangerously assertive national executive.

The composite of Jefferson's beliefs weakened his national leadership in the short run and strengthened it in the long run. Hamilton, with a specific agenda and an itch to move, epitomized the hard side of the new government. Its adherents knew what they wanted—centralized authority—and accepted Hamilton's directions to achieve it. Jefferson expressed a side of federalism so soft that it blended indistinguishably with national antifederalism. No program could have represented the mixture of persuasions that fell loosely beneath this cover, and indeed no sentiment of common purpose united them. Appropriately, Jefferson's ideal was an elusive harmony among society's diverse parts, a felicitous ordering of the whole that he called "happiness." In personal philosophy he inclined toward the "tranquility" of the Epicureans. The ultimate compliment he could bestow on his own presidential cabinet was its "harmony." Even when Jefferson appeared to be tolerating disorder, as in his distant comment on Shays' uprising—"a little rebellion now and then is a good thing"—he did so in the spirit of the prevailing scientific faith in a promptly self-correcting equilibrium—"and as necessary in the political world as storms in the physical."[55] After the storm came the calm. By its nature, Jefferson's ideal set him in a responsive posture. As much as Hamilton took the initiative, Jefferson gave it to him. In 1790, Jefferson had no plan to impose and no inclination to command. His leadership depended on persuasion, not dictation. If in the course of political affairs it was normal "for liberty to yield, and government to gain ground," he would be waiting.[56] In the meantime, the field was Hamilton's.

The long-range strength of Jefferson's federalism lay in its elasticity. Stretching across the entire framework of American government, it accommodated a sturdy executive and a vigorous legislature, a legitimate general government and an extensive role for the states in national affairs. His faith in the gravitational powers of the new national government enabled Jefferson to await the peaceful pull of society's parts into a symmetrical American system. The Hamiltonian precept of enforcing the law with military power appalled him. Because Jefferson missed the convention in Philadelphia, he never felt Madison's emotional attachment to the Constitution's precise, hard-won details. More than any of his colleagues in 1790, Jefferson viewed America's problems in social rather than structural terms. To approach the Constitution in a republican spirit, he thought, would suffice. By the same token, Jefferson carried no grudges against the antifederalists, with whom, after all, he shared many convictions. Such fine gentlemen as Monroe and Gerry were simply guarding America's liberty in the tradition of '76. Jefferson saw himself as the natural friend to everyone of goodwill on either side of a momentary difference of opinion. In all, his vision encompassed a larger proportion of America in a more benign spirit than any among his peers, and it prepared Jefferson to become the most comprehensively national leader of his time.

Madison served as Jefferson's partner in constructing a national society from this design. Alone among the primary actors in the court drama of the early nineties, Madison drew his prestige not from the Revolution but from the creation of the Constitution. Only as recruiter, architect, and advocate for the new government did he qualify for the top ranks of national leadership, and to the end of his life he based both his reputation and his self-esteem on those events. Where Jefferson died extolling the liberties of mankind, Madison departed with the hope that the union "be cherished and perpetuated." Those who worked closely with him developed a deep admiration for his talents. Washington willingly acknowledged Madison's stature, let him shape the first inaugural address, and continued to seek his advice even after they moved well apart on government policy. Nevertheless, in an age when the badges of revolutionary service marked the great leaders, Madison always operated at a disadvantage. The least inhibited by pride among the major figures of his time, he accepted his handicap, assumed the need to function through other men, and attached himself to a revolutionary star—first to Washington, then, in the era's most famous bonding, to Jefferson.

No doubt the subtle effects of his dependence on Jefferson contributed to Madison's long migration from extreme centralizer in 1787 to ideologue of a state-rooted republic in 1800. The steps he took, however, followed logically from his lifelong and almost obsessive commitment to the principle of balance. With a careful hand he distributed the elements of a problem at the two ends of an old-fashioned scale, then adjusted for the slightest tip. A republic could not be too large or too small, a government too strong or too weak, a representative too independent or too servile. When legislative powers waxed in the 1780s, Madison moved to redress them with executive powers. When fears of centralization threatened to stall the experiment in national government, he compensated with greater attention to the states and the people. When Hamilton exuded executive energy, Madison predictably asserted the authority of the House. Then when the entire top level of the national government expanded the scope of its power, he became champion of the states' end of the vertical axis. Even as president he set himself in the

balance, calculating his actions so that they did not outweigh the rights
of Congress or the states or his own cabinet members. More predictably
than Jefferson's, Madison's natural posture was responsive: now add a
little at the other end of the scale.

Where Jefferson's mind took creative surges of speculation without
consolidating what it found, Madison's systematically explored the
boundaries of the customary world and produced monuments of thoroughness. Madison worked best with one issue at a time: the role of
representatives, the meaning of parties, the freedom of speech. Jefferson
cast himself in the role of the great synthesizer who would preside over
a synchronized whole: the first violinist guiding a string quartet, the
builder standing in the great hall of his own design. Appropriately, Madison had little of his friend's passion for music and architecture, and he
had no flair at all for the drama of leadership. In collaboration with
Jefferson, however, the limitations of the balancer worked wonders. To
Jefferson's sanguine faith in such patriotic paragons as Washington and
Adams, Madison countered with stinging appraisals of their actual behavior in the 1790s. When Jefferson floundered before Hamilton's personal assaults and logical skills, Madison, a much better debater than
Jefferson, crafted the essays in rebuttal. Jefferson extended their circle of
support with his vision and charm; Madison fed that support with his
closely reasoned arguments and practical advice. As Jefferson indulged
his tendency to avoid nasty conflicts, Madison, with a remarkable self-
control under attack, infused his friend with some toughness and held
him at his post as leader of an opposition. All the while, with little
touches of deference, Madison reinforced his relation as junior to Jefferson's senior. Here, too, he was the responder.

As Washington took office, none of these gentry leaders questioned the
need for authoritative action to establish the new government. A few
wisps of doubt about executive power in 1789 gathered into clouds the
next year, then broke in a storm over the assumption and funding of
America's revolutionary debt. The temporary consensus around Washington scattered, and with the enactment of excise taxes and a national
bank in 1791 the gentry dispersed even more. Although the policies
themselves mattered profoundly to the government's leaders, they had
only one sure way of understanding the ultimate purpose of a policy.
Always at the heart of gentry government lay the character of the governors, and hence these conflicts translated into intense struggles over
individual honor.

The first rift occurred between Hamilton and Madison. In one sense
their differences over debt assumption simply mirrored their different
casts of mind. With characteristic boldness Hamilton surveyed the ex-

traordinary mess of wartime debts and proposed a relatively simple, workable scheme: gather everything into one pot and fund the whole lot at face value. He was setting the cornerstone for a structure of centralized finance. Just as characteristically, Madison addressed the debts as a distinct problem in equity and countered with a doubtfully practical formula that would have divided payments between the original creditors and those who later bought pieces of the debt at a discount. He followed a particular principle rather than a general plan. Despite pressures from Virginia to resist Hamilton's proposal, Madison remained too much the centralizer—too committed to a clear national resolution of this fundamental issue—to make a prolonged fight exclusively on such dubious ground. Another contest was transpiring beneath the issues.

Hamilton entered Washington's cabinet on a rising curve. A secondary figure at the Philadelphia Convention, he then shot upward by directing the battle for ratification in the pivotal state of New York. Madison's light, on the other hand, was flickering. As payment for his inestimable contributions to the Constitution, his enemies in the Virginia government insulted him by choosing two antifederalists for the Senate and forced Madison into a difficult, demeaning contest for a seat in the House of Representatives. Hamilton, aspiring to become Washington's prime minister, looked upon the House as a body of raw recruits awaiting their commander, and he cast the reserved Virginian as his lieutenant. Madison, acutely sensitive to his uncertain position, expected equality with his peer in the executive branch. Instead, with no more than a gesture toward consultation, Hamilton declared policy and assumed obedience. Although Madison normally conceded a considerable leeway to the executive's "rulers," he could tolerate no further belittlement. What came to him by fiat he rejected. Afterward each of these gentlemen interpreted the rift in the language of betrayal.

Appropriately, Jefferson arrived late to the capital in New York, not dreaming in March 1790 that anything irrevocable could have happened during "a twelvemonth" of peacetime gentry government. With the tasks of diplomacy confronting him and the excitements of France still dancing in his head, he slipped blindly into the morass of the debt debate. A man who automatically thought of the Revolution in American terms —"nine-tenths of these debts were contracted for the general defense"— had no difficulty accepting a thoroughly national solution. Nor could Jefferson muster deep sympathy for the pleas of this or that state, even Virginia: "It is a measure of necessity," and in the name of national solvency conflicting parties had "to give as well as take." Nevertheless, as he admitted with amiable honesty, he was not "very competent" on the issue. "Without pretending to a thorough understanding of the subject, I am apt to suppose difficulties pretty nearly balanced on both sides," he wrote after a survey of gentry characters, "when I see honest and able men so equally divided in sentiment on a question. . . ."[57] He negotiated rather vaguely with Hamilton and Madison, warmly welcomed an eventual location of the national capital on the Potomac, and fretfully awaited a legislative resolution for the debt, which finally came in August with a few modifications of Hamilton's original plan.

Only as the purposes of this debt funding dawned on him did Jefferson see the terrible nature of his defeat. In reckoning with the nation's debts, he began where his European insights had left him. The whole objective of a debt program was liquidation, and the little Jefferson did contribute to the complex discussions in 1790 aimed at that one goal. Anticipating short-term gains in the European financial market, for example, Jefferson happily recommended the use of the proceeds to "[buy] up more principal, and thereby keep this salutary operation going."[58] Finally it penetrated that Hamilton's funding scheme would perpetuate rather than liquidate important parts of the debt. There it stood, the first link in Jefferson's deadly ring of debts-oppression-monarchy-war-debts. A policy that in Hamilton's mind would draw strength and respect to the center of the new government in Jefferson's mind would erode its very foundations. From less apocalyptic premises, Madison sought the same end as Jefferson. In his only opportunity to advise Hamilton on a plan, Madison had insisted on one that "will put the debt in a manifest course of extinguishment," and early in the congressional debates he had alerted Jefferson to the dangers in Hamilton's program to "a final settlement and *payment* of the balance."[59] Yet Jefferson apparently allowed the presence of Hamilton's "sinking fund," which in British precedent and Virginia practice served to retire debts but in this scheme merely sustained their market value, to camouflage the New Yorker's purpose just too long. For this blunder he never forgave himself—but he always blamed Hamilton. He had been duped by a villain. As he realized his mistake, a national bank to secure the debt program was looming, and with Jefferson and Madison now united, the battle was on.

In the usual manner of court politics, the contest began sotto voce with private slanders. Then in 1791 Hamilton extended the range of battle by using the friendly *Gazette of the United States* to attack Jefferson, and the Virginians responded by establishing the *National Gazette*. Keeping the initiative, Hamilton arrayed his charges against Jefferson in two series of pseudonymous essays in 1792, and Madison retaliated that year with equal elaboration. All arguments thrust at the opponent's character: Jefferson the closet antifederalist, the abuser of Washington's trust, the fomenter of sedition within the government; Hamilton the disguised monarchist, the vilifier of the people, the distributor of corrupting government favors. Catiline and Caesar. By pressing more relentlessly than his enemies, Hamilton kept them in retreat. Even their actions were reactions. A matter of bruised honor, not a decision to take the offensive, spurred Jefferson to negotiate for his own newspapers: the *Gazette of the United States* had accused him of heading a "faction"! In a long letter for the record in September 1792, Jefferson was still making his case largely in negatives. He had not opposed the Constitution, not slighted the public credit, not abused his office, not slandered the government, and not interfered beyond the scope of his duties. Other than calling Hamilton an upstart and accusing him of bribery, Jefferson was too busy defending his own reputation to damage his antagonist's.

In an equally long letter for the record that May, Hamilton built a very different case on Madison's duplicity, Jefferson's deviousness, and their joint efforts to destroy his reputation. On the strength of his own character, Hamilton argued, sound government itself depended. Undermine the one and the other would fall. If the new government rested on its financial solvency, then it simultaneously rested on the reputation of the man whose program kept it solvent. Jefferson, knowing that his role in the public criticism of the administration skirted the edge of subversion as the gentry understood it, squirmed mightily to escape such charges. But only once in this long letter did Hamilton slip onto the defensive: "I assure you on my *private faith* and *honor* as a Man that there is not . . . a Monarchical party" in the government.[60] Significantly, while Jefferson wrote his apologia to Washington, hoping to preserve his honor in the great man's eyes, Hamilton sent his brief on legitimacy to one of Madison's former lieutenants in Virginia, hoping to drive a deeper wedge into his opponent's barony.

By gentry standards, nothing better expressed the character of the governors than their styles of governance.* Under all circumstances they had to uphold their own dignity as rulers and hence the integrity of the government they conducted. Assuming that their behavior radiated an influence throughout the nation, the new government's officials self-consciously made their choices on style according to their judgment on a proper republican balance and their sense of America's drift. An accent on the magisterial would counteract popular disruptions. A plain manner would resist the leanings toward monarchy or aristocracy. With a conviction that everything mattered, therefore, they inaugurated a government

---

* Most of the topics that I cover under style the gentry discussed as "forms," often plural with a small "f" to distinguish it from the singular, capitalized "Form"—or basic structure —of government. Even they found the use of the same word for two very important subjects sufficiently awkward to require explanatory asides, and I take my cue from that fact in substituting synonyms for their "forms": style, manner, ceremony, and the like. At the same time, their usage does remind us how subtly the concepts of Form and forms blended in their minds.

with nothing settled. Court politics by its nature was a study in nuances, and gentlemen who thought these early decisions would stamp the national character pondered each turn of procedure with the solemnity of Delphic priests. How should the president be addressed? Every alternative from "His Elective Highness" to "President of the United States" came freighted with republican connotations. Should he report to Congress and gather advice and consent in person from the Senate? After a brief, frustrating experiment, Washington answered with a resounding no. How should Congress, in turn, respond to the president? In acknowledging Washington's first inaugural address, senators with good revolutionary memories rejected the language of the British Parliament—"*his most gracious speech*"—as "the first step of the ladder in the ascent to royalty."[61] How should subordinate officers comport themselves? Not even the president was scrutinized more closely by suspicious republicans, and for his stuffy ways, the obstinate, tender John Adams received round after round of scorching criticism as an agent of monarchy. Should Washington's likeness appear on the nation's coins? ". . . [I]t has been a practice in Monarchies to exhibit the figures or heads of their Kings upon their coins . . . ," declared a watchdog of republican purity, "[and] it would be viewed by the world as a stamp of Royalty. . . ."[62] Congress settled on a replica of Liberty.

Glorification in bas-relief Washington did not covet, but a dignified government he certainly did. Both his personal and his political inclinations placed him firmly at the magisterial end of the spectrum in style. Just as he protected his own aloofness inside a sturdy case of formalities, so he expected the national executive to stand apart from the nation as a beacon of public order. Although he carefully avoided military dress, with its despotic intimations, he adopted the stiff rituals of office and moved comfortably with the trappings of gentry wealth around him. If, on a visit to Boston, it was necessary to have John Hancock carried to Washington's quarters on a litter, so be it. The president of the United States would never degrade his office by calling first on the governor of Massachusetts. In these decisions, Washington received enthusiastic support from many centralizing federalists, who not only encouraged displays of executive authority but also copied them in their own affairs. None of these gentlemen had the slightest doubts about his own republican credentials. Indeed, they thought of themselves as austere patriots. A guest at Jay's palatial home was promised "plain and friendly hospitality" in accordance with the "simplicity of our domestic management."[63] "My manner of living is plain," Washington remarked to a prospective visitor.[64] Europe, after all, offered far more glittering standards.

Jefferson and Madison had just these ominous European models in mind as they expressed their horror at executive pomp. Although Jefferson pictured his presidential hero as a tool of the designing monarchists, he found the plot no less dangerous for that. Madison agreed. As soon as Jefferson joined the administration, Madison warned him—in Jefferson's paraphrasing—that "the satellites and sycophants which surrounded [Washington] had wound up the ceremonials of the government to a pitch of stateliness which nothing but his personal character could have supported and which no character after him could ever maintain."[65] Nothing roused more concern among the critics of executive energy during Washington's first term. One summary of its sins appearing in the Virginians' own newspaper devoted nine of its ten points to style: exalted official titles; fancy and exclusive presidential entertainments; celebration of officials' birthdays; ceremonies on state occasions; ostentatious official parades; credit for the public happiness to government officials; large salaries; "royal and noble vices" such as drinking and swearing; official exclusiveness. Only in the tenth did the national debt appear.[66] When Madison tried to encapsulate the meaning of "anti republican" rule in America, he began with "the pageantry of rank."[67] Sadly, Jefferson concluded in 1793 that Washington himself was no longer an innocent. "Naked he would have been sanctimoniously reverenced," he wrote to Madison, "but enveloped in the rags of royalty, they can hardly be torn off without laceration."[68]

What made the style of governance so momentous was its revelation of a flow in affairs that was carrying the government toward one of those absolute divides in the gentry's architecture of categories, the critical boundary between a republic and something entirely different. Gentlemen who calculated in either-or terms could scarcely bear the implications of their own judgment on an evil turn in the nation's affairs. Every republic had its Rubicon, and after it was crossed, no one could turn back the march. The republic simply perished. Hence, gentry leaders set their lines of defense far in front of its banks and scanned the horizon for Caesars on the move. To a man they decried the terrible "tendencies" toward another form of government because anything more substantial meant irremediable disaster, and these warnings they supplemented with the customary wisdom on a fatal false step: ". . . from what slight beginnings the most extensive consequences have flowed"; "how easy the transition from a republic to any other form of Government. . . ."[69]

A tendency in motion required a Caesar in command. Thus the ultimate focus on character. It was Hamilton's presence as much as his programs that gave coherence to his opponents' thoughts. With their eyes on one evil genius, Jefferson and Madison saw everything following in logical sequence: the use of the debt to corrupt legislators, a national bank to extend the paper "interest," the inevitable demands for a standing army, and, of course, the trappings of monarchic pomp. Much later, when Jefferson had perfect confidence in the republicanism of the executive, he did not even comment on President Monroe's gala entertainments—so fancy, in fact, that they impoverished him. Cato's innocence sanctified Caesar's sins.

During the winter of 1791–92, when Madison mounted a full-scale public campaign against Hamilton's rule, he translated this entire packet of concerns into the language of gentry analysis and directed his attack at the central fears of the antifederalists in 1787 and 1788. As his three basic forms of government Madison offered one "operating by a permanent military force," one "operating by corrupt influence," and one "deriving its energy from the will of the people."[70] The first two were simply the old enemies in transparent disguises. The gentry automatically equated monarchy with militarism and aristocracy with corruption. His particular phrasing, however, linked executive policies with some of the loudest antifederalist alarms—a standing army, a detached elite's illicit profits, patronage, and bargains. Madison's virtuous alternative, a democratically based republic, drew its "energy" not from the executive but from the "people." Praising the states as guarantors of the people's liberty, he raised once again the specter of "consolidation" and cautioned that the national government might yet swallow them. To label the Hamiltonian heresy, Madison selected one of George Mason's favorite terms in rejecting the Constitution, "mixed monarchy." Then to complete the vision of danger he validated the old charge that some delegates at the Philadelphia Convention had been "openly or secretly attached to monarchy and aristocracy, and hoped to make the Constitution a cradle for these hereditary establishments."[71] By then everyone knew that he was fingering Hamilton. Caesar and his cohort had been plotting at the very birth of the new government.

Hamilton started where his Virginia enemies did and came to exactly the opposite conclusions. He made debt funding the core of everything else he proposed, and in his own way he did build a circle of policies from it. Bold as always, Hamilton designed a structure of loans to subsidize the new government's normal operations as well as service the national debt, and in the process he contracted unusually burdensome obligations, even by European standards. Hence he not only needed new taxes; he also demanded their rigorous collection. When western Pennsylvanians balked at an excise tax in 1792, Hamilton advocated a dramatic show of military force to awe the outlaws, establish the national government's supremacy, and ensure its life-giving income. Asserting the national government's authority on such occasions really did require an army of its own, and with the anticipated expense of a standing army, Hamilton came full circle to the centralizing rationale behind his risky debt structure.

Just as Madison interpreted these policies in the framework of 1787 and 1788, so did Hamilton. Then Madison had joined him in defining "the real danger in our system [as] subversion of the National authority by the preponderancy of the State Governments."[72] Hamilton never wavered. Along the top of the national government he moved with a confident authority, viewing the House of Representatives with a touch of disdain and never doubting his ability to master its clumsy impulses. Indeed, the legislation making the secretary of the treasury Congress's agent gave him the special access that he needed to direct its affairs. Against the formidable power of the states, however, Hamilton stood a ceaseless vigil. When the Virginia legislature attacked his debt program in November 1790 as "dangerous to the rights and subversive of the interest of the people" and "repugnant to the Constitution of the United States," Hamilton instantly called it "the first symptom of a spirit which must either be killed or will kill the constitution." Should it not be crushed with "the collective weight" of the national government?[73] What the most powerful of the states pioneered in 1790, lesser ones, including Pennsylvania, then emulated. "I see that influence already penetrating into the National Councils & preverting their direction," Hamilton wrote ominously of these state forays. "Hence a disposition on my part . . . to erect every fence to guard [the national government] from depredations. . . ."[74] If the states pushed into national affairs, he would have to force them back into a passive sovereignty, "circumscribed within bounds." To Hamilton a direct line ran from the Virginia Resolutions of 1790 to Pennsylvania's criticism of the excise law to its own citizens' violations of the law, and he meant to cut that line by isolating the subversive Pennsylvania government and enforcing the tax with a display of national force. Pennsylvania was the convenient target, Virginia the ultimate one. Its Catilines would understand his lesson. Although cautious colleagues stalled Hamilton in 1792, the hunter knew how he would strike.

To Hamilton's inestimable advantage every move, every argument he made rang with legitimacy. Each of his measures passed through republican channels to become the law of the land. When Jefferson and Attorney General Randolph wrote constitutional briefs against parts of the Hamiltonian program, they were awkwardly hacking their way into enemy territory, and Hamilton neatly waylaid them with his applications of a federalist orthodoxy that the president already accepted. By 18th-century standards a persistent criticism of existing laws did threaten a government's foundations, and an open flouting of them did justify their military enforcement. Only "despicable" governments watched impotently as their authority drained away. In opposition Jefferson and Madison were being pushed where they had had no intention of going. Jefferson, the champion of Washington's radiating national authority in 1790, instructed the states the following year to erect "such barriers at the constitutional line as cannot be surmounted."[75] Madison, the exemplary centralizer of 1787, now shaped antifederalist arguments into a rationale of resistance to the government he had done so much to create. In effect, the Virginians found themselves standing among the disjointed parts of the national government's vertical axis without any plan for assembling them. Jefferson favored a defense through state initiatives. Yet the dissenting states were acting on their own, not at Jefferson's command, and the most important of their resolutions actually emanated from his bitter foe Patrick Henry. Madison, on the other hand, retained an old skepticism of state power, despite his recent propaganda in its behalf, and his primary hopes rested in the House. Unless the Virginians promptly built something from these pieces to brace their cause inside the new government, they would be shoved the final step beyond a legitimate opposition.

Jefferson's frustration over the strange turn in his fortunes did not immediately sharpen his insights or improve his tactics. Inexplicably, he was caught in a nightmare. Expecting to be secretary of almost everything in Washington's cabinet, he watched as this role was captured by a man who was his junior by any reasonable standard in a gentry hierarchy. Assuming that all Americans of good faith shared his soft version of a national republic, he became the ineffectual critic of an aggressively centralizing federalism. Anticipating respect from his colleagues, he reeled under persistent attacks on his character. Asking vindication from the hero of the Revolution, he received only cool evasions from his opponents' pillar of authority. Jefferson's last chance to reverse the tide began in December 1792, when William Branch Giles, a Virginia ally in the House, initiated an inquiry into Hamilton's operation of the Treasury. Characters were consistent wholes, the gentry believed, and Hamilton's enemies had not the slightest doubt that mounds of evil lay hidden in the records of his department. Instead, the futile investigation marked one more triumph for Hamilton. A helpless Jefferson condemned the "corrupt" legislature for exonerating a "corrupt" man, spun a fantasy of court revenge that would have legislated Hamilton's office from under him, and prepared to resign as secretary of state.

Every gentry leader cherished a vision of retirement in honor, and from the beginning of his service Jefferson had looked forward to such a gratifying departure. For him to leave in the shadow of dishonor, however, carried a multitude of dark connotations. In the context of court politics, an aggrieved lord's withdrawal from the seat of government was at best ambiguous, at worst incendiary. The taint of sedition for criticizing government policy placed his departure in the worse light. Madison recognized this and begged Jefferson to stay in office. Washington also realized it. With almost as much at stake in appearances as Jefferson, the president first tried to keep him in the cabinet, then worked to convince everybody, including Jefferson, that he was not leaving in disgrace. But Hamilton's circle, following the same train of logic, made no effort to resist its course. Jefferson, who had failed to disorganize the government from the inside, would now pursue his cause through an even more dangerous set of maneuvers from the outside. As "Publius," Hamilton had argued for the perpetual re-eligibility of a president on grounds that in defeat he might roam the land like a deposed monarch. Or in Gouverneur Morris's phrasing: "Shut the Civil road to Glory & he may be compelled to seek it by the sword."[76] So the sullen noble would return to the seat of his "Virginia party," gather his dissidents about him, and wait for his opportunity to renew the attack on legitimate government. Even Jefferson's old colleague John Adams, increasingly suspicious of the Virginian's motives, could not resist a simile of rebellion: "Jefferson thinks by this step to get a reputation as an humble, modest, meek man, wholly without ambition or vanity. He may even have deceived himself into this belief. But if the prospect opens, the world will see and he will feel that he is as ambitious as Oliver Cromwell."[77]

The Politics of Independence

"I could not have supposed when at Philadelphia that so little of what was passing there could be known . . . as is the case here," a disconsolate Jefferson wrote from Virginia immediately after his retirement. "Judging from this of the rest of the Union, it is evident to me that the people are not in a condition either to approve or disapprove of their government, nor consequently to influence it."[1] Court politics cast too shallow a net to reach the many local pockets of opposition to the government's policies, and hence the Hamiltonians had little difficulty dismissing their critics as merely a personal faction. Although Jefferson and Madison recognized the problem and tried to widen the range of support, their personal network, like Hamilton's system of patronage, turned loyalty back to a chief rather than outward toward a common public cause.

The summer before, Jefferson spotted the force that would transform this small web of partisan relationships. "The war [of revolutionary France against Europe]," he reported to Monroe, "has kindled and brought forward the two parties with an ardour which our own interests merely could never excite."[2] After two tentative years, the French Revolution began heating rapidly in 1791. The next year it surged abroad in continental war. At home revolutionaries abolished the monarchy, instituted egalitarian forms of address, and proclaimed a new era in human history. In January 1793, Louis XVI was beheaded, and a month later England and France were at war. As the fortunes of battle turned first against, then for its citizen armies, the French Revolution entered its most radical, Jacobin phase to the accompaniment of incessant decrees, factional struggles, and mass executions. Peaking in 1794, the Terror then subsided, and under a new constitution in 1795 the Directory sought to tame the revolution at home and consolidate its power abroad. Between 1794 and 1796, the reverberations from these momentous European events shattered the old barrier between America's court and its citizenry, reshaped the issues of political conflict, and stimulated a very different mobilization of a national society.

The American gentry responded to Europe's revolutionary tremors as neocolonials who saw their own independence at stake in the outcome. Since 1783 they had pictured their nation as a prisoner on parole, protecting its precarious freedom against international forces that it might elude but could never control. Even the best leaders and the most ingenious measures, they believed, could not stop the great powers from swaying America's citizens, corrupting its officials, or infiltrating its governments, scheming against the nation, allying against it, or warring against it. Jefferson's first thoughts on reading the Constitution went to Poland, plaything of Europe's titans. Partition, absorption: here were the apt analogies for America's jeopardy.

During the 1780s the gentry discussed these threats largely in terms of men and money. As colonies and then as a new nation, America attracted a steady flow of people with gentlemanly pretensions who in the 18th century moved easily across national boundaries in search of better opportunities. They dotted the revolutionary officer corps, the avenues of commerce, and various levels of government throughout the United States, and from a neocolonial perspective they constituted a pool of danger, not merely as ambitious individuals in their own right but as potential agents of a great power. As the gentry contemplated a no-man's-land of national government in 1787, it required no special talent to imagine someone with alien loyalties at the very center of authority. Almost every gentleman accepted Elbridge Gerry's axiom: "Persons having foreign attachments will be sent among us & insinuated into our councils, in order to be made instruments for their purposes."[3] These visions bore directly on the widespread fears of the Society of the Cincinnati, where foreigners mingled in the ranks of the revolutionary heroes, and of standing armies generally. Although Jay chose to remain aloof from the details of constitution-making in 1787, he did send one brief note to Washington: "Permit me to hint whether it would not be wise and reasonable to provide a strong check to the admission of foreigners into the administration of our national government, and to declare expressly that the commander-in-chief of the American army shall not be given to nor devolve on any but a natural-born citizen."[4] Yet could any president avoid seeking a foreign patron? George Mason pictured an American-born chief executive pardoning traitors and preparing the way for British recolonization. Jefferson, envisaging a presidential pawn in office for life, compressed these doubts into a sentence that told worlds about these gentry assumptions of a fragile independence: "A Galloman or an Angloman will be supported by the nation he befriends."[5]

The fear of foreign gold became the standard means of expressing the gentry's feelings of dependence, and here again the vague lines dividing praiseworthy enterprise from subversive activity only aggravated the issue. If a merchant profited from his personal connections in a foreign nation, did he sell his soul or just his goods? When the French, in the process of subsidizing the American Revolution, gave money to members of the Continental Congress, did they corrupt the government or merely distribute purses to deserving patriots? At the heart of these questions lay the gentry's instinctive assumption of weakness, and bribery served as a convenient way of reckoning with it. Bribery's influence could come in only one direction—from Europe to America. The gentry could not conceive of themselves retaliating in kind, as the XYZ affair of 1798 illustrated. If Americans surreptitiously passed money to the French, they were not bribing these officials but paying them tribute, another variation of the same Europe-to-America flow of power. The gentry's deepest doubts told them that America simply could not resist the determined, relentless pressure of a European giant. Translating that general feeling into personal vulnerability, they pictured an American taker for every European bribe, a receptivity to influence so pervasive and so ingrained that they had to build its presence into the structure of their new society.

Appropriately, everybody talked about it in the debate over the Constitution. Federalists made a united front against the European powers central to their campaign, Washington emphasized it at Philadelphia, *The Federalist* drummed on it, and other advocates echoed their arguments. But the simple issue of strength in union barely broached the complex problems of a neocolonial defense. Federalists and antifederalists alike, taking America's dependence for granted, disagreed violently over the Constitution's value in warding off the dangers. For example, would centralization or decentralization provide a sturdier shield? Without a binding union, Jay maintained, "every state would be a little nation, jealous of its neighbour, and anxious to strengthen itself, by foreign alliances, against former friends."[6] To which James Winthrop countered: ". . . it is evidently not of much importance to any foreign nation to purchase, at a very high price, a majority of votes in an assembly, whose members are continually exposed to recall. But give those members a right to sit six, or even two years, with such extensive powers as the new system proposes, and their friendship will be well worth a purchase."[7] The critical relation of numbers to bribery grew so tangled that Hamilton himself, the master logician, stumbled on it in *Federalist* 22 and made his case against the provision for a two-thirds vote on treaties.

Establishing a national government meant locating the United States in a European-dominated universe. The gentry simply could not comprehend the United States as just one nation among many. John Marshall likened countries in America's class to "individuals in a state of nature" who could enjoy the protective benefits of world society only through their proper placement in the scheme of the great powers.[8] With that placement came influence. By the same logic that assigned the superior national government a gravitational pull on state and local governments, Britain or France would radiate its force into a dependent nation. Hence, calculating America's republican balance and weighing attachments to the great powers belonged to the same process.

Some leaders knew exactly where the tip should fall. Such New England gentlemen as Fisher Ames, Rufus King, and Theodore Sedgwick, who had grown up with an inbred suspicion of things French, used the word as an insult during the 1780s. Meanwhile, Jefferson was contrasting the warm and helpful French with those "rich, proud, hectoring, swearing, squibbling, carnivorous animals" across the Channel.[9] Fittingly, the first strains between Hamilton and Madison in 1789 involved regulations for international trade, with Hamilton focusing on the established channels to Britain and Madison seeking to construct broader ones to France. Even the more tentative gentlemen, assuming that others already had their favorites, felt a strong urge to pick a side too.

If neutrality never made sense in the gentry's world, it became an absurdity in February 1793, when France declared war on Britain and Spain. That April the president's Neutrality Proclamation leaned toward Britain. Despite the historic role of the French Alliance, the proclamation gave no hint of a reciprocal concern for France's revolution. Washington, no partisan of Britain, inclined as he did because of his anxiety for the nation's western territory, a teetering appendage that the United States could never defend against Britain and its Spanish ally. Hamilton shared the president's involvement with the western territories, but he brought his own distinctive view to the subject of America in the world. Of all the gentry leaders, he had the fewest reservations about its capacity to demand a place as another great power. He simply did not experience the same nagging emotions of dependence or ponder the same nuances of attachment that preoccupied his associates. Because he also underestimated the problems of mobilizing the nation's strength, Hamilton adopted a singularly cocky style toward Europe. He concentrated on Britain, predominant in the American scheme by colonial heritage, by Atlantic power, and by commercial preeminence. To control its own future, Hamilton reasoned, the United States had to settle matters in each of these areas: assert its independence, extend its base on this side of the Atlantic, and arrange satisfactory business relations with its natural trading partner across the ocean. Ideally he would have eliminated France altogether from the equation, and in 1793 he advocated an immediate termination of the old alliance. Although Hamilton also despised France's radicalism and disdained its American partisans, he wanted above all to keep it in the shadow of his plans for American greatness.

Jefferson and Madison would have resented the tone of the Neutrality Proclamation even more if they had not been anticipating a transatlantic merger of republicanism through the good offices of a new French minister, Edmond Genet, who arrived in Charleston just before the proclamation was issued. Taking America's cheers as his due, Citizen Genet moved slowly northward in a triumphal procession, only to meet a frigid reception from the president's inner circle. With the enthusiasm of a revolutionary and the arrogance of a great power's emissary, the French minister defied the Washington administration, made the United States a staging ground for French plots, and forced a demand for his recall. Jefferson and Madison responded with the kind of impotent humiliation that neocolonial gentry typically suffered whenever they hooked their cause to a European giant. As the enemies of France capitalized on Genet's overbearing tactics, Jefferson tried to salvage what he could within the government and Madison hurriedly organized public meetings in the south. On the defensive, Madison fell back to basics. A break with France at this juncture, he instructed his Virginia allies to declare, would be "one great leading step toward assimilating our Government to the form and spirit of the British monarchy." [10] But no tactics could stop the Genet fiasco from pushing Jefferson and Madison farther to the fringes of Washington's court.

With Genet went Jefferson's dream of using the Old World to redress the balance in the New. As Jefferson retreated before Hamilton's assaults in 1792, the news of France's revolutionary outpouring had worked like an elixir. It would deliver "the coup de grace" to monarchism everywhere, he told his former protégé William Short. Revolutionary bloodshed he dismissed with an impatient wave: "The liberty of the whole earth was depending on the issue . . . rather than it should have failed I would have seen half the earth desolated." [11] Jefferson's memories of European oppression gave him such a vivid image of this transforming miracle that with a missionary's conviction he pressed other gentlemen to see the same vision of an incredible emancipating power sweeping the world. John Adams considered him a man possessed. In his zeal Jefferson had pictured Genet as the agent of those irresistible liberating forces that would crush the Hamiltonian centralizers and purify the American republic. When the swashbuckling Genet only widened the rift between France and the United States, a deflated Jefferson faced instead the terrible prospect of "liberty warring on herself."[12]

What almost all of Jefferson's contemporaries did share with him was a dependent gentry's assumption that the ultimate fate of America lay in Europe. Expressing the underside of Jefferson's initial bright vision, a group of Philadelphia Francophiles warned on the Fourth of July 1793: "Should the glorious efforts of France be defeated ... this country, the only remaining depository of liberty, will not long be permitted to enjoy ... an independent ... republican government."[13] Even the conservative William Barry Grove of North Carolina agreed that if the French had not "blunted ... the fangs of the Lyon" in 1793, "American Blood, would have mingled with the cut throats of Europe in our Country before next Jany."[14] By then the American stakes had risen too high for any gentleman to ignore. Minds accustomed to understanding a nation through the form and style of its government watched France's whole apple cart turn: new constitutions, new calendar, new titles, new dress, new religious ceremonies. Was all this republicanism extending itself, with royalism pressing at its wings? Or was it republicanism destroying itself, with anarchy rushing in its wake?

To the centralizing federalists, revolutionary France, without even a token executive after the king's execution, represented the farthest extreme in legislative, or popular, rule that the 18th-century imagination could reach. "Democracy," once associated generally with legislative excess and social instability, now acquired for them all the lurid particulars of the Jacobin Terror. Predictably, they noted, Genet had fomented treason within the *state* governments and called the people to defy the president himself. Just as predictably, the Frenchman had found his champions in the "Virginia party," whose line of sedition now ran all the way to the National Convention in Paris. Oliver Wolcott, who believed that Jefferson had actually instigated the French Revolution, pictured Hamilton's program as countering the "grand design of an intimate coalition with France, founded on the weakness and degradation of this country."[15]

From Jefferson's "Frenchified" democracy, the centralizers knew, the sequence would move ineluctably to chaos, then despotism. In western Pennsylvania, farmers ignored the distant presidential warnings to uphold the law and continued to ship their surplus grain as liquor without paying the excise tax. When local sympathy for the violators paralyzed national enforcement in 1794, Pennsylvania's government hedged. Hamilton was ready, and this time his colleagues rallied behind him. Under presidential order he marched an army of militia from states adjacent to Pennsylvania into the mountains around Pittsburgh, scattered the thunderstruck farmers, arrested some laggard leaders, and ended what the centralizers called the Whiskey Rebellion. In the summer of 1794, Hamilton's admirers saw themselves saved at the brink. Decisive action had thwarted "a formal and regular plan" for nationwide subversion.[16] Oliver Ellsworth now linked the United States with Britain in a transatlantic barrier against revolutionary upheaval.

The real power behind the Jacobins' pillaging democracy, the centralizers heard, came from a network of political clubs outside the regular government. In 1793, ardent republicans along the east coast responded to the expansion of the French Revolution by establishing a string of democratic-republican societies, modeled in a loose way after the Jacobin clubs of France. That year and the next, they filled the air with celebrations and pronouncements that intermingled enthusiasm for France and advocacy of liberty at home. Sometimes formed around a militia company, often Jefferson's partisans, and seldom delicate in expression, the democratic-republican societies brought the terror of Europe to the very doorsteps of the Francophobes. If the Jacobins of Mainz opened their city gates to the conquering French army, would the Jacobins of Baltimore or New York do less? When otherwise anonymous citizens served as officers of the clubs, a fearful gentry envisaged the Parisian mob. When prominent citizens headed the clubs, they saw domestic Robespierres.

Nothing in Washington's two terms generated such cold fury in the president as these irreverent societies that not only sang a brazen chorus up and down the coast but through a large Philadelphia contingent actually yelled insults into the ears of their rulers. With that echo in his head, an enraged Washington lashed out at the clubs as "the most diabolical attempts to destroy the best fabric of human government and happiness, that has ever been presented for the acceptance of mankind." Their responsibility for "the Western disturbances, admits of no doubt," he wrote Jay.[17] Despite a natural caution and a strong aversion to saber-rattling, the president ordered the march on the western farmers out of his hatred for the eastern clubs. Then to complete "their annihilation," the president used his annual message to Congress to hurl a republican anathema at these domestic Jacobins: the democratic-republican clubs were "self-created societies."

In a narrow sense, "self-created" meant "self-elected," a clear violation of republican principles. More generally, it clashed with the gentry's underlying conception of order. Where everything had its assigned place in a symmetrical arrangement, self-creation had the same jarring effect in the social world that a winged bull would have in the scientific. Its very presence challenged an entire scheme of things. In John Marshall's apt phrase, the democratic-republican societies were "detached clubs," agencies that warred from the outside against the total structure of American society. Through a kindred group of such terms, the gentry identified the gravest evils besetting their republic. In the original draft of the Declaration of Independence, Jefferson accused George III of exercising "a self-assumed power." The confirmed antifederalist James Warren thought the Constitution would produce a "self-created nobility." In 1788, Madison also considered "self-appointed" rights just as dangerous to the republic as hereditary ones, and in 1791, with monarchy on his mind, he warned against the drift toward a *self-directed course* in the national government.[18] By the end of 1794, when Washington set his curse on the democratic-republican clubs, all of France had become a self-created society in the eyes of the centralizers, and they vowed that their republic would not die from the same Jacobin disease. No other country, concluded the cosmopolitan visitor-in-exile Talleyrand, had such a fear of anarchy.

From a Jeffersonian perspective these events in 1794 carried exactly the reverse meaning. Although no gentry leader openly favored tax evasion, Hamilton's opponents knew where the blame actually lay. In the grand tradition of the American Revolution a monarchic tax had inspired the people to defend their liberties, and in the grim tradition of British tyranny a monarchic military force had ridden over a state's sovereign rights to suppress popular resistance. During these years, as Madison wrote to a close associate, an attachment "to the French Nation & Revolution" marked the true patriot, and the democratic-republican clubs simply gave American expression to the worldwide craving for freedom.[19] If they acted as fiery tribunes of the people, so they should in the face of "anti republican" trends at court. Madison called Washington's condemnation of them his "greatest error," and a furious Jefferson pointed at the Society of the Cincinnati, that center of military monarchism, as the real "self-created" menace. The Virginians welcomed the clubs on their own terms: they were both democratic and republican societies, voices of the people asserting their rights in the national republic. Through the House of Representatives, where these sentiments still commanded votes, friends of the societies formally reclaimed their republican legitimacy as "combinations of men."

These events carried a particularly heavy charge in 1794 because they occurred during a war scare. In November 1793, Britain changed the maritime rules for neutral commerce and announced the new order by seizing American ships in the West Indies. Official complaints were simply brushed aside. Although the British softened the rules a bit in January, they did so for their own good reasons, still leaving the United States at the disposal of a great power's whim. Now it was the centralizers' turn to squirm in their champion's embrace. "The English are absolutely madmen," howled the Anglophile Fisher Ames. Yet like Jefferson and Madison, who deplored Genet in private while defending amity with France in public, the same Fisher Ames scorned the advocates of retaliation as speaking "all French."[20] Under executive guidance Congress held its peace and allowed time for Washington's special envoy to get what satisfaction he could from London. In Jefferson's circle, such meekness before the British verified every suspicion of transatlantic intrigue: ". . . the most submissive measures adopted that cod. be devised," fumed Monroe, "to court her favor and degrade our character."[21]

Their worst news came in Washington's selection of an envoy. John Jay was a committed centralizer, an exemplar of the aristocratic style, and a partisan of Britain who spearheaded the public attack against France during Genet's mission. Many southerners and westerners knew him even better as the negotiator who was willing to abandon American access to the Mississippi River in 1786. Reasoning from character to its consequences, they expected Jay to lay their republic before his British master. The opinion that counted in 1794, however, was Washington's, and the president trusted Jay as completely as any of his associates. A fraternal tie from the Revolution grew stronger during the 1780s when both of them worked for a new constitution. If the notoriety of the Spanish negotiations had not disqualified him, Jay might well have superseded John Adams as vice-president, and Washington would have been delighted. The two of them shared common manners and common temperaments. Like the general, Jay behaved with an instinctive caution —nothing rash, nothing premature. Again like Washington, he had no talent for formulating concrete programs. Jay proposed safe generalities, then responded to other people's specifics, and Washington usually agreed with both Jay's banalities and his reactions. Reasoning from character to its consequences, the president gave his envoy the widest possible latitude in negotiating the war-laden differences between Britain and the United States. In that act of faith Washington ignored one critical difference between them: Jay was an Anglophile, and Washington was not.

The treaty that arrived from England in March 1795 put Washington's faith to the test. In exchange for a belated acceptance of American sovereignty in the northwest and a mechanism for settling mutual debt claims, Jay acknowledged wholesale the British rules for Atlantic commerce, sacrificed still more trading rights for the slenderest access to the British West Indies, and capitulated on every issue dear to the southern gentry. As a negotiator Jay failed. Nevertheless, his personal deficiencies

—a desire to appease, a weakness for flattery, an overestimation of British concern for American friendship—scarcely affected the outcome. It was not Jay's treaty. The responsive New Yorker simply took what the British gave him, and any other envoy would have received essentially the same proposal. The meaning of the treaty lay not in its component parts but in its declaratory power as a weak nation's choice between two giants. As Hamilton's lieutenant William Loughton Smith posed the question for his constituents, did they wish to join the British "system" or the French "system"? If the government did not ratify the treaty, Jay reported from London, Britain would treat the United States as a French pawn. "The opinion [in Paris] . . . ," Monroe reported, "is that we are reduced by it to the condition of British colonies. . . ."[22] Although the struggle lasted until April 1796, the United States eventually accepted the British offer.

Objectively, the warring great powers forced a choice on the United States, and it selected the safer and more profitable British camp. Subjectively, America's gentry were fighting once more for the nation's independence. The intensity of the battle, the losing side's perseverance to its last resource, the vulnerability even of Washington's reputation, all marked the contest over the Jay Treaty as an issue of the republic's survival, not its preference. Independence in this neocolonial universe was something America maintained against the pulls of the great powers, and fundamentally, the surge of gentry emotions between 1794 and 1796 was against one of the two titans. Ties to Britain existed in every part of the United States, of course, and so did enthusiasm for the French Revolution. Nevertheless, almost all of the gentry made their abiding commitments in hate. They were seeking shelter from an enemy, and as they cheered one great power to victory, they were thinking primarily of the other's defeat. To their closest friends and family members, the supporters of the Jay Treaty unburdened their feelings about France, not England. "The Barbarians who inundated the Roman Empire and broke to peices the institutions of the civilized world," wrote James Bayard, "in my opinion innovated the state of things not more than the french revolution. . . ."[23] Oliver Wolcott, Sr., flatly told his son: "Of all policies which ever existed among mankind, the French is the worst."[24]

In the other camp Jefferson simply turned away from the Terror at its height. Years later he would designate 1791 as the optimum point in his French Revolution. Instead of picturing France as the advance guard of liberty, Jefferson now recast it as a military arm to destroy British tyranny. After the ratification of the Jay Treaty he spelled out the crisis of American independence as he saw it to a comrade from 1776. When we realize, he wrote Elbridge Gerry, that the British dominate our exports and imports; that they spread their mercantile force throughout the land to corrupt our politics; "that they are advancing fast to a monopoly of our banks & public finances under their control; that they have in their alliance the most influential characters in & out of office; when they have shewn that by all these bearings on the different branches of the government, they can force it to proceed in whatever direction they dictate, and bend the interests of this country entirely to the will of another; when all this, I say, is attended to, it is impossible for us to say we stand on independent ground, impossible for a free mind not to see & to groan under the bondage. . . ."[25] Or in John Taylor's clipped summary: "The English who could not conquer us, may buy us."[26] As Jefferson eagerly traced France's military successes on his European map, he explained why they mattered so much: "Nothing can establish firmly the republican principles of our government but an establishment of them in England."[27]

What made life so difficult for Washington, who agonized for weeks before signing the Jay Treaty, was his powerful aversion to both powers. Like many other southern gentlemen, he found the prospect of a British shelter so distasteful that he could barely slip beneath it. In the end, it required a sharp reminder of the French menace Edmund Randolph's involvement with French bribes—to push him the final inch. And there lay the nub of the American problem: the great powers came as a package. The proud citizens of a new nation fumed at the thought of their rights spread like worms among the robins. At the same time, Americans felt lost without a protector. Their passion for independence arose from equally deep feelings of dependence, and the more profoundly they distrusted one great power, the more eagerly they cultivated the other. In this crossfire of emotions, it was not always easy to calculate how much of their independence they were willing to sacrifice in its name.

From the beginning, American court politics was also a politics of neocolonial intrigue. Usually the representatives of the great powers waited, and the Americans came to them. Almost as soon as Hamilton entered the cabinet, he began passing privileged information to the British and sifting their rumors in return. Not only did Jefferson confide in a series of French diplomats, but as secretary of state he also winked at their clandestine operations. Mirroring Jay in London, Monroe acted the open partisan in Paris and revealed whatever he knew about America's court battles. Another Virginian broke the Senate's rule of secrecy on the Jay Treaty by slipping a copy to the French minister Adet. While Randolph was dickering in private with the French minister, Hamilton's associates were conniving with the British minister, who eventually gave one of them the stolen—or fabricated—letter that undid the secretary of state.

In this elaborate tangle of plots, not one of the schemers doubted that

he was an honorable patriot. By the mid-nineties, as the gentry understood the stakes, the wrong European attachment meant the wrong war,
and the wrong war meant a shattering of the national government, dis-
memberment, recolonization. Could any maneuver be treasonous in
such a desperate game for independence? Hamilton, first into the field of
intrigue, had the last word for all of them. "We are laboring hard," he
wrote Rufus King in London, "to establish in this country principles
more and more *national* and free from all foreign ingredients, so that we
may be . . . truly Americans."[28] As if to justify the riskiest games in
America's defense, both great powers continued to bully the United
States at will. Britain's "domineering spirit" and "the outrageous and
insulting conduct" of its officials left Washington apoplectic after he
signed the Jay Treaty.[29] The French abused the renegade Americans from
Paris, and their minister threatened military devastation if the United
States failed to elect a friendly president in 1796. Yet if London considered Washington's chief adviser a British "agent," why not browbeat
his president into line? If Jefferson's close friend wooed the revolutionaries in Paris, why not expect Jefferson to welcome French interference
in behalf of his election? Weak intriguers only increased the European
scorn for their weak nation.

The new struggle over independence sharpened the old lines of battle
over form and character. Riding the crest of their power, the centralizers
made the Jay Treaty an issue of executive authority and set Washington's
unique prestige against the opposition. Would the father of American
independence now sacrifice it? "Fear not . . . my countrymen," one advocate assured the doubters, "the protecting arm of a Washington is
extended between us and the danger. . . ."[30] In a painful illustration of
the neocolonial's fate, the president found his honor more thoroughly
enmeshed in a treaty he detested than in the many measures he willingly
endorsed. Nevertheless, once he placed his own character in the scales,
he could no longer tolerate the slightest compromise. In fact, Washington's determination to preserve the treaty hardened to the point that the
grim old hero even contemplated another reelection in order to protect
the pact. Moreover, the centralizers stood with the Constitution. Although a bare two-thirds voted for the treaty, the Senate did accept it.
There in a row were all the gentry's sources of legitimacy: the law of the
land, the authority of the government's rulers, the reputation of the
nation's first character.

Everything Jefferson and Madison saw validated their worst fears of an
onrushing monarchy, and they simply refused to accept Caesar's march
as legitimate. By selecting the chief justice as his envoy, the president
violated the separation of powers and subordinated the judiciary to the

executive. The Senate's rule of secrecy allowed executive agents to plot the passage of the treaty before the people could defend their own freedom. The simultaneous pressures for a national army belonged to the same executive campaign against liberty. And all this to bind the United States to monarchic Britain.

Using the only resources available to them, Jefferson and Madison responded by integrating the national government's vertical axis as their constitutional weapon against the enemies of independence. News of the treaty brought an outpouring of angry public meetings and hostile government resolutions. This time the Virginia leaders not only counseled many of these dissenters but also coordinated protests inside the states with a final attempt to block the Jay Treaty in the House of Representatives. Even with Madison's constitutional skills, it required quite an effort to claim equality for the House in completing a treaty. Nevertheless, they managed to make a case. First, they called the Jay Treaty a usurpation of legislative rights, a trick by the executive and Senate to "bind up the hands of the [House] from ever restraining the commerce of their patron-nation."[31] Second, they turned the explicit power of the House to implement treaties into an implied right to pass on them initially. Here Madison stretched to the limit a line of argument he had used in 1788 to soothe the suspicious antifederalists: "I consider the House of Reps. as another obstacle afforded by the new Constitution [to an unwise treaty]. It is true that this branch is not of necessity to be consulted in the forming of Treaties. But as its approbation and co-operation may often be necessary in carrying treaties into full effect; and as the support of the Government . . . must be drawn from the purse which they hold, the sentiments of this body cannot fail to have very great weight, even when the body itself may have no constitutional authority."[32]

For almost a year the newly integrated vertical pole stood against the Jay Treaty, giving constitutional expression to the increasingly fierce struggle over European attachments. If the House established its power over the treaty, Washington was reported as saying, "the government would be at an end, & must *then assume another form.*"[33] "A House that will play President . . . will play mob at last," declared the centralizer Fisher Ames. Seeking to be "omnipotent," it would transform the republic into "a mere democracy" with the president its "master of ceremonies."[34] As Jefferson dug in along the democratic axis, he called Jay's document "a treaty of alliance between England and the Anglomen of this country against the Legislature and the people."[35] More and more of the attacks on a monarchic executive struck directly at the hero himself, softening the core of prestige at the very peak of the hierarchy. Jefferson, unwilling to risk a breach with Washington in 1793, now poured his energies back into politics without any reservations about their effect on his fading idol. The rift did occur, and Jefferson just pushed onward.

As Washington's authority softened, the lines of battle hardened. The pace of events alone was hurrying gentlemen into combat: in 1793 an eruption of revolution in France and its war with Britain, a controversial proclamation of neutrality, the hullabaloo over Citizen Genet, and the prospect of an American war with Britain; in 1794 high tension over the Jay mission, raging Terror in France, and harsh conflicts over the Whiskey Rebellion and the democratic-republican clubs; then in 1795 and 1796 the battle royal over the Jay Treaty, with the great powers rattling at the doors. In gentry government this was uniquely a wartime pace, and they reacted in that spirit. In a crisis of independence, Jefferson declared, "I hold it immoral to pursue a middle line."[36] In 1795 the vote on endorsing the treaty flushed out the neutrals in the Senate. By the following year, when the vote on implementing the treaty forced a division in the House, almost everyone at the center of national politics had separated into camps.

These camps broke past the limits of court politics, spread throughout the United States, and formed two national parties, the Republicans and the Federalists. Matching the neocolonial passions at court, a great upsurge of public involvement in the French Revolution and the European war affected almost every corner of American society from the coast into the mountains. At first, little connected these outpourings at large with the struggles at court. Although national leaders did tap some of the public furor over Genet, they only used it to reinforce their own complex maneuvers inside the government. Considerably more public emotions affected national politics in 1794, as the prospect of war with Britain and the executive's assertions at home drew increasing attention to the national government. But it was the contest over the Jay Treaty that dramatically forged the link, binding these scattered public concerns into nationwide parties. A simple line—neocolonialism stripped to its essentials—divided the parties. To their enemies the Federalists were the British party; to the Federalists the Republican opposition was the French party. The Jay Treaty, pro or con, provided the test of loyalties.

This test worked so effectively that little more than a year later every presidential elector cast a vote either for the Federalist candidate Adams or the Republican candidate Jefferson. In a sprawling country where no national precedent existed and where the interchange of information remained spotty and local, such astonishing discipline spoke eloquently to the strength of a hierarchical habit in matters of basic national and international importance. The more distant the arena of action and the more critical the consequences for an entire nation, the more completely a few national leaders of the highest prestige held the right to define the issues of debate and outline the choices in policy. There was nothing docile about this delegation of authority. Every witness, foreign and domestic, remarked on the fiery popular reaction throughout the United States to the height of the French Revolution, the course of the European wars, and, above all, the Jay Treaty. But most Americans had no natural channels to connect these passions with national politics. If Raleigh, North Carolina, was far from Philadelphia, Philadelphia was even farther from Raleigh, whose residents had no reliable sources of news about momentous national events, let alone a reliable voice in national policy. Their willingness to take direction from the top of a national hierarchy came not from a cowed spirit but from an impassable distance between their lives and the center for national decisions.

What other Americans granted, a national elite grasped. Jefferson, Madison, and a few advisers on one side, Washington, Hamilton, Jay, and their small circle on the other, took as their prerogative the right to explain the crucial links between European forces and America's destiny, and each cluster of leaders mobilized a nationwide hierarchy to contest the politics of independence. At its peak, a party of independence required an authentic hero of the Revolution—not lesser lights such as Hamilton and Madison but a luminary such as Washington, or even Adams or Jefferson. From the top level of this hierarchy came basic policies and their justification. Lieutenants in the national government, sympathetic state leaders, and partisan newspapers distributed these messages, often verbatim, as far down the hierarchy as they could reach, counting on others to spread the messages laterally and then extend the coverage, superior to subordinate. These were the mechanisms of readiness. National elections were the mustering times, and that process relied almost exclusively on a single device: compiling and publicizing lists of notables.

The tactic itself, more or less synonymous with hierarchical politics, rallied voters in practically every disputed cause during the revolutionary era. Now, however, it applied on an unprecedented scale. Extrapolating from the conception of the people as a well-ordered militia, the new parties undertook to gather these innumerable small units into a nationwide muster by a nationwide mobilization of the officer class. Lists of notables constituted the indispensable strands of faith connecting local concerns with central directions. In oversimplified summary, voters trusted local leaders who trusted state leaders who trusted national leaders who issued the call to arms at election time.

Only the parties' stark appeal to a fundamental, popular passion accounted for their extraordinary success. Before the appearance of the Jay Treaty, factional groupings and temporary coalitions circulated around national politics much as they had since the Revolutionary War, and the unusually broad battle over the Constitution did not alter that pattern. Once the national government commenced, the jousting at court produced more of the same old unstable leagues. Even Hamilton, whose organization of a loyal cadre marked a new level of efficiency in national politics, relied heavily on the generalized authority of the government to extend his sway beyond his own small circle. Because the personnel in Congress changed so often, his opponents by necessity negotiated their alliances from season to season. Beyond the court, the United States remained a sea of shifting, provincial interests that offered no coherent or consistent reactions to domestic policy. Before Jay's mission, "cool heads" in New York City described the clashes at court for a visiting Englishman as mere "sparrings . . . [that] will do no mischief."[37] Capturing the essence of national politics as usual, a Georgia Republican later noted that "distant things, you know, make but slight impressions" in local America.[38]

The parties solved the problems of consistency and commitment by avoiding the old issues and focusing on the new. Although the United States continued to form a crazy quilt of interests, its first national parties did not. They cut past those interests and extracted loyalty in the limited, intensely sensitive area of independence. Among the court leaders, old and new fused. The Federalist elite blended antifederalists, disorganizers, democrats, and Jacobins into a single Republican enemy. With the categorizing precision of the gentry mind, Jefferson called his opponents "an Anglican monarchical, & aristocratical party" and William Branch Giles labeled them a "funded gentry–British gentry–land gentry, aristocratic gentry, military gentry."[39] But if veterans of the court wars still talked among themselves about antifederalism and consolidation, to their national audience they concentrated almost exclusively on the codewords of French and British.

That sharp, deep slice into national life also accounted for certain limitations in the new parties. Organizationally as well as programmatically, they stood apart from the rest of American politics. The democratic-republican clubs, which would have had a natural affinity to the Republican party, largely dissolved before the parties emerged. Where state parties existed, as in Pennsylvania and New York, they might support the presidential candidates of the national parties and send representatives to Philadelphia who voted as members of those parties. Nevertheless, an overlap of concerns did not change their distinguishably state character, with a network of loyalties and set of purposes peculiarly their own. More continuously active in a wider variety of political matters, the state parties showed a much greater organizational toughness than their national counterparts. Indeed, the national parties had almost no standing organization of any sort, beyond a few dutifully partisan editors, working lists of notables, and occasional caucuses of like-minded congressmen. Although professional office seekers such as the Republican John Beckley scurried around in an attempt to appear irreplaceable, the parties depended fundamentally on a stable sense of hierarchy and the mechanisms of readiness that would translate hierarchy into votes.

The tightness of the parties' focus kept the range of their discipline narrow. Appropriately, they functioned best in a presidential election, the battle for a first character who secured the national hierarchy and led America's defense against foreign threats. Few other elections had such self-evident importance, just as few other issues had the partisan clarity of the Jay Treaty, and the problems of maintaining a coordinated effort plagued both parties, especially the Republicans in Congress. Adding to their difficulties, a reputation for personal independence ranked high in a gentleman's code of honor. A party member confronted not only his enemies' indictment for slavishness but his own worries about a humiliating obedience. Follow the "interest of your [Republican] majority . . .," one partisan advised another, and then added: "In matters of moment I hope you ever will as you have hitherto done—maintain your independance in spite of all party considerations. . . ."[40] No one could predict the consequences of this gentlemanly ambivalence.

The parties' powerful but restricted appeal meant that their national hierarchies attached an odd assortment of ribs to the backbone of independence and created a curious pair of social mongrels. A few partisans actually did identify with one of the two great powers. A thin string of merchants and lawyers from Charleston to Boston had meshed their lives so thoroughly with England that they composed an authentic British faction. At the height of enthusiasm for the French Revolution, Philadelphia celebrants symbolized their loyalties in the display of "a pike bearing the cap of liberty and the French and American flags entwined, surmounted by a dove bearing the olive branch."[41] Usually, however, partisanship expressed an antipathy to one of the great powers. Inveterate British-haters among the Scotch-Irish, for example, instinctively seized the Republican standard. On the other hand, a number of southern slaveholders who might otherwise have been Republicans turned to the Federalists because the French Revolution had sparked black uprisings in Saint-Domingue. Deeper into their hierarchies the parties became so enmeshed in a bewildering variety of family, religious, and economic concerns that national leaders had no way of fathoming the sources of partisanship or estimating how an interplay among local, national, and international events might alter their base of support. The fact that state and local elections consistently outdrew national ones underlined the limits of party command. Madison's sound social premises in *Federalist* 10 haunted his work as an organizer of the Republican party, and the work of every other national mobilizer as well.

Nevertheless, at that intermediate level where party lieutenants congregated, the many decisions sorting Federalists and Republicans did give each a distinctive cast. Federalists expressed a stronger commitment to social cohesion. They inspected their localities with a disciplinarian's eye, and they applied their prestige to causes that promised a tighter social integration. To a striking degree they sided with the social authority of religion. In 1795, when the French Jacobins' secular substitutes for religion and Tom Paine's revolutionary assault on the churches were common knowledge, a variety of clergymen threw themselves into politics just as the Federalist party was organizing. Appropriately, the ferocious attacks on Jefferson's Deism rose along with Federalism. Although Calvinism and Federalism formed a particularly zealous alliance in New England, the cohesive role of religion also infused Federalism from New York down the coast. Few Federalist leaders anywhere failed to maintain visible ties with a church. In Virginia the desirability of an established church interwove with the dangers from France as the primary bond among the party's leaders, and at the head of South Carolina's most dedicated Federalists stood Charles Cotesworth Pinckney, a pillar of Episcopalianism.

Diversity, on the other hand, characterized the Republican party. When Paine flayed the clergy, for example, the latest sons of liberty in Philadelphia cheered him on while the staid Republicans in New England cringed in dismay. Years later, when Gideon Granger learned that Paine was "about to publish another attack on the Christain Religion," the Connecticut Republican recalled the disastrous consequences in 1795 and begged someone to stop the man.[42] Along with its boisterous seaport partisans, the Republican party included haughty southern planters with special hatred toward their British creditors and bitter memories of wartime devastation. Although it was a commonplace among Federalists to call these southern grandees "Frenchified," they remained sufficiently cold toward France that when it seemed the more threatening great power, a number of them drifted quite easily into an alliance with Federalism. In many areas a considerable overlap between antifederalism and Republicanism helped to account for its diversity. While not every fervently anti-British leader had been an antifederalist, almost every antifederalist leader had been fervently anti-British, and a high proportion of its loose, heterogeneous ranks moved naturally into the Republican party.

To cover its array of constituents, the Republican leadership spread a mist of rhetoric contrasting its popular support with the elitist ambitions of the Federalists. Before many Americans even cared to listen, Madison laid such a claim in 1792, declaring "that the mass of people in every part of the union, in every state, and of every occupation must at bottom be" the opponents of Hamilton's domestic program, and in the mid-nineties the same theme served to gloss over his party's mixture of elements.[43] But the Republican message certainly did not announce a new venture in majoritarian politics. As much as Washington and Hamilton, Jefferson and Madison considered themselves instructors of the nation, whose truths stood unalterable no matter how many voters sided with error. Basically they grounded their case in resistance: the natural American antipathy to British influences and British forms. Moreover, because their strength lay along the vertical axis, they identified their partisans with the democratic elements in the national government and their opponents with its monarchic side. Hence in a scheme where the states spoke the will of the people, the autocratic Pennsylvanian Thomas McKean and the aristocratic Virginian Edmund Pendleton became Republican agents of democracy, while Adams and Jay, their Federalist analogues, became conduits for executive tyranny.

At first glance the Republicans seemed at a hopeless disadvantage. In Hamilton the Federalists had the nation's most skilled political manager, who despite his retirement in 1795 still commanded an able staff of lieutenants. Beyond them lay an echelon of supporters whose commitment to social order sharpened the party's discipline and whose network of mercantile connections facilitated its communications. Federalists controlled all points along the top of the national government except the House, which neither side could control, and by 1796 their treaty with Britain passed its last obstacle to become unquestionably the law of the land. Even under attack and about to retire, Washington gave an immense authority to the cause he endorsed, and until he died in 1799 his aura continued to spread a glow of virtue over the Federalists.

Set against the Federalists' monolith of legitimacy, everything about the opposition seemed "self-created": the public conventions, the assertions of the states, the encroachments of the House, and now a party assault on the social order itself. By continuing to bombard the Jay Treaty, Republicans broke the cardinal rule that distinguished between the legitimacy of criticism before the adoption of a measure and its illegitimacy afterward. That rule had underpinned the hope for a harmonious new government once the Constitution was ratified. John Quincy Adams, an especially dutiful antifederalist, noted in his diary, "I think it my duty to submit without murmuring."[44] In the early newspaper wars Hamilton had stressed the same distinction with charges that his opponents still challenged the Constitution and the funded debt. Hence the

Federalists' accusation that their enemies attacked "government." Applied strictly, the rule would have muffled the Republicans before their party could speak, and throughout the revolutionary era it was honored in the breach at every level of politics. Nonetheless, it remained an important norm in gentry politics and deepened the shadow of rebellion across the Republican enterprise.

Yet appearances did deceive. Hamilton's talents did not turn smoothly to party organization. A far better director than delegator, he found a national party muster less congenial than the close drill of court politics. Even more critical was his emotional removal from the strongest passions of neocolonialism. As his Federalist colleagues slipped deeper into Francophobia, Hamilton continued to pursue the old objectives: executive power, financial stability, mercantile growth. Jefferson was less a spearhead of French subversion than a nemesis of Virginia power, an enemy of the funded debt, and a bar to a general reconciliation with Britain. Basically, the Jay Treaty belonged to Hamilton's long-term domestic program, not to the current clash of revolutionary and counterrevolutionary forces in Europe. Currying France's favor did anger him. "When shall we cease to consider ourselves as a colony to France?" he snapped in reaction to a placating American gesture.[45] Nevertheless, he had no fear of France, and neocolonial fears, after all, were the generators of the national parties. Without that sharp spur, Hamilton never gave his best efforts to the Federalist cause.

Jefferson and Madison took the initiative in party formation because they did believe America's independence was at stake. Feeling what hundreds of other gentry leaders felt, they proved extraordinarily able in tapping the sentiments of their scattered allies and overcoming the early advantages of their enemies. As the battle shifted from court to party, power no longer depended on the particular patterning of satellite gentlemen around Washington's sun. It lay somewhere out there in the American expanse, and no one could hope to reach it through the personal webs of alliance and patronage that prevailed at court. In that quest, the pioneers along the government's vertical axis enjoyed an appreciable head start. Sharing none of the centralizers' aversion to a state-based gentry, Jefferson and Madison by 1796 already had several years of experience in cultivating them and facilitating their protests. The further the state networks fell beyond the surveillance of any one or two leaders, the more Jefferson and Madison reiterated the broad principles of their republicanism and accepted whatever group of local lieutenants would aid their cause. A hierarchy with soft authority over this hard layer of state units admirably suited the requirements of a national muster in a decentralized land.

At the same time, the Virginians' success in rallying such an extensive party only increased the risks of illegitimacy. Coordinating the vertical axis represented a last effort to fight the enemy through the forms of the Constitution. Party mobilization emerged out of failure, and Jefferson and Madison, moderate gentlemen both, recognized that they were raising the stakes in a dangerous game of persistent opposition. Party activity by itself no longer damned anyone. As a league of like-minded gentlemen, "party" had been acquiring more and more respectability and increasing its distance from "faction," once its blood brother, which now bore the worst connotations of selfish, tyrannical, or seditious political combination. During the 1780s a number of gentlemen routinely mentioned the inevitability of party divisions in a republic. Madison, reporting the ratification of the Constitution in Massachusetts, fairly glowed in his praise. "The prevailing party comprized . . . all the men of ability, of property, and of influence," he told Jefferson. "In the opposite multitude there was not a single character capable of uniting their wills or directing their measures."[46] By 1795 the acceptance of parties had become so commonplace that Jay, riding out a ferocious assault on his negotiations with Britain, could take the high ground of detachment: "Differences of opinion, and other causes equally pure and natural, will unavoidably cause parties . . . and [such parties] are probably no less conducive to good government, than moderate fermentation is necessary to make good wine."[47] Anticipating victory in Maryland a year later, another Federalist, William Vans Murray, marveled that he "never knew an election so much on *principles*." It was "a party question," he explained, "not a personal matter."[48]

These benign references to parties rested on an Aristotelian premise of moderation: between static uniformity and violent factions lay mild party competition, the kind of disagreement that Jay once likened to a breeze. But the gales of passion that swirled about his treaty scarcely fit that model, despite his own efforts to minimize their force. Widening the difference, each camp associated the other with the most ominous illegitimacy of all, an attachment to a foreign power. Most gentry leaders, already alert to this susceptibility in parties as the new nation was forming, saw the events of the mid-nineties fulfilling their worst fears. Once again, Jefferson and Madison had to justify a strategy that they chose only under duress.

They began inside the area of general agreement. The two parties that most gentry leaders anticipated had indeed materialized. Only one, however, fell within the requisite bounds of moderation. Madison opened this line of reasoning with an unsigned essay on the parties he identified in 1792, one "republican" and the other "anti republican." Now the distinction separated an American from a British party. Holding government offices gave no respectability to the British party; it simply heightened the dangers of subversion. The real source of legitimacy lay in an adherence to republican virtues—or, more precisely, Republican virtues. At a moment of supreme crisis, party, not government, defended America's independence.

High risks indeed. Picturing the republic itself at issue, Jefferson and Madison came close to declaring war on its government. From pieces of their revolutionary heritage and some neocolonial glue, they built a new framework for legitimacy, starting with the acceptability of moderate, principled parties, shifting the terms of judgment from authoritative rulers/disruptive citizens to good party/evil party, and justifying their attack on both the government's leaders and its policies by assigning their own party a monopoly over republican principles. A choice between parties, not a choice between obedience and disobedience to the government, defined the boundary between legitimacy and illegitimacy. The government, once the antithesis to party, became in its highest offices a mere tool for the corrupt party, and the honest party, once a contradiction in terms, became the primary protection against that corruption. Where small matters divided the parties, good citizens should ignore them, Jefferson told Giles, "but where the principle of difference is as substantial and as strongly pronounced as between the republicans & the Monocrats of our country, I hold it as honorable to take a firm & decided part. . . ."[49]

No one had set out to restructure national politics. A fundamental threat to American independence demanded a grand muster of patriots in the spirit of '76, and the Jay Treaty gave the Republicans an exceptionally effective appeal to a variety of neocolonial fears and revolutionary memories. Neither Jefferson nor Madison was planning beyond the great rally of 1796. After Adams' victory over Jefferson, national parties were nothing more than states of alertness in the minds of the recent combatants, raked emotions that awaited the outcome of crisis under a new president. Nevertheless, the party battle of 1796 marked a dramatic move toward the creation of a national society. As Europe's upheaval shook the United States, gentry leaders connected their own concerns to America's popular reactions and engaged in a truly national politics of independence. Although the parties destroyed neither local attachments nor court politics, at least for a time they transcended both. In the process the two parties advocated competing versions of a constitutional order and modeled them in their hierarchies, the Federalists running lines of authority directly from a central authority through the tiers of citizens below it and the Republicans scaling authority along stairsteps of national, state, and local responsibility.

At the same time, their Janus face showed in bold relief. To achieve national unity, the parties spread a message of national cleavage. Seeking harmony, they flung themselves into battle. Almost equal in strength, they demanded mutually exclusive loyalties in a passionate conflict for independence, with each side predicting recolonization as punishment for the enemy's triumph. The historian Carl Becker once noted that Bismarck united Germany by dividing it into three parts. Here the parties were integrating American society by dividing it in half. But because no one stood above the division to pull the strings, this politics of independence threatened to destroy the very society it was building.

The Edges
of Violence

As John Adams became president in March 1797, international pressures on the United States again increased, this time from the French side. Fulfilling the Republican prophecy that the Jay Treaty would mean war, France interpreted the election of the Federalist Adams as final proof of America's hostility, and declared open season on its shipping. In one sense, the French challenge simply recapitulated the earlier sequence with Britain: a powerful nation's unilateral change in the rules of commerce, a weak nation's need to make concessions or fight. But unlike the threat of war in 1794, when Washington's administration appeared partial to Britain, this confrontation pitted the American opponents of France against the continent's dominant power. The French Directory, alternating contemptuous indifference with insults, refused to accept Charles Cotesworth Pinckney, who replaced the friendly American minister Monroe, and then toyed with President Adams' special envoys, Pinckney, Elbridge Gerry, and John Marshall, who were told in 1798 to meet France's terms or face their republic's destruction.

The Federalists used the trappings of French arrogance—the clandestine code letters X, Y, and Z of the Directory's spokesmen and their imperious demand for bribes—to deepen the American feelings of humiliation and danger, then intensified their preparations for war. In addition to a jerry-rigged navy, Congress now authorized the recruitment of a national army. One great power's minor antagonist was the other's minor ally, and Britain gave the Americans some spare support. Meanwhile, to secure the nation at home, Congress passed the Alien and Sedition Acts, requiring a fourteen-year residency to qualify for citizenship, establishing rules to deport enemy aliens in case of war, and setting stiff penalties for criticism of the government and its officials. Although Adams chose not to request a formal declaration, this quasi-war with France enabled the Federalists to break the political stalemate and become the clear majority party.

All the ingredients for a final, disintegrating explosion of partisanship were stirred into the first thirty months of Adams' presidency. As the French armies battered their enemies on the continent, the American sense of helplessness sank to its depths in 1797. Against the "most powerful" force on earth, Gerry warned his old friend Adams, it was as futile for the United States to resist "as for an infant to resist an elephant." War would transform the states into "meer french colonies."[1] The Bostonian George Cabot pictured the Federalists grappling at the barricades with French invaders. Cling to the French alliance, John Dickinson pleaded, for France's conquest of Britain was as certain as Rome's of Carthage. Exulting in the prospect, a Tennessee Republican predicted that "Tyranny will be Humbled, a throne crushed, and a republick will spring from the wreck—and millions of distressed people restored to the rights of man by the conquering arm of Bonaparte." Yet even as Andrew Jackson savored his vision of cataclysmic justice, he was also expressing the underside of his awe, an alarm over French power in the American west. The fears from vulnerability had no limits, and the Federalists, both feeling them and playing on them, cried out America's jeopardy. Even an American loan to France, John Marshall decided, "would amount to a surrender of our national independence."[2] Rumors of pending coups, surreptitious invasions, and Jacobinical slave rebellions spread among citizens with no way of verifying them. Always the Federalists drummed on the foreign allegiance of their opponents: the Republicans were the French party, and its leaders the minions of the French government. Neocolonial bullying from abroad and neocolonial sensibilities at home combined to make the Federalist campaign so effective that by late 1799 it stripped the Republican party to a skeleton of the faithful.

The president himself vigorously churned these emotions. As soon as "a domestic difference of a serious nature shall break out," he had predicted grimly in 1787, Americans would "call in foreign nations" to fight their battles for them.[3] Anticipating the worst, Adams already sensed this foreign presence by 1792, then saw it flourish in the struggle over the Jay Treaty. As he entered office, he self-consciously planted himself as America's bulwark against the "French party." The more overbearing France grew, the more belligerently defensive the president became. "Is the republic of the United States a fief of the republic of France?" he demanded in outrage. If the terrible power of Europe, with all its "arts and agents," was not "exterminated" throughout the land, it would cause "our total destruction."[4] Adams shared Oliver Wolcott's transmuted Puritan conviction that "The United States are to expect no mediocrity of fortune. They have a good and a bad nature—the principles of both are vigorously contending for mastery" in a mighty, "uncertain" contest.[5] With as exaggerated a belief in his own purity as in other people's corruptibility, the president never doubted that he was leading the angels of American independence against the devils of foreign subservience.

Yet these combustibles never did ignite. The explanation lay in a complex and unpredictable mixture of American restraints and European influences. The initial component was Federalist overconfidence. As French aggression toppled the party balance in the United States, Federalists read these changes as the signs of a disappearing disease. A portion of the people, temporarily deluded, were responding once more to the truth of their real leaders. In June 1797, Hamilton assured Rufus King in London that "the public temper of this Country mends dayly & that there is no final danger of our submitting tamely to the yoke of France."[6] A few months later even the cautious Jay agreed that "the public mind is gradually recovering from its errors."[7] The gentry faith in a natural congruence between their own logic and an invisible public's rationality enabled Hamilton, at the height of tension in the late nineties, to imply "a strong confidence in the good sense and patriotism of the people" in Virginia itself, where his enemies continued to prevail.[8] All the news confirmed these Federalist preconceptions. Whether constituents converted local leaders or those leaders simply reversed themselves, a swelling stream of new recruits came to stand against the French menace. In the public display of cockades, former French partisans discarded the revolutionary tricolors and, at most, sported a neutrally libertarian red. The remaining Republican voices quieted dramatically on foreign affairs, and the party's directorate in Philadelphia became little more than the stalwart Representative Albert Gallatin talking with Vice-President Jefferson. If Jefferson appeared stoical in adversity, he had no choice.

The radical imbalance in party strength dulled the Federalist sense of urgency. No less bitter in their hatred of the opposition and no less committed to its destruction, enough Federalist leaders also felt no special haste in forcing a confrontation. Although most of them anticipated an eventual declaration of war, the pinnacles of Federalist prestige—

Adams, Hamilton, Jay—all counseled delay in the heat of anger over the XYZ affair, when hotbloods like Senator James Lloyd of Pennsylvania talked of war "as necessary to enable us to lay our hands on traitors."[9] Let the French faction dwindle to its final remnant, the leaders at the peak seemed to be saying, *then* crush it. Further Republican losses only strengthened that inclination. In the meantime, Federalists prepared for the day with the Alien and Sedition Acts.

These measures expressed no wild urge to crack every head that stirred. They applied a standard gentry logic of self-preservation to the particular circumstances of 1798. Although gentry rulers always burned under criticism, they still lived with it. Where the critics of the government were the agents of France, however, America's independence demanded that patriots silence the opposition. The president, notoriously argumentative on constitutional questions and tolerant of considerable debate over government "forms," endorsed the Sedition Act because it would quash a deadly foreign influence. By a similar reasoning, Judge Alexander Addison, a moderate in response to the Whiskey Rebellion of 1794, rabidly enforced the Sedition Act as a barrier to Jacobin subversion. Among former colonists with a dim sense of nationality, and among Federalists with an honored leader from the West Indies, the Alien and Alien Enemies Acts carried no general xenophobic message. They focused on the advance guards of French power, especially the revolutionary Irish, whose "organized treason," the Federalists believed, would strike America from within just as French collaborators had done in every fallen nation of Europe.[10] Isolate them now; eliminate them later. No German-born Federalist needed to fear those laws. Significantly, Jefferson, then Adams, identified Hamilton as an "alien" only after each in turn concluded that he was directing a British faction inside the United States.

Nevertheless, these acts did entail risks for the Federalists. By showing their teeth before they were ready to bite, Federalists allowed people time to ponder the implications of these measures. South of New England, the foreign-born mingled everywhere in American society, and not all of them caught the partisan nuances in the Federalist message from on high. Because decentralization and revolutionary ferment had stretched the latitude in public criticism far beyond the limits of the Sedition Act, this measure called upon legal precedent to thwart community practice. Did a quasi-war warrant such a dramatic nationalization of controls in an area that had customarily been the province of the states? Moreover, the Sedition Act still hewed rigidly to the traditional equation between government and legitimacy after party competition had weakened the old norms. Many of the Federalists themselves veered between the standard argument that they were "friends of government" and the new one that theirs was the party of virtue against the party of corruption. Nothing revealed their weaving course better than the exclusion of the vice-president from those government officials who received immunity under the act. An implicit bill of attainder against the Republican Jefferson made it difficult to claim that government, not party, was at issue. Not all Federalist leaders approved the law, and even some of its proponents justified it in a defensive tone.

If the sudden decline of the Republicans saved them from a frontal assault, it still left them in need of a strategy for counterattack. The dangers were obvious enough. Hostilities with France, new taxes, a national army, and the pressures for a formal declaration of war left only a final clamping to complete Jefferson's iron circle of monarchy and degradation. The House Ways and Means Committee, created in 1795 to resist executive domination in financial matters, now did the administration's bidding, and hence the president, Jefferson concluded, could make his own war like a king. Madison concurred. Even as a centralizer in 1787 he had shown a special sensitivity to the war-making powers of the executive and the evils of a standing army, and unlike Jefferson, he had long nursed a basic distrust of Adams the incipient monarchist. Both Virginians recoiled at the Federalist party's mimicry of its London parent —the additional paraphernalia of executive grandeur, then the Parliament-inspired Alien and Sedition Acts. Just a step or two more and the republic would dissolve back into the old colonial tyranny.

Quite clearly, their tactics of resistance had not worked. Early in the 1790s, Hamilton's opponents had become constitutional literalists, a band of scrutinizing lawyers who insisted on a precise phrase in the fundamental law to match each action. The Constitution gave Congress power only to "pay the Debts" of the United States, they argued, not to fund them in perpetuity. And where did the document authorize a national bank? When the Supreme Court assumed the right to judge lawsuits between one state and a citizen of another, the opposition scrambled to check the centralizers with the Eleventh Amendment— new precise phrases. Nevertheless, the more the Virginians explored the implicit powers of a vertical axis in the national government, the more loosely they also had to read the text, as Madison's exceedingly elastic interpretation of the treaty-making process illustrated. Now, in a time of peril, they needed to distance themselves as far from this Constitution as the most detached Hamiltonian and divine its very essence.

With the top of the national government securely in enemy hands, the Virginians retreated down the vertical pole to the states, where the people's last opportunity for a constitutional resistance lay, and here they found themselves on ground that such inveterate antifederalists as John Taylor of Caroline had continued to cultivate throughout the nineties.

What safeguards, Taylor had asked in 1794, did the people still have for their liberties? Perhaps one day the House might come to serve them, but that process would take a good deal of time. Fortunately, there already existed "a security for liberty of the happiest texture which could have been devised. The state legislatures are the people themselves in a state of refinement," and in this huge national republic they "fill up in some measure, the great space between Congress and the people." Not only did state legislatures have "a right to judge every infraction of the constitution"; they had an obligation "as the organs of the people" to supply their own "explanations of the constitution, according with its spirit . . . and republican principles."[11] It was exactly the right prescription for a beleaguered Jefferson, who had little taste for the technicalities of constitutional debate but a great appetite to expound "republican principles" in their moment of jeopardy. So the Republican leaders set about implementing it—not through state secession, Jefferson warned Taylor, with its prospect of fragmentation and recolonization, but by state assertion inside the national framework.

Two strategic problems stood immediately ahead. The lesser one blocked them from striking directly at the primary issues, British domination and war-generated tyranny. In the midst of a conflict with France the merest mention of anyone's subservience to a European power threatened to explode that delicate subject around the Republicans themselves. Hence they chose to attack the Alien and Sedition Acts, a secondary but nonetheless substantial target. If the Sedition Act succeeded, it would muzzle the only voices capable of rallying voters to oust the British party. Then because the Sedition Act contained provisions for punishing its own critics, the very vulnerable Jefferson and Madison resorted to those extremes of midnight conspiracy that 18th-century court politics had a way of inducing: secret authorship, special couriers to the state legislatures, all lips sealed in a pact of honor.

The larger problem in strategy forced them to walk a fine line between using the Constitution to save the republic and citing violations of it so fundamental that they destroyed the compact. Leaning to one side meant relying on the Tenth Amendment and implying from it the power of the states to pass on the constitutionality of national measures that touched their reserved rights. Leaning the other way meant activating the people's ultimate sovereignty, their inalienable right to dissolve a tyrannical government. Madison, more profoundly committed than Jefferson to the preservation of the Constitution, held the two of them in better balance, yet even he pictured the nation perilously close to a state of nature.

Their statements appeared in Jefferson's Kentucky Resolutions of November 1798, Madison's Virginia Resolutions of that December, and Madison's extensive Report of 1800 on the Virginia Resolutions.

Through the Alien and Sedition Acts, they argued, the general government usurped the rights of the states and the national executive stole the rights of the national legislature. That siphoning of power up the vertical axis and across the top of the national government threatened America with "an absolute, or at best, a mixed monarchy." Although the Supreme Court might decide normal disputes under the Constitution, all government units in the compact had "an equal right" to judge those issues directly affecting their interests. In this instance an accumulation of abuses, capped by the Alien and Sedition Acts, created one of "those great and extraordinary cases in which all the forms of the Constitution may prove ineffectual against infractions dangerous to the essential rights of the parties to it," and at the borderland between constitutional government and its dissolution, only the source of all government—the people—could judge whether actions fell in or out of the Constitution that they had authorized. At such moments states and people became identical. The very meaning of the word "states" was "the people composing those political societies, in their highest sovereign capacity": We the People, We the States. Through the states, therefore, "the powers granted under the Constitution, being derived from the people of the United States, may be resumed by them ... [and] every power not granted thereby remains with them, and at their will."

At this juncture Jefferson and Madison took different routes to the same objective. Jefferson's version had the state-people of Kentucky "void" the offending acts. Madison, recognizing how close such a flat assertion of the people's ultimate sovereignty came to declaring the Constitution itself void, simply condemned the violations and moved promptly to the next step: an appeal to all the states—all the people—to mount a common defense of their constitutional rights. Here the Virginians rejoined, with both of them expressing their deep attachment to the union. In fact, they presented themselves as its only true friends. Their doctrines, not the apocryphal ones in Philadelphia, preserved the proper republican balance, and their doctrines, not the consolidating principles of the monarchists, protected the nation from "revolution and blood." Nothing lay further from their minds than splintering the states and pitting them one by one *against* the national government. They wanted all the states—the American people—to demand their rights *in* the national government. In the terminology of 1787, they sought national ends through federal means.

Federalists translated the Republican protests into French and condemned them as treason. Kentucky they largely ignored. What danced before them was the vision of the "Gallic faction" using Virginia, the most powerful of the states and more or less synonymous with Republicanism, as the outpost of French power within the United States. It was

Virginia alone, the president thundered, that must "say whether this country has in it a Faction to be crushed, a faction to be humbled in dust and ashes. . . ."[12] Through those resolutions, cried Jay, the Virginians simultaneously declared "their opposition to their own government, and their devotion to a foreign one!"[13] The prospect of a state's linkage to one of the European giants had obsessed the gentry since the Revolution. Their generous provisions for admitting new western states were designed as much to police an exposed flank against European encroachment as to welcome distant brethren into the union. In 1787, centralizers proposed a national veto over state legislation so that the states could not be "used by foreign powers as Engines agt the Whole," and in lieu of a veto the Constitution included a clause "To guarantee every State in this Union a Republican Form of Government. . . ."[14] As Madison explained the clause in 1788, "the superintending government ought clearly to possess authority to defend the system against aristocratic or monarchical innovations."[15] Or Jacobin, the Federalists now vowed. During these years everybody's answer to an alienated state was swift military repression. Hence the Federalist James Iredell pictured the Virginia Resolutions as the "steps which directly lead to civil war" and the government in Philadelphia as ready "to oppose force to force."[16]

Where his colleagues saw Jacobins, Hamilton continued to see antifederalists. During the heat of the XYZ affair, he remained cool, opposing the Alien and Sedition Acts, a declaration of war, and the blustery threats of force against the Republicans. Hamilton, who understood his enemies better than they understood him, never mistook Jefferson and Madison for French agents. Although he, too, fought a "Virginia faction," its history began with the election of two antifederalist senators in 1788, proceeded through the attacks on his financial program, his character, and the executive's right to direct foreign policy, then shrank into impotence by the summer of 1798. The Virginia Resolutions abruptly changed his mood. Such brazen antifederalist heresy triggered a drive to crush this most dangerous of all challenges to a centralized republic. Indulging his love for the military, he had already roused Washington one last time to serve in name as commander-in-chief while Hamilton became the actual leader of the new national army. Now Hamilton had an immediate use for that army—to camp at the enemy's borders and "put Virginia to the Test of resistance"—and he threw his exceptional energies into creating an effective military force.[17] Obligingly, Congress in 1799 empowered the army to "suppress insurrection." It would probably be necessary, Hamilton thought, to break Virginia into several small states.

As the Virginia Resolutions trapped the most treacherous currents of national politics, 1799 became the year of crisis. No other state took up the Virginia and Kentucky Resolutions. Squeezed at the narrowest base of the vertical pole, even Jefferson grew desperate enough to contemplate the "repeated and enormous violations" that would require secession.[18] If the peak of the government hierarchy could delude the people so thoroughly, his only course was to risk the odds, scale it himself, and as president reclaim the republic. At some point almost every gentry leader indulged the conceit that only his character could save the people from their own weakness. For Jefferson in 1799, however, a salvation through character meant equally a salvation through party. Another grand muster was the republic's sole hope. Adapting his language for the approaching conflict, Jefferson decided that "there must, from the nature of man, be opposite parties, and violent dissensions and discords."[19] In a letter that served as his platform, he opened with the menace of a British-style monarchy and then, with redundant emphasis, raised his banner on the vertical axis: "I am for preserving to the States the powers not yielded by them to the Union, & to the legislature of the Union it's constitutional share in the division of powers; and I am not for transferring all the powers of the States to the general government, & all those of that government to the Executive branch."[20] But Jefferson's declaration came halfway through Adams' term. The Republicans grew weaker by the season, and their weakness no longer protected them. With the Federalists apparently united and thirsting for a confrontation, time seemed an insurmountable obstacle to Jefferson's latest strategy.

As both sides waited for that confrontation, they moved along the line between mock and actual warfare with the consummate skill of men who had played that game all their lives. It came with the gentleman's code, and its origins lay in the elementary commandments of character. Honor required courage; cowardice brought shame. Although courage might take many forms, nothing could compensate for the imputation of physical cowardice, especially after the Revolutionary War identified the highest form of patriotism with military valor. Among the countless attacks on Jefferson's reputation, the most devastating charged that in the face of a British advance in 1780 he had buckled and run. When the indictment was discussed in the Virginia assembly, a deeply depressed Jefferson considered his public career over, and literally to the end of his life he struggled against an accusation that he could neither escape nor refute. In private even Republicans worried about his "weakness" and "irresolution." The intimations of unmanliness that always trailed little James Madison and finally caught him in his own flight from the British in 1814 must have strengthened the bond between the two Virginians.

In layers of protection, gentlemen bedecked themselves in the regalia of personal courage. They learned to handle guns, to glorify the martial heroes, and to interpret the call to war as a test of their own at least as much as their country's honor. If the new republic banned titles of nobility, it did nothing to discourage titles of military distinction. Almost everyone who could possibly lay claim to an officer's rank did so, regardless of any service in battle. In polite address, the Republican Samuel Smith and the Federalist John Marshall were General, Aaron Burr and Timothy Pickering Colonel. At the peak of his political power, even Hamilton's enemies called him Colonel, and long after his death, friends referred to him as General, his paper rank in the attempted mobilization of the late nineties. The higher the rank, the better. Monroe, a captain in the war who failed to return to service as a lieutenant-colonel, became simply Colonel Monroe. Adams, no fool in matters of incremental honor, neatly dispatched his closet competitor of 1796 as "Major Thomas Pinckney." "A man with the title of Major," noted an English visitor to Boston, "sometimes holds your horse. . . ."[21] Quite apart from the status of these titles or their association with the Revolution, they served as common tokens of manly respect. In the 18th century, field officers were expected to court the greatest risks at the head of a battle charge, and the titles alone connoted courage. Despite the absence of a uniform, Jefferson as governor officially commanded the Virginia militia in 1780. When he turned his horse in one direction while the troops were required to fight in another, he guaranteed himself a lifetime's controversy.

These gentry preoccupations with physical courage and personal honor perpetuated the dueling code. A British import, it remained in the United States because it found such a rich market there. From New England to the Gulf, gentlemen lived under the shadow of a formal challenge from somewhere to redeem someone's honor. The tragedies and near-tragedies of the code rent the best families. Hamilton's son died in one duel, and Benjamin Rush's son killed a man in another. With a little less luck Jefferson would have lost his son-in-law to satisfy John Randolph's ravenous honor. Although the gentry might evade an actual encounter, they simply could not ignore the social pressures the code imposed. Many men without the slightest taste for combat felt obliged either to issue a challenge or to deal seriously with one if it came. One pathetic challenger went through the motions of calling Jefferson to account while he was president. To avoid a duel with Hamilton without seeming to shirk it, Monroe labored for days on the precise wording of a note of explanation. Age offered no protection. A young Thomas McKean could boast of his challenge to the 72-year-old Timothy Ruggles and leave Ruggles to struggle like any other gentleman with his quandary of death or dishonor.

The most famous duel of the age demonstrated how intimately the code entwined with a gentleman's qualifications for public leadership. After years of Hamilton's vilification, Burr challenged him, refused a quiet settlement, and killed him on the New Jersey shore in July 1804.

Hamilton, of course, could have refused the challenge. Yet he and his closest associates had lived by the values of the code since the war, and the man who had never missed an opportunity to jab at Jefferson's suspect character reckoned the price. His prominence, "as well in public as private aspects, enforcing all the considerations which constitute what men of the world denominate honor, impressed on me (as I thought) a peculiar necessity not to decline the call," Hamilton wrote in an eleventh-hour explanation. "The ability to be [a leader] . . . in those crises of our public affairs, which seem likely to happen, would probably be inseparable from a conformity with public prejudice in this particular."[22]

Where personal courage stood between honor and shame, the potential for violence hovered around every public dispute. To leash these aggressions, the gentry devised an array of rules and rituals that enabled them to fight for their causes and protect their reputations without turning politics into a bloodbath. The channeling process began with a distinction between public and personal debate. Anything that could be justified on grounds of republican principle, no matter how vicious or destructive to an individual's reputation, fell within a public realm and lent itself only to political or legal redress. To stand as models of impassive self-control in the face of public insults not only exemplified gentry character; it also saved many of those characters' lives. It was on the basis of principled disagreement that Hamilton tried to fend off Burr's challenge, and because the duel smacked of political revenge, it became a scandal. To some degree, this distinction between public and personal did deflect gentry leaders from the field of honor to the law: the libel suits that many of them pursued so passionately, or the Sedition Act that promised Federalists a legal weapon for destroying their personal tormentors.

Nevertheless, as the duel at Weehawken illustrated, the demarcation between public and personal remained so delicately thin that the gentry had to buffer it with additional layers, one of which was public debate through pseudonyms. What a gentleman dared not say under his own name he might risk under one of the stylized aliases of pamphlet or newspaper debate. Although the authors behind these masks were often quite obvious, the persona of a pseudonym still released them from a degree of responsibility for their statements and hence extended another measure of protection against revenge. For public purposes they now became the honorable Brutus, the valiant Wilkes, or the rigorous Old Whig, and words that one gentleman could not utter directly about another, Brutus or Wilkes or the Old Whig could declare in behalf of the republic. The convention of pseudonyms did not simply provide covers behind which gentlemen cast spears at one another. In psychologically subtle but socially crucial ways, these masks actually gave individuals new identities, and as they self-consciously assumed the personae of

Sydney and Catullus and Aristides, they elevated the debates to the level of pure public engagement.

In other words, the masked gentry experienced simultaneously a freedom to indulge in savage personal assaults and an elevation of their cause to the highest realms of patriotic discourse. During the debate over the Constitution when the antifederalist George Clinton, as Cato, ridiculed the arguments of Publius, Hamilton in *Federalist* 67 abruptly dropped his level of discussion to a harsh, personal rebuttal. From behind those masks, anything went in the name of the republic's honor. Fisher Ames, who later lived tolerably well with a Republican administration as Fisher Ames, gentleman from Massachusetts, could scream as Laocoon, sentinel of independence, that "the jacobins, like salamanders, can breathe only in fire. Like toads, they suck no aliment from the earth but its poisons. When they rest in their lurking places . . . it is, like serpants in winter, the better to concoct their venom; and when they are in action, it is to shed it." If the Republicans took power, Laocoon/Ames cried, "the people would be crushed . . . under tyranny more vindictive, unfeeling, and rapacious, than that of Tiberius, Nero, or Caligula, or any single despot that ever existed. The rage of one man [Jefferson] will be tired by repetition of outrage. . . ."[23]

How clearly the gentry understood these masked encounters as ritual duels was revealed by the language they used to describe them. As if the politics of pseudonymous debate were an Arthurian tournament, they talked about it in terms of knightly combat: finding a champion, entering the lists, taking the field, and other chivalric phrases. When Hamilton as Pacificus attacked the friends of the French Alliance during the Genet controversy, Jefferson spurred Madison to prepare his Helvidius essays in response: "For God's sake, my dear Sir, take up your pen, select the most striking heresies and cut him to pieces in the face of the public. There is nobody else who can & will enter the lists against him." "You must, my dear Sir, take up your pen against this champion," Jefferson implored Madison on another occasion when Hamilton had reappeared as Marcellus.[24] In the same spirit a friend urged Samuel Smith "to enter the lists with any champion that can be produced" at a time in Smith's career when pseudonymous slander was threatening to bury him.[25]

Drawing on an equally rich aristocratic tradition, gentry leaders added a final layer of protection between themselves and violent retribution by employing surrogates to fight their gutter brawls for them. As gentlemen maintained a posture of cool detachment, they subsidized or otherwise supported men of lower social rank to fling themselves into the contests of character defamation, rumor-mongering, and generalized vitriol. Vulgar men were expected to use vulgar language. No gentleman could retaliate directly because no gentleman dueled an inferior. For this very reason, forms of legal redress evolved to defend the gentleman's honor against attacks from below. Of all these surrogate warriors, the most coveted were the skilled pamphleteers and newspaper editors, the professional assassins of gentry politics who could reach the widest audience with the fewest restraints and the least personal jeopardy to their sponsors. William Maclay of Pennsylvania called them "gladiators of the quill"—the gentry's slave warriors.[26] What Tom Paine did to the reputation of "the Royal Brute of Britain" the Federalist elite through John Fenno and William Cobbett and the Republican elite through Benjamin Bache and William Duane sought to do to one another. Like fighting cocks, the partisan editors were set in the pit to draw blood for their gentlemanly sponsors.

Gentry leaders, on their part, sustained these rituals of mock combat by internalizing the rules and applying them with meticulous care. Between enemies no ripple was allowed to show on the glassy surface of personal relations. The invariable use of the term "honorable gentleman" for an opponent in debate was no mere courtesy; it offered an essential token of respect where its omission might mean an intolerable insult. During the early nineties, while masked champions and newspaper lackeys were savaging the political reputations of Jefferson and Hamilton, the two gentlemen themselves maintained an impeccable decorum within Washington's cabinet. No matter how acidly the gentry reported these conversations in private, they held rigorously to the bows of courtesy in public, and the failure of the eruptive John Adams to abide by the niceties of these forms contributed to the impression that he might be crazy. The only acceptable alternative to a scrupulous politeness was silence. As the elaborate justifications of Jefferson to Washington and Hamilton to Edward Carrington in 1792 illustrated, each gentleman convinced himself that his enemy, not he, endangered the peace by violating the code of gentry decency. To Jefferson, Hamilton himself had taken the role of a brawling servant; to Hamilton, Madison and Jefferson had deceived him in public and defamed him in private. No doubt Jefferson also believed in some fine distinction enabling him to swear to Washington on his sacred honor that he had no part in the slashing attacks in the *National Gazette*, the political vehicle that he and Madison created for rough combat.

Gentry leaders labored so intently to preserve these shaded gradations because they served so many important functions. As the rituals buffered their bodies, the surrogate voices in particular also ministered to their psyches. The unrestrained delight they took in the most abusive and warped statements about their opponents indicated how much these utterances helped them make it through another day of civility on their faces and hatred in their hearts. The most cultivated New England Federalists, gentlemen such as Christopher Gore and George Cabot who considered themselves bred in the finest English tradition, found the alley language of their editors simply delicious and urged one another to savor the latest morsels. After reading an especially outrageous pamphlet on the Adams administration, Jefferson praised it in phrases that surely must have surprised the unscrupulous author: "Such papers cannot fail to produce the best effect. They inform the thinking part of the nation."[27] Indeed, some of this scurrility was not just beyond gentlemanly bounds; it expressed feelings that gentlemen would not acknowledge in themselves. Before Jefferson could bring himself to believe that the monarchists had captured Washington, lesser men bawled it in public, and Jefferson, still refusing to say the words, rushed to their defense. A free press served deep emotional as well as broad public needs. Categorizing minds and categorizing conventions of political battle enabled the gentry to maintain that critical gap between what they said and what their political agents said without struggling over questions of consistency or hypocrisy. Hence, to the inestimable benefit of their public reputations, they felt no qualms about abandoning those servants who became an embarrassment, a fate that Tom Paine suffered at the hands of Federalists, for example, and James Callander at the hands of Republicans.

Political parties projected these devices for containing personal violence to the country at large. As leaders called a nationwide muster, they also mobilized the apparatus of ritual warfare on a national scale. Scattered tournaments and alley fights were transformed into a full-fledged "Campaign" with a grand array of foot soldiers, cavalry, and cannon deployed across the land. Behind masks and through surrogates, the gentry raged and slandered in the name of America's independence. Newspapers proliferated, following the directions—often the texts—of the primary party organs and providing what Federalists and Republicans alike called each party's "engine," a generic term for the mechanical rams and catapults of old-fashioned battle. As a Republican broadside a few years later illustrated, a call to the polls was a call to arms: "The finishing STROKE. Every Shot's a Vote, and every Vote KILLS A TORY."[28] By 18th-century custom, gentlemen candidates were expected to stand a poll; that is, simply to present themselves to this militia of voters. Like the gentlemen commanders in contemporary European armies, therefore, the leaders of the two parties used no weapons themselves. In the language of the day, each remained at his "post" as a model of courage in the midst of battle, Jefferson self-consciously surrounded by his enemies in Philadelphia and Adams, by his own account, exposed to attack from Republican mobs. Hence even as they led by example, they detached themselves a symbolic step from the clash and clang of war. Others actually exchanged the blows.

Steeped in the customs of ritual violence, the gentry could sublimate their national conflict in mock warfare without ever asking themselves whether they were trying to avoid physical combat. Nevertheless, gentlemen with a yen for real warfare, such as General Hamilton and Colonel Monroe, showed an appropriately low level of sensitivity to the intricacies of this grand national tournament and relatively little sympathy for its unique social value, while those with an aversion to physical encounter, such as the noncombatant Madison and the frail Fisher Ames, indulged the war games most avidly and skillfully. In mock battle, the portly, middle-aged James Bayard could eye "the fury of the Jacobins" with a gentleman's courage and declare in all honesty: "I shall never ask nor expect mercy from them."[29] Along an admittedly fine edge, the parties channeled group aggressions so effectively by raising them so high. In the short run at least, the military trappings of the party muster, the rigidities of party doctrine, and the viciousness of party rhetoric served the cause of peace by heightening the rites of war.

Beyond the short run, peace at home required peace abroad. Given sufficient time, neocolonial pressures—external and internal—would have sucked the life out of these rituals of avoidance. Once again, the interrelated American patterns of character, honor, and independence and the happenchances of European war combined to change the setting, this time relieving the pressures before they became intolerable. The process began with the special dangers of disgrace facing the new president and the peculiar qualities that he brought to the challenge. Elected by a slender margin after the first contested presidential election, Adams knew, as all the gentry knew, that he lay uniquely exposed before the nation. The American Revolution generated only one authentic first character, and while Washington lived, any other president risked appearing an interloper. Although Adams felt in his own mind that he deserved the presidency after Washington and entered office confident that he could serve the nation better than any of his peers, he also expected the worst from an envious mankind, and he steeled himself in perpetual anticipation of malice and intrigue. Seeking honor against impossible odds somehow suited the Adams temperament.

The new president met the challenge to his reputation with a distinctive mix of stubbornness, zeal, and suspicion. Independent to the brink of crankiness, he refused to accommodate his political rhetoric, personal manner, or private conversation to his audience, and hence he actually invited the various accusations that he was incorrigibly monarchic, hopelessly vain, and certifiably mad. Despite his crotchety ways, Adams shared the basic Federalist presuppositions: a commitment to social cohesion, an abhorrence of the atheistic democracy that he identified with the French Revolution, and a conviction that its agents were subverting the American republic. Very much like Washington, he swallowed the Jay Treaty because revolutionary France repelled him just a bit more than Britain. Again like Washington, Adams refused to see himself as a party man even as he presided over one.

What lay beneath this orthodox cover was an obsession with foreign influences so deep and comprehensive that it almost caricatured the neocolonial spirit. In Jefferson's neat summary, "he hates the French, he hates the British."[30] Following those same instincts at home, Adams would leave office convinced that both the Federalists and the Republicans were dominated by "foreign liars."[31] Appropriately, he began his term in a mood of proud isolation: "I am not enough of an Englishman, nor little enough of a Frenchman to please some people."[32] War with France, Adams knew, meant a subservient connection with Britain, and to avoid that deadly package the president took his greatest risk since 1776. After the XYZ uproar one of the American envoys, Gerry, stayed awhile in Europe to maintain a slender tie with France. Adams, who assumed that honest patriots would always suffer slander, ignored the fierce Federalist attack on his Massachusetts friend and nursed his own hope for a negotiated settlement. Hints from Europe encouraged him. Late in 1799, the president sent a new group of envoys to France, escaped to Quincy, and left the militant Federalists in a fury of frustration. The alternative, as Adams later explained it, was "an alliance with England, an endless war with all the rest of the world . . . and, what was worse than all the rest, a civil war, which I knew would be the consequence. . . ."[33] Nevertheless, for a man who lived in dread of public humiliation, another try with the arrogant French constituted a complex and courageous act.

A fortuitous turn in European affairs transformed the president's gamble into an American miracle. After a foolish adventure in Egypt that cost the French their military initiative and Mediterranean fleet, Bonaparte returned to France, overthrew the Directory, and established himself as first consul of a new government just as the latest American envoys were embarking. With Britain secured against invasion and Bonaparte preoccupied with the consolidation of his continental power, the French government was glad to rid itself of a minor Atlantic annoyance and agreed in September 1800 to cancel the obsolete treaty of 1778 in return for a cancellation of American claims against marauding French ships. No war, no alliance, not even a snarl of loose ends. It was an extraordinary coup for a country consuming itself with neocolonial passions.

The immediate result of the president's search for peace was to destroy him as a court leader. Out of deference to the hero, Adams had retained

Washington's cabinet in the expectation that these gentlemen would also serve a new first character. Even in 1797 that decision did him no good, because it surrounded a vulnerable chief executive with men of indifferent reputations. The names of Timothy Pickering as secretary of state, Oliver Wolcott as secretary of the treasury, and James McHenry as secretary of war generated none of the sparkle that Jefferson, Hamilton, and Knox had once radiated, and their mediocrity merely highlighted the drop in prestige from Washington to Adams. More disastrously, this middling trio denied their new president even a minimal respect. In Washington's time members of the cabinet had intrigued against one another; in Adams' time they intrigued against him, debasing his character, plotting against his policies, and generally abusing his confidence. In a manner common to chronically suspicious individuals, Adams suspended critical judgment on those few he chose to trust. As the president moved toward peace, Pickering and Wolcott churned toward war, dragging the phlegmatic McHenry with them, but Adams waited until the evidence of treachery overwhelmed him before he finally repudiated McHenry and Pickering. The conniving Wolcott the president praised and honored to his last day in office.*

When these secretaries had official secrets to divulge, they usually passed them to Hamilton, who remained the premier Federalist after his retirement to New York in 1795. But Adams' failure as a leader did not mean Hamilton's success. The automatic respect that Hamilton received never translated into a predictable obedience. Even through Washington, he had not been able to curb Pickering's abrasive statements on foreign policy. In 1796, when Hamilton schemed to make Thomas Pinckney instead of Adams the next president, he failed utterly. In 1797, rather than dictating national policy, he was writing his former lieutenants in search of basic information about government affairs. Hamilton counseled caution toward France and most Federalists pressed for war. He opposed the Sedition Act and Congress passed it. Although he fumed along with other hawkish Federalists in 1799 and 1800, he never marshaled an effective opposition to the president. Only on financial matters did Hamilton's word remain law. Far more than he realized, his power depended on the subtle persuasions and assessments that face-to-face relations allowed him. Without an intimate role in the procedures of

* Like father, like son. As a way of communicating the most important message of his life, his election as president, the equally jaundiced John Quincy Adams forwarded to his father a personal note of congratulations from the venerable Federalist Rufus King, who in private had expressed these thoughts on the subject: ". . . rather any southern or western democrat than J.Q.A. for President . . . if J.Q.A. become Pr. all of N. England that is virtuous or enlightened, will be persecuted & degraded; manners, laws, principles will be changed and deteriorated." King to Christopher Gore, Nov. 22, 1816, King, VI, 36.

government, Hamilton's voice echoed from a distant chamber and arrived with a muted authority. A style of command that had been impressively brisk in 1790 became merely brusque by 1800.

For opposite reasons, then, neither Adams nor Hamilton was suited to lead a neocolonial party—Adams because he feared both great powers too much, Hamilton because he cared about them too little. Equally obtuse to the requirements of party leadership, the two of them remained free to indulge a final, explosive episode in court intrigue. If Adams blinded himself to the duplicity within his own cabinet, he quickly spotted Hamilton as a dangerous rival whose authority with Washington in particular threatened to humiliate the sensitive president. When the Virginia Resolutions converted Hamilton to the war lobby, the tensions between them mounted. Hamilton dotted his intimate correspondence with contemptuous comments on Adams. Hamilton, the president told his friend Gerry in March 1799, was plotting a coup that would make him king and turn the United States into "a Province of Great Britain."[34] Adams nursed these illusions until mid-1800 when, in apoplexy over his secretaries' disloyalty, he lashed out at the "Creole bastard" he considered their leader and spread the story that Hamilton headed a British faction inside the United States.

With his honor at stake, Hamilton set aside all other considerations to concentrate on a single objective, his accuser's destruction. In a letter circulated among prominent Federalists during the heat of the presidential election, Hamilton struck directly at the heart of Adams' claim to leadership, his character. It revealed "great and intrinsic defects," Hamilton charged, including "the disgusting egotism, the distempered jealousy, and the ungovernable indiscretion of MR. ADAMS'S temper. . . ." Consequently, his official conduct "has sunk the tone of the public mind . . . sown the seeds of discord at home, and lowered the reputation of the Government abroad."[35] Surely Adams' honorable running mate, Charles Cotesworth Pinckney, would be preferable. Climaxing the letter with a defense of his own reputation, Hamilton reminded Federalists of those qualities in Adams that most disturbed them and simultaneously demonstrated that Hamilton could serve them no better.

Hamilton's purposes, of course, were light-years away from Adams' vision of them. Rather than bowing to Britain, he came close to advocating war against it in the summer of 1798. "I take the liberty to express to you my opinion," he wrote Pickering, "that it is of the true policy as well as of the dignity of our Government to act with spirit and energy as well towards G Britain as France. I would *meet* the same measure to both of them, though it should ever furnish the extraordinary spectacle of a nation at war with two nations at war with each other."[36] Hamilton thought about crushing Virginia and even carving a hemispheric empire from the Spanish colonies, but never about subordinating the United States to its old master. He had always held remarkably well to a single proposition: how best to use Britain without being used by it.

Yet Hamilton suffered double jeopardy from the company he kept. Not only did the Federalist Francophobes ignore his recommendations on policy, but their posture of dependence toward Britain perversely hurt Hamilton's reputation as well. A private exchange among Federalists revealed how close to the mark Adams' charges struck. When Republicans fabricated a letter by a British diplomat describing "my bosom friends" Pickering, Wolcott, and McHenry as "all so staunch that I have now no occasion to look after them," Rufus King in London immediately accepted it as authentic and hastened to warn his colleagues.[37] If a Republican parody fit the preconceptions of their friends, the trio simply had no defense against their enemies, and by association Hamilton sank with them.

In one sense this court drama of betrayal, revenge, and vindication had no political effect at all. Federalists who were desperate to "escape the fangs of Jefferson" found it a dangerous distraction, and every one of the party's electors cast his vote for Adams, not because he had won the vendetta but because only his candidacy stood between them and the French menace.[38] In another sense, however, the struggle between Adams and Hamilton foreshadowed the disintegration of a national party. Every gentry hierarchy required its capstone, and the only two gentlemen who might have served at the Federalist peak disqualified themselves. They did not split the party. In effect, they abandoned it to pursue other goals and left the chieftains beneath them to fend for themselves. Self-conscious New Englanders began looking to one another. Southern Federalists, always skeptical of centralized power, turned to their states. New Yorkers resumed their habit of fighting among themselves. And so it went throughout the nation. As a mobilizing mechanism, the Federalist party roughly equaled the Republican party in 1800, but these were the terminal reflexes of a headless hierarchy. Never did the absence of the demigod Washington tell more critically than in 1800.

Under any circumstances the Federalists would have been in trouble by election time. The Convention of 1800 with France contained exactly what the Republicans needed to relieve them of their worst political handicaps. Only the French-hating Federalists could have ended the quasi-war and still avoided the impression of capitulating to this great power. Freed from the shadow of a French war and the incubus of a French alliance, the Republicans could rise and prosper. A general cooling of European hostilities diminished the sense of immediate danger even before the actual settlement with France, and neocolonial politics, based as it was on volatile swings of emotion, responded dramatically to the new prospects of safety. Federalist leaders lashed out in vain to overcome a spreading apathy. Republicans, on the other hand, benefited from the natural centrality of anti-British feelings in postrevolutionary America. A diplomatic miracle, in other words, produced a political miracle. The Republicans, a shrunken minority under siege in January 1800, emerged the majority party in December, and, far more than any other person, John Adams paved the way for that triumph.

The Jeffersonian Resolution

Extending their strength from the south into Pennsylvania and New York, the Republicans Jefferson and Burr slipped past the Federalist Adams in 1800 by eight electoral votes. The victorious party was so proficient as a national mobilizer and so deficient as a political organizer that all Republican electors cast ballots for both of its candidates, created a tie, and sent the election to the lame-duck House, where the Federalists could either block a decision or perhaps choose between the co-winners. Proving once again that Hamilton had a keener eye for character than Jefferson, Burr shocked the Virginian by his hints of interest in the presidency and let some Federalists dream of a Burr administration under their domination. But Federalists in Delaware and Maryland, rather than risk disunion, broke two months of deadlock in Jefferson's favor, allowed his inauguration on schedule, and thereby completed what Jefferson for the rest of his life would call the revolution of 1800.

Because the Republicans did not destroy their rivals' governing system, later generations tended to dismiss Jefferson's claim as the hyperbole of a happy winner. Nevertheless, by gentry standards something profound indeed had occurred. For Jefferson himself it meant triumph after a decade of humiliating defeats, and an incredible reversal from 1799. The same sense of a magnificent turn in fortunes applied to his party, whose first grievance in Jefferson's list of 1798 was that the Federalists "ride us very hard, cruelly insulting our feelings."[1] As the Republican champion in 1800, his victory now spread glory to all its chieftains. The splintering in Federalist leadership only sharpened the image of an enemy fleeing in disgrace before the proud army of Republican conquerors. Above all, the party and its champion had vindicated the nation's honor by saving the American Revolution.

Approximately every decade after 1776—in the late 1780s, around 1800, and finally in the years before the War of 1812—veterans of the original contest sensed a waning of the revolutionary spirit, merged their lives with its vitality, and struggled to save its generative powers. Republicans in the late nineties saw themselves fighting one more round in a continuing revolution against "Anglomen" and "Tory federalism," forces that threatened to smother the last sparks of an independent America. "Not a gun, no, not Even a Pistol was fired in Dover today. . . ," the Republican Thomas Rodney wrote of a fourth of July in Federalist Delaware. "Such Effect has the long Tory rule of Our State produced at last."[2] 1799 was the Republican Valley Forge, a testing time of courage and dedication, and some of them could even take grim comfort in their humiliation, knowing that they suffered once again as true patriots against British tyranny. With a grand muster of the Republican militia, 1800 became their Yorktown and 1801 their Peace of Paris. Appropriately, new bondings expanded their revolutionary fraternities. Wilson Cary Nicholas, Jefferson's co-conspirator in the Kentucky Resolutions, and Albert Gallatin, his lieutenant in Philadelphia, would have his unquestioning affection and trust for a lifetime. Summing up the meaning of these events a decade later, Benjamin Rush wrote to Jefferson, "Our country has twice declared itself independent of Great Britain, once in 1776 and again in 1800."[3]

As Jefferson was battling "the Tory interest" in the late nineties, he described the crisis as "the most eventful ever known since that of 1775," one that would "decide whether the principles established by that contest are to prevail, or give way to those they subverted."[4] When his party reclaimed the Revolution, the new president reached back in his inaugural address to Washington, conveniently dead and deified, and bowed to "our first and great revolutionary character," not simply as a shrewd political gesture toward the hero but primarily as a way to blot Federalism from the record and clarify the line of succession from 1776 to 1801. One after another of Jefferson's associates who had also fought the Federalist Washington made the same efforts to reestablish continuity with the revolutionary hero. In a similar vein, Madison masked the

Virginia Report's sharp break in constitutional doctrine by creating a mythical period of purity sometime during Washington's presidency, obliterating the Adams years as the distortion of "party or personal ascendencies," and linking the Republican interpretation with an "early, deliberate & continued practice under the Constitution."[5] No one was pining for a lost golden age. These Republicans only looked back to move forward, to draw fuel for their continuing revolution.

Without a reprieve from international pressures no one could have preserved for very long the image of 1800 as a redeclaration of America's independence. The good fortune that shone on Adams' peace mission simply showered its blessings on Jefferson's early years in office, which coincided with the only significant lull in the European wars between 1793 and 1814. In international as well as national terms, the new president enjoyed a unique moment of honor: no servile attachments, no bullying humiliations. As a final stroke of luck, Jefferson faced his first international challenge not from Britain, his party's predetermined enemy, but from France, the power to which he reputedly kneeled in vassalage. When the Republican president emerged in 1803 with his head high and the Louisiana territory in hand, he resolved the greatest single fear surrounding his leadership: in Fisher Ames' lurid summary, a "war with Great Britain, a Cisalpine [colonial] alliance with France, plunder and anarchy."[6]

Yet even before the Louisiana Purchase, Jefferson's revolution of 1800 was benefiting from a general shift in America's neocolonial orientation. During the late nineties a merciless buffeting and a callous indifference from the great powers drove gentlemen of both parties further and further into a defensive corner toward everything European. Before hostilities with France fully developed, many Federalists shared Hamilton's anger over Britain's spreading maritime depredations, and as the quasi-war progressed, few of them found much comfort in a preoccupied Britain's erratic attention to a minor ally. In the standard lament of an aggrieved dependent, one frustrated Federalist complained during the summer of 1800: "To me it appears strange that the British ministry have never thought it their interest to try and conciliate this country; they cannot be uninformed of the state of parties here, or insensible to the advantages they derive from a good understanding with us."[7] There were sound neocolonial reasons why Adams, the avowed enemy of a "British faction," was not repudiated by his party in the electoral college.

The Republican disillusionment, of course, was much more severe. "At length the charm is broke," Jefferson bitingly reported to Monroe early in 1798 as he sent news of fresh French assaults on American commerce.[8] With public disclosure of the XYZ affair, even the mild-tempered Madison flared in anger, and a gloomy Monroe, once the leading Francophile in Jefferson's circle, pictured the United States beneath the boots of two enemy giants. Jefferson responded to Bonaparte's rise with the special bitterness of a shattered hope. Never again did the French nation hold a distinctive place in his visions of an expanding republicanism. As he was saving one revolution and Emperor Napoleon —"the great beast"—was destroying another, Jefferson missed neither the parallel nor its lesson. Now America alone was "acting for all mankind."[9]

The most searing lesson, however, came from the helplessness of his cause in the late nineties. As a way of driving that message home, he devised a new calendar: "You know that it was in the year X. Y. Z. that so great a transition from us to the other side took place, & with as real republicans as we were ourselves. . . ."[10] No amount of effort, he reminded his friends, could have won a Republican victory in 1799. To free American republicanism from the mercy of Europe's titans, Jefferson provided an appropriate neocolonial solution, one that at a more optimistic time he had dismissed as unrealistic. The United States would now pull as far into its shell as it could, perhaps breaking all communications with Europe's governments. In the midst of "the year X. Y. Z.," Jefferson stated as part of his political creed "little or no diplomatic establishment." Soon after entering office he reported to a friend abroad: "We have a perfect horror at everything like connecting ourselves with the politics of Europe . . . we wish to let every treaty we have drop off without renewal. We call in our diplomatic missions, barely keeping up those to the most important nations. There is a strong disposition . . . to discontinue these; and very possibly it may be done."[11]

Such a violent swing toward withdrawal reflected as intense an involvement with European might as the grandest schemes for an international connection in the mid-nineties. What emerged around 1800 was not a new cast of mind but a significant shift inside the old one. Although a more confident Jefferson did allow the pendulum to slide back toward the center, an important residue of negativism stayed with him, as his later embargo policy illustrated. The president also accentuated the distance from Europe in little ways. Meeting diplomats in his slippers and inviting these captives of protocol to take seats "pell-mell" at his dinners were delicious acts of neocolonial revenge, and the cosmopolitan president enjoyed them to the hilt. A crude and barbaric land, you say? Bend your stiff backs to the republican manner. The Jeffersonian style suited the temper of the American gentry quite well. It always pleased them to think of their republican culture as distinctive, and even the most passionately partisan among them worried, in Fisher Ames' phrase, about "an *intimate* connection" with either great power. As a general disillusionment with Europe increased their yearnings for detachment, Jefferson's insularity helped many of them identify his victory in 1800 with a revolutionary turn toward true American independence.

In the final reckoning the meaning of a gentry revolution relied on the character of its makers, and no one leaped more happily to that conclusion than Jefferson. Unless circumstances compelled him to reconsider, he swept aside the flaws in those individuals he trusted and pictured their characters as transcendent powers for virtue. Of a staunchly conservative Virginia trio he admired, he once asked blithely "what degree of confidence would be too much for a [judicial] body composed of . . . Wythe, Blair, and Pendleton?"[12] When Robert Morris, the committed centralizer and godfather to Hamilton's financial program, lost control of his speculations and landed in debtors' prison, Jefferson simply mourned a great wartime compatriot: "What a misfortune to the public that R. Morris has fallen from his height of character. If he could get from confinement, and the public give him confidence, he would be a valuable officer in that station & in our council."[13] With Gerry, whose luxurious ways and mercantile interests represented a fair sample of things he feared in government, Jefferson claimed in their long association to have had only a single disagreement. Before he completed his first term, he even claimed to have had just one significant difference with his old comrade John Adams!

If he still found the good in his adversary Adams, Jefferson saw only perfection in his intimates, Madison, the secretary of state, and Gallatin, the secretary of the treasury. Once, far from power, Jefferson had warned his friends that all governors harbored the tendency to become "wolves." When his own administration took office, however, the universal solvent of character removed all doubts. He and Madison and Gallatin could no more become wolves in the national executive than Wythe and Blair and Pendleton on the Virginia bench. With the three of them managing "the great interests of our country," the United States was guaranteed a pure republican government.[14] Even the vicious Hamiltonian system grew benign in their hands. Ideally, Jefferson would have destroyed his enemy's debt structure and national bank; practically, he ceased to fear them under Republican control.

Behind this sanguine view of his associates lay Jefferson's supreme confidence in his own character. While he was still seeking the presidency, Jefferson continued to interpret the contest in structural terms: a monarchic use of executive power, a democratic opposition from the states—and hence from the people. As late as February 1801, with Federalists still blocking his election in the House, he continued to think of his authority as resting on the "democratical" power of friendly state governments and their militia. Once president himself, however, Jefferson used the executive's powers as comfortably as the astute Hamilton anticipated he would. Jefferson had attacked the monarchists only to tame the executive, not kill it, and with a pure republican as president he expected a very compliant democratic base indeed. When Pendleton revived some of the antifederalist amendments from 1788 in order to fix the people's basic rights forever in the hands of the states, Jefferson quietly let the proposals die. The new president wanted no additional constraints on his own leadership. Although Madison, the meticulous balancer, struggled for the rest of his life to reconcile the special need for the Virginia Resolutions in the late nineties and their irrelevance to the honorable administrations that followed, Jefferson, the genial harmonizer, never looked back. He rode the flow of power to the presidency with an absolute assurance that wherever he stood in the scheme of national government, he would always know how to arrange its parts into a republican whole.

Self-confidence certainly did not make him a haphazard president. In fact, Jefferson brought a metaphysician's care to those styles of governance that were supposed to radiate a national influence. There would be no monarchic glitter of "birthdays, levees, processions to parliament, inauguration pomposities, etc." in his government, he had already promised.[15] He labored to strike the perfect republican balance between simplicity and dignity in all public ceremonies. Before his first annual message to Congress, the president had Madison review the manuscript to forestall grammatical attacks from "the purists of New England."[16] To the carping of these same gentlemen, he rode in public without an escort, and, following Franklin's famous model of an ostentatious plainness in personal dress, he cultivated an appearance that one acute observer described as "neglected but not slovenly."[17] Years later, in light of the Virginia Dynasty's manner of governance, Jefferson proudly concluded: "our government is now so firmly on it's republican tack, that it will not be easily monarchised by forms."[18]

Nevertheless, the longer he ruled, the more Jefferson relaxed his concerns about a purified government and acted according to his inclinations. His reading of the Constitution told him that the Louisiana Purchase required an amendment, but his faith in the virtue of his own administration made him an easy convert to quick acceptance, "confiding, that the good sense of our country will correct the evils of construction when it shall produce ill effects."[19] Once Jefferson had fervently defended the rights of the House in the treaty-making process; now he expected the House to authorize millions for his discretionary use without knowing what kind of treaty they might buy. In his second term the president sketched grand plans for a national program of "useful works" that would have satisfied any centralizer's dream. The same republican character that secured the revolution of 1800, in other words, came to justify whatever measures the victor thought were appropriate to it.

As the winners fashioned a gentry revolution from the norms of honor, independence, and character, the losers made an even more striking contribution to the republic by relinquishing power without violence or disunion. Both the stakes in national virtue and the nature of the Federalist faith suggested that it should have been otherwise. To an all-or-nothing battle for the American republic, Federalists brought an all-or-nothing conception of their own alternatives in the contest. The Republicans in opposition had interpreted the control of any state as a foothold in the national government. But Federalists who had spent a decade denying a national role for the states could scarcely legitimize them overnight and make them a base for national power. By their understanding the Republican sweep of 1800 had simply driven them from the national government. Indeed, their sometimes exclusive reliance on executive control left them exceedingly vulnerable to Jefferson's victory alone.

Fundamentally, the Federalists retired in peace because they could not make war. Throughout the crisis of the nineties an impassable buffer of space and diffusion protected the nation from the aggressive impulses of its officials. All gentry leaders carried in their heads a model of the happy society that heard nothing but the truth and nodded in agreement with it. On a national scale, however, a thousand fissures drained every effort to realize that vision. Policies in Philadelphia fell into the vast cavern of American decentralization. During the late nineties, Federalist officials collected few national taxes in the backcountry where Republicans still prevailed and only a few more where they did not. Functionally, the Whiskey Rebels had defeated the Hamiltonians. From their favorite law, the Sedition Act, militant Federalists netted a mere fourteen indictments, and almost any culprit with a good pair of legs and a few friends could go into hiding instead of jail. After more than two years of uninhibited criticism under the law, Fisher Ames, in the very heartland of Federalism, concluded that "the newspapers are an overmatch for any Government."[20] Hamilton's dream of an army fell victim to the same national diffusion. Despite his phenomenal exertions, not even a respectable framework emerged. The United States of the 1790s would sustain only its traditional, locally rooted militia.

Nevertheless, Federalists might have made a show of force against the Jeffersonian Jacobins if gentry conceptions of space had not also facilitated their withdrawal. Although 18th-century gentlemen treasured minute details about the lands that they actually saw, a wider geography quickly became very fluid. William Duane in Pennsylvania, Jefferson in Virginia, and Pierce Butler in South Carolina simply blotted from their consciousness those portions of their states that offended them. The gentry's regional vocabulary reflected the same malleable sense of geography. To both New England Federalists and Virginia Republicans, the meaning of "northern"—or "eastern"—followed the election returns: New England and New York in the early nineties, everything north of the Potomac in 1798, exclusively New England in 1801. Such easy, accordionlike adjustments expressed a habit of mind. Rather than beginning with a determinate block of territory and then considering its nature and needs, 18th-century gentlemen started with a purpose and then shaped their geography to suit it. In broad terms, geography was a dependent variable of ideology. Appropriately, the Constitution originated in a vision of an American republic without a clearly fixed location for it. Nine states, the framers specified, would suffice to form a new union. Although some federalists worked earnestly for an inclusive union, all of them remained open to the possibility of many different Americas emerging. These elastic conceptions trailed the early history of the new nation. During the mid-nineties, Virginia was no more integral to the American republic of most New England Federalists than New England was to the American republic of most Virginia Republicans.

To an adaptable sense of geography, New England Federalists added a unique regional pride. No other gentry group gloried as they did in the purity of their region's society, which they contrasted disdainfully to the lazy, slave-corrupted south and the ethnic hodgepodge of the middle states—"spasmotic, chaotic, and contemptible," as the Connecticut Federalist Chauncey Goodrich described pluralistic Pennsylvania.[21] No other group so consistently presented themselves as a bloc or voted in Congress as a bloc. "You may be assured," Oliver Wolcott wrote his brother in a characteristic conceit, "that the success of the republican system in a great measure, depends on the conduct of the people of New England."[22] No other group questioned the advantages of union simply because of the inferior quality of other regions—a topic of discussion even at the height of Federalist power in 1798. To escape the Republican administration, therefore, New Englanders found it relatively easy to compress their republic and step behind a regional barricade. It was from this vantage point that Ames told his comrades to defend themselves: "The federalists must entrench themselves in the State governments, and endeavor to make State justice and State power a shelter. . . ."[23]

Once inside the shelter, these Federalists might have chosen to bar the door forever. Part of their reluctance to separate altogether stemmed from subtle changes in the meaning of union that were occurring at the end of the nineties. At the peak of involvement with the French Revo-

lution, the gentry's soft sense of distances seemed to dissolve the Atlantic barrier. "The Great Family of Mankind:—May the distinction of
nation and of language, be lost in the association of Freedom and of
Friendship . . . ," rang one toast from the Democratic Society of Pennsylvania; "till the Rights of Man shall become the Supreme Law of every
land," continued another, "and their separate Fraternities be absorbed,
in One Great Democratic Society, comprehending the Human Race."[24]
When England was first threatened with invasion, George Cabot wrote
as if he lived on the outermost British Isle. The greater the disillusionment with the great powers, however, the wider the Atlantic grew and
the more carefully the gentry calculated their domestic resources. Did
they still have the leeway to play with the shape of their union? Jefferson
thought not in 1798 when he discouraged John Taylor's suggestion of a
Virginia/North Carolina republic. North Carolina's fall to the Federalists
the next year underlined Jefferson's message, for no single state could
preserve its freedom in the dangerous world of 1799. The following year
enough Federalists abided by the same logic to defeat schemes in New
York, Pennsylvania, and Maryland that would have reversed the election
returns, set states at one another's throats, and probably splintered the
union.

The immediate alternative to secession was party competition. Like
the Republicans before them, the Federalists responded to defeat by removing legitimacy from the government and assigning it to their party.
"Party," Fisher Ames declared, "is an association of honest men for honest purposes . . . a champion who never flinches, a watchman who never
sleeps. . . ."[25] Four years hence, there would be another grand tournament to determine whether virtue or vice would prevail. Initially the
Federalists were betting on virtue. Jacobin government would falter and
the people would recover their senses. The United States, Hamilton
wrote, was "too young and vigorous to be quacked out of its political
health."[26] After a year of Republican rule an optimistic Oliver Wolcott
reported: "The progress of public opinion towards right sentiments, is as
rapid . . . as ought to be desired:—by the time of another election, the
counter current will be in full force. . . ."[27] These hopes soon faded. The
Republicans, coming to power after one long climb, could interpret their
successes as a permanent revolution in the sentiments of the people. The
Federalists, on the other hand, suffered the anguish of a sudden fall from
grace, and when redemption did not come quickly, many of them soured.
In isolated righteousness William Plumer concluded that Federalism offered "too pure a government for the people—That it presupposes more
knowledge & virtue in the mass of the people than they really have."[28]
Some New England Federalists, including Plumer, finally did hatch a
secessionist plot in 1803 and 1804.

The plot's failure helped to highlight how effectively the surrogate warfare of parties and a slight tightening of the union were reinforcing one another. Originally the Constitution resembled an understanding among gentlemen, a contract of honor that someone's treachery or even malice could void. Now it was assuming the characteristics of a game book, a contract for political conflict that set the parties across from one another in battle array and made the government their trophy. Even within the states the trend ran toward legally squelching the minority before an election, and each of these decisions to play dirty by the rules strengthened the larger contract. During a hopeful moment in the late nineties, Jefferson suggested that if Europe's giants would "show their power just sufficiently to hoop us together, it will be the happiest situation in which we can exist."[29] Early in the 1800s, instead of dividing and then inviting the great powers to sponsor the hostile halves, the United States as a whole adopted the Twelfth Amendment, separating the votes for president and vice-president and preparing the way for countless national tournaments to come. The Constitution certainly had not become a sacred document, but it had stiffened enough to approximate Jefferson's hoop. Sufficient geographical elasticity to return home, sufficient constitutional firmness to remain in the union: these were optimum conditions for a peaceful accommodation to defeat.

Settling the critical issues of form, honor, and independence without tearing the United States apart prepared the way for a Jeffersonian synthesis that momentarily drew maximum advantage from a fifteen-year legacy in creating a national society. It claimed the middle portion of the spectrum that moderate federalists and national antifederalists had occupied in the late 1780s. As if to highlight the continuity, old warriors from either side of that thin line of 1787—Dickinson, Pendleton, Gerry —grew increasingly hostile to the central rule of the late nineties and optimistic that Jefferson's administration would return the republic to its true principles. Where they met, Jefferson stood, then extended his arms. In what he regarded as domestic affairs, Jefferson was so neutral about how the people governed themselves inside their states that it would have taken a coronation to disturb him. Whether they honored or violated the principles in the Bill of Rights, broadened or restricted the suffrage, banged heads or nestled in peace, were matters for them to decide, and as he blandly turned his head, he gave political approval to a reading of the Constitution very much at odds with the suppression of the Whiskey Rebellion in 1794 and the Alien and Sedition Acts of 1798.

Yet the Republicans' vertical axis of government never again looked the same after Jefferson took office. John Marshall, anticipating Jefferson's presidency from the traditional vantage point of centralizing executive versus democratic legislature, predicted that his enemy "will embody himself with the house of representatives. By weakening the office of President he will increase his personal power . . . diminish his responsibility, [and] sap the fundamental principles of the government. . . ."[30] On the contrary, Jefferson attempted to draw the legislature under the president's authority and shrank the vertical pole to its base in the states. As the Federalists shifted ground and called Jefferson a slippery despot, something critical was happening to the Republican vision of government.

What Jefferson and Madison did after taking power was to revive a tradition that they, along with numerous other gentry, had expounded in the 1780s. Make us "one nation as to foreign concerns, and keep us distinct in domestic ones," Jefferson had advised Madison in 1786.[31] "The operations of the federal government will be most extensive and important in times of war and danger; those of the State governments in time of peace and security," Madison had written in 1788 to lull the antifederalists.[32] It was this kind of division that now suited Madison's long argument for state authority in the Virginia Report and made it Republican orthodoxy for the early 19th century. Moreover, it satisfied some of the most cherished convictions that the two of them brought to office. Madison, no longer confident that America's diversity provided its own defense against national tyranny, wanted assurances that the government in Washington would never again suppress free speech, and both men happily watched the Sedition Act die. Jefferson, still obsessed with his iron circle of war-debts-oppression-monarchy, used the dominance of the states in domestic affairs as justification for a frugal, lightly armed national government that would rely on the state militia for its normal protection.

To these modifications in the form of the true republic, Jefferson added contributions that were peculiarly his own. In 1801 he sat atop his party hierarchy with a serene assurance that nobody doubted his credentials as first character among the Republicans. His authority resembled a partisan version of Washington's, virtually untouchable in public whatever the secret Republican grumblings. In an example of private frowns and public smiles that would be repeated year after year, Thomas Rodney reported after Jefferson's inaugural address that militant Republicans "were not Pleased with it & that great damped their Joy—but the Aurora"—the militant Republicans' paper—"says otherwise."[33] Jefferson embodied the continuity in their battle for independence from 1776 through the trials of the nineties to their present triumph. To repudiate him would break that continuity and unravel the party fabric. Moreover, the president sought harmony as earnestly as his followers did. Although he continued to soothe state Republicans and assure them of his personal concern, he remained as aloof as possible from their factional squabbles. Fight among yourselves, he seemed to say, but within my hierarchy bury your differences and unite. With an even grander neutrality, Jefferson accepted the religious animosities that beset local America because he refused to believe that a good republican would ever place his sect above his country. Hate thy neighbor, but love thy nation.

After the model of Washington, Jefferson aspired to be the nation's, not just the party's, first character, and the ritual of partisan warfare helped him to cultivate that illusion. Just as all gentlemen engaged in their seamiest political fights through surrogate bully boys, so by extension Jefferson could interpret the actual, nasty encounters of the recent election campaign as beneath him. Over the years Madison had provided no greater service to Jefferson than to preserve this sense of removal. Although Jefferson might sketch the partisan argument, Madison put on the mask and argued it in the newspapers. Madison, not Jefferson, exposed himself to defend their resolutions of 1798 and scrupulously hid his senior's participation. Jefferson outlined the party platform, but Madison directed the party mobilization. Sincerely grateful to his loyal legions yet peculiarly detached from their labors, Jefferson set himself above the battlefield and stretched his mind to encompass as many Americans as possible within the republican fold.

He drew in the people without the slightest difficulty. Almost exactly paralleling the Federalist analysis between 1795 and 1798, Jefferson had continued to regard the people as "essentially republican" even while his own party's fortunes sank. Like all gentry leaders, he maintained a sharp distinction between honest dupes and calculating enemies, the deluded and the seditious. With virtuous leaders to tell them what they thought, the people still spoke for republicanism, as one body of them had, for example, from Jefferson's script in the Kentucky Resolution. Lacking such guides, the people were "decoyed into the net of the monarchists by the X Y Z contrivance," he later explained.[34] When victory in 1800 fulfilled his faith, Jefferson effortlessly absolved the people for their temporary desertion.

Although the people's seducers posed a more complicated problem, the president approached them with confidence that superiors in a gentry hierarchy usually showed toward second-echelon gentlemen. As the greatest dangers of the nineties were lifting, Jefferson prepared the way with a revealing series of terminological shifts. When Adams broke with the war Federalists and sent a new delegation to France in November 1799, Jefferson responded by splitting the original "Anglican monarchical aristocratical party" into the "pure Monocrats" who followed the president and the "Anglomonocrats" who followed Hamilton. In neocolonial terms that denoted a profound separation, literally an ocean of difference between the two branches of Federalism. By 1801 most of the "pure Monocrats" turned benignly into "the federal sect of republicans," and the remainder of his opponents merely a "little party" of "desperadoes." The man who continued to praise the *Federalist* essays after he had repudiated half their judgments slid easily through these adjustments.

To such battle-bruised captains as McKean of Pennsylvania and Giles of Virginia, who wanted to pursue the retreating enemy and eliminate them one by one, Jefferson's miracle of shrinkage suggested an ominous lack of resolve, and the new president tried to appease them with assurances that all of those "covering under the mask of federalism hearts devoted to monarchy" he would "abandon as incurables, & will never turn an inch out of my way to reconcile with." But the indecisive Federalists below the top rank he did expect to convert. These waverers, Jefferson told the militant Monroe, "look with a certain degree of affection and confidence to the administration, ready to become attached to it, if it avoids in the outset acts which might revolt and throw them off. To give them time for a perfect consolidation seems prudent." Before the crisis of the nineties he had described the middling levels in "both parties" as "federalists and republicans." With an eye to these lesser figures he declared in his inaugural address, "We are all republicans—we are federalists."[35] Jefferson was offering a public balm, not a partisan blend. By repeating in the balance of his address the main tenets of the party platform that he had outlined in 1799, he made it plain that as a magnanimous first character he anticipated turning basically good Americans into good Republicans.

Presiding in catholic majesty, then, Jefferson pursued the great dream of American happiness by expanding his hierarchy to cover as much of the nation as he could in a soft envelope of peaceful accommodation. He promised his defeated enemies the right to attack him in peace. Lower taxes eased the anxiety among his southern allies that northern interests would use the national government to milk them dry. When the Louisiana Purchase worried some because it might lead to a divided nation and others because it might produce a western-dominated one, Jefferson painted a beatific picture of small republics multiplying across the continent and settling in their own fraternal ways how they would group together. And so it went in small as well as large matters. To manage the sticky business of protocol between the president and the state governors, for example, Jefferson set rules that secured everybody's honor. Mollifying with a masterful hand, he prepared the way for Madison's later summary of the revolution of 1800. The doubters, Madison wrote, "overlook the overbearing & vindictive spirit, the apocryphal doctrines, & rash projects, which stamped on federalism its distinctive character; and which are so much in contrast with the unassuming & unavenging spirit which has marked the Republican Ascendancy."[36]

Acting through a political party, Jefferson had at his disposal the most powerful nationalizing force of his time. By the early 1800s, Federalists and Republicans agreed that a party brought legitimacy to the government rather than drawing legitimacy from it. That much the revolution of 1800 proved beyond question. Even those victors who dreamed of a government perpetually legitimate under perpetual Republican rule thought of the source of legitimacy as honest men, not honorable offices. As a prize of party battle the national government attracted a new kind of intense, purposeful attention. Never again would a presidential candidate toy with the idea of bowing to his opponent as Jefferson did in 1796. Nor would the gentry ever again consider the Senate as a gathering of wise men. Political leaders came out of the nineties counting heads in the legislature, not admiring their contents. When the judiciary emerged dramatically as a partisan arm of the Adams administration, the full range at the top of the national government lay exposed as the spoils of war. Now both sides needed to believe in the inevitability of competitive parties. "Wherever there are men there will be parties . . . ," Jefferson wrote as he took office.[37] On their part, the Federalists who were suffering under "the *present* state of parties" had to conclude that "other parties will & must succeed them."[38]

As Jefferson won the battle of parties, however, he lost the cement for a national society. Once he had astutely noted the international stimulus for America's parties; now he mistakenly assumed that these neocolonial vehicles could be transferred to a general domestic service. Their strength lay precisely and specifically in an attachment to the powerful passions for independence. Although taxes aroused anger, they did not generate national parties. Nor did the Jeffersonian model of a stately simplicity, the sterling character of a Republican leadership, the natural loyalty of a yeoman citizenry, or anything else. America's first parties had no potential for development. Their impressive nationwide musters responded to just one kind of signal. As that alarm grew fainter, the captains and sergeants and privates simply ceased hearing it and went about other business.

In some ways the hopes of the centralizing federalists and the fears of their antifederalist opponents offered a remarkably good guide to the function of parties as society-builders, even though neither side in 1787 had anticipated their central role in the creation of a national hierarchy. The centralizers' plan depended on releasing a natural elite from their provincial bonds in order to act for the whole nation, and the parties, by channeling an unprecedented energy from local to national concerns, did indeed empower a handful of leaders to set national policies. At the same time, the parties also fulfilled the prophecies of irresponsible rule that so deeply disturbed the antifederalists. As the parties funneled authority to the top of the hierarchy when political tensions were most severe, they fed the very evils that the antifederalists had predicted: foreign entanglements, a standing army, the suppression of dissent, the imposition of direct taxes, the risks of civil conflict. Significantly, it was in the area of the parties' prerogative—the protection of American independence—that Jefferson, generally so mild in domestic affairs, shrugged off his constitutional restraints and assumed the power to make rules for the good of the nation: the Louisiana Purchase, the prosecution of Burr's alleged treason in the west, the enforcement of an unpopular embargo.

In a narrow sense the antifederalists had the better of the argument, and during the nineties they won an increasing number of former federalists to their general point of view. In a larger sense, however, both sides erred in underestimating the force of inertia in a distended society. By issuing the parties such narrow grants of power for such short spans of time, provincial America collapsed the standing army, frustrated the suppression of dissent and the collection of taxes, and dissipated the risks of civil war. Localism, maligned by most of the gentry and the historians who would follow them, saved the new national system by killing its worst excesses with indifference. Madison did capture an essential truth in *Federalist* 10 when he predicted that a multiplicity of small interests would protect America from the evils of party.

If Jefferson had not been so enmeshed in the process, he might have appreciated the signs of a cosmic harmonizer redressing the errant tendencies of America's leaders and maintaining a certain symmetry in their national enterprise. To correct their brittle, categorizing involvement with government forms, the harmonizer gave the gentry faith in the efficacy of little readjustments and the omniscience of great characters. To manage their conceits of character, it gave them the high road of national revolution to satisfy their honor and the low road of party warfare to save their lives. To counter the destructive thrust of their parties, it gave them enough power to compete avidly for the national government but too little power to act out their desires for vengeance. Above all, it gave them the neocolonial passions to construct a national framework, then relief from those passions before they could consume the entire structure. At critical points, Europe held America's destiny in its hands, but it was too preoccupied with its own problems to squeeze. As the great powers released their grip, they left America with a Constitution, a residue of national habits, and a president who aspired to govern the whole nation in peace. At the same time, their withdrawal undermined the authority of the revolutionary gentry, set the grand plans for a national society in decline, and allowed an entirely different range of enterprises to take its place.

Part Two

BEGINNINGS AND ENDINGS

BY 1840, millions enjoyed what had forever eluded the revolutionary gentry, an easy faith in the distinctiveness of their society. The heart of their unique America was its democracy, a term that no longer identified the popular element in a republican balance but now covered all the essentials in American life. Among the winding routes that people followed to reach this level of confidence, only two ran the full distance from the turn of the century to the 1840s. One turned away from the past, pioneered a revolution in individual choices, and beckoned to all white Americans who had at least a modest base of property. By contrast, the other trail sought to maintain a connection with tradition. It began with an acceptance of elite privileges, distributed them more broadly among well-situated citizens, and adapted these changes to the rapidly extending contours of western settlement. The leaders along this second route, including Henry Clay, Daniel Webster, Nicholas Biddle, Lyman Beecher, and Joseph Story, became the new notables in national affairs. In retrospect, it looked as if these two alternatives to the gentry hierarchy —one driven every which way by popular impulses, the other still reined from above—were racing neck and neck to see which would replace the old order.

Actually, the meaning of the long passage to the 1840s lay not in a simple race but in a complex interplay of ambitions, and those who worked the hardest to mediate among these conflicting inclinations served as the best guides along the way. On two counts the agents of continuity earned the right to that place. During the first twenty years of the 19th century, while the push toward greater popular choices remained inchoate, the most vital interactions occurred between the revolutionary gentry themselves, who still held many of the nation's important public offices, and these rising younger leaders who considered themselves the old gentry's direct heirs. Where 18th-century leaders sought honor, their apprentices looked for both honor and enterprise. Where the veterans of the Revolution fought to free themselves from Europe, the new men expected both national independence and continental greatness. Where the old gentry prized hierarchy, their immediate successors coveted both social stability and expanding opportunity. From the tension between these 18th-century traditions and their modifications came changes in national policy that surfaced sporadically between Jefferson's inauguration and the War of 1812, then burst forth dramatically after 1815 to sweep away the old gentry visions.

The dynamic between seniors and juniors revealed itself initially and worked out its implications most thoroughly in state affairs. Appropriately, it was also at the state level that the modifiers of tradition first encountered the full force of a popular revolution in choices during the 1820s and won their badge as mediators a second time, in this case more as conservators of tradition than as innovators within it. Inside the states and then across the nation, another set of tensions mounted during the twenties and thirties, entwining the adaptors of the old ways with a widespread and increasingly insistent demand for new freedoms. This latest interplay between old and new was at least as intricate as the one between the revolutionary gentry and their apprentices. Perhaps nothing better illustrated the subtlety and the prolonged inconclusiveness of the entire process than the role of Andrew Jackson, the last of the Revolutionary War veterans to assume high office, who emerged as the first national leader to direct a frontal assault on the carriers of the revolutionary tradition. Across the full span of four decades, only one strong thread bound together these many, tangled alternatives: a common preoccupation with the lure of America's magnificent domain and the chase of authority to catch up with the people who were filling it.

Space

As Jefferson was purifying his republic and preparing the way for the quarter-century reign of the Virginia Dynasty, the gentry's national hierarchy was already pulled taut across the United States. By 1800 it was clear that the Constitution could not fulfill the centralizers' original goal of hardening a "weak and relaxed civil Authority" and mobilizing "a very sparse and extending population." Nor could the new political parties, organized to preserve the United States from European subversion, contribute much to the day-to-day governance of the nation. Jefferson's loose rule marked the peak of national control over such a large domain of restless citizens. During the early 19th century, space and movement destroyed that hierarchy. A dramatic expansion of territory and a perpetual migration of people snapped its networks of personal authority, stretched its base beyond tolerable limits, and finally toppled the entire structure.

Behind the process of destruction lay one of the fundamentals of American history, the world's most favorable ratio of arable land to people. By the end of the 18th century, statesmen already saw in their abundance of land an eternal fount of revenue, ideologues a guarantee of republican virtue, climbers an invitation to wealth, planters a family patrimony, and ordinary farmers a birthright. The Louisiana Purchase, doubling the nation's size, expanded the range of those visions magnificently. After filling out to the south and southwest in a treaty of 1819 with Spain, the national government then seized another huge domain in 1848, this time increasing the total area by more than 60% and completing a solid American block from coast to coast. Despite a population growth of about 450% during the first half of the 19th century, the proportion of people to territory did not significantly rise.

The initial challenge to the gentry hierarchy came with the first heavy crossing of the Appalachian Mountains. Although the push into the interior paralleled the history of white settlement in North America, it required almost two centuries before an appreciable number of these migrants breached the Appalachian barrier to pioneer its western side. With carts and wagons little better than their distant ancestors', along hacked and trampled routes, the opening surge of this extraordinary folk movement followed the disruptions of the Revolutionary War and established a base for the new states of Kentucky in 1792, Tennessee in 1796, and Ohio in 1803. Slowed again between 1807 and 1814, it rushed forth after the next war and in approximately two more decades spread through the nation's original domain, the most accessible portions of former French and Spanish territory, and a piece of Mexico that in 1836 became the independent state of Texas. If the broad thrust of the movement was westward, the actual flow of people traced the curves and bends of the river systems. Some pioneers flanked the Appalachians to the south and entered through the river outlets along the Gulf of Mexico. By the early 1830s a significant number were using the Erie Canal to slip through the mountains in the north. Under the stimulus of persistent migration, hunks of territory divided to form states and new territories, then more states: Missouri from Louisiana, Alabama from Mississippi, Illinois from Indiana, Arkansas from Missouri, Wisconsin and Iowa from Michigan. As the union grew during this second surge from seventeen to twenty-five states, its western flank enveloped most of the Mississippi Valley.

Once across the mountains the migrants lived in fluid societies of strangers. In 1810 about 70% of the inhabitants in the old northwest had not been there a decade earlier, and in 1820 over 50% were newcomers since 1810. Not only did children constitute a high percentage of the ten-year veterans, but these figures registered none of the ceaseless movement from place to place within the region. In such a kinetic setting, hierarchical tiers had no chance to form. Although many of the same economic inequalities materialized in the new areas, the sense of a contained, personally integrated whole never did. Nor did westerners retain respect for the distant seats of authority they had left on the other side of the mountains. In combination with an unprecedented rate of growth in towns and cities everywhere, this human flux, churning decade after decade, eroded the foundations beneath the gentry's social order.

•   •   •

To reckon with the meaning of the trans-Appalachian west, 18th-century gentlemen commonly used the term "empire," denoting an extensive country and a diverse population. Although "empire" might also suggest a great nation, it never lost the taint of concentrated power, imposed law, and military authority—the rule of the mighty few. Hence during the debates over the Constitution, only the brashest of the centralizers publicly described the existing states as an "American empire." Far more often the word expressed fears of a threatening despotism. Avoid consolidation, one partisan of state sovereignty wrote John Adams, so that America would "remain a collection of Republics, and not become an Empire, for then freedom will languish and die."[1] By equating a central government with empire and empire with force, the antifederalist James Winthrop set the term at the heart of his proof that the proposed constitution would destroy American liberties.

None of them, however, doubted the term's applicability to their trans-Appalachian lands, and initially very few of them balked at its colonial connotations. "Settlements in that Western Country" should be regulated for the benefit of the home "States," one of the New York Livingstons noted matter-of-factly in 1783.[2] To this end the government under the Articles of Confederation, which secured national rights over the area from its member states, fixed stages of territorial development under an autocratic eastern rule that Monroe, one of the architects of the Northwest Ordinance of 1787, described with refreshing frankness as "a colonial government similar to that which prevail'd in these States previous to the revolution."[3] Naturally the American gentry thought that they, unlike the British, would be good colonial governors, and in that spirit they held out the prospect of eventual statehood within the union. Nevertheless, no national leader during the 1780s seemed eager for the day. Richard Henry Lee called the trans-Appalachian pioneers "the Sons of Violence," and Washington welcomed the prospect of Indian attacks winnowing out the worst of them.[4] John Jay, ready to relinquish America's navigation rights to the Mississippi, justified his policy as a check on random movement "through the Wilderness" without "those Advantages of Education, Civilization, Law, and Government which compact Settlements and Neighbourhood afford[.]"[5] Edward Rutledge of South Carolina agreed: ". . . it will stop migration, it will concenter force. . . ."[6] Another architect of the Northwest Ordinance, Nathan Dane of Massachusetts, hoped no new states would ever form in the west. At Philadelphia, Madison defended his Virginia Plan as a guarantee of eastern dominance over the west's "objectionable minority," and delegates of a variety of persuasions urged some limitations on a barbaric western influence. They lost largely because a populous west seemed too remote a prospect for the bother. Hence it was quite possible to harbor ambitions of a grand western empire without contemplating any significant enlargement of the United States. The Constitution's guarantee of equality for entering states might have been nothing more than a paper promise to the west.

At the same time, the eastern gentry wanted profitable colonies. Scarcely any of them failed to envisage a miraculous pitcher of public revenue, a personal fortune, or both from the sale of western lands. Such implacable enemies as Hamilton and George Clinton could at least agree on the fundamental purpose of empire: sell to large-scale speculators and fill the public treasury. Caught in a tension between economics and ideology, some, like the British before them, played with schemes to control the flow of migration. Washington proposed settling a state at a time, pushing squatters to the far edges of the frontier, and thereby civilizing the west in regulated sequence. In the end, however, the salesmen prevailed. Although Washington's plan was "the wisest and the best," Richard Henry Lee replied with due deference, who could resist the rapid use of "this fine fund for extinguishing the public debt"?[7] Talk of stemming the migratory tide sounded good, George Mason admitted. "But go the people will. . . ."[8]

At the end of the 18th century most western settlers and eastern gentry were still glowering at one another across the mountains. The widespread eastern willingness in 1786 to bargain navigation rights on the lower Mississippi for trading privileges in Spain rankled as a bitter memory in the west. Small wonder that almost any separatist scheme around the turn of the century found some western support and that none of these adventurers lost favor at home. The eastern centralizers, on their part, correctly perceived western settlement as inimical to hierarchical order. If it required their best efforts to maintain control over western Massachusetts in the late 1780s and western Pennsylvania in the early 1790s, how could they ever tame those "ragged, dirty, brawling, browbeating monsters" beyond the mountains?[9] Every cultivated traveler returned from the west with stories of public jostlings, casual rudeness, and rampant disorder. As a rule, eastern leaders thought as little as possible about this lawless land. The first western state was the only one whose spelling they never bothered to standardize: Kaintucky, Kentuckey, Kentucke, Kentucké, and Kentucky served them equally well.

The most creative effort to stretch the hierarchy, span the mountains, and cover the continent with traditional republicanism came from Jefferson and his circle of associates. It originated in a basic principle of all gentry hierarchies, a paternal concern downward and a filial respect upward. Kentucky, initially dominated by an offshoot of the Virginia elite, served as their first experiment in familial control. Madison and Jefferson both cultivated these second-echelon gentlemen, who in turn invited Madison and Jefferson to shape their state constitution, and like proud parents the Virginians watched the new state develop during the 1790s into a Republican stronghold. They could scarcely quibble with the Federalist judgment that the Kentucky Resolutions of 1798 echoed Virginia sentiments, for Virginians not only wrote them but even delivered them to the Kentucky legislature.

It was an auspicious start for an expanding vision. From Kentucky's example emerged the Jeffersonian model of endlessly recapitulating republican structures spreading across the continent, each with the essential characteristics of their eastern brethren and each bound by republican sympathies into a single American system. A socially frozen uniformity always accompanied this vision. Jefferson pictured Eli Whitney's cotton gin, for example, integrated into the same kind of yeoman household economy that he had known in Virginia and now expected to flourish unchanged in the west. So did the invariable principles of hierarchy. During his first term, Jefferson expressed no objection to Arthur St. Clair's autocratic rule as governor of the Northwest Territory and showed no hesitation in imposing a colonial tutelage over the long-established French-speaking society in Louisiana. "In proportion as we find the people there riper for receiving these first principles of freedom," the head of the national family told Gallatin in 1803, "Congress may from session to session confirm their enjoyment on them."[10] In time Louisiana too would join the western progeny.

The Jeffersonian formula invested the revolutionary republic with a vague, serpentine extendability. After the Louisiana Purchase the great Republican father refused to predict how "the elder and the younger son" —the western domain divided by the Mississippi River—might live together. He hoped for unity, Jefferson wrote, but he would never insist on it. "God bless them both, & keep them in the union, if it be for their good, but separate them, if it be better."[11] Borrowing a leaf from Adam Smith, he pictured the peaceful workings of commerce strengthening this loose continental league of friendship and freedom. The softness of Jefferson's image reflected the nature of his constitutional commitment, so deeply rooted in its vertical axis that it opened the possibility of multiplying states without rending the national hierarchy. From premises similar to Jefferson's, the grizzled Republican Matthew Lyon declared in 1816: "I have long considered that our mode of Government by states confederated for national purposes only, will fit a larger empire than ever yet existed. . . ."[12]

Jefferson's singular passion for space, however, rose out of his horror at Europe's congestion. Abandoning Montesquieu for his own reasons in the 1780s, he substituted a yeoman imperialism as the indispensable outlet for a swelling republican population. "Our confederacy," he wrote from France, "must be viewed as the nest from which all America, North and South is to be peopled."[13] While other Republicans cheered the Louisiana Purchase as America's security against its European enemies, Jefferson thrilled at the sheer grandeur of the nation's boundaries, and when Burr seemed to threaten that prize, the president struck instantly. In a scheme where only space could preserve America's republicanism, any seizure of land from a despotic European power justified itself. His lieutenants Monroe and Charles Pinckney mimicked the master perfectly when they wrote about grabbing territory from Spain out of a "love of peace." As he left office, Jefferson summarized his solution to the problem of the republic's size. By assuring his successor that whatever territory America held would be "an empire for liberty," he deftly coupled the old term of authoritarian danger with the essence of republicanism and, in a phrase, purified the continental dream.[14] Until all hierarchies disappeared, Jefferson's vision of innumerable pioneers pushing westward to farm in freedom, his obsession with more territory, and his permissive approach to national governance most effectively spanned the gap from Montesquieu to Manifest Destiny.

Initially the Federalist opposition fought each step in Jefferson's imperialism. When the Mississippi bounded the nation, Fisher Ames wrote in response to the Louisiana Purchase, "we were confined within some limits. Now, by adding an unmeasured world beyond that river, we rush like a comet into infinite space."[15] Repeating the time-honored strictures against diffusion three years later, Timothy Pickering described a nation "so scattered that we have no strong *point* anywhere."[16] Although these concerns did reflect a distinctive need among northeastern Federalists for a tight, comprehensive hierarchy, they found echoes among veteran Republicans as well. Opposing any white expansion into the Louisiana territory, James Jackson of Georgia exclaimed: "In the name of God have we not land enough for a settlement without this!"[17] As Jefferson and Madison maneuvered to push the Spanish into the Gulf of Mexico, John Dickinson, the patriarch of Delaware Republicanism, considered it appalling to struggle "for Wildernesses beyond the River Mexicano, or on the remote waters of the Missouri. . . ."[18]

As more and more of their own sons and daughters emigrated beyond the mountains, however, conservative easterners unbent their stiff hierarchy and extended it westward in their own version of a paternal connection. Rufus King's metamorphosis was exemplary. A particularly haughty judge of the barbaric west in the 1780s, King considered its settlers lost to the nation and wanted to block further migration there. Although he later approved Hamilton's scheme to conquer Spanish territory, he still viewed the entire west as no more than a colonial hinterland. Boston, New York, and London, King's centers of honor and friendship, triangulated his interests. Then in the sharp upswing of northeastern emigration after the War of 1812, his son Edward moved to Ohio, and King, always a dedicated father, continued to advise him and solicited support for his banking career in Chillicothe. To a skeptical John Adams he wrote warmly about the western movement, assuring him that human ties would cement the new region to the nation. Now King's sense of a family network extended from Britain to the Mississippi. "We are the powerful descendants of England," the elder statesman told the Senate, "desiring perpetual friendship . . . with her," but at this stage of life the American branch had other pressing obligations. The eastern father must concentrate his "most vigilant attention" to secure a proper patrimony for his children in the west.[19]

How seriously King took his own charge surfaced dramatically in 1819 with a thunderous attack on slavery in the trans-Mississippi territories. By then a familial model for America's expansion had wide currency among the old gentry. Countering King's demand that the eastern head of the family force its obstreperous Missouri offspring to abandon slavery, Nathaniel Macon of North Carolina responded in horror: "Will you for this order the father to march against the son . . . ? God forbid!"[20] Even John Randolph, disdainful of everything western, treated its settlers like whining, greedy children. Asked "what have we done for the West," he threw up his hands: "Sir, let *me* reverse the question. What have we *not* done for the West? Do gentlemen want monuments?"[21] From this familial consensus the immediate successors to the revolutionary gentry —John Quincy Adams, Henry Clay, John C. Calhoun, and their associates—adapted their approach to American space. Acutely conscious of their place as sons of the founders, they took as a basic part of their heritage a responsibility to preserve the family's cohesion. With the Appalachians still looming as the most formidable barrier to its unity, they set out to build actual links across the divide. "We are . . . rapidly, [I] was about to say fearfully, growing," declared Calhoun in 1817. ". . . We are under the most imperious obligation to . . . bind the Republic together with a perfect system of roads and canals. Let us conquer space."[22] "Look at the line of the Atlantic, and that of the Mississippi," Clay instructed Congress a year later, "—look how nature invites you to make perfect . . . the two great lines by means of [connecting] roads and canals."[23]

Playing the eldest brother rather than the father, these men took a less rigid stance than their predecessors toward family relations. Nevertheless, they did assume the privileges of the firstborn, the right to plan from the east what would be best for the "young west." At most, their minds reached the Kentucky foothills, then peered toward the Mississippi as they calculated their conquests of space. They too sought to contain the union, and in this important regard they sounded much like their gentry mentors. "There are limits within which our federal system must stop," King stated as a matter of course in 1819; "no one has supposed that it could be indefinitely extended. . . ."[24] Three years later Monroe spoke of a "just limit" to forestall the dangers from "expansion over a vast territory."[25] By the same token, when Calhoun marveled at the size of the United States in 1817, he thought immediately of the "tendency to disunion." "Are you not large and unwieldy enough already?" John Quincy Adams asked the younger Americans who coveted Texas. The consequences of annexation, he warned them, "would be weakness, and not power." "Instead of aiming to enlarge [the nation's] boundaries," echoed Daniel Webster, "let us seek, rather, to strengthen its union. . . ."[26] Clay would link the Mississippi with the Atlantic coast, but he wanted no part of an empire on the Pacific.

During the 1820s, in the heyday of national authority for Clay, Calhoun, and John Quincy Adams, a critical change in these bounded attitudes was breaking loose across the nation. Its origins lay in new relations between enterprise and land. Among the gentlemen of the 18th century perhaps no activity came closer to approximating a common denominator than land speculation. Prospects from their grand domain dangled like golden apples, and they harvested so avidly that even the wealthiest found themselves periodically strapped for funds. These ventures ranged indiscriminately across the country. Although the gentry did invest in nearby plots, they plunged just as effortlessly into speculations far beyond their ken: Boston merchants in the Yazoo of Georgia, Robert Morris in far western New York, Madison in the Mohawk Valley. The more deeply they engrossed themselves in land speculations, the more ethereal their sense of geography became. Morris and John Nicholson, princes of the breed, played with huge chunks of territory from New York to the Carolinas much as they would have shifted tokens on a game board. Philadelphia defined their only geographical reality; the rest was an essentially spaceless, placeless quest for wealth to draw home for their greater glory, no more earthy than the bank stock and treasury paper that also enticed so many of the gentry.

During the 1790s the momentum of these involvements increased with the commercial prosperity accompanying the early wars of the French Revolution, for in some fashion foreign commerce underwrote almost all speculations. Watching the American gentry in the mid-nineties, one Englishman concluded: "Were I to characterize the United States, it should be by the appellation of the *land of speculation*."[27] Stretched exceedingly thin by an ever-expanding ambition, the whole skein snapped in 1798 and 1799 when the tightening of British maritime controls and naval warfare with France more or less froze American finance. From the Yazoo through the Shenandoah Valley to the banks of Lake Erie, large land speculations collapsed, dethroning Morris and Nicholson and sending a great many lesser lights for cover in the new nation's most extensive panic. So much gentlemanly distress even inspired a brief experiment in national bankruptcy legislation.

An activity as indigenous to gentry life as land speculation did not disappear just because one big bubble burst. As commercial profits soared once more after 1803, the adventurers returned along with them. Yet the general pattern of land speculation never again looked the same. Although some investors continued to stay home and manipulate tokens, many others either tied their land speculations to particular transportation enterprises or put their funds in the transportation enterprises instead. Wherever transportation became central, investors acquired a new geographical sharpness, a sense of specificity about terrain and distance that clearly distinguished them from the homebound plungers of the nineties. A focus on roads, bridges, and canals not only pulled their attention to earth; it also involved them in a multitude of details on the spanning of space, mortgaged their ambitions to the numbers of people who used what routes to carry how many goods from where to where, and often sent them inland in search of indispensable support, both financial and political.

The building of turnpikes and canals was already a thriving British enterprise by the middle of the 18th century, and the American gentry copied the British model in thinking about their own territory. Before 1800, however, very few of them set these ventures at the center of their concerns. Morris and Nicholson did promote the first overland stone road, a turnpike from Philadelphia to Lancaster that opened in 1794; but it got lost among their grandiose land schemes, and their minds rapidly drifted elsewhere. Although a number of relatively simple road improvements followed in the wake of the Lancaster Turnpike, neither lotteries nor private subscriptions collected sufficient funds for another big enterprise. Washington's pipe dream of channeling trade from the Northwest Territory through the Potomac River encouraged one of several complicated waterway projects that soon sank in debt and confusion.

Entrepreneurial interests shifted at the turn of the century because perceptions about land and opportunity were changing just as the gentry accumulated a new surplus to invest. In part, this reorientation simply followed the pattern of neocolonial attitudes. The greater the disenchantment with Europe, the wider the Atlantic grew and the larger the American interior loomed. The simultaneous collapse in free-form land speculations greatly accelerated the arrival of a new consciousness. Hence years after the Lancaster Turnpike had proved its worth, it sud-

denly became the sparkling example to emulate, and companies of investors pressed their legislatures for similar charters. In the next two
decades, more than 80 of these companies completed over 1,800 miles of
turnpikes, with another 700 in progress, and the National Road, authorized amid this enthusiasm in 1806, crossed the mountains during the
1810s and pushed into Ohio. Webs of roads interwove the major port
cities with their hinterlands; twisting networks ranged across the eastern
backcountry. As the large eastern states swelled—Pennsylvania grew
from 35 to 51 counties and almost doubled its population between 1800
and 1820, and New York filled out even more amply—a coastal elite
discovered a whole new meaning in these upcountry areas. In 1787, a
voice of Philadelphia had declared: "Happy would it be for Pennsylvania
if her boundaries were comprised by the Susquehannah: we should then
be more compact and united."[28] Four decades later, the Pennsylvania
legislature appropriated almost a million dollars of transportation subsidies in a massive effort to attach Pittsburgh's commerce firmly to Philadelphia. Although disputes still abounded between westerners and
easterners in the old states, they were now joined in a nexus of particular
roads stringing specific towns a determinate distance from one another
—a common conception, in other words, of a geographically concrete
world.

As the passion for more turnpikes waned after 1820, an even greater
surge of enthusiasm for inland water transportation replaced it, and with
the new wave came a revolution in open-ended visions across space. The
steamboat, basically freed from monopoly control by 1818, quickly
proved its amazing power by mastering the currents of the Mississippi-
Ohio river artery through the west. Where a keelboat averaged about six
miles a day going upstream, a steamboat in the early twenties could
travel all the way from New Orleans to Louisville in a little more than a
week. Meanwhile, the Erie Canal, authorized in 1816, was cutting
through western New York, repaying Governor DeWitt Clinton's pride
with revenues as it proceeded, and preparing to explode the meaning of
transportation development on its completion in 1825. If some scoffed at
"Clinton's Big Ditch" in its complicated planning stages, not many
doubted the potential of canals, which were being built on a small scale
throughout the turnpike boom and enjoyed a burst of popularity after
1815 from Georgia to Massachusetts. Then a combination of the steamboat's radically reduced transportation rates and the Erie Canal's immediate, stunning profitability triggered a nationwide scramble to secure
these heavenly benefits at home. Within another decade, investments in
canals already doubled the grand total for turnpikes, with far more to
come. Steamboats spread eastward, increasing their tonnage tenfold between 1820 and the early thirties. Although no Atlantic port matched

New York's success, Baltimore and Philadelphia persevered with their canal projects and expanded their interior trade. By the early thirties, Ohio carved two large systems to feed Cleveland at the north and Cincinnati at the south, and a canal around the falls at Louisville cleared river passage from Pittsburgh to the Gulf. Comparable quests for the dream beckoned to Americans from Illinois to Florida.

The pace of development never seriously slowed. Although mistakes and hard times blighted many of these hopes in the late 1830s, railroads were already sweeping past canals to become the great American inspiration. As leaders in Charleston and Boston recognized in their initial response to the Erie Canal's triumph, here was a mechanical marvel that could finally emancipate them from fate's distribution of navigable rivers. Now human ingenuity would dictate its own terms. "Free from the inundations, the currents, the rapids, the ice, and the sand bars of [the Mississippi River]," a promotional appeal for the Atlantic and Michigan Railroad envisaged in 1829, "the rich products of its widespread valley would be driven to the shores of the Atlantic, with far greater speed, than if wafted by the wings of the wind. . . ."[29] By 1833, 136 miles of track, the longest run in the world, connected Charleston with Hamburg, South Carolina, and Baltimore, projecting an eventual connection with the Ohio River, had three feeder lines serving the city. In 1843, as the depression lifted, the nation's investment in a multitude of railroad projects already equaled its total for canals and in the next six years more than doubled that impressive amount.

In one sense, the effects of each new thrust in transportation built on the last. The geographically hard orientation of the turnpike era deepened decade by decade, gluing minds ever more firmly to earth, multiplying the demands for exact topographical information, and stimulating a phenomenal improvement in cartographic precision. Within their lifetimes the method that Jefferson and Gallatin used for charting "the great and important [national] road" would seem incredible. "Why should not the guide-line from St. Louis to Vincennes be direct, instead of bending . . . ?" the president asked his colleague. "I like your idea of straightening the guide-line from Vincennes, although it may pass through a corner of the Indian lands. But . . . should not the guide-line go thence direct to Cincinnati, as I have penciled it, or to Dayton, if that be the shortest way to Chillicothe? . . . the post-office map (the only one I have here) must be egregiously wrong if Dayton is not much out of the direct road from Vincennes to Chillicothe." A series of spurs must connect to Cincinnati, Jefferson thought, "or do such roads exist already?" At a time when it required about five weeks to travel from the nation's capital to Nashville, he insisted that "the line being completed, we must have a horse-post which will effect it in six days, say from Washington to St. Louis."[30] With the increasing geographical concreteness of the early 19th century also came a sharpened meaning for the dots on the map. Even the grandest dreams began somewhere in particular. Place-centeredness, long the mark of provincialism, now characterized the ambitions of the nation's most enterprising promoters. If 19th-century Americans retained the gentry term "internal improvements," they rapidly abandoned its lofty sense of the general good and left only a multitude of conflicting, place-serving demands.

The revolutionary impact of canals and railroads came as these innumerable schemes left their points of origin. Turnpikes, usually reworking the familiar, heavily traveled routes, tended to have precise endings as well as beginnings. Canals and railroads, on the other hand, spun visions into space, sending the mind's eye down the Mississippi into the Gulf, through the Great Lakes across the Atlantic, or, by the 1840s, from ocean to ocean. Railroads in particular turned promoters into scanners who swept the terrain for as many possible connections as the imagination would register, then turned back to their maps to trace an ever more complicated filigree of feeders, intersections, and extensions. At their outer edges, these patterns increasingly faded past the limits of settlement or shaded toward other people's faintly sketched plans for construction. From the Euclidian aspirations of the turnpike era, visions were transformed into a fanning projection of indeterminate lines that incorporated future growth into present reality. Like the nation's population, the lines flowed, forming magnificent pictures of "a continuous and eternal stream of commerce." The pursuit of happiness, once a felicitous ordering of the whole, became a race to catch the elusive dream as it was disappearing over the horizon.

By the 1820s these waves of change were washing relentlessly at the foundations beneath a tottering national hierarchy. By the 1840s no traces remained. Conceptually, Americans flattened the world that gentry leaders had tried to see whole into an indefinitely extending plane for movement and enterprise. "The pride and delight of Americans is in their quantity of land," the Englishwoman Harriet Martineau reported after her visit in the mid-thirties. "I do not remember meeting with one to whom it had occurred that [the United States] had too much."[31] A decade later Americans had no spatial logic, no vestige of Montesquieu versus Madison, for deciding how much of Mexico they would take. No longer looking upward within a contained system, they looked outward, saw the land stretching endlessly ahead, and followed it. The old imagery of father and son, older brother and younger brother, dissolved into these fluid, earthbound lines of growth. The "young west" became the "new west" and the entire nation a perennially "young America" that reached out to span *the whole unbounded continent.*[32]

Revolution
in Choices

As new conceptions of space spread across the United States during the 1820s, a transformation in individual rights was pushing just ahead of them to prepare the way. Already a nationwide force when the Erie Canal opened in 1825, it provided the popular thrust behind the destruction of a hierarchical order. This democratic surge covered the basics of American life—the nature of economic opportunity, the structure of political authority, the future of the soul, and the state of the body—and as it moved, it infected individuals everywhere with a heady feeling of command over their destinies, a sense of marvelous potential in their own lives that they came to project onto the nation as a whole.

In each of these four areas—opportunity, authority, salvation, and health—significant changes were stirring well before 1800. The imperial domain from the peace treaty of 1783, the freedom from colonial restraints over commerce, and the trading possibilities from the wars of the French Revolution quickened the dreams of a prosperity that Americans themselves could control. The very essence of the American Revolution was political self-determination, with the right to construct governments, allocate sovereignty, and select officials according to America's own republican lights. Around the middle of the 18th century, evangelical outbursts throughout the colonies generated new urges toward religious separatism that challenged the established churches and drew the dissenters apart into bands of equals before God. Meanwhile, Arminian ministers within the Calvinist churches diluted the stern doctrines of predestination to the point where their upright parishioners had no need to fear that God would deny them the eternal salvation they had earned. The most comfortable of the Deists simply set to rest the entire issue of a hereafter. Asked for his thoughts on the afterlife of the soul, Jefferson replied: ". . . I have for many years . . . reposed my head on that pillow of ignorance which a benevolent Creator had made so soft for us, knowing how much we should be forced to use it."[1] In a comparable spirit of self-confident secularism, scientific medicine stripped supernatural influences from the problem of disease, placed its causes firmly inside each individual's body, and prescribed cures according to rules of reason rather than dictates of folklore.

None of these changes, however, did appreciable damage to the main structure of hierarchy. In most cases the already privileged elite monopolized the primary benefits from these trends toward a greater personal freedom. The bonanzas of land were sold in large tracts that only the wealthy could afford, and only merchants with substantial capital or credit could pursue the risky new maritime opportunities. Arminianism catered to the successful few, ratifying the superior holiness of a small minority and distinguishing them from the multitudes too weak to save themselves. Rationalism in science and religion had similar uses. Only the handful capable of understanding the principles of the universe, an elite assumed, could master their own lives and govern the rest. Where this rising faith in self-determination did spread in the late 18th century, it often affected whole families, softening their authoritarian tone, infusing young men with a greater sense of their importance, and encouraging women to seek a wider autonomy in their lives. But a leavening at the top of American society did nothing to democratize its ranks.

The American Revolution contained a far higher democratic potential. Nevertheless, it scrambled the hierarchical order in only a few areas, notably around Philadelphia and New York City, and even there challengers had great difficulty consolidating their gains. Rough-hewn revolutionary committees generally had short lives, and aspiring new leaders tended to seek traditional privileges for themselves more than innovative rights for their followers. In large portions of the United States the Revolution actually strengthened gentry rule by channeling popular ferment toward the British and the American Tories, seeming to purge society of its worst aristocratic sins, and exalting the patriot gentry as protectors of a purified republic. What preserved America's hierarchical order above all else was a looseness and resilience that had characterized it throughout the 18th century. Always more open and fluid than its European models, it had given the impression of a system forever in crisis, and hence it had inspired incessant warnings about "turbulence" and "decay" from those perched uneasily at the top. Yet this very lack of firmness had necessitated qualities of adaptability that weathered each apparent collapse, leaving a hierarchical standard intact and functioning decade after decade. Indeed, the endless repetition of the same complaints about lesser folk who were affronting their betters suggested how firmly the hierarchical norms held during the 18th century, and how ritualistic many of these laments came to be. If the Revolution eliminated some visible symbols of elite power, these had rarely been crucial to a society as decentralized and discontinuously governed as America's. If the upheaval of the 1770s spread exciting new ideas about the people's rights, their greatest tribune, Tom Paine, found himself a strikingly isolated man after his return to the United States twenty years later. In the 1790s gentry leaders were still directing the governments that they had designed.

Not surprisingly, most Americans in the nineties invested their energies in local or private affairs and showed little interest in those areas where an elite hoarded the benefits. Only a minority of the eligible voters —sometimes an exceedingly small one—cast ballots for high, distant offices. A large majority ignored the churches that usually damned them and the doctors who generally regarded them as a menace to the public health. Detachment did not mean indifference. The issues of republican independence roused far more enthusiasm than its electoral politics, and the traditions of Protestant Christianity retained vastly more authority than its churches. Nevertheless, when poorer Americans did assert their beliefs, they tended to bypass established institutions and speak immediately to their own needs: a public gathering of protest, a fervent response to an itinerant preacher. In 1786 a group of Philadelphians who sensed evil spirits affecting their health took to the streets, trapped a woman with the reputation of a witch, and knifed her to death. This pattern of direct, sporadic actions left the broad structure of society in other hands. Even those who mounted a frontal assault on authority, like the Whiskey Rebels, did not try to alter the framework of government. The powers above—God, gentlemen, fate—made the rules; they took the risks of breaking them.

Yet little beyond the gentry's fiat preserved their claim to exclusive privileges and unique freedoms. Eighteenth-century America had none of the fixity that reinforced an acceptance of fate, and its hierarchy had no formidable superstructure of nobility, church, and army to sustain its authority. Weakening the theological framework of Calvinism in behalf of a few elite souls and placing control over the body's health in a few superior minds opened the way for others to do as well by their own souls and bodies. Beginning in 1803, more and more Americans began to explore the possibilities of these benefits for themselves. There were no giant shackles to break. They pushed a little, found room, and probed for a direction. At first they tended to mimic the gentry, seeking to share their privileges and generally staying in dialogue with the existing traditions of authority. Then around 1820 came the critical transition when an exploration of possibilities turned into a declaration of rights, the mimicry of old ways ceased, and a multitude of Americans no longer acted as if elite monitors were watching over them. After 1825 an extraordinary popular passion for personal freedom fought to extend the range of these exhilarating new rights in a self-fueling process that propelled the participants as fast and as far as their impulses drove them. In each area their objective was self-determination, and in sum they generated a revolution in choices that transformed the character of American society.

By 1800 the equation between opportunity and space was already a platitude of national pride. When Nathan Appleton visited Britain in 1802 and encountered the slums of Manchester, he automatically contrasted their dismal congestion with "Happy America! where the poorest of your sons *knows* that by industry & economy he can acquire property. . . ."[2] Yet as the young Bostonian crowed for his countrymen, larger numbers of them were following the familiar westward paths to improvement without striking root. In his own state an increasing flow of propertyless seekers passed through the line of western towns from Worcester to Northampton, only to find nothing and move on again. As farmers left the older sections of Virginia for fresh soil, more than half the state's counties lost population between 1790 and 1800; at the turn of the century one-third of the adult males who had pushed as far west as the Shenandoah Valley still found themselves landless. From Vermont to Georgia, feelings of rural crowdedness and decline were stirring the urge to migrate.

The next step was the radical one. The Appalachian chain formed such an imposing wall between east and west that the lands on the far side acquired the reputation of a world apart. Traveling the rudimentary routes of commerce, word trickled back, then spread in folk fashion, of a uniquely open domain, a vacuum waiting for anyone with the energy to fill it. Here, in mythic fashion, opportunity was free: good land either literally for the taking or so cheap and plentiful that labor alone set the limits to a family's holdings. The image of a bountiful backcountry, of course, had existed since the 17th century. Nevertheless, scaling a mountain wall made the Appalachians a symbolic divide of a special sort and, for people of small means, invested the crossing with a commitment to make a new life. Once there, thousands found it too expensive to farm in this free land and failed. Thousands more became mired in title disputes and, with thousands of others, moved again—often again and again —in search of the elusive vacuum. Yet like other enduring myths this one contained enough truth to retain its magic decade after decade.

Expecting a certain kind of freedom, the migrants behaved in ways that helped them secure it. Wherever they met restraints, they pulled against them. Although speculators increasingly located the best western land, they discovered that unless they lived in the vicinity or hired a conscientious local agent they could not regulate its use or sometimes even its sale. When the speculators' own ambitions did not overextend their resources, the costs of a protracted struggle against local resistance often did, and prices fell accordingly. Government land was little safer. Squatter uprisings considerably more extensive than the notorious rebellions of Daniel Shays and John Fries lit up the west after the War of 1812, and no trans-Appalachian Hamilton appeared to crush them. Resident officials generally found it the better part of wisdom to tolerate a good deal of evasion rather than sacrifice their own local reputations to a rigid legal standard. In effect, their superiors in Washington left this thin network of officialdom to its own devices. The spread of settlement far outstripped the scope of centralized communication or even the range of solid economic prospects. While the new steamboat was still being tested on the western rivers, Indiana, Illinois, and Missouri were already states. The first great land rush from the southeast to the Mississippi River preceded the first great cotton boom. For decades, per capita farm income in the northwest remained well below the national average, including the income from those supposedly crowded or worn regions the migrants had left behind.

Despite such a dramatic diffusion of people across the nation, the nature of economic opportunity changed very little until around 1820. Every year more migrants moved farther from the centers of government, faced a wider array of decisions, and showed less respect for the established authorities in making them. Nevertheless, seizing opportunities still meant battling the rules that others set from on high. Although Congress lowered the price of public land from $2 to $1.25 an acre in 1820, a depression year, the government sold it for cash in large units that only a wealthy minority could afford. The western model remained squatters versus speculators, already an old story in the 1780s, when Washington discovered that even a hero's commandment did not budge them from his Ohio land.

The critical shift occurred when the ambitions of merchants joined those of the settlers in creating a new framework for the nation's interior commerce. Traditionally, American merchants looked to sea for their opportunities. Forced outside the British system by the Revolution, they spread their activities around the world in a quest for profitable trade wherever it might appear. Their ships roamed the Baltic and the Mediterranean, penetrated the markets of China and touched ports in South Asia, explored the fissures in Spain's empire and the cracks in Britain's throughout the western hemisphere. Often the voyage itself—buying, selling, and bartering at intermediate stops en route—added substantially to their profit. Marketing at home engaged very little of these merchants' attention. If they got the goods into port, customers came to them. Carrying goods inland and even collecting much of the interior surplus for export fell to other traders—very often British commercial agents, just as Jefferson had feared. It was a risky but lucrative system for the port merchants, especially after 1793, when the European wars opened an array of new opportunities, legal and illegal, to the adventurous shippers. Between 1790 and 1810, New York and Baltimore almost tripled in size, Philadelphia more than doubled, and even Boston, the laggard, grew an impressive 85%. From the exceptionally high profits of this neutral trade came the precious surplus of capital that not only funded almost every other American enterprise but greatly increased the nation's ocean fleet. Shipping tonnage doubled during the first decade of the 19th century.

After 1807, however, these prospects dimmed. Shifting government restrictions at home and unpredictable waves of repression abroad made commercial profits very erratic until 1812, when war with Britain blighted them. By 1815, peace returned everywhere, eliminating America's peculiar advantages as a neutral and bringing severe competition from a massive British fleet that carried cheap manufactured goods from its own backyard, enjoyed ample financing, and quickly secured a worldwide network of trading routes. In America's major Atlantic ports, British agents sold a flood of inexpensive British goods at auctions that underpriced the established mercantile houses and forced more and more of them out of what had once been a staple source of wealth. Then a panic in 1819 turned into a depression that did not lift until the mid-twenties, and in highly atomized fashion American firms fell back on their own dwindling resources. Little wonder that in the census of 1820 the big port cities barely held even for the decade.

Between 1815 and 1825, two ways of resolving this crisis in opportunities beckoned to the port merchants. One lay eastward. They could join the competition they could not beat and link directly into the British system, either as its suppliers or as its selling agents. The burgeoning cotton export trade offered the best prospects; import specialization, particularly in metal products, added some more. Nevertheless, the British system did not have an abundance of such cozy spaces. Of the relatively small number of firms that assimilated effectively, most operated from New York, with New Orleans a distant second.

The alternative lay westward, following the flow of migration. At first, however, the enticements of interior commerce came into conflict with a new caution about the risks that American merchants were willing to run. In the early decades after the Revolution, they more or less took for granted the random, scrambling nature of their enterprise. When ships put to sea in search of goods and markets, their itineraries and lists of reliable foreign contacts served as no more than rough guides. Inevitably, captains and supercargoes enjoyed a wide latitude not only in assessing the quality of goods they purchased but even in deciding what goods to exchange at an unanticipated stop for an indeterminate market somewhere else. From the vantage point of the merchants in port, commerce was necessarily a form of speculation, and almost as a matter of course these gamblers also tried their luck in distant real estate, dubious bills of exchange, and similar plunges. Until 1807 the returns usually dulled the concern about the risks. Then between 1807 and 1814 the scrambling grew increasingly desperate as they shaved the laws, listened for the rumors, played roulette with maritime insurance, sent one ship to intercept another with instructions to put in at Lisbon or Montreal, and counted ever more heavily on a kind providence. Even the best of these jugglers, such as Nathan Appleton, tired of the game before the war was over.

More scrambling in the face of British competition after the war only deepened the merchants' desire for a new kind of control over their affairs, a regularization of transactions that would replace the unhappy gambling of recent years with a set of predictable calculations. In other words, they were determined to widen their range of choices. Lunging blindly into a new commerce with a wild west held few charms. As scramblers they already had too many experiences with strangers, and strangers were expensive. Between the early nineties and the early twenties, Thomas Perkins' Boston firm averaged about $5,000 a year in bad debts, a price no one felt free to pay in the increasingly tight postwar years. The port merchants were equally averse to stocking every kind of ware, like overgrown peddlers, and trying to sell an infinite assortment in an unknown western market. As a first step toward rationalizing their business they were already limiting the range of products that each one marketed.

This deadlock between need and caution broke quickly in the years after 1815 because thousands of individuals between the coastal cities and the agrarian interior shared the urge to increase their opportunities, seized pieces of the extensive interior trade, and cumulatively formed lines of commerce linking merchant and jobber, jobber and storekeeper,

storekeeper and farmer, farmer and drayman, drayman and packing house, packing house and boatman, boatman and merchant, on and in and around a giant web of limited, autonomous transactions that enabled each of the participants along the way, almost always managing a little fraction of the trade, to maintain personal connections with the individuals on either side of him. Prosperous eastern merchants did not have to go west and mobilize a new trade with its settlers. Countless mutual ambitions joined west and east in an ingenious popular solution to the challenges of space and anonymity. Nobody tried to integrate these chains of commerce. Each concentrated on a personal control over his own affairs. During the 1820s, family ties dominated the business firms in a growing center of western trade such as Rochester, New York, even more than in an older maritime city such as Salem, Massachusetts. As Alexander Brown's extremely successful commercial house—later Brown Brothers—expanded its operations along the coastal ports, it remained a string of family branches until Alexander ran out of sons. New branches were then entrusted to outsiders only after each had undergone such a long, intensive apprenticeship that the newcomer might well have considered himself adopted.

The desire to make every business decision a matter of self-conscious choice placed a much stronger emphasis on consolidating a firm's activities, and transformed the leading merchants from shrewd speculators into calculating managers. The contrasting styles of two great merchants, Thomas Perkins of Boston and Erastus Corning of Albany, illustrated the change. Perkins, who made his primary fortune in the China trade during the European wars, also invested in a Vermont ironworks, a Massachusetts lead mine, a local land and bridge enterprise, a gold speculation in France, and myriad odds and ends. At no time could he expect to do more than assess, invest, and rely on a friendly fate and a scattering of associates. Corning, who first prospered in the 1820s, started in hardware merchandising, developed his own iron foundry and nail factory, promoted a New York canal to enlarge his markets, entwined banking and land speculation with the canal venture, supported transportation and bought land in the northwestern states as his marketing extended there, and climaxed his career as president of the New York Central Railroad. Everything fit with something else, and Corning, unlike Perkins, stretched his hands to control it all. Like Alexander Brown, he granted authority outside his family with a reluctance bordering on the obsessive.

Connecting these innumerable units of personal control throughout the American domain would have been utterly impossible without an equally endless proliferation of credit. Land-rich but capital-poor, dispersed loosely across vast spaces that swallowed up the scant supply of hard money, Americans conducted their continental business on paper promises. Nothing else worked. Hence they generated credit as they proceeded, using it to lubricate each transaction in the sequence and settling accounts annually when the farmers' surplus, the ultimate basis for these long strings of inland trade, had been marketed. Whatever satisfied the two parties to a transaction constituted an acceptable form of credit. Banks supplied relatively little of it in the interior. A young thriving city such as Syracuse, for example, managed quite well without any bank until 1830, and the flourishing state of Ohio had no more bank paper circulating in 1831 than it had had in 1819. Personal notes, ledger accounts, local bills of exchange, anything with a recognizable stamp of personal reliability would do. The indispensability of these splinters of credit, in turn, kept the links of commerce small and guaranteed their multiplication as the chains expanded, for nothing backed such credit except the faith that one individual had in another's eventual payment. "Credit is morality," one economic commentator aptly concluded.[3] This kind of trust could extend only to the next link. As a result, commercial dealings actually became more personal as they spread over America's impersonal space. To ensure credit, individuals returned again and again to the same places of business—farmers to the same storekeepers, inland buyers to the same city merchants. An otherwise irrational fragmentation in urban merchandising made excellent sense in this personally grounded commercial scheme. British auctioneers doing a cash business at the Atlantic ports might destroy the importing American merchants, but only those American merchants who gave credit to their inland buyers succeeded in the western trade.

By 1825 a new grillwork of credit covered the nation, and the prospects it excited released the great public force behind the canal boom commencing that year. In combination, steam power, canals, and credit democratized a magnificent range of opportunities. Steamboats, carrying freight on the inland waterways at one-tenth the old rates, were an immediate bonanza to everyone within their scope who had anything to sell or buy. Canals, capable of reducing freight rates to as little as one-hundredth the cost of a mountainous overland route, promised miracles for the areas they opened. All an enterprising American needed, whether he sought a farm, an artisan's shop, a country store, or an iron foundry, was credit, and Americans now demanded it as their right—not a privilege to be granted but a right to be claimed by every individual whose reputation earned it. Behind the American's "firm faith in paper," so bewildering to European visitors, lay his belief that credit formed "the lever by which he governs nature."[4] Credit alone could open this bottomless cornucopia of personal choices. In 1837, when a Missouri legislative committee recommended a "policy of compelling the banks . . . to lend

money, in small sums, . . . to every merchant, every mechanic, and every
farmer who may desire it" and could justify it, the legislators spoke the
revolutionary new language of popular self-determination.[5]

As a corollary to the sweeping insistence on popular choice, the government's sale of land, still the ultimate objective for most Americans,
was also democratized. The minimum plot, which had been 640 acres in
1796 and 320 in 1820, fell to 40 in 1832. Nine years later Congress let
the outer wave of settlers select their own farms: the Pre-emption Act
offered squatters as much as 160 acres of the land they had occupied
before the surveyor caught up with the population. When squatters commanded the right of choice from the national government, the era of
gentry privilege had passed beyond recall.

The emergence of a popular politics of choice not only paralleled the rise
of economic self-determination but also entwined with it at crucial
points along the way. That meshing was particularly close at the beginning of the 19th century when between 1803 and 1805 a new politics of
development infected one state legislature after another and quickly
came to dominate their proceedings. Originating in the ambitions of elite
promoters, it focused initially on banks and turnpikes, privileges that the
legislatures granted one by one through special acts of incorporation. In
theory each legislative decision represented a time-bound bestowal of
public powers to private interests in the name of the general welfare. As
theory translated into practice in a hierarchical society, those general
interests were gentry interests, and the gentlemen who received such
public rights used them with a free conscience, mining whatever advantage they could during the duration of the grant. At Jefferson's inauguration about 30 incorporated banks, varying considerably in size and
significance, dotted the coastline from Portland to Charleston. Unlike
later institutions of the same name, they served no general financial
functions. Each facilitated the business of a small circle of insiders, issuing short-term credits, discounting bills, arranging maritime insurance, and the like on a personal, exclusive basis. More conveniently and
safely, banks offered services that other agencies—private commercial
houses, insurance pools, even wealthy individuals—were also providing
friends and relatives in the gentry's informal cliques of character. In other
words, they strengthened the existing economic advantage of their prosperous members.

In two ways the meaning of bank charters changed with the new century. Rather than gilding privilege, they became devices for generating
opportunity, centers for investment that accepted as large a debt as they
dared from their own officers and allies and acted as agencies of promotion in a capital-starved economy. From the outset most of these banks

were tied by charter or private ambition to expansive enterprises in turn-pike or bridge or canal construction, auxiliary land speculation, manufac-turing, or some combination of these. Second, banks multiplied astonishingly. In the decade after Jefferson's inauguration the number of charters tripled, then more than doubled again by 1816. Even those fig-ures significantly understated the case. Because companies for turnpike construction and other public works, like banks, granted loans to insiders and issued their own paper credit, it made only a technical difference what name appeared on the chartering act. Altogether during these years state legislatures authorized about 1,500 such promotional corporations.

This explosion of promotional charters scattered sparks of opportunity down the hierarchy and across the land. More members of the gentry, more marginal gentry, then more men with no claims at all to gentry standing entered the competition for these charters. As the social base for promotion was broadening, ambitions spread to towns and counties that suddenly caught glimpses of a wonderful prosperity in charters to serve them too. Where a major city dominated the state, the initial con-tests usually pitted factions of the gentry over access to elite privileges: in New York the Manhattan Company Bank for the Clintonians versus the Merchants Bank for Hamilton's old circle; in Baltimore the challenge of the Union Bank, allied with Samuel Smith's associates, to the gentle-men ensconced in the Banks of Maryland and Baltimore; in Philadelphia the new Bank of Philadelphia against the old Bank of Pennsylvania. Over-lapping these bank wars and intensifying as the decade proceeded, smaller or newer towns attacked the domination of the cities or the first-favored centers and demanded banks of their own. By 1808, Powles Hook (Jersey City), Trenton, and New Brunswick had institutions to match Newark's in New Jersey, and in 1808 and 1809, Marietta, Chillicothe, and Steubenville joined Cincinnati as banking outposts in Ohio. Mean-while city groups were winning charters with such popular names as the Mechanics' Bank of 1806 in Baltimore and the Farmers and Mechanics Bank of 1809 in Philadelphia. Between 1810 and 1815 these rising pres-sures gathered strength in even smaller towns and more remote areas and pried open system after system of state privilege. State banks with extensive branches spread through North Carolina and Georgia. About a dozen charters shattered Baltimore's monopoly in Maryland banking, and after 1811 a host of new institutions appeared in Ohio. Six more New Jersey banks arrived in 1812 and an additional ten in New York between 1810 and 1812. In 1814 Pennsylvania authorized an astounding 41 charters, primarily to serve its western counties.

Promotional charters tapped those wells of energy that were generally exploring a new range of economic opportunities early in the century and attracted a unique public intensity to the politics of development.

"It is impossible for you to imagine how popular the measure is," one gentleman reported to another on the campaign among New York City mechanics in 1810 to establish their own bank.[6] Communities, not factions, mobilized in the battles for growth, as the charter petitions of 1804 and 1814 for a bank in Lynn, Massachusetts, illustrated. In the sometimes ferocious competition for a turnpike connection, backcountry settlements swallowed old prejudices against coastal exploitation, jockeyed for eastern favor, tolerated the tolls, and even connived with outside land speculators who were investing in the road. In spurts, state elections now attracted an unprecedented participation: 82% of Delaware's eligible voters in 1804, 64% from Massachusetts in 1809, 80% from Vermont in 1812 and New Hampshire in 1814.

Yet the framework of political authority and its corporate favors did not change radically during the early years of the 19th century. While the first round of charters was engaging such widespread enthusiasm, the companies themselves remained exclusive clubs that pursued the specific ambitions of their small inner circles. Ostensibly popular enterprises such as the Mechanics Bank of New York, which roused high hopes in 1810, quickly fell under merchant domination. Although membership in these clubs did come from farther down the hierarchy, the new recruits continued to emulate the established gentlemen. Backcountry petitioners for turnpikes were left waiting for the elite companies to trickle their benefits into the remote settlements. In its early stage, in other words, the politics of development kept the initiative, the agenda, and the control of promotional ambitions—the power of choice—at the upper reaches of American society. During these years it was still common to visualize electoral politics as one commentator did a gubernatorial contest in Ohio: no voters, just three gentlemen—Thomas Worthington, Edward Tiffin, and Return Jonathan Meigs—and as this particular partisan of Worthington and Tiffin put it, "two Virginians" should never "suffer a single Yank to oust them."[7]

Panic and depression cracked this framework. Hard times after 1819 not only punctured the universal faith in corporate promotions; they also left a residue of bad credit paper that company insiders had issued as they saw fit. Private banks and comparable note-issuing corporations never regained their general, buoyant reputation as the advance agents of prosperity. But bitterness alone was no longer enough. Coming off a curve of rising expectations about the popular benefits from politics and the popular availability of credit, Americans who a few years earlier had been willing to receive from above now demanded the right to set their own terms. If there had been alternative routes to prosperity, there should be alternative ways out of adversity, and in several states grass-roots movements for legalized debt relief dominated the politics of the early twenties. From an effort to determine the economic agenda these assertions broadened to a reshaping of the structure of political authority. Wherever privilege seemed to bestow unregulated power, an angry popular force hammered away at it.

One target of this furor, the legislative caucuses that nominated party candidates, had originated in state politics around 1800 as a more liberal and open replacement for the purely private selections by gentry cliques. With Madison's nomination in 1808, a national counterpart became the standard Republican technique for authorizing the party's presidential candidates as well. Before the 1820s the only effective criticism of caucus nominations emphasized decentralization, not democratization. Hence when DeWitt Clinton's New York allies attacked Madison's nomination by a national caucus in 1812, they presented their candidate through a state caucus. Early in the twenties, however, an entirely different, wholesale attack condemned caucuses as a denial of the people's right to choose. One after another the caucuses crumbled like rickety shacks, and in their place emerged new methods of nomination, usually some kind of special convention, that could claim a direct connection with the will of the people. Informal circles of party management at the various state capitals faced a similar hostility as secret thefts of the people's power to decide for themselves. Rising rapidly with the decade, these stirrings of self-determination in politics swept states as diverse as Alabama, Kentucky, and New York into a full-blown national movement by 1824, when a campaigner in New York epitomized its spirit with a call to battle "between the *Albany Regency* (the machine of *King Caucus*) and the PEOPLE."[8] That year a record percentage of New York's electorate voted.

The urge for popular control also spilled into constitutional revisions and amendments. Since the late 18th century, gentry leaders, seeking a tactical advantage over their opponents, had expanded the franchise in one state after another, and in most cases little remained by 1820 to complete the victory for universal white male suffrage. Nevertheless, the drives of the 1820s came with a new explicitness about popular sovereignty, a new assertion of the people's right actually to rule. A variety of indirect elections, the time-honored republican method for sifting popular opinions through elite minds, fell before the demand that the people themselves should choose their judges, their governors, their presidential electors. Property qualifications for high state office met a similar fate. Voice voting—reporting to one's superiors—was repudiated. If many of these attacks had a largely symbolic meaning, symbol and substance blended to a single end: empower the people to shape their own politics so that they, in fact, governed. Until the 1820s old theories of republican balance kept these democratic impulses on the defensive, fighting against aristocracy, against monopoly, against cabals and plots. Now they broke loose to give a wide and undifferentiated array of citizens the initiative. Although the battles against privilege never ceased, they became police actions more than countermoves, the sovereign people's eternal vigilance to determine their own destiny.

By the mid-twenties, a demand for the power of self-determination had transformed the style and tone of American politics and opened the way for a continuing quest to broaden these popular rights of choice. The eruption of an Anti-Masonic party late in the decade marked a dramatic example of a new local initiative in both the organization and the agenda of politics. So did the simultaneous appearance of Working Men's tickets in the eastern cities. During the exploratory years of a new freedom, associations of urban workers suffered from a particularly heavy hand of elite control. "Shall all others, except only the industrious mechanic, be allowed to meet and plot . . .?" an outraged lawyer for the New York cordwainers cried in 1809.[9] Until the twenties the answer was basically yes. Then in a surge of independence local unions and workers' parties mushroomed along the coast. "We . . . do not ask to have our grievances redressed as a favor," declared a group of Boston workers, "but we demand it as a right."[10] During these same years state constitutions and election-day ballots grew longer in an effort to squeeze the discretionary authority out of government offices. Successful politicians increasingly adopted the rhetoric of mere reflection, as if their voices really came from the electorate. It was no longer possible for a few gentlemen to claim society's responsibility for instructing the untutored masses. "Every man's example is, in a greater or less degree, a leading influence [in public opinion]," William Leggett wrote in the New York *Evening Post*; "and it is . . . the undoubted right" of each one to try his skills at persuasion in a marketplace of equals.[11]

When prosperity returned in the late twenties and the passion for canals revitalized the politics of development, it operated in striking contrast with the era of turnpike promotions. Instead of private enterprises borrowing public authority, canals expressed government policies, relied on government credit, and consequently acquired the aura of public causes, the people's projects to serve their own needs. Turnpikes, despite their proliferation, still had a zero-sum quality: one string of towns lost as another won. The potential for canals—and even more for the railroads trailing close behind them—seemed almost limitless, and their advocates demanded government aid for extensions and feeders and additional lines as a fundamental American right to participate in a boundless material progress. Now the people decided how many and how far. Here as elsewhere in the new democratic age, anything political had to appear as the people's choice.

• • •

At the turn of the century the obstacles to a popular choice in spiritual matters were more generalized than in political affairs. Gaining control over one's eternal life required the breaking of three monopolies: God's over the distribution of souls between heaven and hell, a professional ministry's over the translation of his terms, and a minority's over their immortal benefits. The first suggestion of new possibilities struck wildly in an extensive western revival that started in 1800 at the Gasper River in Kentucky, swelled the next year at the Cane Ridge camp meeting, then spread through the rugged pioneering country on either side of the mountain ranges from Georgia to Pennsylvania until it finally subsided in 1805. Initially this great outpouring of religious sentiments seemed to raise no new questions about who governed the individual's immortal soul. Revivals had flared fitfully in the backcountry for decades, and Baptists in particular had turned their converts into holy bands who proclaimed their separation from a surrounding corruption and urged a godly life on their neighbors. Despite their leveling of worldly distinctions and their challenge to established authority, however, these zealous sectarians only reinforced the Calvinist keystone of predestination, which exalted God's omnipotence and presumed his selections for salvation. Against this background the latest fervor during the first years of the 19th century looked like a grander version of a familiar story. Almost all the western revivalists, a mix of Presbyterians, Methodists, and Baptists, preached a frontier variant of the traditional message: the sovereignty of God, the sinfulness of humans, and the providential moment when those who opened their hearts might receive a miraculous blessing. Vivid images of hellfire provided the necessary lever of persuasion. The western upsurge did little to encourage a more popular appeal from the settled eastern clergymen. Coastal Presbyterians who went west to participate in God's work returned to repudiate the revivals as barbaric emotionalism and to feed the stories of a howling, jerking mob whose behavior denied every canon of a genuine salvation. It had been the Devil's work after all.

Nevertheless, the Great Revival, as it came to be called, did mark the critical point of change, stirring impulses that, once released, never slackened. Baptists and Methodists who recognized these raw westerners as their natural recruits did respond enthusiastically and dispersed rapidly through the west to harvest them. Both relied on itinerant messengers of the faith who shared the everyday experiences and spoke the ordinary language of backcountry Americans. During the next few years, both adopted the revival's camp meetings as a way of attracting scattered settlers, winning new messengers, and sending them home to plant congregations in their neighborhoods. The Baptists, with no denominational superstructure and no fixed requirements for the ministry, spread more easily, soon abandoning the camp meeting in favor of a simple multiplication of independent local churches. It was the Methodists, however, who made the major contribution to a growing popular control over salvation. Unlike the Baptists, the Methodists rejected predestination, placed Christ's atonement at the heart of their doctrine, and offered at least the potential for anyone's salvation. With every year of expansion an urge toward greater spiritual self-determination increased the tension in their churches.

These pressures for personal choice rose predominantly in the west, where the distance from established authorities and their unresponsiveness to local needs generated a general skepticism toward outside power. Methodism, a hierarchy capped by a self-styled bishop, Francis Asbury, and regulated through a general conference of ministers, had felt the pulls of western resistance almost as soon as it began to marshal its resources to expand in the 1780s. Appropriately, the first of the Methodist secessionists, James O'Kelly of Virginia, likening Bishop Asbury to the pope, had justified his rebellion in the contemporary idiom of anti-federalism: "A consolidated government is always bad."[12] Early in the 19th century these continual pulls against central power were joined by new pushes toward theological liberalization, challenging the traditional Wesleyan assumption that only a few in the sinful human race could find the strength to accept God's offer of grace. As a stimulus westerners heard an exciting message of hope from a handful of mavericks, including Alexander Campbell, Barton Stone, and Elias Smith, who emerged from the Great Revival with visions of a pure, primitive Christianity and offered a thoroughly democratic grace to all who would accept it. Although barely connected to the existing churches, they found western audiences eager to receive such glorious news under any auspices. Whoever brought a similar message met an equally enthusiastic response, and the Methodist doctrine, above all others, adapted most readily to this popular demand. By the 1810s, disputes over infant damnation, simplified creeds, spontaneous ministries, and much more were besetting the entire western region.

Until 1816, Bishop Asbury managed to contain these churning forces. A tenacious, resourceful fighter, he viewed the American continent as his personal domain, a missionary kingdom that he had sacrificed the comforts of his British home to conquer. To preserve his empire, Asbury battled relentlessly against Anglican absorption from the outside and anarchical dissent from the inside. Those who challenged his hierarchy he subdued or drove from the church. Over those who submitted, the bishop laid a kindly, paternal hand. It was the church's "duty," he said, "to condescend to men of low estate," and he drove himself unstintingly in that missionary calling.[13] Although Asbury immediately sensed the importance of the Great Revival—"The work of God is running like fire in Kentucky"; "Great things have been done in the western states"—he remained throughout his life a conservative 18th-century Wesleyan, concerned about shallow conversions and humbled by the awful powers of God and the Devil. "Knowing the terror of the Lord," he emphasized a year before he died, "we persuade men."[14]

With the death of Methodism's old-fashioned patriarch in 1816, the liberal western forces broke free and merged with other democratic impulses around them to tame the Lord's terror. Bowing routinely to Asbury's memory, Methodist circuit riders proceeded to abandon his cautions, use whatever techniques would rivet an audience, and eliminate the last doctrinal restraints to a popular appeal. In 1822 one of the most successful, Peter Cartwright, simply brushed aside yesterday's complex question of infant damnation: "If all hell was searched, there would not be a single child found in it. . . ."[15] Meanwhile, a significant proportion of Baptists and a scattering of Presbyterians had softened their craggy Calvinism to suit a broad, diversified public.

Rather than just welcome the glad tidings about human control, as the first audiences in the 1800s had, Americans increasingly demanded it as their right. Now they created their own spiritual opportunities—opportunities limited only by the energy of the ministers and the commitment of the people, any people. Humans, not heavenly messengers, sparked religious revivals, and everyone with the will to act could find the way to salvation. ". . . God meant by his promises just what a plain, common sense man would understand them to mean," declared the Presbyterian-Congregationalist Charles Grandison Finney, an alert student of the Methodists and the most famous among the swelling interdenominational band who carried the new message. Instead of waiting to receive God's grace, individuals had to discover it within themselves. Each one chose for eternity. "Talking in general terms against sin will produce no results," Finney warned his fellow ministers. "You must make a man feel that you mean *him*."[16] But would people recognize the moment of grace? "A real Christian has no need to doubt," Finney assured them.[17] "Conversion . . . is a plain, common-sense, practical business, intelligible to all," echoed one of Finney's contemporaries.[18] Hence when the decision to follow a Christian life was made, no one had to feel humble before God's priceless gift. Individuals could exult in their personal triumphs. No mystery there: no inscrutable Lord on high, no cryptic Word that required a theologian's skill, no prolonged uncertainty that only a minister could interpret.

With the passing of the transition from an exploration to an assertion of spiritual rights, the message of individual control spread through the towns and cities along the coast. Rolling in from the west on a wave of revivals, it isolated the old learned orthodoxies in a few pockets of strength and established a new religious tone for the nation. The traditional doctrines seemed so utterly obsolete that one minister after another tried to purge them from memory. The earnest itinerant John Finley found it impossible that he had ever accepted a Presbyterian predestination, and the irrepressible Lyman Beecher made the outrageous claim that since 1800 no "approved Calvinistic" authority had "believed or taught" infant damnation.[19] This sweeping triumph of popular choice bore almost no relation to the earlier pioneers of an elite freedom. The 18th-century vanguard of Arminianism ended in the cul-de-sac of Unitarianism, thoroughly radical in its theology but equally indifferent to a popular appeal. Some ministers of New England Congregationalism, the original center of a liberalized Calvinism, continued the struggle, but their leaders in the early 19th century were still wrestling with the old orthodoxies and looking to the old constituencies. Nathaniel Taylor, for example, fought to keep a qualified "moral agency" free from the heresy of "self-determination," and his associate Asahel Nettleton aimed his revivals in the 1820s at the small outposts of well-to-do Unitarianism.[20] Probably the most effective connection between the republican past and the democratic present came through a subterranean stream of Deism, now rechanneled from a source of gentry self-confidence into a way for various workingmen to express their social and intellectual independence from elite authority.

Although the expansion of religious choices interlinked with all areas of the new democracy, the closest ties bound a self-determination for the soul to a personal control over the body. Spirit and flesh were united in the Christian tradition through the titanic war between God and Satan over human destiny, and the mundane weaknesses of the flesh made it the Devil's special province. In that awesome battle, mere human specks could do little more to relieve the afflictions of the body than pray to the one and propitiate the other. As the Lord's arbitrary and unfathomable powers diminished, however, so did Satan's. The forces of evil certainly could not be allowed a mightier commander than the forces of good. Shrinking the scope of these powers also meant secularizing their battle-field—bringing them from the imponderable heights and depths and confining them to a more familiar terrain. The more earthbound the contest, the higher expectations rose that humans themselves might influence the outcome.

One way of humanizing the contest was to translate it from theological into natural terms, view good and evil as balance and imbalance, and claim the ability to understand its many tips by means of universal laws

governing each action and reaction. In this scheme, rationality secular-
ized the cosmic forces by compressing their meaning inside the superior
human mind. If rationality could not actually control these forces, it
could at least demystify them. Most of America's gentry and their physicians favored this course. In Satan's old realm of the flesh, doctors
objectified human diseases, assigned them to imbalances within the
body, and relied on an elite intelligence to prescribe the corrective. Functionally, scientific medicine served a general American population no
better than the learned ministry. Just as the minister's theology left an
overwhelming majority of their souls on the same old road to hell, so the
physician's medication left an overwhelming majority of their bodies in
the throes of the same old diseases. Whatever psychic advantages derived
from a faith in the doctor's authority were canceled by the damaging
effects of his cures: harsh purgatives, mercury compounds, systematic
bleeding, misapplied quinine, and their companions in the increasingly
orthodox "heroic" treatment. "My nerves, my digestion, and my head
were seriously affected," John Marshall reported after prolonged doses of
the standard medication. ". . . I at length resolved to take no more medicine, after which I was slowly restored to my former self."[21] In addition,
doctors simply cost more than most Americans could pay.

The popular route to control over the body paralleled the one for controlling the future of the soul. It retained the traditional cast of characters
—God, Satan, human—but gradually changed the human's role from a
pitiably weak recipient to the powerfully determining actor. Instead of
requiring superior minds to comprehend the contest, it simplified the
battle into terms that anyone could understand. As the Lord's message
became accessible to ordinary common sense, so did Satan's influence,
and in the process the competing forces circulated more and more closely
around the individual until their orbit ranged somewhere between the
arm's reach and the body's interior. The evangelist Peter Cartwright
wrestled with his Devil as if he were a country bully. The more sedate
Charles Finney located the battlefield inside each human being. At this
stage the outcome depended exclusively on individual strength—not a
trained intelligence to comprehend but a committed will to triumph. In
matters of flesh or spirit, people could if they would.

Nevertheless, popular confidence in the ability to rule the body clearly
lagged behind other areas of democratic assertion. During the first two
decades of the 19th century, official medicine, rather than slipping onto
the defensive as did orthodox religion and gentry statesmanship, actually
tightened the licensing laws for physicians. Only when the transition
from an exploration to a declaration of rights occurred in other areas did
the demand for a personal control in health also erupt and spread into a
broad range of choices for determining the state of the body. The first

thrust for a new freedom came from Samuel Thomson's immediately successful *New Guide to Health* (1822), a formulation of time-honored botanical remedies into a simple set of rules that anyone could grasp and apply. By the end of the decade, bands of Thomsonians, drawing support from the evangelical ministry, disdaining the aristocratic pretensions of regular medicine, and attacking its monopoly privileges, carried his message nationwide under the motto "Every man his own physician." A variety of popular health programs then moved through the broad gap that the Thomsonians created and expanded their clientele during the 1830s: homeopaths with a more elaborate botanical system imported from Europe, Sylvester Graham and his followers, hydropathy specialists, and sundry eclectics. Although these schools differed on how much guidance their patients required, each made individuals the sovereign centers of their own health and stressed the accessibility of their cures. Like the popular evangelicals in religion, they showed Americans how they could save their bodies with means that lay readily at their disposal. All that Sylvester Graham's regimen required was the will to enact it: diet, exercise, fresh air, cold water, sexual restraint. While the popular evangelicals told individuals to purify their souls by choosing a godly way of life, the Grahamites instructed them to purify their bodies by choosing a healthy way of life.

As the Thomsonians struck, regular medicine was entering a decline that eventually left it in disarray. Fighting each new group's legal right to practice on one hand, elite physicians bent with the competition on the other. Folk medicine always hovered around the edges of their science. For example, Benjamin Rush, the father of heroic medicine, had advised Jefferson to treat his rheumatism by "drawing an iron comb, or three or four forks over the parts afflicted" or bathing them "with a liniment composed by adding two ounces of scraped Castile or Venice soap, an ounce of camphor, half an ounce of opium, and two drams of solid volatile salt to a quart of spirit of any kind. . . ."[22] Under attack for their destructive cures, the official doctors now dispensed less mercury and antimony and relied more on natural remedies and recoveries. If John Marshall still suffered the rigors of the orthodox poisons in the early thirties, the sick John Randolph received a diet of milk, "sarsaparilla . . . and unleavened bread." Jefferson Davis received a more imaginative mix of "Colchium [tea], opium, hot water & chloroform," with perhaps a bit of "Holland gin."[23] Some regular doctors even let patients set their own dosages. But retreat turned to rout as state after state across the nation, beginning with Ohio and Alabama in 1833, either weakened or eliminated the legal protections for an orthodox, self-perpetuating medical profession and allowed an open field for individual choice.

During the 1830s, lecturers and writers of all sorts adopted health as one of their staple subjects, treated it as a matter of elementary common sense, and made each person morally responsible for its care. There was nothing esoteric about doctoring, the genteel Reverend George Burnap of Baltimore assured his audience. "Medicines have no creative or healing power. They only arouse or direct the natural functions of the human system."[24] In fact, as Dr. William Alcott wrote, medicines "are liable to sow the seeds . . . of numerous other diseases"; but "where *Nature* succeeds, we simply cure the disease." The solution lay in a "steady obedience . . . to all laws, physical and moral"—a basic understanding of the human body, which Alcott outlined in simple terms, and then the self-discipline to care for it.[25] Proper habits in eating and drinking and the salutary effects of early rising, regular exercise, and fresh air dominated these popular discussions. Hence Horace Mann, following the common wisdom of the day, placed good health first among every young man's moral responsibilities, and defined willpower as his crucial resource. Burnap called good health a "religious duty." During these years physical training joined the causes of evangelical reform.

In an age when women held special obligations for keeping the family's morals, a good deal of this advice went to them. First, they were told, they had to improve their own health, which some of them from personal laziness and social flightiness had allowed to deteriorate scandalously. Then they should tend to their children. Lowering infant mortality, Burnap concluded, was specifically their moral responsibility. A stream of literature on pediatrics instructed women not only on the care of their children but even more on the daily habits of good health they must inculcate in the young. As women's range of duties broadened, so did their horizon of choices. The Thomsonians argued that wives and mothers, not the aristocratic regular doctors, could best decide on matters of family health, and the many alternative schools of medicine following the Thomsonians included a significant number of women practitioners. With the flood of advice on health came basic guides to female physiology, and women demanded more. By the 1840s, graphic public lectures on the reproductive system supplemented the multiplying array of informational literature. Implicitly through this general diffusion of knowledge, explicitly from a few radical voices, an increasing number of women received the revolutionary message that they could determine the sexual and reproductive uses of their own bodies. Even the women's groups who mounted attacks on prostitution were speaking in their own way to the individual's right of control over her body.

Two national shifts in popular behavior between 1830 and 1850 suggested how powerfully this democratized right of choice was affecting American society. During those two decades, as the doctrines of self-determination in health were sweeping the nation, the average number of births among white women in their years of fertility took a dramatic drop, the equivalent of one child per woman and double the decline over the preceding thirty years. Neither the techniques of birth control nor the precision of reproductive knowledge improved. What did change was the environment of choice, including the greater availability of abortions, the public distribution of physiological information, and, above all, the popular belief in a right to choose. Now, according to the new values, it required only the will to decide—and many more couples did.

This same setting had an even more abrupt influence on the consumption of alcoholic beverages. Rising slightly from the Revolution to around 1830, it plummeted in the next twenty years to about one-fourth the average alcoholic intake per person. As part of the nationwide concern over health came a new preoccupation with the "poisons" that individuals thoughtlessly or stupidly inflicted on their bodies, and among these alcohol ranked first both in the attention it received and the disastrous consequences it brought. The militant temperance—or abstinence—movement that emerged in the late twenties gave the issue of health an emphasis equal to its religious appeal, as the guiding statement for the American Temperance Society illustrated: "Alcohol, when used as a beverage, causes death to the bodies and souls of men."[26] The body's disintegration served as the movement's standard way of proving the immorality of liquor, and the opponents of "TeeTotalism" struggled mightily to defend its medicinal value. Nevertheless, the Thomsonians and their offshoots railed at the evils of alcohol, and innumerable lecturers and writers cited its use as the most fundamental—and sinful—violation of nature's way. Americans, in other words, were inundated with arguments that placed alcohol at the core of a personal responsibility for their bodies, and made temperance tantamount to an acceptance of the new right of choice. People could if they would—and strikingly large numbers did.

By 1840 a process that originated in an effort to stretch the range of traditional possibilities had transformed them. From age-old impulses to find better farms and higher profits, Americans developed unique popular schemes of land distribution and internal commerce. From the continuing attempts to widen access in republican politics, they fashioned a democratic politics. From a familiar Protestant quest among the damned souls of the west, they devised a universally available salvation. From the long, gradual decline of supernaturalism, they made the body's health everyone's personal responsibility. Although elite competition for public favor facilitated the early stages of this transformation, in the end it was a popular assertion of rights that created America's society of choices. As the critical turn from spreading hopes to popular rights was occurring in the 1820s, the various strands were weaving a common pattern of trans-forming change: commercial and evangelical innovations entwining along the route of the Erie Canal, debtor politics and Thomsonian medi-cine strengthening the general assault on privilege, pressures everywhere reinforcing a nationwide movement for self-determination. The personal anger of young men at their patriarchal fathers and the public anger at patriarchal politics and patriarchal religion echoed one another during these transitional years.

What emerged, as Alexis de Tocqueville recognized in the early thir-ties, was a society resting on a new premise of equality. Now fathers relinquished control "without a struggle," he reported; "the son . . . en-ters upon his freedom . . . without effort, as a possession which is his own and which no one seeks to wrest from him."[27] During the revolu-tionary era, equality had been an essentially defensive concept, one that protected the status of free men by defining their residual human rights. Now equality thrust aggressively forward into a field of action, empow-ering Americans to decide their individual destinies from a panorama of choices that spread before them all. "The feeblest and most obscure do not now despair of exerting influence . . .," the temperance leader Justin Edwards stated proudly in 1834.[28] More grandiloquently, Horace Mann declared: "The idea and feeling that the world was made, and life given, for the happiness of all, and not for the ambition, or pride, or luxury, of one, or of a few, are pouring in, like a resistless tide, upon the minds of men, and are effecting a universal revolution in human affairs."[29]

The limits that a hierarchical container and a commitment to balance had placed around human actions in the 18th century dissolved. For Americans everywhere it meant that *you may be whatever you resolve to be. Resolution is omnipotent.*[30] Benjamin Franklin, once honored as the artisan's friend among the gentry, became a legitimate model for the artisan's own aspirations. "Who can tell how many Franklins may be among you?" asked the president of New York City's Mechanics Society at the beginning of the new era; ". . . your opportunities are great and liberal."[31] "This is a country of *self-made men*," boasted an American in the early forties, "than which nothing better could be said of any state of society."[32] Than which nothing worse could have been said about the revolutionary gentry's—an anarchy of "self-creation"!

Where the gentry had once monopolized public communication, a bab-ble of voices now competed for attention. Although the leaders of the late 18th century had written a great deal about the people, they had not written to them. They had informed one another and waited for the effects to percolate downward. Public discourse broadened along with the democratization of choices. As early as the Great Revival in the west, a shrewd Francis Asbury was planning to use the network of country stores to distribute Methodist tracts. By the 1820s a simple popular language of persuasion suffused a nation of decision makers. Where 18th-century leaders had written their statements at home and awaited the results, the agents of the new order found their inspiration on the move and took their messages to the people. Sylvester Graham worked out his science of health while on tour; the vision behind the American Home Mission Society came to its founders in a "stage-coach." Revivals and camp meetings became the standard Protestant road shows, and distributors of religious literature pursued the "way-faring man" and the "weary pilgrims" throughout the land. Now Americans everywhere were making choices, and anyone with a message had to seek them out.

A surge of interest in education swelled school enrollments and broadened the base of a literate citizenry who saw information as personal power and spurred the popular writers to their tasks. Between 1800 and 1840, the proportion of illiterates among white Americans dropped in the north from around 25% to around 5% and in the south from around 45% to around 20%. Oratory, once the pride of gentry character, also became a popular art, and speaking skills entered the school curriculum as essential training in a democratic age. In 1833 a college-educated Bostonian marveled at the "easy rhetoric" in the west, "avoiding all cant phrases and solemn phraseology," that "in every way surpasses Eastern oratory." An Ohio politician was less flattering: "Everything that can put three words together is on the stump."[33] America was a talking society where millions, not hundreds, shared the responsibilities for maintaining connections, spreading information, and persuading one another of the truth. Women who were struggling to extend their democratic range considered the right to a public platform about as precious as the right to vote. "Oh, if I was a man, how I *would* lecture!" exploded Lydia Maria Child in 1837.[34] The meaning of the world now lay within everybody's ken and invited everybody's views.

Although members of the old gentry and their immediate heirs complained bitterly about the course of change, they had no weapons for resisting it. Their own values endowed the people with certain rights of choice—usually a yes or no to the truths issued from above. As these expanded beyond the range of hierarchical control, gentlemen watched them grow without knowing how to define their boundaries. Against a backdrop of Jacobin Terror, an emerging democracy seemed a terrible risk, and a sprinkling of events such as the mob murder of Baltimore Federalists in 1812 reinforced those fears. But the keepers of the old hierarchy could only insist on an obedience that others refused to give. In the end many of these gentlemen joined what they could not check. If they could no longer export their authority, they could export their wealth, and when they did, they usually flowed at the top of the new streams of enterprise. In fact, the most stubborn resistance to the revolution in choices developed outside of those streams, among predestinarian Baptists and authority-bound Mormons, for example, whose greatest strength lay in the backwashes of economic opportunity.

These dissidents pointed up a crucial characteristic of the new democracy. Millions still lacked the freedom to choose. Perhaps a majority of Americans did claim a personal control over their souls and bodies. With white women, native Americans, and almost all blacks denied the right to vote, however, only about a third of the nation's adults participated in the new politics, and only by visualizing every wife as her husband's partner in the quest for economic opportunity did half the adult population enjoy any range in those choices. Abundant land, the opiate of the American masses, remained an illusory choice to countless seekers who could never afford the steep initial costs of establishing a farm. Nevertheless, the rights of individual self-determination that unprecedented numbers did seize set a national norm, and the battles of the future would circle around who should exercise which of them. They proved extraordinarily infectious. Overwhelmingly, Americans grasped the power of choice as soon as they spotted it and protected it jealously once they had it. The doubters almost always challenged somebody else's capacity to decide, not their own. As the old gentry discovered early in the century, the power to choose, once released, was exceedingly hard to contain.

The Last Tournament

If President Jefferson had realized that he was presiding over the decline of gentry society, nothing could have consoled him. As it was, his confidence rose biennially with each round of elections, particularly his own victory against token opposition in 1804. Relaxing in the comforts of success, Jefferson anticipated an early liquidation of the public debt and sketched a magnificent national program in transportation, manufacturing, education, and the arts. As the president's vision broadened, however, his connections down the national hierarchy weakened. Conducting an executive branch of little more than 100, mostly clerks, he had only the thinnest lines of communication beyond his own network of correspondents, and after 1804 he allowed those critical private lines to slacken. Although he continued to cultivate congressmen at regular White House dinners and occasional open houses, he devoted less energy to recruiting good Republican candidates for the legislature and less care to maintaining strong Republican leadership in either branch. His grand scheme for nationally funded "useful works" would have required extraordinary efforts to enact, yet instead of focusing his impressive talents on the plan, the president presented it as a theoretician rather than a politician.

The states reciprocated by occupying themselves with their own concerns. Each of them had an ongoing pattern of politics that the crises of the 1790s disrupted but never destroyed, and in the absence of a compelling foreign danger the snarled threads wove themselves once more around state issues. Despite the renewal of war between Britain and France in 1803, nothing in Europe's struggle immediately intruded on America's sense of peace. Even more important, the new politics of development rose simultaneously to operate by a logic that bore very little relation to the old national parties. Although "Republican" and "Federalist" continued to be worn proudly as badges of honor, these labels made less and less sense out of state politics. It always mattered where a person stood on the issue of independence, but the issue of independence often did not matter at all in the affairs of a state.

By 1804 the sharpest effects of the old partisanship had already passed in most states, and from a national perspective the results looked like moderation. During 1805 and 1806 one after another warrior from the nineties talked as if an age of republican tranquillity were finally arriving. Virginia's Senator William Branch Giles found Congress "the most harmonious" since the adoption of the Constitution, and the Federalist James Bayard noted with surprise how "extremely civil and friendly" the prickly Republican Giles had become.[1] William Plumer, a Federalist who had recently plotted New England's secession, now accepted Jefferson as his president and hoped for an amalgamation of the two parties. One Pennsylvania commentator, dating the arrival of parties with the Jay Treaty, declared them gone a decade later, and the North Carolina Federalist John Steele referred to his party "as *having been*, because it was in my opinion dissolved at the conclusion of the late general peace [in 1802] when the French revolution terminated. . . ."[2] Neocolonial at birth, the parties were dying from Europe's neglect.

Jefferson blandly mistook a decline of the old party spirit for a triumph of Republican harmony. Those state leaders who found national partisanship an inconvenience to their politics of development spoke a language of accommodation that blended with Jefferson's own image of national felicity under a virtuous ruler. By contrast, the fervent keepers of the Republican faith seemed needlessly contentious. As chief of a beleaguered opposition during the late nineties, Jefferson had applauded their ringing truths and stinging attacks; but he was the president now, and the party of principle prevailed. Those quarrelsome "high-flyers" even circulated unpleasant rumors about his own republican dedication. Should the party's first character be required, as Jefferson felt obliged in 1806, to defend his record to William Duane, the editor of his own party's newspaper? In the president's little world of Washington the party's real enemies were the unreconstructed monarchists of Boston or such powerful Federalist senators as Bayard of Delaware and Uriah Tracy of Connecticut, who from time to time gulled enough wayward Republicans to disrupt Congress. The feuds "between conflicting friends," he complained, only disturbed the peace without furthering the cause of republicanism.[3]

Hence Jefferson's appointments favored those lukewarm partisans whose personal inclinations and political associations drained the administration's energies into strictly state-based feuds, weakened party discipline, and sapped the base of his leadership. In his cabinet, for example, the New England crowd of Secretary of War Henry Dearborn, Postmaster General Gideon Granger, and Levi Lincoln, the first attorney general, all had strong ties to land speculators and entrepreneurial businessmen, and all defended Federalist appointees against high-flying Republicans. Robert Smith and Jacob Crowninshield, his two secretaries of the navy, came from prominent merchant families whose tepid Republicanism expressed an essentially expedient party allegiance. Caesar A. Rodney, Jefferson's legislative lieutenant and then attorney general, cherished an intimate friendship with the president's enemy Bayard, who considered his own political principles the same as Rodney's—unless perhaps his friend was "a little more *peopleick*."[4] Above all, the president's two intimates, Madison and Gallatin, consistently sided with the accommodating subverters of the old parties—Madison from temperament, Gallatin from an active involvement in Pennsylvania's politics of development.

As colleagues, these intimates were indispensable to Jefferson. With Madison he relaxed in a collaboration that had almost become instinctive. Gallatin not only covered Jefferson's exposed flank in public finance but also criticized his proposals in an unusually blunt and useful manner. The Swiss-born secretary's ingrained distrust of the great powers steadied him against the strongest neocolonial swings between dependence and isolation, and he offered particularly sharp assessments in international affairs, where Jefferson and Madison generally thought too much alike to improve one another's perspective. But neither lieutenant strengthened the administration's party leadership. As secretary of state, Madison retired from his earlier role as Republican strategist and left party management to the president's soft, distant judgment. Gallatin was an outright liability in party affairs. The dogged, driving traits that Jefferson admired for their salutary effects on the public debt others experienced as a narrow, stabbing assertiveness. Not even John Adams had Gallatin's knack for alienating so many potential allies. Southern Republicans who might have honored him for his dedicated party service in the late nineties resented his opposition to slavery and his eagerness to tax it. Despite his sympathy for the commercial needs of the coastal cities, an exceptionally large number of their merchants came to despise him. Washington veterans like Nathaniel Macon, newcomers like Henry Clay, and just plain agreeable souls like Caesar Rodney at least had in common a hearty dislike of the secretary of the treasury.

Only in foreign affairs did the administration maintain its authority to command. The more Jefferson detached himself from domestic affairs, the more he concentrated his talents in the area where his conception of republicanism justified a thoroughly national government. The guideline that he had stated to Madison in 1786—make us "one nation as to foreign concerns, and keep us distinct in domestic ones"—became a touchstone during his presidency and a summary of constitutional orthodoxy in retirement: "Seventeen distinct states, amalgamated into one as to foreign concerns, but single and independent as to their internal administration. . . ."[5] What he failed to realize as his second term began was the way in which this separation of functions was isolating him from the flow of American life. With no foreign menace to alert them, former line officers from both national parties gladly turned to their own affairs. "Republican," once the banner of independence from Britain, increasingly served as little more than a loose cover of convenience for the people across the nation on whom Jefferson chose to rely. The president, who thought he was riding a wave of success, sat instead on a cloud of apathy. By early 1807, American politics had left him in preeminence.

That June off the coast of Maryland a British warship, refused the right to search the American vessel *Chesapeake* for British deserters, attacked it, took four sailors from its crew, and left it to limp home and signal a new round of international crisis. This flagrant example of impressment fitted into a tightening pattern of maritime controls that the British imposed as the long contest with France came to depend almost exclusively on their sea power against Napoleon's domination of the continent. The turn in policy began in May 1805 with a British ruling—the *Essex* decision—that denied neutrals the right to engage in specifically wartime as distinct from normal peacetime lines of trade. Accelerating in 1807, the new policy completed its first cycle that November with orders-in-council requiring neutral trade to pass through British ports and be licensed. Shades of the old colonial system! France retaliated by defining a licensed ship as a British ship and hence fair game for confiscation. Each side declared a comprehensive blockade of the other.

Once again, the great powers fixed the United States in their vise: follow British rules or face seizure on the sea, follow French rules or face seizure in the ports of Europe. Eliminating the middle ground, they forced a choice, for or against. Once again, the revolutionary gentry viewed their situation in a warped mirror of European power. As the squeeze began, they saw themselves shrink into dependence. William

Plumer, a gentleman of considerable courage and no friend to France, wrote of Napoleon in his journal: "His name is a host—The world trembles before him. . . . Who can set limits to his conquests!" So that nothing would "tempt him to reek his vengeance on my country," Plumer favored removing from the congressional library a book particularly offensive to the emperor.[6] John Randolph, picturing a global British power that could prevail "against the United flags of the Universe," called any thought of American retaliation absurd.[7] As they swung erratically between such feelings of helplessness and an equally exaggerated belligerence, they searched futilely for a dignity that neither Europe nor their own predilections allowed them to achieve.

Monroe, Jefferson's favorite protégé and his roving ambassador in Europe from 1803 to 1807, illustrated the neocolonial dilemma in action. After receiving Bonaparte's gift of the Louisiana territory, he tried his hand at negotiating for Spain's Florida territory that covered a strip along the Gulf from Louisiana to the peninsula on the Atlantic. Fearing contamination from another XYZ affair, Monroe refused to ease his way with bribes, and his mission failed. During these frustrating months, he accepted a fantastic rumor that France and Britain were on the verge of making peace in order to combine forces and divide the United States between them. Moving to Britain, where he had been treated with peremptory rudeness during an earlier stop, he reacted to the new pressures on American commerce in 1805 with sabers rattling. Risk war "in defense of our rights honor and interests," he told the president, or "All will insult us."[8] Yet the longer he stayed in England, the more at home he felt. Making the critical gentry distinction, he decided that its form of government was "more republican than monarchical" after all, and as he negotiated a major treaty with the British, his growing sympathy led him to sign unacceptable terms.[9] To his president, Monroe offered the inevitable American justification for a bad bargain: "It is important for us to stand well with some power."[10]

Jefferson had been experiencing his own swings of sentiment toward the European titans. After the searing events of the late nineties, his first impulse as president was to hide the American chrysalis in a cocoon of diplomatic isolation. Only the French threat in New Orleans jarred him into playing the old game. If France occupied that port, Jefferson wrote for Bonaparte's eyes, it would immediately dissolve the "fund of friendship" between the two nations and force the United States to "marry ourselves to the British fleet and nation."[11] But his heart remained at home. As he basked in his new Louisiana empire, he wrote comfortably late in 1803 about the distant "battle of lions and tigers" in Europe that might neutralize "their power of tyrannizing."[12] After the coronation of Emperor Napoleon completed his alienation from France, he turned his attention in 1805 to a relatively benign Britain and indulged his own fantasy of a lopsided alliance that would use the lion's jaws to help him devour Spanish territory. Madison gently scotched the passing thought.

Nevertheless, the appearance of an ostensibly friendly British government the next year buoyed Jefferson's optimism even higher. This government, he hoped, would replace the lapsed Jay Treaty with a truly equitable one that ended impressments and guaranteed America's commercial rights under a cover of British naval power. Reviving the neocolonial's inflated sense of America's importance—"the first wish of every Englishman's heart is to see us once more fighting by their side"—the president pictured the British eager to buy peace with the United States as their European war intensified.[13] The record should have told him otherwise: the hotter the wars, the harder the hearts of the belligerents. Monroe and the American minister in London, William Pinkney, like Jay before them, sent home what the British chose to give them, the exchange of a few murkily phrased and elaborately hedged commercial concessions for America's abandonment of economic retaliation, its active resistance to Napoleon's decrees, and no satisfaction on impressments. Even Rufus King called it devastating to "the national honour."[14] The ultimate indignity Jefferson and Madison scarcely recognized. To understand the document's opaque prose, they had to speculate on how the British admiralty courts would construe it, for Britain alone would interpret and enforce its own fiat. Now Jefferson suffered the pangs that Washington had felt eleven years earlier. This time the president discarded the treaty instead of submitting it to the Senate.

That humiliating deflation of hope served as backdrop to Jefferson's almost welcoming response to the *Chesapeake* incident. As public cries of outrage erupted everywhere, he sought to hold that mood in readiness for a final confrontation with the British bully. Leave the French tyrant to Europe, he declared; Britain is our enemy and "I say 'down with England'. . . . "[15] Memories of all those accumulated, festering grievances, national and personal, poured into a single sentence: "Now then is the time to settle the old and the new."[16] But the time passed. There were the forms of negotiation with Britain to fulfill and the fleet of merchant vessels to warn home. His advisers reminded him that with no American navy or fortifications worth the name, Britain would ravage the coastline. Lacking an army of more than a few thousand, the president relied on the state militia, but that summer it failed to answer the government's call to arms. Although Jefferson's romantic vision of the republic's spontaneous mobilization for actual battle might have eliminated these obstacles, he could not escape his iron circle: wars generated debts which caused mass degradation which produced tyrants who made wars. Were not France and England verifying its terrible truth that very day? In 1803, when the Federalists demanded a military solution to the closing of New Orleans, the president had known why: their "object is to force us into war if possible, in order to derange our finances. . . ."[17] In his second inaugural he had dreamed of a time when ample government revenues would pay for wars without creating new debts. That prospect, however, lay in the future. Now Jefferson needed a cheaper, safer alternative.

The republic's tradition and the president's temperament supplied it. Since colonial days the limitless powers of commercial coercion had charmed countless gentry who were not themselves merchants, and Jefferson, Hamilton, and Madison, among many others, had spoken grandly of its possibilities during the 1780s and 1790s. Usually they contemplated some regulation of imports, after the example of the European powers. This approach represented the perspective of the port cities, where the influx of European goods dominated American commerce, and from that angle of vision Congress passed a partial restriction on imports in 1806 as retaliation against the British. Jefferson, however, viewed commercial policy from an agrarian perspective. Europe relied far more on America's surplus, he had told Washington in 1788, than America did on Europe's finished products. Hence Jefferson sought leverage through exports, and he soon converted an already sympathetic Madison to that agrarian strategy. In fact, Madison was suggesting a ban on exports as early as 1805.

Moreover, neither Virginian thrilled to the glory of battle. Although Jefferson's opinion on the merits of a just war vacillated, he usually thought of it as the failure rather than the fulfillment of a country's virtues, "the consequences of a want of respectability in the national character."[18] A comprehensive scheme of economic coercion required far higher qualities of resolution and control. Not only would such a policy pinch the enemy by withholding goods; it would elevate the nation's character through common sacrifice. The crux of the matter in this latest crisis was the lucrative re-exportation of other countries' goods that slipped in and out of American ports and accounted for the nation's recent surge of commercial prosperity. Jefferson would gladly exchange it for a higher virtue. Even while his administration defended that trade against the *Essex* decision of 1805, the president did not consider it fully moral or at all necessary for a frugal republic's happiness. In addition, eliminating the re-export trade would remove one more possible excuse for war.

As usual, forces from Europe finally pushed the United States into a decision. Britain, following its familiar maritime policy of seize now and pay later, issued stiff new rules and unleashed its navy to sweep America's unsuspecting ships from the oceans. Napoleon quickly followed suit, and by December 1807 no American vessel abroad was safe. At the president's behest the government clamped a total embargo on foreign trade. The full meaning of this dramatic response floated in limbo. In the short run, it protected shippers from their own daring, provided a test of Jefferson's proposition about European dependence on America's supply system, and built an incentive into negotiations with the great powers. The first to repeal its maritime restrictions, the administration instructed its ministers in London and Paris, won the United States as an ally. Ideally, of course, both would yield. But how long should America wait? Early in the test, Jefferson considered eleven months the nation's limit. At some point, he realized, "the embargo, continued, becomes a greater evil than war."[19] Hence the embargo might be an alternative to war or a preliminary to it. As the months passed, nobody helped Jefferson in weighing his choices. Although Madison wrote the best public defense of the embargo, he remained otherwise quietly obedient. At the opposite extreme, Gallatin bombarded the president with contradictory judgments. After the *Chesapeake* incident, he cheered the prospect of war. Then he demonstrated that the United States could not fight one. Next, in a cogent attack on a long-range embargo he favored war again, without demonstrating how it had suddenly become practical. In the end, Jefferson was left to commune with his own character.

He never had qualms about applying the government's power in behalf of American independence. During the 1780s when he was expressing so many concerns about domestic centralization, Jefferson declared on the subject of foreign affairs, "I love energy in government dearly."[20] In a crisis he automatically assumed that the gentleman atop the American hierarchy must "direct the whole public force to the best advantage of the nation."[21] At those moments his treasured distinction between foreign and domestic affairs disappeared, the rule of law dissolved into the rule of men, and the president's word became the voice of the nation. All the way down the hierarchy he expected obedience, and just like the Federalist gentry before him, he interpreted resistance as proof of a great power's subversion.

A preview of this frame of mind appeared early in 1807, when Aaron Burr fell into a morass of intrigues that he had helped to create and emerged the leading villain in a plot to carve a new empire out of the western United States and Mexico. Jefferson, who already despised Burr as an unprincipled adventurer, read his guilt from his character, demanded his trial on charges of treason, and approved the net of arbitrary arrests that gathered suspects indiscriminately into jail. Although Jefferson lost much of his interest in Burr's fate after the attack on the *Chesapeake,* he simply shifted that orientation to the struggle over the embargo.

Month after month as neither European giant budged, evidences of public hardship, evasion, and anger multiplied, and Jefferson's government responded with greater stubbornness, harsher laws, and sterner enforcements. The president chafed at the recent changes in state law that shifted libel from a criminal offense against the government to a civil offense against an official, and he vented his wrath on judges, especially Republican ones, who refused to interpret the embargo legislation as he did. With no apparatus of its own for halting general violations of a law, the national government resorted to occasional authoritarian forays against a few offenders, all the more arbitrary for their unpredictability. Neither sea captains nor mountain traders, both a tough, freebooting lot, were intimidated, and the embargo became a sieve. Vows of poverty taken in other people's behalf rarely elicit widespread enthusiasm. Walking the circle of logic that said the people mirrored the virtues of their leaders and the leaders expressed the wishes of the people, Jefferson utterly misread the nation's willingness to accept his regimen and live self-sufficiently in the name of freedom. Surely the most unfair charge against him during the entire ordeal was that he clung to this policy for a "love of popularity."[22]

As the embargo passed its anniversary in the winter of 1808 and 1809, Jefferson clutched a failing policy. The British, whose troops mortified him in war, whose king humiliated him at court, and whose ministers insulted him in diplomacy, had done it again, for the president had no place to go: his government could not maintain the embargo and his nation could not fight a war. Always far better at creative thinking than at systematic administration, he drifted. Partly Jefferson was relinquishing the initiative to Madison, who had just been elected his successor, out of a conviction that he must not embarrass his friend as John Adams' so-called midnight appointments had embarrassed him. The forms of a good ruler included his correct passage into retirement. Nevertheless, Jefferson was also repeating a pattern of withdrawal from adversity that had marked his whole career. While he was packing for Monticello, Congress ended the experiment.

It was a sad conclusion to a reasonable gamble. Nobody during the era of gentry government could mobilize the United States for war. Although Jefferson had some foolish ideas about the efficacy of little gunboats, he had no hope whatsoever of building a navy to challenge the British at sea. His very credentials as a Republican depended on his rejection of a standing army. Neither his nation nor his party, in other words, would allow effective preparation for war, and if Jefferson had tried one in 1807, the results would have been far more disastrous than the embargo. Moreover, commercial coercion emerged naturally from the central place of commercial freedom in the gentry definition of independence. The federalists made it integral to their arguments for the Constitution, and commercial regulation became the first item of business for the new government in 1789. A commercial treaty triggered the formation of national parties; then a quasi-war over commercial rights almost destroyed one of them. By 1807 even a number of old Federalists saw Britain's primary objective as the destruction of its commercial rival. Hence the embargo was no evasion. It lay at the heart of America's neocolonial battle. If it expressed the cocoon side of that mentality, it at least had the merit of clarity. The muddle of selective restrictions that followed the embargo transformed a domestic sieve into an international sluice-way of violations that only the European powers could regulate.

The embargo failed because it had quicker, sharper political consequences in the United States than in either France or Britain. Like the rest of their generation, Jefferson and his colleagues could not grasp America's insignificance in Europe's calculations. Napoleon had utter disdain for everything about that bastard republic. Although the United States asked only that France repeal those ocean rules it could not enforce in any case, Napoleon still would not bother. As Madison wrote half-plaintively in July 1808, "It would seem as if the Imperial cabinet has never paid sufficient attention to the smallness of the sacrifice...."[23] Various British governments on their part decided that they could get what they needed from American commerce without conceding anything to its government. When the special British envoy George Rose arrived in the heat of patriotic fervor over the embargo, he had instructions not to discuss even the attack on the *Chesapeake*, let alone the big cage of maritime restrictions, until the United States gave more ground in negotiations. Only Spain respected the power of the United States, and Spain's opinion no longer counted in 1808. At home, on the other hand, the inertia of deductive reasoning behind the embargo drove the administration's lofty major premises deeper and deeper into an impenetrable thicket of resistance. Gallatin's final contribution to Jefferson's policy was a demand for despotic controls from a government that could not even enforce republican laws. In the end, however, these failings were no more than minor variations on the dilemma besetting an entire generation of gentry leadership. Caught between intractable domestic conditions and unyielding international circumstances, the president took a creative leap and fell short.

If this latest crisis wreaked havoc with gentry diplomacy, it worked wonders with their partisanship. After a brief interlude of general anger over the *Chesapeake* incident, the national parties awoke to divide the nation and dominate its political debate. In rising crescendo during the campaigns of 1808, Federalists accused the administration of playing lackey to its master Napoleon, courting war with Britain, and plotting to destroy American freedom. Resistance to the embargo, the administration responded, was a direct consequence of British "intrigues" and "English agitators." According to a spokesman for Maryland's Republicans, Anglomonarchic Federalists would "permit the English king to seize all American property . . . and impress every seaman into his service. For say they, is not the ocean his, does not America belong to him, and has he not a right to the services of his subjects?"[24] After visiting the United States in 1807 and 1808, a puzzled Englishman reported that Americans were still fighting the French Revolution with parties that made "jacobinism and anti-jacobinism" the line of battle. French party, British party: the same old rhetoric would respond seismographically to every international eruption until the end of the War of 1812.

To some degree neocolonial rhetoric simply matched neocolonial realities. The rapid increase in European bullying and the sudden confrontation with choices for war, embargo, or capitulation spotlighted the nation's jeopardy and sharpened the need to define its real enemy. The larger meaning behind the parties' miraculous return from the dead, however, lay in the contrast between a gentry tradition's ability to explain international crisis and the failure of a new politics of development to compete with that explanation. During the lull after 1800, while others were shifting their attention to state affairs, a scattering of veteran partisans clung stubbornly to their politics of independence. Fisher Ames nursed remnants of the Federalist party specifically to stop the Gallic Jefferson from precipitating war with England. "I have long considered england as but the advance guard of our Country . . . ," wrote another sturdy Federalist, John Rutledge, Jr. "If they fall we do. . . ."[25] The minute France threatened the United States in New Orleans, old warriors raised the cry of Jefferson's subservience to Bonaparte. Meanwhile a handful of them in New England were hoping to secede from the union with British support. Jefferson, on his part, traced every Federalist move in Congress as the work of monarchists, and a band of militant Republicans continued to find British influences corrupting their states. When the *Chesapeake* incident shattered America's peace, these were the people with an instant explanation. Duane's *Aurora* immediately linked it to a chain of abuses dating from 1793. Because Federalists still maintained an impressive network of newspapers throughout the country, they could enter a nationwide debate without delay. Faced with an international crisis, the gentry hierarchy still functioned effectively, and by late summer of 1807 a tenacious old leadership filled the public vacuum with a partisanship from the nineties.

The resurrection of the old politics disrupted the new. State-based promoters who watched their entrepreneurial alliances suddenly crack and their surplus funds disappear with the embargo had no ready response other than howls of unhappiness. A factional politics of development that only confused the hidebound partisan made perfect sense to them, and the politics of independence that made perfect sense to the old warriors only confused the very different conflicts over charters and speculations. In their indignation the state-oriented leaders tended to curse the entire mess and everyone associated with it—British and French, Federalists and Republicans alike. Yet nobody could ignore a prolonged international crisis that rocked the economy and threatened war. Lacking a way of their own to reckon with these basic issues, the politicians of development drifted uneasily into the old party camps and contributed to the illusion of a clear-cut national partisanship that simply renewed the battle of the 1790s.

In fact, the parties with the old labels of Republican and Federalist had to be remade after 1807, and in their new dispensation they revealed far less vigor, far less of the comprehensive coverage, programmatic unity, and internal discipline that had characterized the originals. Age was one important contributor. In an electorate dominated by young voters, men in their twenties like Nicholas Biddle and Washington Irving had no bitter memories of the 1790s and no emotional roots in those battles. Although they were also outraged by the lordly behavior of the great powers, they found the neocolonial conceptions of their elders absurd. Biddle called them "childish notions." "One day I am dining with a knot of honest, furious Federalists," Irving wrote in 1811, "who are damning their opponents as a set of consummate scoundrels, panders of Bonaparte, etc. etc. The next day I dine, perhaps with some of the very men I have heard thus anathematized, and find them equally honest, warm, and indignant; and if I take their word for it, I had been dining the day before with some of the greatest knaves in the nation, men absolutely paid and suborned by the British government."[26] Voting patterns zigzagged after 1807. Moments of international crisis shot the old parties into prominence and produced sharp voting shifts from North Carolina to New England. Just as abruptly, moments of lull released people to their local pursuits, revived state factionalism, and allowed a vapid Republicanism to dominate national politics.

Good memories weakened the old party loyalties almost as much as dim ones. Many gentlemen who had once glorified France or Britain as a champion of freedom followed France's despotism on the continent and Britain's tyranny on the seas into deeper and deeper disillusionment until their negative cast made any firm party attachment impossible. Such models of an earlier Republicanism as John Randolph, John Taylor of Caroline, and Nathaniel Macon of North Carolina came to hate Napoleon so bitterly that they began a long, futile search for a president who would talk like a Federalist but claim to be a Republican. In South Carolina, William Loughton Smith, Hamilton's tough-minded lieutenant from the 1790s, declared the old Federalism archaic and became a Republican. The Federalist Bayard, who thought the attack on the *Chesapeake* justified war, emerged from the embargo almost neutral. "It seems left to us only to chuse our enemy," he wrote his cousin, "—I will not say our friend for that is a choice which does not exist between [Britain and France]."[27] Finding enemies everywhere, John Quincy Adams inched cautiously toward the Republicans. Although he was convinced as late as 1806 that Jefferson was a French pawn, a year later he found the servility of the Federalists toward Britain even more horrifying. By 1808 he supported the embargo, identified the Federalist leadership as "political descendants in direct line from the tories of our Revolutionary war," and prepared himself to join Madison's administration.[28]

If nobody could have built much of a party from such material, Madison made almost nothing of it. For the first time a man without the credentials of a revolutionary hero held the highest office in the national hierarchy. Even Charles Cotesworth Pinckney and George Clinton, the ancient generals who had been propped like tottering Cids in front of Madison's opposition in 1808, qualified better than a minor figure in the Continental Congress. His role as a creator of the Constitution was still a well-kept secret. A quiet presence who had operated for more than fifteen years in Jefferson's shadow, Madison shone so dimly that a striking number of gentry leaders, including his own secretary of war, William Eustis, spelled his name "Maddison." While Jefferson reigned, dissident Republicans who dared not attack him used Madison as a scapegoat for whatever angered them about the government, and once Jefferson retired, a variety of closet rebels, barely contained by his public eminence and personal diplomacy, broke openly with his successor's administration. Madison, the least moved of all the gentry leaders by pride and competition, was also the least forceful in commanding allegiance and punishing defectors. He just let the party splinters fly. With a superb logical mind, he still had no flair for dramatic adaptations of policy, and as president depended instead on a firmly fixed view of proper republican government. The same sensitivity to balance that blessed his writings cursed his administration.

Balance meant moderation, and during Madison's first term moderation in party affairs meant a reliance on the men least likely to feel a passionate commitment to any national cause. The new president missed what Jefferson had quickly sensed in 1807: in a crisis "highflyers" made the best allies. Continuing to favor the preoccupied leaders of development politics in the states, Madison also filled his cabinet with the same type of Republicans, then added to his woes by doing nothing to create cohesion among them. He maintained such poor communication with his lieutenants that three weeks after he appointed a new attorney general, his secretary of the navy had not heard of the change. Gallatin, who remained as secretary of the treasury, refused to grant his former equal a leader's deference and largely went his own way. The president's attempt to use cabinet appointments to balance party factions gained him nothing. As long as he kept an unsympathetic Robert Smith as secretary of state, Madison had an inept officer in an important post; when he dismissed him in 1811, he enraged Smith's powerful brother Samuel.

Like every president before him, Madison needed at least one confidant whose loyalty and dedication he could take for granted. Oddly, he found his answer by enticing the proud, suspicious Monroe from his tent in Virginia to become Robert Smith's successor as secretary of state. These Virginia neighbors of radically different talents and temperaments had struggled for years to maintain a friendship that seemed fated to collapse. When the Virginia assembly failed to make Monroe a delegate to the Philadelphia Convention in 1787, he bitterly and erroneously blamed Madison for plotting "arrangements unfavorable to me," opposed the Constitution, and embarrassed its chief architect by running against Madison in the first election for a seat in the House.[29] Eventually Jefferson reconciled his two favorites. That very patronage, however, stirred feelings of competition in Monroe that he could neither acknowledge nor manage, and when the administration rejected his treaty with Britain in 1806, Monroe blamed Madison quite personally for the humiliation. Returning home, the wounded Monroe allowed Madison's enemies in Virginia to use him as their candidate for president in 1808. Wait your turn, Jefferson gently pleaded, but Monroe quit only after the power of Madison's Virginia support stopped him. There matters stood until Madison's call in 1811. For once, another man's weaknesses and Madison's strengths combined to surmount a troubled past and solve a presidential problem. Monroe's ambition led him to accept Madison's offer. Madison's superior intelligence enabled him to get a new secretary of state on the president's own terms and hold an invaluable colleague in subordination. Bonded in these years of crisis, they remained warm friends for the rest of their lives.

The president harnessed his new secretary of state so successfully because in international affairs Madison revealed a clarity and tenacity quite at odds with his oblique direction in domestic politics. With remarkable steadiness he held to the belief that Britain stood alone as America's nemesis, and his hand was always there to correct a friend's misguided course—to deflect the optimistic Jefferson's scheme for an alliance of conquest with England or reverse the erratic Monroe's lapse into partiality for the British cause. He brought an equally sharp focus to the basic issues. Although impressment stirred the public wrath, Madison recognized how ambiguous it was to negotiate. The underside of British impressing was American enticing of British deserters or at least acquiescing in their presence on its ships, and according to Gallatin, about half the new nation's seamen fit America's own definition of British citizens. These sailors, by the prevailing rules, the British navy had a right to reclaim. But since the 1780s, Madison had looked past such issues as impressment and seen a single, overriding goal in British policy: subjugating the United States by swallowing its commerce. Unlike Jefferson, he neither balked at the thought of war nor let it slip from the front of his mind. A month before he took office he called war "inevitable" if Britain maintained its maritime policies; in the middle of his first term he predicted that "we shall ultimately be at issue with [Britain] over her fictitious blockades"; and by late 1811, with Monroe in tow, he was preparing for the event.[30]

Madison's was the quintessential clarity of the neocolonial mind. Just as a good Federalist saw American independence at stake only with France, so an exemplary Republican such as Madison saw it at stake only with Britain. Actually, British seizures peaked in 1807, when its navy caught a far-flung fleet of American ships unaware of a change in the rules, and in dollar value French seizures probably exceeded British ones before war finally came. Both governments justified their confiscations by sneeringly informing the United States that they were enforcing America's own laws of nonintercourse. Both sent to Washington a series of ministers who were cut from the old cloth of the colonial governors: inexperienced, arrogant, disdainful, or a combination thereof. Nevertheless, Madison carefully distinguished between the two powers. French violations abused American rights, but British violations threatened the nation's freedom.

Obligingly, Britain eased the new president's task by opening his administration with a fresh humiliation. In 1809, a new envoy, David Erskine, foolishly exceeded his government's instructions and gave Madison exactly what he wanted, a cancellation of America's latest trade restrictions for a cancellation of Britain's most onerous maritime rules. As Americans were celebrating the triumph, Erskine's superior, George Canning, angrily repudiated the agreement, blamed Madison, and left his administration with an insulting reminder of its international helplessness. A year later, when an equally unauthorized French official declared that his government would now repeal its harshest controls, Madison chose that as the occasion to push French issues aside and narrow the contest to its basics: an independent United States versus a tyrannical England. By the spring of 1811, new legislation imposed an embargo on the British trade. Muting Napoleon's persistent violations and demanding concessions from London, the president started the final march to war.

Later generations, unable to recapture his logic, would find only a muddle of issues and obscurely label the conflict the War of 1812. But neither Madison nor his opponents suffered from any confusion. As the leader of the national hierarchy, the president carried the responsibility for defining foreign dangers and deciding how to meet them, and Madison approached the war like a sound Jeffersonian first character, patiently drawing the people toward their duty and carefully explaining the meaning of the contest as America entered it. No Federalist doubted that the president bore that responsibility. "When the President has made the war," Bayard wrote rather mildly to his friend Caesar Rodney at the eleventh hour, "I presume Congress will not be too modest to declare it."[31] Federalists called it "Mr. Madison's War." Where each side identified the other as the tool of a great power, the war was just as automatically construed in party terms. As one Pennsylvania Republican noted on the eve of the conflict, "The honor of the Nation and that of the party are bound up together and both will be sacrificed if war be not declared."[32] A Federalist victory in the elections of 1812, Monroe concluded, would quite literally end the American republic. "For," as Jefferson wrote, "the republicans are the *nation*."[33] From the opposite side, Rufus King condemned it as "a war of party, & not of the Country."[34]

Across a divided nation, however, lay the inseparably entwined themes of independence and honor to give the war a common meaning for Americans of all ages and persuasions. If they did not always accept the same definition of these issues, they could still use them to form their alliances, frame their debates, and explain the course of events. The ways of construing independence created the most pronounced differences in interpretation, and the meaning of the Revolutionary War marked the line between them. Those who had experienced it as the shaping event in their lives never stopped fighting it. "Are we upon the eve of a declaration of our independence upon G. Britain being repeated a third time . . . ?" Benjamin Rush asked in 1811.[35] Invariably they measured the republic's health against their memories of the original patriotic upsurge. William Duane could find no better way of ingratiating himself with Jefferson than to tell him: "The Whigs in your native State are as full of zeal as in any period of the Revolution."[36] Signs of squabbling brought the standard response: "How different were the feelings and conduct of our citizens in 1774. . . ."[37] When Congress temporarily reopened America's foreign trade everywhere, a stern Mercy Warren demanded that the nation's leaders "revivify the principles of the Revolution."[38] Even the most entrepreneurial among them could not comprehend the narrowly economic preoccupations of the new development politics. "We are degenerating into a mere nation of traders . . . ," the prosperous merchant Gerry complained. "We must be roused by some great event that may stir up the ancient patriotism of the people. . . ."[39] Hence when John Adams reacted to America's victories during the war as "sublime . . . immortal, eternal," he spoke from the deepest feelings of his generation.[40] As the revolution survived, so did they.

Those too young to remember the Revolutionary War began with America's independence as their premise. They would protect it and reassert it, but they could not comprehend that it had yet to be won. "Our Fathers fought for and bequeathed liberty & Independence to *us* their children," declared Felix Grundy of Tennessee. A new war "will enable us to transmit to *our children* the rich inheritance unimpaired."[41] Out of the same orientation, John C. Calhoun referred to the "sovereignty and independence of these states, purchased and sanctified by the blood of our fathers, from whom we received them, not for ourselves only, but as the inheritance of our posterity. . . ."[42] Although these self-conscious sons of the fathers learned to parrot the neocolonial phrases of their elders, they could never enter into their spirit. Rejecting the familiar arguments about the need for a great power's shield, Henry Clay declared: "I protest against the castigation of our colonial infancy being applied in the independent manhood of America."[43] Privately the shrewd Charles J. Ingersoll called the entire idiom of French and British parties one of "the diseases of colonization."[44] Josiah Quincy could no more understand the leniency of many older Federalists toward British violations than young Republicans could understand Madison's blandness toward French confiscations. In fact, their impatience over the government's caution in the face of these indignities gave some of them the name of War Hawks. Nevertheless, they only saw the nation's enemies across the Atlantic. At home, their opponents might be fools, but they were not traitors.

No word recurred more often in the discussions preceding the war than "insult," the red flag to gentlemen whose code bound them to preserve their honor at the cost of life itself. Indeed, honor defined independence. Without it nations, exactly like individuals, became the despicable objects of anyone's abuse, mere creatures who had sacrificed their rights to freedom. "The man or the nation without attachment to reputation or honor, is undone," John Adams had told his countrymen during the quasi-war with France. Yet only "great" nations had "character to lose," as Jefferson reminded Adams. Would the new United States, still undergoing an initial test of honor, take its place as a gentleman among the nations or declare itself a cringing menial? The gentry could not even consider the alternative. As a prominent Virginian wrote Jefferson on the subject of impressment, "But, by the great God in heaven, I had rather not exist as a man or nation than to suffer such violations. . . ."[45]

An aspiring gentleman needed to attend the forms of honor with unusual care. Despite their "contempt" for the Spanish government, Jefferson counseled Madison in 1807, "respect to ourselves requires that [our diplomatic correspondence] should be decent."[46] Precisely on such grounds of gentlemanly behavior Britain challenged the United States with an unrelieved string of insults. Whatever the ambiguities of impressment, the manner surrounding it revealed an utter contempt: the haughty abuses of the American flag at sea, the disdainful assertions of Britain's right to act as it pleased. Like the agents of a colonial master, British commanders took seamen indiscriminately from American ships as if anyone who spoke English were automatically a British subject. Reviewing the Jay and Monroe-Pinkney treaties, Jefferson and Madison agreed that what made them fundamentally unacceptable was their "form," the insufferable language of imposed terms.[47] And when Madison then negotiated an honorable agreement with Erskine in 1809, the British government repudiated it with fresh insults. In his second inaugural address, Jefferson, citing a truism about a gentleman's character, noted that "as with individuals . . . a just nation is trusted on its word." "Her good faith!" he exploded after the British rejection of the Erskine agreement. ". . . Of the nation who never admitted a chapter of morality into her political code!"[48] Under such persistent, intolerable bullying, a gentleman either abandoned his sacred honor or fought for it. More precisely, the aggrieved gentleman had the right to demand a formal settling of accounts. As Rufus King stated for his generation, ". . . the Honor of the Nation is the only legitimate cause of war."[49]

War in this sense was quite literally a duel, and gentlemen of all ages from all parts of the United States understood it as such. The dueling code still permeated the nation in the early 19th century. Although fewer northerners than southerners or westerners actually dueled, gentlemen everywhere hovered like moths around the light that the code shone on their own and other people's characters. Nothing in the affairs of the national government fascinated William Plumer of New Hampshire more than the personal details of the dueling threats, challenges, and negotiations that repeatedly dotted the course of congressional business, and none of the many principals in these encounters dismissed the matter as absurd or inconsequential. DeWitt Clinton, bent on avoiding a duel with Jonathan Dayton of New Jersey in 1803, tried first to settle the issue through a private exchange but finally made a public apology in the House to satisfy his adamant challenger. Among those who refused to duel, it was particularly important to avoid the intimation of cowardice.

Commenting on John Randolph's pursuit of the much older Samuel Dana, Plumer wrote in his journal: "Why attempt to practice on Genl Dana? does he think this gentleman living in Connecticut dare not accept a challenge—Mr. Dana has nerve."[50]

The formal illegality of dueling deterred no one. To defend his family's honor in 1805, the son of a leading Boston Federalist rode a well-worn path across the border into Rhode Island, New England's favorite outlet. Nor did the gentlemen who refused to duel condemn it as immoral. In 1808, when Congressman George Campbell of Ohio challenged and seriously wounded Congressman Barent Gardenier of New York, Josiah Quincy in a blow-by-blow account to his wife saved his only strictures for the curiosity seekers who had intruded on the gentlemen's private affair. Daniel Webster, facing one of John Randolph's numerous challenges, simply denied Randolph's "right to call me to the field" on whim. "I do not feel myself bound, at all times & under any circumstances, to accept . . . an invitation of this sort," Webster explained, adding that he was "always prepared" to fight under provocation.[51]

In a gentry environment sensitive to the nuances of this code and to its critical role in defense of a gentleman's honor, Madison meticulously led the nation through its preliminary rites into war. No dramatic event triggered the sequence. Each gentleman had to decide for himself when an accumulation of insults demanded a challenge. As guardian of the nation's honor, Madison took this responsibility, made the judgment late in 1811, and that November told Congress to ready for war. There could be no crude rush for the pistols, however. Just as gentlemen moved in perfect control through their final negotiations, Madison carefully went through the motions of offering Britain a last chance to retract and waited out the months of diplomatic protocol with no unseemly show of haste. In this eleventh hour of dead calm, Bayard reported: "One can discover very little war spirit in either House of Congress. And yet the members will tell you very coldly, that war is inevitable."[52] The proper forms fulfilled, the president called for an official declaration of war in June, and Congress enacted it.

At this point Madison could state the case of an aggrieved nation whose exemplary behavior satisfied every canon of the gentleman's code and established its right to take the field of honor. "Anxious to make every experiment short of the last resort of injured nations," the United States had shown "a patience without example under wrongs accumulating without end." To each "inviting opportunity" for a just settlement, Britain had "heaped on our country" greater "injuries and indignities." The requirements of honor and independence merged in only one solution. "To have shrunk under such circumstances from manly resistance would have been a degradation" of the United States "from the rank of a sovereign & independent Power," an announcement to the world that "the American people were not an independent people, but colonists and vassals."[53]

Some hotbloods among the younger Republicans found Madison's "patience without example" excessive. "A man receives a fillip on the nose," a restless Clay wrote in 1810, "and instead of instantly avenging the insult, inquires of the person giving it what he means!"[54] As Clay's language demonstrated, however, these War Hawks understood perfectly the fusion of honor with independence and the applicability of the gentlemen's code to their nation's situation. With "the American Eagle struck and insulted" by the attack on the *Chesapeake,* declared Calhoun in his first public statement, "it would disgrace our character Abroad, and exhibit us a degenerate and pusillanimous people" if the United States failed to defend its honor.[55] Once the president had begun the final round of negotiations with Britain, there could be no failure of nerve. ". . . [A]fter the pledges we have made, and the stand we have taken, are we now to cover ourselves with shame and indelible disgrace by retreating from the measures and ground we have taken," Clay exhorted the House. ". . . And what would you think of one individual who had thus conducted to another, and should then retreat."[56] Responding to Madison's call for a formal declaration, Calhoun echoed the president's justification in a report to the Senate: "But the period has now arrived, when the United States must support their character and station among the Nations of the Earth, or submit to the most shameful degradation. Forbearance has ceased to be a virtue."[57] Like the older gentry, these gentlemen prepared to raise pistols with Britain as the last calculated step in a logical sequence deriving from the fundamentals of their personal lives. Honor absolutely demanded it, and without honor there would be no independent United States.

As an expression of the dueling code, otherwise inexplicable events surrounding the declaration made perfect sense. Dueling wars were contained, structured forms of violence, not a total commitment of community resources to a battle for survival or annihilation. Hence the Federalists who cast France in exactly the role that the administration placed Britain, as well as those marginal Republicans who saw no distinction between the oppressive great powers, sought—and almost won —a simultaneous declaration of war against both European enemies, as if a gentleman were calling two bullies to the field of honor on successive days. Clear-eyed gentry such as Madison and John Adams opposed twin wars neither as an absurdity nor as a military impossibility, only as a crucial error in assessing the nation's requirements for honor and independence. By the same token, the New England Federalists who hoped for a quick British victory were not anticipating a devastated nation, only a salutary humiliation of Madison's administration and an escape from the dishonor of allying the United States with Napoleon. Because a dueling war had such limited scope, its advocates could be economizers without also being hypocrites, and the Republicans in Congress, lacking determinate guidelines, endlessly debated how much or how little military preparation they should authorize. To assuage Jefferson's fear of the iron circle, Gallatin, a dedicated wartime leader, vowed to conduct the nation's finances so that "at its end the United States may be burdened with the smallest possible quantity of debt, perpetual taxation, military establishments, and other corrupting or anti-republican habits or institutions."[58]

On June 23, six days after the United States declared war, Britain repealed its most offensive maritime orders, and four weeks later the news reached America. The time that it always took information to cross ocean and mountain barriers made such overlapping patterns of action a normal part of gentry life. More important, however, a duel in progress contained its own strict rules. Second thoughts after the pistols were cocked brought instant disgrace. In 1809 when Clay left the dueling field with a wound, the overwhelming concern among his friends was not his health but an assurance that Clay had not buckled before the participants officially settled the affair. Two months before the actual declaration, Monroe announced that the time for reconsideration had already passed: the next "step is WAR." The nation's reputation left no other "question for freemen and patriots to discuss. It exists; and it is by open and manly war only that we can get through it with honor...."[59] Even Jefferson, who had cautioned against a war on "false estimates of honor," understood the commandment to proceed now: "... the sword once drawn, full justice must be done."[60] Under somewhat comparable circumstances in 1804, he had hastened American warships to an attack on Tripoli before peaceful mediators could intervene, leaving "our just desires for vengeance disappointed, and our honor prostrated."[61] Although Madison's administration began seeking a negotiated settlement as soon as the war commenced, no gentleman among the nations could flinch in the field until every last form of an honorable adjustment had been completed.

At one level the war proceeded disastrously. To begin with, the Jeffersonians had responded so well to the temper of American republicanism that they had almost no resources to mobilize for a war. National taxes per person were about one-fifteenth of Britain's. Those Americans who funded a piece of the war from their own pockets could expect no reimbursement from the parsimonious government, and its skeleton of officials could not even provide Washington with basic information. Never did the orthodox Republican division between national and state realms prove more telling. In reaction against Hamiltonian tyranny, state laws hemmed in the national uses of the militia. The Jeffersonian illusion of a patriotic groundswell to do battle for American independence shattered into an array of self-centered state units and the private interests they sheltered. State taxation underwrote the state's development projects instead of the nation's war aims, and a burst of new banking and manufacturing charters channeled credit toward the secondary benefits of the war rather than its military requirements. It was the cool guardians of these enterprises, not the patriotic Hotspurs, who still dominated state government. In 1814, with British forces hovering off the coast and the national government virtually bankrupt, a friendly commentator could only say of the national war effort that it survived "by the *mere forces of genius.*"[62]

At a level more basic to the war's meaning, however, the record actually improved during these difficult years. Once underway, the war became a tournament, during which the various military champions of each nation engaged one another in separate combat. No responsible Republican expected to triumph in every battle, and certainly none of them anticipated driving the mighty British fleet from the seas. They fought for respect, not for the fatuous dream of destroying their enemy. By the tests of control and courage under fire, the war opened miserably with General William Hull's ill-calculated surrender of his army outside Detroit without giving battle. Monroe could scarcely believe the initial report: "We have just heard . . . that Genl Hull has surrendered by capitulation. . . . The circumstances attending this most mortifying & humiliating event are not known. . . ."[63] Privately Clay declared that for "so shameful, so disgraceful a surrender . . . [Hull] deserves to be shot." Publicly he demanded that through some other engagement "the disgrace of Detroit . . . be wiped off."[64] And in a series of isolated battles along the coast and in the Great Lakes, so it seemed to be. Where the goal was honor, the record in combat improved considerably as the war continued, despite Britain's obvious superiority and its increasing menace to America's coastline. In fact, the more effectively the British navy attacked along the coast, the more it violated the code of gentlemanly warfare and the more Americans it converted to the administration's cause. If some Federalists still took pleasure in the British raid on Washington and Madison's flight from a burning White House, they were outraged by the parallel attack on Alexandria, Virginia, a sturdy bastion of Federalism. Neocolonials forever, the revolutionary gentry could never fathom Britain's indifference to the details of their party geography. As British warships threatened the northeastern ports, Rufus King finally acknowledged that the nation's honor was in jeopardy, and the old Hamiltonian Oliver Wolcott became so zealous for the war that he opened

correspondence with the Devil himself, President Madison. State governments from Massachusetts to South Carolina organized separate armies
of their own. In a disjointed version of the Jeffersonian groundswell,
Americans now appeared ready to fight for their honor.

The climax to these hopes came stunningly at New Orleans, where in
January 1815 Andrew Jackson's militia crushed a large, veteran British
force. It was the last engagement of the tournament, sandwiched between the negotiation of a peace treaty at Ghent and the blare of the
final, official horn, and to American gentlemen everywhere it guaranteed
precisely what they had sought, a magnificent vindication of their valor
in combat. "Peace has come in a most welcome time . . . ," the hardheaded Joseph Story wrote to a close friend. "Never did a country occupy
more lofty ground; we have stood the contest, single-handed, against the
conqueror of Europe; and we are at peace, with all our blushing victories
thick crowding on us. If I do not much mistake, we shall attain to a very
high character abroad. . . ."[65] Although the Treaty of Ghent solved no
technical issues, it was an honorably phrased settlement, and it could be
construed as a crucial token of respect for the American character. Reviewing the treaty, Calhoun declared: "I feel pleasure and pride . . . in
being able to say, that I am of a party which drew the sword on this
question, and succeeded in the contest; for, to all practical purposes, we
have achieved complete success."[66]

Peace in Europe, of course, automatically ended impressments and
confiscations, and proud Americans never had to test their claims to a
new respect. Nevertheless, they felt its presence deeply. "Let any man
look at the degraded condition of this country before the war. The scorn
of the universe, the contempt of ourselves . . . ," Clay declaimed. "What
is our present situation? Respectability and character abroad—security
and confidence at home." For any doubter, he rang off the names of
America's victorious wartime champions—"Hull of the Constitution,
Jackson, Lawrence, Perry . . ."—irrefutable proof of the nation's elevated
character.[67] To these satisfactions of an honor redeemed, the remaining
revolutionary gentry added the inestimable benefits of a united republic,
a submerging of factions in this latest round of the continuous struggle
for independence. Even at the outset of the war, Monroe thought that its
common trials had already "diminished the influence of foreign attachments. . . ."[68] Afterward, Gallatin declared that it "has renewed and reinstated the national feelings and character which the Revolution had
given and which were daily lessening."[69] With the Battle of New Orleans, Jefferson concluded, the British party died in America.

These men found honor and independence because they needed to find
them. From a successful duel came a new equilibrium in a gentleman's
relationships—respect from his peers, perhaps even friendship with his

opponent, as Clay had predicted for Anglo-American relations just before the hostilities. Believing they had won the right to an honorable gentleman's rank, they declared its existence. Through British eyes the sequence of affairs looked very different indeed. Rather than a gentleman's challenge, Britain treated America's decision for war as a kick from a dirty little sneak. While the war still raged in Europe, it scarcely mattered. As Napoleon's armies collapsed, however, the British talked of the United States in language that disdained its gentlemanly pretensions. Now they would give the upstart a "good beating," a "thrashing" appropriate to the village ruffian. Only Napoleon's return, then a general warweariness, produced a peace of convenience at Ghent.

The neocolonial struggle for independence had an equally ambiguous outcome. If freedom from the traditional, closed systems of commerce measured American independence, the postwar changes were dramatically emancipating. After 1807, Jefferson and Madison had good reason to picture Britain as an omnivorous monopoly. Holland, which had floated the national debt and the Louisiana Purchase, disappeared as an alternative source of credit. The British navy threatened to plug the last holes in a wall enclosing the West Indies and Europe, and the importation of British goods only deepened the pit of debt and dependence. Hence the sudden withdrawal of the British fleet and the reopening of the European trade lanes lifted an immense burden of neocolonial fears. But Britain emerged from the prolonged European wars as a new kind of imperial power. While invasions and blockades were stifling its continental competitors, Britain integrated an internal credit structure, catapulted ahead of its rivals in manufacturing efficiency, and dominated the seas as never before. As the world's paramount banker, producer, and carrier, it began to shape a global economy immediately after Napoleon's downfall.

Hence if economic autonomy measured independence, as Jefferson and Madison believed it should, America's freedom remained as elusive as ever. The percentage of American imports from Britain rose during the next two decades until it reached about half the new nation's total, with the percentage of American exports to Britain trailing close behind. It was a classic imperial relationship: American agricultural products—above all, cotton—for British manufactured goods. Underwriting the entire scheme of American development lay British credit. Fast, regular packet service, beginning in 1818 between New York and Liverpool and spreading in the next few years to America's other primary ports, both symbolized and facilitated the assimilation of America's transatlantic trade into the British system. As cotton was coronated, the factors who managed its movement from the plantations into the market relied ultimately on British credit. By the mid-twenties Britain was also serving as America's investment banker. Shrinking opportunities on the European continent turned the attention of British capitalists to the United States just as the canal boom began, and in little more than a decade after the opening of the Erie Canal the amount invested in America's various transportation enterprises equaled the total of the nation's state debts. Again, a tight reciprocity between commodity exports and capital imports underlined the imperial relationship. Before 1815 the American economy had been jerked up and down by general conditions in Europe; after 1815 it responded specifically to the capital markets of London, which precipitated the panics of 1819 and 1837 and held the United States in depression for years following them.

"We have hated those most who oftenest make us feel [our] impotence," Fisher Ames finally recognized at the end of his life. "The British have done this. . . ."[70] Because the new imperialism generated a sense of broadening opportunities rather than narrowing freedoms, it no longer aggravated those feelings of an oppressive dependence that led to the War of 1812. The only carriers of the old tradition were a handful of gentlemen with their roots still stuck in the Revolution. One of them succeeded Madison as president, and in the Monroe Doctrine he wrote a final postscript to the era of neocolonialism.

After a lifetime's effort Monroe's near-unanimous reelection in 1820 relieved him at last of the struggle to preserve his reputation and left him surveying a republic that, as he stated in his second inaugural, "will soon attain the highest degree of perfection of which human institutions are capable. . . ."[71] No member of the revolutionary gentry could have envisaged this republican paradise without a simultaneous faith in the disappearance of foreign factions. So it was with Monroe: "the destruction of the federal party" in national affairs, he told Madison, signaled the "new epoch in our political career."[72] Secure as America's first character, Monroe moved more comfortably into a gentry president's special realm, foreign affairs. His message to Congress in 1822 extolled the glories of Greece and praised its current fight for independence. French repression in Spain stirred the same feelings of attachment to a universal battle for liberty. When Prime Minister Canning suggested the possibility of an Anglo-American statement to warn the continental powers against interference with the new governments in Latin America, the president already had momentum toward an expansive response. From his Virginia colleagues he received familiar advice. Although Jefferson referred grandly to "our hemisphere," he recommended slipping under Britain's wing to secure American objectives, much as he had envisaged in 1805. Madison wrote more cautiously but also favorably, adding his plea to support Greek independence as well.

From his secretary of state, however, the president received another line of advice. John Quincy Adams kept alive his father's ingrained sus-

picion of every European intention and argued for an independent declaration. That, after all, was the prerogative that the United States had won
in the War of 1812. Monroe, alert to the slightest indignity from a great
power, shared more with his secretary of state than he did with his
Virginia colleagues. In 1815, for example, that acute sensitivity covered
the exact placement of the American and British signatures to the Treaty
of Ghent so that the United States would not slip into another humiliating subordinance to Britain. With Adams holding Monroe's focus as
tightly as possible to this hemisphere alone, the two of them prepared an
exclusively American statement for the president's annual message in
1823. It swept the subject of the western hemisphere with the grand
strokes of an 18th-century document: no European intervention, no
transfer of territory between European powers, no new colonization.
Negatives all, they set a neocolonial barrier against the traditional
sources of intrigue and subversion across a stretch of territory appropriate
to America's new stature as a gentleman among the great powers.
In 1823, however, not many Americans cared. It would take time before American capitalism in an age of development inserted its own meaning into this epilogue to the era of gentry pride and neocolonial
independence.

The Era of
State Power

The national parties that contested the War of 1812 died with the arrival of the treaty concluding it. After almost forty years' preoccupation with danger from the great powers, European peace destroyed the Republican party just as totally as the Federalist. Occasionally someone sent up the old cry. Only a fool would doubt "that we are destined to have war after war with Great Britain," Clay declared in 1816.[1] "Take my word for it," Vice-President Daniel Tompkins told his New York associates in 1817, "we shall have another war within two years."[2] Once alarms like these had brought the national parties rattling back to the field. Now all the talk in the world could not pump life into either one. During the next quarter-century a diffusion of American political energies brought the golden age of state authority.

The sources for this new era came from the politics of development that spread rapidly after 1803 and strained against the national politics of independence. The one glorified principles of government, the other profits from enterprise. The one made politics a mirror of society, the other a subdivision within it. The one tried to mobilize a nation, the other a band of allies. The one saw its causes as eternal and immutable, the other as tactical and contingent. When the passions for national honor and independence did not interfere, the politics of development had crisscrossed the old loyalties to serve its own ends. Left to their own devices, Federalists on the coast of South Carolina and Republicans in the interior merged into a statewide elite that by 1808 dominated its economy from Charleston. Federalists led the early phase of banking in Republican North Carolina. In New York's bitter political battle between the camps of Morgan Lewis and DeWitt Clinton, the Republican Lewis allied himself with the Federalist Merchants Bank, while the Republican Clinton was leaguing with Federalists to form the Oneida Manufacturing Company. In many states the natural alliances were regional or territorial ones. East versus west or north versus south defined development politics in New Jersey, just as coast and interior did in New Hampshire and North Carolina. Vermont's legislature divided not along the old party lines but according to its Canada-oriented and American-oriented commercial sections. In the major cities, Philadelphia Republicans fought separate banks for Republicans in western Pennsylvania by the same self-serving logic with which Boston Federalists resisted bank charters for Federalists in the surrounding Massachusetts towns.

In states with a high intensity and wide distribution of development issues, the governors tended to be men who represented a middle ground, a point of accommodation in a complex field of old party loyalties and new economic promotions. Joseph Bloomfield, a Federalist turned Republican who was the only governor of New Jersey from 1803 to 1812, nimbly maneuvered its partisan divisions, showed in his own business activities a keen appreciation for the opportunities in development, and facilitated charters for banks, bridges, and turnpikes throughout the state. In Massachusetts, where old party lines retained considerable significance, the perennial Federalist governor was Caleb Strong, a muddier of issues and muffler of conflicts who hated to decide for or against the Constitution in 1787 and refused to choose between the Adams and Hamilton Federalists in 1800. His Republican counterpart, James Sullivan, disarmed moderate Federalists just as effectively as Strong did the moderate Republicans. Although Sullivan attacked the speculative banks that he identified with British influences, the entrepreneurial Republican had no objection to the patriotic American banks and development corporations in which he invested extensively. Pennsylvania's German-rooted community, several of whose leaders had teetered between Federalism and Republicanism since the mid-nineties, generally stocked the governor's office in that state until the late 1820s. Simon Snyder, a former tanner's apprentice who served from 1808 to 1817, looked like an enemy of elite enterprise until he took office, abruptly moved to the center, and presided encouragingly over the swarms of Pennsylvania projects. Even those state governors who generated fierce hatreds—McKean in Pennsylvania, Lewis and DeWitt Clinton in New York—relied on state coalitions of Federalists and Republicans. City governments, which were largely opened to a popular competitive politics by the 1800s, often replicated this model of accommodation in their own development politics. Going directly against the grain of national partisan trends, Baltimore elected a Federalist mayor between 1804 and 1808, then shifted smoothly to a Republican for the next eight years as its government concentrated unerringly on the city's ambitions.

By no means did this new style of politics have the states to itself. Not all gentry leaders nor even gentry banks plunged into promotions. Where the cultural roots of a party ran deep, as among the Connecticut Federalists, a rhetoric of sedition and crisis predominated well after 1803. The ruling Virginia Republicans would not compromise with the state's Federalists. At a minimum, however, the consciousness of the state—not just its coastline or its gentry but its geographic and jurisdictional whole —sharply increased. Political organization spread and systematized in such states as Massachusetts, New York, New Jersey, and Pennsylvania, revealing a much stronger continuity than it had in the days of the grand party muster. It was no longer tolerable to contest state elections with lists of notables drawn almost exclusively from their eastern strips. Politically, the center of gravity shifted from major cities to state capitals. The regular pilgrimages that DeWitt Clinton as United States senator and then mayor of New York City took to Albany before he himself became governor symbolized the change, as did the movement of Pennsylvania's capital in 1812 to Harrisburg, a hundred miles inland from Philadelphia. In 1807 a promoter of New York turnpikes sensed the trend: "But as it belongs peculiarly to each individual state to encourage and patronize its own domestic works of utility and convenience, every state may be considered in relation to matters of this kind as a distinct country and people."[3]

From the perspective of the politics of independence, the most visible practitioners of the new state politics were derisively called "tertium quid"—a third sort of elusive something—or commonly just quids.* Unable to understand the quids on their own terms, party purists attacked them as deviants who at their worst qualified for Hamilton's ultimate insult about Burr, men with no principles whatsoever. Because the quids expressed a tendency rather than a doctrine, because that tendency spread so extensively after 1803, and because it adapted to the peculiarities of a state's politics, the label came to have an indeterminate, shifting

---

* John Randolph, by appropriating the name "quid" for his own very different rebellion against Jefferson's administration, has complicated the historian's terminological problems. Because almost all contemporaries used "quid" as I do here, I feel justified in denying Randolph his borrowed title and reclaiming it for its original purposes.

application appropriate to the term's literal meaning. Most of the attention focused on a few leaders, gentlemen who had already assumed important roles in the politics of the 1790s and who had often foreshadowed the drift into quiddism in their avid business activities and uncertain party attachments. Tench Coxe, an inveterate promoter who coined the term and still followed its spirit, switched allegiance from Hamilton to Jefferson in the mid-nineties out of ambition, not doctrinal convictions. The New Jersey Federalist Jonathan Dayton, an avid land speculator, called for revenge against the British in 1794, barely accepted the Jay Treaty, maintained good relations with such renegade Federalists as Samuel Smith and Joseph Bloomfield, and cheered the Louisiana Purchase. Even before 1803, Smith, James Sullivan, and Thomas Law, a prominent land speculator, were pining for a new party of moderate Federalists and moderate Republicans.

Yet as these histories revealed, the most visible quids had feet planted in both centuries. They never fully escaped the partisanship of the nineties, remained sensitive to both national and state politics, and continued to wrestle with the incongruities between the two levels. While they took the brunt of attack for the new style of politics, younger men of lesser fame were pursuing it with fewer qualms. Thomas Worthington, the rising power in Ohio politics, apparently became a Republican because the primary opponents of Ohio statehood were Federalists. A local expert for the Ohio land speculations of the Republican Gallatin and the Federalist James Ross, equally solicitous of such grim party warriors as the Republican Giles and the Federalist Robert Goodloe Harper, Worthington made decisions during his many years in Congress with eyes fixed on the rapid settlement of his state, the business prospects of his territorial base in the Scioto River Valley, and the needs of his own investments there in land, banking, and manufacturing. William Plumer, while still a committed Federalist, remarked of the chameleon Worthington: "But I know the man, *his smiles are the smiles of deceit.*"[4] Joseph Ellicott, resident agent for the Holland Land Company, and Peter B. Porter, prosperous shipper on the Great Lakes, vied for political dominance in western New York, promoted regional transportation, and looked to Albany for aid as if the world ended at the Hudson River. Beneath the publicized affairs of gentry notables, the brothers Mahlon and Silas Dickerson were fashioning an alliance of politics and enterprise that would eventually make Mahlon governor of New Jersey. So, in muted ways, it went wherever development politics thrived during the early 19th century.

When a resurgent politics of independence swept through their states after 1807, these coalition builders struggled on as best they could. Some tried to keep the two levels of politics separate, as the Ohio Federalists did when they chose the state's Grand Sachem of notoriously "Jacobin" Tammany Hall as their candidate for governor. Or like the ingenious Governor Snyder of Pennsylvania, they continued to promote the same state schemes in transportation and manufacturing under the patriotic guise of independence from Europe. Indeed, a good deal of the state support for war came from motivations of honor-and: honor and the acquisition of native American land, for instance, or honor and calculations of economic advantage against British competitors. At best, however, the revival of national partisanship broke the rhythm of the new politics, and at worst, it wiped out years of carefully wrought accommodations. In Massachusetts, for example, Federalists now tightened their grip on the banks, met the wrath of the Republican Governor Gerry, who considered them "british federalists," and engaged in a partisan bank war that obliterated the emerging quiddish alliance in finance and development.

The new politics repaid the old in kind. State-oriented quids responded reluctantly to national problems, organized halfheartedly for presidential elections, and never disciplined their colleagues to support President Madison's policies in Congress. When the United States Bank's petition for recharter came before Congress in 1811, it was every state faction for itself, and the president, who badly needed the bank's services, watched his chosen allies contribute to its defeat. By then development politics had so scrambled the old lines of partisanship that Michael Leib, a professional British-hater, presented the petition to recharter the largely British-owned U.S. Bank; William Duane, the high-flying enemy of bipartisanship, served as bipartisan chairman of Pennsylvania's Committee on Roads and Internal Improvements; and DeWitt Clinton, manager of a national campaign against quiddism in 1808, came to Washington with the arch-Federalist Gouverneur Morris to seek funds for the Erie Canal.

Through Clinton the fractured condition of American politics revealed itself with striking clarity in the elections of 1812. The ambitious and manipulative New Yorker became the first catchall candidate in presidential history. He carried no revolutionary credentials of any kind and no party label that held from state to state. To some, Clinton was a northern man who would overthrow the Virginia Dynasty, and as geographical consciousness hardened, that prospect attracted a body of supporters from New York northward. To others, he was remembered for his earlier diatribes against quiddism, and scattered Madison-haters rallied to him for that reason. In the parlance of state politics, however, he was a "peace Republican," the dead center of quiddish compromise, and his immersion in the factional alliances and development projects of New York linked him to other state leaders who also found national and international pressures disruptive of their governments' primary goals. Finally, his dislike for the war, however muted after the declaration, made him palatable to most Federalists. Simply by presenting himself in 1812, Clinton captured all the seaboard states from New Hampshire to Delaware plus a share of Maryland and totaled an impressive 89 electoral votes to Madison's 128.

With the ending of the war, the barely contained forces of a state-bounded, coalition-based, development-oriented politics shucked off its national constraints, swept the field, and left the old parties in rubble. Under whatever names made local sense—Federal Republican, Independent, New Ticket, and an abundance more—state leaders took the legacy of quiddism and translated it into an American style of politics that now prevailed without national competition of any kind. "We talk here . . . of the perfect Extinction of the Party Spirit," the veteran Federalist Christopher Gore reported from Boston, "and there are not a few of our first rate Patriots, perfectly willing . . . to take Sides with any man in any party, and approve & promote any Measures, however contrary to former Conduct & former Professions. . . . "[5] The old spirit, lamented another diehard in Maryland, had drowned in a "Torrent of *Moderation*."[6]

A history of loyalty to the Republican party did not help a politician's chances any more than an identification with the Federalist party hurt them. Thomas Worthington, who had dismissed the national parties with something approaching incomprehension in 1811 and voted against war in 1812, now became Ohio's governor. Clinton, in open alliance with former Federalists, reigned as the most powerful politician in New York. Soon after the accommodator Simon Snyder, the quid Joseph Hiester served as governor in Pennsylvania. In the search for a middle ground some link to the Federalist party was often a valuable asset. Roger Taney, war Federalist and postwar governor, emerged as Maryland's leading politician. Another war Federalist, Isaac H. Williamson, followed the quid Mahlon Dickerson as governor of New Jersey and held office for the next twelve years. In the New England states a Federalist heritage seemed mandatory for success. William Plumer, a secessionist who then lost his "credit as a *party-man*" during Jefferson's administration, served four terms as governor of New Hampshire on either side of the war.[7] When the opposition in Connecticut finally won the governorship in 1817, they elevated—of all people—Oliver Wolcott, partisan of partisans in the 1790s who had drifted into quiddism as a bank president, converted to war Federalism, and finally abandoned his party connections. John Quincy Adams stood as the ranking political figure in Massachusetts, and as Maine sought to separate itself from Massachusetts, William King, a brother of Rufus and a former Federalist, led the movement and became the state's first governor. As far south as North Carolina a number of ex-Federalists prospered. Even in Virginia, a particularly bloody battleground of the old partisanship, the ruling Republicans extended a hand to their enemies in 1816, allowing new bank services in their territory and drawing former Federalists into the administration of the state's transportation enterprises.

By contrast with the vibrancy of state politics, the national government seemed lifeless. When the Treaty of Ghent saved an impotent national government from collapse, it created the aura of a United States that had met a powerful enemy and prevailed through the strength of an indigenous American spirit. Madison's ineffectual wartime administration faded so rapidly from memory not because it was too embarrassing to recall but because it became irrelevant to the way in which victory was perceived. The whole nation, abstract and undifferentiated, had triumphed, and in the celebration the national government shrank into inconsequence. From a local perspective the most controversial issue in national affairs between 1815 and 1819 was a law raising congressional salaries, the one action that forced the legislators into an elaborate justification of their votes.

Monroe, who succeeded Madison in 1817, epitomized the new meaning of the national government. In powdered wig and buckled breeches, he entered office with political values as obsolete as his dress. Jefferson, who thought of him as an American Lafayette—ardent, innocent, gallant—once wrote to Madison of "our friend Monroe; turn his soul wrong side outwards, and there is not a speck on it."[8] "Purity of heart," Kierkegaard noted, "is to will one thing," and for Monroe that one thing was reputation. An exceeding sensitivity to slights and criticisms pushed him along a twisting course from a fiery Republicanism to a tacit alliance with Federalism, then back again to passionate Republicanism. Yearning for military honor in the War of 1812, he desisted only after he was accused of angling for the presidency. When he finally won the coveted prize of first character, he held rigidly to the Republican prescription that placed domestic affairs in the hands of the states, monitored his cabinet officers to protect his administration from any taint of corruption, and left Congress to its own devices. Veterans such as Rufus King and Henry Clay marveled at a president who functioned "without friends in Congress; by which I mean no one offers himself to explain or support those measures wh. are supposed to have the recommendation & favor of the Extive. . . ."[9] By the old values of honor, hierarchy, and Republican orthodoxy—but only by those values—everything Monroe did made sense.

Yet there he stood, a living artifact, a costumed embodiment of the revolutionary glory that for almost all Americans belonged to legend. The qualities of *gravitas* that Monroe had developed to compensate for a slow mind added to his dignity as a chiseled symbol of the nation, a fine statue to contemplate in a decorative public office. For ceremonial purposes the president did matter. When in the most imaginative act of his first term Monroe toured New England in 1817, citizens of all ranks and persuasions cheered his procession, competed to honor him, and marked his visit as a great occasion—precisely because, as one Bostonian commented, "the People seem to feel no Interest or Concern in the acts of the National Govt."[10] During the 1820s, younger Americans carefully set other such artifacts on display: a nodding John Adams at the constitutional convention in Massachusetts, a deaf James Madison at the Virginia counterpart. Otherwise, few Americans could think of anything for Monroe to do. The scores of state-oriented newspapers scarcely mentioned his remarkable reelection with only one dissenting electoral vote. The president reciprocated with official silence on their most important issue, the Panic of 1819 and the subsequent national depression.

How far the divorce between these levels of politics had proceeded in such a short time was revealed in the contrast between two clashes over state and national authority, the Hartford Convention of 1814 and the conflict surrounding Missouri statehood in 1819 and 1820. At the nadir of Madison's administration late in 1814, leaders from the New England states gathered at Hartford to reconsider the union in light of a pending British attack on their territory. Not unreasonably, they saw no hope in Washington. "The General Government as the head, for the defense of the country, is dissolved," one delegate wrote during the convention to a colleague in Washington. ". . . If the war continues, the States must defend themselves. . . . " He added stoutly: "We mean to fight the British if they come . . . [and] we shall acquire the ways and means."[11] For emergency purposes, the convention decided, these required state control over revenues and the militia, in the long run constitutional amendments to reallocate federal powers; and its representatives left Hartford for Washington to set their proposals before a hapless national government that an earlier resistance from these very same states, of course, had helped to paralyze.

Nevertheless, as the delegates traveled, they were still following the traditional vertical axis that bound the states into national government and invested their actions with a meaning for the entire republic. Although extraordinary times demanded extraordinary measures, the New England dissenters pictured themselves preserving "the union of the states . . . through the present critical exigency." In their cloudy crystal ball they saw "the dying struggles of democracy" on the verge of destroying the United States. "The national union—the most delicate of all ties —if once severed is gone forever." Their measures would save it at the brink, then leave it "firmly established" for the future.[12] As heartily as they hated Madison's administration, they had to extract authority from it without toppling the national government in the process. "No one will more sincerely rejoice than myself," the Connecticut Federalist Chauncey Goodrich wrote, "if these proceedings shall be the means of arranging . . . the questions in controversy . . . in a manner most consistent with the honour of the general Government."[13] Both in spirit and in strategy the analogue to the Hartford Convention lay in the Virginia and Kentucky Resolutions, another gentry attempt to meet a crisis, clarify the republican balance, and strengthen the union through a broadly conceived assertion of state power. John Jay was no more inconsistent in approving the later effort than Madison had been in sponsoring the earlier one.

In February 1819, four years after the arrival of the Treaty of Ghent swamped the Hartford resolutions, Congressman James Tallmadge of New York moved an amendment to the Missouri statehood bill that made the gradual abolition of slavery a condition for its admission to the union. The flood of attacks, recriminations, and justifications that spread over the next year covered a whole range of constitutional and customary rights governing relations between the states and the national government and once more forced political leaders to calculate the price of union. Among the surviving revolutionary gentry the subject fell momentously on the scale of a life's work, and they responded to it out of the depth of their past. To the extent their debate had a core, it was the Constitution's peculiar link between slavery and national political power, the three-fifths clause. Rufus King, never reconciled to the compromise he had signed at Philadelphia in 1787, led the fight for the Tallmadge amendment in the Senate, hoping that the vicious constitutional clause might still be repealed. Monroe traced the issue a year farther back to the Jay-Gardoqui negotiations of 1786 when "The same men, in some instances"—King in particular—had first plotted to block southern influence at the Appalachians.[14]

But the real danger to the union in 1819 and 1820 was apathy. So few people cared deeply about these issues, as the perceptive Martin Van Buren gently told King during the contest. In Missouri itself, debtor relief rather than statehood dominated local politics. The three-fifths clause affected only national politics, not the interior workings of state government, and not even most congressmen, who came and went as spokesmen for their states and localities, considered it very important. When the roll was called, they voted according to the presence or absence of slavery at home, a matter of great economic and social consequence there but not one that shaped clear convictions about good or bad national policy. From Washington, Clay reported that "the topic of disunion is frequently discussed and with as little emotion as an ordinary affair of legislation!"[15] They were speaking the language of their constituents. Back home, as the young John Tyler reported of Virginia, "Men talk of a dissolution of the Union with perfect nonchalance and indifference."[16] Even those who were seeking some compromise, such as Senator James Barbour, often acted less like national officials than ambassadors of a foreign power as they alternated between their negotiations for a settlement and proposals to disband the United States. Significantly, Barbour still went by the title "Governor," an essentially honorific post that he had held years before in Virginia. During the era of neocolonial conflict the national government had mattered so much to the parties of independence that their battles threatened to tear the union apart. Now the national government mattered so little that irrelevance threatened to dissolve the union. When compromise finally did resolve the Missouri question, its issues dropped immediately from sight. The same diffusion of interests that made the controversy so dangerous in the first place assured instant success to its settlement.

Economic ambitions absorbed what the old national politics lost. The release from international crisis freed pent-up drives for development across the country: states with an agenda such as New York and Pennsylvania rushed on with their plans, laggards such as South Carolina and Georgia now threw their energies into elaborate programs, and newcomers such as Indiana and Mississippi entered the union with schemes of their own for banks, turnpikes, and canals. Although hard times after 1819 stalled some of these enterprises, the states maintained a strikingly high rate of investment in transportation even during depression. Indiana, for example, laid plans for 24 new roads in 1821. When the Erie Canal opened in 1825, no promoter in a triangle from Boston to Cincinnati to Baltimore needed a guide to its implications. As the development spirit accelerated into the early 1830s, its range spread enormously, and no state or territory escaped its version of these intense, complicated preoccupations.

In one sense, these were the centrifugal forces in American life that the long battle for independence had held in check. In another sense, however, they revealed a new set of state checks against these same forces of decentralization. As development proposals elbowed each other in competition for the same resources, state governments tried to coordinate them. After 1815, bank charters more often mandated assistance for some transportation project that the legislature rather than the stockholders decided to support. The Erie Canal inevitably became the backbone for transportation development in New York, and other states, including South Carolina, Ohio, and Pennsylvania, designed their own comprehensive plans for transportation. Virginia, already a stockholder in two canals, a turnpike, and two major banks by 1816, invested through a central Board of Public Works in 56 transportation companies during the next two decades. Elsewhere states legislated specific compromises among conflicting claims, as Maryland did in the "Eight Million Dollar Bill" of 1836, which broke a deadlock among the Chesapeake and Ohio Canal, the Baltimore and Ohio Railroad, and their lesser competitors. Although the results of these integrating efforts were exceedingly uneven, legislatures everywhere still acknowledged the standard of serving development ambitions for the entire state. The whole state and nothing but the state. In fact, a desire to siphon business from "foreign" states supplied one of the important motivations for legislative planning.

In this setting of expansive provincialism, each state capital served as a nucleus to order local energies so that they did not smash one another in wild ambition. The regulating power fell to small groups of men, more or less permanent fixtures at the capitals, whose enemies named them to reflect their size, their cohesion, and in gentry terminology their "self-created" authority: the Richmond Junto, the Albany Regency, the Chillicothe Junto, the Concord Regency, the Nashville Junto. Like the contemporary business firms, they remained small because they relied on a depth of mutual trust. "It is part of my political creed," declared Silas Wright of the Albany Regency, "always to act with my political friends, and to let the majority dictate [the] course of action."[17] As the particularly stable Richmond Junto demonstrated, family connections forged the strongest links inside these political firms. Usually, however, the partners cemented their ties through an accumulated record of reliability. Again like their commercial counterparts, these men extended their activities by networks of personal exchange, using patronage or other government favors instead of credit. Where their knowledge of individual reputations ended, their bargaining stopped. More distant connections they left to allies who were constructing personal networks of their own throughout the state.

Politicians and merchants behaved so much alike because they had been encountering such similar problems. Before 1815, state leaders also suffered from the confusions of international crisis, and after the war they too found that a broadening range of interests exceeded the limits of face-to-face arrangements. Just as the merchants integrated their activities to achieve a greater personal control, so did the politicians. The parallel ended there, however, for these political leaders became the center for a self-contained state system rather than the anchoring link in an indefinitely extending line of commerce. Initially these differences benefited the politicians. As the indispensable hubs of state communication and brokerage, the shrewdest among them seized the opportunity to systematize their command. Through legislative caucuses, they organized their allies into voting blocs. Through careful slatemaking, they matched offices with state districts in a way to reinforce some local loyalties and attract others. Through links of mutual interest with newspaper editors, they guaranteed a favorable public hearing for their causes, promotional or electoral. Businessmen needed them more than the converse. So did fledgling politicians. Before the war the ambitious Mahlon Dickerson had drifted between Pennsylvania and New Jersey in search of better fields for advancement. Now each state sealed itself from its neighbors, formed its own exclusive club, and tightened discipline over all those who sought entry.

Managing development politics at a state capital required skills and credentials very different from those of the revolutionary gentry. As brokers the new leaders relied on a mastery of details and an adaptation to shifting local interests, not a command over first principles and comprehensive explanations. Parochialism was now a virtue. Of that perennial power in the Richmond Junto, Thomas Ritchie, an associate remarked: ". . . [his] horizon is limited to the State of Virginia. . . ."[18] A sharp focus on objectives was equally essential. Although state chieftains threw every resource into a political contest, they rarely mistook the contest over a transportation route with a battle over the eternal verities. As soon as the Erie Canal proved its success, Martin Van Buren's Albany Regency switched from its critic to its champion and prepared for the next fight. The height of a broker's social standing had little relation to the breadth of his power. If few had very humble origins, not many had a gentry lineage either, and they showed no compunctions about making politics their profession. By the same token, they assumed a natural compatibility between their political and personal fortunes. It never dawned on Thomas Hart Benton, a rising star in Missouri politics, to disengage himself from the banking and trading allies whom he aided and who aided him in turn. Indeed, many citizens welcomed a politician's stake in their promotion both as a public announcement of the project's worth and as a private surety for his commitment. Partners in common, all of them would succeed or fail together. To an aristocratic observer such as Alexis de Tocqueville, it seemed a sad declension from the founders' lofty contests over principle, but to the participants everything meshed neatly into a pattern of bargain and enterprise.

Development politics, like its gentry predecessor, also gravitated toward a two-party division, this time over the access to government resources that a dominant junto controlled to the exclusion of others. During the early 1820s, losers in these battles for the state capital followed two strategies in an effort to strengthen their own coalitions. One took them deeper into the society of their state, where hard times between 1819 and 1825 inspired bursts of a new democratic spirit: demands for debtor relief and constitutional reform, attacks on corporate monopolies and any other evidence of elite privileges. It was during these years that the name "Federalist" became a curse, not for its war record but for its reputation as an enemy of "the people." Although regency managers recognized the need for aggressive statewide electioneering, the reigning ones preferred the quiet procedures of the back room, and the more effective they were in this setting, the slower they usually were to catch the leveling tone of the new, free-swinging democracy. Van Buren, for example, tried to dismiss its spokesmen simply as "wild men." As insiders lagged, outsiders increasingly mobilized these inchoate attacks into a formidable opposition.

The outsiders' second strategy led into national affairs. Ruling brokers generally followed the axiom of Silas Wright: "Love the state and let the nation save itself."[19] National issues almost always meant trouble for the group in power. The tariff, for example, touching different interests throughout the state, stirred conflicts that they had absolutely no means of controlling—the broker's nightmare. Presidential elections might pose similar problems. In this respect Monroe's victory in 1820 represented the ideal type, an uncontested election of a passive president by an indifferent populace. With no automatic successor to Monroe, however, 1824 looked more threatening, and as early as 1822 a fretful Van Buren was already complaining about "the distractions which are produced by the approaching contest for president."[20] Many of the ablest junto leaders thought they saw a safe solution in William Crawford of Georgia: he carried the gloss of legitimacy from a national legislative caucus, and he, like Monroe, believed in minimal national government. There would be competition, of course. New Englanders demanded a northern man, and some across the Appalachians called for a westerner. Important interests in such states as Ohio and Pennsylvania wanted more national help for internal improvements than Crawford promised. Nevertheless, such shrewd brokers as Van Buren, Ritchie of Virginia, and Dickerson of New Jersey estimated that a symbolic nomination, a scattered opposition, and a bored electorate would ease Crawford into office with the least possible fuss. His qualities as a leader simply did not matter. When Crawford suffered a stroke early in the campaign, state managers inquired about his health only to learn whether he was still a plausible candidate, not a competent one.

What happened in 1824 jolted the leading state managers into a wholesale reconsideration of national politics. Andrew Jackson, the candidate whom most of them held in the slightest regard, received the largest popular and electoral votes. Moreover, the last became first in ways particularly offensive to the canons of orderly junto politics, a mysterious diffusion of popularity for the hero of New Orleans among whooping and hollering local enthusiasts. Even worse, Jackson's appeal, apart from his military glory, struck the high notes of the "wild" new democracy: the people's candidate versus the tool of an aristocratic caucus, a friend of the common man versus the monopolies. Because no candidate received a majority of the electoral vote, the House chose among the three leaders —Jackson, Adams, and Crawford—and through an arrangement familiar in every state capital, the supporters of Adams, who had ranked second, and of Clay, who had limped in fourth, negotiated a victory for the chilly New Englander. A "corrupt bargain" to defy the people's will, the Jackson men now cried. Worst of all, these Jackson men were usually outsiders who seized on the general's popularity and used it to gain state power—rising newcomers in Ohio, declining old-timers in North Carolina, but challengers to the ruling clique in either case. Jackson's cause, in other words, combined in a single package the sharpest fears among successful brokers: an incalculable disruption from national affairs that swelled the dangerous democratic tides and channeled them to the benefit of their enemies. From New Jersey to Alabama, the election of 1824 hardened a competitive, two-party politics inside the states.

Adaptable as always, the canniest of the insiders tried to tame this threatening movement by stealing its candidate. Before the next election, Van Buren, Ritchie, and Dickerson were all Jackson men. Where presidential candidates served as nothing more than tokens, the state-oriented politician felt quite free to shift his bets at will. When conditions in Missouri required it, for example, Thomas Hart Benton effortlessly switched in the midst of the 1824 campaign from Clay to Jackson. Benton's old feud with the general was no more relevant than the office he sought. In that same spirit other alert politicians were making the same choice. David Henshaw, a wealthy Massachusetts promoter whose railroad from Springfield to Albany was denied state aid, proceeded to rally the enemies of monopoly into a Jackson camp. James Buchanan, responding to the ratio of twenty votes for Jackson to one for an opponent in his Pennsylvania district, organized a similar statewide coalition of democratic and antimonopoly enthusiasts to challenge the rulers at Harrisburg.

Although Van Buren and Ritchie did exchange views on presidential politics, almost nothing beyond a common expediency united these various maneuvers. In each instance the line of concern ran straight from the state capital to the White House and back to the state capital again. Nor did Jackson himself unify them. The old general was just another catchall candidate, a shiny wrap for the ambitions of assorted politicians whose interests turned inward to their states. What distinguished the

Jackson campaign from its predecessors was a new seriousness among the state brokers. Never again would they make the mistake of 1824 and belittle the significance of a presidential election. Glad to be rid of the national caucus or any other check on their personal control, they approached 1828 as a test of their skills to turn a presidential election to state advantage.

Comprehensive
Programs

The Constitution, which could not have survived a major war at any point between 1789 and 1815, emerged so cleanly from the last tournament with Britain because it had been so little used. To the inherent limitations on any wartime president's power, Madison added a philosophical appreciation for America's diversity and a temperamental aversion to the domestic use of force. He lectured the recalcitrant states on their constitutional obligations, but he never tried to coerce them. No hint of a Sedition Act came in response to the seditious activities in New England. Thanks to a timely treaty of peace the United States had to endure only a bit of a war, and its national structure looked remarkably healthy after the ordeal. It was not clear, however, who would care enough about the union to maintain it.

A handful of men rose rapidly during the second decade of the 19th century to assume that responsibility. Clay, the oldest, established his reputation first as a powerful congressman before the war and a member of the peace commission that ended it. Calhoun, Van Buren, and Webster, all born in 1782, quickly followed him: Calhoun as a War Hawk and a prominent member of Monroe's cabinet, Van Buren as a political wizard in New York and its senator in 1821, and Webster as a national spokesman for the Boston establishment and an outstanding constitutional lawyer who brought his fame with him to Congress in 1823. By then friends of all of them except Van Buren were discussing their presidential possibilities, while Van Buren's associates expected him to make presidents. No shaping event welded them into a political generation as the Revolution had their gentry predecessors, and no dramatic moment transferred national power into their hands. Nevertheless, they did seem to be heirs to the founders, and they did share enough similar experiences to give them certain common qualities.

As a group they expressed a national version of the original quiddish spirit. Coming of age to the clang of national party battles, they then contributed to the muffling of those wars in their states after 1803. Clay apprenticed in Kentucky politics as a supporter of promotional banking. Webster, an admirer of the quiddish Governor Plumer in his home state of New Hampshire, attached himself as a new Boston lawyer to the city's business developers. When Calhoun from the upcountry of South Carolina married into a prominent coastal family, he was smoothing both sectional and partisan divisions in his state. Quiddism and politics were almost synonymous in Van Buren's New York. Each man felt the quiddish urge toward limiting political contests, a tendency that encouraged Calhoun to conciliate the New England Federalists in 1812, that led Clay to become the Great Compromiser, and that established Van Buren as a model of the new professional politician. Although Webster's skills as a broker did not shine, his mind played constantly with political alliances that might further his national ambitions. By containing their public encounters, these men maintained civil, often cordial private relations with their opponents. In 1826, Van Buren, the silkiest of the four, spent the Christmas holidays with a man he had recently repudiated as a turncoat. Clay, the most abrasive, made his enemies on temperamental far more than partisan grounds. As stiff as Webster and Calhoun often were, both expected to hold a firm line between political and personal affairs. The evening after Webster's thunderous reply to Hayne in 1831, the two senators shook hands and exchanged pleasantries at a Washington party. At about the same time, Jackson dumbfounded Calhoun by drawing the South Carolinian's social feud with another cabinet member into administration politics.

Yet—again like the original quids—these men never fully extricated themselves from gentry politics. Too young to feel a personal identification with the Revolution or even with the creation of the Constitution, they sank their roots in the issues of the late 1790s. For them, as for a wide range of political leaders their age, the sequence of events from 1798 to 1800 defined the origins of their United States. Where the revolutionary gentry saw an unfolding crisis of independence in these events, the younger men, looking back from the early 19th century, found an exclusively domestic lesson, a dramatic revelation of the Constitution's meaning that served as a touchstone throughout their careers. By the end of the War of 1812, anyone who claimed a place in the Republican tradition also inherited Madison's Virginia Report of 1800 as the bible of republican orthodoxy. Like bibles generally, this one lent itself to the varied interpretations of many ingenious minds. Clay, for example, struggled mightily in 1818 to square Madison's Report with a bill for internal improvements that Madison himself had vetoed, and Van Buren asked Jefferson to bless his policies as true to the principles of '98 while he was supporting Rufus King as senator from New York. Through such misty uses the Republican doctrines of the late nineties came to saturate political discourse so thoroughly that in the mid-1830s Harriet Martineau was taught to date the arrival of democracy in the United States from Jefferson's election in 1800.

For most politicians this creed simply validated state authority in an era of state dominance and quickly became a litany. Among the handful who committed themselves to national affairs, however, the gentry heritage had a far subtler shaping effect. As self-conscious successors to the founders, they could not rely on state power alone to maintain the union they inherited. Ranging from Webster, a former Federalist who repudiated the Republican orthodoxy, to Van Buren, a founder of the Albany Regency who treasured his state, all of them sought ways of overcoming the centrifugal forces that distributed American energies among its many provincial capitals. The more deeply they invested themselves in a national cause, the weaker their state ties became. By 1812, Clay's career had taken a national turn that he never reversed, and when he returned to Kentucky at various times in his career, he merely perched there. After the war, Calhoun's immersion in executive duties and his ambitions for the presidency worked similar results on his orientation. Between 1819 and 1825 he barely touched base in South Carolina, and even after state affairs engaged him again in the late twenties, he spoke through the state to the nation. Webster's lifelong preoccupation with the structure of the national government originated during these same years. Each labored persistently to transcend a regional identification; none fell willingly into the currents of his state's political life. Although Van Buren's continuing attachment to the Albany Regency marked him as the exception, he too relied increasingly on secondhand summaries of New York politics as he devoted more and more of his attention to national affairs.

Drifting away from the vital centers of postwar political life, first Clay, Calhoun, and Webster and finally Van Buren lost touch with the changes that churned through the states. As the demands for credit democratized, Clay decried the motley mess of local banks, and Calhoun extolled the virtues of a strict specie standard. Webster's attachment to vested prop-

erty rights was already a fixed passion. None of them sensed the democratic ground swell against the national caucus. Late in 1824, Clay was
still hoping that if he could just place third in the electoral balloting, the
House would make him president. Although all four spoke warmly about
the benefits from internal improvements, none of them shared the era's
racing ambitions to plunge across space, and not a single adventurous,
growth-obsessed leader emerged from the lot. It was as if their sensitivities to the drive for development had been arrested sometime before
1820.

Instead of responding to the dynamics of popular politics, they engaged
in a dialogue with the last of the revolutionary gentry, and inside this
little world of national leaders, passing and rising, they fashioned their
approaches to public policy. On the one hand, they looked to the old
leaders for acceptance: Webster to John Marshall, Van Buren to King,
Calhoun to Monroe. On the other hand, they chafed at the revolutionary
gentry's limitations, their preoccupation with ancient issues and their
caution in meeting new needs. While they apprenticed, therefore, they
took lessons on the changes that they, as the next keepers of the nation,
would have to make. For the three of them who witnessed the War of
1812 from Washington, Madison's administration epitomized the evils
of passivity and diffusion. Short of a miracle, "the Govt. will die in its
own weakness," wrote a disgusted Webster in language only a bit more
blunt than Clay's and Calhoun's. "It cannot enlist soldiers. It cannot
borrow money—what can it do?"[1] Although they would never again rely
on a president alone, their nation did require an operative center of authority and a clear source for its policies. In the years immediately after
the war, as they cooperated with such veterans as Gallatin, King, and
Alexander Dallas to strengthen the government against bankruptcy at
home and discrimination abroad, they found the old gentry unable to
recognize the urgency of stretching the nation's authority across its western domain. Finally, in the Missouri controversy of 1819 and 1820, they
concluded that only they cared enough about the union to save it—even
from the aging gentry themselves.

Three groups comprised the cast of characters in the Missouri drama.
A few unbending old gentry gave it form, large and loosely engaged
congressional majorities gave it substance, and a handful of younger nationalists eventually swung the balance to compromise. In the Senate,
King, 65 years old in 1820, took the lead against slavery in Missouri, and
his shrillest public support came from such vintage Federalists as Elias
Boudinot of New Jersey, a revolutionary patriot and now 80, Theodore
Dwight, former secretary to the Hartford Convention and 56, and their
agents among the veteran party editors. King's most eloquent opponent
in the Senate was William Pinkney of Maryland, a prominent partisan

since the 1790s and 56 years old, and behind him the angriest cries rose from such Virginia stalwarts as John Taylor, 67, and Spencer Roane, 58. From the sidelines the patriarchs of the old parties—Jay at 75 and Jefferson at 77—added their dogmatic voices of support.*

What these anomalous Nestors brought to the debates was a legacy of geographically vague but emotionally potent sectional antipathies that predated the Constitution, deepened during the party battles of the 1790s, and lingered on to affect their understanding of the nation's dangers and prospects. Slavery occupied an uneven, often murky place in these sectional tensions. Periodically southern gentry did fear a northern attack on their human property, most notably during the formative years of the Constitution, and at times northern leaders did express their hostility toward this institution. Nevertheless, Charles Cotesworth Pinckney of South Carolina saw a greater threat to the slave system from Virginia than from New England, and the hero of slavery's northern critics, Washington, owned scores of slaves. It was difficult for northern Federalists who attacked their southern enemies as Jacobin democrats to picture them simultaneously as aristocratic slave masters. At most, slavery in the northern image served as one index to a repellent culture led by corrupt men. It was equally difficult for such Republican luminaries as Jefferson and Madison, who mistily anticipated the eventual disappearance of slavery everywhere, to set it at the heart of their sectional concerns. At most, slavery in their southern scheme belonged to a group of vulnerable interests that required special protection against intriguing outsiders.

After 1803 these ill-focused involvements blended with the gentry's equally imprecise but strong responses to American space. Although some of them abandoned the west to barbarism, others tried to assimilate it into their visions of a healthy republic. With the Louisiana Purchase, for example, it became standard doctrine among southern gentry to picture slavery growing more benign as it expanded. According to the traditional conception of a hierarchical society, the diffusion of any institution over a wider and wider area softened it, and these southerners now looked to the west as the east's safety valve for congestion, rebellion, and race war—even as the source of eventual emancipation. More concretely, many northerners as well as southerners welcomed the prospect of adding friendly western states to their balance in the national scale. In all of these visions the west served the east, not itself. Sons following the fathers, the western states would enter a union defined and directed by interests east of the Appalachians.

---

* These ages have been rounded at their birthdays in 1820. Old age, of course, is a relative matter. In 1820 about 88% of the white males in the United States were under 45.

It was from this vantage point that the old gentlemen dug in and fought the battle over Missouri. Not many of them could stretch their sense of a national hierarchy farther west than that. In Missouri, therefore, the eastern fathers would make a decision with profound consequences for a union about to be wrapped in space and fixed in character. King, whose antipathy for southern slave power extended back to the 1780s, saw this moment as the nation's last chance—his last chance as an elder states-man—to protect the republic from the permanent dominance of "the slave Legion." Let slave interests prevail here, he told his sons, and they "will determine all questions respecting the general & common welfare and, in a word, will rule us as they have done in contempt of our rights."[2] Hold the line and the balance would tip northward, the pressures to revise the Constitution's three-fifths clause would mount, and the repub-lic might yet be purged of its greatest evils. Southern gentry, working with the same components, also defined it as the crucial moment with irreversible consequences. Not only would the abolition of slavery in Missouri pit an enlarged north against a beleaguered south, but, as Spen-cer Roane told Monroe, it would reverse the "humane" policy of "dis-persing [slaves] throughout the country" and force "the Eastern people . . . to be dammed up in a land of Slaves," with all the pending horrors of racial slaughter.[3] Invariably these gentlemen were using Missouri as a means to fulfill their eastern-based conceptions of policy. In one of those personal glosses that the revolutionary gentry always felt free to issue on the meaning of the Constitution, King concluded that as a state beyond "our original territory" Missouri had fewer rights of self-determination at the time of its admission than previous western states had enjoyed. For this western son, Father could set all the rules.

The locally rooted majorities whose votes deadlocked Congress month after month neither followed nor cared about this complex accumulation of gentry concerns. In fact they seemed to treat it as an issue with no past whatsoever, just one to address and settle by its own lights, and those lights in almost all cases reflected the labor system, free or slave, of their particular constituencies. Without obedience to a party or defer-ence to a leader, they simply projected these home truths into universal truths. As younger men with a new faith in personal choice, they exer-cised it with an easy dogmatism that introduced a different kind of moral tone into the Missouri debates.

Inflexible old hatreds, inflexible new truths—no setting could have been less attractive to the handful of emerging national leaders who felt that only they wanted to preserve the union. Unless the issue of Missouri was "satisfactorily adjusted," an appalled Clay wrote to a Kentucky in-timate, "it will form the basis of the most alarming parties that ever distracted this Country."[4] Taking the southern side, Clay cleverly hooked the admission of Maine, which was also applying for statehood, to that of Missouri as a way of extracting northern votes for a southern solution to the matter. Placating the northern side, Senator Jesse Thomas of Illinois, who like Clay was 43, proposed that west of Missouri slavery would be banned "for ever" above a line at 36°30′ latitude. It worked, in part because a scattering of congressmen anticipated personal benefits from a shift in their votes. The 36-year-old John W. Taylor of New York, for example, who had seconded Tallmadge's original antislavery motion, now championed the compromise, and in the next session of Congress he was rewarded with election as speaker of the House.

In one sense, settling the Missouri question ended an era. Never again would the old gentry play a significant role in shaping domestic policy. Among them only Monroe, whose presidential reputation hinged on some resolution of the issue, accepted the compromise. Jefferson pictured it dooming the union. From their opposite poles, King and Spencer Roane each gave an impatient eastern glance to the divided territory beyond Missouri, and each concluded that the enemy had received the better land. One of Roane's associates, reflecting an eastern gentry's general disdain for this strange western wilderness, described the south's portion as "intersected with mountains in one direction, destroyed by Earthquakes in another, and interspersed in a third with swamps and bayous, and infected with mosquitoes and bilious diseases. . . ."[5] Yet the overwhelming inclination among the younger men who dominated American politics was to accept, forget, and move on. In a broker's spirit of limited political conflict, the anger from the long Missouri battle dissolved almost instantly in the latest business at hand. Northern votes gave Monroe, ostensibly a slave president, his virtually unanimous reelection. The three-fifths clause, yesterday's pivot of debate, abruptly slipped from public discussion as the promoters of development, to whom it meant nothing, avidly pursued their plans. The line at 36°30′ that disgusted King, perplexed Monroe, and depressed Jefferson made good sense to them. Rather than a way of balancing power within a contained national hierarchy, they saw it as a means of opening space for everybody's ambitions. Even the Virginian Thomas Ritchie, an opponent of the compromise, understood its new logic of growth and argued immediately for more American territory in the southwest. The adamant old gentry were simply left behind to nurse their ancient hatreds and doubts.

In another sense, however, the gentry's final contribution to national politics precipitated consequences that would have a profound effect on the decades to come. Before 1820 the clearest geographical divide in the minds of American leaders was the Appalachian chain. The fuzziness of north and south in their conceptions left a large bloc from New York to

Maryland nowhere in particular. Now the Missouri Compromise established a line that, once traced back to the Atlantic Coast, neatly sorted
the United States according to a simple formula: slave or free. This sudden sharpening of another sectionalism sounded the alarm among the
handful who aspired to direct their nation's future. The separation of east
from west was their challenge, of north from south their nemesis. Clay
treated the new sectionalism as shocking and unnatural, a distraction
that he continued to hope would somehow just disappear. In something
of the same spirit, Webster evaded the subject of slavery in his search for
a holistic union. Applying his own lesson from the Missouri debates, Van
Buren devoted his considerable talents as a national politician to muting
the conflict between slave and free states. Even those who drew a different conclusion found themselves exceedingly uneasy with the implications. Out of a deep respect for Rufus King—"there is not a man in the
Union of purer integrity"—John Quincy Adams rethought the issues
separating north and south during the Missouri crisis and decided that
"the bargain between freedom and slavery contained in the Constitution
of the United States is morally and politically vicious."[6] Nevertheless, it
was a judgment that he kept exclusively in his diary until he had left the
presidency. Calhoun, the first to act on the centrality of the north-south
division, wrestled for a lifetime with ways to contain it inside a more
perfect union. Like the rest of this small band, he never ceased to believe
that he had a special calling in public life to transmit the national legacy
of the Revolution to all future generations.

By the mid-1820s, these self-styled keepers of the union, along with men
of similar persuasions in business, law, and religion, emerged as leaders
for an array of comprehensive programs that addressed the basic challenges of their apprenticeship years: the strengthening of a national center, the formulation of nationwide policies, and the harnessing of a
growing west to eastern authority. Clay, the first of the new leaders to
focus his ambitions on the presidency, was the first to issue an integrated
political statement. Rejecting the cautious constitutionalism of Madison
and Monroe, and expanding on the big dreams of Jefferson and Gallatin,
Clay asserted the right of the national government to point the broad
path of America's development through an interlinked series of proposals
that came to be known as the American System: a tariff to protect its
industries, a government investment in transportation to move its goods,
and a sufficiently high price for public lands to fund the subsidies. Although Calhoun and Webster had better theoretical minds, it was Clay
who gave clear, imaginative expression to their common postwar concerns. In the quiddish spirit, Clay's program appealed to the elites who
already dominated America's development enterprises. By encouraging

their growth while regulating the pace of the popular western movement through land prices, the American System struck a middle ground between the gentry's contained hierarchy and a harum-scarum rush for new opportunities.

Losing the election of 1824 denied Clay his chance to preside over this program, but the winner, Adams, shared so many of his convictions that the American System did, in effect, have its trial. Every Adams was a singular figure in national politics. An antifederalist who sought a cohesive new nation, a Federalist who turned Republican without trusting either party, and an opponent of slavery's expansion who negotiated a wilderness empire for its growth, John Quincy placed such a compulsive emphasis on his own moral integrity in a career of political ambition that no one could possibly have predicted the many curious turns in his long public life. At the same time, he was a sharper observer of men and affairs than his father and a much more alert participant in the give-and-take of elite politics. By subordinating his innumerable reservations about southern and western ethics, he managed to work effectively first with Madison and Monroe, then with Clay. When John Randolph in 1825 likened the alliance between the prunish Adams and the rakish Clay to a union of "the Puritan and the black leg," he let the wit of an old character politics obscure the reasonableness of an arrangement between a president and a secretary of state who agreed on fundamentals in both national and international affairs.

Adams' distinctive contributions as a national leader netted him only trouble. Twenty-two years old as Washington became president and already a precocious aspirant for public leadership, he retained the vision of an exalted first character too vividly for mere experience to dim, and in his own term he saw himself filling that obsolete role. Congressmen too should act for the nation, he announced, and not be "palsied by the will of our constituents." Out of that gentry tradition, Adams drew up a set of proposals that reflected his sense of the national government's supervisory function in a great republic, including sponsorship of a national university, the metric system, and scientific inquiry. Congress, paying no attention to any of this, snickered at the chilly president's strange ideas and went its own way. Nevertheless, the American System made considerable progress. Public land prices remained high and tariff levels increased. Breaking the Virginia Dynasty's dike of resistance, national funds for transportation moved westward. Segments of the National Road proceeded across Ohio, and that state, along with Indiana and Illinois, received land grants in return for liberal schedules of construction on their canals. In 1828, under the appropriately comprehensive and paternal banner of National Republicanism, the president who had approved these measures automatically stood as a candidate for reelection, with wide support in those states north and west of Maryland that contained industries in need of protection and transportation enterprises in need of subsidies.

Initially the Second Bank of the United States belonged within the general conception of the American System. Clay and Calhoun sponsored the legislation chartering it in 1817 specifically to impose order on a sprawling, irresponsible multitude of note-issuing banks. During its first two years, however, it functioned like a bigger version of any other promotional bank, allowing insiders at each of its dispersed branches to invest its capital for their own benefit. This rich fund quickly became entangled in a mass of private development, and when the Panic of 1819 blighted those enterprises it threatened to destroy the Bank as well. Relentless austerity under a new president, Langdon Cheves of South Carolina, saved it. Taking a broadax to the problem of the Bank's solvency, he demanded immediate repayment of its extensive, loosely monitored loans in sound money and instantly drained the life out of those portions of the economy that depended directly or indirectly on the Bank's liberal infusions of credit. Even Clay, no friend of the ordinary debtor, found the cure too harsh.

The draconian policy that Cheves applied like a desperate merchant on the verge of bankruptcy was altered by Nicholas Biddle, who succeeded him in 1822, to serve a comprehensive economy in good times as well as bad. By establishing uniform procedures among the Bank's branches, gearing its activities to the nation's main line of commerce—the cotton trade—and thereby hooking the Bank into the British credit system, Biddle organized a nationwide network for transactions of almost any size or complexity and made the Bank's own notes a universally acceptable currency in commercial exchange. In gratitude, eastern elite circles treated the Bank as sacrosanct, no longer just an arm of government policy but an untouchable constant in their good society. Richard Rush, secretary of the treasury under Adams, feared that a mere mention of the Bank in his annual report might tarnish it with politics.

For this adulation Biddle himself was primarily responsible. The gifted and charming son of a successful Philadelphia merchant, Biddle came of age in a quiddish household where his father's brand of Federalism never inhibited warm family friendships with Republicans. Appropriately, the young Biddle went abroad as a private secretary for one of them, established a cordial relationship with Monroe there, then returned to become a war Federalist and effortlessly abandon his party as it disappeared in the postwar politics of amalgamation. Never deeply immersed in state affairs, Biddle looked nationally after the war, cheered the comprehensive policies of Washington's rising leaders, and as the Bank's new president found natural allies in Clay, Webster, and Calhoun, all of whom considered Biddle a valued colleague.

Although the youngest in this group by several years, Biddle had the deepest commitment to the old gentry values. A gentleman of broad interests and learning, he relied on the intrinsic qualities of his superior character. The first requirement for the presidency of the Bank, Biddle wrote in a barely disguised description of himself, was a "*talent* for business rather than what is commonly called a man of business," for "the mere men of business" lacked the breadth of mind for wise judgment.[7] Jefferson the "philosophical statesman" was his ideal, and much like Jefferson the party leader, Biddle the Bank president created a network of personal lieutenants in the Bank's many branches. Despite the charter's provision for a decentralized governance of these branches, Biddle himself selected their presidents and boards of directors. The officers who managed the daily affairs of the branches all apprenticed first in the home bank at Philadelphia and dispersed only after they had passed Biddle's rigorous testing. Soothing, flattering, and recruiting like a gentry master, he presided over this institutional kingdom with Jeffersonian grace.

The Bank, Biddle liked to say, was a "passive" agency for the immutable principles of sound finance. In classic gentry fashion he assumed a perfect compatibility between his judgment and these truths, and he directed the Bank as his personal firm with absolute confidence in its impersonal public virtues. Indeed, in the spirit of Jefferson's equation between the Republican party and the nation, Biddle's mind merged the operations of the Bank with the central functions of national governance, picturing it as the one dependable source of stability for the entire United States. To fulfill the Bank's grand purpose, he entered office with plans for "a more enlarged development of its resources and a wider extension of its sphere of usefulness," more than doubled its notes in circulation between 1823 and 1826, then doubled them again between 1826 and 1831.[8] Apart from specie itself, the bedrock in financial exchange everywhere, these Bank notes, including some illegal ones of Biddle's own devising, provided the United States with its only uniform currency. Reining the greediest tendencies among the Bank's insiders and holding its officers to a loyal pursuit of his policies, Biddle ruled with the Olympian vision and Aristotelian moderation of an exemplary first character. But as always, the problem in assessing a powerful gentry leader was to determine whether he would become a Solon or a Caesar.

The answer depended largely on where a person fit in the chains of commerce that were extending through the American interior as Biddle took control of the Bank. Most of these transactions were conducted through primary credit—that is, arrangements based on personal reputations. Within the ranges of reputation, currency was whatever bore a trusted name: notes endorsed by a wealthy merchant, bills issued by an established local corporation, vouchers backed by government taxation, or one of many comparable substitutes. The inland trade, however, developed along with a proliferation of incorporated institutions and private firms whose credit paper circulated more widely than their good— or bad—names did. These were the "foreign notes" that plagued every way station in American commerce. If the nation's decentralization made them inevitable, the recipient's ignorance made them anathema. Not even the finest individual reputation in the land could add a penny's value to the piece of alien bank paper in his hand.

Where personal trust could no longer define the exchange, transactions moved to a secondary level. Here credit arrangements were formal and payments in almost all cases were made in specie or the equivalent. In the end, the economic prospects of every aspiring American depended on which level he had available to him. The most obvious anomaly that the subordinance of American commerce to Britain's financial system created was the disjuncture between America's normal twelve-month cycle of payments and Britain's reliance on short-term issues of credit. The American economy rested on a base of agricultural customers whose costs and income required approximately a year to balance, the British economy on a distribution system with a relatively rapid turnover of finished goods. At the intersection between the two, America's inland commerce evolved a fairly standard formula: an initial credit for six months with three-month extensions that accrued more or less automatically to a total of twelve months and sometimes several months beyond that. These terms established the norm for primary credit. Occasionally individuals had to shuttle from firm to firm, keeping old debts aloft with new loans, but within the circle of their reputations, even such "kiting," as it was called, tended to follow relatively predictable patterns. Although this assortment of primary arrangements often hid the costs of credit in various service fees and odd terms of renewal, it formed the lifeblood of America's uniquely diffuse scheme of interior trade. Secondary credit, on the other hand, hewed to the letter of the agreement, forced a renegotiation at each interval, and threatened to break the year-long skein at any point. Survival itself hinged on those extensions, for very few along the commercial chains had the reserves of hard money to liquidate their debts before the end of the farming season and a final settling of accounts. Secondary credit meant perpetual jeopardy beneath the blade of bankruptcy.

Seekers after primary credit found no friend in the Bank. Viewing the economy in the impersonal terms of long-distance commercial flows, Biddle ran it as a national domain of secondary credit. The Bank's branches regularly forced local and state banks to redeem their paper in specie or Bank notes. Consequently, the price of facilitating long-range transactions with a uniform currency was a consistently deflationary and constraining policy. At about the time a British observer noted that most American banks actually "prefer accommodation paper, resting on personal security," Biddle called "accommodation paper" a "melancholy" error and defined precise "business loans" as "the legitimate object of Banking."[9] Six-month extensions of credit were as far as Biddle would stretch his liberality, and these only came grudgingly. Hence the Bank's most prominent admirers were those wealthy businessmen who had their own ample sources of primary credit, cheered the Bank's disciplinary effect on the "foreign notes" of some other locality, and profited from a regularization of long-range transactions. The situation looked very different from the perspective of those small businessmen represented by the New Bedford merchant Charles Morgan, who in hard times dreaded going to the "Boston banks where there is no sympathy for me and where they only give me money when their own people do not want it so I never feel safe for a moment."[10] Biddle remained totally oblivious to the new democratic faith among the innumerable Charles Morgans that in a land of enterprise they had a personal right to such credit.

Like the gentry models he emulated, Biddle saw the nation from the perspective of the eastern seaboard, or more precisely in his case, a composite of the major ports from Boston to New Orleans. "We have had enough & more than enough of banking in the interior," he declared as his first order of business in 1823. ". . . It is time . . . to make . . . the large commercial Cities the principal scene of our operations."[11] From that urban base the Bank expanded its activities. Especially after 1828, its notes laid a thick cloud of secondary credit over the Ohio Valley and cotton south, placing much of its long-distance trade under a shadow of strict, contractual terms and threatening to extinguish countless local pockets of primary credit in the event of a sudden contraction. In other words, a comprehensive national policy to Biddle's Bank—and it surely was *Biddle's* Bank—meant subordinating west to east, interior to seacoast, town to city, farmer to merchant. Moreover, Biddle's blurring of Bank and nation meant that what hurt the Bank hurt the nation, and in a pinch he would sacrifice all other considerations to the health of his institution, secure in the belief that his decision to exchange general distress for the good of the Bank served the fundamental needs of his country. Then the elite's Solon would become the multitude's Caesar.

The gentry norms that Biddle adopted John Marshall acquired by birth. An officer in the American Revolution, an active proponent of the Constitution, and Virginia's leading Federalist by the late 1790s, he was already 46 when John Adams submitted his nomination for chief justice as Congress was breaking the tie between Jefferson and Burr. In 1825, with ten more years to live, Marshall remained the last of the revolutionary gentry in high national office and the only leader of a comprehensive program with those almost mythical credentials. From Marshall's 18th-century origins came the values that shaped his extraordinary career on the Supreme Court. Like his gentry contemporaries, he assumed an orderly universe with basic principles that a cultivated intelligence could grasp. At the heart of Marshall's social order lay property rights. The responsibility of government—and hence his task as a public leader—was to maintain those rights through the correct application of fundamental principles. Although Marshall had great respect for legal learning, he never allowed the limits of his technical knowledge to govern the breadth of his decisions. In determining the law, as in judging poetry or farming practices or European revolutions, he relied on the same clear sweeps of deductive logic. As chief justice, therefore, he defined his role by the same lights that William Plumer used to dismiss one batch of judges with a snort: "Who of them can resort to first principles?"[12]

In theory, first principles stood immutably above all men. "Courts are the mere instruments of the law," Marshall declared, "and can will nothing." In practice, of course, he never doubted his capacity to define those principles and translate them into legal rules. No gentry leader carried the burdens of office more effortlessly or, in general, lived more comfortably with himself. Accustomed to casual dress as a young man, Marshall retained the habit without affronting his powdered peers or limiting his own effectiveness. He moved easily in any social setting, gave the most relaxed parties of his time, and enjoyed the pleasures of the good life with an unaffected delight. Yet, like another Virginian across the way in Washington who also dressed simply and charmed irresistibly, the chief justice knew, and his colleagues knew, that he was the first character of the Court. Just as Jefferson fashioned the executive branch into a model of gentry harmony, so Marshall drew the other justices beneath his gracious wings, responded to their opinions with what Joseph Story called an "unwearied patience," and for a quarter-century gave the Court a single, authoritative voice. Unique to its history, he transformed it into an agency for one man's vision.

In Marshall's world, gentlemen prized unity out of their fear of subversion. However genial his temper, Marshall indulged the passions of the 1790s as thoroughly as any partisan. The French Revolution chilled his soul, and his unyielding opposition to Jacobinism in America eventually led him to endorse Hamilton's plan to seize the government of New York in 1800 and deny the presidency to a Republican. Writing in 1808 to a kindred Federalist, Timothy Pickering, Marshall analyzed the embargo in language characteristic of the unregenerate neocolonial: it "will impel us to a war with the only power which protects any part of the civilized world from the despotism of that tyrant [by] whom we shall then be ravaged."[13] The War of 1812, he believed, came in response to Napoleon's dictate. No doubt the depth of Marshall's particular hatred toward Jefferson nourished these convictions. The two turned on each other the special venom they reserved for the defilers of their native soil. Marshall's Federalism forever polluted the purity of Jefferson's beloved Virginia; Jefferson's Republicanism banished Marshall to the corners of his cherished homeland.

If Jefferson won the battle for Virginia, his enmity brought inestimable benefits to Marshall's career as chief justice. He inherited a Court that the federalists had initially assigned a rather low priority. Although such early justices as James Wilson, John Jay, and Samuel Chase had issued grandly centralizing decisions, neither gentry party paid much attention until the Sedition Act, when the national judiciary suddenly emerged as a strong arm of Federalist order. In 1801, it stood high but exposed, a vulnerable salient whose authority could have been neutralized by a little legislative pruning and a lot of Republican indifference. Jefferson and his allies, however, mismanaged both strategies, fumbling awkwardly toward a new judiciary act in 1802 and flattering the Supreme Court with a bitter, ineffectual attack through the impeachment process.

"It appears to me," William Branch Giles wrote Jefferson at his inauguration, "that the only check upon the Judiciary system as it is now organized and filled, is the removal of all its executive officers indiscriminately."[14] Originally Court appointments for life had rested, in Madison's explanation, on the "well-founded maxim, that . . . the smaller the power, the more safely may its duration be protracted." When the judges arrogated the right to impose Federalist doctrine on the people, Republicans turned to the other half of Madison's maxim—"the greater the power is, the shorter ought to be its duration"—and sought to oust the usurpers.[15] Hence the Republican leadership embarked on what it thought would be a sequence of impeachment trials to convict overweening Federalists of "high crimes and misdemeanors." Their failure to net more than one minor judge came not from the weakness of their constitutional logic, which followed standard 18th-century principles, but from the slowness of their gentry pace, which allowed almost all of Jefferson's first term to elapse before their first target on the Supreme Court, Samuel Chase, stood trial. By then, the republic had suffered no peril from several more years of a Federalist judiciary, partisan loyalties had softened, and new sources of support for the Court had developed in the states.

These latest allies rallied during the first years of the 19th century in response to wholesale assaults on lawyers, the common law, and the state judiciary. A popular antipathy to lawyers long predated the American Revolution. Shays' rebels drew on this tradition, and so did William Plumer's father, who, when his son chose the law, tried to bribe him into an honest profession. Lawyers in this scheme of things were practitioners of the black arts whose "dark, intricate, antiquated formalities" and "obsolete phraseology" robbed the people of their money and their rights.[16] At first these popular sentiments crossed the party lines of the 1790s, infecting backcountry Federalists and Republicans alike in such states as Massachusetts, New York, and Pennsylvania. They became partisan issues only in the late nineties, when the Federalist judiciary rested its new claims to power on the nationwide applicability of British common law—"the glorious birthright of every American," in the ominous boast of Chief Justice Francis Dana of Massachusetts.[17] That turned the dark mysteries of the law into an issue of freedom from Anglomonarchic rule, and Republicans made it a dogma of national independence.

Growing Republican majorities after 1801 did not, however, doom the common law. In most states the attacks on British precedent merged with other battles over court jurisdiction and judicial autonomy, and together these assaults challenged the traditional elite privileges of most Republican and Federalist leaders interchangeably. Even in the case of the common law, a Jeffersonian gentry sponsored it in Kentucky's first constitution, and Republican votes protected its authority in the Northwest Territory after 1801. As Republicans at the top of their state hierarchies strained credibility with their claim that the common law had grown Americanized and therefore free from British control, they joined bipartisan blocs of privilege to defeat all except a few cosmetic changes in the state legal systems. In fact, defending the judiciary from men of lesser wealth, education, and prestige cemented some of the firmest quiddish alliances in the early years of the 19th century. With a sharpened consciousness of their interests, these quids provided the Senate votes necessary to acquit Justice Samuel Chase, eliminate the possibility of future trials, and leave the national judiciary with the Jeffersonian gift of a markedly increased stature.

Marshall made the most of his new opportunities because he had a plan and he bided his time. Although the Republican triumph destroyed the Federalist dream of a national hierarchy capped by the president, Marshall saw in the Constitution itself an alternative source of national order. After all, it had originated as the superstructure for a national society, and if the Court could lay exclusive claim to its interpretation, a just society might yet materialize inside it, with the chief justice instead of the chief executive as its first character. Marshall knew precisely where the enemy camped: at the base of the vertical axis where Madison's Virginia Report, the holy writ of the Republicans, assigned the ultimate power to define the limits of the federal compact. In his own mind the chief justice was equally clear about the enemy's objective: a Jacobinical attack on property rights and hence on all public order. Marshall's strategy followed logically from his premises: subordinate the states, secure property rights, and spread the Constitution as a protective cover over the entire republic.

After lying low for a decade, Marshall struck out on his quest. In *Fletcher* v. *Peck* (1810) and *Dartmouth College* v. *Woodward* (1819), he gave the most dangerous of the democratic agencies, the state legislature, one chance and one chance only to dispense a particular property right to its citizens. After that, the bargain was inviolate—in the case of an open-ended corporate charter, it endured forever "like one immortal being." In *Sturges* v. *Crowninshield* (1819), Marshall placed private contract rights beyond the legislature's reach. Like the corporation, a debtor's liability extended into eternity. Through his colleague Joseph Story in *Martin* v. *Hunter's Lessee* (1816) and personally in *McCulloch* v. *Maryland* (1819), the chief justice elevated the centralizers' most extreme—and erroneous—construction of the constitutional compact into the law of the land: it had derived exclusively from the whole people, in no way from the states. If Jefferson thought the revolution of 1800 had securely planted the Republicans' vertical pole, the Federalist Marshall now yanked it up from its base. To his free-floating Constitution, Marshall then imputed the characteristics appropriate to a transcendent sovereignty. *Cohens* v. *Virginia* (1821), in combination with *Marbury* v. *Madison* (1803), declared the Constitution "permanent." Together with *McCulloch* v. *Maryland*, the *Cohens* decision made the Constitution the overarching law of "one great empire" and endowed it with whatever powers it required to fulfill its purposes. In these two cases—the climax of his campaign—he pinioned the state legislatures and their defenders in the state judiciary to those inferior places in a national hierarchy that the Court would define for them.

Only his gentry adversaries with memories as deep into the 18th century as Marshall's understood exactly what the chief justice was doing. In Virginia, Spencer Roane and John Taylor could set the Federalist Marshall of 1821 against the federalist Marshall of 1788 who had issued such honeyed assurances of a limited national judiciary and a large state sovereignty. Along with Jefferson they recognized the paraphrase of Hamilton's arguments for the first Bank of the United States in Marshall's decision in *McCulloch* v. *Maryland* upholding the second. They remembered him as the leading instigator behind the XYZ crisis, and they knew him as a Tory to that day. As Marshall sought to reverse their revolution of 1800 and reimpose a "consolidated" government, they countered with a call for the "revival of the spirit and principles of 1799." Roane, branding Marshall's judicial assault far more dangerous than the Missouri controversy, defined the conflict in the fundamentals of the vertical axis: ". . . the liberties of the people will fall with the State governments."[18]

The chief justice, for his part, was just as immersed in the old battles. He had been battering away at Madison's Virginia Report since the *Marbury* decision in 1803, and his ultimate enemy remained the old Hamiltonian nemesis, "antifederalism." "The attack on the judiciary is in fact an attack upon the union," he informed Story. Roane and his ilk Marshall brushed aside as "minor gentry," mere lieutenants for the real commander, Jefferson, who "obviously approved & guided" the entire campaign against the Court.[19] There the Virginia enemies stood in Marshall's mind: first character against first character in a contest between opposing hierarchies. In this sense it belonged to the same battle of old men that swirled simultaneously around Missouri. King and Marshall versus Jefferson and Taylor: it might have been 1794—and in many ways for them it still was.

Marshall's authority, of course, relied on a much broader base of support. Eternal corporate rights surely pleased those who held them, and eternal debtor liability certainly gave creditors comfort as the economy was falling into a depression. Partisans of the Bank realized that Marshall at least as much as Langdon Cheves had saved it at the nadir of 1819. In general, Marshall's undying struggle against the Jacobins sounded remarkably contemporary to the opponents of a new assertive democracy in the early 1820s. Yet Marshall's limitations became more and more evident even in these circles. The stark, unyielding quality of the old Federalist's Euclidian proofs at law formed a box of truths, where an evolving 19th-century enterprise required flexibility. In an age of state dominance, too heavy a hand on its legislature would pall development. Land speculators as well as ordinary farmers, respectable merchants as well as shop mechanics, went bankrupt in a chancy economy. Nothing in Marshall's 18th-century background prepared him to understand corporate procedures in a promotional era. How a corporation functioned did not matter in the *Dartmouth College* case; only the sanctity of property did. Why the Bank needed its branches was equally irrelevant to *McCulloch;* only the constitutional authority to maintain them counted. The proliferation of various currencies to serve an expanding commerce deeply disturbed Marshall. In 1827, when the Court endowed corporate officials with broad discretionary powers, the skeptical chief justice dissented. That year, he also issued his only dissent in a constitutional case to protest the majority's liberalization of bankruptcy law. Although the legislature still could not tamper with past debts, it could now set formulas to adjust future ones.

What saved the chief justice from sliding into obsolescence was his remarkable collaboration with Joseph Story, a gregarious Massachusetts quid who joined the Court in 1811, quickly became Marshall's junior partner, and during his own long tenure bridged the gap between the Virginian's 18th-century obsessions and the development ambitions of the early 19th. No laying on of hands between a gentry mentor and his successor occurred more smoothly or proved more significant. As conservative as Marshall, Story had a deeper knowledge of the law and a much richer acquaintance with contemporary business. Deferring to his senior when he could and differing as a loyal colleague when he could not, Story served as an intermediary both between the chief justice and other justices and between the old Virginia gentleman and such new national leaders as Story's friends Webster and Biddle, always in a manner that preserved inviolate Marshall's standing as the Court's first character. It was Story, the sometime bank president and enthusiast for commercial expansion, who led the way in adapting American law to greater leniency for developers in damage suits, wider rights in the uses of their property, broader freedom in corporate management, and easier escape through bankruptcy proceedings. As Marshall's power dwindled, Story was spreading the word across the nation. Beginning in 1832, Story published a set of massive *Commentaries* on various subdivisions of the law, an encyclopedia of privilege-protecting jurisprudence that supplied a common reference for elite lawyers and responsive judges everywhere. In particular, his *Commentaries on Equity Jurisprudence*—the last resort from an otherwise unresponsive body of law—built into 19th-century procedures a critically flexible resource for thriving business enterprise.

In only one area did the old Virginian's caution keep the Constitution more adaptable and more acceptable to elite interests than Story would have made it. Unlike the adamant centralizers from James Wilson to Daniel Webster, Marshall always retained a strong concern for state power and never welcomed the prospect of a consolidated nation. As he propounded the sweeping authority of the national government, he continued to reiterate the distinctive rights of the states—"for some purposes sovereign, for some purposes subordinate," he noted at the height of his nationalism in *Cohens* v. *Virginia*. Even in reaction to the South Carolina Nullifiers whom he despised, he emphasized the same principle: "In fact, we have always been united in some respects, separate in others. We have acted as one people for some purposes, as distinct societies for others."[20]

Slavery lay at the heart of this seemingly odd element of moderation. A distinguishably southern Federalist, Marshall remained alert throughout his public life to the peculiar needs of the peculiar institution, and he resisted any national encroachment that might threaten his region's stake in its human property. The most dramatic concentration of his nationalizing decisions appeared early in 1819 just as the storm broke over Missouri, and the juxtaposition of the two strained Marshall's contrary impulses to their limit. Publicly he denied the right of special state interests to alter uniform national rules. Privately he gave very high priority to the reelection of Monroe, his inveterate constitutional enemy, for fear, an associate reported, "that the non-slaveholding States might determine to place no man in the chair who would object to the [most sweeping antislavery] restrictions."[21] Later, in an effort to ward off further antislavery attacks, he warned an old northern associate that the "Southern States . . . view with immovable prejudice & dislike everything which may tend to diminish [slavery]."[22]

Virginians as diverse as Madison, John Randolph, and Marshall understood that the most dangerous weapon in the hands of unsympathetic northern centralizers was the Constitution's commerce clause, which the forthright Madison acknowledged gave "Congress [the] power to prohibit the internal slave trade" and which might also be used to free slaves as they crossed state boundaries.[23] Use that power, Randolph exclaimed, and you "blow up the Constitution in ruins."[24] As chief justice, Marshall could not avoid the dilemma of the commerce clause, but as a Virginian he did his best to evade its consequences. When *Gibbons* v. *Ogden* (1824) offered him the ideal opportunity to establish a blanket national authority through that clause, Marshall seized it in principle, then relinquished as much as he could in practice. Yes, he declared, the Constitution invested Congress with exclusive powers over interstate as well as international commerce. No, he decided, he would not actually apply this rule to the canals and steamboats of domestic trade. Looking southward, he chose instead to eliminate state restrictions on America's interior commerce with a tortured use of national rights at sea. Story, whose aversion to slavery raised precisely the danger Marshall feared, was deeply disappointed. Five years later the chief justice carefully distinguished the national nature of interstate commerce from the "police" powers of the states, a particularly useful term in a slaveholding society. For the benefit of that society Marshall maintained an ambiguous tension to the end of his life. By then he probably shared as much constitutional ground with Madison as with the younger breed of centralizers. Fittingly, after long conversations with those two aging constitutional giants in 1835, Harriet Martineau reported "their hearty admiration of each other."[25]

Together, in other words, Marshall and Story designed a comprehensive framework of American law for a divided society in an age of development. By making the Constitution a national bulwark for vested property rights and spreading the message among the elites who held those rights, they created a nationwide network of state and local strength to implement their comprehensive law. Without such support the Court could have achieved very little. Unlike the European nations that were also seeking cohesion through the law, the United States had no administrative hub radiating approximately uniform rules of procedure and enforcement. Especially across the mountains, national judiciary officers manned their isolated outposts with scarcely any assistance from Washington. There, as the Ohio legislature quite reasonably declared in its challenge to *McCulloch* v. *Maryland*, if the state chose to ignore the Bank, it could not conduct even a minimum business—whatever the Court said about its constitutionality. The Bank's Savannah branch, in fact, was withering under just such treatment from the Georgia government. To succeed, therefore, this venture in a comprehensive law relied on the very jurisdictions that, in theory, the Supreme Court was disparaging, and it was the genius of Marshall and Story to turn that apparent contradiction into a functioning system. At the same time, of course, a good many people of solid local standing with development ambitions of their own saw Marshall's eternal corporations as infernal monopolies and Story's dense legal prose as monopoly's barricade. Stretching from east to west, this elastic legal cover would only carry authority in the long run for those who had access to it.

For Clay and Adams, Biddle and Webster, Marshall and Story, these comprehensive programs were ultimately moral matters, visions of a virtuous society that they set about implementing in competition with threatening forces of evil. In both impulse and logic, therefore, they came from the same general sources as the church-based ventures in national comprehensiveness that also flourished during the 1820s. The organizers of these religious enterprises were the national quids of American Protestantism, evangelical promoters who broke across the constraining lines of denominational exclusiveness and collaborated to impose cohesion on a growing, sprawling country. Here too the emphasis rested on harnessing the west to the east, with a conscious muting of differences dividing north from south. Imaginative enough to devise new policies for their purposes yet conservative enough to demand national integration on their own terms, they sought to modify the traditional hierarchy so that it could accommodate but still contain an expanding nation.

In 1801, at almost the same time that the political quids were emerging, Presbyterians and Congregationalists in the north—nicknamed "Presbygationists"—prepared a Plan of Union to cooperate in spreading the faith westward. It took time, however, before these urges for development translated into an effective program. The natural scope of church control was local, and the initial response to changing values in a mobile society was to concentrate on order at home. During the second decade of the 19th century, new ordinances to preserve the Sabbath, laws to suppress gambling, campaigns to banish transients, and the like dotted New England and New York. Most of the interdenominational activities that did materialize sent missionaries to the poor citizens of the cities, distributed Protestant literature among them, and organized Sunday schools for their children. Yet these stiff local hierarchies were beginning to loosen as the sons and daughters of the moral monitors themselves embarked in quantity for the west. Much as Rufus King stretched the scope of his concern during the postwar years to cover his migrating son, so parents everywhere in the northeast came to acquire a different perspective on the barbaric west. In a speech to just such people, "On the Importance of Assisting Young Men," the rising Presbygationist light Lyman Beecher looked westward in 1815 and declared: "The integrity of the Union demands exertions to produce in the nation a more homogeneous character, and bind us together with . . . habits and institutions of homogeneous influence."[26] From this perspective it now mattered very much, for example, that an increase in western whiskey production was flooding the market with cheap liquor and threatening to make drunkards of all comers.

As these evangelical concerns deepened, leadership passed from older men who exhorted to younger men who acted. In the 18th century the best that locally bound eastern Protestants could devise for the wild west was an export of virtuous forms, such as the quixotic legal codes of 1788 and 1790 that banned drunkenness, profanity, gambling, and Sabbathbreaking throughout the Northwest Territory. In something of that same spirit the Connecticut general assembly of 1816 commissioned a plea to the state's emigrants to keep their virtue and faith wherever they might go. Yet some in the older generation were also issuing pleas for a religion of good works, one that softened the doctrinal code of salvation and urged young people to seek God through an extensive benevolence. Timothy Dwight, three years older than John Marshall and president of Yale from 1795 to 1817, exemplified those gentry tutors, and Lyman Beecher, four years older than Joseph Story, belonged to the group of apprentices who converted their message into programs for a growing nation. The younger men never slackened their attention to local control. Many years later the Frenchman Michel Chevalier would find nothing "more melancholy than the seventh day in this country; after such a Sunday, the labour of Monday is a delightful pastime."[27] In addition, however, they projected that same vision of a systematic morality across the nation. Now they included the entire "young west" among their dependents.

The hallmark of these activists was organization, broadly interdenominational, largely indifferent to theological doctrine, and always

"American" to convey their comprehensive purpose: the American Tract Society, the American Temperance Society, the American Sunday School Union, the American Bible Society, the American Home Mission Society, and a host of lesser ones. Together they composed what came to be known as the Benevolent Empire, and by the early twenties their common focus fell on the stream of settlers into the west—that is, everyone beyond the Appalachians. Ingeniously, they adapted their centralizing purposes to a decentralized country by recruiting countless local groups and individuals, leaving local finances as much as possible to them, yet establishing a single, concrete goal to unify their activities—a minister in every community, a Bible in every home, a religious message in every hand. They felt none of the repulsion of Timothy Dwight's generation for the flood of cheap publications that broke the old ministers' monopoly on communication at home. The new promoters simply turned the Devil's weapon to the service of the Lord, duplicating and distributing millions of their own Protestant exports for the same market.

Like the parallel ventures in comprehensiveness, the Benevolent Empire shaped its activities to the spreading revolution in commerce and relied on an expanding web of vested interests for its strength. Prosperous merchants funded its enterprises. Organizational managers, operating much like the cashier of a bank or the chief clerk of a commercial house, oversaw the business of moral reform at the home office, and field agents, functioning much like jobbers, followed the main arteries of interior trade to peddle their pamphlets and Bibles. Along the route prominent local firms often served as depots for distribution. Appropriately, New York City, the dominant channel for American commerce, became imperial headquarters. There and in the field the various organizations cooperated with one another to blanket the nation with virtue. The most impressive of the lot, the American Tract Society, stretched its reach across the south and past the Mississippi River through about 100 "Depositories," each with its own manager, budget, and subsidiary agents, that were distributing close to a million pamphlets a year by 1825. At the same time, like the long chains of commercial credit, the Tract Society's network depended on innumerable small links of personal trust. "Many of the Tracts, I distributed with my own hands," one agent reported; "but by far the greater part, I sent for distribution into various places in the southern and western states; confiding them to faithful and judicious men, with whom, for the most part, I am personally acquainted."[28]

"We want a NATIONAL SOCIETY," cried the founders of the American Home Mission Society.[29] Despite its array of affiliates in the south and west, however, the Benevolent Empire remained fundamentally a northeastern enterprise. During one five-day span in 1834, 22 of its societies held conventions in New York City. Like their counterparts in Washington and Philadelphia, the imperial leaders looked westward from that perspective, serving those "destitute regions" in eastern board meetings, writing messages in eastern studies, and training field agents and missionary ministers in eastern schools and seminaries. Westerners who played their appointed role got a hearing. "The claims of the new states upon the old are the claims of children upon their parents," read the shrewd appeal of the New England migrants to Jacksonville, Illinois, in behalf of a new college. "They are sensible of their need, and now ask for aid. Let parental sympathy extend to them the means of education, and you secure their gratitude and affections forever—withhold these means and the children grow up in ignorance and alienation, and forget the institutions of their fathers, and cease to venerate their character and to cultivate their virtues."[30] Western innovators such as the revivalist Charles Finney, on the other hand, seemed dangerously disruptive. The imperial directors sought converts, not colleagues, across the mountains. It was their hierarchy, and like the American System, the Bank, and the Supreme Court, the Benevolent Empire could never function if followers decided that they too should be leaders.

In 1825, as King died and Monroe sank abruptly from public life, each of the new comprehensive programs stood mobilized for action. The leaders of the American System ruled the executive, Biddle's policies spread the Bank's power south and west, Story began to adapt Marshall's Constitution for a developing economy, and Beecher prepared to add a militant American Temperance Society to the legions of the Benevolent Empire. The men in charge of these ventures ranked among the most creative of their time. Fighting off the reactionaries who wanted only to clutch the old ways and overcoming a nationwide inertia toward diffusion and fragmentation, they often moved ahead of the currents to channel them toward national unity. Clay's American System arrived before the revolution in steam power and the Erie Canal; Biddle's vision of uniform financial transactions preceded the richest developments of an interior trade; the Benevolent Empire's flood of religious literature anticipated by about a decade the new printing technology that would encourage so many others to copy its campaigning tactics. If these men did not sense the revolution in choices that was transforming their society, they at least participated in it with striking results.

In place of the gentry vision that integrated all of society within a single hierarchical structure, the new leaders took the dream of national unity and divided it into slices of economic, legal, and religious concern. Except for Marshall, none of these men saw himself at the pinnacle of an inclusive national order, and even the chief justice had to admit in 1832 that his comprehensive "union has been prolonged thus far by miracles."[31] Although mutual interests, common allies, and numerous friendships overlapped their boundaries at many points, each of the comprehensive programs had its own rationale and mission. No Hamiltonian would have tolerated the autonomous powers that Biddle gained for the Bank. But then no counterpart to revolutionary republicanism now spanned the breadth of American life. Neither Clay nor Adams felt a special affinity for Marshall's Court, and Story pursued his legal goals as if they had no relationship with parties and elections. Some of the benevolent imperialists found the workings of government downright offensive; Clay, for one, returned the compliment. Hence as these leaders operated in their little worlds—the same handful of lawyers arguing before the Court, the same directors encountering one another on the boards of the moral societies, the same wealthy cliques reinforcing Biddle's sense of virtue—they were doubly threatened with isolation: from one another's peculiar interests and from the nation at large. The initiative in national policy that they held in the late twenties depended in large measure on the willingness of everybody else to leave them alone.

The Jacksonian Resolution

When the assault on comprehensiveness did come, it gathered momentum until it eliminated all pretensions to central control and left Americans to find their way alone. That process originated during the very years when the comprehensive programs seemed destined for preeminence. Both the revolution in choices and the plans for national direction —the one with many scattered voices, the other with a few guiding ones—reached new levels of assertiveness simultaneously in the midtwenties, but at first only the comprehensive programs focused clearly on their objectives. Evidences of a mobilized competition for public leadership did not appear until the movement to elect Andrew Jackson president.

After the general's popular success in 1824 an array of tough-minded, state-rooted political leaders from New Hampshire to Louisiana lined up behind him and prepared the way for the first nationwide presidential contest between two candidates since 1800. This time, however, national candidates preceded national parties. Despite the use of "National Republican" to designate Adams' cause and "Republican" or "Democratic" to identify Jackson's, these were merely labels, not political organizations. The battle belonged to the states, whose political power was approaching its peak in 1828.

National issues did figure in the campaign, especially the tariff and transportation subsidies that accounted for Adams' primary sources of strength. Charges of "corrupt bargain" plagued the president, and charges of incompetence beset his challenger, who in bits and pieces had served a few undistinguished years in Congress. These accusations, in turn, were embellished with outrageous tales about the prim, penurious president's immorality and extravagance, and equally lurid attacks on Jackson's brutality in the bush. Nevertheless, the state politicians who were jealously guarding their domains passed each national issue through their own filters. If the American System suited their state politics, they praised the president's judiciousness and experience. If Jackson's personal popularity suited them better, they exalted the general's courage and purity. Accounts of a great political debauch during the Adams administration became a standardized way of rousing fears about too much activity in a capital city that still seemed very distant and alien to most Americans. Calhoun, who had rediscovered his roots in South Carolina, grandly elevated just such hostilities into an ideological slogan when he called the contest one "between *power* and *liberty*."[1] Shrewdly, Jackson's campaign concentrated on its cold, controversial opponent and avoided any commitment that could not be contradicted from locality to locality. What, if anything, the general really did favor, no one knew. Hence the architecture of Jackson's victory was a row of state blocks that neither disturbed the popular base beneath them nor revealed what might rise above them.

Those hardheaded sponsors who pictured the general as a paper dragon in a parade of state leaders showed much less insight than the opponents who feared him as a wild destroyer. Only a handful of gentlemen as old as Jackson himself understood the sources of this strange invader's drive. As the last of the presidents who had fought in the Revolutionary War and the first who came without gentry standing, he was twice removed from the circle of leaders who dominated national affairs before his election. Unlike Adams, who was also born in 1767, Jackson experienced the Revolution as an underaged soldier, suffered a wound and imprisonment, lost two brothers in the war, and cultivated those memories for a lifetime. Bringing a personal neocolonial passion to the politics of the 1790s, he voted in Congress to repudiate Washington's Farewell Address, cheered the prospect of England's destruction, and in 1815 took sweet revenge at New Orleans for his humiliations thirty-five years before. Jackson needed no revolutionary tutor to identify the Hartford Convention as a hotbed of "monarchists and traitors."[2]

Jackson, however, never had access to his party's inner councils. From middling origins in South Carolina, he struck west as a soldier of fortune to hack a place for himself in a land that welcomed fighters and tolerated schemers of all kinds. In his circle of parvenu plungers, adventurers, and filibusterers, Jackson scrambled well, and like any skillful, determined climber, he studied the terrain at the top with the intensity of someone who was pulling himself there a foot at a time. The code that the gentry internalized he memorized. If honor was sacred, he would repay every slight in whatever time and with whatever weapons it required. If character meant control, he would become an iron man of self-possession— paying the inevitable price, of course, in eruptive outbursts of fury. Gentlemen from the region of his birth named their estates and worked them with slaves. Jackson prized the Hermitage as the jewel of a fierce quest, and he no more questioned the legitimacy of slavery than the legitimacy of his title to former Indian land. Adopting the litany of Cincinnatus, he took particular care to sound it during his avid pursuit of the presidency: ". . . as you know the Hermitage is my delight, and my only ambition to dwell on it."[3] Gentry rhetoric was suffused with references to universal rules. "On the Tariff," he explained to a perplexed following in 1824, "I am Governed by principle alone. . . ," and so he would claim for each stand he took in public affairs.[4] Above all, Jackson rested his credentials for national leadership on the revolutionary generation's respect for military fame. No sane man dared criticize his predilection for military attire or call him anything other than "General."

When Jackson emerged as a presidential candidate, the surviving revolutionary gentry knew just what he was. He was their wilderness fighter, one of those far-flung agents who followed the rules of the jungle for the higher good of the republic. Recognizing Jackson's tactics as "violent & irregular, to say the least," the patrician Spencer Roane then added indulgently: "I could not forget that the old fellow 'had done the State some service,' nor that these enormities, were, perhaps, inseparable from that boldness of character which had made him so useful."[5] But, much as Madison privately encouraged the filibusters who seized West Florida from the Spanish in 1810 yet publicly dissociated his government from their action, gentry leaders expected these conquistadors and their dirty work to stay a world apart. Jackson no more suited their qualifications for a president than Cortez did their model of a philosopher king. A visitor to Monticello reported an "alarmed" Jefferson calling Jackson "one of the most unfit men, I know of for such a place . . . merely an able military chief . . . a *dangerous man.*"[6] The old Republican Gallatin condemned Jackson's movement as "monarchical." The old Federalist Marshall pictured him leading the "furious passions" of the age, and his fellow partisan King thought immediately of a military despotism. Jackson knew what they knew. The gentry class, he informed a friend in

1824, expect "to see me with a Tomahawk in one hand, and a scalping knife in the other. . . ." Unlike such apprenticing leaders as Webster and Calhoun, the general sought no benediction from the venerable fathers. He would take the office. *"You must risque to win,"* he counseled his ward, Andrew Jackson Donelson.[7] Appropriately, Jackson's hero from an earlier era was the greatest military climber of them all, Napoleon Bonaparte.

In two ways Jackson's singular route to the White House freed him for the tasks ahead. First, a cunning man on the rise learned to create and dissolve his alliances easily. Like the chief of a military junto, he did not check backgrounds or discriminate against idiosyncrasies; he required only absolute loyalty. Hence he could accept the perpetual flux of his supporting coalitions and advising associates and extract the greatest benefit from them. Second, his struggle against the grain of the gentry hierarchy made him an alert and implacable enemy of gentlemanly privilege in all forms. Among the candidates in 1824, he alone recognized that "nomination by a congressional caucus would dam politically any man it might name."[8] As president he declared the government's offices open to any citizen of elementary talent not because he wanted to demean these posts—his appointments matched previous standards—but because the memory of losing to someone with a gentleman's credentials still burned inside him. Just as Marshall's ancient battle against the Jacobins had a modern sound to the vested interests of the twenties, so Jackson's old fight against gentry exclusiveness had a contemporary ring to the far more numerous advocates of a democratized opportunity. Climbers were never levelers. The general and his ambitious followers shared a religious devotion to their own accumulations of property. But no climber would tolerate a message from on high that he was going too far too fast. From a dead past, in other words, Jackson acquired a remarkably lively sympathy for America's rampaging new revolution in choices, a perspective in striking contrast to the coastal provincialism of the national quids.

The jumble of interests that had collected behind Jackson's candidacy came to Washington in 1829 with a jumble of inclinations but no policy, not even a concerted desire to undo the American System. Schooled in a state politics of advantage, their strongest habits told them to take something and carry it home. The president, with no plan of his own beyond an urge to purify the government, concentrated on setting his house in order, and he went about it not like a gentry first character but like a junto chieftain. His great obsession was the social acceptance of Peggy Eaton, a tavernkeeper's daughter who married his secretary of war and suffered slanders in genteel circles similar to those that Jackson's own wife, Rachel, had faced before her death in 1828. But Jackson himself, not Peggy Eaton, stood at the center of this prolonged and seemingly peripheral struggle over a shady lady's reputation. His demand for an obligatory courtesy to her became a test of personal obedience to his command. As he repeatedly insisted, an attack on her was an attack on him, and no one—not even the intimates in his own household—who denied fealty to the general could serve faithfully in his administration.

It was the distinct misfortune of the national quids to understand this apparently formless mulling and squabbling so poorly. To the keepers of a comprehensive union everything about the Jacksonian crowd marked them as untutored, and the veterans in national affairs moved confidently to instruct them. Inside the administration, Vice-President Calhoun saw only Van Buren, the kind of man he could recognize as an authentic competitor, standing between him and a prime minister's role beside the old general. In Congress, Clay, the master parliamentarian and imperious commander, assumed that he could lay the authority of his reputation and experience over the band of newcomers. From Philadelphia, Biddle traveled to the White House and left convinced that this westerner could be taught the principles of national finance. Webster, who considered the president a "novelty," would eventually toy with the possibility of harnessing Jackson to his own national aspirations.

None of them realized that the vacuum in leadership existed only in their imagination, that none of the new arrivals, beginning with the president, felt any need for an established elite's mediation because they felt no need to govern in the elite style. Veterans in their own right, they expected to conduct national affairs as they had their state affairs. Instead, the overweening efforts to solve an imaginary problem created a real one for Jackson. Where the general construed issues as personal challenges, he wrestled them indefatigably for his honor. The more he saw them as the affronts of patronizing superiors, the more passion and skill he brought to the battle. Fueled by his hates, he was a canny, relentless antagonist, far more than a match for Calhoun or Clay or Biddle. Fighting Jackson made them angry, impatient, precipitate. Jackson knew the breed, waited for the mistake, then skewered the opponent on his own pike of pride. The stakes in these encounters ran high, for through them came the sharpened definitions of national policy.

Politically, the crucial confrontation pitted Jackson's administration against Biddle's Bank. In a society where credit determined opportunity, the nation's most powerful bank could not avoid becoming a political issue. The particular form of the issue, however, emerged from the interaction between the two leaders, each demanding a proprietary right over his domain and each certain that he alone protected the paramount interests of the United States. Biddle took the initiative. Although the Bank did not require another charter until 1836, its proud president wanted an early reaffirmation, and he probed for the new president's inclinations. Jackson hid them in a mist of cryptic compliments and muted threats as Biddle, through his many Washington connections, gathered advice: shrewd from insiders who watched the combative president at close range, bad from outsiders of Biddle's own persuasion who reported the latest rumors about the particular men controlling the backwoodsman's mind. Because the bad advice was more congenial, Biddle chose it and pressed for recharter in 1832, an election year. Times were flush, with land booms in the west and farm prices strong, and in respectable business circles the reputation of the Bank stood at its zenith. An institution embodying right reason and impartial virtue, Biddle believed, simply had to prevail. Clay, Jackson's opponent in the coming election, made recharter his cause, a full complement of national quids—Webster, Calhoun, Adams, Story—endorsed it, and the bill glided through Congress.

The president watched these self-assured patricians file into the narrow pass, then struck. Taking the counsel he wanted, he issued a veto message of total war on the Bank as an alien, irresponsible monster of monopoly. Jackson, the outsider who designed all of his major state papers "so that the people may fully understand" them, encouraged his draftsmen to attack the exposed nerves in a society of popular choices and unfathomable chances.[9] Where should the terms of opportunity be set? Never, Americans agreed, beyond the range of their own control. Yet the sources of credit for most of them, the veto message declared, only "exist by [the Bank's] forbearance." What part should the government play in setting those terms? Ideally it should "shower its favors alike on the high and the low . . . but when the laws undertake to . . . grant titles, gratuities, and exclusive privileges, to make the rich richer and the potent more powerful, the humble members of society—the farmers, mechanics, and laborers—who have neither the time nor the means of securing like favors to themselves, have a right to complain of the injustice of their Government." And the larger consequences of such favoritism? Here the old partisan from the 1790s spoke for himself: "Should [banking power] become so concentered, as it may under the operation of such an act as this, in the hands of a self-elected directory whose interests are identified with those of the foreign stockholders, will there not be cause to tremble for the purity of our elections in peace and for the independence of our country in war?"[10] Biddle called it "a manifesto of anarchy," and well he might have in light of the popular response.[11] Where little evidence of a focused hostility to the Bank existed before the veto message, that document now raised vengeful public cries as it spread across the country. The Bank's friends still commanded a majority in Washington. Jackson, however, relied on his strength in the states, and there the votes lay. He won reelection handily.

The Bank's one chance of survival was to lull the concerns that the Jacksonians had just roused. To flex the Bank's muscles and fatten its reserves, however, Biddle chose to increase its hoard of scarce specie by 50% between 1833 and 1834, dramatically shrank the national base of credit, and demonstrated in the midst of boom times precisely what people had to dread from an external power. Not many transactions dealt in hard money, but without some specie to settle distant accounts, not many transactions of any sort could occur. Whether citizens defined their range of affairs in local, state, or regional terms, thousands of converts could now see the vivid outlines of that monster in Philadelphia. The Bank's contraction simply fed the wellsprings of fear about omnipotence and conspiracy that the veto message had tapped and that once flowing proved impossible to check. The Jacksonians could have asked for no better cooperation. In 1834 the president on his own authority withdrew the government's deposits from the Bank, an act as controversial as the veto but again one that the steely Jackson, prepared to kill or be killed, was able to sustain. Two years later the Bank as a comprehensive, national institution died with its charter.

Wherever Jackson could focus on an individual, he drove himself with that same tenacity toward his objective. Fighting Clay, whom he somehow linked with Burr as "traitors to their country," always worked like an elixir on him, and battling Calhoun came to have a similar effect. The primary beneficiary of the general's vendetta against Vice-President Calhoun was Van Buren, the only prominent national quid with the wit not to instruct Jackson.[12] Early in 1832 when the South Carolinian broke a tie in the Senate to defeat Van Buren's nomination as minister to Great Britain, Jackson took a characteristically personal revenge "by placing Van Buren in the chair, that give the casting vote for his rejection."[13] As the new vice-president, the unwaveringly loyal New Yorker then received his chief's blessings for the presidency.

Without personal combat to direct his energies, however, Jackson became erratic or indifferent. Although the drift was clearly running against the American System and the president hurried it with a veto on funds for a Kentucky road, he continued to tolerate a good deal of congressional support for internal improvements. On the one hand, Jackson's inclinations led him to transfer responsibility to the states, as he did by shifting the government's funds from the Bank to various state banks. On the other hand, his fears of a corrupting central government, rooted in an old anti-Hamiltonian republicanism, led him to veto a bill that would have distributed surplus national revenues to the state governments. A similar passion for purity lay behind his stunning order in 1836 to receive only specie as payment for government obligations. Not only did the Specie Circular undercut the more liberal land law from Jackson's first administration; it sucked hard money from the very people who had hated the Bank for draining their precious reserves. Finally, it was the enemy Clay, not the Jacksonians, who arranged the compromise tariff law of 1833, setting year-to-year schedules for a gradual reduction of duties. The president had a vision of the national government "discharging unfelt" its broad "superintending functions," but he was not the kind of leader to translate vision into policy.

Only after Jackson left office did the drive against comprehensiveness acquire direction, then systematically sweep the field during the next decade. Even Biddle's Bank, operating under a Pennsylvania charter, made one more effort to regain its national power before it finally expired in 1841. Fresh leaders with a keener sense for policy added considerably to this purposeful campaign against comprehensiveness, and so did the spur of hard times that began with the Panic of 1837 and hung on until the mid-forties. Above all, however, it was the spreading, cumulative effects of a democratic revolution that pressured the leaders, powered the drive, and eventually obliterated the eastern centers of control.

The American System, even at its peak of importance under Adams, had never been a model of centralized direction. Dickering groups jerry-built the tariff laws, state factions shaped the national legislation to aid transportation enterprises, and local standards dictated the administration of the land laws. Before Jackson's election, Clay already sensed these forces sufficiently to soften the centralizing tone of his program and incorporate both a greater latitude for state discretion and a wider margin for congressional compromise. In this sense the pulling and hauling over tariff, land, and transportation policies during Jackson's tenure simply continued a trend. Against this background, Van Buren's inauguration in 1837 marked a significant turn toward the conscientious neutralization of the national government and the calculated diffusion of its powers. Although the Little Magician was properly famous for his deftness in human relations—in the midst of the Bank War both Jackson and Biddle praised him—he harbored beneath this velvety surface a firm commitment to preserve the heritage of the founders. Far more than Jackson, Van Buren was Jefferson's self-conscious legatee, and as president he set out to adapt that heritage to the circumstances of the late thirties. Then after an interim, ineffectual administration by the opposition party, President James K. Polk, a Tennesseean as stubborn as Jackson and as dedicated as Van Buren to the national government's detachment, completed the new framework. By 1846, national funds sat in an isolated Independent Treasury, the flat, low Walker Tariff freed the American market to the streams of international commerce, and liberal land laws, no longer encumbered by the Specie Circular, opened the way to a popular expansion. As if to wrap up all loose ends, Washington abandoned the old National Road, the government's first grand gesture toward union through transportation, and parceled it among the various states it crossed. Scattered cries of resistance sounded a requiem over the bones of the American System.

No center of control slid more gracefully into its new subordinate role, or salvaged more authority as it did, than the Supreme Court. How it managed so well related partly to power, partly to policy. As the Court's enemies reminded it, the national judiciary could settle almost nothing without the cooperation of the states, and, as illustrated by Jackson's dismissal of a ruling to protect Cherokee rights against the state of Georgia, the Court also required cooperation in Washington. "The authority of the Supreme Court," Jackson inserted pointedly in his veto of the Bank charter, must rely on "the force of their reasoning."[14] Unlike the Bank's intrusive influence on the credit system, the Court's word alone did not necessarily affect anyone. The Bank fell; the Court survived intact.

The Court's majority did not, however. Death and retirement enabled the Jacksonians to alter its orientation and in 1836 give it a new chief justice, Roger B. Taney, who had earned Jackson's favor through conspicuous valor in the war against the Bank. In his style of leadership, Taney was thoroughly contemporary. Instead of seeking harmony beneath a first character, Taney presided like the chairman of a contentious committee. The Court now spoke with many voices expressing many interests, and its chief justice looked for working majorities, not a monolithic authority. These changes, along with less Olympian prose, muffled the magisterial boom of Marshall's Court and placed the justices in dialogue with other government bodies around the nation. The phantom of a Court-directed national hierarchy disappeared forever.

In one area of substance, Taney's Court also broke sharply with Marshall's. The new chief justice's first major decision, *Charles River Bridge v. Warren Bridge* (1837), reinstated the corporation's public purpose and allowed the state government to curb its privileges in light of a changing social interest. "While the rights of private property are sacredly guarded, we must not forget that the community also have rights . . . ," Taney declared with an eye to the bustle of innovations around him. "And in a country like ours, free, active, and enterprising, continually advancing in numbers and wealth; new channels of communication are daily found necessary, both for travel and trade. . . . A state ought never to be presumed to surrender this power . . . to promote the happiness and welfare of the community. . . ." Eleven years later a supplementary decision enabled the state to cancel obsolete charters and encourage those late-coming entrepreneurs whom Marshall's immortal monopolies had frustrated. Although Story and Webster found any dismissal of vested rights shocking, they had no reason to fear Taney's democracy. Like Story, Taney brought excellent quiddish credentials to the Court. An early advocate of corporate enterprises in Maryland, he moved in the stream of development politics during the twenties and joined Jackson's cabinet with no more of a leveling instinct than Story himself. In the drive to legitimize the latest commercial practices, Story now had an eager companion in his chief justice, and in tandem, Taney and Story invested the corporation with the legal rights of an individual in order to free its interstate activities, enlarged the procedural leeway of its directors, and certified the legality of those standard mercantile notes and bills that served as the currency of a nationwide commerce.

The difference between them lay in Taney's far more tender, circumspect approach to the rights of the states. When Story declared the existence of an overarching mercantile law in *Swift* v. *Tyson* (1842), Taney could accept it as a useful fiction. He had not wrecked the Bank to create chaos, and no one state could be allowed to clog the channels of a nationwide commerce. Nevertheless, the chief justice showed no desire to carve exclusive national domains in the grand tradition of Marshall and his apprentices. Jackson's ringing unionism in response to South Carolina nullification, for example, struck Taney as excessive. He much preferred soft accommodations with state authority, and he almost always carried a majority of the Court with him. Like Marshall, Taney displayed his greatest caution skirting the edges of the Constitution's commerce clause, potentially so lethal for slavery. In extending national power over the inland waterways, Taney also used the government's admiralty jurisdiction, not the commerce clause, as if the Ohio River were just a narrow variant of the high seas. Moreover, in a compromise to suit the new age, the Court certified concurrent national and state jurisdictions over commerce and implied a generous leaning toward the powers of the states. In sum, Taney's Court adapted to the prevailing currents. In an era of flourishing commercial capitalism, the Court ratified its rules and encouraged its growth. In an era of jealous state sovereignty, it diminished its supervisory authority and pacified all but the extreme advocates of states rights. By the mid-forties the Court sat modestly and securely in the new scheme of government.

For its zeal in the area of the Court's caution, the Benevolent Empire suffered a much more jagged decline. During the Jackson years, as the Court largely marked time, the moral imperialists increased the pace of their activities, and the most ambitious among them, led by the New York merchant Arthur Tappan, extended their scope as well. Driving directly at the issue that the Court evaded, Tappan and his allies sponsored a new American Anti-Slavery Society in 1833, subsidized abolitionist agents in the sensitive regions bordering the slave states, and even organized a massive mailing of abolitionist tracts into the south itself. From the outset the Benevolent Empire had stirred local resentment as rapidly as it grew. Now this resistance acquired not only a focus but also a powerful band of recruits wherever word about the antislavery society spread. Like Biddle's strategy for the Bank, Tappan's enterprise was verifying the worst accusations of the empire's enemies.

The consequences extended in two directions. First, the latest New York crusade inspired sharp, often violent confrontations in the field, blighting the empire's reputation in the slave states, disrupting its use of a commercial network, and generally identifying it with commotion rather than a new moral peace. Second, the intrusion of this controversial cause encouraged Protestant denominations to go their separate ways in missionary work. Support for the pioneering interdenominational societies came initially from a sense of confusion about methods for managing religious problems over a vast western territory. The more familiar the problems, the less critical these special organizations seemed. A denominational restlessness was increasing in the early thirties quite apart from the abolitionist issue. When the Presbyterian Church split north and south in 1837, the legitimacy of the entire northeastern program, not just its most radical component, divided the denomination's leaders. Hence the panic of that year and the depression following it provided an occasion as much as a cause for an abrupt narrowing of support, and with the return of prosperity in the mid-forties only a routinized version of the least controversial societies was still thriving. Otherwise each denomination devised its own evangelical program to seek its own goals. Serving the church replaced saving the nation. Like railroad builders with eyes solely on their own routes, the agents of religion headed west as Presbyterians or Congregationalists, not as representatives of Christian morality, and the empire's vision of comprehensiveness dissolved in the concrete pursuit of denominational growth.

Under normal circumstances some other structure of authority should have benefited from the collapse of these national programs. Yet by traditional standards each of the logical alternatives—the state governments, the constitutional union, the national political parties—showed signs of losing cohesiveness during the very years when it might have been filling the vacancies of power. In the 1840s everything seemed to decline all at once.

The most obvious candidates to profit from the fall of comprehensiveness were the states—the basic frameworks for economic development, the building blocks beneath Jackson's election, the customary repositories of American loyalty. Nevertheless, the same economic difficulties that hurried the decline of the Benevolent Empire also undercut the power of state governments. In good times, state legislatures, like other optimistic developers, accumulated debts in the expectation that their investments would always yield a maximum return. A contracting economy, especially after 1839, left most of them embarrassed for funds, and by 1842 nine states had ceased to pay interest on their bonds. In a number of cases, the states indebted themselves to support enterprises that private investors actually controlled. But in such mixed enterprise, too, the shortsightedness of the private sector became the sin of the public sector. That proposition applied with particular force to the state banks that crumbled in most of the defaulting states—Michigan, Mississippi, Florida, Illinois, Indiana, Arkansas, Louisiana—and several more as well. Any corporation chartered by the state carried the state's reputation, and countless citizens, still obliged to pay for the wreckage, came to see these state creations in the same light that had shone on Biddle's monster. The record usually sustained their charges, for state charters did, after all, legalize promotional playthings for a few insiders. How widely these sentiments spread became clear when the governor of South Carolina, as hidebound an elitist state as the union contained, declared in 1839: "All charters which confer exclusive privileges on certain persons intrench upon the equal rights of the rest of the Community."[15]

Antimonopoly always ran a fine line between multiplying the opportunities for corporate development and denying them altogether as special privileges. During the depression some militant Jacksonians tried to close these doors of opportunity, not open them wider, and where they prevailed, the restrictions on new incorporations grew exceedingly tight. By the mid-forties some states chartered no banks at all. Even a swing in the other direction to enact free incorporation laws diminished the importance of the state legislatures, for those laws stripped the government of its discretionary authority. When the economy revived and the pace of enterprise quickened again, state governments never regained their centralizing powers. Although some latecomers continued to finance transportation projects, most of the funds for the railroad craze came either from governments beneath the state level—cities, counties, towns —or from private sources beyond it, especially those British investors who would never in their lives buy another American state bond. The pulls of decentralization that such states as Pennsylvania, Ohio, and New York had neutralized at the peak of their little American systems now triumphed everywhere. "Exchanges of local advantage are the levers that move the whole commonwealth," a veteran of Pennsylvania politics declared for all of them.[16]

Simultaneously the general political authority of the state legislatures was slipping. In the heyday of state power, senators served as obedient ambassadors who felt obliged to vote on important matters as the legislatures instructed them or to resign immediately. At the time of a new senator's election it was common to acknowledge this binding power, as James Buchanan did in 1834, and thereby declare himself the voice of his state. Thomas Hart Benton, a fulminating enemy of the Bank, still assured the Missouri legislature that "if my state is for it, I shall not *frustrate* her will."[17] During the late 1830s, however, the ambassadorial scheme began to unravel. Political parties or even factions within the parties now demanded the primary allegiance of the state's officials, and as they won it, they placed senators in an impossible position. A shift in the legislature's party or factional balance at any time during his six-year term guaranteed voting instructions that would contradict a senator's partisan loyalties and, by the old rules, force his resignation. When states such as Tennessee and Virginia used these incompatible commandments to yank their senators out of Washington year after year, one loyalty or the other had to prevail. By the early 1840s the parties supplanted the legislatures, and the once taut leash to the state capital lay slack. In succeeding years, as constitutional revisions increased the autonomy of county and city governments, filled more offices by popular election, and specified less frequent legislative sessions, the state capitals increasingly became dots on a map of diffused power rather than magnetic cores for their jurisdictions.

The apparent beneficiary of the decline in state power was the union. Along with the sharpening 19th-century consciousness of geography came a hardened sense of the nation as a bounded whole, and the weaker its interior centers of power grew, the more this encompassing shell seemed the lone barrier to an endless scattering of pieces. Hence when South Carolina issued its Nullification Proclamation in 1832, denying the legality of the tariff law inside the state, Jackson's harsh response was the most uniformly popular action of his administration, and over the next fifteen years the glorification of the union reached an apogee. Like so many of Jackson's victories, this was essentially a personal one. For the eight years of his presidency it was his union to defend, and anyone who defied it defied him. He would march into Columbia and hang the rebels himself, Jackson fumed. Behind the Nullification Proclamation stood Calhoun, and like so many of his defeats, this was essentially a tactical one. To his knack for political blundering he carried the additional handicap of a home state peculiarly insulated from the currents that were changing American politics. There the nation's best-integrated elite held remarkably fast against a rising democracy. When all other states selected presidential electors by statewide popular vote,

South Carolina still refused. When all but one other state employed conventions to nominate candidates, South Carolina still refused.

Apart from these contingencies of personality and position, however, Jacksonians and Calhounites shared large areas of agreement about the nature of the union. Almost to a man they claimed the principles of 1798 as their heritage. Both camps drew a line between national and state sovereignties and showed a tender solicitude for state autonomy. "[The General Government's] true strength consists in leaving individuals and States as much as possible to themselves," the Bank veto message declared, "in making itself felt . . . not in binding the States more closely to the center, but in leaving each to move unobstructed in its proper orbit."[18] More formally, Calhoun wrote: "Our system then consists of two distinct, and independent governments. The general powers, delegated to the General Government are subject to its sole and separate control, and the States cannot without violating the constitutional compact interpose their authority to check or in any manner counter act its movements, so long, as they are confined to the proper sphere; so also the peculiar and local powers reserved to the States are subject to their exclusive control, nor can the General Government interfere in any manner with them without violating the Constitution."[19] Very few agreed with Calhoun that a protective tariff exceeded the constitutional powers of the national government, and even fewer showed any interest in his cumbersome scheme of redress: a state veto suspending application of the law until three-fourths of the states—the proportion necessary to change and hence to judge the Constitution—could pass on the dispute. Nevertheless, Calhoun himself considered the tariff merely the "occasion" and the danger of "consolidation" the true cause of the conflict. The Jacksonians, as enemies of comprehensiveness who repeatedly called the union a "Confederacy," were fighting the same threat, and Jackson's declaration that all branches of the government had equal rights to decide a constitutional dispute offered no more practical guidance than Calhoun's procedure. Both leaders, in other words, sincerely sought to preserve a decentralized union.

Their similarities stood out even more sharply in contrast to their profound differences with Madison, the man everyone honored as his constitutional guide, and those differences, in turn, marked the transformation of the union during the first third of the 19th century. Calhoun in particular thought that he was simply restating the principles "in Madison's famous report" to meet new problems, and, always the careful student, the South Carolinian wove its phrases into his own argument.[20] As he borrowed the master's language, however, he jettisoned its framework, stirring Madison to a public attack on state nullification. Only at its starting point could the venerable Virginian accept Calhoun's argument: yes, Madison agreed, the people had authorized the Constitution in state units, not as an undifferentiated whole. From that point the two diverged beyond recall, for Madison's Constitution created a stable, orderly national hierarchy. By ratifying the Constitution and establishing a new government, the people at the base of the hierarchy exchanged a portion of their sovereignty for a set of procedures, specifically the elections and amending process that the document detailed. These, in sum, regulated the activity of the vertical axis. To emphasize its integral role in a thoroughly national structure, Madison stressed the necessity for the people in the several states "to *co-operate*," never to strike at "will." A "diversity of independent decisions" by the state governments—nullification—would violate the Constitution's binding rules, "decompose the Union," and throw the people back on "the law of self-preservation" —"a natural not a *constitutional* Right." Dissolving a hierarchy represented the most solemn decision in gentry statesmanship: a revolution. Only the "failure of all these Constitutional resorts" and the most extraordinary accumulation of "usurpations and abuses" could justify the perils of a state of nature.[21]

Madison, seeking to preserve a nation's existence rather than exalt a state's rights, saw the crisis of the late 1790s as essentially counterrevolutionary, an attempt to undo everything that had been accomplished since 1776 and, in retrospect, an utterly aberrant moment in the long, triumphant emergence of the American republic. After 1800 he, like Marshall, treated the constitutional compact as sacred, a permanent set of arrangements to keep the nation whole. Fittingly, Marshall now cheered Madison's gentry rebuttal: "He is himself again. He avows the opinions of his best days. . . ."[22] But Calhounites and Jacksonians alike simply lacked the ability to grasp the revolutionary gentry's logic. Madison's moment of aberration became their norm. Instead of ordering relations in a hierarchy, they set the national and state governments, in the neat phrase of the democratic theorist Frederick Grimké, "side by side"—one here, one there—to debate and bargain over the boundary between them. Although Calhounites interpreted these exchanges in adversarial terms and Jacksonians in accommodating ones, both pictured a flattened union of distinct governmental realms that the Constitution girdled but no longer integrated. "Dual federalism," this relation came to be called. Without a hierarchy's interplay, Madison could see no union at all. "This idea of an absolute separation & independence between the Govt. of the U.S. and the State Govts as if they belonged to different nations" simply destroyed his generation's work.[23]

In the new, flattened conception of federalism, the vertical axis—the revolutionary gentry's most ingenious contribution to a national governing system—finally and forever collapsed; and as it did, it floated away on a sea of people that lapped indiscriminately at politics everywhere. From the gentry's distant reservoir of ultimate authority at the bottom of the national hierarchy, the people became an omnipresent mass who, it was claimed, had an immediate call on all public officials. Ideal leaders now had good ears, not independent minds. The weakening of the state centers, coupled with a rising presidential vote that increased three times faster than the total population between 1824 and 1840, dissolved the last vestige of a uniquely intimate link between the people and their local representatives. The New Yorker James K. Paulding, who thought of himself as a follower of pure Republicanism, managed in a single sentence to repudiate the entire Republican theory of a special democratic axis to the national government. The only clear expression of the people's will occurs "in the great national Election for President," Paulding wrote in his enthusiasm for Jackson and Van Buren, "and in my opinion the results will show, as on former occasions, that the voice of Congress, and the State Legislatures is not that of the People."[24]

How thoroughly an amorphous people dominated this latest version of the union was revealed in the dialectical process that created the new national parties, Democrats and Whigs. The dialectic began with the Jacksonian reaction against the Bank in particular and comprehensiveness generally. Between 1832 and 1836, as the Bank War ran its course, the passions of the battle drove those early Jackson men who favored some central controls into an agglomerate Whig opposition and gave the two camps a certain cast that they never completely lost. Substantial citizens who appreciated the containing goals of comprehensiveness and resisted a hurly-burly expansion gravitated toward the Whigs, leaving the most thoroughgoing enemies of privilege to the Democratic party. Whigs found their most natural home in the northeast; Democrats drew their greatest strength from the south and the west.

Politically, however, the parties emerged from the first round of the dialectic speaking a very similar language. Both directed their attacks against unregulated centers of power, both mobilized as the champions of the people's rights, and both promised to further the autonomy of the states. In 1836 the Whigs even allowed the states to pick their own assortment of presidential candidates. This common ground became the point of departure for a second round of the dialectic. Like the Jacksonians a few years before, the Whigs now capitalized on what they were against. Jackson, never shy about justifying any personal decision in the name of the people, left a record of autocratic acts that proved vulnerable in a climate hostile to centralized authority. Van Buren absorbed the consequences. Through the novel device of a national party convention Jackson rammed through Van Buren's nomination first as vice-president and then as the party's presidential candidate. No nomination could have roused more resentment in the south and the west. Like Madison for Jefferson, Van Buren already served as the lightning rod for Democratic anger that could not be directed at the party hero. Suspect as a regency manipulator in both Albany and Washington, the discreet, fastidious New Yorker lay exposed to a great burst of assaults on his secretive ways and aristocratic tastes.

These attacks were preliminary to the Whigs' wholesale popular challenge in 1840. At a nicely orchestrated national convention, Whig leaders avoided the appearance of dictation in any area—party candidates, party issues, party organization. Instead of a strong man with a long record like Clay, they ran William Henry Harrison, until recently a nobody who, like Jackson, had a reputation for killing Indians. No distracting program intruded into a campaign that sought solely to identify the party with the values and aspirations of ordinary citizens. This time the Democrats were unprepared. Van Buren and his party's veteran managers still assumed the right to present their chosen slate of candidates to the electorate, and issues still mattered to these carriers of the principles of '98. The hoopla of a vapid nationwide appeal affronted their beliefs in a rational political order and left them in confusion. But they too learned. Four years later the Democrats nominated a nonentity at a freestyle convention, promoted him with slogans in a noisy, popular campaign, and completed the second round of the dialectic by regaining the presidency.

The political synthesis of the early 1840s offered a scene curiously devoid of winners. The Harrison campaign, by gearing its appeal to the whole body of voters, marked a further decline in the authority of the states. For the first time a presidential election outpolled the contests for state offices. Yet the presidency itself was gutted of authority. If Jackson demeaned the office by pushing his unpopular favorite into it, the Whigs practically destroyed its significance by carting their aged bush fighter into the executive chair. Polk's brief success in forceful leadership represented a fluke of personality, not a shift in political values. It was the much-admired Silas Wright, not the much-hated Polk, who modeled the Democrats' conception of a chief executive as the neutral, decorative governor of New York. No other branch of the national government took charge. From the time that Clay in the Senate and Jackson in the White House battled one another in almost every area of foreign and domestic policy, warfare between these government units became chronic. The House, elected over a span of about fifteen months, rarely showed even the pretense of a national body as its members scrapped and scrambled for local advantage. Systematic programs tended to disrupt rather than unite parties. In the early forties when Clay tried to revive a thin version of the American System, he splintered the Whigs, and Polk did much the same to the Democrats as he completed the Jacksonian policy of government withdrawal. By the mid-forties Whigs and Democrats across the nation no longer differed clearly over such issues as transportation subsidies and banking policies, matters that a decade earlier had helped to divide them into recognizable camps. "We still know aged men," a bemused commentator wrote in 1840, "who firmly believe that all the federal party were identical with the Tories of the revolution, and others who associate their democratic opponents with the Jacobins of France."[25] The gentry's polarized parties with their exact sense of mission did seem quaint indeed in the nebulous world of Whigs and Democrats.

By the standards of the revolutionary gentry an entire society emerged formless in the mid-forties. As if the reel of history had been run backward, Americans dismantled the old structure down to its 18th-century foundations: the comprehensive programs of the 1820s, the hierarchical parties, the presidential first character, the vertical axis of an integrated national government, and hence back to the bare words of the Constitution itself. Citizens rarely needed to notice the national government. Almost none of its measures touched their lives. Even the momentous Bank War scarcely affected the operations of the economy. Hard times in 1837 came from external sources; survival during the depression depended on private arrangements; and a new ease in long-range transactions during the 1840s rested on a purely fortuitous increase in the supply of precious metals. As the Frenchman Michel Chevalier reported even while "King Andrew" reigned, ". . . there is no government here in the true [European] sense of the word; that is, no directing power." "The Federal government," echoed Tocqueville, "is . . . naturally so weak that, more than any other, it requires the free consent of the governed to enable it to exist."[26] Appropriately, life in Washington was a buzz of transients and seekers who treated it like an open port, an American Constantinople of political profiteering. To sharpen that image of a city without a country, officials in Washington developed no program for preserving their records comparable to the ones at state capitals.

The centrifugal whirl that left the national government in isolation spread its effects outward. State governments struggled against these same winds to protect their slipping authority. The major eastern cities, swelling grandly in population, dwindled as national nerve centers just as their European counterparts were drawing in more and more central powers. Even those changes that suggested a greater urban consolidation actually followed the currents of diffusion. During the 1830s and 1840s as city halls acquired increasing responsibility for services and safety, their capacity to rule declined with their expansion. Political clusters in their booming, sprawling wards and districts decided how portions of the city would, in fact, be governed. Behind these dispersals of urban power lay the acceptance of an open-ended grid in land development that allowed flocks of real estate speculators to set the pace and pattern of growth. At best, cities approximated their own federal system. At worst, city dwellers went their own ways. In such settings across the nation most politicians simply abandoned the pretense of mobilizing energies that no center could coordinate.

Yet it was a formlessness that worked. By the mid-forties the new synthesis enjoyed a remarkably bipartisan acceptance. Only a few diehards still mourned the Bank and the American System. Both parties fell into a routine of boisterous, predictable competition. A Constitution widely resented and tentatively adopted in 1788 now ringed a union that stretched westward beyond the most sanguine imagination at Philadelphia. Instead of the despotism that so many had predicted from an empire a fraction of this size, most white Americans enjoyed far better protection against tyranny than the gentry governments had ever provided. Without threats from abroad or teeth at home, the national government presided over a citizenry that boasted of its unique democracy to any European who would listen. A revolution in choices had triumphed nationwide, and whatever enabled America's apparent chaos to function lay somewhere inside this revolution, for the original gentry venture in a structured republicanism had evaporated with scarcely a trace.

Part Three

DEMOCRATIC SOCIETY

BY THE TIME that the comprehensive programs disintegrated, a new democratic society was already meeting the needs of America's curiously diffuse nation. The passing of the one and the arrival of the other occurred with so little conflict because they had so little contact. Comprehensiveness, drawing on an 18th-century heritage, assumed the existence of a nation, planned for the whole of it, and placed leaders in a strategic location to direct affairs everywhere. Americans of that persuasion relied as a matter of course on superstructures: a national administration, a centralized banking system, the Constitution, an enlarged version of the patriarchal church. The new democratic society, on the other hand, originated in family life, invested ultimate responsibility in individuals, and expected them to determine their own affairs. Any structures larger than the family extended its functions, reinforcing the obligations of individuals and enabling them to fulfill their destinies.

Along these two planes, in other words, two histories had been unfolding contemporaneously. In the 1820s, as the comprehensive programs mobilized to regulate America's growth, a democratic society was just beginning to form out of the revolution in choices. In private rather than in public, often too elusively to catch the observer's eye, the values of this revolution reshaped families, fanned outward as sons and daughters left home, and spread nationwide by the 1840s through an intricate weave of institutions that accepted the ceaseless dispersal of people as the American way. The authority that citizens refused to concentrate in an eastern leadership they distributed as they moved, spreading it so evenly and extensively that it covered the entire nation. Now space and authority joined in a natural partnership.

The particular timing of this society's arrival mattered as much as its particular qualities. Maturing just as the hardships of propertyless Americans were increasing, it doubled as a class barrier against democracy's outcasts: blacks, native Americans, immigrant Catholics, and the poor generally. Because this new society was already operating when a full-scale contest over slavery's expansion commenced in the late forties, it gave common national qualities to the sectional struggle that deepened in the next decade. Secession and civil war, rather than signaling an internal failure of America's democratic society or a strange deficiency

in its leadership or a wholesale collapse of its mechanisms, grew naturally out of the new order. Its protean institutions shaped themselves
rather easily for sectional conflict, and its values, common to southerners and northerners alike, motivated and then justified the steps that led
to war. Finally, the new society settled into place just as the potential for
industrial growth was heightening—a burst in iron production, an integration of railroad lines, a start toward an organized money market. Instead of reorienting American society toward an industrial revolution,
however, these economic activities slid into the grooves of a far-flung
commerce that had been so recently and firmly established, and a space-
spanning approach to growth continued to prevail well after the Civil
War. Only an appreciation of how long the new society was aborning and
how successfully it resolved the most bedeviling problems of freedom
and space from the early 19th century could explain how tenaciously
Americans in the late 19th century clung to it when they were finally
inundated by a tidal wave of industrial change.

13

Economy

After the War of 1812 a few proud optimists had envisaged their nation soaring past Great Britain during the next generation to become the world's industrial center. Around 1820 the United States did, in fact, contain the essential ingredients for an industrial revolution: a productive, freehold agriculture, a mobile, softly stratified population, an ambitious and reasonably well-educated citizenry, an expanding domestic market, and a public policy that neither inhibited enterprise nor drained resources into government pomp and military might. The distance from Europe's markets posed no insurmountable problem, as Britain's record in the Atlantic trade illustrated. Nor did America's late start, for by the early 19th century, technological changes allowed a newcomer to slip into competition whenever it was ready. But the lure of American space had drawn the patterns of growth elsewhere. Between the 1820s and the 1840s, a commercial economy that had been hugging a narrow coastal strip was converted to cover a continental empire. People, capital, information, and authority all diffused much too rapidly to mobilize and systematize. In this setting, a free and thriving agriculture, a mobile and ambitious citizenry, and a rich and growing domestic market actually eroded the possibility of an industrial revolution.

By contrast to the European models for progress in the early 19th century, the American economy had no core. As financial direction, technical information, and scientific exchange increasingly concentrated in London and Paris, Philadelphia and New York were losing what strength they had once had as America's nerve centers, and the nation's capitalist energies spun across space with less and less resistance each decade. The most pressing problems in British enterprise were intensive and integrative, those in American enterprise extensive and distributive. Where British capitalists were experimenting with better ways to combine and coordinate the elements in an industrial process, their American counterparts were stretching the range of commercial activities as far as they could possibly go. Every year the accent fell more sharply on horizontal networks rather than vertical structures.

Viewed nationally, the consequence was a crazy quilt of economic transactions. Most of them followed the stubby-fingered links of the interior roads, which continued to bear the heaviest burdens of American transportation. Around the cities more intricate webbings connected hinterlands to their hubs. Two curving vines of commerce hooked the ends from many of these myriad strands: one, following the Ohio and Mississippi rivers, extended from Pittsburgh to New Orleans; the other, tracing the coast, ran between New Orleans and Maine. A third line from New York City along the Great Lakes developed more gradually. Ten years after the completion of the Erie Canal, 80% of the tonnage it carried to the Atlantic still came from within its own state. By 1846 the volume from the western states finally exceeded New York's total. As these changes in the northwest illustrated, flows were constantly shifting, not only across the Appalachians but also within the eastern hinterlands and among the Atlantic ports, where a bustling intercity trade reminiscent of the years before 1815 began to thrive during the 1840s. In no sense, however, did this tangle of links and lines form a national pattern. A mercantilist mentality continued to prevail in state capitals, where governments used their powers to discriminate against the enterprises of neighboring states, and in cities, where other domestic centers were no less "foreign" than Liverpool or Le Havre. The initial burst of railroad construction only accentuated the decentralization by creating many short pieces under separate owners with different track gauges and incompatible equipment. The proliferation of banks, each a little bailiwick of its own insiders, had the same effect.

As the range of inland commerce broadened, the volume of business increasingly justified a national system of specialization, but decentralization and diversification still predominated. No matter how great the economic incentives, business firms chose to remain small and personal. Even cotton, the basis for America's biggest business, exemplified the standard process. At the growing end, successful factors who arranged the passage of cotton to market limited their portion of the business by maintaining simple partnerships and responding to the demands of their best customers like all-purpose businessmen. As the planter's sole channel to the marketplace, the factor supplied his credit and insurance, purchased his jewelry and hardware, organized his occasional visits to the city, and stood ready to profit from any other request he might make. Much the same applied at the weaving end. Jobbers who specialized in the sale of textiles often served as the local storekeeper's lifeline to the city and performed their own array of services in negotiating, purchasing, and shipping that bore no relation at all to cotton cloth. Specialization followed local or private rules of advantage. When the prospering Phelps, Dodge and Co. decided to discard its secondary activities and concentrate its business, it chose to export cotton—and import metals. Characteristically, it also bounded its growth by remaining a family-based firm. Layer upon layer of commercial styles, each a reasonable response to immediate circumstances, operated comfortably together in an economy of infinite adaptations. While one broker in the iron trade bought and sold, another bartered like a farmer at the county fair. Between 1845 and 1847, in the heyday of the steamboat, landings of the old-fashioned flatboats, which still carried about a third of the traffic on the western rivers, reached a new peak at New Orleans.

By a comparable logic of adaptation, almost every city, old or new, cast its economy to serve the needs of its commercial hinterland, and these parallel responses tended to replicate the same mixture of small-scale activities in each largely autonomous region: processing farm products and manufacturing for local markets, wholesaling and jobbing, financing and transporting. Within the cities, specialization often meant fragmentation. For example, the division of urban merchandising into specialized outlets, already well established in the east by the early 1820s, endured decade after decade despite the obvious inconveniences of such splintered purchasing because urban commerce continued to rely on a multiplication of personal, credit-linked connections between buyer and seller. Two cities deviated most noticeably from the general standard of diffusion: New York, the dock for over half of the nation's imports, and New Orleans, America's great cotton emporium. They, however, specialized as extensions of the British economic system. For the American economy they functioned primarily as depots from which a life-giving British credit entered the endlessly branching channels of the interior trade. Appropriately, when the nation's first financial exchange developed in New York City during the 1850s, it served above all to distribute European investments among America's railroads.

Hence very little in the American economy built upward toward a national pyramid of functions. Almost everything spread outward. Although distinctive concentrations certainly appeared—cotton in the south, grain in the northwest, merchandising and manufacturing in the northeast—they developed amid a ceaseless duplication of economic activities for local and regional markets. The southern states continued to produce enough food for their own needs. The northwest spun its own network of manufacturing and merchandising. Farmers in the northeast, adapting to the growth of towns and cities around them, pursued the most prosperous agriculture outside the deep south. At the same time, only a few pieces of this economy functioned in isolation. In addition to the visible arteries of commerce that joined its local and regional clusterings, countless capillaries of labor-intensive trade pushed over the mountains and moved in and out of half-navigable streams to form an important, if incalculable, portion of the interior traffic, especially from the original eastern states into the west. The bits of capital that came west with the migrants fed these backdoor passageways of trade, for the newest settlements often lay beyond the range of cheap transportation. Before the pioneers had much to sell, they still had to buy, and in this regard the Erie Canal, which carried far more goods westward than it brought eastward during its first two decades, proved a bonanza for the northwestern settlers.

Through these many linkages, large and small, emerged an intricately interconnected but essentially unintegrated array of subdivisions that did business with one another without merging into a common economy. Beneath the interregional flows of credit, for instance, Americans still counted the currency of everyday transactions in a local idiom: dimes and half-dimes in Alabama, bits and half bits in Florida, levies and fips in Philadelphia, shillings and sixpence in New York, ninepence and fourpence in Boston. By rounding off their values, the British shilling served as a reasonable common denominator; by adding them up, the Spanish dollar provided an approximate unity; but by the higher laws of regional custom, Americans retained a variety of separate ways that had no purpose except serving themselves.

The meaning of speed and schedules altered from place to place in a somewhat similar fashion. Long trips that people had calculated in weeks around 1800 were now measured in days, and many Americans not only showed an immense excitement over this evidence of progress but also acquired a hurrying, hustling manner that was noted by numerous foreign visitors. In a few centers along the coast, where merchants entered a transatlantic system of fast packets, and even semaphore messages on the latest cotton prices in Liverpool, days broke down into hours and minutes. Along the main interior routes of commerce, however, a day remained a day. Travelers arose, ate, and departed not by the clock but by the innkeeper's gong. Inland steamboating, a characteristically atomized American business, prided itself on speed without either following fixed schedules or coordinating arrivals and departures. At the primary ports boats came and boats left. ". . . [We] reached Cairo about 3 P.M.," the Illinois lawyer Orville Browning noted in his diary. "No boat for either N O or St. Louis, and no telling how long we may be detained." And the next day: "Still at Cairo."[1] Farther from the main routes, the days grouped in larger and larger bunches until, for most farmers, they merged into the traditional seasons of the annual cycle. Fittingly, clocks sold throughout the countryside as mechanical novelties rather than as devices to discipline a daily life. Even in manufacturing towns, time did not impose an abstract, inexorable order. Workers struggled with employers over control of the factory bells because a victory would give them at least some control over the meaning of time in their lives. Time, in other words, was locally negotiable. In commercial America, people hurried, and making the right connections mattered; but no common rules united the many ways that localities and regions construed these common values.

As the American economy was transformed, it rose to second place among the world's manufacturing nations—still far behind Great Britain but equally far from its own standing in 1820. Apart from the New England textile mills and a handful of other exceptions, production was spread among small shops that interspersed themselves within the cities, dotted the towns, and sprinkled across the countryside. With a flexibility that the big British firms had lost, American operators stopped and started production more or less as they chose, both because the capitalization of these plants was so low and because so many of them were secondary or tertiary investments that could sit idle without ruining the owners. According to one account, nine out of ten manufacturing establishments along the seaboard states closed in response to the Panic of 1837, only in many instances to reopen the next year—and shut again the following one. Neither costly production machinery nor expensive steam generators made sense in such an on-again, off-again scheme. Despite the prominence of New England's textile factories, a larger amount of cotton and woolen goods came from numerous little mills that were scattered across the northern states, and iron manufacturing, the other basic in early-19th-century industrialization, was fragmented among small firms that normally handled just one part of a sequence—smelting or refining or processing.

America's dispersal of economic activities discouraged advances in production and technology. Only where steady demand or concentrations of factories—the firearms and textile industries in Massachusetts, for example—established good preconditions for innovation did American ingenuity have a systematic impact on production improvements, and even among these exceptions the so-called American system of manufacturing interchangeable parts arrived slowly and unevenly. Elsewhere the diffusion of small plants and the dissipation of knowledge across space retarded changes and left local experimenters to repeat the same trial-and-error processes. Technologically, nothing distinguished the cluster of industries in Syracuse, a growing center of production for up-state New York, from the scattering of rural shops around it. Canal boats and labor reserves, not plant investments and productive techniques, accounted for the collection of many manufacturing firms at the port city. Much the same comparison applied to Cincinnati, the major indus-trial center in the west, and the manufacturing towns throughout Ohio, Indiana, and Illinois: more of the same kind of shops operated in the city than in the countryside. Appropriate to the American way in manufac-turing, firms used whatever sources of energy lay at hand: water, wood, people. The only comprehensive comparison for the antebellum years revealed that in 1838, Louisiana—not New York or Pennsylvania or Ohio —led the states in the industrial uses of steam power, the heart of large factory production in Britain.

The dictates of two masters—competition and credit—reinforced this pattern of manufacturing. One issued from the British factories, whose efficiency drove down American import prices about 60% from 1815 to 1840 and drove out almost every seaboard competitor that tried to chal-lenge them. East of the Appalachians, American manufacturing sought the areas that Britain did not fill. The textile firms of New England specialized in a coarse cloth that fell below the quality of the British mills, and many small shops along the coast manufactured leather, glass, or household goods that in the early 19th century lay between the levels of handicraft and mechanized factory production. Only in the 1840s did the output from these eastern centers include a significant amount of heavy machinery, including railroad engines. Across the mountains the same principles, once removed, also prevailed. What neither Britain nor the Atlantic cities could make and ship cheaply enough the western firms manufactured. Even after the iron-hungry railroad expansion of the forties and fifties, stoves, relatively simple to produce but relatively bulky to transport, still headed America's list of iron goods and came from an assortment of shops throughout the west and the east. Mean-while, Wales dominated the production of American rails. As a rule of thumb in filling cracks and gaps, small was sophisticated. That maxim applied with special force when a firm relied on the tariff for its survival, because import duties fluctuated too often between the 1820s and 1840s to justify a large investment in any protected area. Even the large New England mills that hazarded a move into a finer grade of textiles had to retreat in a hurry when the tariff dropped. By the same token, inexpen-sive British chemicals and dyes quickly eliminated their American com-petitors in anything approximating an open market. Revealingly, the low

Walker tariff of 1846 forced some eastern manufacturers back to a simpler, cheaper technology than they had been employing in the previous decade.

The manufacturer's second master was the American merchant, who determined the allocations of credit. In Britain, where factories produced the primary goods for sale, industry and commerce meshed in a continuous enterprise. In the United States, where farm products dominated, the manufacturer's requirements clashed with the annual cycle of credit that moved goods in an agricultural economy. Merchants and their banks needed special incentives to redirect funds from their normal channels of profit into risky long-term plant investments or short-term payroll loans. Although manufacturers occasionally joined together to help themselves, most of them simply took what little capital they could command, remained small, and depended that much more on the merchants' services. Without a bevy of merchant brokers, for example, the iron industry could not even combine its fragments of smelting, refining, and processing, let alone market a finished product.

Unusual investments required a particularly deep personal trust that in depression approached a heavenly faith. Not surprisingly, merchant and manufacturer often fused in the same individual, who borrowed as a merchant to act as a manufacturer or in a few cases became a merchant to market his own product. Erastus Corning, who decided to make some of the hardware he sold, and Phelps, Dodge, which began to manufacture some of the metals it was importing, illustrated a standard sequence. The most successful of these fusions merged a group of merchant-manufacturers into a capitalist club, the Boston Associates, which functioned like a joint-stock company and applied its impressive reserves of primary credit—especially through its affiliate, the Massachusetts Hospital Life Insurance Company—to develop New England's large textile mills. Yet even the biggest operators around Boston had difficulty finding enough credit in their merchant's pocket to fill their manufacturer's pocket. In a commercial economy geared to moving goods, not making them, American manufacturing, already forced to complement Britain's superior industry, also complemented the dominant mercantile thrust of the nation's business. If, in an oversimplified distinction, manufacturers produced goods and sought the markets to sell them, merchants found markets and sought the goods to supply them. As various merchants weighed the profitability of local manufacturing in their commercial schemes, they turned America's many small units of production into another set of links for their marketing chains.

Hence the new rank of the United States as a manufacturing nation expressed a statistical fact, not a wholesale upheaval. Investing capital for mercantile purposes, benefiting from the isolation of inland markets, and always channeling their primary energies into the chase across space, Americans accumulated their industrial strength inside a commercial framework—that is, without the massive demographic, social, and economic changes denoted by industrialization. A decade after the Civil War, the average number of wage earners in a manufacturing and mining establishment still barely exceeded eight. Between the 1790s and the 1850s the broad occupational structure in America's premier city, New York, altered remarkably little, and throughout the nation the shift away from agricultural pursuits sent about three times as many workers into commercially related jobs as into manufacturing. The antebellum economy never took off toward industrialization. Rates of growth remained quite steady over the decades. Although household production for the market dropped drastically by 1830, the far larger household output for its own consumption declined much more gradually. In other words, the kind of economic activity did not change fundamentally during the early 19th century. The United States had been a commercial nation since its origins. What transformed the economy was an extraordinary expansion in the scope of its commercial activity.

Following a uniquely rapid rate of urbanization, the lives of most city dwellers did change dramatically during the early 19th century. Despite their backyard garden plots and their sprinklings of livestock, they had severed ties with the countryside and found themselves impelled to create new social patterns to suit an unfamiliar city setting. Especially in clusters around Boston, New York, and Philadelphia, industrial workers composed an important component of these Americans, and they shared the distinctive coloration of their cities' societies, jostling in closer competition, interacting more intensely, and revealing a greater consciousness of their common lot. Nevertheless, manufacturing firms themselves did not significantly reshape this environment. They just contributed additively to it. Although factories with more than 100 employees did concentrate here, most urban establishments remained small. Moreover, relatively few Americans experienced any of this urban transformation. With cities defined as settlements over 2,500 and no more than three of them larger by 1840 than Peoria would be a century later, a qualitatively different urban society characterized only a few dots on the American map. On the contrary, the overwhelming majority of Americans were caught in a flow of human interactions as extensive as the lengthening strands of commercial enterprise, and while their economy was stretching farther across the continent, Americans remade their values to reckon with space.

14

Democratic Culture

During the 1820s and 1830s a new conception of the family, specializing the responsibilities of men and women and specifying their obligations to their children, laid the groundwork for America's democratic society. Men, as husbands and providers, linked the family with the wider world, acting for it in public affairs and tending to its economic welfare. Women, as wives and mothers, held sway over the household, including its nurturing atmosphere as well as its routine operations. Within the home, children passed through a series of stages that prepared them to face a lifetime of decisions. Although the 19th-century model significantly altered relations between husbands and wives, its primary bond joined mothers and children, and the meaning of this connection derived from the expectation that at a crucial moment these fledgling adults would snap their ties to the family, embark into the unknown, and rise or fall on the merits of what they had acquired during childhood. Abruptly and irreversibly, they entered a world of choices as sovereign individuals. From that pivotal redefinition of adulthood came an entire life cycle to fit it: the formative sequence of childhood, the testing time of youth, the harvesting years of maturity. Around the adult emerged a setting of supports to soften the starkest effects of a lonely sovereignty. And beyond the individual stretched a universe of larger groupings—

communities, states, nations—that replicated this same pattern of choices and consequences. By the 1840s what originated in family life had been elaborated into a complete democratic culture.

Certain elements in the new family model traced far back in time. Husbands traditionally held a monopoly on the family's worldly affairs. Household operations, including the care of young children, customarily fell within the ken of women, and by the end of the 18th century, publicists were exhorting mothers to prepare their children for the demanding tasks of republican citizenship. Nevertheless, the contrasts between old and new were far more striking than their similarities. The model for the 18th-century family, despite some evidences of weakening, remained a patriarchy. The father, as master of the family's property and keeper of its honor, ruled according to a code that subordinated the individual interests of his dependents to the welfare and reputation of a perpetuating patrilineal name. Franklin and Jefferson played out this role as naturally as the New England Calvinists. No special merit attached to the wealth that a gentleman himself earned. Hamilton, for example, simply acquired the status of his aristocratic wife, absorbed her wealth as his own, and proved his right to high station by his behavior, not his income. Because an ill-governed household reflected on the patriarch's character, the scattering of advice literature that came from British and American authors at the end of the century told fathers to tighten the screws of discipline in a revolutionary era, diminish the authority of flighty women, and curb unruly children. Wives, denied wills of their own, hopelessly shamed themselves if they failed to obey their husbands. When the political battles of the 1790s set the Jays against the Livingstons, Sarah Jay, a Livingston by birth, had no alternative to an abject, total repudiation of her father and brothers. Although affection certainly wove its way through these relationships, it was not an essential ingredient. With reasonable exaggeration Jonathan Dayton could remark axiomatically that "no heir apparent ever loved his father."[1]

In the 18th-century family model, as in the hierarchical society that reflected and reinforced it, a basic set of superior-inferior relations remained constant during the patriarch's lifetime. Beneath him his wife, sons, and daughters were perpetual dependents and he their perpetual overseer. Not only did fathers feel obliged to arrange apprenticeships and marriages for their sons and daughters and settle them in adult life through gifts and dowries; adult sons and daughters tried to draw further on those resources and even to return to the parental home. The Polonius-like advice that fathers gave sons at their majority belonged to a lifelong continuum of counseling and monitoring, a seamless attachment that lasted until the father's death. Throughout his life, Rufus King never for a minute doubted either his right or his responsibility to guide his adult sons, including the one in Ohio. Even at a distance, therefore, parents pictured their migrating sons and daughters in a setting that would come to mirror the society at home and allow them to reenact the same kind of life. It was in this spirit that Jefferson spoke of western states as the republican sons of their eastern fathers. The patriarchal family, like the hierarchical society, depended on a containment of patterned human relations, even among its mobile members.

A revolution in choices broke the container and spilled sons and daughters into an unpredictable environment that they alone would have to meet. Hence the crucial new image in the early 19th century set these emerging adults at the point of a departure from which there could be no return, a dramatic separation from their parents that sent them questing into an indeterminate future. In practice, of course, countless deviations from the norm occurred on both sides of the divide between the late 18th and the early 19th centuries. Particularly in the older agricultural regions along the coast where a shrinking patrimony would no longer support a father's claim to dominance, sons did leave home suddenly in the late 18th century and strike out on their own. Moreover, many young adults in the early 19th stayed under the family wing. Well into the new century some prospering elites continued to maintain a patriarchal style, and even more respectable families continued to invest heavily in apprenticeships and subsidies for their sons and daughters. Although increasing numbers of them did migrate far from home, their moves were often mediated through networks of kin and family friends. Nevertheless, the new image of youth's irreversible departure expressed social and psychological truths for all of them that fundamentally altered family relationships during the 1820s and 1830s.

Whether sons and daughters settled down the road or across the continent, they now carried their own destinies with them as sovereign individuals: "There *is* no limit to personal responsibility."[2] Metaphorically, all of them packed a precious store of parental gifts in their wagons and drove over the horizon, keeping a good face as they waved goodbye to the somber father and weeping mother at the homestead gate. From this new meaning of adulthood came the reconception of childhood as unique and irrevocable and the redefinition of motherhood as the source of every new generation's lifetime pattern of choices. On the one hand, women in the early 19th century were boxed all over again in a dependent domestic sphere, leaving the legal powers for a patriarchy more or less intact. What relatively small adjustments did occur between the rights of husbands and the rights of wives did not necessarily favor the wives. On the other hand, women acquired obligations in their domestic sphere that no one dared to call less significant than the men's. If the picture of the pious woman tending her family had an ageless quality to it, the new 19th-century image featured morally independent women with wills of their own, making the decisions that set all human beings under their care on paths toward a good or an evil life.

The end of life began in infancy, the cultural counselors of the new age repeated in an earnest, monotonous litany. Along with the bombardment of advice that struck women during the second quarter of the 19th century came the essential premise that the minds of the newborn were putty and their souls clean. "How entire and perfect is this dominion, over the unformed character of your infant," Lydia Sigourney told the nation's mothers. "Write what you will, upon this printless tablet. . . ."[3] The promise of power, however, was also a warning of dangers. Something or someone would commence to write on the tabula rasa, for babies had no way of resisting the unavoidable impress of experiences. Consequently from the infants' earliest days mothers had to envelop them in a protective, prescriptive regimen of wholesome influences.

How long the stage of utter plasticity lasted varied with the numerous experts on the child's inner state. Horace Bushnell, whose writings on "Christian nurture" around midcentury attempted to synthesize a cultural revolution, declared that the truly critical years ended at three. Sigourney extended the "waxen state" through "the first seven years of life."[4] Four or five was a common divider. Sometime during these years child-rearing moved into a second, more explicitly instructional stage, one dedicated to the endless repetition of a few, simple truths—"*very easy*, as well as of *invariable and universal application.*" Through Bible readings, didactic tales, motherly commentaries on the day's events, aphorisms, and any other available device, the child should receive a relentless hammering of elementary moral absolutes that, as one writer phrased it, "will endure as long as life endures."[5] "The lessons [the mother] teaches are never forgotten," another guaranteed. "They will recur . . . to the remotest years."[6] Memory in children appeared before reason, the standard psychological wisdom declared, and these carefully simplified truths, implanted in receptive minds that were still soft enough to take the impression, would eventually bake into the mind's clay as the inflexible guides of a lifetime. During the years of indoctrination, in other words, children internalized a few very general yet immutable propositions: above all, the virtues of dependability, diligence, and honesty, with a trailing set that included frugality, charity, and courtesy. If all went well, parents riveted into their children a panel of buttons that would give immediate, certain responses to any of the future's unpredictable pressures.

During a final stage that began around age ten, boys and girls were allowed more and more latitude in testing life's broad principles on their own. These trial runs of freedom elicited the most comment and the least comprehension among Europeans. If Harriet Martineau found the "independence and fearlessness" of American children delightful, most visitors, misinterpreting a measured leash for parental incompetence, judged them something between unpleasantly assertive and downright undisciplined. In fact, each preceding stage in child-rearing prepared the way for these simulated life experiences. Even in their very early years children were presumed to have will, and parents raised them in an effort to channel but never destroy this prerequisite to an adulthood of individual choices. Jacob Abbott, an early, widely read adviser to parents, emphasized the need to ease children gradually into greater and greater temptations; all of the counselors warned against a prolonged period of dependence. Later, parents themselves would ritualize the stories of the little boy packing his bandanna to run away, then losing his courage around the bend, as if to validate the urge even before its time had come. By their early teens, well-raised children were expected to understand how a handful of internalized absolutes applied to their mix of daily affairs. Somebody inside would always be watching them. What the Protestant God had lost in a majestic sovereignty, he and his parental agents gained in an insidious presence.

Now these fledgling adults stood at the threshold of character. Only when they took complete command of their lives did they finally acquire a character, for character related exclusively to the full, free choices of adulthood. A structural term in the late 18th century, connoting the internal arrangement of human components, became utilitarian in the early 19th, connoting a piece of equipment that had no meaning apart from its ability to perform tasks. A ship had been carefully built at the dock, went one of the common metaphors of character. Would it survive the uncertain voyage ahead? In time, the seasoning of the lumber and the caulking of the cracks would matter immensely, but until the ship actually went to sea, no one could judge it as a ship. Read from the day of embarkation backward, the individual's character collapsed, stage by stage, into a jumble of parts that eventually disappeared altogether. Infants, however beautiful, were mere things. Advice books generally identified the young child as "it." From this perspective the thought of a child's damnation was unconscionable. If humans went to hell as a consequence of their decisions, children, without the wherewithal to make those decisions, simply could not be punished for what they could not do. Condemn the ship when its planking still lay in the forest? As a Puritan's justice changed into a Yankee's abomination, Horace Mann bitterly recalled his mother's anguish over the prospect of a dead little

brother roasting in hell. The popular literature of Mann's generation whisked the souls of dead children to heaven with scarcely an explanation.

Before the crucial moment of departure from home, not a great deal
distinguished the standards for rearing girls and boys. Although they had
radically different apprenticeships for a woman's sphere or a man's
sphere, the guides for raising "it" presumed the same kind of indoctrination, the same core of values, and the same sequence of development
for both sexes. Moreover, through the first two stages, the same mother
employing the same personal style monopolized the care of all the children. What divergence did occur came with the final stage when for the
first time the father acquired some significance. Until then he functioned
largely as the symbol of a hard external world. As male children approached their teens, however, fathers were expected to instruct them in
those worldly matters and to encourage them toward some risk-taking
in a land of opportunities. Between the 1810s and the 1840s, custody law
adjusted to this division between a mother's time and a father's time,
marking the line at about age ten. Yet as foreign commentators noted,
mothers were also slackening their hold on teenage daughters. To a striking degree, boys and girls continued to proceed toward adulthood under
a single regimen for a single reason: to prepare them to act as sovereigns
in a society of individual choices.

In adulthood, however, the lives of women and men abruptly separated. For many young women their first free choice, a marriage partner,
sent them circling back to repeat the story of their childhood, now recast
as the domestic rulers and nurturing mothers. With an authority that the
Swedish visitor Fredrika Bremer contrasted with the greater dependency
of their European counterparts, they reigned as "the center and lawgiver
in the home," and they received public honors appropriate to their important new station.[7] A German immigrant concluded that in the United
States "a woman who is the wife of only a tradesman has it better than
the richest farmer's wife at home." Rather than trailing her husband in
public, "the woman walks *beside* him."[8] Nevertheless, the sudden slam-
ming of the household door not only gave her domestic palace the qualities of a tomb but also forced a severe repression of thoughts and feelings
that just yesterday had met a warm welcome. Husbands, however they
may have bent the rule, were charged to leave the sordid business of the
world at the doorstep and by silence, evasion, and euphemism seal their
wives from the hurly-burly of the street. Figuratively, the father took his
son outside of the home to discuss the realities of a man's life. Hence
from an impressive openness in expression as growing girls, they were
suddenly expected as wives to swallow their feelings in saintly self-
sacrifice and play dumb about the wider world, creating an impression of

shallowness that appalled the bright, critical Harriet Martineau. Little wonder that marriage often brought more trauma than fulfillment.

In one sense, the abrupt change in a married woman's lot reflected the general sobriety that so many young adults showed as soon as they struck out on their own. After watching young men in American cities, a British observer remarked: "The principal business of life seems to be to grow old as fast as possible."[9] By contrast to the young woman's sudden calm, however, the young man was supposed to become an engine of energy. "Man was made for action . . . ," the Reverend Joel Hawes exhorted his youthful audience.[10] Every foreign visitor commented on the extraordinary bustle of Jacksonian America, especially among young men on the make. Life in America was "delightful," the touring Michel Chevalier decided, "in the eyes of him who prefers work to every thing else, and with whom work can take the place of every thing else."[11] No ambitious male in the early 19th century would have assumed, as the elite in Jefferson's generation did, that successful citizens took dinner in the early afternoon and allotted the balance of the day to personal cultivation and social pleasures. "The American lives twice as long as others," an Englishman decided in the 1830s; "for he does twice the work during the time that he lives. . . . He rises early, eats his meals with the rapidity of a wolf, and is the whole day about his business."[12]

The images of physical movement that suffused American culture— the children leaving home, the wagons moving westward, the trains trailing smoke in their wake—communicated more than the literal truth that countless people did migrate, that fresh opportunities did lie in new lands, and that technological innovations did expand the possibilities of both. They merged with a larger metaphor of life's course—its inherent dynamic, its hopeful vista, and its relentless drive integrated in a statement about the modern pilgrim's progress.

Young males, it was assumed, had at most a decade and probably less to reveal their talents for the race. With independence an authentic ship hit the water, but it still had some of the "pliability of youth." Married or not, each of these young men was pictured alone, a sovereign atom in a sea of alternatives, and his task was to stay afloat as he turned an indeterminate quest into a fixed destination. Fundamentally the test lay in the instincts rather than in the intelligence of the young navigator. He was not assessing alternatives; he was translating deeply embedded truths into actions. The real meaning of the individual's much vaunted will, commentators made clear, was habit. "All the qualities which constitute character [are] subject to the will . . . ," the Reverend George Burnap told his Baltimore audience. "The instant the young man commands sufficient force to utter the fiat, I WILL, the chaos is reduced to order. . . . " And how did will shape character? "It is only by the formation of habits," Burnap explained, "that principles can be converted into character."[13] According to another adviser, habits turned those principles into a "second nature, fixed and permanent."[14] "Habit," the cultivated politician Charles Sumner was quoted as saying, "is everything." Hence such zealous character-builders as Horace Mann and Henry Barnard set habits at the very foundation of a child's education, habits so powerfully established that they left the young "actually feeling" those essential truths "as plainly as we feel the earth beneath our feet."[15] Where the 18th-century gentry had relied on control, respectable Americans now counted ultimately on a reflex, an inexplicable rush of an answer from their unplumbed depths.

Ideally, therefore, child-rearing had taken the chance out of choice. Knowing that their children would face an incalculable range of decisions, parents tried to equip them with the instincts for virtue in a changing world. Remove the margin for error in childhood, the popular advisers told them, and guarantee a future of respectability and success. For young males the high tension came from learning all at once how to apply those aphoristic absolutes in every area of their lives, and the early-19th-century schedule of maturity marked an end to this frantic period of choose, choose, choose sometime in their middle twenties, when their characters solidified and they settled into a steady course—"for life and for eternity." In retrospect they attributed the stabilization to a flash of insight, often a response to some happenchance circumstance that suddenly congealed their uncertainty into a clear, long-range goal. They were looking for it to happen—indeed, they needed it to happen—and so it did. Or if it did not, they rearranged their memories to create it: Theodore Dwight Weld, Wendell Phillips, and Lewis Tappan compressing a gradual commitment to abolition into the electric reaction to one event, Harriet Beecher Stowe transforming a vaguely encouraging letter from her sister-in-law into the inspiration for *Uncle Tom's Cabin*, Horace Mann tracing his entry into public education to the catalytic effect of an unexpected offer. Something had to touch the crucial button.

After the consolidation of a man's purpose the balance of his life, it was assumed, would more or less fulfill the qualities of character that had hardened along with his goal. The possibility of a terrible mistake never disappeared, of course, but its likelihood diminished sharply with the comforts of a fixed way. Those who managed the transit and emerged with successful careers not only commanded the respect of their society but also won the right to pass their wisdom back to the struggling youth on the other side of the divide. Indeed, the longer they lived, the more purely they exemplified a triumph against the hazards of limitless choices and responsibilities that everyone faced. Biographies and memoirs as simple, congratulatory moral tales became a natural and increasingly popular means of spotlighting the path of virtue, and young men commonly picked one of these paragons as a model to emulate. It was no accident that a seniority system slipped so easily into the procedures of the Senate during the 1840s. At times, respect verged on worship. Democrats made Old Hickory literally an object of veneration. During Horace Mann's final hours, townspeople in Antioch gathered at his bedside as they might have around a dying saint to catch his last words.

Successful old men received such adulation because the chances of matching their record seemed so slender. Beginning with children's tales that almost always sketched the wider world in shadowy, ominous tones, the heavy lines in the picture of life's course depicted the multitude of dangers threatening simultaneously on many fronts. The youth's ship embarked on "a sea where many dark nights and furious storms are to be encountered; where you are liable, on the one hand, to be allured into fatal gulfs; and, on the other, to be dashed upon hidden shelves."[16] "Place yourself in an attitude of defense," ran a characteristic warning to youth. "Insidious foes lurk around your path."[17]

To express an omnipresent jeopardy, Americans in the early 19th century elaborated upon an image of crowded, chaotic cities that suggested the normless anonymity of jungle warfare. Here resided the gaudiest concentrations of temptation and the starkest evidences of success and failure. Even their own spokesmen made city life sound like chronic social crisis. In a culture that envisaged life's promise as a line moving into open space, the picture of a lonely youth engulfed by evil enticements and jostled by unscrupulous strangers compressed the perils of a fledgling adulthood in their most vivid form. When Thomas Jefferson and Oliver Wolcott deplored the 18th-century city, they had stood apart to condemn the "mobs" at its bottom layer. Neither had feared for his own character. Now an enveloping urban environment endangered everyone who entered it.

As a mere diatribe against America's Sodom, these warnings would have quarantined the cities and instructed young men to go elsewhere or simply stay home. On the contrary, everyone assumed that a stream of ambitious males, raised to quest for success, would flow naturally toward these centers of opportunity. Avoiding the challenge would have denied the imperatives of an adult's freedom and life's test. Hence as the moral spokesmen of the early 19th century painted their horrible picture of urban corruption, they were designing a metaphor to reckon with the complex, conflicting requirements of moral certainty and economic risk inside the same mobile youth. Through the image of the city they communicated the most dramatic version of an inevitable journey into the unknown, the challenge of choices in an environment of strange people following strange ways. In sum, the city epitomized all the hazards of a social change that no one could stem—and relatively few thought should be stemmed. The metaphor really covered all young men regardless of their origins or destinations. Even if you plan to "live in rural districts, in villages or towns," Henry Ward Beecher told his youthful readers, pay special heed to the terrors of the city, for you are "migratory, restless people" and you know so little about the dangers ahead.[18]

What the temptations of the city communicated to men, encounters with men expressed to women. As a new decorum barred all but the faintest allusions to the body and its functions in the exchanges between men and women, an obsession with women's vulnerability to lecherous men was reinforcing this network of proprieties. From the young widow's helplessness before her leering landlord in the popular melodramas to the nun's seduction by the passionate priest in the anti-Catholic tracts, the vision of a lone woman facing a lone man symbolized the ultimate female jeopardy. In tales of the young man's fall, illicit sex, if it occurred at all, came well along the slide after drifting or gambling or drinking had already sealed his doom. For women, sex alone defined the fall. In one sense, males used both the protective social customs and the images of danger to emphasize a husband's property right to his wife: neither she nor any other man should ever forget who owned her. A literal, logical extension of these strictures, like the warnings to young men, would have frozen women in the home. Yet the elaboration of dangers and proprieties neither lessened a woman's freedom of public movement nor blocked her access to far more basic physiological information than earlier generations could have imagined receiving.

Once again, the image of a sexually charged confrontation between an aggressive male and a defensive female communicated a complex message of inevitable encounters that would challenge a woman's capacity to choose virtue and fulfill her life's obligations. In its extreme versions, it merely reminded women to domesticate themselves. Sensible young widows married again. By Protestant definition, nunneries invited promiscuity. More generally, however, the image commanded women to battle for the sanctity of the home against the destructive worldly forces around it. Males, everyone knew, were the carriers of this corruption. A pimp, not a prostitute, accosted the homesick youth in the city. In place of the 18th-century stereotype of the sexually active flirt endangering the patriarchal family, it was male invaders who threatened domestic virtue in the 19th century. With the purity of the home as her charge, a woman could scarcely stay inside and hide. Like an armored figure of liberty with a chastity belt as her buckler, she was enjoined to meet the worldly host at the garden gate, cow them into retreat, and save the innocent babes within. It required only a slight extension of this notion to turn women into the natural protectors of community virtue as well.

The most complicated portion of the message set wives in tension with husbands and women's obligations in tension with one another. Potentially the most dangerous contaminant was the husband himself, the daily infiltrator whose drive for success required traits very much at odds with the canons of domesticity. Always a kind of alien in the woman's sphere, he might shed his worldly ways each evening or, more likely, he might trail some of them in with him. The unflattering portrait of men by popular women novelists certainly suggested the latter. Hence the real battle might well pit the wife against her husband's passions, and during the early 19th century these encounters acquired a number of standardized forms, each with its own symbol of the wife's triumph: the abandonment of the bottle, the religious conversion, the pure family Sabbath. In this formulation, the rising public pressure on husbands to curb their sexual demands in marriage operated at the heart of the struggle between the aggressive male and the taming female for control over the home.

Nevertheless, the woman rarely had the leeway to choose between her husband and her children, for she had simultaneous obligations to both. Could she serve everyone without sacrificing someone? The answer fell under the same cloud that covered the lonely male searching for success, and nobody had cause for optimism. Men and women alike carried an impossible commandment to keep inviolate the few and simple truths from their childhood in a changing world of ambiguous choices. If the expectation behind these absolutes enabled them to accept human perfectibility as an ideal, the strain of living with them guaranteed a gnawing self-doubt.

A prosperous male knew that success by itself never proved a man's virtue. What means had he used? In fact, what thoughts had he harbored? "Let the result of an action be what it may," declared the popular moralist Francis Wayland, "we hold a man guilty simply on the ground of intention. . . ."[19] Did a man ever harbor "a profane and immodest curiosity"? "SEXUAL DESIRE . . . LASCIVIOUS DAY-DREAMS, and amorous reveries," the health reformer Sylvester Graham warned, disease the body as thoroughly as the acts themselves.[20] No sooner did Charles Finney hint at a more liberal doctrine than he quickly retracted: "impure thoughts . . . fester in your soul"; as your own master you must "*turn your thoughts away instantly.*"[21] Over and over again Americans were taught the same linear logic of failure. From the first sin the second ineluctably flowed, and so it ran in an irreversible sequence. "Beware! young man," one moral adviser exclaimed as he pictured a lively sociable group approaching the tavern door. "This is the moment for the resistance of temptations; here the first steps are taken in that downward path, which leads by a more and more rapid descent to the precipice of perdition."[22] Hence Henry Ward Beecher did not have to explain why after one try at gambling a young man's remorse did him no good. "Good God!" Beecher had him cry, "what a wretch I have been. I am not fit to live. I cannot go home . . . Oh! that I were dead!" There would be no second chance: ". . . a parent's training and counsels for more than twenty years, destroyed in a night!"[23] As Mann emphasized, there was no middle ground. An individual chose "moral life or moral death."[24] In the face of these extraordinary risks in the new freedom, Finney's advice rang a bit hollow: ". . . *learn to say, No.*"[25] Although the old Calvinism had scarcely been a cheery faith, at least it had recognized the inevitability of human flaws. God had been the only sovereign then, and the Old Deluder had had his uses.

When a man slipped, he failed both himself and the mother whose truth he violated. A woman, however, faced multiple jeopardy. In addition to herself and her own mother, she failed the husband whose worldly welfare depended on his domestic retreat. Above all, she failed the helpless children who would pay the consequences forever. As she worked with their waxen minds, "It follows of course then, that every moral obliquity of the mother is almost sure to be reflected in the character" of her offspring.[26] A common assumption of prenatal influences with their own indelible impact added a particularly mysterious set of burdens. If the standard domestic tableau of the early 19th century depicted just one child to a mother who sat slim and serene in her parlor dress, daily life mocked the image. Almost always caught in a long schedule of household work, often beset by one life-threatening pregnancy after another, sometimes charged with the care of several small children, mother had no chance to be the infinitely attentive parent that she was commanded to be.

The values of the early 19th century left these men and women with no place to hide their flaws. The human formed a simple whole, with body, mind, and soul merged into a single expression of character, and a weakness anywhere permeated the entire person. It was not happenstance that during the 1820s a revolution in choices swept simultaneously across so many areas. Unitary individuals felt the need to control the entire terrain of a unitary life. As they understood their own lives, so they judged other people's, watching in particular for the telltale flaw that would expose the whole story behind it. In the standardized morality tale, the false reasoning of the city sharper revealed his corrupt soul, and in the standardized account of a religious conversion, the troubled soul ate at the body "till, from a state of robust health, I was reduced almost to a walking skeleton."[27] As Horace Bushnell reminded his readers, sin "uncentralized" a person. ". . . Cain was only branded on the forehead," Mann told the nation's youth; "but over the whole person of the debauchee or the inebriate, the signatures of infamy are written. How Nature brands him . . . : BEHOLD A BEAST!"[28]

The most visible manifestations of character, in other words, became windows into its core, and appropriately the condition of the body—the character's public display—received a rush of attention. Diet, hygiene, and exercise entered the regimen of proper mothering and the curriculum of proper schooling. Advocates of health reform flipped quickly between an interior morality and an exterior vitality to emphasize the critical importance of their message. Advice on sexual matters, for example, ranged easily across the whole of life and tied masturbation to insanity, salacious thoughts to eternal damnation, marital infidelity to career disasters, and frequent intercourse to mental torpor. By the 1830s, European visitors were routinely struck by these curious American mixtures of the private and the public, the spiritual and the secular. What they missed was the utter nakedness of Americans, to their own eyes at least as much as to others'.

Although no cosmic account registered greater psychic strains in the 19th century than in the 18th or 20th, the new democratic culture did bring special kinds of stress, especially from guilt. Rising parallel with the pressures of personal responsibility came new ways of easing them— sometimes by momentary releases of tension, sometimes by more substantial offers of a reprieve. Weeping won unprecedented acceptance, and the deeper the guilt, the greater the approval. "Many a hard face did I see wet with tears," ran a standard male description of a speaker's simple eloquence, "as he struck the chords of feeling to which God made the soul to respond."[29] The popular melodramas of the early 19th century struck at those same chords in an endlessly repeated ritual of everyone's guilt: the abandoned mother, the wandering son, the intruding villain, the tender reunion, the triumph of virtue. Which sons or daughters had not deserted mother, strayed from her truth, and yearned for a reconciliation? Which mother, in fact, had not betrayed her lost son, deserved her isolation, and yearned equally for a reconciliation? Everybody cried, then returned to do it again and again in response to the same eternal verities. The buncombe style that P. T. Barnum raised to a showman's art and the tall tale that humorists made an American hallmark won their immense popularity as safe, cathartic versions of the sharp trading and warped truth in the male world of affairs that clashed with the inflexible childhood commandment to honesty. The inner knots relaxed in laughter, and men hurried to the next carnival or roared over the next outrageous story.

Cultural spokesmen also supplied Americans with more routinized ways to reaffirm their essential goodness. One was a strict observance of the Sabbath, a subject of increasing public controversy but a matter of considerable relief to many an overtaxed conscience. "No young man, who habitually keeps this day," Joel Hawes promised his uncertain audience, "is in much danger of having his principles undermined, or his morals corrupted."[30] Regular Bible readings, a custom in numerous families that never joined a church, served much the same reassuring purpose. So did the growing horde of lecturers who followed the circuit, specialized in the reiteration of familiar virtues, and left their audiences with a thinner but serviceable sense of recommitment to the simple truth.

No custom provided as critical a reaffirmation as the effusive paeans to mother. Every respectable American looking back to childhood had to find the perfect mother there, for the very roots of a successful, moral life depended on her existence. If mother actually drank and cursed and broke up the furniture, she had to be replaced or invented. A kindly neighbor or teacher, an aunt or older sister, might then become the true mother, ensuring the childhood impress of the indispensable absolutes. If mother died in a child's infancy, the right to an imaginative glorification of her memory expanded accordingly. Here as elsewhere the florid sentimentality of the early 19th century was a very practical matter. Fathers offered no competition or compensation in this scheme. With growing girls the father was judged helpless. "But she lacked a mother's care," Nathaniel Hawthorne wrote of the ill-starred Zenobia in *The Blithedale Romance*. "With no adequate control, on any hand (for a man, however stern, however wise, can never sway and guide a female child), her character was left to shape itself." Even with their sons, fathers had only a peripheral effect. Later in the century, when the prosperous merchant John V. Farwell recounted his version of the poor country boy succeeding in the city, he recalled arriving in Chicago at 19 with perfect tokens of each parent's influence, $3.25 from his father and a Bible from his mother. Whatever the sacrifice behind the cash, no one doubted which gift had carried him further. Behind every prominent man of Farwell's generation loomed the giant force of a mother's love and no more than the shadow of a father's hand. At best, fathers demonstrated the comforting possibility that a sprinkling of sins and mistakes did not necessarily destroy the individual. Fittingly, when the wagon carried the young adults over the horizon, it was the mother who wept and the father who consoled the mother.

At the far end of the spectrum beyond the rites of release and reaffirmation lay the chances for renewal, the best that troubled Americans could find in their new culture. They appeared in two forms: reaching the new west and rediscovering the old truths. Both allowed a sharp discontinuity in the otherwise steady cause-and-effect sequences of adult life, a suspension of the normal rules that abruptly canceled an accumulating record of failure. In one sense, moving west symbolized the flow of life toward opportunities in an expanding nation. After waving goodbye and passing over the hill, the departing sons and daughters would enter the westward caravans and fulfill their destinies in an inviting new field of choices. But the newness of the west also suggested a formlessness analogous to the child's, a setting of innocence where thwarted adults could start afresh. "The farther West one goes, the less will he find . . . of a well-defined and fixed character . . . ," one evangelist wrote encouragingly.[31] In this sense, the move west became a transcendent leap rather than a linear progression, an erasure of the past rather than an extension of it. Western settlers cultivated this myth of renewal with declarations of a uniquely open opportunity and a demand that all arrivals prove their worth anew. By an imaginative reworking of the myth, a city filled with newcomers could be made to serve much the same purpose. Americans did not have to talk literally about a recaptured innocence to seize the chance for another start and experience an immense relief at laying the past to rest. Indeed, it felt so good that some repeated the process again and again.

So did some of the repentant sinners at religious revivals, and to skeptical observers they seemed little more than the evangelist's alternative to an evening at the melodrama. Actually they offered a means for renewal so important that by the 1840s the revivalistic style served as a model for almost all public appeals. What the revivalist offered was a chance for beleaguered sinners—and who, after all, had not bent the childhood absolutes?—to discard their shabby old lives and begin again with new ones. Once more, renewal meant a transcendent leap, not a logical next step. Unlike the sudden solidification of a young man's decision on his career, the revival conversion broke an existing process of life. Using the standard 19th-century figure of life's path, one man recalled the preacher who " 'struck the trail' of my experience some distance back . . . [until at] length he came right up to me," worked his miracle, and vaulted the convert to an entirely different road.[32] Fundamentally, of course, the path was an interior course, and lostness a feeling about oneself. Without a deeply drilled conscience, no guilt would stab the listener, and without a lively sense of guilt, no conversion would occur. Hence revivalists addressed themselves not to the obviously corrupt but to the apparently upright, the people of solid upbringing most eligible to these sharp pangs of doubt. Conversion, rather than a release from the terrors of eternal damnation, was basically an escape from self-damnation. By contrast to the 18th-century revivalist who stressed the

utter pettiness of his audience in the eyes of God, his 19th-century counterpart emphasized the moral ugliness of his audience in their own eyes.

With these attacks the evangelist probed for the buttons of immutable
childhood truth. Methodist and Baptist hymns evoked a longing for the
bliss of "home," linking heavenly peace with childhood purity. Congregationalists and Presbyterians envisaged a distant mother's prayers mediating between her lost children and God. At the receiving end of the
barrage the guilty convicted themselves as sinners, then waited for the
moment of explosive release, the sudden gush of feelings that washed
away the old sins and marked the beginning of a new life. "Afraid of
sudden conversions!" snorted that master of the inner keyboard, Charles
Finney. "Some of the best Christians . . . were convicted and converted
in the space of a few minutes."[33] By their nature, in fact, conversions
were "instantaneous," another revivalist declared. No one could "reckon
a passage of time in the sinner's being born again. He was unborn—he is
born."[34] Who had forgotten Saul on the road to Damascus?

But Pauls appeared rarely. The lot of the sensitive conscience in the
early 19th century was a recurrent sense of lostness, for the interior
absolutes always set an impossible standard. As foreign visitors noted
with some surprise, Americans came to anticipate revivals—to make
them regular occurrences—and they expected a similar style in their
Sunday sermons. Repeated often enough, these instances of renewal became a somewhat jagged Protestant variation on the Catholic confessional. Although such rhythmic sequences disturbed the serious
evangelist—"Heartless confessions," Finney called such short-lived conversions—he still responded to the need. Heaping special doses of self-
hatred on the backsliders—*"the most unhappy people," "the most guilty
people," "the most despicable of all people"*—the revivalist promised in
the end that they too would be forgiven by a merciful God.[35]

From a restricted set of alternatives evangelical Protestantism offered
women their most serviceable setting for release, reaffirmation, and renewal. If women traditionally formed the bulk of church membership,
they had not always been expected to keep the family morals, and this
responsibility created a deepening alliance with the ministers who in
turn came to depend upon them. During the long battle against the old
orthodoxies, women had a vested interest in the overthrow of infant
damnation and the sentimental ascent of children into heaven, not simply from affection but also as a reflection of their maternal care. By the
same token, mothers worked actively for the conversion of their older
sons and daughters in order to ratify the quality of their nurture. Rearing
children for religion was like "raising a crop of corn," and as the common
expression went, revivals were the harvest. Where they could also draw
their husbands into the church circle, they completed their familial task,

consolidated their domestic domain, and rested about as comfortably as their culture allowed.

In collusion, ministers and women labored to take the chance out of choice by invoking a consciousness of community. Although the moment of conversion resolved an individual's guilt, its setting expressed community values and expectations. Not only did religious gatherings replicate communities in session; their organizers also made certain that everyone felt an incessant group presence. Hymns sang of "we," "the band of saints," and other felicitous collectivities. While the minister preached, his audience echoed its affirmations. Perhaps for several days running, revivalists packed the schedule with activities. "It is important," Finney emphasized, "that the time should be fully occupied. . . ."[36] As individuals stirred in response, they found themselves encircled with common prayer, bombarded by the cries of male and female "exhorters," clustered in the camp meeting's "pen," or displayed on the "anxious seat." In the throes of conversion, they validated the group's norms and won its hosannas for their virtue.

The convert's responsiveness emerged directly from childhood training. Mothers instructed their children to believe that the good people around them—never indifferent, always knowing—would shun the vicious and welcome the virtuous. When they left home, they expected eventually to settle with such people, and if it did not happen, they looked for their community. As a matter of course, Baptist and Methodist congregations in the west, like Presbyterian and Congregational ones in the east, policed the behavior of their members, not only affirming the absolutes that they held in common but also easing the strain of individual decisions on the details of daily life. As the Cambridge *Chronicle* approvingly noted, nothing eluded "the eye of the community."[37] These communities were extensions of the home as much as the church, and hence women, in league with ministers, figured prominently in them. But men's affairs also required a community. No farm survived without credit, every business rooted itself in a place, and only the smallest speculations drew on a family's own surplus. Because worldly opportunities relied on a man's reputation inside some community, males too came of age seeking a group to support their enterprise.

Although tensions certainly existed between individual and community authority, the culture of the early 19th century minimized them. Raised to expect an identity between their values and those of some right-thinking group, adults anticipated a frictionless relationship. Unlike the hierarchies of an earlier time, these communities had the appearance of a collection of equals where authority diffused so evenly that no one was bowing to a superior power. Just this kind of homogeneous pressure lay behind a temperance triumph that was reported in 1833: "And when this solitary drunkard looked around and saw not an individual, who would touch the drunkard's poison, except himself . . . [he] resolved to be like other people."[38] Emerson, the ringing champion of the individual will, accepted whatever menial offices the Concord town meeting assigned him and wrapped himself in the traditions of his community when "young foreigners" criticized his judgment. Robert Rantoul, an ideologue of Jacksonian individualism, referred to the nation's towns as "little democratic corporations." It was not even a contradiction to see individual freedom in a highly regimented Fourierite community. "The highest civilization," the economic publicist Henry C. Carey declared out of this common wisdom, "is marked by the most perfect individuality and the greatest tendency to union, whether of men or of nations."[39] Particularly in times of community crisis the most individualistic Americans had to search deep into their feelings before they challenged their group's truth.

To express the natural affinity between individual and community, Americans attributed precisely the same characteristics to both. Like the individual, the community had a will to direct it and a destiny to fulfill its inner virtues or vices. "The township, taken as a whole, . . . is only an individual, like any other to whom the theory [of self-determination] I have just described is applied," Tocqueville reported as the American canon.[40] The same implacable lines of cause and effect, making each step the inevitable consequence of the ones preceding it, determined the courses of both. Communities also awaited flashes of insight to consolidate their purposes and save them from their errors. What linked the individual to the community then proceeded along a sequence of state to region to nation, and what characterized the smaller units applied in turn to each larger one: inherent values and linear destinies, times of trial and bursts of opportunity, the horrors of corruption and the wonders of conversion. Evoking the image of a "young America," for example, placed the nation in that peculiar condition of energy, hope, tentativeness, and jeopardy that marked the testing period of the adult male. The invariable laws of life remained exactly the same as this reasoning moved from microcosm to macrocosm. "Individual character is the combined result of early impressions," the westerner James Hall wrote. "The same is true in regard to national character."[41] "Man, as an individual, is capable of indefinite improvement," Charles Sumner told an audience at Union College. "Societies and nations, which are but aggregations of men, and, finally, the Human Race, or collective Humanity, are capable of indefinite improvement. And this is the Destiny of man, of societies, of nations, and of the Human Race."[42] More concisely, the publicist

Calvin Colton declared that "what is possible for a small community, is possible for a larger, is possible for the world. . . ."[43]

The replication of an individual's life process in the course of each larger social unit suggested the existence of a natural unity, a single universal logic enveloping all of them, and so in various ways Americans concluded in the early 19th century. Appropriately, many of them used a simple organic model to encompass the entire human experience. Unlike the essentially static and heavily anatomical organicism of earlier centuries, the 19th-century version emphasized growth and wholeness, a vital organism that evolved as it acted. Americans thought of their society as "a body progressing," Tocqueville commented. The next step blended humans with all other elements of life and change into Nature's comprehensive scheme for the universe. From strikingly similar urges, scientists and theologians collaborated to synthesize the findings of science, including geological data on the age of the earth, with a reasonably orthodox Biblical account of God's work. Poets and artists discovered in the beauties of the butterfly and the mysteries of the forest a natural drama that spoke directly to the human situation. "What I have observed of the pond is no less true in ethics," Thoreau concluded at Walden. The standard promotional sketches of the factory placed it in a sharply three-dimensional setting of lovely fields and woods and asked viewers to see an easy harmony between industrial growth and bucolic peace.

Nature's grand cover with its own inexorable logic of development did raise some basic questions about the scope of human choices inside it. Through ingenuity and adaptation, however, Americans did their best to mute the conflict. Robert Winthrop, indifferent to the future of agriculture in his state, gave Nature's sovereignty a quick bow as he dismissed the farmer's prospects: "Nature has marked and quoted [Massachusetts] for a different destiny."[44] From European organic thought Emerson among others borrowed only the portion that empowered the human mind to create its own order. While European romantics were turning the mystical union of the social body into a reactionary message, their conservative American counterparts merely cautioned against too hasty a progress. At midcentury, when Horace Bushnell sensed too great a strain between scientific evidence and his Christian beliefs, he just severed empirical from intuitive knowledge—as if that closed the issue. Meanwhile, to ease the tension between an organic whole and a free-wheeling pursuit of opportunities along infinitely varied paths, Americans granted themselves full freedom to construct whatever unities, large or small, suited their circumstances. Community leaders who saw themselves moving in harmony with the nation one year could imagine themselves striking out on their own the next, then picture a union with their state the next, and feel no incongruity as they shifted among these settings for enterprise. Without a mandatory nationalism that compelled all parts of America to merge, holistic thought had no inherently swallowing tendencies to it. A natural unity was whatever various Americans chose to declare one.

Only a few pockets of the nation broke cleanly enough from the values of a flowing, linear change to offer a clear alternative. In almost all cases they drew their authority from heavenly instructions, whether the time-honored ones of the Amish or the fresh ones of the Latter-Day Saints, and set themselves as islands of virtue in an ocean of sin. Beyond these defensive communities, however, many other Americans felt at least some kind of pull toward a belief in the apocalyptic second coming of Christ—premillennialism. According to this orientation, the changes in American society verified a rapid spreading of evil that the Bible had foretold, and a premillennialist's understanding of these events depended on an ability to decipher those cryptic Biblical prophecies. Mundane choices testing ordinary human character paled before the awesome gathering of forces that would plunge the world into the day of judgment. Premillennialists took their satisfaction not from the evidence of today's success but from the anticipation of tomorrow's sudden reversal of fortunes when the reign of corruption would end, the worldly sinners would receive their terrible punishment, and the faithful few would rise to glory. As the thousands of Millerites who set aside their goods in 1843 to await Christ's arrival demonstrated, this dramatic counterpoint to the assumption of a steady cause-and-effect progression in human affairs had considerable appeal, even among those who operated from day to day on a belief in life's continuity. It could represent the ultimate reprieve, the total destruction of an entire maze of pathways and glimmering opportunities that was generating nothing but frustration and guilt.

Nevertheless, an apocalyptic settlement did remain in counterpoint to the major theme of a ceaseless flow. In its broadest terms that irresistible movement meant progress, an inherent and universal force that was impelling human society on an upward course. Where the revolutionary gentry had calculated improvements as carefully adjusted weights on a scale, Americans in the early 19th century saw progress pressing forward at an ever-accelerating pace toward a dazzling future. "We believe that human improvement is indefinite," stated a usually cautious Unitarian journal in 1834, "that no almighty fiat has set limits to its progress."[45] "Our country . . . is great already . . . ," Timothy Flint wrote after a review of a decade's growth. "What will it be in half a century to come?"[46] "Each succeeding generation ought to be, and, in a normal state of society, will be, richer than the preceding," the moderate Amasa Walker concluded.[47] Their nation, Americans liked to believe, was leading the way. "The Progress of Centuries in other lands, is here realized in as many years," announced a group of Michigan's leaders.[48] Little wonder that Americans overlooked Tocqueville's many cautions and applauded the general message of *Democracy in America*. Instead of making them a caricature of the present, as so many Europeans did, this perceptive Frenchman called them the wave of the future.

At the same time, progress moved in a strikingly impersonal fashion. In effect, it was the unfolding of Nature's own interior truths. As slow as gentry improvement seemed by contrast, at least it had represented the self-conscious creation of the gentry themselves. Now progress became a torrent that no one controlled. It was a *"law,"* Sumner emphasized, and men had to "act in conformity with it."[49] By obeying what Mann called the "sublime" laws of progress, "all the resistless forces of Nature become our auxiliaries and cheer us on to certain prosperity and triumph; but, if we act in contravention or defiance of these laws, then Nature resists, thwarts, baffles us; and, in the end, it is just as certain that she will overwhelm us with ruin. . . ."[50]

Getting right with progress, then, became the task of every enterprising unit from the individual to the nation. Once aboard the train, the rest would be relatively simple, for the first move along the right track at least pointed a straight course to success. In this conception lay the basic source of comfort from a young man's consolidation of purpose. The same logic justified every transportation venture in the early 19th century, and a common tendency toward hasty, slipshod construction reflected a similar faith in the inevitably prosperous outcome. Even if a particular canal or railroad failed to balance its accounts, its defenders still claimed that it was somehow initiating a flow of wealth across the rest of the state. Northerners who wanted to send freed blacks to Africa presented their program as the first step in an irresistible sequence: a contented black society in its natural environment, a thriving cotton production in Africa, an intolerable competition for the southern states, and an end to slavery. Abolitionists used "immediate emancipation" to express the same compression of a process: immediately starting and inexorably finishing merged into a single vision. In the 1780s, Jefferson had proposed the periodic elimination of debts as a long-range holding operation against Europe's corruption. In the 1830s, Thomas Skidmore made a roughly comparable proposal in anticipation of a total American renovation. From a central change, waves would rush to cover the entire society. "Banish ardent spirits—banish intemperance from among us, and our almshouses would fall to the ground—our jails would become empty . . . ," went another familiar reform litany.[51]

The trick, of course, was catching the right train, and that required an exceptionally keen vision both ways down the track. Looking one way,

Americans needed a bit of clairvoyance to spot the dominating trends of tomorrow as they peered into today's clutter of activities. Technological experiments became one of those peepholes into the future, and a great variety of inventors, tinkerers, and promoters played on this new faith in technology as fortune-telling. On these grounds Americans gained their reputation as worshippers of innovation. At the same time, every track not only went somewhere; it came from somewhere, and its origins told as much about its destination as the direction in which it pointed. Appropriately, the 1820s and 1830s witnessed a rush of interest in history. The past had become prologue in a new sense, and during the second quarter of the 19th century the proofs of history routinely appeared to demonstrate the progressive thrust of proposals as small as fixing a town site and as large as organizing a western territory. The nation's founders emerged as the perfect anticipators of America's future, and getting right with progress now required getting right with their heritage. Phrased in another way, the founders were the nation's parents, exemplifying the unalterable truths in their own lives—"I cannot tell a lie"—and transmitting them to their sons and daughters of the next century. Sentimentalizing their purity authenticated the existence of those few and simple absolutes at the heart of a growing young America. So, in smaller compass, did the idolatry of a locality's founders. State and local historical associations mushroomed in the west, where community leaders glorified their predecessors much as they were glorifying home and mother—and for much the same reasons.

If the complexities of getting right with both past and future argued in favor of slow decisions, the imperatives of growth insisted on speed. The guiding principle of the universe, Henry Ward Beecher declared, was "the law of growth," and growth in the early 19th century forced all units of society into the pressure box of incessant responses to incessant changes.[52] "Life only avails, not the having lived," Emerson told the nation. "Power ceases in the instant of repose." "There is no such thing as standing still in religion," Charles Finney reminded his audience. "The conditions of the people can never be stationary," echoed a Massachusetts leader. "When not improving they are sinking deeper and deeper. . . ."[53] More bluntly, the Cleveland *Leader* concluded, "One may as well be dead as idle," and in the standard morality tale a business failure usually did mean a quick slide from sloth into death.[54] Even to pause was to lose ground. "Under a good government enterprise is kept perpetually upon the stretch," a Baltimore clergyman lectured. "Every hand capable of producing is kept constantly at work, every brain capable of contriving is kept continually employed to invent new methods. . . ."[55] Michel Chevalier pictured respectable Americans warning one another that disaster would follow the slightest slackening of pace: "Your country will be ruined, and you will be ruined with it." The motto of the driving, plunging westerners, he decided, was *"Victory or death!"*[56] Hence the exuberance of local boosterism and the wail of local catastrophism issued from the same mentality, and the jerky swings between them derived from the most nerve-wracking commandment in the new culture: grow or die.

What kept these strains tolerable was the equally powerful assumption that each social unit had a right to its own testing lane. There it would pit its special inner qualities, its distinctive application of the truth, against the challenges of progress. Clearly some towns, cities, and states grew faster than others, all of them knew it, and that knowledge bore on the assessments of their own health. Nevertheless, a fanning array of parallel ventures, each with monopoly rights on its own track, mitigated the effects of comparison in a number of ways. Laggards could picture themselves gathering momentum at a steadier pace to pass those hares later in the race. At midcentury, investors in Superior, Wisconsin, could still assure one another that their site "must outstrip Chicago within the next 20 years."[57] Indeed, no two tests of merit involved exactly the same elements or circumstances, and the inclination to accentuate the differences allowed an almost limitless variety of explanations for the slower runners. Most important of all, an exclusive field for each racer opened the way for a self-generated reprieve, a flash of insight that would reveal the errors of the past, clean the slate, and enable it to begin again with the truly progressive plan. Such fresh starts abounded in the early 19th century and marked the commitment to parallelism as America's greatest source of renewable optimism.

Parallelism also accounted for a degree of mutual tolerance in a culture that had no other way to deal with conflicting truths. As long as other people's sins and stupidities operated safely apart in their own realm, they could only prove fatal to themselves. By the late thirties it required the most dreadful moral violation or the most egregious example of an unjust reward to stir Americans into an attack on some distant test of error. The reverse of such tolerance was a confident indifference to the lessons that one group might have learned from another. If each unit was testing a unique merit, it could assume that a failure elsewhere had no necessary application whatsoever to its own try. Because the urge to leap aboard the right train drove them so hard, Americans proved highly susceptible to fads that disappeared only after the same flaws had been demonstrated over and over again. During the 1830s and 1840s, countless farm families had to conduct their separate experiments in cultivating silkworms before that craze finally died a redundant death. A passion for plank roads stayed alive between the mid-forties and the late fifties through a comparable conviction that rotting lumber on the roads in one area did not preclude success in another. The same errors in railroad construction appeared in one venture after another—even if the same gauges and equipment rarely did. Like the railroad entrepreneurs, individual steamboat builders followed their own lights in design and construction, preparing the way for a scandalous record of deadly boiler explosions.

The entire parallel scheme rested on the premise of an open America, ultimately a subjective matter but substantively a corollary to the nation's expanse of land. With more space than anyone could span and more people than anyone could reach, the natural American impulse was to declare enough leeway for everyone's test. "Let the American direct his career to any goal he pleases, his energies are unshackled. . . . There is room for all . . . and all may receive the reward due for their labor." When the young Rutherford B. Hayes noticed "many of my early friends and acquaintances of no greater promise than mine evidently outstripping me in the race of life," he showed no desire to surpass them, only to drive himself onward. "There are no conflicting interests between Green Bay, Milwaukee, and Chicago," a Milwaukee promoter concluded in 1836, "each has its own appropriate country. . . ."[58] Following the success of the Erie Canal, it never dawned on the leaders in other coastal cities that New York had captured the west. Ample space remained for each city to meet its own challenge of growth. Although Finney considered the Methodists both crude in manner and wrong in doctrine, he still looked admiringly at their success and used it as a spur to his own associates. "We must have exciting, powerful preaching" too, he declared, or the Methodists "will run away from us."[59] Among such an abundance of souls to save, do thou likewise. Where head-to-head competition did exist, Americans assumed that superior virtue would quickly triumph, redraw the boundaries of a monopoly track, and oblige the loser to try again elsewhere.

At the same time, no one could measure a sufficient openness, and these tolerant assumptions always lay exposed to sudden changes of heart. If the commandment to grow or die turned anxieties inward, the need for parallelism directed them outward. When Americans saw someone else's shadow falling across their private lane of progress, they would fight for their very lives to clear the path.

A cover as broad as this democratic culture stretched over a host of differences. In the northeast, where a tradition of homogeneous Calvinism had its firmest grip, the prescriptions for child-rearing, the concerns for wandering youth, and the specifications for a moral life found their fullest expression. The sanctimonious Yankee was a stereotype among millions of Americans who refused to regard a little pleasure as a sin.

Deeply rooted elites along the Atlantic coast expressed strong doubts about a national scramble after progress. Although not even the most optimistic spokesman declared America perfect, Boston's leading Unitarian, William Ellery Channing, simply "groaned" under the nation's "low, selfish, mercenary" state: "Our present stage of society is one which must be passed through. A true civilization lies beyond it."[60]

Nevertheless, the main lines of the culture did have a national scope. By the second quarter of the 19th century, respectable southerners as well as northerners revealed a new self-consciousness about child-rearing that gave women sovereign powers over the malleable years, and foreign visitors were complaining equally about the loose discipline over their sons and daughters. Chevalier found white southerners constrained in roughly the same way as New Englanders by the invisible authority of their absolutes. As Frances Trollope reported a guilty southerner crying that "when I was fifteen my mother died, and I backslided, oh Jesus, I backslided! take me home to my mother, Jesus!" she might just as well have been recording a northern revival. The autobiographies of such southern ministers as Peter Cartwright and Jacob Young employed the same images of saintly mothers, wayward sons, and instant conversions that Charles Finney and Henry Ward Beecher used in their writings.[61] Domestic and worldly spheres, along with the rituals to protect women and the home from aggressive, contaminating men, appeared as fast in the west as in the east. The McGuffey readers and their didactic imitators spread everywhere, and the metaphor of the evil city echoed nationwide. While theater-hating Protestants shed tears over their sins in church, thousands of others shed tears over the same sins at the melodrama. European comments on the extraordinary bustle of ambition in the United States made no significant distinctions between north and south or east and west.

By the 1840s, in other words, respectable families across the nation raised their children to internalize a set of simple absolutes and relinquished them as adults into a full-blown democratic culture of choices. To survive they required evidence of growth; their growth required them to move with the impersonal flow of progress. Usually the first firm step prefigured the outcome—success or disaster—and the responsibility in either case rested solely with the individual. Nevertheless, because even good people slipped thoughtlessly into the wrong path, they might still gain a fresh start by responding to a flash of recognition and reversing directions immediately. Attributing the same qualities to groups as to individuals, Americans interpreted the behavior of communities, states, regions, and nations according to an identical scheme of interior values, choices, and their consequences, and individuals sought to link their future with some larger collectivity that would validate their values, support their choices, and share their consequences. The responsibilities of freedom were lonely enough without having to experience them alone.

Nothing gave this culture a more distinctive quality or lubricated its operations more effectively than the commitment to an open field for each of life's tests. These separated arenas might be visualized in a number of different ways. Some utopian communities pictured their truth spreading in concentric waves from a pure core. Women were said to rule a domestic sphere. To some degree, however, every version made use of free space. Women, too, were taught to abhor the crowded city, with its encroaching males and enticements to youthful sin, and to visualize the ideal home in an expansive, private setting. The most characteristic image projected life's tests along an array of parallel lines. In that pattern of tracks resided the essence of American democracy—its definition of liberty and its prerequisite for equality. By pitting individuals and groups against themselves rather than against one another, parallelism minimized the frictions of competition and maximized the hopes for new opportunities and fresh starts. Much as a flexible sense of geography had functioned for the revolutionary gentry, parallelism allowed mutual hatreds to survive inside the same society. If parallelism meant laissez-faire, it was laissez-faire of a special kind, for monopoly—an exclusive domain for every enterprise—defined these lanes no matter how broad they might become. At the same time, parallelism only accentuated the nation's looseness and diffusion. For an American society to cohere, an extraordinary scattering of people had to accept a common set of rules, then abide by them for their own ends without benefit of an umpire.

The Institutional Web

From the internalized absolutes that respectable Americans carried along their parallel tracks came a multitude of institutional strands that gave their society its tensile strength.* Many contemporary observers and later historians, looking for clear centers of authority and formal schemes of organization, surveyed early-19th-century America and found only bursts of atomized behavior, a kinetic confusion that was undermining the last pillars of an old order. But social institutions then as now depended fundamentally on the continuing patterns of behavior that people followed to manage social responsibilities in mutually acceptable ways, not on the massive buildings that later housed institutional headquarters or on the systematic organizations that grew from them. Unlike Americans in the 20th century, those in the early 19th wove such patterns on their own from long, thin threads of human connectedness that spread

---

* Here I have chosen "respectable," a term of self-designation in the 19th century, to identify the broad stratum of Americans who used the new democratic values to create a network of institutions. In the next chapter I return to the same issue as a problem of social class.

outward with their nation and functioned without elaborate superstructures.

The development of this institutional webbing trailed just behind the
revolution in choices and gave social expression to the democratic culture that the revolution inspired. During the 1820s the revolution had
its greatest initial impact on a democratic redefinition of adulthood and
the new conceptions of child-rearing that accompanied it. From the mid-
twenties to the mid-thirties, as eastern leaders designed their comprehensive programs, their mechanisms of order became increasingly entangled with an aggressive but still diffuse demand for personal choice.
Between the mid-thirties and the early 1840s, as these comprehensive
structures were dissolving, Americans adapted the substance inside them
to suit an endless dispersal of decision makers: nationwide popular parties without the centralized campaigning of Jackson's coterie in Washington, extensive skeins of personal credit without Biddle's Bank,
movements to abolish liquor and slavery without a benevolent imperi-
alist's guidance. By the early 1840s an entire generation that had been
raised in the democratic ethos came of age to provide a mass base for
these adaptations and maintain them, along with many new strands, as
an intricate, almost invisible stitching of institutional behavior throughout American society.

Democratic institutions began where democratic individuals began:
the reliance on a few, simple truths, their application in highly varied
settings, their periodic reaffirmation, and their operation along separate
lanes. Trained to function from a handful of simple truths, Americans
were already attuned to follow some fixed star in every part of their lives.
Accustomed to the voice of an interior police, they needed no more than
an occasional reinforcement to hold an internally directed course. Confident of an uncomplicated line running from individual wills to public
results, they asked only that nothing interfere with the drive toward
their objective.

By the 1840s there was scarcely an area of activity that lacked its
convenient package of elementary truths to regularize American behavior. Etiquette books collated rules on a range of public behavior from
conversation and entertainment to weddings and funerals. Men read instructions on the essential principles of business management, and
women on the essential principles of a domestic economy. *Cushing's
Manual* (1845), stating primary guidelines that were then adapted in
countless local variations, became the standard reference on procedures
in a public meeting. A basic plan for the cheap balloon-frame house
appeared everywhere. For well-to-do Americans, Andrew Jackson Downing combined a model home with a model landscaping to create a model
aura of reclusive tranquillity. By midcentury there were ideal types avail-

able for an assortment of public buildings, including schoolhouses and hospitals. At greater risk to the borrower, designs for a universal bridge —rational, economical, and infinitely applicable—circulated widely. Indeed, the instinctive receptivity to a formula was sometimes hard to distinguish from mindless mimicry. Learning that a rehabilitative workhouse was evidence of community progress, for example, certain towns built one even though there were virtually no indigents to occupy it.

Although popularization certainly had its precedents, a critical difference separated the simplification of elite messages in earlier decades from the distribution of democratic truths in the 1840s, and the nub of it lay in the assumption of free choice. The most successful of the new institutions operated as if their immutable principles either arose in spontaneous generation—parties enunciating the people's will—or reflected the eternal verities—denominations articulating the Bible's essence or business transactions following the laws of trade. Rules could never descend from a higher human authority; they had to move naturally across a flat plane of equality. What was later expressed in the myth of Johnny Appleseed—the humble itinerant who spread growth and health and virtue as he traveled about the land—exemplified the ideal distribution of democratic truths. As an egalitarian carrier the popular orator served even better than the popular manual. By the 1840s, speakers furthering every imaginable cause in simple summary and common language poured across the nation. Like the best of the revivalists, they took their messages to the people and merged with them to reaffirm the absolutes and ratify the faith. The very act of lecturing became institutionalized in the lyceum system that blanketed the northern towns with public speakers during the 1840s. Most of this swelling band of orators also wanted to take the chance out of choice, but they filtered through American society in a way that seemed to enhance the individual's right to a free decision.

Yet a golden tongue was not enough. An orator entered the new institutional mesh only if he persuaded his audience that he and they held a common stake in a common cause. In a culture of sovereign atoms, institutional connections depended on personal trust, and in a society of moving particles, personal trust depended on mutual interests, bonds that interlocked people's welfare in the same economic enterprise or political contest or moral crusade. Reviewing his lifetime in the south, J. D. B. DeBow concluded that since the 1820s the values of the commercial town had "quietly and almost imperceptibly" spread to cover the entire region. This exceptionally shrewd observation applied to the north as well as the south and to the city as well as the countryside. By the 1840s the norms of the town prevailed among respectable Americans everywhere. Relations were both regularized and personalized: no trust without a tacit contract, no contract without a tacit trust. Hence to the internal discipline of hugging one's truth, institutions added the external constraint of maintaining one's reputation in a scheme of shared ventures and entwined consequences.

Stretching the values of the town across America's space required some means of extending the sense of a personal connection far beyond the limits of anyone's actual acquaintance. Most institutions overlaid the authentic familiarity of local life with a synthetic familiarity that simulated feelings of a direct human connection between individuals who, in fact, were strangers. The common practice of printing lectures and writing books in which authors told the simple truths to "you" the reader invited them to become "your" intimates. Parties publicized their presidential candidates as neighborly heroes, and commercial networks used trickles of gossipy information about distant firms to create circles of artificially personal relations. Already personifying the wider world, respectable Americans took naturally to such personalized impersonality.

In all, these interconnecting devices worked remarkably well. Simple absolutes moved lightly with a mobile population. Quickly assimilated and easily reinforced, they not only regularized the behavior of individual Americans but also sent clear signals of mutual recognition as groups gathered for common enterprises. Viewed broadly, the nation still revealed an extraordinary diversity. Local adaptations of the same immutable truth remained the essence of every successful institution, and those local translations, taken one step further, produced countless breaks and offshoots: splinter parties, denominational schisms, new credit networks, branching bands of reformers. Yet, as Tocqueville marveled as early as the 1830s, the "social machine" continued to run itself.

The most important institutional networks—politics, business, religion —followed three prongs of the revolution in choices: authority, opportunity, salvation. Of these the national parties, the Whigs and Democrats, were the most visible, largely because the structure of the federal government required them every four years to focus a national scattering of partisans on a common event, the presidential election. Add to that the rising passion for politics generally and the parties emerged with a set of traits that caricatured the reliance on simple slogans, enthusiastic rallies, and hero worship. Persuading close to four out of every five adult white males across the United States to vote for one of two men in 1840 certainly did require a lot of hoopla.

Even more than other institutions, therefore, the parties devoted a very high proportion of their energies to communication. The host of local newspaper editors served as such important transmitters that they could command some of the parties' finest rewards. Another network of communication extended from Congress, where a small amount of business left an abundance of time for partisan oratory, and these rhetorical replays of party principle, so different from the learned arguments of the revolutionary gentry, were then distributed as reinforcements for the faithful. By the 1840s each national party also gathered in convention every four years to stage a partisan revival and readjust the party's truth. From the conventions—or just as often from a chain reaction within the party webs—came the slogans that spread through placards, parades, and papers to draw millions to the polls: the Union against the Nullifiers, Tippecanoe and Tyler Too, the Re-occupation of Oregon and the Re-annexation of Texas. Neither the mighty nor the lowly could function without them. After disdaining the "abstractionisms" of the Democrats in 1844, the wealthy Whig Abbott Lawrence countered with a ringing "Let us go for Clay and Freylinghuysen—and the American System—and the Union as it is!"[1]

Although these activities absorbed a great deal of time during campaigns, they generated no permanent national organization and little apparatus of any kind. So-called central committees for aspiring presidential candidates did little and died soon. The important flurry of committees and speeches and picnics accompanying every election arose from local networks of mutual interest, and consequently party responsibilities diffused among hundreds of autonomous centers, each dependent on its own lines of trust and each free to shape its own portion of the campaign. To accommodate this decentralization, party slogans needed to be more than just vague; they also needed to be plentiful enough for a local option. In 1844, Democrats could contest New York with "Polk, Dallas, and the Tariff of 1842" but definitely not with "the Re-annexation of Texas."

Even the slogans, however, usually relied on a final link in the chains of trust, a sense of personal attachment to the candidate himself. In the old gentry parties, trust had to ascend only one level of the hierarchy: trust the local notables to select trustworthy men above them. Although a few reputations, especially Washington's, had national currency, they also revealed the great chasm separating leaders from followers. The power of Washington's image derived from his reputation as a veritable demigod of virtue and resolve, someone utterly unlike any other American. In the democratic age, trust ran laterally. No intermediary layers or qualitative distinctions divided voters from leaders, who now represented a quintessential version of the same characteristics that the voters prized in their own lives. This kind of leader was simultaneously a paragon and a familiar. To call Jefferson "Tom" or Madison "Jemmy" meant to declass the gentleman and declare him unfit to lead. Hence the Federalist vision of "the Jacobins raising Thomas to the Executive Chair."[2] Partisans who called Jackson "Old Hickory" or Taylor "Old Zach" personalized his connection with ordinary citizens and ratified his trustworthiness as a democratic leader.

A bit of genius lay behind the slogan of 1832: Jackson or the Bank. Trust the man, not the thing. Leaders were presented as the embodiment of the simple truths that Americans everywhere accepted unquestioningly. Isaac Hill's tableau of the aging Jackson with a tenacious grip on his life, and his Bible and hymnal at hand, captured a crucial image of unyielding inner strength and virtue. Even the preacher Peter Cartwright could set aside Jackson's dueling and swearing and describe him as inherently moral. Variations on this theme abounded in the politics of the forties and fifties. Huzzas for Harry of the West—invariably "the self-made man"—expressed the same kind of synthetically familiar feelings among Clay's partisans, and the frequency with which parents named their sons after some distant political figure suggested how intimately he had entered into their everyday lives. When Webster turned against a portion of his New England constituency by supporting the Compromise of 1850, the response resembled the shock over a prominent neighbor's sudden denunciation of God.

At the same time, these personal loyalties often pulled against party loyalties. Every time Calhoun hopped between parties, he carried a constituency with him. Some feared that a failure to nominate Clay in 1844 would alienate enough of his personal partisans to defeat the Whigs, and the failure to nominate Van Buren in 1848 did cost the Democrats his New York contingent. As best they could, party managers smothered these attachments under a blanket of party loyalty. With the exception of Clay in 1844, parties came to avoid the magnetic men and nominate the mediocrities and nonentities instead. Now only the dead or nearly departed could qualify as party heroes. By definition, every Democratic nominee was Jackson's man. To satisfy the need for personalized leadership, each new candidate received a gush of acclaim as the people's friend, then disappeared in favor of a fresh familiar four years later. Party, not personal, standards waved over this passing parade. Out of this tradition, Wisconsin Republicans in 1860 would fall enthusiastically behind the latest man of the people, "Abram Lincoln." A similar tightening occurred down the ranks. When senators violated their voting instructions from home, the party rather than the state legislature disciplined them. During Jackson's presidency the old gentry principle of patronage as a personal bond to a superior finally gave way in the largest branches of government administration, and the officeholder's obedience to party doctrine replaced it. Defections at any level increasingly became treason to the group.

Yet to a remarkable degree the sequence of party forming and fracturing, forming and fracturing, proceeded into the 1850s as if nothing had changed. The vital force inside both parties remained a volatile mass of little parts with a bewildering variety of factional names, now clashing, now bargaining, now separating over local, state, and regional issues that in most instances only the participants themselves understood. Although party labels stood for a machinelike regularity, nobody had blueprints for the gears inside, and predictions of an imminent disintegration trailed both parties through the years. Even the most skilled party managers, trying to comprehend a far larger domain than their 18th-century counterparts with a similar mix of rumors and reports, knew less about the substance of American politics at midcentury than Hamilton and Jefferson had in the 1790s.

Instead of engineers running a big machine, managers served as a multitude of mechanics who periodically wound the springs on a host of little devices. Because party affairs occupied only bursts of their time, many of them used the balance to turn politics into a personal lane of opportunity, securing contracts, promoting private investments, expanding their legal practices, or doing whatever else might advance their careers. Giving or taking payment for votes on those legislative issues that the party absolutes did not cover occurred as a matter of course. Were they diligent and dependable in all of their dealings? Were they still dedicated to their party's principles? Then they were honest men with clear consciences.

Party politics, therefore, had two distinct sides requiring very different styles and skills. One turned inward to a circle of associates, the other outward to the voting public. One emphasized bargains and arrangements, the other principles and divisions. One relied on trust among friends, the other on trust among strangers. Only a few, including Stephen A. Douglas of Illinois and William Henry Seward of New York, proved equally adept in both areas. Most excelled in just one. The Massachusetts Whig Charles Sumner, for example, modeled the orator of principle but lacked any capacity for compromise. The Kentucky Whig John J. Crittenden, on the other hand, epitomized the moderate, reliable accommodator but had little flair for partisan campaigning. Similarly, the Democrats contained their own mixture of warriors and peacemakers. When Jackson and Calhoun challenged each other with toasts over the issue of nullification, Felix Grundy of Tennessee followed with one of his own: "The [Democratic] party throughout the nation: May they be as harmonious in action as they are united in principle."[3] Please, gentlemen, no fighting! Van Buren, the master of personal relations, failed even to comprehend the need for a trustworthy national image.

It required both kinds of talents to maintain a semblance of parallel competition between parties that always seemed on the verge of making it a free-for-all for the same goal—the same voters. While the men of principle tried to sharpen the line between them, the managers worked as best they could on just one side of that line. Campaigners, like revivalists, concentrated on rallying a natural constituency, not converting an incorrigible opposition. In this spirit, the Democrat Van Buren and the Whig Clay reached a tacit agreement in 1844 to avoid the issue of Texas, a subject that might disrupt the entire pattern of party competition. Nevertheless, party battles were never shams. Almost every manager cared deeply about his party's absolutes and thrust himself zealously into the campaigns. Many a loser took solace, along with the Whig Orville Browning, in a conviction that his party was "contending for the immutable principles . . . [and in] a trustful hope that truth will ultimately prevail."[4] More help was needed in containing these bitter clashes.

As a final step in minimizing the risks of an outright brawl, managers came to think of electoral politics as a game—deadly serious as such contests often were, but a sporting event nonetheless. Appropriate to the image of parallel tracks, they commonly pictured it as a form of horse-racing, a popular yet respectable sport in the early 19th century and one peculiarly associated with the inner merits—the breeding and training— of the racers. Hence prospective candidates were "in the running," and Polk emerged as America's first "dark horse" nominee. After the conventions came the presidential "race" itself. Calhoun "bolted" from one party, then from the other. Managers deepened the sense of sport with a splurge of gambling on the outcome. "Don't forget to bet all you can," Van Buren reminded a friend on the eve of Jackson's initial victory.[5] The Democratic chieftain Francis P. Blair of Missouri won a small fortune on his "dark horse" in 1844. The bets always crossed party lines: a manager never wagered against his own slate. In this way, men who were fierce competitors, such as the Whig Thurlow Weed and the Democrat Edwin Croswell, became regular betting partners, channeling their animus into a tense but contained rivalry in the grandstands as the candidates raced to the pole. Hamilton and Jefferson would have turned away in disgust.

By contrast to the parties, America's interior commerce operated with no national focus of any kind. Nor did this most radically decentralized of all institutional networks have slogans or conventions or heroes to give it any obvious points of reference. With the commercial turn inland around 1820, hundreds of thousands of people spun a web of credit connections that grew as Americans pushed westward and functioned as if it had no beginning or end. In very general terms, it did originate with British finance, America's underwriter, and terminate with American agriculture, the ultimate customer, and at those ends credit moved only one way—the British firm giving, the American farmer receiving. Never-theless, the essential characteristic of this continental network was its multiplicity of intermediate participants who both took and granted credit and in the process kept the webbing intact. It was an expensive scheme, with its profusion of middlemen drawing profits at every little bend in the stream of commerce. But thanks to the reserve of British credit sustaining them, Americans enjoyed the luxury of doing an inland business their way.

Their way was the way of the town. Because no one—farmer, store-keeper, boatman, jobber, teamster, merchant—wanted to take responsi-bility for business affairs beyond his own ken, everyone negotiated with someone who would. Except for the minority who bartered or paid cash, credit forged each of the links that extended the range of buying and selling and moving. Credit, in turn, depended strictly on a personal rep-utation. In a sprawling land of mobile people the confidence man was the Devil himself to commerce, for once he ducked around the corner no one would ever find him. By appropriating the language of 18th-century piety—a granting of "grace" in the payment of debts, for example, or their final "redemption"—the commercial web revealed its intimate in-volvement with those internalized absolutes that meant salvation in this world as well as the next. "We esteem good moral character . . . as our most valuable capital . . . ," a group of Oneida's aspiring young men as-tutely declared in the mid-thirties.[6] Because almost everybody both gave and took credit in this scheme, almost everybody shared a mutual inter-est in its individualized morality. The jobber did not want the country merchant's store, and the storekeeper did not want the farmer's land. Each wanted to keep a sound customer in his own business and hence still a customer, still the next determinate link in the chain. Any defaul-ter rattled the entire chain, and credit went only to those who seemed tough enough to hold their places.*

At the same time, these arrangements were also regularized. Credit through reputation built into this network a powerful bias toward con-tinuing relationships. Year after year, the same buyers returned to the same sellers, attempting to deepen trust into a mutual dependence that would make additional services to the steady customer as important as

---

* The standard historical judgment, that between the 1780s and the 1840s the personal business procedures of eastern merchants disappeared into the impersonal world of conti-nental commerce, rests on a classic example of comparing apples and oranges. The apples in this instance are the intimate elite circles that functioned in the 18th-century ports, and the oranges are the entire chains of 19th-century commerce. Of course, no 19th-century merchant could hope to know everyone along the full length of a chain. If we set an orange next to an orange, however, he had far stronger personal connections into a long flow of commerce than his counterpart under the old methods of commerce, where coastal shippers and inland traders alike relied on a knowledge of their goods, not of their customers.

additional sales. What cemented these bonds above all else was the standing contradiction between an agricultural economy's annual cycle of debt settlement and a commercial world's short-term turnover in transactions—the root cause for America's reliance on informal, or primary, credit. Only an endless series of personal accommodations bridged the gap. The institutionalization of these transactions in primary credit involved two formulas, which expressed the simple truths of American commerce. The first set the calendar for credit: an initial grant for six months, then extensions by three-month intervals to complete the year. The second fixed the interest rate at 6%. Like all absolutes in the new culture, these lent themselves to countless variations. Extensions sometimes came in multiples of three months and not uncommonly stretched to a total of fifteen. Creditors might increase their return above 6% by adding service charges or offering extensions at a higher rate. A sudden, severe financial stringency such as the Panic of 1837 threw the entire scheme haywire. Yet the norm of 6% remained inviolate, a measure of the truth in business that rolled off tongues in the north, south, and west as if it were a Biblical maxim. On this matter at least, Lewis Tappan, George Fitzhugh, and Abraham Lincoln could agree, and a half-century later Missouri townspeople would still be using 6% as the sacred figure.

During the prolonged crisis that began with the Panic of 1837, this intricate institutional webbing proved its maturity. America's structure of secondary credit shriveled to the point of collapse. The Bank was gone. The national government, which had redistributed its funds to state banks before the panic was preparing to hide them in the mattress of the Independent Treasury where no one could abuse—or use—them. Domestic banking contracted to the narrowest limits for survival, and at the hub of the international system, London's financiers restricted their activities to the transatlantic essentials for the British economy. In their initial responses to this radical tightening, Americans instinctively turned inward to their smallest personal circles of support. Yet when depression then settled across the nation, America's interior commerce continued to flow briskly. With failure as their alternative, merchants and jobbers, steamboat owners and overland haulers, storekeepers and meat packers maintained their links of primary credit, two by two, because these had worked before and there was no other choice now. Applying the same principles of a personal contract in bad times as well as good, they sustained the commercial economy in the midst of a massive deflation.

Nevertheless, times did remain hard between 1839 and 1843. Manufacturing establishments along the Atlantic coast suffered severely from British competition. Importing eastern merchants who now operated on a tight tether of British credit had less leeway in carrying their jobbers or inland customers, and the closing of so many interior banks inevitably disrupted a number of local economies. As the commercial networks strained through these trials, two adaptations developed in response. First, groups of city merchants sought more precise information about the reliability of scattered inland firms that could no longer be trusted to pay their debts simply because they had paid them in good times. Among various efforts to acquire this information, the abolitionist Lewis Tappan devised the most serviceable model in 1841 by using his own extensive commercial connections to compile reports on firms around the country and then allowing New York's merchants to see them for a fee. Tappan's Mercantile Agency and several imitators spread during the 1840s to provide commercial centers in every region with at least rudimentary credit ratings. The second adaptation softened the attitude of state legislatures toward bankruptcy proceedings. Most strikingly, Massachusetts set uniform rules in 1838 that allowed a bankrupt to retain up to $500 of assets for a fresh start.

Although credit ratings and bankruptcies smoothed some edges of uncertainty from American commerce, neither changed the fundamentals of the institutional web. Credit agencies, rather than evaluating the state of a firm's balance sheet, evaluated the state of the businessman's character. Their files collated a community judgment on his personal reputation, and in a self-fulfilling fashion they encouraged a denial of life-giving credit to those men whose interior qualities, according to their immediate associates, should cause them to fail. Hence every conscience-nagged merchant had reason to worry about these gumshoe reports: a "vile stigma on our character," a nervous group of midwestern merchants called one such *"Black Book."*[7]

Moreover, despite Massachusetts' example, most states retained their punitive laws on bankruptcy and then liberalized the consequences through special legislation that dealt with one person's hardship at a time. Once again, a local reputation for good character served as the basis for such individual petitions. Each man sought to establish himself as an exception to the revealing general term for the defaulter—a business "failure." These characterological reprieves from the legislature were a formal analogue to the informal techniques by which wealthy creditors were easing their most reputable debtors past a temporary insolvency. Among the Appletons and Lawrences and Jacksons and Lees in Boston's circle of merchant-bankers, for example, a technical bankruptcy was little more than an awkward pause in a prosperous career. In similar fashion a handful of manufacturers in Philadelphia and New York stayed afloat from 1837 to 1843 because their merchant creditors simply held the debts year after year out of a basic faith in their characters and an enduring hope of better times to come. The values of the town remained triumphant.

What hard times did not generate was a demand for more banks. As Michel Chevalier told his French audience, much as he might have explained any curious barbaric rite, the founders of the standard American bank "have, on their own authority, opened a credit for themselves, and generally admitted their friends to share in the privilege . . . [or] discounted no paper but their own. . . . " In 1857 an American authority could still offer as "a proverb, that banks never originate with those who have money to lend, but with those who wish to borrow." Because the existing banks only served insiders, each group of needy capitalists had "to create a new one."[8] Against a background of widespread hostility toward such irresponsible privilege, the American economy flourished during the late 1840s and the 1850s with a fund of bank capital roughly comparable to that of a poor agrarian nation a century later. A few states operated with no banks, and most of them at least tightened the rules to discourage new creations. Nevertheless, a skepticism about banks did nothing to inhibit primary credit generally. Even Jackson, the great champion of specie, called the many varieties of personal credit *"bona fide* exchange" for almost all purposes and only balked at considering these "promisory notes" government-sanctioned *"money."* John Catron, the man whom both Van Buren and Polk expected to champion hard money on the Supreme Court, explained the realities of "paper, and credit, in our fiscal system" to his sponsors this way: "The public mind in the cities & Towns knows nothing else, and in the planting states, little else. On Earth has there never been a people so weded to paper . . . [and political leaders] must flex themselves to it, or *fall. . . ."*[9] These private commercial networks actually benefited from the disappearance of the weakest bank paper and, in fact, scarcely noticed the absence of Biddle's Bank. While the Bank was sinking, people as diverse as the austere John Quincy Adams, the business-minded Democrat George M. Dallas, and the radical theorist William Gouge had accurately predicted that in a scheme of personal transactions "credit must and will regulate itself."[10]

The greater accent on personal reliability strengthened the tendency toward continuous business relationships and hence toward parallel enterprise. Short of a private feud or an unusually bad reputation, even apparent rivals in the cutthroat cities responded to one another's misfortunes with a kind of self-involved compassion. As fellow competitors against the same hazards and opportunities, they saw a failure next door as an ill omen at home, not as a chance to seize another firm's customers. An open America offered ample business for all good men, and one good man's insolvency only signaled trouble for other good men in the same line of business. Appropriately, the small set of iron manufacturers who supplied America's railroads shared secrets and exchanged patents as a normal business practice. Eastern jobbers commonly pooled their knowledge about unreliable firms in the interior. In an ideal world each man should have an exclusive track to test his own merits in the race for profits.

Across this nationwide pattern of transactions the Supreme Court laid its blessings in *Swift* v. *Tyson* (1842). The issue before the Court was the use of a personal note between two parties as a means of payment to a third party—that is, the use of a personal note as currency. Joseph Story took the occasion to declare an open national arena for such primary credit transactions, noting that they composed the bulk of America's actual medium of exchange. A unanimous Court supported him. Because *Swift* v. *Tyson* simply ratified prevailing practice, commercial spokesmen scarcely commented on it, and in the coming years a Court often divided on other matters routinely reinforced this institutional cement. These declarations of legitimacy served equally as a declaration of independence. During the 1840s and 1850s, a thriving inland commerce that the British had largely abandoned after 1815 broadened and deepened as the base for an autonomous American economy. Although London could still yank the longest rope of credit, Americans now had their own devices to keep the many strands of domestic commerce intact and the flow of interior trade on its way. This time Jefferson and Hamilton would have been delighted.

The national parties of the 18th century, saddled with a need to mobilize every four years, proceeded to collapse after 1815 under the stress of space, mobility, and democracy and had to be rebuilt during the thirties and forties. Commerce, thoroughly decentralized, could reckon with these challenges by expanding a tradition of personal exchange until, cumulatively, it had revolutionized its operations. Religion fell between those extremes. Like parties, the Protestant denominations claimed to have national frameworks, but like commerce, none had a fixed territory to cover or a national timetable to follow. The denominations, in other words, enjoyed considerable latitude in adapting to the same triad of challenges—space, mobility, democracy.

By all odds the most successful were the Methodists and Baptists, minor denominations in the late 18th century that surged with the early westward movement to become the Protestant leaders by 1820. Both met the opportunities of expansion by deploying an army of preachers among the dispersed western settlers. Initially the Methodists suffered from too sharply peaked a hierarchy. During the 1820s and 1830s, however, eastern Methodist leaders ceased to view the west as the Devil's playground and relaxed their surveillance over its affairs. By contrast, the radically decentralized Baptists threatened to fragment as they spread westward. Meeting the Methodists on a middle ground, the Baptists tempered their extreme particularism by the 1830s with state or district conventions that resolved sundry doctrinal disputes and local quarrels.

The heart of the appeal for both denominations was their elementary religious truths. Ironing the complexities out of John Wesley's thought, Methodists broadcast a simple message of a sinful world, a saving Christ, and a heaven open to all who had the faith to seek it. Although Baptists retained a Calvinist heritage, they made it immediately accessible to everybody. One Baptist minister translated its doctrine into a "five-finger exercise": faith in God, repentance of error, baptism by immersion, remission of sins, and infusion of the Holy Spirit. Neither denominational message waited on ceremony. When carnivals tented next to their meetings, preachers just yelled their simple truths louder than the barkers. Neither denomination required special training for the pulpit. Both of them stressed the individual's responsibility to God, both expected congregations to police that responsibility, and both allowed congregations to form almost instantly. A jealous lay power prevailed in these congregations, and as local values varied, so did their orientations. Some were reformist, others conservative, but comeouter or stayinner, they remained Baptist or Methodist by a strict adherence to a simple core of doctrine.

Because Congregationalists and Presbyterians refused to distill their doctrines into five-finger exercises, they fell behind in the race for souls. Structurally they were geared for expansion; doctrinally they were not. In two ways, however, they sought to widen their appeal without lowering their standards. Through the Benevolent Empire, basically their joint venture, they pioneered in the mass distribution of simple religious literature and the multiplication of popular Sunday schools. Nevertheless, as they passed out more Bibles and tracts, the Methodists and Baptists continued to gather in more members. Revivals offered a second means of reaching a broader public. Despite a stubborn resistance from denominational conservatives, Presbyterian and Congregational ministers labored earnestly to stir the coals of enthusiasm within their churches. Grow or die was a nervous matter for the laggards. By engrafting a spontaneous emotional appeal onto their church doctrine, they managed a moderate rate of growth and entered into the dominant spirit of early-19th-century Protestantism.

Just as the conservatives feared, however, revivalism did take its toll from the Presbyterian and Congregational orthodoxies. By the 1840s, the softening of their doctrines in combination with the hardening organization of the more popular denominations fixed an institutional pattern for most of American Protestantism. Except for the Congregationalists, periodic state, regional, and national conventions enabled the keepers of the denominations to make certain adjustments in the prevailing absolutes and reaffirm the faith among a diverse membership. Denominational journals, published sermons and tracts, and traveling ministers provided an occasional finger pressing the button of an internalized truth. Even the Disciples of Christ, once the deadly enemy of church organization, relented in 1849 to form state and national conventions. By then, almost all of the Baptist congregations had replaced their lay preachers with paid ministers, and almost all of the boisterous Methodist camp meetings had disappeared. Revivals everywhere followed a roughly common formula standardized by a group of simple manuals. Each denomination now operated its own complement of Sunday schools, missions, and other benevolent activities.

The firming of these denominational schemes coincided with a time of interdenominational peace. As usual, the sharpest conflicts were intradenominational, pitting members against one another over the interpretation of the church's simple absolutes. During the first third of the 19th century, splinter after splinter broke from the largest denominations in the name of a purer, often a more democratic faith: western Presbyterians shucking off the remnants of original sin and eastern authority, Baptists following Alexander Campbell's commitment to the redemptive power of baptism and the egalitarian congregation, and many more. As Campbell's group illustrated, a magnetic individual often gave the defection its coherence. Then, as the institutional patterns were settling, the major denominations simply cleaved in two: the Presbyterians in 1837, the Methodists in 1844, the Baptists in 1845. Earlier schisms had usually expressed the strains of an east-west tension. With east and west more or less connected, the divisions from 1837 to 1845 came from pulls north and south.

Nevertheless, in the largest as in the smallest of these fractures, once the internal debates ended in separation, rancor almost always ceased. A new truth, a new track, a new test, with ample space and an abundance of souls for everyone, underwrote a remarkable toleration among parallel competitors, each convinced of the others' errors but each preoccupied with its own cause and its own growth. No final tally, like a presidential election, measured the cost of a defection. Everyone's path remained open. To keep the hatred alive required something as horrible to the immutable truths of Protestantism as the Mormons' claim to an altered Bible. Otherwise competitors went their own ways. Characteristically, a British visitor at a Methodist revival "heard nothing which could be offensive to any other sect."[11] Peter Cartwright referred to "the contemptible business of proslyting members of other Churches."[12] When rival preachers clashed in a new territory, someone was expected to win quickly and secure a monopoly, as an admiring account of the Methodist Lorenzo Dow's contest with Presbyterians and Baptists in Mississippi illustrated: "All he asked was an open field and a fair fight. In about three months he completely silenced them, and we had nothing to do but go on and preach the Gospel. . . ."[13] In response to the denominational cleavages between 1837 and 1845, Presbyterians, Methodists, and Baptists acted in much the same way. Only the Methodist division left a lingering bitterness, and that concerned the distribution of church property, not the struggle over members. In retrospect, these sweeping slices of north from south, all related to differences over slavery, seemed to prefigure a bloody, winner-take-all civil war. At the time, however, they represented a natural allocation of territory for parallel paths, east to west.

Like the political parties, the denominations institutionalized around immutable yet adaptable truths, networks of reinforcement, and parallel competition. Again like the parties, the Protestant churches had a distinctive domain, and one of its defining characteristics separated it from the worldly rough-and-tumble of politics or business. Religious territory turned back toward the home rather than out toward the lanes of opportunity. Following the family division between morals and enterprise, the church belonged next to the women and children. Hence, the churches added Sunday schools but subtracted election-day sermons. When some denominations rotated ministers as a way of minimizing personal influence and maximizing doctrinal trust, church laymen often welcomed the turnover: ministers who stayed too long tended to dabble too widely in public affairs. Even the ministers who did influence politics joined their colleagues in a self-consciously spiritual, otherworldly description of their calling. Charles Finney, whose revivals churned the forces behind abolitionism, never mentioned the Civil War in his memoirs.

Statistics on actual church membership seemed to shrink the ministers' domain even more narrowly. Although the numbers grew impressively, increasing about ninefold in the first half of the century, only about 15% of the population belonged to a Protestant church at midcentury. What the exact size of the church sphere obscured, however, was the atmospheric authority of Protestantism, an influence that floated above the denominations and pervaded American life. States that denied public offices to ministers simultaneously demanded that the men who did hold them believe in God. Merely displaying a Bible in his hand offered a token of trust for the itinerant preacher in a strange town. Biblical names served as the family staple, and Biblical references dotted all manner of public address, on the assumption that everyone would simply know them. Indeed, the entire concept of early-19th-century progress—the ascending and descending paths, the flashes of insight and surges to greatness—merged themes of Christianity and secular enterprise into a national creed.

In an intellectually amorphous but psychically powerful way, respectable Americans sensed in that atmospheric Protestantism the essence of their internalized absolutes, the broad, immutable values on which each of them relied for a lifetime's guidance. "There are many ways of professing Christianity in the United States," Harriet Martineau observed; "but there are few, very few men . . . who do not carefully profess Christianity, in some form or another."[14] "The simple *practicals* of religion, *these, these* are the Alpha and Omega," declared Theodore Weld in his impatience over theologies.[15] To explain the meaning of religion that he had found among Americans of "real wisdom, worth and independent sincerity" in his wide travels, Timothy Flint used the standard imagery of the youth on trial, wandering and then affirming. They search and doubt, he wrote, "until finally they have settled to rest, not in a creed of numerous articles—but of a few simple truths, to which the mind clings more closely, the more they are examined; which fluctuate not with our temperaments, hopes and fears. . . ." These, Flint concluded, they found applicable "under all changes and circumstances."[16]

In other areas that shared the ministry's claim to be a profession, the principle of a few and simple truths also predominated. By the 1830s, restrictive legislation that attempted to preserve the practices of medicine and law for an elite had either softened, atrophied, or disappeared throughout the United States, and the local medical and bar associations that policed them had withered along the way. Regular medicine, confronted with a popular demand for self-determination in bodily health, now shared its field with an array of alternatives, most of which by the 1840s formed their own institutional strands through elementary rules, journals and lectures for reinforcement, and various centers for treatment and training that ran parallel to the path of the regulars.

Law democratized from within. Beginning in the western states and then spreading through the east, admission to the bar fell into the hands of local judges whose highly mixed qualifications set Gresham's Law to work on the quality of new applicants. As a common cover across this assortment of legal practitioners lay a few basic truths that had been distilled from the leading experts on Anglo-American law. Although custom still specified a reading of Blackstone and perhaps Coke as well, apprentices who found the British masters too formidable turned to popular guidebooks that provided a shortened course of study and a convenient reference for the future. One of the first of these, Francis Hilliard's *The Elements of Law* (1835), assured its readers that the law contained

"certain broad and fixed principles, which embody the essence of the
system, and remain unchanged . . . a few comprehensive, elementary
maxims of which [all the] details are merely the occasional modification,
while the maxims themselves remain of the same general truth and
applicability as before."[17] Endeavoring "to be clear and simple, rather
than to seem profound or erudite," wrote Timothy Walker, the author of
the most successful popularization, " . . . I have crowded as many general
principles as I could into the smallest compass. . . ."[18] Hence long before
the conservative Lemuel Shaw's famous defense of the common law in
1854 as "a few broad and comprehensive principles . . . modified and
adapted to the circumstances of all the particular cases which fall within
it," innumerable self-made lawyers throughout the nation had been taking that axiom for granted. "The common law," Hilliard told his students, much as Finney said of the Bible at the same time, "has no more
characteristic feature, than its *strong common sense*. . . ."[19] In addition
to these general simplifications, lawyers could also find summaries of
state statutes in the legal periodicals and digests of the Supreme Court's
record in the publications of its reporter Richard Peters.

Beneath this national veneer, lawyers, clients, and courts created local
networks where the rewards of the law followed the lines of personal
trust. In order to draw the greatest benefits from such communities,
lawyers tended to attach themselves to one court, appearing again and
again before the same bench and, when necessary, following the court on
its circuit. Judges, raised from the same values, often made a lawyer's
reputation the certificate for a sound legal argument. For clients who
sought legal services at a distance, the American Legal Association,
founded in 1849, tried to duplicate the success of the mercantile credit
agencies. The association's goal, it announced, "is to furnish professional
and business men with the name of at least one prompt, efficient and
trustworthy Lawyer in every shire-town and in each of the principal
cities and villages in the Union. . . ."[20] The task exceeded their grasp,
however. Most legal reputations remained local, as did the varied applications of the law's immutable principles. The actual working of the
law, one popularizer noted, "does but adapt itself to the community."[21]

The law, if not the oldest profession, was one of the older ones, and its
democratic adjustments came hard. Public education, on the other hand,
developed along with the new culture, spread through much of the nation
during the 1840s, and automatically mirrored prevailing values. The urge
to educate citizens so that they could follow the guidance of their leaders
had a long history in America, and the Revolution stirred an even deeper
interest in creating what Benjamin Rush called "republican machines"
from the sovereign people. In this hierarchical spirit, free schools for the
poor had appeared in the major cities very early in the 19th century,

cropped up in more and more towns and cities as the nation expanded, and joined with the original movement for charitable Sunday schools. By the 1830s, however, a very different logic was powering a new drive for mass education. With the democratic right to choose came declarations of "the *absolute right* to an education" that would prepare Americans for those choices.[22] Spokesmen such as James Carter and Horace Mann now promoted free public education as a crucible of democracy, a blending of all children to function from a common set of values. Unevenly but inexorably, the existing schools broke their ties with private philanthropy, new ones multiplied during the 1840s, and a network of common schools formed.

As a preparation for choices, public education acted as an extension of the family. During the most malleable childhood years, female teachers as surrogate mothers were expected to instill the immutable absolutes and leave on the nation's youth "the imprint which the sense of truth stamps indelibly upon the character."[23] The readers and spellers and geography texts communicated the same moral lessons and patriotic messages between different covers. Literacy, once a way of preparing the people to follow their gentry instructors, now helped them internalize their culture's simple truths. From such popular manuals as *The School and the Schoolmaster* (1842), teachers also had a basic model of personal conduct and classroom procedure. Mann's writings and Henry Barnard's journal reiterated year after year the themes of a moral vocation with an urgent mission. Teachers' institutes provided—in Barnard's phrase— an "educational revival agency," and by the late forties, handbooks standardized these gatherings wherever they met. Infusing the entire educational process were Timothy Flint's "few simple truths" of Protestantism. "There is enough—thank God there is enough—of common Christian ground in the Bible, for all sects to meet on and cultivate . . . the great fundamental principles upon which Christians are agreed," educators in the northwest declared.[24]

Of all the new institutions, public schooling most exactly reflected the community it served. The number of classes, the timing of the school term, even the language of instruction, expressed the wishes of a local leadership. No external standards inhibited the hiring and firing of teachers strictly on the basis of local reputation. As superintendent of schools in Massachusetts, Horace Mann had no powers of coercion and still saw his post eliminated as too intrusive. The city systems also adapted to local control. Introducing the law that would resolve an angry controversy over religious instruction in New York City's schools early in the forties, its sponsor explained: "The practical consequence is, that each district suits itself, by having such religious instruction in its schools as is congenial to the opinion of its inhabitants. . . ."[25] Alone with a gaggle of children, the committed teacher had to take comfort from the purity of the absolutes that were guiding her, for they often seemed to elude her employers and her pupils alike.

The cultural centrality of the family also influenced another, thinner institutional network relating to the management of deviants—the criminals, the insane, and to a lesser degree the chronically poor. In the 18th-century social order, these outcasts fell into a residual category below the level of the true people—that is, those with a modicum of property who stuck to their work. Where local ties sustained them, the insane and the indigent had lived in the dingy corners of their communities. Otherwise they, like the criminals, had belonged to the eternal problem of society's dregs. Those judged vicious had been expelled, maimed, or in persistent cases executed. Those judged benign but incorrigible had in some way been imprisoned. Without devoting a great deal of attention to the subject, gentry leaders had tried to extract a return for the prisoners' keep through various programs for coerced labor. Republican reforms had extended no further than a more sensitive categorization, separating the quarters for the insane and the debtor, for example, from those for the most despised criminals.

By the 1820s and 1830s the new culture was affecting the response to these groups, especially the criminals and the insane. If individual choices determined individual destinies, deviancy became a matter of individual failure rather than social inevitability. Moreover, if all functioning members of a society enjoyed equal standing, those unable to assume the responsibilities of equality simply had no place in that society. A half or a third equal was a democratic absurdity. Hence, instead of shuffling deviants about at the bottom of society, the reformers of the early 19th century insisted that they be taken out of society, placed in segregated facilities, and treated as wayward individuals. If they rehabilitated themselves, they could return one by one to their communities as full-fledged equals. They had chosen to divorce themselves from society; now they could choose to reenter it.

What the new scheme envisioned was a wholesale character reformation, an interior reconstruction that would dig out the bad impulses and implant the standard virtues in their place. The only available model for inculcating basic values was the family shaping the child. Reformers proposed, in effect, to infantilize their isolated sets of deviants and subject them to a rigorous family discipline, one that would compensate through its incessant pressure for the fact that these deviants were already adults. Fortunately, the common connotations of a weak character were softness and flabbiness, by contrast to the firm stuff of a virtuous character. In prisons, insane asylums, and almshouses, therefore, administrators set detailed schedules to cover the inmates' movements and activities all day, every day. Useful labor now served to train character, not produce a pittance of social profit. Particularly for criminals, the riskiest subjects of rehabilitation, the daily schedule sought to intensify each inmate's concentration on his or her own psychic state, driving every lesson home with the least distraction and the greatest interior force. New York's Auburn Prison, which separated inmates at night and had them work side by side in silence during the day, provided the most generally copied penitentiary system of the early 19th century, one that took the chance out of choice with a vengeance. The objective always remained a socializing one. By hammering the essential community values deep into the inmates' minds, one by one, the reformers, like the parents and teachers and ministers who trained real children, believed that they were best equipping these individuals to function as citizens of the good society.

The institutionalization of these reforming enterprises followed the standard scheme of overarching truths, local adaptations, and occasional reinforcements through journals, books, and conventions. At the same time, where so few had a vested interest in a special area of knowledge, the urge to band together, transform that knowledge into an insiders' monopoly, and create a profession found its clearest expression. The handful of leaders in the Association of Medical Superintendents, for example, claimed that only they knew enough to prescribe for the insane and tried to drive the casual copyists from their field. In an equally small specialty, administrators of urban welfare such as Robert Hartley in New York and Franklin B. Sanborn in Boston also sought to separate themselves as professionals from the amateurs. So did the Lazzaroni, self-appointed chieftains of America's small establishment in the natural sciences, as well as small groups of engineers. By husbanding bodies of information and sharing them among insiders, these efforts did minimize the dissipation of knowledge so characteristic of early-19th-century America. Nevertheless, with the exception of the natural sciences, none of these fields developed effective means for convincing others of their exclusive competence, nor did they establish effective centers of training as visible monuments to their expertise. Europe remained their magnet, and along with their amateur rivals the American specialists hurried across the Atlantic in a search for the best knowledge.

Fields that attracted a great deal of attention and a great many practitioners were irresistibly spread across the American web of simple truths, popular reinforcements, and idiosyncratic adaptations. Although Henry Barnard held aloft the same torch of professionalism in public education, almost no one accepted his minutely detailed models for schoolhouse construction and wall decoration as privileged knowledge. Like the self-styled experts in education, the small band of serious theologians converted one another while the popularizers were serving the public needs. "You read books," Peter Cartwright had the successful evangelist tell the learned minister, "but I read men."[26] Among the fields blanketing American society, only lawyers managed to create an effective layering of specialization and popularization, and their unique accomplishment reflected the distinctiveness of their field: the practice of law was democratized, but the law itself was not. The movements early in the 19th century first to compile and then to codify a labyrinthine accumulation of British and American precedents made the law more specific, not simpler. During the 1820s, well-to-do citizens and their legal allies not only protected a complex law against the democratic codifiers; they also adapted the law to serve their own needs in economic development. From there the law branched along two paths, one marked by the popularization of a few, simple truths and the democratization of practice, the other charted by the multivolume compilations of Nathan Dane and James Kent in the 1820s and Joseph Story in the 1830s and 1840s—flinty conservatives all—that maintained a sturdy bastion for elite privileges. Wealthy Americans paid high fees to those few lawyers who could manipulate the intricacies of such a law. These legal experts, clustering city by city around their prosperous clients and demonstrating the value of a specialized education at the Litchfield or Harvard law school, established small but solid outposts of professionalism in a nation of self-made advocates and circuit riders. Tocqueville called them America's aristocracy.

The tension between simplicity's coverage and complexity's exclusiveness had no bearing at all on the bands of Americans who consciously set out in the early 19th century to transform their society. These men and women knew that they wanted to reach everybody. If, as the Democrat Robert Rantoul claimed, all people harbored the "instinct for perfectability," or as the Whig Charles B. Haddock argued, "moral energy is irrepressible," then Nature was already enlisted on the reformers' side, and they needed only to bring human decisions in line with human nature. Although most respectable Americans did not share such a grand optimism about the prospects for improvement, the reformers were as firmly planted in their culture as those who pictured endless prosperity from the construction of a particular canal or those who promised general political harmony from the adoption of a legal code. Reformers simply drove the logic of everyday life more relentlessly and envisaged the consequences more universally. The difference lay in their most characteristic exhortation: "What ought to be done can be done."

Hence the reformers, like any other Americans with a message, pushed at the interior buttons of their fellow citizens in an effort to rouse their commitment to the immutable truth. Scarcely a reform failed to identify its cause with those atmospheric absolutes from the Bible. At the same time, reformers offered their converts the comforts of a like-minded group with whom they would share the burdens of personal responsibility. Reform causes institutionalized just as other areas of social activity did. Some of them, originating inside the Benevolent Empire, adopted its pioneering procedures—the "simple, serious, practical" messages, the network of "faithful and judicious" agents, the restatement of guiding absolutes in annual conventions and published addresses—and then operated through a decentralized network in the 1840s after the superstructure of eastern controls disappeared. Even the Millerite movement in preparation for Christ's second coming in 1843, then in 1844, spread the word in the early forties through the usual apparatus of newspaper, lectures, and conventions, with a handful of insiders adjusting the absolutes. Other reforms also relied on their newspapers as founts of truth flowing indeterminately outward, converting and reaffirming followers wherever they moved, and extending the range of reform through the evangelical work of these converts. Much of the noise associated with early-19th-century reform came from a passionate preoccupation with getting its messages abroad. A fount of truth placed an unusually high premium on the faith in a single leader's purity—William Lloyd Garrison among northeastern abolitionists, for example, or William Ladd in the peace movement—and personalized truths increased the probability of personalized factions. Countless little pieces snapped from these reform networks. Indeed, many reforms covered so little ground or spun their webs so finely that they shaded into the realm of fads. In the case of the underground railroad for fugitive slaves, the web relied so exclusively on one individual's faith in the next that it actually was invisible.

Among men and women in search of their audience, the cultural commandment to grow or die pressed with a special insistence. If transportation promoters could benefit from a popular association between progress and their enterprises, few reformers enjoyed a similar advantage. To fix attention on their cause, they presented highly dramatic versions of the standard linear logic that ran from a root cause to a comprehensive effect. A variety of reforms, including temperance and public education, guaranteed an end to all human poverty. More than one enthusiast saw world peace as the inexorable result of the new telegraph. In addition, the reformers, unlike businessmen and politicians, had no obvious intermediary checkpoints to measure their success, nothing comparable to the struggles for credit or the tallies at the ballot box. Here in its purest version was the new American faith in the efficacy of the individual will, for nothing seemed to stand between the truth and a total transformation. The "law of Love," Elihu Burritt declared in that spirit of a world to remake, was the "law of Gravitation in the moral world," Nature's irresistible force in the cleansing of human relations.[27] Zeal feeding on zeal in their own reform circles scarcely dampened these dreams. Nevertheless, great hopes that brought no early returns stirred a number of reformers to take another leap, to experience yet another conversion to a new cause with even more dazzling consequences to follow. Such men as William Lloyd Garrison, Samuel Gridley Howe, and Samuel B. Woodward became addicted to progress, and they required regular doses of a fresh vision as the effects of the older ones were subsiding. Many causes, after all, meant many means to the one great end, human perfection.

These lunging qualities in reform's march of progress reflected the failure of parallelism to ease the heaviest pressures for growth, growth, growth. If reformers had lived exclusively in a world of competing moral causes, they might have developed very different characteristics, for in most cases they showed a standard tolerance of one another's ventures. Instead, they saw themselves surrounded by moral indifference, and one after another of them decided that they had to convert the entire unregenerate mass. Building a railroad or winning an election, by contrast, required a finite number of allies for a limited objective. Only the most wide-eyed Protestant ministers shared the reformers' infinite ambition, and the major denominations, exceedingly leery of distracting enthusiasms, held these zealots in check. Fittingly, reformers often condemned the clergy as obstacles to progress. Hence when reformers framed their issues in the normal language of glory or catastrophe—grow or die—they, far more than the advocates around them, spoke about all of life for all people. In the advanced stage of many reforms, the only proper testing lane was the universe.

The reforms best adapted to the values of parallelism were the scores of communitarian experiments, ranging from Robert Owen's New Harmony to John Humphrey Noyes' Oneida community, that in various ways modeled the perfect society. In an effort to save society, these groups of reformers left it. In time, many of them believed, their irresistible truth would spread through a flawed, unhappy world and reshape it. For now, however, they required separate testing spheres. In effect, they created their own segregated asylums, committed themselves, and through precise sets of rules sought to reconstruct their characters for perfection. As a whole, these many model communities revealed the essential qualities of American parallelism, each imputing uniqueness to its own efforts and almost none drawing on the experiences of comparable ventures.

The drive to expand women's rights also remained within the bounds of American parallelism, largely because men kept it there. As a distinctive movement, it originated in a meeting at Seneca Falls, New York, in

1848 and developed institutionally through a platform of fundamental truths, a series of conventions to adapt and reaffirm them, and a cadre of lecturers to propagate them. Its primary thrust came from the heart of the new democratic culture, freedom of choice. By barring the American woman from public life, man had rendered her, in Elizabeth Cady Stanton's telling 19th-century phrase, "an irresponsible being." Women were charged to shape the characters of the men who did rule, then banned as incapable of sharing their rights. The suffrage laws even elevated "the most ignorant and degraded men" above them.[28] By taking his wife's property and wages, the husband made her a slave during his life and left her helpless at his death. If, according to the prevailing values, a man had no money because he lost his virtue, a woman lost her virtue because she had no money—and men were conspiring in her fall. Nature commanded women as well as men to progress or decline. "Very early," wrote Margaret Fuller, "I knew that the only object in life was to grow."[29] "Why should not woman seek to improve elevate and raise higher her standard of moral and intellectual worth, in order to keep pace with the age in which she lives?" Huldah Stone, a labor leader at Lowell, demanded in 1846.[30] To replace their man-made cul-de-sac, reformers sought a genuine path of progress with full opportunities to speak and act and vote in their own behalf. Time and again they turned to the simple truths in the Bible to prove their case. Could men argue, asked a group of Wisconsin reformers, "that the Creator of man is not her Creator; that she has not the same evil to shun, the same heaven to gain; in short, the same grand, immortal destiny . . ."?[31]

Men did manage to argue a good deal of that. Recognizing the assertion of women's rights as an encroachment on their monopolies, men responded with a mixture of anger, ridicule, and praise. The last proved the most suffocating—a rebuttal to the charge of inequalities that glorified them. While equal in an abstract sense, it went, men and women were perfect opposites—the one endowed with "energy, enterprise, and courage," the other with "sensibility, tenderness, patience"—and hence "it was intended by God that they should move in different spheres."[32] Caught in their own belief in basic gender differences and unwilling to add the entire marriage arrangement to their cause, the reformers gave away too much to win that debate. Meanwhile, their logical allies, the male reformers with whom they were already collaborating in other causes, appealed to that God-given attribute of patience and told women to wait. In a natural sequence of events, the men assured them, the success of the great reforms at hand would bring women's freedom in their wake.

Blocked by enemies and friends alike, reforming women channeled most of their energy into causes that dealt only indirectly with their own situation. The usual avenue ran from the domestic sphere through the church into the wider world of sin. If no male in the 19th century doubted God's gender, many a minister must have thought that all the angels in heaven were female, because women provided both the bulk and the strength of their congregations. From the church it was a relatively short step to an auxiliary organization and then possibly an independent association that offered members considerable freedom in directing their own campaigns and expressing at least some of their feelings along the way. The most impressive of these independent associations, the Female Reform Society, originated in 1834, spread from New York City across a network of over 500 affiliates, and by 1840 diffused its truths through a standard institutional pattern.

Attacking worldly sins meant attacking men—dissolute males overrunning the west, drunken males abusing their families, lustful males using prostitutes, brutal males degrading slaves. Reforming women assailed these man-made evils with a venom that was legitimized by their culture's absolute separation of right from wrong. In a high proportion of these moral crimes, the immediate victims were women, and reformers used the acts of victimization to highlight the ways in which men making vicious decisions preyed on women lacking the right to a free choice. Defending the prostitutes in their charge, for example, the Women's Prison Association of New York City declared in 1849 that rarely "has there in truth been any such deliberate choice—any such insane election! Our experience has shown us conclusively that in nine cases out of ten, no choice was ever made, for none was ever offered."[33] In the 18th century, marriage had forced respectable women into a defense of the family names they acquired. They took what they got. After the 1820s, however, the revolution in choices individualized reputations to a far greater degree, and reforming women could turn the aggrieved wife, suffering at the hands of a squandering, drunken, violent husband, into an increasingly sympathetic figure.

Of course much more was at issue in these causes than the redirected anger of the reforming women themselves. Wives obviously had a deep stake in the gambling and drinking and assaulting habits of their husbands: their well-being in every sense hung in the balance. The solid male values of frugality, sobriety, and dependability, even the sentimental courtesies toward the gentler sex, doubled among women as the rules of elementary self-defense. Moreover, destructive patterns of behavior did tend to recur, often with disastrous consequences for entire families, and hence female pressures for perfection also had their practical side. A good deal of worldly wisdom intermingled with the moral absolutism of such statements as Elizabeth Cady Stanton's in 1852: "Let no woman form an alliance with any man who has been suspected even of the vice of intemperance; for the taste once acquired can never, never be eradicated. Be not misled by any pledges, resolves, promises, or tears."[34]*

Stanton's stern advice carried the authority of the most successful reform movement in the early 19th century. Under the inappropriate name of temperance, the enemies of liquor transformed an earlier appeal for moderation into a drive for total abstinence that expanded after 1826 into a nationwide crusade. Justin Edwards, a Massachusetts minister, presided over its major clearing house, the American Society for the Promotion of Temperance, with an army of agents distributing millions of tracts, over a million and a half members, and more than 8,000 local affiliates by 1835. When the Benevolent Empire deteriorated, temperance generated its own dispersed institutional network. From the beginning, separate state societies such as those in Virginia and South Carolina conducted their own campaigns; in 1836 the American Temperance Society itself split; and in the early forties new groups, particularly the Society of Washington and the Sons of Temperance, flourished on their own. The more fragmented its organizational pattern, the more the crusade relied on the elementary truths of its doctrine and the ready availability of its reaffirmation.

These truths formed an argument as comprehensive as it was simple. Liquor violated the body's laws of Nature, the soul's laws of God, and the economy's laws of Progress—in sum, the very foundations of civilization. Between the 1820s and the 1840s its advocates broadened their picture of alcohol's effects from individual self-destruction to a whole-

---

* Heterosexual anger and revenge were certainly not a female monopoly in the 19th century, as we learn in G. J. Barker-Benfield's account of the cruelties inflicted on women in the name of medicine and Michael Paul Rogin's brilliant analysis of the assault on Biddle's "Mother Bank." But as Rogin's topic also demonstrates, hate and love came in clusterings as ambivalent and subtle in the 19th as in any other century. While Jackson's legions attacked the Bank as a devouring mother who would annihilate her children, Biddle's allies, including Joseph Gales and Levi Woodbury, used exactly the same term, "Mother Bank," to express their affection for this nurturing center of economic virtue. As our store of fairy tales reminds us, mother and stepmother have always been the reverse sides of a single image, and no collection of males had stronger reasons than the respectable men of the early 19th century for flipping it now this way, now that. If every one of them simply had to have an idealized mother as surety for his virtue, every one of them had also been cut from the warmth of the home and thrust alone into a society of fearsome risks with steel-trap consequences. Mother had stroked and guided them, but mother had also abandoned them to the wicked world, making every man in his frightened moments a Hansel in the woods and every mother a sometime stepmother-witch. Mother Bank, Stepmother Bank: in the turmoil of the early thirties, a striking number of men changed their minds quite abruptly, as Biddle's intimate, Charles J. Ingersoll, did in his conversion to Jacksonianism in 1832. Protecting fathers, abusing fathers: in the reform movement around midcentury, many women experienced the same oscillating emotions toward the male authorities around them.

sale dissolution of family life, social morality, and national prosperity, and during these same years their reform tactics evolved just as impressively: from moderate drinking to a ban on hard liquor in 1826, to total abstinence from all alcoholic drink a decade later, to a wider assault on the liquor business in the forties, and finally to a legal prohibition of its sale. At each step, the scent of success and the spur of growth drove the crusaders to demand more and expect more as a consequence. Although this escalation cost the movement some supporters along the way, it more than compensated for the losses by gilding the image of temperance as the pacesetter in the march of progress. The more converts the movement attracted, the more it sought to reach the weakest-willed members of society, those whose vulnerability to sin made a mandatory ban the only sensible policy. The same logic that had long condemned state lotteries for enticing the weak to gamble condemned state authorization of liquor for enticing the weak to drink. At its peak between 1851 and 1855 the movement inspired prohibition laws in thirteen states from Maine to Delaware and New York to Iowa, with three others hovering on the brink. Appropriate to the spirit of an immutable truth, the initial Maine law became the model for legislators everywhere.

Then the movement collapsed. A free society's aversion to legal solutions could not explain it, for the widespread urge to take the chance out of choice gave such prohibitory legislation as much of an emancipating as a coercing cast. It freed the way to virtue. Nor could the angry resistance of its opponents explain the collapse—sinners always howled at the bar of justice. Nor could the turmoil in the mid-fifties over slavery— as the success of a later drive during the disruptions of the First World War illustrated, prohibition might well have drawn strength from other militant concerns. The movement disintegrated because it could no longer sustain the impression of growth. Only in this sense did the problems of enforcement and the divisions over slavery contribute to the rapid repeal of the prohibition laws and the general dissolution of the reform network. It had ridden the rails of progress to the final station, and the promised land was not there. Much like the Millerite movement without a second coming or the campaign for plank roads without a passable route to town, the crusade abruptly lost its popular following. Where the alternative avenues to an elusive progress were almost infinite, Americans had no inclination to fan life into a dying cause. So they looked elsewhere for the signs of growth.

In the mid-fifties many northerners who had once supported prohibition found their alternative in a broad, diverse antislavery cause. Within that cause, the sharpest set of simple truths belonged to the advocates of slavery's immediate abolition, whose movement originated in 1831 with Garrison's trumpet call for a relentless campaign against the sin of slaveholding. Between 1835 and 1837 it looked as if abolitionism might be absorbed within the Benevolent Empire when the most ambitious of the imperialists, Arthur Tappan, subsidized its expansion and organized a mass distribution of abolitionist literature from his New York headquarters. With the empire's passing, however, Garrison still stood firmly by his press in Boston, and local abolitionist societies still dotted the northwest along the paths of a crusade that Theodore Dwight Weld and his band of Oberlin evangelists had conducted during the 1830s. A split between the Garrisonians in New England and Tappan's New York circle, then further divisions, destroyed all vestiges of central control and allowed the movement to shape itself to the America of the 1840s: an extensive network of local groups, voices of truth adjusting and reiterating a simple, moral message, a flock of lecturers to reaffirm the absolutes, and occasional conventions to ratify the faith. Although a particularly lively conflict characterized the movement's leadership, the essential clarity of immediate abolitionism enabled its scattered followers to maintain their sense of a common cause beneath a simple cover. The towns of Weld and Phillips in western Maine could live comfortably side by side, even if those crusaders could not. By the 1840s the abolitionist movement was institutionalized.

In many ways abolitionism was just one reform among many. It spoke the familiar language of total contrasts between virtue and sin. Instead of a debauched drunkard who wallowed in his passions and destroyed his family, it pilloried the bestial slavemaster, lashing and fornicating, flounting the commandments of God and crushing the souls of his victims. Like the enemy of liquor who declared that the "man's hands are RED WITH BLOOD, who stands aloof from the temperance cause," abolitionists castigated neutrality as an evil equivalent to the act itself.[35] They rested their faith in the power of truth to convert all those who were free to choose. As the vanguard in the movement of truth, they would be the ones who, in Wendell Phillips' phrase, "broke up the crust of an ignorant prejudice, roused a slumbering conscience, shamed a proud sinner," and they banged away at the buttons inside their fellow citizens, knowing that these people too could be vaulted to the path of virtue.[36]

Yet abolitionism was also unique among American reforms. Demanding total change on the most sensitive issue in white American society, the movement marked itself immediately as the most dangerous—the most disreputable—of all the reform causes. Where temperance neatly reflected the standard virtues of self-discipline in early-19th-century culture and attracted support from a wide variety of businessmen, ministers, and wage earners, abolitionism did indeed promise to break the crust of customary ways all around it and inspired a ferocious anger in response. Respectable citizens remembered their conversion to the cause in unusu-

ally melodramatic terms because a commitment to abolitionism threatened to destroy their claims to respectability, and other Americans
further darkened the atmosphere with their acts of violence—the mob-
bing of Garrison in Boston, the murder of Elijah Lovejoy in Alton, Illinois, and a host of less publicized assaults against the itinerant crusaders.

Most striking of all, the abolitionists predicated their cause on massive
changes in a stretch of land that often lay thousands of miles from them.
Standing in one part of a distended society, they commanded a distant
part to transform itself. The lone analogy in the early 19th century—and
an exceedingly strained one at that—was the Protestant mission movement in the west. Abolitionism, in other words, made such a bold, blunt
thrust at the basic preconceptions about parallelism in American society
that only a widespread belief in the collapse of parallelism could justify
the cause. By the 1840s the feelings of growth sustaining abolitionism
depended on a perception of decline rather than advance, a steady worsen-
ing of conditions that would convince more and more northerners that
the tentacles of slavery were moving from their base in the south and
choking American opportunities everywhere. Rather than a culmination
of the reform spirit, the abolitionist movement was in many ways the
scavenger among its blighted hopes. When prohibition failed to ring in a
new age, abolitionists stood ready with an explanation that turned disillusionment into the source of recruitment. By feeding on a sense of
adversity, the abolitionists shared a singular affinity with premillennialism: the lonely virtue of the few, the deepening crisis, the apocalyptic
judgment immediately at hand. Well before the Civil War, it became
evident that abolitionism would never emerge naturally out of an unfolding progress. In some fashion its truth would have to come marching
with a "terrible swift sword."

A Society
in Halves

As America's institutional web spun itself across the country in the 1840s, it mobilized the values of the new culture into a nationwide standard for inclusion and exclusion, a class line that separated those who were qualified to participate in a democracy of free choices from those who were not. Viewed from above the line, it set the most significant of all the nation's parallel tracks, dividing virtue from vice, growth from decay, and hope from despair, and respectable Americans found themselves devoting more and more attention to the maintenance of this crucial distinction. In the process, their institutional networks gave structure to the class division. As they interconnected respectable Americans, in other words, they simultaneously formalized the separation between the respectable and the disreputable. Appropriate to the culture it expressed, the class line relied on a few simple truths that in an extensive nation could then be adapted to local circumstances. Inevitably, these truths were rooted in judgments of character, and to make the judgments generally applicable in a society of mobile people, they were shaped into stereotypes that allowed a quick categorization into acceptable or unacceptable. Acceptability meant equality, unacceptability ostracism.

"Democracy everywhere has no soft words, no suppleness of forms. . . ,"

Michel Chevalier wrote of Jacksonian America, "it is apt to con-
found moderation for weakness. . . ."[1] So it seemed by 18th-century
American as well as 19th-century European standards. The gentry hierarchy, by grading authority down its tiers, had dispersed responsibilities
among national, state, and local elites, blurred the division of rights
among its ranks of citizens, and shaded the boundary between a republican people and society's residue. Lacking gradations in a flattened
society, respectable Americans now drew a line—in or out—and
concentrated on preserving their one significant distinction. What
emerged were two models of life, partly the product of an upper-class
imagination but in a self-fulfilling fashion partly a reflection of the actual
prospects in American society.

Above the class line lay the paths of progress that adults could choose
if they would. Here, it was claimed, no one enjoyed privileges that others
could not share, and everyone achieved a success equivalent to merit.
Much of the tone of American society sustained that image of homogeneous enterprise. When Tocqueville marveled at the universality of the
American scramble for wealth, his point of contrast was an idle aristocracy in Europe, so strikingly absent in the United States, where respectable citizens of all kinds took a common code into a common arena of
enterprise. Even the prosperous Chicago merchants who "retired from
active business" around midcentury avidly pursued land development,
not a gentleman's leisure.[2] Because of the economy's rate of growth during the forties and fifties, the few who did rely on safe investments paid
the penalty of a relative decline in wealth. Respectable Americans everywhere condemned any signs of aristocratic aloofness—"exclusiveness"
—among the very rich. Moreover, enough abrupt falls and dramatic rises
in fortune occurred to support the impression of a characterological justice in the world of affairs. If almost no one went from rags to riches, a
good many did go from modest to quite substantial wealth.

Below the class line the poor were expected to stay in rags, and most
of them did. Barred from the opportunities to advance, they fulfilled the
prophecies of doom that respectable citizens hurled at them. Large numbers of them joined the vast flow of Americans that made a turnover in
excess of 50% of a community's population every five or ten years a
common occurrence, particularly along the main routes of migration. As
propertyless floaters, a reputation did them no good, and the staple virtues of sobriety, dependability, and perseverance brought them no returns. Left with society's hardest work and lowest security, they learned
to take pleasure where they found it and let tomorrow care for itself. In
a rough world they presented a rough appearance, spoke a rough language, and expected a rough response. By and large, they got one. They
were "the dangerous classes" of the cities and the contaminants of the

towns. A settled Baptist and Methodist ministry no longer served them, and respectable citizens openly despised them. Hence the alternative model of life in America: a rootless, shiftless people whose interior flaws destroyed their prospects along with their morals and hurried them to a pauper's grave.

By midcentury the boundary between these models was hardening. A vague, grandiose language of inclusiveness that suggested the possibility of progress catching everybody up in its current and rushing all people toward perfectibility slipped out of fashion. Advocates of segregated disciplinary centers for criminals, the insane, and the indigent no longer talked glowingly about reshaping the adult character. Misshapen wax in the crucial childhood years, it seemed, did harden in grotesque forms, and on this basis a whole range of adult outcasts, including the feeble-minded, were increasingly abandoned to custodial rather than rehabilitating asylums and prisons. With a new urgency, school reformers such as Henry Barnard insisted that the children of the poor "must be taken at the earliest opportunity"—preferably at three—"if the seeds of good are to be planted before the seeds of evil begin to germinate."[3] Others took the final small step, located the seeds of evil in heredity, and absolved everyone except the parents of responsibility. Equating the deeply drilled truths from childhood with an inborn capacity to distinguish right from wrong, these conservatives concluded that Nature had bestowed this inestimable benefit only on some humans and that society now must reckon with a fundamental separation between those who did have a moral sense and those who did not.

Yet pessimism at the borders of their class seemed to enhance the optimism of respectable Americans about their own lives. Evidence abounded at midcentury of a growing ease with the drive for wealth, the prospect of achieving it, and the right to enjoy it. Perhaps never before had the visions of a boundless progress appeared more glittering. Fewer successful Americans talked about getting right with Nature, more about being there already. Emersonian self-reliance became a happy national creed. In both the quantity of investment capital and the spread of public enthusiasm, the railroad promotions of the 1850s far exceeded anything preceding them. In 1849, as Barnard was pleading for a last chance to save the impoverished three-year-olds, Horace Bushnell described sound character evolving effortlessly out of America's comfortable homes and marked the age of three as the end of the formative stage. The earlier the better in this vision, for it made the transmission of respectable virtues in the families where they already existed that much closer to an automatic process. Around midcentury, children's literature diminished the importance of charity for the poor and ratified the morality of grand material rewards. Fashion advisers who had once condemned gaudy displays encouraged their readers to indulge in the pleasures of the latest high style. To those who had, more would be given, for America was indeed the promised land of the godly.

Two tracks, two prescriptions, two largely self-perpetuating life pro-cesses: everything depended on which side of the boundary. The most critical variable in locating white Americans was property—either its outright ownership or, in the case of women and of sons who were await-ing an inheritance, access to its benefits. At midcentury close to 60% of the free adult males did not have anything more substantial than an assortment of personal belongings that they could cart along with them. Millions in this majority, especially the young men, joined the stream of migrants in order to gain that essential property, and they sought above all the American standard for independence and equality, a farm. The national obsession with land—getting it and keeping it—expressed far more for these young men than a simple urge for improvement; it marked the crucial difference between something and nothing. Some-thing meant an avenue to reputation and credit, family and stability, opportunity and growth. Nothing meant the drift from place to place with America's floating population.

To commence independent farming required for each 50 acres approx-imately $1,000, cash or credit, more if the land was fresh and timbered. Those who began the quest with a capital stake—a team of oxen, a wagon, and some tools, for example—might achieve their goal in a few years of intensive hire in plowing and hauling. But that strategy, of course, presupposed a home base to shelter the oxen and repair the equip-ment. For the man on the move who started with nothing and hired only his labor at the prevailing rates, sweating and scrimping might net him $500 a decade, or something close to his life expectancy as time enough to secure a minimal farm of his own. If he broke from the migratory flow, settled, and built a local reputation, credit might enable him to escape that hopeless cycle of working, saving, and dying. Here, however, he encountered a scarcity of credit that plagued marginal farmers in the 1840s and significantly widened the economic gap to respectability by midcentury.

After the depression of the early forties, credit in agricultural America never regained its former flexibility. Funds that had once gone into farm mortgages, the bane of bankers and other creditors during those hard times, now went to a shorter range of safer bets, the more liquid trans-actions within the commercial networks. Louisiana's Forstall Act of 1842—appropriately named after a specialist in international exchange —exemplified the trend by requiring banks to rest their primary business on short-term commercial paper and segregate farm mortgages in a back corner. Large areas of rural America had no banks at all in the mid-forties, and the ones that did survive the depression often refused to touch a mortgage. In one sense these credit policies simply reinforced the time-honored principle of farmers sowing, others reaping. But at the margin between nothing and something, it meant in addition a far lower chance for newcomers to receive any of those scarce funds. Moreover, a general tightening of agricultural credits also affected the country storekeepers, so often the farmer's de facto banker, and once again a credit shrinkage at the store hurt the untried beginner in the field most of all. Hence, even though wages for farm labor held strong during the 1850s, the rural credit squeeze more than counteracted their effects on the aspiring homesteader.

Retaining these propertyless migrants in a labor pool resolved one of the economy's central problems of growth during the early 19th century. If America's chains of commerce were suspended from a ceiling of British capital, they were anchored to a floor of agricultural productivity, the basis for the nation's commercial expansion throughout the early 19th century. In broad terms, the farms had to raise enough to provision the people who lived there, feed those who resided in towns and cities, and supply the export trade. Because the population of towns and cities increased at more than twice the rate of the countryside after 1820, and the volume of exports, never less than 80% agricultural, rose faster than the total population, the crucial component in sustaining this pattern of growth was the capacity to generate a larger and larger agricultural surplus beyond the requirements of the farm families themselves. In fact, the size of that surplus needed to be even greater than it seemed at first glance. The cotton fields also provided the raw material for America's own textile mills, which ballooned from a quarter of a million spindles in 1820 to nine times this number in 1840. In effect, the south also exported to the north. The more one part of the countryside used its gains in productivity to grow inedible cotton, the greater the burden elsewhere to grow an excess of food.

Although American agriculture began the 19th century with certain advantages, these did not account for its impressive increases in productivity. Despite the inheritance of Europe's most advanced agriculture from Britain, the United States failed to build on it. On balance, Americans probably lost as much in wasteful extensive farming practices as they gained from experiments with crop rotation and stockbreeding. Since colonial times, a high proportion of American farmers had learned to respond well to changing markets. Those habits spread and sharpened in the early 19th century with the faster movement of market information. But alertness alone only made the most of an existing productivity; it did nothing to increase the output. Finally, farmers found an abundance of rich land as they moved westward, and these fresh fields brought higher yields per acre. At the same time, virgin land required the slow, grueling work of ringing trees, axing trunks, and hacking stumps. In the area from Tennessee and Missouri northward, the losses from clearing land more than canceled the gains from its fertility.

Before agricultural machinery began to make an important difference in the 1850s, the answer to a sufficient production of food lay in the labor supply. From the pool of propertyless adult males, even younger than the national average, came the muscle that enabled farmers to plant and above all to harvest much more than their own families' labor could have managed. Often with elementary farm skills from childhood and with a penchant for job-hopping, young transients took the short-term employment that farm owners offered at good wages but at a far lower cost than the year-round maintenance of their own family members. The balance was the farm owners' profit. Although they grumbled about the unpredictability of seasonal labor, they located it, used it, and benefited from it. Northern agriculture could feed the cities and contribute as much as 20% of the export surplus because it, like southern agriculture, had access to cheap labor.

Making it in the pool of propertyless laborers required shuttling between the countryside and the town or city whenever better employment opportunities appeared. Where strength or simple farm-related skills were the entry requirements, as in harvesting, lumbering, hauling, building, and much of manufacturing, the migratory wage-earners could continue to shift from job to job and place to place as long as the demand for manual labor generally ran high. For some years the shuttle worked reasonably well. While the percentage of propertyless adults rose in the first half of the century, so did real wages, leaving open the appearance and sometimes the possibility of accumulating enough money to settle, learn a trade, and establish a respectable life in the town or city. But conditions in the labor pool also changed markedly around midcentury. Outside of agriculture, real wages sagged for unskilled and semiskilled work. A glut of impoverished immigrants, particularly from Ireland, crowded the cities, and neither newcomers nor veterans had the information or perhaps the inclination to distribute themselves in a nationwide match with job opportunities. The common impression that "a much larger number of laboring people congregated in the seaboard towns, than can find constant and profitable employment" now fitted the facts.[4] In the textile centers around Boston, that surplus encouraged more speedup and stretchout in the work and drew in a lower-paid, heavily Irish proletariat to replace the female Yankee millhands. Agriculture provided no new outlets, for by the 1850s mechanization was bounding the number of jobs in the countryside. The flow of labor backed up to fill the city reservoirs, creating a larger and larger body of wage earners who were completely dependent on the urban job markets.

Skilled workers, self-employed artisans, and small shopkeepers suffered very little direct competition as this pool swelled beneath them. Indeed, real wages for the skilled workers continued to rise, and the ranks of the self-employed continued to grow, suggesting that many of those with roots and a reputation could actually benefit from an abundance of greenhorns at the bottom layers of the urban economy. Nevertheless, the percentage of the self-employed dropped as strikingly as their numbers increased. The burgeoning cities simply grew much faster than they did. For city dwellers the analogue to the family farm was the independent business, and a relative shrinkage of opportunities here narrowed the passageway to respectability at its most sensitive urban juncture. Even a strong wage scale for the prospective owner's skills could not compensate for the dimming dream of independence. Once again, the crux of the problem was credit. Although owning the means of production and employing a few workers still lay well within the realm of possibilities in an economy of small shops, securing the credit to sustain an independent business decreasingly did. The same emphasis on commercial transactions, the same caution about untried newcomers—in other words, the same credit squeeze that frustrated aspiring farmers in the forties and fifties—also caught hopeful citizens at the class margin in the cities and completed a nationwide pattern that was deepening the economic divide between ins and outs.

In their darker moments, respectable Americans watched the endless flow of migrants and envisaged total inundation, communities simply drowning in strangers. Yet a substantial minority among the propertyless would either inherit some wealth or earn enough to settle and acquire a community stake. Who within that stream deserved a chance to enter the circle of respectability? Who had to be excluded from the community's track of progress? If all societies faced the task of sifting and selecting new members, none had ever reckoned with such a fluid population. In the less peripatetic 18th century, settled communities often told strangers to move on—and moved them on if they did not go voluntarily. But almost all people were strangers in the new territories of the 19th century, and almost no place in the United States lacked a high percentage of them. The urge to grow, let alone the need to profit from transient labor, eliminated that 18th-century rule of thumb. Now the challenge was to maintain a boundary of integrity for the community while acknowledging the inevitability—even the desirability—of a perpetual human flux.

Raised to enter a society of strangers, the sons and daughters of respectable Americans learned to judge one another through a set of readily observed or readily inferred qualities of character. The most important evidence lay immediately on the surface. "Every Christian makes an impression by his conduct, and witnesses either for [virtue] or [vice]," Charles Finney told his audience in the mid-thirties. "His looks, dress, whole demeanor, make a constant impression on one side or the other."[5] "Only extraordinary circumstances can give the appearance of dishonesty to an honest man," echoed Henry Ward Beecher a decade later. "Usually, not to *seem* honest, is not to *be* so."[6] Although the 18th-century gentry also relied on appearances for an initial screening, they had kept a constant watch for those invisible flaws that might take years to reveal themselves. Benedict Arnold had looked for all the world like a patriotic gentleman. By the early 19th century, respectable Americans assumed such a perfect communion between body and soul that everybody's true self stood nakedly on display. Villainy acquired its sharp physical stereotype—the dark look, the shifty manner, the harsh voice —and no one at the melodrama needed a program to spot it. Oliver Wendell Holmes was convinced that an unmistakable "physiological type" characterized his superior Brahmin associates. When the European science of phrenology arrived in the United States, it made such automatic good sense to thousands of Americans that they transformed it into one more quick, invariable guide to character. In its German origins, phrenology explained the unique qualities of genius through a detailed examination of the cranium's shape. During the 1830s its American advocates democratized the science into a test for all people, and by the 1840s its most successful partisans, notably Orson and Lorenzo Fowler, were instructing their readers on the proper ways of scanning the contours of the skull for an evaluation of the passing parade. Popularized phrenology won converts among an impressive assortment of thoughtful, sober citizens. Appropriately, one enthusiast blessed it as the first "means of deciding, with anything like certainty, the talents or character of a stranger."[7]

Beginning with judgments at a glance, respectable Americans proceeded across a spectrum of public behavior. Violence provided one index. Male brawls and fights, usually free-for-all and often brutal, qualified as a national pastime throughout the United States. Nevertheless, respectable men not only condemned these encounters but even altered the role of honorable violence in their own lives. Among the revolutionary gentry, dueling had borne a resemblance to cockfighting, a sport many of them shared with men in the lower orders. Specially bred to the event, 18th-century gentlemen had gone to the dueling field to kill or at least draw blood for their honor. After the War of 1812, however, only an aging generation held fast to that deadly code. During the transition years

the classic confrontation pitted murderous older aggressors against reluctant younger participants. One younger man, finally trapped by a relentless older challenger, tried farce as his defense. As weapons for
gentlemanly combat, he proposed that they sit together on a powder keg
with two fuses and light them when ready. After the older man's second
recoiled in horror, he substituted muskets with buckshot at three paces.
Another younger man foiled his grim elderly challenger in North Carolina by choosing broadswords too heavy for the old man to lift. Fittingly,
the one duel that Harriet Martineau mentioned in her account from the
mid-thirties involved a nineteen-year-old whose father and uncle forced
him into the field. By then the deadly tradition had more or less disappeared. In the west, bluff was replacing bloodshed, as an irate Captain
David Hunter illustrated in 1839 when he cowed the Chicago editor John
Wentworth with a brace of empty pistols. In elite southern circles where
dueling retained some currency, it followed such an elaborate and refined
book of rules that the forms of honor tended to overwhelm the substance
of violence. Those who did duel usually avoided bloodshed as best people
could with lethal weapons in their hands. In general, physically damaging an equal became the mark of outsiders.

So did a range of related public behavior: swearing, carousing, and
above all drinking. In the 18th century a drunken gentleman had reeled
by his inferiors indifferent to their judgment; his 19th-century counterpart stumbled the gauntlet of his equals. Some variation on temperance
enjoyed such wide acceptance by the 1840s because of the utility of
public drunkenness as a quick test of character. The proliferating guides
to behavior in almost every kind of social situation played upon this
same simple equation between the surface record and the substance of
respectability. In fact, a similar utilitarianism permeated the entire Protestant ethos that enveloped American society. Social behavior alone, no
longer cloaked in a mysterious alliance with God or Satan, now distinguished the true Christians from the sinners, and immediate social consequences, no longer tempered by the prospects of eternal salvation or
damnation, should mete their rewards and punishments. As one spokesman for this practical Christianity stated, it preserved "the social
fabrick."

In all except the newest areas of settlement some families of property
anchored themselves against the tide of migration, shaped their definitions of public virtue into tests of respectability, and attempted to regulate the flow. Newcomers who passed an initial sorting were pressed
with a persistent, utilitarian friendliness, a probe for more information
under the guise of a democratic openness. "You are in a house of glass,"
one appalled object of scrutiny reported.[8] Acceptance showed America's
generous side. Not only did it mean an almost instant equality, but a

local familiarity over the years also softened many of the rigid rules on tolerable behavior. Innumerable communities lived comfortably with their closet drinkers and dissenting cranks. Nevertheless, the hard side of community protection clearly predominated by the 1840s. In an era of immutable absolutes, no community met the homogeneous ideal of its keepers. Where the commandment to grow or die merged individual fates with a community's future, it never required much imagination to see an influx of evil strangers irreversibly tipping the balance toward failure. The classic image of community subversion became one of the era's clichés: "that Trojan horse" to Thoreau, "the Grecian horse" to Buchanan, and—stubborn to the end—"the Roman Horse" to Jackson. Against the threat from outsiders community members adopted any convenient tactics. "We believe that we have a right to pass all those laws that we deem necessary to the quiet and peace of our community," declared Stephen A. Douglas, and throughout the United States local law was whatever local judges and local leaders said it was, including arbitrary arrests and vigilante violence.[9]

In the long run, however, the challenge was to live in the presence of evil without being corrupted by it. Nothing slowed the torrent of migrants, and nothing transformed propertyless laborers into model community members. Ultimately, the keepers of the community wanted a class line not to define their social relations with outsiders but to avoid them altogether. Hence their Sabbath laws, often unenforceable, served as a banner to which the virtuous could repair, a rallying point for the respectable to set themselves apart from the disreputable. No image better suited this sense of a ceaseless struggle than the standardized account of the camp meeting: an inner band of the godly surrounded by a ring of rowdies, saints and sinners holding separate ground in an ongoing contest that the righteous would win only if they never faltered.

Cities displayed an exaggerated version of all these problems. The most common ports of first and last resort for transient job seekers, they compressed a particularly powerful flow of America's propertyless into tight spaces with indeterminate boundaries. Outside the richest plantation areas in the south, cities revealed the widest economic gaps and the sharpest evidence of self-perpetuating tracks for winners and losers. Already identified as unique repositories of sin, cities also came to be seen as uniquely threatened by an engulfing evil mass. As if to validate these fears, they were struck with rashes of group violence during the thirties and early forties that conjured images of a powder keg in a room of flying sparks.

Inside the cities, however, the elite assumption of an ultimate control at the top died gradually. During the 1820s and 1830s, urban philanthropy remained a proud service, with an impressive number of propertied men playing an active role in all of its operations. Purified models of factory life, ranging from Robert Owen's New Harmony venture to the Lowell community for female millhands, inspired adaptations in a variety of manufacturing centers, where the desire to "convince the enemies of domestic manufacturers that such establishments [unlike their British counterparts] are not 'sinks of vice and immorality,' but, on the contrary, nurseries of morality, industry, and intelligence" expressed a common merger of employer righteousness and self-interest.[10] With the larger cities subdivided into approximate neighborhoods and many of these sections dependent on relatively small numbers of stable residents, the wherewithal for community cohesion had not entirely disappeared. Several of the so-called riots during the early thirties were led by established elites who, after the gentry fashion of community leadership, mobilized lesser citizens like an informal militia to drive out some hated intruders —the abolitionist crusaders, for example.

Nevertheless, the relentless pace of urban growth and diversification was clearly outstripping these traditional mechanisms of control. A rising number of violent outbreaks erupted from below, set their own targets, and followed their own course. In 1844, when the venerable patrician Horace Binney called for an end to the protracted anti-Catholic riot in Philadelphia and nobody listened, the old order declared its bankruptcy. Experiments in factory paternalism dwindled, and by 1850 the work rules, the arbitrary stretchouts, and the manipulated wage scales looked about the same on either side of the Atlantic. City governments handled more and more of such tasks as street paving, policing, fire protection, and public health that had once been the informal responsibility of civic leaders. Residential patterns increasingly reflected class lines, and by the 1850s, policemen in special uniforms appeared as the agents of a respectable order in the city's poorer districts. Philanthropy too was passing into the hands of salaried managers, who dispensed charity on a business basis and relieved their wealthy donors of any direct contact with the poor.

The upper-class drive for public schools belonged with these mounting demands for protection. Rooted in a tradition of charity education, the city schools always had a flavor of benevolence that was missing from their small-town counterparts, and it was still not clear around 1840 what roles church and state, private philanthropists and public officials, would play in an expanding educational network. Some Protestant leaders in New York, Pennsylvania, and Maryland, for example, sought a public subsidy for parochial schools on the assumption, as Governor William Henry Seward of New York phrased it in 1842, that it was better for the Catholic church "to educate the offsprings of the poor, than to leave them to grow up in ignorance and vice." As respectable city dwellers wrestled with their worries about urban disorder, however, they settled on a full-blown public system as their best protection. Its "primary objective," Henry Barnard explained at midcentury, was not the cultivation of the intellect but "the regulation of the feelings and dispositions, the extirpation of vicious propensities." "No one at all familiar with the deficient household arrangements and deranged machinery of domestic life, of the extreme poor, and ignorant . . . and all the vicious habits of low-bred idleness, which abound in certain sections of all populous districts," he argued, could possibly doubt the need for public agencies to mold the next generation of the lower class.[11] By midcentury the perceptions of an urban elite had come full circle: a capacity to live near the poor without bothering about them in the late 18th century, a fear of inundation early in the 19th century, and finally a series of intermediary agencies that allowed them once more to live with a neighboring poverty. If each agency did its job, respectable citizens would now ring the rowdies.

As this barricade for the respectable rose during the forties and early fifties, the difficulties of staying on the right side of it increased for skilled workers and marginal shop owners. Caught at the edge of the class line, they jealously prized their own traditions of respectability: the right to a reasonable division between work and leisure, a place as active, informed participants in government, and above all the independence to determine their future. Even in an economy of small shops, some craftsmen had been losing their battle against the machines, more of them had been slipping into dependent contracts with merchant capitalists, and almost all proprietors of very modest enterprises had been suffering the consequences of tighter credit. To ameliorate their lot around midcentury, these city dwellers might draw upon three traditions, each originating in the first flush of the revolution in choices.

One turned their attention outward. In its most common expression it demanded free public land as a foundation for free individuals, and it rested its case on the popular belief in an American birthright to a farm. Phrased in the new democratic idiom, it demanded "the Freedom of the Public Lands, as a means to abolish the Monopoly of the Soil. . . . "[12] "Vote yourself a farm," the urban reformer George Evans declared. More diffusely, this tradition looked westward as the place for a fresh start upward. Although these spacious ambitions confused the opportunity to move with the opportunity to rise, they contained their kernel of reality. Wealth in the free-soil countryside was, in fact, more equitably distributed than in the cities, and the newer western centers did have more open social structures than the eastern cities. These visions continued to attract thousands who found their urban paths blocked, and land reform remained a staple in the workingmen's reform movements of the forties and fifties.

A second tradition turned their attention to each other and pursued freedom through collective action. As the revolution in choices exploded during the 1820s, groups of urban workers formed organizations "to raise the mechanical and productive classes to that condition of true independence and equality which their . . . utility to the nation and their growing intelligence . . . demand."[13] In addition to cheap land, they sought free public education, sound banks and currency for the thrifty worker, and an end to imprisonment for debts, by now almost exclusively a poor man's trap; and sometimes with great passion they attacked the "useless" merchant capitalists, elite lawyers, and speculators. A labor theory of value that defined the swelling wealth at the top of American society as stolen from honest laborers provided a common rationale, and the ten-hour day a common objective. A longer working day, they argued, was "at war" with Nature—"with the real interest of man's physical, intellectual, social, moral and religious being."[14] During the 1830s, "daughters of freemen" in the textile mills joined them in demanding an independent worker's wage and swelled the ten-hour movement in Massachusetts. As a simple set of truths that spread from city to city through pamphlets and lectures, these principles wove an institutional connection that some skilled workers then activated during the 1850s in a renewed effort to cross the class gap.

A third tradition turned their attention inward. Drawing directly on the values of respectability, it told urban workers at the class margin to rely on their inner resources and by strength of character alone draw themselves upward. Since the 1820s, conservative voices from above had been exhorting them to shun the false gods and recognize inner merit as the sole basis for improvement. "The Temperance Union is the best of all unions," declared a report from the American Temperance Society.[15] Obedience always ranked very high on such lists of virtues. Women who challenged their employer's rules became Amazons and men rioters. Sometimes the very meaning of a wage contract pivoted on a proper respect, as the Ohio Canal Commission made clear when it refused to guarantee payment to workers who were "insolent or disobedient to their employer—Such men do not deserve their wages."[16]

By far the most powerful incentives in this tradition, however, came from the standards of respectability that workers had internalized. The interior drive to meet those standards—and to convince others that they met them—shaped lives all along the urban class margin. One of the first consequences of rising real wages for the husband in a workingpeople's family was the withdrawal of the wife as a wage earner and her retirement into the home where by respectable norms she belonged. When data gatherers for city directories came around, a number of wives who could not afford to leave the work force still claimed that, in fact, they had. Many workers' groups phrased their objectives in a carefully calculated language of decency and moderation, assuring the world of their strict moral standards, their strong commitment to self-cultivation, and their personal distress over public conflict. "[We] assail no one . . .," read a characteristic petition. "Detraction and calumny form no part of our proceedings. . . ."[17] No doubt a twisted common law that continued to single out the organizations of urban workers as conspiracies added a practical reason for setting themselves apart from rioters and dressing their appeals in a rhetoric of peace and order. Nevertheless, in their confrontations with the merchant capitalists, artisan leaders braved the courts with an almost foolhardy courage. An urge for respectability far more than a fear of reprisals determined these tactics.

Hard times between 1837 and 1843 significantly deepened the appeal of this individualized, internalized tradition. Although wage earners and shop owners of all kinds suffered from the abrupt opening and closing of urban businesses, the unskilled workers absorbed by far the heaviest losses. As commerce flowed steadily through the depression, those skilled workers who did stay on the job fared quite well. Looking down from the margin's edge, they saw below them the cavern of "vice and immorality" inhabited by a mass of propertyless, degraded laborers. What kept them from falling? Not land policies or antimonopoly campaigns, and certainly not collective action against employers. Read in immediate, self-evident terms, the lessons of the depression pointed directly to the arguments for respectability. It was the individual's sobriety and reliability and perseverance that made the critical difference between winners and losers. Unprecedented bursts of enthusiasm for evangelical Protestantism erupted in the cities' working districts, and the temperance crusade suddenly swept up thousands along the class line. Founding their own organization, the Society of Washington, workers gathered converts among their fellows by telling a simple moral tale of a dramatic personal change and an escape from the floaters' pit. The buttons were there to be pushed, and by midcentury temperance belonged with the staples of respectability along the class divide.

As they issued from above, the arguments for temperance in the 1840s emphasized social control, but at the class margin temperance meant self-control: the personal discipline for independence and progress. In much the same way, the commitment along the class line to public education also gave it a very different cast. Urban public schools, enrolling over half the school-age population at midcentury, drew pupils from the middle economic ranges and, in a city such as New York, duplicated in their student body almost exactly the percentage of the families of skilled workers, small shopkeepers, and independent tradesmen. For parents in these families the schools carried the hopes for a training that would secure the next generation's place within the circle of respectability. The simple truths of virtue and conduct that echoed in these classrooms meant jobs, property, stability, reputation, everything that distinguished the honest worker from the outcast. If impoverished immigrants swamped some other portion of the city's school system, it scarcely mattered, just as long as their own sons and daughters still had a ladder of escape from the pit.

As tensions along the class line mounted, such de facto segregation of immigrants into their own overcrowded, understaffed schools came to reflect a deepening animus among skilled workers toward their mere presence. Rioters who set their own targets during the thirties and forties made the Irish their most common victims, and the mobs who attacked them ranged from day laborers to those artisans, shopkeepers, and clerks who were living at the margins of respectability. Newcomers did crowd the labor market and accept lower wages, and around midcentury their sheer numbers did contribute to the hardships of the urban work force. More than a million destitute Irish landed during the famine years of the late forties and early fifties alone. Nevertheless, skilled workers rarely experienced direct competition from these immigrants. Rather than an immediate economic threat, they represented above all the horrors of the bottomless, propertyless pit. A Protestant standard of virtues blamed their impoverishment on individual vices, and workers who had internalized those values engaged in an increasingly bitter vendetta against the swarms of sinners who were polluting the world around them.

These class-sharpened antagonisms, in turn, belonged to a long, broad tradition of hostilities that enveloped the Irish in particular as soon as they arrived in America. Their Catholicism tapped wells running deep into the colonial years: the fear of annihilation by Catholic France or Spain, the strict Calvinist identification of the Pope with the Antichrist, the general Protestant terror of Catholicism as a consignment to hell. As if the lot of Irish Catholics were not bad enough early in the 19th century, they also inherited an elite aversion to their enemies, the Protestant Scotch-Irish. While Federalists had condemned one set of Irishmen as Jacobin terrorists, Republicans had attacked another set as "foreign adventurers who come here to speculate in politics & raise themselves in office. . . ."[18] Catholic or Protestant, they had been called simply "Irish," the common term for all kinds of antipathy. That amalgam was still fogging the mind of the Massachusetts patrician in 1829 who pictured Boston's Catholics rushing to Washington to celebrate the inauguration of Andrew Jackson, "the *Irish* President."[19]

By the mid-thirties, however, a transformation of values had reshaped this tradition to suit the new American society. Now Irish meant exclusively Catholic, and Catholicism, rather than conjuring geopolitical or theological terrors, elicited images of personal behavior that bespoke a corrupt character. Appropriate to a culture that relied on a handful of immutable truths, these assumptions about behavior—sometimes singling out the Irish, sometimes covering all Catholics—formed stereotypes that enabled Protestants to understand the lot of them without actually knowing any of them. The Irishman was a broad-backed, light-skinned, loud-mouthed brawler, strong enough for brute labor, feckless enough to squander everything he earned, and drunken enough to keep him in society's gutter. Left to themselves, the Irish would labor a bit and sink, perhaps taking more from society as they went than they had ever contributed. Feeding those doubts, a specialist in mental illness, Edward Jarvis, informed the Massachusetts legislature in 1854 that the Irish carried inherent inclinations toward insanity and poverty and hence would inevitably pack the state's asylums.

But the even more ominous stereotype of Catholicism warned that the Irish were not left to themselves, for all good Catholics belonged to an authoritarian army, drilled by the American hierarchy and directed from Rome. Hopelessly flawed in character, the Irish marched to the orders of their church—"human priest-controlled machines," Samuel F. B. Morse called them. As a corollary, respectable Protestants often assigned them the qualities of arrested children, incapable of free choices and therefore unfit for a democratic society. Would individuals with an ability to choose decide to pollute their bodies and souls with alcohol and priest-craft? Yet precisely because the Catholic church had such slavish members, its power vastly exceeded its mere numbers. In a society particularly hostile to centralized authority and chronically unable to mobilize its scattered citizens for a general purpose, the Catholic church loomed as a uniquely threatening force. During the 1830s it did not require a crazy leap of imagination to picture this supposed monolith in competition for control of the trans-Appalachian west. The winner quickly took all in the American conception of such head-to-head encounters. The sudden flood of Catholic immigrants in the late forties and early fifties chilled the hearts of many urban Protestants who operated from these same assumptions. It was equally natural to turn the basic stereotype of authoritarian priests and supine followers into a spotlight on the most intimate human relations: priests seducing helpless women in the confessional or helpless nuns in the monastery. Corruption in one area always meant corruption everywhere.

These Irish and Catholic stereotypes varied greatly in intensity and detail across the range of American Protestants, many of whom simply dismissed the lurid elaborations as foolishness. Nevertheless, no one could fault the essential logic behind them, for even the skeptics carried the same cultural convictions about holistic characters and grow-or-die competition. In the end, enough of this hostile imagery hung in the air to keep almost all the Irish and the Catholics on 'he far side of acceptability. Although Protestant promoters of economic growth welcomed Irish muscle, they never invited an Irish presence into the ranks of the respectable. William Henry Seward, an ostensible ally of the Catholics, made it clear, for example, that he collaborated with their church "less from sympathy, than because the welfare of the state demands it."[20]

Respectable Americans, in other words, drew a line and generated a social conflict of their own choice. How thoroughly the decision came from above emerged in the record that the Irish and the Catholic church actually made. In a society that used the drive for wealth as a measure of virtue, the Irish emigrated from material motives and scraped for work wherever they could get it. They understood the implacable force of grow or die better than most American citizens. In a society that expected homogeneous communities to mark off their own territory for a test of virtue, the urban Irish clung together as best they could to preserve their church, protect their culture, and sustain one another in the American struggle. Where institutions relied on a simple catechism of absolutes across a decentralized network, the Catholic church, largely ignored by the Vatican as a backwash, spread through an array of more or less autonomous units as effectively as any Protestant denomination, and even sponsored its own itinerant revivalists to gather in the strays and strengthen the local parishes. Where moral education underwrote both personal and social virtue, Catholics sacrificed more dearly to establish such a school system than any Protestant group in the nation. Give or take some alcohol, the Catholics might have been praised as exemplary Americans.

In fact, some Germans and Irish did merge with their fellow citizens. By the American standards of a homogeneous community, the entry requirement was ethnic invisibility, an erasure of all distinguishing traits that later found expression in the image of the melting pot, and members of these immigrant families had the choice of paying this price because they did not face the great chasm of race. White Americans, approaching a unanimity that they showed on no other subject, made skin coloring the most important single determinant in their human relations. Even those few who escaped the overwhelming white aversion to dark skin had to fight the issue on racial terms. Nobody could be indifferent. Out of that consciousness, race became the insoluble problem for the egalitarian community of the 19th century. Screening by readily observable characteristics and assuming an interior that mirrored the exterior, almost all whites saw a dark skin as irrefutable proof of Nature's hard side, evidence of flaws so fundamental that nothing could correct them. Catholics might change their religion, drunks their taste, and criminals their vocation, but no conversion could turn black into white. According to America's democratic norms, anyone who joined the community enjoyed equal rights with the rest, and according to the prevailing logic of irresistible cause to effect, intermarriage would follow inevitably from entry. Membership and "amalgamation," in other words, formed a single issue, and in this grow-or-die world the spreading of an indelible stigma of color signaled death for any family or community that suffered from it. No other problem of their own making carried such profound consequences for white Americans or such terrible ones for their victims.

Race had not always opened such a yawning chasm in American society. The 18th-century hierarchy, predicated on gradations of human inferiority, left those with dark skin in a blurred bottom group and offered neither guidance nor incentive to examine the issue further. Only the existence of black slavery in a revolutionary republic pressed the gentry to think more deeply on the subject, and even then, only a few leaders probed the question of race with any seriousness. Particularly in South Carolina and Georgia, where slavery had its strongest hold, almost all slaveholders accepted its presence as perfectly compatible with their republican experiment and talked openly about brute black labor as indispensable to their way of life. Coerced labor drew on a long Anglo-American tradition. As late as the 1810s, for example, the impressment of seamen into the British navy brought cries of outrage as a violation of the rights of free Americans, but not as a way of extracting useful labor from the bottom of society: the wrong people from the wrong country, but not necessarily the wrong policy. Jefferson, along with some of his southern associates, did deplore slavery both as a curse and as a contradiction, and in the first bloom of revolution he did fret over the problem of race. Where along the bottom layers of human inferiority did blacks belong? Were their deficiencies inherent? If they were freed, where could they live without endangering the republic? Jefferson's primary commitment, however, lay with social harmony, and the more fundamental a disruption he perceived from emancipation, the less attention he gave it. In the end he could only wish the problem away.

Northern leaders legislated away their far smaller version of slavery, and a few of them favored emancipating slaves everywhere. Nevertheless, northern legislatures approached emancipation with no surge of revolutionary fervor. They were carefully amending their republics, not radicalizing them. Very few gentlemen seemed to care where the blacks would land after emancipation. Indeed, the northern programs for gradual emancipation at least opened the possibility of selling slaves in the south during the transition years. What little heed the freed blacks did receive fell in the category of charity for the destitute, and the most publicized manifestation of that spirit, the American Colonization Society, which the immediate successors to the revolutionary gentry founded in 1819, argued persistently that blacks had no acceptable place in a white society. In the gentry tradition, northern antagonism to southern slavery concentrated on its corruption of the whites: its creation of black harems for debauched white males, its encouragement to laziness, and other characteristics incompatible with republican leadership. Even such confirmed enemies of southern slavery as Rufus King and Timothy Pickering did not consider freedmen—those in Haiti, for example—capable of self-government.

This mixture of disdain and indifference toward free blacks disappeared along with the gentry hierarchy. Egalitarian Americans, sensing an infinite jeopardy, drove them out with a vengeance. Beginning around 1820, as the revolution in choices was just bursting nationwide, northern states enacted law after law restricting black rights, communities hardened their policies of exclusion, and urban whites reacted with increasing violence against the proximity of blacks. Now the question of race became a matter of general concern to which white Americans applied a full complement of Biblical exegesis, scientific analysis, and intuitive understanding.

To justify banning blacks from their democracy, white spokesmen employed two primary lines of argument. One changed the gentry conception of a stairstep inferiority into a simple separation that suited the 19th-century division between ins and outs. It transformed inferior into subhuman and dropped those with dark skin to a ledge below the authentic human race of whites. Humans and beasts could never be equals. Cartoon figures depicted blacks as clothed gorillas. One white educator, explaining why blacks had no need for his services, asked: "Would you do a benefit to the horse or the ox, by giving him a cultivated understanding, or fine feelings?"[21] A second justification for exclusion adapted the new distinction between children and adults. Assigning blacks the qualities of children, it denied them the capacity to make responsible decisions in a society of equals. A much softer argument, it left a host of ambiguities. If insouciant Irish and docile Catholics were also children in the same sense, was this a racial or a class distinction? What responsibilities did whites have for these children? Might they under some circumstances develop into adults with actual characters that would qualify them for a democratic society?

Most of these uncertainties evaporated in the south, where slavery always controlled the issue of race. Slavery was a profitable labor system for white owners, and both the policies and the theories regarding blacks derived from that essential fact. When Jefferson speculated about emancipating Virginia's slaves and relocating them in the western wilderness, he failed as usual to grasp the subject's hard economic core. The owners wanted guaranteed cheap labor, and Jefferson's scheme offered them nothing. The same deficiency crippled the American Colonization Society, which talked about compensation but never about a labor replacement for the slaves. Even such a rare soul as Edward Coles, Madison's former secretary who went west to emancipate his slaves, postponed freeing them until they had cleared a large Illinois farm for him. Logical contradictions abounded inside slavery: blacks as natural, contented slaves who had to be kept from rebelling or escaping, for example, or slaves as capable of adult decisions in criminal but not in civil law. Nevertheless, the higher logic of preserving a labor system straightened each twist of reasoning. Those who held slaves and those who aspired to hold them made slavery the prerequisite for their own right to economic choices—their own imperative to grow. When slaveholders dealt with the potentially ambiguous analysis of the child-black's mind as "plastic clay, which, may be moulded into agreeable or disagreeable figures, according to the skill of the moulder," they never doubted their lifetime rights as the potter.[22] Slavery did not prolong the subtle shadings of paternalism and interdependence from the 18th-century hierarchy. It created the most fundamental division between ins and outs in 19th-century America, and all the anomalies in human affection between whites and blacks had to work out their meaning across this determining property line.

Unlike white northerners, who identified skin color as a problem in its own right, southern slaveholders subordinated race relations to the perpetuation of slavery. If those northerners who hated dark skin wanted to drive blacks as far away as possible, those southerners who equated blacks with slave labor wanted to maintain surveillance over every dark-skinned person in the vicinity. By the 1850s that meant almost half the total population in the lower south. No matter what regulations held slaves in their workplaces, white southerners lived with a constant need to protect themselves against retaliatory violence. Slave codes and black courts, demanding subservience above all, set their harshest penalties along a scale of verbal to physical aggression against whites. An evasive disobedience signified none of the danger of a direct assertiveness. The broad pattern of southern race relations, therefore, followed the changing white perceptions of potential black violence. As the risks seemed to increase, so did supervision and repression; as the risks seemed to wane, so did the controls.

The first sharply rising curve of concern came with the prolonged black struggle against enslavement on the sugar island of Saint-Domingue. For a decade after 1794, as the bloody battle for freedom proceeded in the Caribbean, the American slave states responded by strengthening the state militia system, restricting the movement of free blacks, and forcing them to register and give evidence of good conduct. In this atmosphere, the Methodist church withdrew its declarations in favor of emancipation, then dropped all mention of slavery. In 1800, Gabriel Prosser's plan for a slave rebellion in Richmond simply heightened the prevailing spirit of danger, but Denmark Vesey's scheme twenty-two years later in Charleston spurred a new repressive drive. Black gatherings of all sorts, including church activities, came under the ban, loose rules of evidence to prove an individual black's freedom disappeared from the southern courts, and new laws restricting an owner's right of manumission spread among the slave states. During this round, southern Presbyterians fell silent on slavery. In 1831, Nat Turner's uprising through Southampton County, Virginia, triggered a final burst of controls: legal bars to the education of blacks, tighter slave patrols, and more systematic uses of white Christianity to pacify slaves.

Nevertheless, the protective framework around slavery changed noticeably in the early 1830s. From a primary involvement with the internal sources of jeopardy—free blacks, embittered slaves, secret gatherings—slaveowners now redirected their attention to external sources of attack, especially those northern abolitionists who opened their militant campaign just as Turner was plotting his rebellion. Although the initial southern reaction to this evangelical onslaught involved a good deal of internal repression, slaveholders sorted out their responses during the 1830s and emerged in the 1840s with a confidence about the slave system that expressed their own sense of inner merit on its own path of progress. The tension over separate black churches with black preachers abated. Slave artisans enjoyed considerable freedom of movement in the towns and cities. Slave literacy, even slave gatherings on a holiday, ceased to be pressing public issues.

What had materialized was one more institutional network to join those forming everywhere in the nation. A clear explanation of slavery as a virtuous system supplied the few and simple truths that permeated the south. In an endless litany of reinforcement, newspapers, ministers, publicists, and politicians reiterated the same elementary absolutes about God's curse on Ham and Nature's special endowment of blacks for field labor, the slaves' contentment with their lot and society's benefits from their enslavement. Both the laws governing slavery and the devices for enforcing them spread a generally uniform cover over the region: bans on trafficking with free persons or marrying outside the slave system, evening curfews, passes to regulate movement beyond the owner's premises, special white patrols, and special black courts. Appropriate to one of America's extensive institutional webs, communities then applied these truths to suit their local differences. Slaves at hire in the towns and cities worked out their own peculiar patterns of leeway. None of the legal formulas to determine "white" and "negro" could change the thousands of community judgments about which children of what near or distant interracial unions were considered white and which ones black. In some parts of the south a local reputation could even sustain an interracial marriage.

Unlike any other institutional network of the 1840s, this one blanketed an entire region, but that region alone. In the process of protecting slavery, it enveloped all blacks and institutionalized a racial line, pushing free blacks only a step away from slavery and defining genuine freedom by skin color. Willy-nilly, southern whites of all sorts came to have a vested interest in slavery, however much some of them hated its economic consequences and its chief beneficiaries. As participants in a culture that could distinguish only between ins and outs, slaveless white farmers and townsmen recognized that slavery alone blocked a flood of blacks from spreading through their egalitarian world. Who at midcentury could envisage simply walling off three million former slaves? In a forthright application of the democratic creed, one white Alabaman told a touring northerner: "I wouldn't like to hev 'em freed, if they was gwine to hang 'round. . . . Now suppose they was free, you see they'd all think themselves as good as we; of course they would, if they was free."[23] Although Jefferson in the 1780s had feared the blacks' bloody revenge and deplored the distasteful consequences of interracial marriage, he gave only the vaguest mention to the prospect of black equality. Seventy years later, the threat of equality was precisely the issue among slaveless whites. Slavery neither softened the day-to-day conflicts among these whites nor made them deferential to the great planters, but it did give them a common stake in an institution that seemed intimately related to every white man's opportunities.

As this institutional network formed, its spokesmen entered into a loose, prolonged debate with the growing number of northerners who in some fashion deplored slavery. Exercising such direct control over another person's life and benefiting so brazenly from another person's labor clashed too boldly with the new democratic values to escape northern condemnation. Self-determination and slavery were the 19th-century antipodes. It required only an intimation of the black's humanity to touch northern white emotions with descriptions of pain under the lash, misery in chains, and grief at the auction block. As Richard Henry Dana's famous account of a seaman's flogging in *Two Years Before the Mast* (1840) illustrated, nothing symbolized human degradation in a democratic age more shockingly than an individual's helplessness before the arbitrary blows of a whip. Nor could anything strike closer to the core of the new culture than the picture of families torn and scattered by the slave trade. The very sources of morality dissolved with them. Even so sympathetic a character as Topsy in *Uncle Tom's Cabin* (1851) would suffer lifelong consequences for having just "grow'd" when she most needed a mother's care. What blacks might do with their lives if they had the right to live them mattered far less in this argument than the fact that slavery denied them the right. Hence the reformer Gerrit Smith could appear as a militant champion of both women and blacks with the statement: "I make no claim that woman is fit to be a member of Congress or President; all I ask for her is what I ask for the negro, a fair field."[24]

It was a small abolitionist minority who extracted the richest moral message from the widespread image of the blacks as children and in the process contributed far beyond their numbers to altering the terms of debate between northerners and southerners. Although these men and women never freed themselves from the assumptions of black inferiority, their premises clustered at the far end of the white spectrum: an authentic humanity for the blacks and an absolute condemnation of their cruelly enforced dependence. What possible relation, they demanded, did the systematic brutality, the endless humiliations, the imposed ignorance, the smashed human wills, and the shattered families of slavery have with preparation for the God-given right to an adult's life? An entire package of early-19th-century values surrounding the responsibilities of parents, the needs of children, the rights of choice, and the simple truths of a democratic society came together in an impressive argument that made immediate emancipation the only solution. For the doubters, they pointed to showcase models of the free and transformed black, especially to the imposing, eloquent Frederick Douglass, who joined the abolitionist crusade as lecturer and editor after his escape from slavery in 1838.

What this antislavery appeal lacked was a way of linking the evils of slavery with the opportunities of northern whites. As a picture of moral corruption, it argued more logically for separation than action. On those grounds it eventually impelled the Methodists and Baptists to split from their southern brethren, and many others shared the urge to keep clear of slavery's contamination. Nevertheless, for those northerners who expected a close correlation between morality and economic success, the proponents of slavery had the better of the debate, for King Cotton underwrote the nation's economic growth in the early 19th century. Moreover, a longstanding American concern as powerful as the immorality of slavery pointed to the teeming, chaotic city as the greatest danger to American virtue, and southern spokesmen from John C. Calhoun to George Fitzhugh proudly contrasted the harmonious progress of the agrarian south with the class-ridden strife of the urban north. As long as slavery did not block their own avenues of opportunity, the millions of white northerners who simply despised blacks had little difficulty accepting their bondage somewhere to the south.

In the hands of the new democracy, progress was an awesome two-edged sword indeed. One side cut the way to an extraordinary vision of human potential: perfectionism. The other side hacked down the people who were obstructing that vision: genocide. Among the 18th-century gentry the same tendency that tempered their expectations of human improvement also checked their extremes of ruthlessness toward other human beings. Now in the name of progress anything might go. The American circle of logic allowed them to remove people who stood in their path of progress and simultaneously told them that those who fell along the way were merely fulfilling Nature's decree. Above all others, native Americans learned how literally whites could apply the principle of grow or die, and how futile their efforts were in affecting the outcome. For them, progress was the most dangerous doctrine imaginable in a period of rapid white expansion.

Superficially the white stereotype of native Americans did not carry the same devastating message as the stereotype of blacks, and, appropriate to the early-19th-century concentration on visible traits, the critical differences lay in a physiognomy and skin color closer to that of the whites. Since the late 18th century a number of white Americans had talked vaguely of an absorption of native Americans through intermarriage—the ultimate white compliment—and writers from Jefferson to James Fenimore Cooper had attributed qualities of perception and courage to red men that no contemporary white author assigned to blacks. Nevertheless, what whites gave for appearance they took away for culture. That portion of the stereotype defining native Americans as savages —the very antithesis of a civilized people—left them helpless before the onslaught of white progress. From that premise all else followed. Where progress itself meant a higher and higher civilization, those who clung to savagery were by definition killing themselves. Purported friends of the native Americans could only lament their inevitable passing and attempt to ease their way. Whites with fewer compunctions justified their own passions and interests through their elastic definitions of savagery. Calling the native Americans treacherous, they cheated them. Calling them ferocious, they murdered them. Calling them barbaric, they paraded their defeated chiefs in public like freaks, then sent them off to die. To label the offspring of intermarriage, whites borrowed from their livestock nomenclature: "half-breeds." As losers without a chance for redemption, the native Americans had no recourse against this cavalry of progress.

The fundamental cause for their vulnerability was the absence of an exchange, comparable to black labor, that might have tempered the most ruthless white impulses. On the contrary, their primary asset, land, became their heaviest liability, for the increasing numbers of whites who coveted it viewed the native Americans solely as a frustration, a superfluous mound of rocks on their road of opportunity. Hence the fate of their nations—the Seneca, the Miami, the Fox, and the Saux in the north, the Creek, the Cherokee, the Choctaw, and the Chickasaw in the south— hinged on the state of white ambitions and the willingness of white governments to support them. For a time, the preoccupation of the national government with the European powers and their North American bases and its cautious attitude toward western settlement buffered the native Americans. With Washington's secretary of war, Henry Knox, setting a tone of judicious paternalism, the administrations of the 1790s promised the western nations that the United States would change no existing boundaries "unless by their free consent, or by the right of conquest in case of a just war"—the terms of international law.[25] Even Jefferson, who viewed white expansion much more favorably, anticipated an abundance of time for the gradual adjustment of white and native American territories.

Beneath this cool gentry exterior, however, stirred a hot anger over native American savagery that indicated how weak the restraints actually were. Nothing roused more fury in Jefferson during the Revolutionary War than native American attacks, and during the War of 1812, Madison singled them out for similar vituperation: "merciless savages . . . ruthless ferocity . . . carnage and torture."[26] Following Jefferson's grim dictum of 1780—"The same world will scarcely do for them and us"—the Virginia Dynasty funded military expeditions and pressed native Americans to migrate at about the same rising rate as the mounting white demands for their land.[27] Although Marshall, who opposed a pellmell western movement, tried to protect the old fabric of treaties, the imposition of white contract law on western land disputes trapped native Americans in a complicated set of rules that would only be used to dispossess them. Under Crawford and Calhoun, the War Department readied its machinery to drive out the southern nations, whether they had adapted to white ways as impressively as the Cherokees or resisted them as impressively as the Seminoles. Just as white missionaries saw even their converts as savages at heart, so equally sympathetic white observers saw even the Cherokees as barbarians practicing the civilized arts. Not surprisingly, the voices of charity sounded very much like the voices of greed. "It need not be regretted, since it is the order of providence," the philanthropic Nicholas Biddle declared in 1826, "that tribes of savages should gradually yield to the progress of civilized men."[28] Through government removal, the impatient Thomas Hart Benton argued in 1824, "the day of their final extinction would be deferred."[29]

By the late twenties, Jefferson's slowly ticking clock no longer told the time in grow-or-die America. Everything preliminary to a wholesale seizure of native American lands sat in place except a national administration as committed to an immediate resolution as the white speculators and settlers. Jackson was their man. Relentless in any contest, he entered office with a first priority to sweep the southwestern nations across the Mississippi River and, playing the 18th-century patriarch who demanded absolute obedience to his will, he wrenched his "children" from their lands, drove them to the strange desolate plains above Texas, then forgot them as abruptly. The forced march of the Cherokees alone killed a quarter of their population. Meanwhile, an exterminating little war against the Potawatomis, Chippewas, and Ottawas fully cleared an equally rich stretch of northern Illinois and southern Wisconsin for white settlers. Land speculation soared in the early thirties. Although some of Jackson's enemies used the occasion to attack his dictatorial ways, most whites responded with silence. Whatever their sensibilities, their stereotypes told them the inevitable was now happening. In the east a sense of the native Americans as romantic curios from the past—as if they had already died—was jelling as a characteristic 19th-century attitude. "Yet they have vanished from the face of the earth," one easterner had announced as early as 1825, "—their very names are blotted from the pages of history. . . ."[30] There was no tragedy here, just brutal destruction. If the design and acceptance of policies pointing toward the death of an entire people was genocide, white America stood defenseless against the charge.

A long cycle that originated in the gentry hierarchy and traced the rising expectations and democratized prospects of the early 19th century culminated at midcentury in a society that preserved a culture of equality in its upper half at the expense of its lower half. Below the class line lived an agglomeration of white Protestant floaters and outcast religious sects, white Catholics, blacks in and out of slavery, and native Americans. Above it was a relatively homogeneous Protestant stratum comprising perhaps as much as two-thirds of the nation's white population. Like the other indeterminate lines in America's spreading society, this one had no beginning or end. It threaded its way through the cities and towns and countrysides to mark whatever division made sense in each locality, and along its interminable course it defined the contrasting characteristics of the two classes.

Life above the line was geared to the requirements of a growing, decentralized commercial nation. A web of institutions resting on a common set of values enabled respectable Americans to move freely and transact a wide variety of affairs with relative ease across great stretches of space. Although increasingly subdivided by the specialized tasks of occupation and gender, they had no difficulty picking up the cues of one another's respectability and merging into community groups. The very essence of America's lower class was its fragmentation. Extending from the Mexicans in California to the Irish in Boston, from the Shakers in Ohio to the slaves in Texas, its members had no effective means of interconnection. Only the Catholic church had the qualities of a strong lower-class institution. Urban workers, despite their tradition of protest, were still struggling with a legacy of particularism that separated them in myriad ways by cities, crafts, and skills. The increasingly hardened subdivisions that mattered below the line scattered people into mutually hostile bands, ceaselessly competing for space and work and self-respect. In the city streets, poor Protestant and Catholic boys came of age fighting one another for territory. Among the seasonal farm laborers as well as in the urban pool of the unskilled, free blacks were already the last hired, the first fired. When they did find niches in the work force—providing menial personal services, for example—male immigrants refused to demean themselves by contesting those jobs, just as Yankees largely abandoned the bottom ranks in the New England textile mills to the Irish. Although black and red intermarried and even combined as guerrillas in the Seminole Wars of the 1830s and 1840s, their causes rarely linked. A handful of native Americans were themselves slaveholders, and the Mormons, despised themselves by respectable Americans, called slavery a "divine institution."

An upper class existed because respectable Americans constructed it from common values and institutions; a lower class existed only because an upper class created it by exclusion. As respectable Americans learned to use their new social system more effectively, they consolidated the division of privileges between the classes. By midcentury, for example, the democratization of legal training and the simplification of pleading procedures meant that almost all citizens with a modicum of property had access to a lawyer who could at least represent them in local court. The propertyless and the floaters remained essentially defenseless in any court. Appropriately, courts showed an increasing concern for the solidarity of respectable families and even for the rights of its individual members. On the other hand, courts treated those families whom they judged disreputable more and more callously, splitting them at will, dumping their old and sick members into other jurisdictions, binding their children through otherwise obsolete apprentice laws, and generally acting on the assumption that they had no substantial rights whatsoever. For those who started with some property, the prospects of preserving it improved each decade. The bankruptcy formula that enabled commercial defaulters to retain a core of assets spread during the forties and fifties to cover farmers as well, guaranteeing the protection of their homesteads and a portion of surrounding land against their creditors. At the same time, the hazards of speculating with lower-class labor increased, especially through court rulings that shifted the burdens of risk in dangerous jobs from the employer to the worker.

In almost all cases the flow of American lives moved laterally along class channels. Only at the capillary ends of society—in some country stores and churches, for example, or in some city factories and public conveyances—did a little interaction occur. It was against this dominant flow that America's most inclusive institutions, the political parties, had to conduct their electoral affairs in an era of the democratic franchise. The miracle of universal white manhood suffrage sprang from the miscalculations of many leaders who periodically enlarged the electorate on the mistaken assumption that the new voters would remain their gratefully loyal followers. By the time the gentry and their successors recognized their errors, almost everything had been given away, with some notable exceptions in Rhode Island and South Carolina. If additional leverage was needed, the new western states, adopting the most liberal standards for suffrage to entice settlers, contributed their growing pressure to the cause. The response of the broadened electorate was astonishing: 80% voting in New Hampshire in 1814, Tennessee in 1817, and Mississippi in 1823, almost 90% in Ohio five years later, and a breathtaking 97% in the Alabama elections of 1819. Presidential balloting took two dramatic leaps: from 27% of the adult white males in 1824 to 58% in 1828, and from 58% in 1836 to 80% in 1840. Although neither census takers nor voting officials could possibly keep track of the entire cascade of migrants, these returns even as estimates revealed a significant penetration into the ranks of the propertyless floaters.

Initially, the new mass of voters confused many political leaders. Nevertheless, by attending camp meetings and holiday celebrations and by sponsoring picnics and rallies, they devised a working set of techniques. Always appear transparent and open to the ordinary eye; always make opponents seem opaque and cabalistic. In a bit of advice that was already commonplace when he offered it, James Graham, a North Carolina Whig, told a friend in 1840: "I have always accomodated by *habit* and *Dress* to the People when electioneering. . . ."[31] Treating the voters to some liquor, once a way for the gentry giver to affirm his superiority over the yeoman receiver, became an almost impersonal means for party equals to gather and celebrate. With an egalitarian style also went some egalitarian substance—a leveling of standards in the professions, for example, and above all a decentralizing of authority from the judiciary in the lower south to the governments of the northeastern cities. Never cost-efficient, these trends were reasonably community-efficient instead.

By Jackson's time, politics differed from any other pattern of respectable behavior. However exposed the reputable merchants or ministers were to public scrutiny, they maintained a pose of dignity, a public decorum that set a social distance between themselves and the cruder folk. Only politicians mingled willingly along the class margin, mimicking its language and mirroring its ways. The price was a tarnished reputation. "There never was a period in the history of our country," wrote the westerner James Hall, "in which its public men have sought popularity, power, and office, with so much avidity . . . [and] display a dissoluteness altogether incompatible with the genius of a sober-minded people."[32] "Offices, in the United States, seem to be *legal tender*," Horace Mann disdainfully commented in 1839, "for nobody refuses them."[33] A year later the Reverend George Burnap advised: "But above all things, the young man has need to be warned against turning politician as a business and profession. Of all employments this is one of the most wretched. . . ."[34] "Pontius Pilate," Horace Bushnell acidly remarked, "was a politician. . . ."[35] These were the judgments that led Tocqueville to report a great decline in American political life since the gentry era.

The ultimate danger, of course, lay in those lower-class voters whom the politicians were incorporating into public life. Unlike the 18th-century gentry who invariably blamed leaders for misguiding the people, 19th-century respectables feared the people themselves, the massive exercise of choices among voters incapable of making the right ones. The floating riffraff in the west and the Irish rabble in the east ruling a moral nation? From these images came one of the most famous fictions in American history, the myth of a barbarian orgy in the White House celebrating Jackson's inauguration. They also provided one of the most telling arguments in behalf of public education: "The theory of our government is,—not that all men, however unfit, shall be voters,—but that every man . . . shall become fit to be a voter."[36] "This country is filling up with thousands and millions of voters," Emerson heard conservatives cry, "and you must educate them to keep them from our throats."[37] "Loco-Focoism," derived from an aggressive popular faction of the New York Democracy, became a scare word in some elite circles roughly comparable to Jacobinism in an earlier era and Populism in a later one.

What actually developed, however, was a critical new division between electoral and legislative politics, with political managers serving as liaisons between the two. It was their task to draw voters to the polls from both sides of the line while preserving the legislature as an arena for just one class. Although politicians had two clienteles, they belonged to only one, and in the end they acted much more as class buffers than as class brokers. During the 1830s and 1840s, in settings as different as Worcester, Baltimore, and Cumberland County, North Carolina, democratic politics drew in activists and officeholders closer than ever to the margin but never actually from the lower class, and these men, rather than becoming conduits across the line, helped to guard the moat. As exemplars of a democratic openness, they reinforced the faith of the poor; as participants in government, they preserved the domain of the upper class. In sum, politicians were expected to take the legislative chance out of the electoral choices.

Legislative politics focused on the economic issues of class privilege—that is, the acquisition, distribution, and use of property. In this tier, factions fought vigorously over questions of development and opportunity. Electoral politics concentrated more and more on the cultural issues of class division—that is, race, religion, nationality, and such related matters as the preservation of slavery and the appropriateness of temperance. In this tier, groups contested their claims to respectability, asserted their right to follow their own customs, and echoed their pride in the symbolic egalitarianism of the ballot box. Here, for example, it mattered a great deal that democratic politics tapped only whites below the class line, but whites who were both Protestants and Catholics.

Cultural differences of some kind had always entwined themselves in American politics. Religion and nationality bore directly on the separation of revolutionaries, Tories, and neutrals during the Revolutionary War, then in different arrangements on the separation of Federalists and Republicans. From a gentry perspective, however, these divisions were subsumed under a republican politics common to everyone. When New Jersey Federalists appealed to Dutch voters in 1801, for example, they emphasized the French devastation of their homeland. When Jefferson appealed to the New England Baptists, he shaped the message in the standard language of republican freedoms. One argument, many audiences. Even the recipients seemed bent on securing their place in a traditional politics following traditional principles. Self-conscious Germans in Pennsylvania prepared their own federalist and antifederalist slates late in the 1780s and formed their own democratic-republican society in 1793 so that "Germans [would have] that station which their industry, their integrity, and their patriotism merit."[38] They wanted a German presence in gentry politics, not a distinctive German politics. By the 1840s, styles and motivations had changed drastically. In 1844, Ohio

Democrats, stinging from recent attacks in their state on Van Buren as a closet Catholic and a friend to the blacks, circulated German-language leaflets that accused Clay of cheering anti-Catholic rioters and plotting forced marriages between Germans and blacks. In this as in countless comparable instances, it was no longer a German presence, but a German prejudice that powered the new electoral politics.

What 18th-century leaders managed to integrate, in other words, 19th-century politicians consciously separated. Just as the gentry strained down the hierarchy to make a connection with the people, the solid citizens of the 19th century labored in a flattened society to barricade the unacceptable from the acceptable people. The result was a division of politics into two spheres that usually had no relation with each other. In almost every state across the country during the late thirties and forties, banking and transportation dominated the affairs of the legislature, sometimes pitting Whigs against Democrats in a sharply drawn party battle and sometimes one region of a state against another but always reckoning with the economic preoccupations of those creditors and debtors, investors and farmers, who stood above the class line. During the same years, these economic issues increasingly drifted out of electoral politics. After the "Whig Saturnalia" of 1840, the continuing legislative struggles over railroads and bank charters operated quite apart from the Protestant versus Catholic rhetoric in northern campaigning or from the southern debates over which party better loved the common white man. Even the act of voting came to reflect the differences between these spheres. The model among upper-class Americans made it the solemn, discrete choice of the individual citizen. The more deeply a campaign penetrated into the lower class, however, the less distinct the act of voting became and the more broadly social it grew. Migrants with no stake in the communities, often not even in the states, where they happened to vote joined others at the fringes to make it an outing—a holiday gathering, a boisterous march, perhaps some singing and fighting along the way. Going to the polls and taking a drink blended the spirits of a happy occasion.

These two tiers did not create a real and a sham politics. Cultural identities and antipathies expressed the values of American life as well as economic opportunities did. But one kind of politics ended at the polls, while the other proceeded to make government decisions. Significantly, the reward that New Hampshire Democratic leaders gave their Catholic supporters at midcentury removed their electoral disabilities, plowing the legislative results back into the electoral process. No one ever discovered how strong the interest in economic policy actually was in lower-class America because the upper class kept economic policy as its own monopoly. At the same time, the United States by contemporary standards had an astonishingly large electorate, a remarkably large upper class, and a strikingly loose social structure within that class, justifying the general European estimate of America as an unprecedented experiment in democratization. Around 1850, the percentage of Americans with at least a modest base of property and the right to vote was probably more than double that in Britain, where a far smaller percentage than in the United States sat at the very top of society and held the nation's great wealth. But which of America's two classes was the growing half of this new democracy? As the line between them hardened, the uncertainty of the answer added significantly to the strains that at midcentury were already besetting American politics.

17

A Crisis in Parallelism

As America's web of institutions was forming, it neither affirmed nor denied the existence of a nation. Unlike the 18th-century venture in building a society from the top down, this one originated in a multitude of everyday needs that responded to the long lines of settlement and enterprise, not to the imperatives of union. The most comprehensive of the institutional networks—the political parties and the commercial chains—lay across the nation without integrating it. Additively they covered immense stretches of space; substantively they allowed countless citizens to live with no more than passing attention to the rest of the United States. The national government's decline as a center of authority nicely complemented these free-form creations. Jefferson at his most insular could scarcely have found fault with its apparatus in the early forties: no bank, no military worth mentioning, no taxes that a growing majority of citizens could remember paying its officials. The General Land Office atrophied. Eight clerks assisted the Department of State in its international affairs, and no pressing foreign danger mobilized a demand for more than these men could manage. Around midcentury the government even allowed the nation's vaunted ocean shipping to decline for lack of a subsidy. Speculations about a political alliance between south and west or north and west resembled talk of an international arrangement, with Washington cast as headquarters for an ag-glomerate league.

This wisp of a nation found its most natural expression in essences—God's chosen vehicle for human progress, for example, or the people's agent for continental conquest. Adapting a Federalist tradition of homo-geneity to the new age, Daniel Webster won great fame as the spokesman for a mystical wholeness that arched softly above America's sprawling, diversified life. Along with the belief in a distinctively egalitarian society came the many, similar calls after 1820 for a truly independent American literature or painting or even science as manifestations of this unique nation's spirit. The neocolonial Noah Webster, born in 1758, had re-vealed his sense of America by rooting its language deep in a bed of strict British usage. Those 19th-century Americans who still measured their arts, institutions, and economy against Britain's now set the two coun-tries on their separate paths, each with its own intrinsic qualities work-ing out its own future. If Americans still trailed the British in the march of civilization, the New World, with its special vitality of a free people ranging across an open continent, had the sources for an ultimate victory. America had the best track all to itself.

These national conceptions warmed respectable Americans in a blan-ket of commonality without determining how they lived or thought. Their firm loyalties began at home and extended from the community through its surrounding area no farther than the state, the most distant unit that actually fed their enterprises and influenced their local environ-ments. Beyond these hard, practical loyalties lay a nation that they cre-ated in their own image as a comforting reinforcement for their personal or community choices, a destiny for the whole that could be seen as consonant with each of their many destinies within it. The clearest expression of this sense of an enveloping support came in the glorifica-tions of the union that rang out in nationwide celebration from the 1820s to the 1840s. Older leaders such as Clay and Jackson made the union's preservation their proudest claim. Younger men such as Abraham Lin-coln and Stephen Douglas came of age taking its permanence as a given, and for them the Constitution, divested of its legal intricacies, became one of America's sacred truths. The symbols of the union—its flag, its holidays, its heroes—had tremendous emotive power not because they reasserted a government's presence but because, in effect, they were its presence. Mourning the passage of the familiar postage stamps, a south-ern unionist wrote in March 1861: "Maybe this is the last letter you'll ever get with one on it. The Union is gone and all those things follow.
. . ."[1] Yet in the end, such feelings were optional. Lines of loyalty might connect with the nation or stop with the community, and nothing com-pelled one choice over the other. Even the nation's heroes slid easily into

smaller spaces: Jackson the western man, Patrick Henry the Virginian, the Adamses of Boston.

Sections had the least claim on American loyalties. Without governments to aid people's enterprise and without benign symbols of wholeness to match the Constitution and the revolutionary tradition, sections lacked the attraction of both the hard local attachments and the soft glow of the union. Hence nothing foreordained the arrival of southern sectionalism as a powerful competitor in the late forties, even though some kind of sectional consciousness had existed for a long time. The common use of "northern" and "southern" to designate leaders and interests dated from the 18th century, and the white settlers in the early 19th retained these labels as they followed the lines of western migration. They also transported different models of township and county government. Above all, whites from the south took slaves with them, generating special characteristics in the style and structure of their societies. With slavery came the laws and patrols and preoccupations of policing it. When a fear of abolitionism struck in the early 1830s, it chilled the attitudes in slave territory toward some of the reform ferment that was then bubbling to the north. Moreover, in the richest southern lands slavery brought a distinctive pattern of agriculture, with farms of a much higher capitalization and far larger acreage than elsewhere in the United States, and atop those holdings reigned a small, distinctive agricultural elite, misnamed planters, who stood apart not only because of their wealth but particularly in the southeast because of their aristocratic ways and their affinity for the old gentry values of honor and shame.

Neither singly nor in clusters, however, did these characteristics bind the south into a section before the late forties. The "isms" that southerners singled out for attack tended to be the same ones that almost all respectable northerners also abhorred: the challenges to private property and capitalist profits, or the adventures in a new kind of community freedom such as Fanny Wright's Nashoba and John Humphrey Noyes' Oneida. Although slaveholders dug in with a renewed vigor after 1831 to protect their labor system, they generally pictured themselves at war with a crazy, vicious band of abolitionists, not as section battling section. Certainly southerners had ample northern company in their hatred of abolitionists. Just as abolitionists attacked at a distance, so southerners defended at a distance, rendering the southern restrictions on a debate over slavery largely a symbolic ban on phantom outsiders.

The basics of early-19th-century democracy swept the south and the north indiscriminately. In schooling and literacy, for example, southern whites improved their relative standing in the nation during the very years when the northern common schools were spreading, and as far north as Wisconsin migrants from the south led the way in promoting public education. In much of the south a rough separation of areas dominated by plantations from those dominated by small farms kept politics feisty and diverse. Indeed, significant stretches of it were effectively free soil. The small farmer's urge to acquire slaves derived not from an idolization of the southern grandee but from the obvious logic of economic opportunity. If great planters served an exceptionally large number of terms as governors, the powers of those offices were also notably weak, and such men did not control southern legislatures. No greater gap separated the styles of poor and rich in the plantation south than in the urban north. Commenting on "the household economy" among South Carolina's elite, one knowledgeable northern visitor reported "a style appropriate to a wealthy gentleman's residence—not more so, nor less so, that I observe, than an establishment of similar grade at the North."[2] For every Charlestonian who bowed to the glories of British culture, there was a Bostonian to match him; for every southern attack on the evils of Yankee industrialism, there was a northern counterpart.

Attempts to translate southern peculiarities into a functioning sectionalism produced only frustration until the late forties. Nullification left South Carolina stranded in a sea of praise for the union, and advocates of a cooperative southern politics—the Calhounites—remained a noisy but largely ineffectual scattering of minorities. The support that nullification did receive applied to states rights, not southern rights, and on matters relating to slavery, individual states continued to serve as the natural units of decision and action. In fact, a good deal of the rhetoric spilled in the south's behalf expressed the longstanding enmity in Virginia and South Carolina toward Massachusetts, state-based rivalries that at most pitted southeast against northeast. Although northern politicians sometimes found the values of southern politicians quite strange, easterners often felt the same way about westerners. When James Buchanan's niece Harriet Lane gossiped about the Lincolns of Illinois who were coming to occupy the White House—"They say Mrs. L. is awfully *western*, loud & unrefined"—she was playing upon familiar old prejudices.[3] A number of the northeastern stereotypes about drinking and gambling and killing applied generally to the west and the south: everybody else.

The impersonal differences that presumably divided north from south blurred in much the same fashion. Towns and cities, for example, clustered heavily in the north. So did bank capital. In the early forties, however, these differences separated the areas around the major northeastern cities from the rest of the nation far more than they distinguished a north from a south. In the percentage of citizens in settlements of 2,500 or more, the ratio of retail stores to population, and the proportionate investments in those stores, Alabama stood side by side with Illinois around 1840; in roughly comparable ways Mississippi paired with Indiana and Georgia with Ohio. All of these states had more capitalist characteristics in common than any of them did with Massachusetts. If sharp differences distinguished the growing and marketing of cotton from wheat, the same was true of wheat and livestock. Moreover, everything relied on essentially the same credit networks that lubricated American commerce. Arguments that the north sucked profits from the south dissolved in the general rule that the people who had the credit to dispense got the biggest profits. Farmers everywhere suffered as a consequence. At some level of abstraction it was possible to claim that the south had a thinner, less variegated web of institutions and the north a more industrial, diversified economy—but only by first creating an artificial south and north to house the generalizations.

When sectionalism did appear in the late forties, it began to shape all this information toward its special ends, and during the next fifteen years, as towns and industrial shops spread more densely through the northwest and its flow of trade turned increasingly toward the northeast, the contrasts between north and south deepened. Nevertheless, the sharp, initial turn toward a southern sectionalism did not wait for the trends. It arrived at a time of indeterminacy. If the Methodist and Baptist churches were dividing along sectional lines, the political parties and commercial chains continued to spread grandly across the nation. Slavery, the one region-wide, region-specific institution, did underlie southern sectionalism, but then slavery had always accompanied the territory, with or without a sectional mobilization. No sudden breakdown in national authority impelled its presence. In fact, as southern sectionalism emerged, it shored up the frameworks of authority around it, strengthening the importance of state sovereignty and investing the national government with a greater significance than it had enjoyed since Jackson's first administration. What made the critical difference, what elicited a new sectionalism, was a crisis of growth in a grow-or-die society.

As the national government became less visible inside the United States, its external responsibilities stood out in sharper relief, and with economic recovery in the early forties, pressures mounted to push the government along its appointed track. An independent Texas, separated from Mexico since 1836 by American settlers bearing American arms, invited absorption. Following the first of the popular overland trails, migrants flowed into the Oregon Territory, where their presence not only caused friction with the British to the north but also stirred interest in the Mexican coastal lands to the south. In both Texas and Oregon, disputed boundaries added to the possibilities for an adventurous foreign policy, especially after the Tyler administration maneuvered the annexation of Texas early in 1845 and bequeathed to the expansionist President Polk its dubious claims to more Mexican territory. Using unsettled debts and boundaries as camouflage, Polk precipitated a war of conquest with Mexico in 1846, and in little more than a year American forces penetrated to the Mexican capital, staked out a new western empire, and inspired talk of annexing the entire enemy country. Instead, the government in 1848 settled for a Texas extended to the Rio Grande, a vast stretch of land west of Texas and the Louisiana Purchase, including most of Mexican California, and a payment of $15 million for the seizures.

Who would benefit from this new domain? In a loose sense, all enterprising Americans. "Land," Harriet Martineau reported from her visit a decade earlier, "was spoken of as the unfailing resource . . . the great wealth of the nation; the grand security of every man in it . . . and the cure for all social evils. . . ."[4] The earlier continentalism of Jefferson and John Quincy Adams had construed such imperial wealth as a magnificent patrimony to be set aside for future generations. But the lines of the 1840s that thrust indeterminately across space generated an almost limitless appetite for land. What amount of it would ever be enough for a progressive nation of progressive citizens? A chorus of liberals and conservatives, northerners and southerners, joined in defining more land for the United States as inherently good for everybody—Americans, Mexicans, the human race. Calling for "an indefinite" extension of the national domain, William Greenough presented the inevitable rationale: Nature demands "progress and development, and attaches her curse on all inaction."[5]

East of the Appalachians, however, a number of citizens still found ample room for their enterprise inside the old national boundaries. Some firmly rooted local elites felt quite comfortable in their own environments, and at the class margin many more looked to the towns and cities for their opportunities. The louder the cries of Manifest Destiny around them, the more restrictive they became in defining a healthy growth. On the eve of the war the Georgia Whig Robert Toombs announced that he did not "want a foot of Oregon or an acre of any other country"—then added, "especially without 'niggers.' " A vocal group of New England Whigs was apoplectic over the prospect of more slave territory. Even large Democratic constituencies in New York and Pennsylvania would tolerate Mr. Polk's war only if it brought additional free soil—"a creed suited to the latitude in which we live," the New York Democrat William Cullen Bryant coolly wrote with his back to the south.[6] It was from these eastern areas rather than from the more permissively expansionist western states that the demand originated to specify a meaning for this hazy bonanza of land. Early in the war a Van Burenite, Congressman David Wilmot of Pennsylvania, moved an amendment to an appropriations bill that would have excluded slavery from the war's territorial acquisitions. A fire struck in the east rapidly spread nationwide, and for over three years it swirled around the issue of the Mexican conquest.

The debate over the Wilmot Proviso and its successors catalyzed southern sectionalism: a challenge to slavery that state government could not and the national government would not meet, a mobilization of sectional loyalty in response. Before 1846 slavery, always present, rarely dominated political discussions even among Calhoun's followers. Two years earlier one of them, Francis W. Pickens, cheered Polk's nomination with a characteristic mix of concerns: "He is a large Slave holder & plants cotton—*free trade*—Texas—States rights *out & out.*"[7] Now slavery's needs would dictate southern responses to homesteads, railroads, constitutional interpretations, and the rest of national policy. Before the Wilmot Proviso, war and expansion were party issues, with all the prospects of transience that accompanied party sloganeering. Now section would dictate to party. In this framework it did matter that the southern states contained a relatively thin pattern of institutions, for it simplified the assimilation of these strands into a sectional network. As party spokesmen adapted to the primacy of sectional interests, so did evangelical leaders, who shifted from a mild chastening of their misguided northern critics to a fiery attack on them as incendiaries. Only the web of commerce was too extensive and too finely spun to be drawn into the new sectionalism. All of this developed over time, of course, and never created a southern monolith. No large portion of such a diffuse nation could have become one. Nevertheless, by midcentury the preponderance of public authority in the slave states expressed this increasingly self-conscious interlacing of sectional loyalties.

The real whip in the process was the future dictating to the present—slavery where it did not exist defining slavery where it did. The commandment to grow or die drove southerners as mercilessly as northerners. "To sell cotton in order to buy negroes—to make more cotton to buy more negroes, 'ad infinitum,' is the aim and direct tendency of all the operations of the thorough going cotton planter," a Yankee visitor to the southwest commented in the 1830s; "his whole soul is wrapped up in the pursuit. It is, apparently, the principle by which he 'lives, moves, and has his being.' "[8] Where Caleb Cushing of Massachusetts considered it axiomatic that growth was "the very necessity and condition of existence," John Slidell of Louisiana cited exactly the same self-evident truth: ". . . the law of our national existence is growth."[9] The omnivorous American appetite for land, in other words, gnawed just as fiercely in the south. Throughout the 1840s and 1850s, large stretches of cotton land continued to lie at hand in the slave states, prompting a trained British observer to note that "the territory at the disposal of the South had [consistently] been much greater than its available slave force has been able to cultivate. . . ."[10] Nevertheless, an abundance by the standards of his tight little island looked increasingly like a deficit to American eyes, and those eyes turned naturally westward.

Alternative paths of growth did attract some southerners. As depression lifted in the forties, old dreams of a trans-Appalachian trading empire revived in the southeast. Once again, Charlestonians looked across the mountains toward Cincinnati and through Tennessee into Alabama. Virginia, Missouri, and Alabama plunged into a variety of transportation enterprises, and during the fifties railroad mileage, increasing threefold in the north, grew fourfold in the south. But three or four times what? Among the most sectionally conscious southerners, the scramble to excel in an economic race for which northerners seemed to have been born just accentuated their weakness. In the 1850s, New York and Boston still held about as much bank capital as the entire south. A second route to growth led into Latin America, and schemes to seize this or that portion as a fresh field for slavery dotted the late forties and fifties. Yet the Mexican War not only destroyed the possibility of conquering more slave territory as national policy; it also revealed how many southerners, like white Americans everywhere, balked at the thought of incorporating millions of dark-skinned Hispanics into their nation. Race, which had never inhibited the old gentry imperialists, cooled the conquering ardor of a good many white democrats in the middle of the 19th century. Although this path of progress continued to stir discussions throughout the 1850s, it produced nothing more substantial than a few filibustering expeditions.

Perforce, the southern need to grow thrust toward the western territories, where it immediately encountered the Missouri Compromise line at 36°30'. In the years after 1820 the new values of parallelism turned this simple line into the ideal means for managing competitive enterprises. To the degree that there were composite slave and free-soil interests, each had a lane of its own in the drive westward, and the longer this dividing line endured, the more it acquired the qualities of a natural separation, as if fate had dictated both its placement and its consequences for the competing labor systems. Hence when California, with its expanse of territory straddling 36°30', poised to enter the union as a free state, the automatic southern response was outrage—slavery belonged in southern California—and the combination of measures that became the Compromise of 1850 sought to compensate for this breach, particularly in their vague prospect of slavery's growth within the rest of the Mexican conquest as far north as the 42nd parallel.

Older leaders such as Webster, Clay, and Calhoun had already read the future of slavery in a higher law. Nature ruled that it would soon reach its limits. Zachary Taylor, inaugurated as president in 1849, agreed: ". . . nature has so arranged matters as regards the ceded Territory, which will prevent the existence of Slavery in any portion of it."[11] Not one of them, however, was an ardent expansionist. They belonged to an earlier era when eastern-based leaders often calculated in terms of slave and free balances within a broadly contained nation, and they sought in their various ways to stabilize the results of Nature's decree. When Webster justified his support for the territorial compromises in 1850 with a magisterial "I would not take pains to reaffirm an ordinance of nature nor to re-enact the will of God," he spoke with a supreme northern confidence but no special malice toward the south. After all, these men had risen to prominence at a time when many still thought slavery's extension meant its dilution and gradual disappearance.

But Calhoun, Clay, and Webster were at the end of their long careers. To the younger men who dominated public affairs, the pace of growth— the vital, pushing pursuit of progress—defined the terms of a healthy policy. Movement was overwhelming all plans to contain it, and the stark distinction between growing or dying gave an imperative message to each turn of affairs. Among sectionalists, the statistics on northern manufacturing, northern population, and the northern surge into Iowa, Wisconsin, and Minnesota set the beat for comparison, and these southerners calculated their prospects accordingly. Calhoun did catch the central theme in their argument when he declared that slaveholders wanted only "equality" in the west. But equality was no longer a matter of balanced growth. It meant an equal chance to move and seize and expand now, to "test our rights, and opportunities . . . by the law of nature" in an open west, Jefferson Davis declared, and put the lie to Webster's vision.[12] Unable to grow, slavery would die. Even essentially cautious northerners taunted the south with this basic, midcentury logic. "We will establish a cordon of free states that shall surround you," declared Columbus Delano of Ohio; "and then we will light up the fires of liberty on every side until . . . all your people [are] free." Horace Bushnell, a bellwether of moderate respectables, pictured a "northern tier of states, from one ocean to the other . . . pressing down thus more and more heavily on the confines of slavery . . . till finally it will be discovered that the laws of population are themselves abolitionists. . . . And the time is much closer at hand than many suppose."[13] White southerners, already feeling that heat and that pressure, demanded instant relief.

Northern sectionalism came gradually and unevenly in response to the southern initiative. To a large majority of northerners, slavery in any guise simply could not be made compatible with their visions of progress, and they wanted nothing to do with it in the western territories. The Wilmot Proviso did strike a responsive chord throughout the north. The south's promotions of its cause only sharpened this consciousness. Nevertheless, bits and pieces of the same trends that spread doubts through the south led many northerners to believe that they were already hooked to the train of progress, and confidence encouraged a preoccupation with their own enterprises. Moreover, just as a relatively simple web of institutions hastened cohesion in the south, a more complex one delayed it in the north. Most northern churches, even most northern reforms, tried to ignore the south, and the standard texts in the northern common schools purveyed a happy nationalism that just blinked slavery out of existence. A maze of business connections ran between the regions. Why choose among the larger frameworks for loyalty? Everybody's natural inclination was to interchange or combine attachments to state, region, and nation, and most northerners preferred to keep it that way.

Everything hinged on the maintenance of parallelism. "To our country," rang a toast of 1838, "—The whole must prosper when every part takes care of itself."[14] To the eve of secession, northern and southern unionists alike saw no contradiction whatsoever between national harmony and the autonomy of those parts. Advocates of the state liberty laws that tried to undermine the Fugitive Slave Law of 1850, for example, defended them as necessary to the perpetuation of the union. "To render Virginia commercially and socially independent of the Northern States will in no way injuriously affect the Union," one of the state's Whigs declared in 1860.[15] Both Jackson and Calhoun would have understood. Just as long as sin stayed there and did not come here, most northerners could tolerate slavery. That saving sense of a separation between slavery and free soil benefited immeasurably from a buffer zone extending between the Atlantic and the Mississippi. Along it lay those states with only a small minority of slaves in their population: Delaware, Maryland, Kentucky, Missouri. Next to them stretched those portions of Pennsylvania, Ohio, Indiana, and Illinois that had the least aversion to the institution and the most intimate interconnections with slaveholders. Together they insulated the heart of slavery to the south from the centers of its harshest opposition to the north, protecting each from the feeling of a direct impingement by the other.

In 1854, parallelism broke down in the western territories—the cutting edge of a linear progress—and from there the consequences spread eastward to muddy its effectiveness everywhere. To organize the next stretch of territory beyond Missouri and Iowa, Senator Stephen Douglas presented legislation that, in the spirit of America's decentralized democracy, left the question of slavery or free soil to the settlers themselves. In theory, Douglas' popular sovereignty offered the reasonable prospect of reversing the trend toward southern sectionalism and dispersing the loyalties that it was mobilizing. Only slavery guaranteed a congressional split into antagonistic sectional blocs. A low tariff, for instance, had substantial northern support. The question of government-sponsored railroads westward lent itself to various parallel solutions, and the issue of a homestead law contained nothing irrevocably sectional in it. Yet as long as the passions over slavery flared, they did indeed consume everything else, feeding the flames of sectionalism as they raged. Dampen those emotions and Americans could again scatter along their sundry paths of progress. "The great principle of self government . . . the principle upon which our whole republican system rests," Douglas concluded, was the natural corrective to an artificial crisis.[16]

In response to southern demands for an equal field for growth, the Illinois senator agreed to the outright repeal of the Missouri Compromise line. Then to assuage northerners, he repeated the commonplace wisdom that Nature had already committed the Kansas and Nebraska territories to free soil. Parallelism did not preclude every element of face-to-face competition. It only required a quick resolution and ample space for the loser to try again. During these very years of debate over the future of the west, Douglas was witnessing a model example in his own backyard. As Chicago enterprise pushed southward along new lines of transportation, it encountered St. Louis enterprise, overmatched it, and redirected the lanes of St. Louis' growth westward. It was more a fluid turning of paths than a clash, and it left both cities with grand vistas of progress.

Douglas' gamble failed not only because it dissolved the buffer between slavery and its fiercest enemies but also because it opened lanes of development to slaveholders that had been allotted to northerners. In the south the repeal of the Missouri Compromise line sparked little comment. It merely fulfilled the expectations raised in 1850 and reinforced by the Democratic landslide in 1852 that the national government would give slavery its due in the west. But in the north, more than three decades had enshrined the line at 36°30' as an immutable truth for the old Louisiana territory, and the maintenance of parallel growth now demanded it. No matter that years of doubt had clouded its legality and that compromises over the Mexican conquest had misted it further. Old Jacksonians from the slave states understood. Both Thomas Hart Benton and Sam Houston predicted in 1854 that the obliteration of this magic line would end the union. So did another old Jacksonian, James Buchanan, who as late as 1850 had urged his Democratic colleagues to extend it through the middle of California. Even Calhoun, a sincere unionist and no fool in these matters, had voted in 1848 to run the line to the Pacific. A union of autonomous parts required precisely this kind of etched division to sustain its strength.

Kansas became the nation's battleground, and the winner would take all. In the early fifties both slave and free economies showed abundant signs of energy. A burst of success in Kansas would propel one of them toward a great sweep of the spoils. If the south triumphed there, David Atchison of Missouri predicted, "we carry slavery to the Pacific Ocean[;] if we fail we lose Missouri Arkansas and Texas and all the territories"—and, by a simple extension of this logic, the entire slave system behind that tier.[17] Hence, as Roger Baldwin of Connecticut announced, the future of "the whole American people" lay at stake in the west. Once construed as an issue of national growth, what happened in Kansas mattered everywhere—in Charleston as much as St. Louis, in Boston as much as Chicago—and thousands of easterners, including many a cautious, wealthy Whig, suddenly sensed a personal connection with the whirl of events around such strange places as Lawrence and Topeka. *"Kansas must come in as a slave state or the cause of southern rights is dead,"* one of them from Georgia declared.[18] Exclude "slavery from the Territories," a conservative South Carolinian warned a business associate in Boston, and "I am prepared for a dissolution of our government rather than yield a *right which is essential to the very existence of the South."*[19] If southerners felt blocked, northerners now felt invaded. In reaction to Douglas' move, local political coalitions formed throughout the northern states, combining as opponents of the Kansas-Nebraska legislation and presaging the development of a sectional Republican party.

The one potential competitor for the politics of sectionalism was the politics of class, and as Kansas bled the ailing old parties, the prospects for class politics rose sharply. Constricting opportunities at the class margin squeezed Americans nationwide. Throughout the north the step across the divide to independent farming or shopowning continued to lengthen, and those who managed it found their footing on the edge of respectability more slippery than ever. Before midcentury, the costs of development in this high-risk economy had spread rather broadly among entrepreneurs, mechanics, farmers, taxpayers, and public creditors both here and abroad. Now the price of progress fell more and more leadenly on small farmers and wage earners. Agricultural credit was at least as tight in the south, where only the large planters had hopes of financing growth from their own resources. White farmers had traditionally seen the path upward marked by the acquisition of slaves. But the price of slaves, now more or less uniform across the entire section, soared during the prosperous fifties. The slave system, instead of following the ideals of white democracy and distributing its benefits more broadly, concentrated them more narrowly during the decade, as the percentage of white households owning any slaves dropped dramatically from just over 50 to just under 40. Talk of reopening the African slave trade came to nothing. Beneath these slaveless farmers flowed the stream of propertyless poor whites, whose chances of making a start in the settled areas dwindled just as their northern counterparts' did. Before midcentury, the costs of southern development had been extracted overwhelmingly from black labor. Now they began to spread more generally among whites as well.

At the same time, the cultural sensitivities that most directly expressed mounting tensions along America's class margin were following one of the repetitive patterns in early-19th-century politics: the tactics that political leaders first used to manipulate voters turned into the tactics that voters then used to influence political leaders. During the late forties and early fifties, the cultural issues from electoral politics increasingly pushed their way into the rest of American political life. Centers of anti-Catholic, anti-immigrant political activity were growing in a range of cities from Philadelphia to Milwaukee, and the movement for legal prohibition rose to its peak between 1851 and 1855. The major parties had considerable elasticity in adapting to such currents. Nationwide in scope and polymorphous in form, they aimed their appeals as widely as they dared and gambled that they could attract more new groups than they lost in old ones. Their shifting bases accustomed them to shifting policies. In successive legislatures, majorities calling themselves Democratic might curse, then sponsor, then curse development corporations. If Whigs recruited more Sabbath-keeping, teetotaling Protestants than their opponents, they also introduced hard cider as the keynote in a national campaign. Because party managers always had to struggle to maintain an approximate parallelism, they were already versed in the problems of a messy interaction, and they prided themselves particularly on their adeptness in bridging the class line.

Hence when Whig leaders found their old appeals wanting and their party fracturing even more than usual after 1852, they had little to lose in experimenting with a politics that transformed their electioneering rhetoric into a full-fledged organization, and many of them joined with an aggressive lot of newcomers to form the American, or Know-Nothing, party in open opposition to Catholics and immigrants. It had the advantages of a high pitch, a ring of simple truth, and in many parts of the north an immediate resonance with an array of popular demands for purer communities and wider opportunities. In a number of ways, therefore, the Know-Nothings represented an extension of politics as usual. Among wealthy citizens the new party had the additional attraction of deflecting antagonisms from them toward the struggle at the class boundary. In this sense, it provided an excellent defense against another kind of class politics. Yet despite a striking initial success in the elections of 1854, the experiment faded rapidly after 1855 for two primary reasons: the inherent limits of its doctrine and the ready availability of a more suitable alternative.

By the 1840s the crucial test of a national party was its ability to span the gap between cultural and development issues. The Know-Nothings failed that test, except in those coastal cities where a sufficient quantity of Catholic immigrants encouraged Protestant voters to merge the culture of respectability with the economics of opportunity. Even in those areas, the party's success left it confused over how to translate electoral appeals into legislative programs. State governments were equipped only for symbolic warfare against the cultural enemy, and veteran managers found it very awkward to mix the nativist anathemas that they hurled during elections with the economic bargains that they struck in the legislature. Although the impulses behind Know-Nothingism certainly remained strong after the party's collapse, they worked themselves back into local politics along the class margin.

In the slave states, where the American party survived to contest the elections of 1856, it served almost exclusively as a home for wandering Whigs. Here the party's slogans bore almost no relationship to local circumstances and presented no challenge to its legislators. "We strive for our native-born sovereignty, our native born supremacy in that land which a beneficent God has given us," John J. Crittenden declared from the safety of Kentucky.[20] Throughout most of the south, therefore, it was as sectional a party as the newly founded Republicans, in this case calling back to northerners with the demand that they cleanse *their* domain of sin in the national interest. It might have worked if enough poorer southern whites had envisaged the rising power of an immigrant-infested north as more threatening to their opportunities than the rising power of an antislavery north. Not nearly enough of them did.

In the north, where so few blacks lived, whites along the class margin could combine free soil in the west, the perpetuation of slavery in the south, and a pox on all blacks in the vicinity without contradiction. Taken together, these policies would preserve their world of opportunities for whites only. In the south, however, an aversion to blacks and a fear of their competition almost invariably came to focus on the single issue of slavery's perpetuation, the poorer whites' surest protection. Hinton Rowan Helper, the North Carolinian whose fierce attack in 1857 on the haughty slaveholders won him loud applause in the north, undoubtedly expressed a widespread bitterness among the south's slaveless farmers, but his call for slavery's abolition lost him that audience. Keeping blacks in their place belonged to class politics everywhere. In the north it justified sporadic mob violence; in the south it justified an obstinate defense of slavery. Along the class line in the south, accepting slavery in the settled areas meant equating opportunity with new lands somewhere beyond the shadow of the planters who already held the best tracts, an open western domain where poorer whites could make a fresh start in a friendly setting. In the mid-fifties, land and space still prevailed nation-wide as the magic wands of progress. No alternative appeal could keep these dreams, laden with the implications of free soil and slave soil, from tunneling westward and spilling with a great popular force into the contested territory beyond the Mississippi.

Both the politics of class and the politics of sectionalism were nourished by assumptions of conspiracy that had infused an American understanding of public affairs since at least the 1760s. In the personal, hierarchical, neocolonial world of the late 18th century, conspiracies issued from abroad and worked through their gentry agents in America. As insidious as these plots were, they almost always had a sharp human focus—a Thomas Hutchinson for the Boston radicals, a Hamilton for the Virginia dissidents—and toppling their leadership, it was assumed, would destroy even as widespread a force as Jacobinism in the 1790s. In the early 19th century, as the hierarchy dissolved and authority scattered, conspiracies became increasingly diffuse, acquiring the characteristics of a generalized, evolving process much as all American activities did. It was the Monster Bank with its myriad tentacles, not Biddle himself, that Jackson's followers attacked. In the eyes of their enemies, the Masons or the Catholics dispersed and plotted everywhere. The conspiratorial orientation of the early 19th century also lost the Manichean neatness of the late 18th: monarchist-republican, Jacobin-republican. Nothing inhibited the citizens of an expanding decentralized democracy from picturing numerous conspiracies, major and minor, operating simultaneously in economic, cultural, and political activities, in local, state, and national governments, in neighboring communities and foreign capitals.

These assumptions about hidden corruptions and conspiratorial intentions affected enough people of diverse temperaments and persuasions to qualify as cultural norms. To say, for example, that John Quincy Adams believed in a Masonic plot because an Adams always saw conspiracies obscured a larger truth with a smaller one. So did Jackson and Calhoun, Lyman Beecher and Joseph Smith, Thomas Hart Benton and William Lloyd Garrison, Lincoln and Douglas. No decade stood apart from another in either the range or the intensity of these conspiratorial alarms, and almost no legislation or election of any consequence escaped their influence. Alabama farmers, Cincinnati clerks, and New York mechanics responded equally to their appeal. They pervaded America not because, generation after generation, a mass paranoia afflicted the millions, but because such assumptions related reasonably to their lives. Hidden actions in distant places did affect them, and it made sense to ask who was doing what where. In a society of spotty and unverifiable information, Americans did what others in their situation would have done: they constructed answers from what they believed in general about human ambitions and political processes, the consequence of bad values and the growth of unregulated power.

Where the most prized possession was the right of choice, those Americans who sensed that right disappearing looked for the people who had stolen it. Enemies took predictable forms. Reversing the standard public virtues, they were aggrandizers rather than equalizers, aristocratic rather than democratic, and secretive rather than open. In other words, they were greedy, autocratic conspirators, and Americans in the normal course of their lives kept alert for rumors and signs—their basic sources of information—to spot these enemies before their wickedness spread. As any good American knew, each step in an ineluctable sequence of cause and effect carried momentous consequences for the outcome, and no detail, no apparently trivial action, lacked meaning within the iron-bound logic governing human affairs. Americans found themselves scanning events without knowing exactly what a pivotal one would look like. Necessarily the tension mounted until the issue was somehow resolved: Jackson, not the Bank, prevailed; Protestantism, not Catholicism, won the new west; the United States, not Britain, took Texas.

The firming of American society around midcentury affected these norms in slight but significant ways. During the 1820s and 1830s, some Americans continued to assign a European base to such amorphous conspirators as the Masons and the Catholics. By midcentury this neocolonial legacy almost completely disappeared. Despite occasional southern references to the complicity of British abolitionists and northern ones to papal dictation, the real sources of American corruption now lay in America. No one charged that the Irish immigrants had been sent to the United States in the sense that New England Federalists once imagined the Jacobins had sent them. Pressures also increased on society's leaders to maintain a clear domestic divide between the virtuous and the vicious. If in a local setting this charge applied specifically to issues of class, in a national setting the principle translated more generally into an obligation to draw the line between a pure nation and the sources of its corruption. Respectable Americans who located about as many people below as above the class line had little difficulty visualizing about as many people outside as inside the true nation.

With a sufficiently clear line, parallelism still offered the prospect of insulation against such dangers, for it did not matter a great deal what connivances or corruptions worked themselves out on another set of tracks. Americans might hate these evils almost casually. Hence even the arrival of a second sectional institution, the free-soil, free-labor Republican party in the north to match slavery in the south, did not guarantee a national binge of conspiratorial assumptions. After more than half a century of coexistence, no heavenly writ said that slavery and free soil could not continue to function side by side. Moreover, the Republican party by no means signaled the arrival of a single-minded north. Mobs attacked antislavery spokesmen there to the eve of the Civil War, and throughout the region mutual ignorance and suspicion marked relations between country and city, northwest and northeast, and above all the more northerly stretches of free soil and those bordering on slave states.

Nor was the prospect of one section living with a president from another section inherently intolerable. It all depended on preserving distinctive paths of enterprise. The presidents elected in 1856 and 1860 seemed ideally suited to that purpose. Buchanan of Pennsylvania and Lincoln of Kentucky and Sangamon County, Illinois, both had their roots in the buffer zone between intense sectionalism and both reflected its concerns—Buchanan's desire to enforce the Fugitive Slave Act, for example, and Lincoln's interest in colonizing freed blacks abroad. Buchanan's career from its quiddish origins in Pennsylvania politics through its Jacksonian development revealed an unwavering attachment to the rights of autonomous, state-centered enterprise and a powerful aversion to the national government's intrusion into these separate spheres of growth, free or slave. At the heart of his creed, Lincoln stated in 1858 that "each individual is naturally entitled to do as he pleases with himself and the fruit of his labor, so far as it in no wise interferes with any other man's rights—that each community, as a State, has a right to do exactly as it pleases with all the concerns within that State that interfere with the right of no other State, and that the general government, upon principle, has no right to interfere with anything other than that general class of things" beyond individual and state rights.[21] Neither man was inclined toward precipitate action. Both revered the Constitution, and in crisis both preferred to let events unfold and pitch their appeals to preserving the union.

Nevertheless, the crucial prerequisite to a parallel sectionalism—defusing the conflict in the western territories—lay beyond reach. As they did with all social groups, Americans assigned a core of character to each section, a simple, immutable guide to its actions and their moral meaning. By 1856, self-conscious northerners had set slavery at the core of the south and self-conscious southerners had set abolitionism at the core of the new northern party. Following these lights, each side interpreted—or anticipated—the other's moves, and in their glare, the old Jacksonian formula of more land as "the cure for all social ills," the answer to "those intestine animosities . . . which burn more fiercely the narrower the bounds within which they are confined," disappeared in the shadows.[22] Only if an undifferentiated assortment of Americans on the make, not slaveholders and free-soilers, met in the west did the various applications of the old formula have a chance to work: John M. Clayton's use of the judiciary to settle the question of slavery's presence or absence, or Douglas' use of popular sovereignty. These solutions suited basically homogeneous communities that were resolving problems inside the framework of their common agreement, not hostile groups that came to the territories to battle for their lives. Hence in Kansas popular sovereignty became a mirror trick, a sleight-of-hand to dismiss the issue of slavery that now ate at the heart of an open American society—movement, growth, opportunity, choice. At the climax of his debates with the champion of popular sovereignty, Lincoln laid bare the emptiness of Douglas' solution in 1858: "Is it not a false statesmanship that undertakes to build up a system of policy upon the basis of caring nothing about *the very thing that every body does care the most about?*"[23] Douglas remained master of an old bargaining, expansive politics, but Lincoln better understood the dilemmas of the new—and Lincoln's argument prevailed.

All of the conditions now existed for a nationwide fear of conspiracies at their most virulent and sectionwide responses at their most adamant. Two incompatible, expansive forces met in unstructured competition at the dynamic edge of American opportunity, each certain of its inherent American right to grow and of a diabolical enemy's determination to defeat it. Each enemy, in turn, acquired the standard characteristics of the conspirator: insatiably aggrandizing, hostile to the people's rights, and nourished by its hidden, systematic uses of power. In retrospect, the Fugitive Slave Law of 1850 appeared to northerners as an insidious southern wedge into their territory. Indeed, they came to see actions in Washington as evidence of a plot to foist slavery on the entire nation. Chief Justice Taney's decision in the Dred Scott case of 1857, defining slaves as property, placing them under federal protection, and thereby denying Congress the right to exclude slaves from any territory, marked the most dramatic twist in the plot, while President Buchanan's struggle to keep slavery alive in the Kansas Territory repeatedly underlined its purposes. Southerners on their part watched the abolitionist conspiracy extend from a ceaseless agitation that stymied slavery's growth in Kansas and threatened its survival in the border states to John Brown's outright attack in 1859 at Harpers Ferry and his public glorification in the north. As a consequence, countless people had a reasonable explanation for fragments of otherwise inexplicable information: shadowy events in Washington, violence and deception in Kansas, the gratuitous sweep of

Taney's decision, the seeming madness of Brown's raid. To a striking degree northern and southern congressmen did vote as blocs on territorial issues. Voices in both sections did cheer their bloody partisans in Kansas and did justify any political manipulations in their behalf. Buchanan did court the south and Taney did come from a slave state. Respectable northerners did aid Brown's plot.

The protective wall of a sectional parallelism, once breached in the west, had crumbled across the nation. Surely the Court's next step would open the free states to slavery's expansion. Surely Brown's raid prefaced more and larger forays to come. When Lincoln needed a speech in 1858, he drew naturally on the simple truths relating to formless competition. Now the nation itself was at stake, and it could not remain "permanently half slave and half free. . . . It will become all one thing, or all the other." A few months later Seward repeated the same standard principle: ". . . the United States must and will . . . become either entirely a slave-holding nation, or entirely a free-labor nation. . . ." Lincoln then proceeded to show how close a total victory for the slave power conspiracy actually was. Equally conservative southerners applied the same logic in reverse. If the Republicans gained as much as a foothold in the national government, Robert Toombs of Georgia wrote, they "would abolitionize Maryland in a year, raise a powerful abolition party in Va., Kentucky and Missouri in two years, and foster and rear up a free labour party in [the] whole South in four years. . . . Then security and peace in our borders is gone forever."[24] The turn in any face-to-face encounter came swiftly, sweeping even the most vital progress into decline. Was it just coincidence that economic depression struck the north right after the Dred Scott decision?

Politicians and parties adapted themselves to sectionalism because they had no means of taking another direction. Although political leaders had a considerable play in their powers to legislate, they had very little slack in their powers to persuade. Parties had no effective centers of strategy, no mechanisms for redirecting trends of opinion or combating popular convictions. Citizens, on the other hand, had the profoundest commitment to their immutable absolutes. Party slogans worked if they touched the right buttons and acquired the sound of democratic truth. By the late fifties too many Americans north and south knew exactly what the truth should sound like, and they waited until they heard its ring before they responded. Opposing party leaders, as culture-bound as any other Americans, almost never trusted one another's virtue. Even inside their own party, factional compromise meant apportionment, not consensus, and across party lines the one prospect more heartening than an electoral victory was the opposition's utter annihilation. Hence they also reacted to the breakdown of parallelism with the usual assumptions of a conspiratorial enemy and the standard reliance on an unsullied absolute. Rather than shaping sectionalism, politics served as its carrier throughout the land.

Even more, politics became the vehicle for the resolution of a direct confrontation, first in the west and now nationwide, that was simply lasting too long. Great forces operating in human affairs—an earthquake, an epidemic, a depression—always kept alive the possibility that on the grandest scale, God and the Devil still struggled for the world. At these moments sacred and secular tended to merge into a single inclusive vision—"a contest for the advancement of the kingdom of Heaven or the kingdom of Satan—a contest for an advance or retrograde in civilization," as one Illinois farmer combined them in 1858.[25] In "the fulness of time," such conflicts had their Armageddon and, anticipating its arrival, Americans made it happen. Only elections offered the means for a massive popular choice between good and evil, progress and decline. By widespread agreement the final answer was invested in the presidential election of 1860. Between 1856 and 1860, advocates of southern secession described the success of their sympathizers as steps toward "liberty"; Republicans calculated results in terms of the states won or lost for "freedom." At the climax in 1860, Lincoln and the Republicans in the north and John C. Breckenridge and his wing of the Democratic party in the south expressed the sectional spirit, each running only in one region and speaking only to that constituency. Against them stood Douglas, a second Democratic candidate, who attempted to straddle the sections, and the Whiggish Constitutional Unionists, who nominated John Bell to contest the deep south and its buffer zone. Sectionalism triumphed north and south. Although Lincoln won with a minority of the total popular vote, the message was no less clear to victor and vanquished alike.

Resolution in both sections took the form of a reprieve, a purging of sins and a saving leap back to the path of progress. In midcentury idiom the American democracy was always young, always in the process of becoming and hence always open to those flashes of insight that exposed error and allowed a hairbreadth escape from its terrible consequences. Among avid Republicans, victory meant a sudden reversal of the slave power's march toward disaster and a return to the road that the founding fathers had set toward a limitless development. In identifying the overriding Democratic sin Lincoln among many others had stressed the theme of wandering, of straying from the truths of the parental generation. Now at the critical moment a free people had made their choice for virtue, and in the euphoria of success not many Republicans doubted that the flow of progress would catch the south in its eddies and, however reluctantly, draw it along with the rest of the nation.

In the deep south, on the other hand, Lincoln's victory announced the triumph of Black Republicanism. Gentry politicians with their focus on the character of the leader had always been free to speculate on his possible change of heart. Some Republicans had thought John Adams might join them in 1797; some Federalists had thought the same about Aaron Burr in 1801. But in 1860, people spoke in an election, and their voice carried a simple, irrevocable message. Lincoln brought a section's abolitionist commitment to power. What did a promise to guarantee slavery's existence mean from a party that would seal it forever from the west and thereby set it, in Lincoln's stabbing phrase, "in the course of ultimate extinction"? At the initial Democratic nominating convention of 1860, southern leaders rejected a far more sympathetic Douglas when his northern partisans would not commit themselves to preserve slavery's avenue of growth into the west. After Lincoln's election, northern votes promptly admitted Kansas as a free state and organized new territories to the Rockies, sounding slavery's death knell as they proceeded. "Politics defines what the inhabitants of a state think should be the problems to be solved," Bernard Crick wrote a century later. "They may not all be capable of solution."[26] So the agents of compromise discovered after Lincoln's victory. By then it was too late to exhume the old formulas for a parallel growth: too late to enact the Missouri Compromise line as a constitutional truth, too late to embark on a war of conquest and open new slave lands for the south.

In the heart of the slave south, stopping the downward spiral into decay required an even more titanic leap to a fresh beginning. Its leaders had watched the coming victory of Black Republicanism as if they were waiting for an alarm to sound, and when it did, the states in the lower south moved to create their own union, one based on a purified constitution and a return to what the Confederacy's founders saw as the true path of the fathers. If slavery was the core of the south, it came wrapped in cotton. Rhetoric of the king's triumphal procession and the south's irresistible growth toward the tropics resounded during the secession conventions. The decisions to secede in the lower south, breaking sharply from the partisan patterns of the 1850s, produced a remarkable general élan, a great surge of release from the burdens of uncertainty and error and a reprieve to begin anew. Before the spring of 1861, each side in a divided nation had flushed sin from its land and stood once more on a track of progress. Caught between these renewals of virtue, whites near the boundary between slave and free soil had no agenda of their own other than delay. When others refused to wait, they too had to choose.

Just as sectionalism did not necessitate secession, so secession did not dictate war. Nevertheless, the creation of the Confederacy did not resolve the tensions that had been building in the north. A league of enemies, still vigorous and still pressing to expand, now moved beyond any semblance of control. Although some northerners joined the New York Democrat Samuel Tilden in predicting that Nature would keep the two nations separate, many others felt that Nature had been doing nothing to encourage parallelism during the fifties. If, as Martin Conway of Kansas claimed, Nature had endowed a superior northern society with the "right to rule this continent," then secession perverted progress by blocking its natural course of advancement.[27] Certainly those northerners who had come to believe the worst about the slave south found it intolerable to contemplate this hateful power left unpunished next door. Was there no retribution for a rebellion against the laws of heaven and earth? Now was the moment to eradicate forever "a barbarous & inhuman institution," Samuel Gridley Howe declared, before it could "make of us all barbarians & monsters."[28] Northern and southern soldiers who expected to be killed upon capture revealed how widespread the assumptions of an utterly unredeemed enemy had become by 1861. Moreover, northerners who were convinced that they fought for democracy against an aristocratic slave cabal not only carried with them a faith in the people's invincibility but also expected a welcoming reception from the south's oppressed white farmers. And, of course, in a setting of violated parallelism, northerners would be waging a defensive war—"for self-preservation," the converted pacifist Garrison announced. To waver in a grow-or-die world meant decline. "Indeed the moment a nation ceases to extend its sway," William Gilmore Simms wrote for his generation of Americans, "it falls a prey to an inferior but more energetic neighbour."[29] A reluctant Lincoln also understood this, and for his party, his section, and his nation he acted, precipitating the Civil War.

A good many northerners, including Lincoln, continued to believe in the midst of the world's most concentrated bloodbath that the invisible bonds of union still held. The Constitution's history refuted them. Flimsy since its origins, a union survived as a hierarchy, then a comprehensive cover, then an agent of parallel growth, only because too few people found compelling reasons during its several crises to break it. The marvel was that it had lasted this long. At the level of culture, however, history sustained Lincoln's mystical nationalism. Following the same values about virtue, vice, and their just rewards, about enterprise and growth, about the danger of outsiders to the true community, like-minded people across the land turned a common culture on one another and fought savagely for truth, freedom, and opportunity as their culture defined those fundamental terms. In this sense it was indeed a civil war. Although it broke the tacit rule of a merely rhetorical warfare between large groups of antagonistic whites, it did so only after each side had gradually, systematically defined its opposition as barbaric and hence eligible for slaughter.

Many 20th-century Americans found the self-righteous, absolutistic style of the secessionmongers and warmongers offensively alien and sought to escape the implications of such a passionate, popular clash of truths. Had everyone except a few moderate souls gone insane? No, the troubled or indecisive souls were the aberrants, for all good Americans were expected to feel the simple truth deep inside themselves, choose virtue, and pursue it unflaggingly. To fight, even to die, for the immutable truth had a peculiarly powerful relevance to mid-19th-century Americans. Had the moral absolutists obscured deeper economic and political conflicts that actually forced the contest? No, all issues in the mid-19th century were fundamentally moral, and a common culture fused these issues into one or another moral unity. Nor, by the same token, did southerners and northerners go to war simply over slavery. They fought over conflicting needs for growth in a formless competition that spread its jeopardy into politics and enterprise, community preservation and personal ambition—liberty and democracy in the most inclusive senses. A common culture did not determine each action on the road to war; but it set the bounds of reason around each actor's understanding and provided a justification for the choices that made civil war one natural expression of its values.

Epilogue

America's democratic culture, along with the institutional web that it spun and the class line it drew, survived the Civil War to dominate the balance of the 19th century. By the test of endurance, therefore, it succeeded far better than the first venture in building a national society. As a consequence, America proceeded to industrialize with a social system that had emerged from the needs of a distended, commercial people and their economy. The United States would be the world's premier industrial nation before this 19th-century foundation crumbled. Until then Americans made do with a society geared to extensiveness, individualized responsibility, and parallel opportunities.

Rather than destroy the old ways, the Civil War exposed basic problems that Americans then tried to resolve with the traditional means at hand. According to the original northern logic of the war, the Confederacy's military defeat and the adoption of the Thirteenth Amendment abolishing slavery drained the south of its power to damage the nation and readied it for wholesale democratic changes. Despite the terrible record of wartime casualties, very little sentiment surfaced in the north to draw a final, vindictive measure of blood from the south. Nevertheless, northerners did demand assurances that their nemesis would not return in a thin disguise. Because none of the filigree connections in America's network of institutions linked north and south in 1865, the formative months of Reconstruction became a study in garbled messages, missed cues, and short-circuited communications. Visions of a south led once more by the same old aristocrats astride a new variant of slavery prompted a loose military rule over most of the former Confederacy and a renewed attention to protections for the blacks. What would establish them as genuinely free? Over their souls, they and their ministers would have to preside. But over their bodies and their enterprise—life, liberty, and property—they required a guarantee of self-determination: the Fourteenth Amendment. With more reluctance northerners added the franchise—the Fifteenth Amendment—and hence the final plank beneath the basic rights of democratic choice.

By that route, the old abolitionist heresy of expecting full citizenship for blacks entered the Constitution, even though almost all northern whites still saw the former slaves as children. The northerner who came south as a planter and viewed free blacks as a "plastic mass" spoke a standard idiom that arched over the war years and united whites in both sections. Equating the capacity to choose with literacy and literacy with a moral education, some northerners sponsored common schools for these fledgling adults, but a small missionary effort did little to allay the general white doubts. The more time passed, the more northerners sustained a black franchise solely to check southern whites. Although northern officials oversaw the creation of new state constitutions in the south, they had no place to go after they had taken the essentially self-fulfilling steps of empowering blacks with the rights of citizens and mirroring a northern truth in the south's legal framework. To dally forever in the old Confederacy risked the ultimate irony: a north victorious in its war for progress straying from the true path in the defeated enemy's land. Depression in the early seventies underlined precisely this danger of growth stalled in a futile enterprise. By then slavery did appear quite dead. If blacks remained children, perhaps they had no inner resources to be anything else. To extricate themselves, northern white leaders had only the standard 19th-century guides. They allowed a southern sphere to reemerge and left northerners and southerners, whites and blacks, to their parallel enterprises. The freedman's dream that blacks would "be considered as men, and allowed a fair chance in the race of life" would not come to pass.[1]

Once more, the levels of government became separate tracks of activity, with Republicans as eager as Democrats to guarantee the autonomy of the states. In fact, a large majority of Republican leaders never abandoned that faith even at the height of Reconstruction, and the greatest vigor in northern political life during those years still sparked its state and local governments. Governments continued to establish the preconditions for opportunity, parties to negotiate their terms, and citizens to seize their chances. Wartime laws for homesteads, a transcontinental railroad, and tariff protection all were understood as facilitators for private enterprise, and the rest of the wartime apparatus to mobilize wealth and manpower, often inoperative, disappeared with the assurances of peace. Despite a significant realignment of voter loyalties, the political parties that stabilized in the mid-1870s emerged essentially the same as their prewar counterparts: diffuse, state-based networks that sought to maintain the separation of their popular, slogan-filled campaigning from their bargaining in the legislatures. Elected officials still traveled to Washington as state and local ambassadors, largely dedicated to the benefits they could extract in the neutral zone. During the 1870s, returning southerners found that little had changed in their absence.

Just as politicians continued to drum the same simple truths, so popular writers in all fields of knowledge employed the familiar mix of sound morality and basic information in an effort to persuade their audience of sovereign decision makers. Mystifiers and complexifiers, denying adult Americans the right to choose, were fundamentally undemocratic. Mothers and fathers held fast in the traditional spheres, and boys, dreaming of Huck Finn but learning to emulate Tom Sawyer, prepared for a departure into the unknown by internalizing the truths necessary to cope with it. Character—unitary, visible, constant—rooted all enterprise, and businessmen small and large ran their names to the top of the mast as proof of their firms' strength. Exterior still mirrored interior, as the pioneer sociologist Edward Alsworth Ross illustrated in his professional assessment of the immigrants from southern and eastern Europe: "To the practiced eye, the physiognomy of certain groups unmistakably proclaims inferiority of type . . . lips thick, mouth coarse, upper lip too long, cheekbones too high, chin poorly formed, the bridge of the nose hollowed, the base of the nose tilted. . . ."[2] Inside a union that was everybody's inviolable framework, presidents served explicitly as moral exemplars for the nation. Free enterprise remained monopoly enterprise, whether it covered the merchant's territory in a southern county or the Union Pacific's domain across the Rockies. Along these exclusive lanes each unit worked out a fate according to its unique merits. "A civilization like ours," wrote Henry George, "must either advance or go back; it cannot stand still."[3]

At the same time, changes in tone and emphasis, many of them dating from the 1850s, did affect the composite qualities of this culture. With each decade in the second half of the 19th century came a higher and higher premium on stability, both personal and social. Guides to individual behavior increasingly stressed a disciplined moderation, the kind of inner orderliness that could maintain a lifetime's steady course in the middle of the road. Neither the young male's conversion to a career nor the mature adult's electric encounter with the blinding truth struck with anything like the predictable frequency of the early 19th century. The magnate Tom Johnson's memory of an instant conversion to *Progress and Poverty* in the 1880s now represented the exception. Appropriately, the revivalist style settled into a businesslike litany. Although Dwight Moody and his contemporaries still probed for the interior buttons with their simple absolutes, minister and audience alike managed the experience with a notable calm, and tears slipped out of vogue. Solid, sober gentlemen, monuments to a record of temptations avoided and responsibilities met, sat stiffly for the photographs that depicted the essence of the late-19th-century male character.

These gentlemen, in turn, argued the case for a society as free from bounce and commotion as their own lives had been. An aging Emerson spoke to the past in 1867 when he envisioned a postwar unity that would emerge from "striking a new note. Instantly the units part, and form in a new order, and those who were opposed are now side by side."[4] Instead, the spokesmen for respectable America talked about the stabilizing influences of an immutable legal structure, a machine of human progress geared to the slowly turning "wheels of justice." The *State* as a reification of the social order crept into American usage. Social Darwinism, welcomed for its resonance with the traditional values of growing and testing, collected the units of competition into such large groups and implied such a stately pace for progress that it threatened to drain the last drops of dynamism out of American society. As the leaders of the American Social Science Association used the fashionable term "science," it communicated the same impression of a measured, orderly change. Only when all data were gathered, arranged, and studied would the whole of society move forward. By the 1870s, thoroughness had replaced urgency as the watchword for respectable reform.

Where science meant order and control, those who claimed its mantle took increasing pride in their detachment from the hurly-burly of American democracy. Although aspiring professionals in medicine, law, and other areas of specialized knowledge still had not prevailed over the popular demands for information and choice in a decentralized society, their cause was gradually gaining. Regular medicine began to build a new wall of legislative defenses, technical law grew more lucrative in a diversifying economy, and a few universities developed as havens for the withdrawn scholar. Detached experts presided over the custodial institutions for society's deviants much as sanitary engineers managed the unsavory problems of society's garbage. Indeed, the trend toward separate enclaves spread far wider than the professions. Wealthy Americans of all kinds demarcated little worlds for themselves through exclusive residences, clubs, schools, and resorts, and gentlemen who had once pictured themselves as leaders of their cities distanced themselves sufficiently to pro-

mote state controls over those governments. Not surprisingly, more and
more of them expressed deep doubts about an indiscriminate franchise
that threw all government to the ignorant, alien wolves. Even prominent
politicians found the customary campaign immersions in public opinion
increasingly distasteful, delegated as much of the electioneering as they
dared, and prized a clublike atmosphere at the centers of government.

In one sense, all of these efforts to rein American democracy served as
preconditions for a second significant shift during the last half of the
century. Economic opportunity, always crucial to a society of choices,
now rose to dominate it. Tied ever more directly to the nation's thriving
urban centers and increasingly dependent on the spread of railroad transportation, it generated imperative demands for city connections in the
countryside, set city against city in hotter and more complex competition, accentuated the horizontal, earthbound thrust in economic development, and extended the geographical range of American dreams.
Southern leaders, looking for new paths of progress after a disastrous
war, quickly picked up the cues, joined in the splurge of railroad construction, and scanned the nation for profitable lines of growth. The
National Banking Act, passed during the Civil War to create a market for
government bonds, proved so useful as the source of a uniform currency
that it became a fixture in economic policy and also encouraged the
extension of commercial enterprise. The nationwide movement to syn-
chronize railroad gauges followed this same expansion of visions. As the
hubs of these churning activities, cities had much less need than before
to reckon with their moral image; they simply received the economic
ambitions that poured their way. In 1895, when Booker T. Washington
counseled blacks to place economic opportunities ahead of all others, he
expressed priorities that countless respectable whites had long since
fixed in their own lives.

It was the single-minded pursuit of economic opportunities in wider
and wider geographical domains that finally set the 19th-century society
on its way to collapse. The imperial consequences of these quests
strained intolerably against the standards of personal merit, community
rootedness, linear expansion, and parallel enterprise that continued to
justify them. J. Pierpont Morgan may have believed that his financial
kingdom expressed nothing more than the sum of the individual characters creating it, but the results bore absolutely no relation to the isolated
lanes of growth that had initially inspired such an explanation. The
mammoth corporations of the late 19th century, blanketing economic
activities everywhere without anchoring themselves anywhere, belonged
nowhere. Yet by law—and the 19th-century custom of personifying all
units of enterprise—they too were "individuals." Placed in head-to-head
competition with a rival, Standard Oil promptly swallowed it and pre-

served a monopoly along one track of enterprise. John D. Rockefeller might see his success as a classic expression of parallelism, but if Rockefeller was right, the whole scheme was somehow fundamentally wrong, a conclusion that dawned gradually on Americans at every social and economic level. Major railroads had no luck parceling "natural territory" among themselves. The United States in the early nineties still had no national bankruptcy law. Indeed it still had no national government of note. The Sherman Act of 1890, a statement of the simple truth about parallel enterprise, contained all the ambiguities of yesterday's immutable absolute in today's new era. Americans had rushed headlong into an industrial revolution and tried to cope with a culture that they had inherited from the age of trans-Appalachian expansion.

What increasingly confused successful Americans infuriated the losers, and their numbers rose as the century wound down. Especially after 1873, as the economy followed a long curve of deflation, uncertainty, and tightening markets, the proportion of the propertyless, the futilely mobile, and the sweated grew accordingly, drawing a larger percentage of whites below the class line and exposing more and more ostensibly solid citizens to the hazards of the class margin. The loudest cries of outrage came from these newly vulnerable people. Where were the opportunities now for a fresh start? Interest rates did not soar in a deflationary era, but credit simply became harder and harder to command. The national banking laws, in effect, reestablished a nationwide system of secondary credit, offering scant encouragement to the newcomer and actively discouraging agricultural credits. Only the emerging centers of finance capitalism provided an ample source of primary credit. The traditional dream of a homestead in a new land, dying hard in the hearts of many a city worker from rural Europe or rural America, shriveled to a mere longing by the 1890s. That left the urban labor pool, now swollen to an ocean, where American hopes seemed to drown without a trace.

By traditional reasoning, a great fraud had occurred. Somebody somewhere had stolen the democratic rights of choice. Governments no longer responded to the people's wishes. The test of personal merit had been perverted into an exclusive right of the rich to grow richer and flaunt their wealth in the gaudy displays of a leisured aristocracy. The vastness and omnipresence of these aggrandizing forces left individuals and their communities not just at bay but seemingly in jeopardy of oblivion. Drawing on the values available to them, groups of angry citizens demanded the destruction of these impinging powers—the land monopoly, the money monopoly, the transportation monopoly—and the reopening of American society. Above all, they struck to the heart of 19th-century opportunity, a people's primary credit, and in various combinations they rallied behind such proposals as Alexander Campbell's convertible greenbacks and Charles Macune's subtreasury plan that would automatically transform ordinary people's assets into the funds for ordinary enterprise. Appropriate to a battle at the 19th-century class line, these dissidents in the antimonopoly leagues and farmers' alliances, the Knights of Labor and the American Federation of Labor, bent every effort to establish their respectability as sober, God-fearing citizens who spoke a simple truth that all Americans could recognize and asked only a fair field to prove their merit. Utopias as soft and gentle as William Dean Howells' and as structured and grandiose as Edward Bellamy's pictured a new day when the old verities would once more bring real choices into the lives of all worthy Americans. If elites disparaged the franchise, these beleaguered Americans did not, and they turned to politics with a passionate conviction that the people's voice, in full chorus, could reclaim the nation for virtue. 1896 became the time—the Bible's "fulness of time"—for a final confrontation of good and evil, ending forever this conspiracy against democratic rights.

No victory, no secession, no war; only failure. In fact, the failure was total. Severe, lingering depression in the nineties highlighted a massive impoverishment of opportunities by any 19th-century standards. Parallel growth had crossed the continent, turned back on itself, and crowded even the most successful entrepreneurs. Although some received a momentary lift from the vision of new openings across the Pacific, the fundamental answers had to come at home, where general feelings of disconnectedness signaled a fatally ailing culture. The prospect of class warfare spread a siege mentality among successful Americans whose willingness to use violence in their own defense gave them little comfort in the face of so many enemies. Countless small communities, including a sprinkling of rural utopias, lost a sense of attachment to any larger environment and turned permanently inward. When Frederick Jackson Turner tried to recapture the basic 19th-century process of leaving home and community to venture westward, he found no continuity in values that might have softened the shock of migration. In a stark version of cultural rootlessness, his individual pioneers stood with little more than their animal instincts to grow or die on the frontier. In a similar vein, the writers of children's literature now pictured the world beyond their young readers as an essentially normless, often terrifying fantasy land with no character models, no prudential lessons of any kind, to guide them into adulthood.

With the new century came, once again, a wholesale renovation in American life. The paths of opportunity turned upward into a vertically structured industrial society instead of outward along the routes of geographical expansion, and a successful passage now required the willingness to live by whatever fluid sets of values suited the management of this society's intricate operations. Hence parents were encouraged to rear adaptive children who could shift their standards as adults—"other-directed," David Riesman called them—rather than children who would hold forever to a set of immutable absolutes. Group efficiency and coordination replaced individual guilt and achievement as the spurs to advancement. In this society's upper levels, power was consolidated according to the many functional requirements of an urban, industrial nation and the services that its citizens came to expect. Specialization and professionalization marked each of these subdivisions. Only through the mediation of experts could ordinary Americans expect to care for their bodies and souls—or psyches, as their transmuted souls became. The division between voting and governing was increasingly formalized to place the complexities of public policy far beyond the average mind's comprehension, and appropriately the proportion of the electorate who went to the polls declined.

The important lines of demarcation in this society no longer ran parallel across space; they separated the enclaves of managers and experts above from the uninitiated below. Across the new divide, interactions depended on roles in an economic process: managing the production and distribution of goods, laboring at the production and distribution of goods; dispensing goods and services, consuming goods and services. Such a society was no longer moving and growing in the old linear, geographical sense. It progressed or declined according to abstract measures of its economic interactions—Standard of Living, Gross National Product. Basic units from the corporation to the city concentrated on systematizing fields of activity and perceived their primary challenges as intensive rather than extensive. Eventually the national government also committed itself to a systematic management of many American problems. There were no longer empty spaces where strange or despised people might work out their own destinies. New rules defined how to apportion the same spaces and resources: immigration restriction and anticommunist purges on the one hand, civil rights and civil liberties on the other.

Nevertheless, the values of the 19th century survived in modern America. Strains of antimonopoly sentiment kept a variant of the old parallelism alive. So did the stubborn champions of community autonomy and states rights. By and large, the old values belonged to the lower levels of 20th-century society. In this national system of power and prestige, a majority of people in the cities, towns, and countryside lacked any realistic prospect of sharing its privileges, looked elsewhere for their values, and found many of them in tradition. While elite Americans lost a sense of life's wholeness in a scheme of subdivided expertise and malleable values, the losers by these new national standards commonly retained their commitment to a world where behavior still revealed a unitary character and simple truths still applied to all human beings in all combinations and situations. Women still ran the home, men still threatened to contaminate it, and children still learned moral absolutes that were valid for a lifetime. Given a fair chance, males continued to believe, they could go it alone. The universe of these Americans, unlike the universe of the elite, was still going somewhere, often still going to heaven or hell. Their souls generally remained souls, and they preserved recognizably personal choices over their eternal fates. Skeptical in most cases of distant, patronizing experts, they sustained enough popular lore about the health of their bodies to keep a wider latitude of personal choices there also.

Yet old values in a new society had a radically different meaning, not only because of their many subtle adaptations to a range of modern opportunities but even more because of their social coverage. Once the common property of all respectable Americans, they increasingly became the special province of those who could not or would not compete for the big prizes in a national system. Now they stood explicitly, often fiercely, at odds with the values of those who did hold society's most favored positions. In this fashion, a culture that had served in the 19th century to distinguish America's upper class became in the 20th the common ground for a significant proportion of the nation's under class.

Notes

These notes cite sources for quotations, except those that are very brief or come from readily available documents. In almost all instances I have followed these sources literally in my text. However, I have omitted editors' brackets and the italics that denote coded words so that these would not appear to be my brackets and italics.

Part One:
THE REVOLUTIONARY REPUBLIC

Introduction

1 Lee to Patrick Henry, Feb. 14, 1785, *The Letters of Richard Henry Lee*, ed. James Curtis Ballagh (New York, 1911–14), II, 331. Hereafter cited Ballagh.

2 Jay to James Lowell, May 10, 1785, *The Correspondence and Public Papers of John Jay*, ed. Henry P. Johnston (New York, 1890–93), III, 143. Hereafter cited Johnston.

3 Washington to Jay, May 18, 1786, *The Writings of George Washington*, ed. John C. Fitzpatrick (Washington, 1931–44), XXVIII, 431–2. Hereafter cited Fitzpatrick.

4 Jefferson to Elbridge Gerry, Jan. 26, 1799, *The Writings of Thomas Jefferson*, ed. Paul Leicester Ford (New York, 1892–99), VII, 329. Hereafter cited Ford.

5 A South Carolinian quoted in J. Franklin Jameson, *The American Revolution Considered as a Social Movement* (Princeton, 1940), 20.

6 Thomas Rodney to Jefferson, Sept. 1790, *The Papers of Thomas Jefferson*, eds. Julian P. Boyd et al. (Princeton, 1950–), XVII, 548. Hereafter cited Boyd.

Chapter 1:
Leadership

1 *The Federalist* Number 17, ed. Benjamin Fletcher Wright (Cambridge, 1961), 168.

2 Ibid. 20, 185.

3 Albert Gallatin to Louis F. Delesdernier, May 25, 1798, *The Writings of Albert Gal-*

latin, ed. Henry Adams (Philadelphia, 1879), I, 16.

4 *The Records of the Federal Convention of 1787*, ed. Max Farrand (New Haven, 1937 [1911]), I, 431. Hereafter cited Farrand.

5 *William Plumer's Memorandum of Proceedings in the United States Senate 1803–1807*, ed. Everett Somerville Brown (New York, 1923), 6.

6 Jay to Washington, Mar. 6, 1795, Johnston, IV, 170.

7 Francis Hopkinson to Jay, Jan. 12, 1785, ibid., III, 136.

8 "Speech Delivered on 26th November, 1787, in Convention of Pennsylvania," *The Works of James Wilson*, ed. Robert Green McCloskey (Cambridge, 1967), II, 772. Hereafter cited McCloskey.

9 *Federalist* 39, 280.

10 *The Complete Anti-Federalist*, ed. Herbert J. Storing (Chicago, 1981), VI, 160. Hereafter cited Storing.

11 "Letters of Agrippa," *Essays on the Constitution of the United States*, ed. Paul Leicester Ford (Brooklyn, 1892), 54.

12 Adams to Mercy Warren, April 16, Jan. 8, 1776, *Warren-Adams Letters* (n.p., 1917–1925), I, 222, 202.

13 Jefferson to Thomas Nelson, May 16, 1776, Boyd, I, 292.

14 Thomas Emmet quoted in *A Documentary History of American Industrial Society*, eds. John R. Commons et al. (Cleveland, 1910), III, 329. Hereafter cited Commons.

15   Madison to Washington, Feb. 21, 1787, *Letters of Members of the Continental Congress,* ed. Edmund C. Burnett (Washington, 1921–36), VIII, 546. Hereafter cited Burnett.

16   Jay to Silas Deane, Feb. 23, 1784, Johnston, III, 114–15.

17   Adams to Samuel Adams, May 4, 1784, "Letters of John Adams and John Quincy Adams, 1776–1838," *Bulletin of the New York Public Library,* X (1906), 237–8.

18   Jefferson to Horatio Gates Spafford, Jan. 10, 1816, Ford, X, 12.

19   Jefferson to Madison, June 20, 1787, Boyd, XI, 483; to Francis Hopkinson, Mar. 13, 1789, ibid., XIV, 651.

20   Robert Troup to Jay, May 6, 1792, Johnston, III, 423.

21   Washington to Madison, Feb. 16, 1789, *The Papers of James Madison,* eds. Robert A. Rutland et al. (Chicago and Charlottesville, 1962–   ), XI, 446. Hereafter cited Rutland.

22   The Diary of Thomas Rodney, Mar. 29, 1801, Manuscript Division, Library of Congress.

23   Jefferson to William Short, Dec. 14, 1789, Boyd, XVI, 27.

24   Oliver Wolcott to John Marshall, June 9, 1806, *Memoirs of the Administrations of Washington and John Adams,* ed. George Gibbs (New York, 1846), I, 244. Hereafter cited Gibbs.

25   "The Anas" (Aug. 2, 1793), Ford, I, 254.

26   *The Journal of William Maclay,* ed. Charles A. Beard (New York, 1927), 7.

27   John R. Mercer quoted in Joseph Charles, *The Origins of the American Party System* (New York and Evanston, 1961 [1956]), 96.

28   "A Plebeian," Storing, VI, 142.

29   June 24, 1788, Rutland, XI, 173.

30   "To the Students of New Jersey College," 1798, *The Works of John Adams,* ed. Charles Francis Adams (Boston, 1856), IX, 206. Hereafter cited *Works.*

31   Jay to Robert R. Livingston, Dec. 14, 1782, Johnston, III, 7; Lee to Samuel Adams, Nov. 18, 1784, Ballagh, II, 294.

32   Jefferson to Jay, Aug. 23, 1785, Boyd, VIII, 427.

33   *Federalist* 11, 139.

34   Madison to Edmund Pendleton, Feb. 24, 1787, Burnett, VIII, 548; to Robert R. Livingston, Aug. 10, 1795, *The Writings of James Madison,* ed. Gaillard Hunt (New York, 1900–10), VI, 236. Hereafter cited Hunt.

35   Resolution of a Meeting in Lexington, Aug. 28, 1795, Box 12, Breckenridge Family Papers, Manuscript Division, Library of Congress.

36   Jefferson to Monroe, June 17, 1785, Boyd, VIII, 233.

37   *Federalist* 11, 142.

38   Ibid. 84, 533.

39   "To the Inhabitants of Arlington and Sandgate, Vermont," June 25, 1798, *Works,* IX, 202.

40   *The Papers of Alexander Hamilton,* eds. Harold C. Syrett et al. (New York, 1961–1979), V, 483. Hereafter cited Syrett.

41   Livingston to Jay, Nov. 23, 1782, Johnston, III, 2.

42.   Lee to Samuel Adams, Mar. 14, 1785, Ballagh, II, 345.

43   Hamilton to Carrington, May 26, 1792, Syrett, XI, 439.

44   Monroe to Jefferson, Sept. 3, 1793, *The Writings of James Monroe,* ed. Stanislaus Murray Hamilton (New York, 1898–1903), I, 274. Hereafter cited *Writings.*

45   Jay to Jefferson, Aug. 18, 1786, Boyd, X, 272.

46   Morris to Jay, Jan. 10, 1784, Johnston, III, 104–5.

47   Jefferson to Madison, Mar. 15, 1789, Boyd, XIV, 661.

Chapter 2:
The Politics of Form

1   Charles Pettit to Wilson, July 2, 1786, Burnett, VIII, 399.

2   King to Gerry, April 30, 1786, ibid., 347.

3   Farrand, II, 35.

4   Ibid., 110.

5   Washington to Jay, Aug. 1, 1786, Fitzpatrick, XXVIII, 503.

6   Jay to Washington, Oct. 27, 1786, Johnston, III, 213.

7 Jay to Washington, Jan. 7, 1787, ibid., 229.

8 Lee to Francis Lightfoot Lee, July 14, 1787, Ballagh, II, 424.

9 Farrand, I, 324.

10 Ibid., 483 (Wilson), 489 (King).

11 Ibid., 532.

12 Daniel Carroll in ibid., II, 292.

13 Ibid., 150.

14 Lee to Samuel Adams, Aug. 8, 1789, Ballagh, II, 495–6.

15 Storing, II, 233–4.

16 Lee to Thomas Lee Shippen, July 22, 1787, Ballagh, II, 427.

17 Melancton Smith in Storing, VI, 157.

18 "Brutus" in ibid., II, 369.

19 Ibid., V, 257.

20 Ibid., II, 232–3, 300, 304, 282.

21 *Federalist* 26, 217.

22 Farrand, I, 49.

23 "Federal Farmer" in Storing, II, 331.

24 *Federalist* 17, 167.

25 Storing, VI, 166–7.

26 *Federalist* 2, 94.

27 "Speech 1787," McCloskey, II, 767.

28 Madison to George Nicholas, April 8, 1788, Rutland, XI, 13.

29 "Letters of Fabius," *Pamphlets on the Constitution of the United States* (Brooklyn, 1888), 207, 179.

30 *Federalist* 39, 282–3.

31 Ibid. 45, 328.

32 Madison to Washington, Feb. 15 [1788], Rutland, X, 510.

33 Madison to Randolph, April 10, 1788, ibid., XI, 19.

34 Madison to Jefferson, Oct. 17, 1788, ibid., 297.

35 "Amendments," June 8, 1789, ibid., XII, 196–7.

36 Madison to Jefferson, Dec. 8, 1788, ibid., XI, 382; "Amendments," Aug. 17, 1789, ibid., XII, 344.

37 Storing, II, 282.

38 Jefferson to Madison, Mar. 15, 1789, Boyd, XIV, 660.

Chapter 3:
The Politics of Character

1 Jay to Washington, June 27, 1786, Johnston, III, 204.

2 Wilson, "Speech 1787," McCloskey, II, 759; Farrand, I, 423.

3 Jefferson to John Norvell, June 14, 1807, Ford, IX, 72.

4 Jefferson to Pendleton, Aug. 26, 1776, Boyd, I, 503.

5 *Federalist* 63, 419.

6 Ibid. 65, 427.

7 Storing, II, 142.

8 Tracy to Oliver Wolcott, Aug. 7, 1800, Gibbs, II, 399.

9 Draft of Address, 1798, Papers of Wilson Cary Nicholas, Manuscript Division, Library of Congress.

10 "General Defense of the Constitution," June 6, 1788, Rutland, XI, 79.

11 Oliver Wolcott to Frederick Wolcott, Mar. 3, 1794, Gibbs, I, 129–30.

12 Hamilton to James A. Bayard, April [16–21], 1802, Syrett, XXV, 605.

13 Washington to Jay, May 18, 1796, Fitzpatrick, XXXVI, 37.

14 King to John Adams, May 5, 1786, Burnett, VIII, 355.

15 "Letters of Agrippa," *Essays on the Constitution*, 73.

16 Harry Ammon, *James Monroe* (New York, 1971), 177.

17 *Federalist* 49, 351.

18 Jay to Washington, Mar. 16, 1786, June 1788, Johnston, III, 186, 346.

19 Madison to Jefferson, Oct. 17, 1788, Rutland, XI, 296.

20 Wolcott to Oliver Wolcott, Sr., Feb. 14, 1792, Gibbs, I, 73.

21 Jefferson to William Findley, Mar. 24, 1801, Ford, VIII, 27.

22 Charles C. Rogers, Jr., *Evolution of a Federalist: William Loughton Smith of Charleston (1758–1812)* (Columbia, 1962), 156–7.

23 Roane to Philip Aylett, June 26, 1788, "Letters of Spencer Roane, 1788–1822,"

Bulletin of the New York Public Library, X (1906), 167.

24 Jefferson to Philip Norborne Nicholas, April 7, 1800, Ford, VII, 440.

25 William Pierce quoted in Robert Allen Rutland, *The Birth of the Bill of Rights 1776–1791* (Chapel Hill, 1955), 132.

26 William Smith to Ralph Izard, May 23, 1797, "South Carolina Federalist Correspondence, 1789–1797," ed. Ulrich B. Phillips, *American Historical Review*, XIV (July 1909), 787.

27 Storing, II, 44.

28 Jefferson to John B. Colvin, Sept. 20, 1810, Ford, IX, 279.

29 Hamilton to Jay, May 7, 1800, Syrett, XXIV, 465.

30 Lance Banning, *The Jeffersonian Persuasion* (Ithaca, 1978), 61.

31 "Notes on the State of Virginia," *The Portable Thomas Jefferson*, ed. Merrill D. Peterson (New York, 1975), 165–6.

32 John Marshall, *Life of Washington*, 2 vol. reissue (Philadelphia, 1848 [1804–7]), II, 127.

33 John R. Howe, Jr., *The Changing Political Thought of John Adams* (Princeton, 1966), 96; *Works*, VI, 255.

34 *Federalist* 10, 134.

35 John Mitchell Mason quoted in Richard Buel, Jr., *Securing the Revolution* (Ithaca, 1972), 233.

36 Jefferson to Lafayette, April 2, 1790, Boyd, XVI, 293.

37 Jefferson to Edward Coles, Aug. 25, 1814, Ford, IX, 479.

38 Washington to Jay, Aug. 1, 1786, Fitzpatrick, XXVIII, 502.

39 Rush to John Adams, Feb. 12, 1812, *Letters of Benjamin Rush*, ed. L. H. Butterfield (Princeton, 1951), II, 1123.

40 Hamilton to Washington, July 30, 1792, Syrett, XII, 137–8.

41 Washington to Jay, May 8, 1796, Fitzpatrick, XXXVI, 37.

42 *Federalist* 37, 265.

43 Hamilton to Washington, Nov. 5, 1795, Syrett, XIX, 396.

44 Jefferson to Madison, June 20, 1787, Boyd, XI, 482.

45 Jefferson to Benjamin Rush, Oct. 4, 1803, *The Writings of Thomas Jefferson*, eds. Andrew A. Lipscomb and Albert Ellery Bergh (Washington, 1905), X, 421. Hereafter cited Lipscomb and Bergh.

46 Jefferson to Francis Hopkinson, Mar. 13, 1789, Boyd, XIV, 651.

47 Jefferson to Philip Mazzei, April 24, 1796, Ford, VII, 76.

48 "The Anas" (Oct. 1, 1792), ibid., I, 203.

49 Jefferson to Edward Carrington, May 27, 1788, Boyd, XIII, 209.

50 "The Anas" (Feb. 7, 1793), Ford, I, 215.

51 Jefferson to Luis Pinto de Souza, Aug. 7, 1790, Boyd, XVII, 117.

52 Jefferson to Edward Carrington, Jan. 16, 1787, ibid., XI, 49.

53 Jefferson to Adams, Nov. 13, 1787, ibid., XII, 350–1.

54 Jefferson to Madison, Sept, 6, 1789, ibid., XV, 397, Dec. 20, 1787, ibid., XII, 442.

55 Jefferson to Madison, Jan. 30, 1787, ibid., XI, 93.

56 Jefferson to Edward Carrington, May 27, 1788, ibid., XIII, 208–9.

57 Jefferson to John Harvie, Jr., July 25, 1790, to Francis Eppes, July 25, 1790, ibid., XVII, 271, 267; to George Mason, June 13, 1790, to David Howell, June 23, 1790, ibid., XVI, 493, 553.

58 "Jefferson's Opinion on Fiscal Policy," Aug. 26, 1790, ibid., XVII, 426.

59 Madison to Hamilton, Nov. 19, 1789, Rutland, XII, 451; to Jefferson, Mar. 8, 1790, Boyd, XVI, 213.

60 Hamilton to Edward Carrington, May 26, 1792, Syrett, XI, 443.

61 *Journal of William Maclay*, 9–10.

62 *Annals*, 2 Congress, 1 Session (Mar. 24, 1792), 484.

63 Jay to Washington, April 14, 1789, Johnston, III, 367.

64 Washington to George William Fairfax, June 26, 1786, Fitzpatrick, XXVIII, 470.

65 Jefferson to Madison, June 9, 1793, Ford, VI, 293.

66 *National Gazette*, Dec. 12, 1792.

67 "A Candid State of Parties," Hunt, VI, 115–6.

68 Jefferson to Madison, June 9, 1793, Ford, VI, 293.

69 Dickinson quoted in Gordon S. Wood, *The Creation of the American Republic 1776–1787* (Chapel Hill, 1969), 39; Gerry quoted in George Athan Billias, *Elbridge Gerry* (New York, 1976), 110.

70 "Spirit of Governments," Feb. 20, 1792, Hunt, IV, 94.

71 "A Candid State of Parties," Sept. 26, 1792, Hunt, VI, 112.

72 Hamilton to Edward Carrington, May 26, 1792, Syrett, XI, 438.

73 Hamilton to Jay, Nov. 13, 1790, ibid., VII, 149.

74 Hamilton to Carrington, May 26, 1792, ibid., XI, 438.

75 Jefferson to Archibald Stuart, Dec. 23, 1791, Lipscomb and Bergh, VIII, 2.

76 Farrand, II, 53.

77 Merrill D. Peterson, *Thomas Jefferson and the New Nation* (New York, 1970), 516.

Chapter 4:
The Politics of Independence

1 Jefferson to Madison, Feb. 15, 1794, Ford, VI, 499.

2 Jefferson to Monroe, June 4, 1793, ibid., 282.

3 Farrand, II, 268.

4 Jay to Washington, July 25, 1787.

5 Jefferson to Madison, Dec. 20, 1787, Boyd, XII, 441.

6 "An Address to the People of the State of New York," Johnston, III, 316.

7 "Letters of Agrippa," *Essays on the Constitution*, 88.

8 Robert Kenneth Faulkner, *The Jurisprudence of John Marshall* (Princeton, 1968), 90.

9 Jefferson to Abigail Adams, June 21, 1785, Boyd, VIII, 239.

10 Madison to Jefferson, Sept. 2, 1793, Hunt, VI, 193n.

11 Jefferson to William Short, Jan. 3, 1793, Lipscomb and Bergh, IX, 10.

12 Dumas Malone, *Jefferson and His Time* (Boston, 1948–81), III: *Jefferson and the Ordeal of Liberty*, 126.

13 Circular Letter, The Democratic Society of Pennsylvania, July 4, 1793, *The Democratic-Republican Societies, 1790–1800*, ed. Philip S. Foner (Westport, 1976), 66.

14 Grove to John Steele, April 2, 1794, *The Papers of John Steele*, ed. H. M. Wagstaff (Raleigh, 1924), I, 113.

15 Wolcott to Oliver Wolcott, Sr., April 14, 1794, Gibbs, I, 133.

16 William Bradford quoted in Richard H. Kohn, *Eagle and Sword: The Federalists and the Creation of the Military Establishment in America, 1783–1802* (New York, 1975), 159.

17 Washington to Henry Lee, Aug. 26, 1794, Fitzpatrick, XXXIII, 476; to Jay, Nov. 1, 1794, ibid., XXXIV, 17.

18 Marshall, *Washington*, II, 269; Paul Goodman, *The Democratic-Republicans of Massachusetts* (Cambridge, 1964), 26; *Federalist 47*, 336; "Consolidation," Hunt, VI, 67.

19 Madison to Archibald Stuart, Sept. 1, 1793, ibid., 189–90.

20 Ames to Christopher Gore, Mar. 26, 1794, *Works of Fisher Ames*, ed. Seth Ames (Boston, 1854), I, 140 (hereafter cited Ames); Winfred E. Bernhard, *Fisher Ames* (Chapel Hill, 1965), 222.

21 Monroe to Jefferson, May 4, 1794, *Writings*, I, 293.

22 Ammon, *Monroe*, 145.

23 Bayard to Richard Bassett, Dec. 30, 1797, American Historical Association *Annual Report* (1913), II: *Papers of James A. Bayard, 1796–1815*, ed. Elizabeth Donnan, 47. Hereafter cited Donnan.

24 Oliver Wolcott, Sr., to Oliver Wolcott, Nov. 21, 1796, Gibbs, 397.

25 Jefferson to Gerry, May 13, 1797, Ford, VII, 121–2.

26 [John Taylor], *An Enquiry into the Principles and Tendencies of Certain Public Measures* (Philadelphia, 1794), 24.

27 Jefferson to Edmund Randolph, June 27, 1797, Ford, VII, 156.

28 Hamilton to King, Dec. 16, 1796, Syrett, XX, 446.

29   Washington to Jay, Aug. 31, 1795, Fitzpatrick, XXXIV, 293.

30   Walter R. Fee, *The Transition from Aristocracy to Democracy in New Jersey 1789–1829* (Somerville, 1933), 66.

31   Jefferson to Madison, Sept. 21, 1795, Lipscomb and Bergh, IX, 310–11.

32   Madison to George Nicholas, May 17, 1788, Rutland, XI, 48.

33   "The Anas" (April 9, 1792), Ford, I, 191.

34   Ames to Thomas Dwight, Jan. 5, 1797, Ames, I, 213; to Hamilton, Jan. 26, 1797, Syrett, XX, 488.

35   Jefferson to Edward Rutledge, Nov. 30, 1795, Ford, VII, 40.

36   Jefferson to William Branch Giles, Dec. 31, 1795, ibid., 43.

37   *Henry Wansey and His American Journal, 1794,* ed. David John Jeremy (Philadelphia, 1970), 87.

38   Noble E. Cunningham, Jr., *The Jeffersonian Republicans in Power* (Chapel Hill, 1963), 191.

39   Jefferson to Philip Mazzei, April 24, 1796, Ford, VII, 75; Dice Robins Anderson, *William Branch Giles* (Menasha, 1915), 49. Giles, who spoke in the idiom of southern planters, meant land speculators by the term "land gentry."

40   David Townsend to William Eustis, Mar. 4, 1802, Papers of William Eustis, Manuscript Division, Library of Congress.

41   Charles Downer Hazen, *Contemporary American Opinion of the French Revolution* (Baltimore, 1897), 172–3.

42   Granger to William Eustis, Nov. 18, 1802, Eustis Papers.

43   "A Candid State of Parties," Hunt, VI, 119.

44   "Diary of John Quincy Adams," *Proceedings of the Massachusetts Historical Society,* XVI (1902), 378.

45   Hamilton to William Bradford, June 13, 1795, Syrett, XVIII, 374.

46   Madison to Jefferson, Feb. 19, 1788, Rutland, X, 519.

47   Jay to Henry Lee, July 11, 1795, Johnston, IV, 178–9.

48   Bernard C. Steiner, *The Life and Correspondence of James McHenry* (Cleveland, 1907), 200–1.

49   Jefferson to Giles, Dec. 31, 1795, Ford, VII, 43.

Chapter 5:
The Edges of Violence

1   Billias, *Gerry,* 254–5.

2   Andrew Jackson to James Robertson, Jan. 11, 1798, *The Papers of Andrew Jackson,* eds. Sam B. Smith and Harriet Chappell Owsley (Knoxville, 1980), I, 165; Paris Journal, Feb. 26, 1798, *The Papers of John Marshall,* eds. Herbert A. Johnson et al. (Chapel Hill, 1974–   ), III, 204.

3   Adams to Jefferson, Oct. 9, 1787, Boyd, XIII, 221.

4   "To the Students of Dickinson College, Pennsylvania," 1798, "To the Citizens of Baltimore and Baltimore County, Maryland," May 2, 1798, *Works,* IX, 204, 186–7.

5   Wolcott to Noah Webster, July 5, 1799, Gibbs, II, 245.

6   Hamilton to King, June 8, 1797, Syrett, XXI, 103.

7   Jay to Timothy Pickering, Nov. 13, 1797, Johnston, IV, 233–4.

8   Hamilton to Theodore Sedgwick, Feb. 2, 1799, Syrett, XXII, 452.

9   James Morton Smith, *Freedom's Fetters: The Alien and Sedition Laws and American Civil Liberties* (Ithaca, 1956), 110.

10   John C. Miller, *Crisis in Freedom: The Alien and Sedition Acts* (Boston, 1951), 45.

11   *Enquiry,* 55, 64–5.

12   Smith, *Freedom's Fetters,* 18.

13   Jay to Jedediah Morse, Jan. 30, 1799, Johnston, IV, 253.

14   James Wilson in Farrand, I, 172.

15   *Federalist* 43, 311.

16   Iredell to Hannah Iredell, Jan. 24, 1799, *Life and Correspondence of James Iredell,* ed. Griffith J. McRee (New York, 1858), II, 543.

17   Hamilton to Sedgwick, Feb. 2, 1799, Syrett, XXII, 453.

18   Jefferson to Wilson Cary Nicholas, Sept. 5, 1799, Ford, VII, 391.

19 Jefferson to John Taylor, June 1, 1798, ibid., 264.

20 Jefferson to Gerry, Jan. 26, 1799, ibid., 327.

21 *Wansey Journal*, 56.

22 "Statement on Impending Duel with Aaron Burr," June 28–July 10, 1804, Syrett, XXVI, 280.

23 "Laocoon No. I," Ames, II, 111–13.

24 Jefferson to Madison, July 7, 1793, April 5, 1798, Ford, VI, 338, VII, 231.

25 John Henry quoted in L. Marx Renzulli, Jr., *Maryland: The Federalist Years* (Rutherford, 1972), 203.

26 *Journal of William Maclay*, 252.

27 Jefferson to James Callander, Oct. 6, 1799, Ford, VII, 395.

28 Howard B. Rock, *Artisans of the New Republic* (New York, 1979), 62.

29 Bayard to Andrew Bayard, May 26, 1800, Donnan, 111.

30 Jefferson to Madison, Feb. 14, 1783, Boyd, VI, 241.

31 Adams to Benjamin Stoddert, Mar. 31, 1801, *Works*, IX, 582.

32 Adams to Abigail Adams, Dec. 12, 1796, ibid., I, 495.

33 Adams to James Lloyd, Mar. 31, 1815, ibid., X, 155.

34 Billias, *Gerry*, 297.

35 "Letter from Alexander Hamilton, Concerning the Public Conduct and Character of John Adams, Esq. President of the United States," Syrett, XXV, 186, 196, 207–8.

36 Hamilton to Pickering, June 8, 1798, ibid., XXI, 500–1.

37 King to Timothy Pickering, Mar. 24, 1800, *The Life and Correspondence of Rufus King*, ed. Charles R. King (New York, 1894–1900), III, 213. Hereafter cited King.

38 Richard E. Welch, Jr., *Theodore Sedgwick, Federalist* (Middletown, 1965), 215.

Chapter 6:
The Jeffersonian Resolution

1 Jefferson to John Taylor, June 1, 1798, Ford, VII, 263.

2 Thomas Rodney Diary, July 4, 1801.

3 Rush to Jefferson, *Letters of Benjamin Rush*, II, 1099.

4 Jefferson to Edmund Pendleton, April 2, 1798, Lipscomb and Bergh, X, 22.

5 Madison to M. L. Hulbert, May 1830, Hunt, IX, 372.

6 Ames to Oliver Wolcott, June 2, 1800, Gibbs, II, 369.

7 Thomas FitzSimmons to Oliver Wolcott, July 24, 1800, Gibbs, II, 389.

8 Jefferson to Monroe, Mar. 8, 1798, Ford, VII, 213.

9 Jefferson to Joseph Priestley, June 19, 1802, Lipscomb and Bergh, X, 324.

10 Jefferson to Giles, Mar. 23, 1801, Ford, VIII, 26.

11 Jefferson to William Short, Oct. 3, 1801, ibid., 98.

12 Jefferson to Madison, Mar. 15, 1789, Boyd, XIV, 659.

13 Jefferson to Madison, Mar. 12, 1801, Ford, VIII, 14.

14 Jefferson to Larkin Smith, Nov. 26, 1804, ibid., 337.

15 Jefferson to Madison, Aug. 3, 1797, Lipscomb and Bergh, X, 414.

16 Jefferson to Madison, Nov. 12, 1801, Ford, VIII, 180n.

17 *The Papers of Daniel Webster*, eds. Charles M. Wiltse et al. (Hanover, 1974–   ), I, 370. Hereafter cited Wiltse.

18 Jefferson to Lafayette, Nov. 23 [1818], *The Letters of Lafayette and Jefferson*, ed. Gilbert Chinard (Baltimore, 1929), 396.

19 Jefferson to Wilson Cary Nicholas, Sept. 7, 1803, Ford, VIII, 247–8n.

20 Charles Warren, *Jacobin and Junto* (Cambridge, 1931), 160.

21 Goodrich to Oliver Wolcott, Nov. 18, 1799, Gibbs, II, 288.

22 Wolcott to Frederick Wolcott, June 11, 1793, ibid., I, 100.

23 Ames to Christopher Gorc, Dec. 13, 1802, Ames, I, 310.

24 *Democratic-Republican Societies*, 103, 104.

25 Ames to Theodore Dwight, Mar. 19, 1801, Ames, I, 293.

26 Hamilton to Henry Lee, Mar. 7, 1800, Syrett, XXIV, 298–9.

27 Wolcott to John Steele, June, 1802, *Papers of John Steele*, I, 289.

28 *Plumer's Memorandum*, 199.

29 Jefferson to John Taylor, June 1, 1798, Ford, VII, 265.

30 Marshall to Hamilton, Jan. 1, 1800, Syrett, XXV, 290.

31 Jefferson to Madison, Dec. 16, 1786, Boyd, X, 603.

32 *Federalist 45*, 328.

33 Thomas Rodney Diary, Mar. 14, 1801.

34 Jefferson to Thomas McKean, July 24, 1801, Ford, VIII, 78.

35 Jefferson to Dickinson, July 23, 1801, to Monroe, [Mar.] 7, 1801, to Giles, Mar. 23, 1801, Ford, VIII, 76, 9, 10, 26; to John Wise, Feb. 12, 1798, *American Historical Review*, III (July 1898), 489.

36 Madison to William Eustis, May 22, 1823, Hunt, IX, 136.

37 Ford, VIII, 1n.

38 *Plumer's Memorandum*, 63.

Part Two
BEGINNINGS AND ENDINGS

Chapter 7:
Space

1 William Gordon to Adams, Sept. 7, 1782, *Proceedings of the Massachusetts Historical Society*, LXIII (1930), 469.

2 Philip V. B. Livingston to Jay, Feb. 22, 1783, Johnston, III, 32.

3 Monroe to Jefferson, May 11, 1786, Boyd, IX, 511.

4 Lee to Francis Lightfoot Lee, July 14, 1787, Ballagh, II, 424.

5 Jay to Jefferson, Dec. 14, 1786, Boyd, X, 599.

6 Rutledge to Jay, Nov. 12, 1786, Johnston, III, 218.

7 Lee to Washington, April 18, 1785, Ballagh, II, 349.

8 *The Papers of George Mason 1725–1792*, ed. Robert A. Rutland (Chapel Hill, 1970), III, 973.

9 Willie P. Mangum quoted in R. Carlyle Buley, *The Old Northwest* (Indianapolis, 1950), I, 97.

10 Jefferson to Gallatin, Nov. 9, 1803, Ford, VIII, 275–6n.

11 Jefferson to John C. Breckenridge, Aug. 12, 1803, Ford, VIII, 243–4n.

12 Arthur Preston Whitaker, *The United States and the Independence of Latin America, 1800–1830* (Baltimore, 1941), 185.

13 Jefferson to Archibald Stuart, Jan. 25, 1786, Boyd, IX, 218.

14 Jefferson to Madison, April 27, 1809, Lipscomb and Bergh, XII, 277.

15 Ames to Christopher Gore, Oct. 3, 1803, Ames, I, 323–4.

16 *Plumer's Memorandum*, 418.

17 Ibid., 139.

18 Alexander DeConde, *This Affair of Louisiana* (New York, 1976), 233.

19 King, VI, 127, 703.

20 *Annals*, Senate, 16 Congress, 1 Session (Jan. 20, 1820), 224.

21 *Annals*, House, 18 Congress, 1 Session (Jan. 30, 1824), 1298.

22 *The Papers of John C. Calhoun*, eds. W. Edwin Hemphill et al. (Columbia, 1959–), I, 401. Hereafter cited Hemphill.

23 *The Papers of Henry Clay*, ed. James F. Hopkins (Lexington, 1959–), II, 458. Hereafter cited Hopkins.

24 King, VI, 703.

25 "Views on the Subject of Internal Improvements," *Writings*, VI, 274, 273.

26 *Register of Debates*, House, 24 Congress, 1 Session (May 25, 1836), 4044; Robert F. Dalzell, Jr., *Daniel Webster and the Trial of American Nationalism 1843–1852* (New York, 1975 [1972]), 85.

27 William Priest quoted in Robert D. Arbuckle, *Pennsylvania Speculator and Patriot: The Entrepreneurial John Nicholson, 1759–1800* (University Park, 1975), 93.

28 Philadelphia *Independent Gazette* quoted in James Weston Livingood, *The Philadelphia-Baltimore Trade Rivalry 1780–1860* (Harrisburg, 1947), 8.

29 *Western Monthly Review*, III (July 1829), 22–3.

30 Jefferson to Gallatin, Aug. 31, 1806, Ford, VIII, 467; July 14, 1806, *Writings of Albert Gallatin*, I, 305.

31 Harriet Martineau, *Society in America* (London, 1837), II, 29.

32 A toast quoted in Albert K. Weinberg, *Manifest Destiny* (Baltimore, 1935), 120.

Chapter 8:
Revolution in Choices

1 Jefferson to the Reverend Isaac Story, Dec. 5, 1801, Ford, VIII, 107.

2 Frances W. Gregory, *Nathan Appleton* (Charlottesville, 1975), 143.

3 [Calvin Colton], *The Junius Tracts* (New York, 1844), II, 21.

4 [Michel] Chevalier, *Society, Manners and Politics in the United States*, trans. T. G. Bradford (Boston, 1839), 350, 304.

5 *House Executive Document* 227, 25 Congress, 3 Session, p. 607.

6 Mathew Davis quoted in Rock, *Artisans*, 166.

7 Alfred Byron Sears, *Thomas Worthington* (Columbus, 1958), 141.

8 John Arthur Garraty, *Silas Wright* (New York, 1949), 36.

9 William Sampson in Commons, III, 279.

10 Ibid., VI, 84.

11 *Social Theories of Jacksonian Democracy*, ed. Joseph L. Blau (Indianapolis, 1954), 83.

12 James O'Kelly to Jesse Nicholson, Dec. 1792, *The Journal and Letters of Francis Asbury*, ed. Elmer T. Clark (London, 1958), III, 114.

13 John B. Boles, *The Great Revival, 1787–1805* (Lexington, 1972), 169.

14 Asbury to Mrs. John Dickins, Sept. 12, 1801, to Charles Atmore, June 3, 1803, *Journal and Letters*, III, 226, 261; "Journal" (Aug. 13, 1815), ibid., II, 788.

15 *Autobiography of Peter Cartwright*, ed. W. P. Strickland (New York [1856]), 228.

16 Charles Grandison Finney, *Lectures on Revivals of Religion*, ed. William G. McLoughlin (Cambridge, 1960 [1835]), 83, 161.

17 Ibid., 387.

18 Calvin Colton, *History and Character of American Revivals of Religion* (London, 1832), 218–19.

19 *The Autobiography of Lyman Beecher*, ed. Barbara M. Cross (Cambridge, 1961 [1864]), II, 103.

20 Taylor to Lyman Beecher, Jan. 14, 1819, ibid., I, 284–6.

21 Marshall to Joseph Story, Oct. 21, 1831, "Letters of John Marshall," *Proceedings of the Massachusetts Historical Society*, XIV (1900), 347–8.

22 Rush to Jefferson, Aug. 26, 1811, *Letters of Benjamin Rush*, II, 1098.

23 Randolph to Andrew Jackson, Feb. 26, 1832, *Correspondence of Andrew Jackson*, ed. John Spencer Bassett (Washington, 1926–33), IV, 411 (hereafter cited Bassett); Samuel A. Cartwright to Davis, Oct. 12, 1852, *The Letters of Jefferson Davis*, eds. Haskell M. Monroe, Jr., et al. (Baton Rouge, 1971–   ), IV, 303.

24 George W. Burnap, *The Spheres and Duties of Woman*, 3rd rev. ed. (Baltimore, 1848), 170.

25 William A. Alcott, *The Young Woman's Book of Health* (New York, 1857 [1850]), 131.

26 "Introduction," *Permanent Temperance Documents of the American Temperance Society* (New York, 1972 [1835]).

27 Alexis de Tocqueville, *Democracy in America*, ed. Phillips Bradley (New York, 1945), II, 203.

28 "Seventh Report," *Permanent Temperance Documents*, 2.

29 *Horace Mann on the Crisis in Education*, ed. Louis Filler (Yellow Springs, 1965), 154.

30 Joel Hawes, *Lectures to Young Men* (Hartford, 1831 [1826]), 23.

31 Rock, *Artisans*, 283.

32 *Junius Tracts*, VI, 111.

33 James Freeman Clarke to William H. Channing, Nov. 8, 1833, James Freeman Clarke, *Autobiography, Diary and Correspondence*, ed. Edward Everett Hale (Boston, 1892), 103; Benjamin Wade quoted in James Brewer Stewart, *Joshua R. Giddings and the Tactics of Radical Politics* (Cleveland, 1970), 158.

34   Child to Louisa Loring [Mar. ? 1837], *Lydia Maria Child: Selected Letters, 1817–1880*, eds. Milton Melzer et al. (Amherst, 1982), 64.

Chapter 9:
The Last Tournament

1   Anderson, *Giles*, 102; Bayard to Richard Bassett, Feb. 3, 1805, Donnan, 162

2   Steele to Nathaniel Macon, Jan. 17, 1805, *Papers of John Steele*, I, 445.

3   Jefferson to Wilson Cary Nicholas, Mar. 26, 1805, Ford, VIII, 349.

4   Bayard to Rodney, Feb. 24, 1804, "James Asheton Bayard Letters, 1802–1814," *Bulletin of the New York Public Library*, IV (July 1900), 230.

5   Jefferson to Madison, Dec. 16, 1786, Boyd, X, 603; to A. C. V. C. Destutt de Tracy, Jan. 26, 1811, Ford, IX, 309.

6   *Plumer's Memorandum*, 521, 559–60.

7   Ibid., 370.

8   Monroe to Jefferson, Nov. 1, 1805, *Writings*, IV, 352n.

9   Daniel C. Gilman, *James Monroe* (Boston, 1883), 99.

10   Monroe to Jefferson, Jan. 11, 1807, *Writings*, V, 2.

11   Jefferson to Robert R. Livingston, Mar. 16, 1802, Ford, VIII, 138, 145.

12   Jefferson to Benjamin Rush, Oct. 4, 1803, Lipscomb and Bergh, X, 422.

13   Jefferson to Madison, Aug. 27, 1805, Ford, VIII, 378.

14   King to Gouverneur Morris, Mar. 30, 1807, King, V, 13.

15   Jefferson to Thomas Leiper, Aug. 21, 1807, Ford, IX, 130.

16   Jefferson to William Duane, July 20, 1807, Lipscomb and Bergh, XI, 291.

17   Jefferson to Madison, Jan. 13, 1803, ibid., X, 343.

18   Jefferson to Madison, Feb. 8, 1786, Boyd, IX, 264.

19   Jefferson to Levi Lincoln, Mar. 23, 1808, Lipscomb and Bergh, XII, 21.

20   Jefferson to Abigail Adams, July 7, 1785, Boyd, VIII, 265.

21   Burton Spivak, *Jefferson's English Crisis* (Charlottesville, 1979), 75.

22   Josiah Quincy, Jr., to John Adams, Dec. 15, 1808, Edmund Quincy, *The Life of Josiah Quincy of Massachusetts* (Boston, 1867), 146. Because this Josiah Quincy is the only one who figures in my account, I have omitted "Jr." in the text.

23   Madison to John Armstrong, July, 22, 1808, Hunt, VIII, 37.

24   Renzulli, *Maryland*, 248.

25   John Rutledge, Jr., to Harrison Gray Otis, July 29, 1806, Samuel Eliot Morison, *The Life and Letters of Harrison Gray Otis* (Boston, 1913), I, 282.

26   Bernard Mayo, *Henry Clay* (Boston, 1937), 379.

27   Bayard to Andrew Bayard, July 3, 1809, Donnan, 177.

28   Adams to Ezekiel Bacon, Nov. 17, 1808, *Writings of John Quincy Adams*, ed. Worthington Chauncey Ford (New York, 1913–17), III, 253.

29   Monroe to Jefferson, July 27, 1787, Boyd, IX, 631.

30   Madison to Caesar Rodney, Sept. 30, 1810, Rodney Family Papers, Manuscript Division, Library of Congress.

31   Bayard to Rodney, May 6, 1812, "Bayard Letters," 237.

32   Sanford W. Higginbotham, *The Keystone in the Democratic Arch: Pennsylvania Politics 1800–1816* (Harrisburg, 1952), 253.

33   Jefferson to William Duane, Mar. 28, 1811, Ford, IX, 313.

34   King to Christopher Gore, July 17, 1812, King, V, 254.

35   Rush to Jefferson, Aug. 26, 1811, *Letters of Benjamin Rush*, II, 1100.

36   Duane to Jefferson, July 1, 1807, "Letters of William Duane," ed. Worthington C. Ford, *Proceedings of the Massachusetts Historical Society*, XX (1906–7), 299.

37   Rush to John Adams, Feb. 8, 1808, *Letters of Benjamin Rush*, II, 960.

38   Billias, *Gerry*, 312.

39   Ibid., 309.

40   Peter Shaw, *The Character of John Adams* (New York, 1976), 301.

41   Roger H. Brown, *The Republic in Peril: 1812* (New York, 1964), 72.

42 Hemphill, I, 68.

43 "Speech on Proposed Repeal of Non-Intercourse Act," Feb. 22, 1810, Hopkins, I, 450–1.

44 I am indebted to Alan Zachary for this quotation.

45 John Tyler quoted in Bradford Perkins, *Prologue to War* (Berkeley and Los Angeles, 1963), 94.

46 Jefferson to Madison, Aug. 16, 1807, Lipscomb and Bergh, XI, 326.

47 Jefferson to Madison, April 27, 1809, ibid., XII, 276.

48 Jefferson to John Langdon, Mar. 5, 1810, ibid., 375.

49 King to Porter, Dec. 10, 1811, King, V, 254.

50 *Plumer's Memorandum*, 271.

51 Webster to Randolph, April 1816, Wiltse, I, 198.

52 Bayard to Andrew Bayard, Feb. 13, 1812, Donnan, 193.

53 Special Message to Congress, June 1, 1812, Fourth Annual Message, Nov. 4, 1812, To the Republicans of New Jersey, July 25, 1812, Hunt, VIII, 196–8, 230, 205.

54 Clay to Caesar Rodney, Aug. 6, 1810, Hopkins, I, 481.

55 Aug. 3, 1807, Hemphill, I, 34–5.

56 "Speech Urging Passage of the Embargo Bill," April 1, 1812, Hopkins, I, 641.

57 "Report on the Causes and Reasons for War," June 3, 1812, Hemphill, I, 110.

58 Gallatin to Jefferson, Mar. 10, 1812, *Writings of Albert Gallatin*, I, 517.

59 [James Monroe], "Newspaper Editorial," April 14, 1812, Hopkins, I, 645.

60 Jefferson to Monroe, May 5, 1811, Ford, IX, 324; to Robert Wright, Aug. 8, 1812, Lipscomb and Bergh, XIII, 184.

61 Jefferson to Robert Smith, April 27, 1804, Ford, VIII, 301.

62 *Southern Patriot* quoted in John Harold Wolfe, *Jeffersonian Democracy in South Carolina* (Chapel Hill, 1940), 282.

63 Monroe to Clay, Aug. 28, 1812, Hopkins, I, 722.

64 Clay to Monroe, Sept. 21, 1812, Speech Jan. 9, 1813, ibid., 728, 770.

65 Story to Nathaniel Williams, Feb. 22, 1815, *Life and Letters of Joseph Story*, ed. William W. Story (Boston, 1851), I, 254.

66 Speech Feb. 27, 1815, Hemphill, I, 282.

67 Speech Jan. 29, 1816, Hopkins, II, 148.

68 Monroe to Clay, Sept. 17, 1812, Hopkins, I, 727.

69 Gallatin to Matthew Lyon, May 7, 1816, *Writings of Albert Gallatin*, I, 700.

70 Ames to Josiah Quincy, Nov. 6, 1807, Ames, I, 405.

71 *Writings*, VI, 173.

72 Monroe to Madison, May 10, 1822, ibid., 289.

Chapter 10:
The Era of State Power

1 Speech Jan. 29, 1816, Hopkins, II, 152.

2 Dorothie Bobbé, *DeWitt Clinton* (New York, 1933), 210.

3 Benjamin DeWitt, "A Sketch of the Turnpike Roads in the State of New-York," *Transactions of the Society for the Promotion of the Useful Arts, in the State of New-York*, II (1807), 191.

4 *Plumer's Memorandum*, 202.

5 Gore to King, Jan. 26, 1817, King, VI, 48.

6 Renzulli, *Maryland*, 318.

7 *Plumer's Memorandum*, 574.

8 Jefferson to Madison, Jan. 30, 1787, Ford, IV, 368–9.

9 Rufus King to J. A. King, Jan. 19, 1821, King, VI, 378.

10 Christopher Gore to King, Oct. 9, 1816, King, VI, 32.

11 Chauncey Goodrich to David Daggett, Dec. 25, 1814, "Letters of Connecticut Federalists, 1814–1815," ed. William E. Buckley, *New England Quarterly*, III (April 1930), 325.

12 Roger Minot Sherman to David Daggett, Feb. 4, 1815, ibid., 329–30.

13 Goodrich to Daggett, Jan. 17, 1815, ibid., 327.

14 Monroe to Jefferson, Feb. 7, 1820, *Writings*, VI, 114.

15 Clay to Horace Holley, Feb. 17, 1820, Hopkins, II, 781.

16 Oliver Perry Chitwood, *John Tyler* (New York, 1939), 48.

17 Garraty, *Wright*, 31.

18 Peter V. Daniel quoted in Charles Henry Ambler, *Thomas Ritchie* (Richmond, 1913), 206.

19 Garraty, *Wright*, 31.

20 Robert V. Remini, *Martin Van Buren and the Making of the Democratic Party* (New York, 1959), 23.

Chapter 11:
Comprehensive Programs

1 Webster to Ezekiel Webster, Nov. 29, 1814, Wiltse, I, 177; Webster to Moody Kent, Dec. 22, 1814, *The Writings and Speeches of Daniel Webster* (Boston, 1903), XVI, 32.

2 Rufus King to J. A. King and C. King, Feb. 2, 1820, King, VI, 279.

3 Roane to Monroe, Feb. 16, 1820, "Letters of Spencer Roane," 174–5.

4 Clay to Martin D. Hardin, Feb. 5, 1820, Hopkins, II, 775.

5 Henry St. George Tucker to James Barbour, Feb. 11, 1820, "Missouri Compromise," *William and Mary College Quarterly*, X (1902), 11.

6 *Memoirs of John Quincy Adams*, ed. Charles Francis Adams (Philadelphia, 1874–7), V, 13, 11.

7 Biddle to ———, Oct. 29, 1822, *The Correspondence of Nicholas Biddle*, ed. Reginald C. McGrane (Boston, 1919), 27. Hereafter cited *Correspondence*.

8 Biddle to Calhoun, Dec. 6, 1822, ibid., 29.

9 Biddle to John McLean, Jan. 11, 1829, ibid., 71.

10 Francis X. Blouin, Jr., *The Boston Region 1810–1850* (Ann Arbor, 1980), 101.

11 Biddle to Robert Lenox, Feb. 3, 1823, *Correspondence*, 31–2.

12 Lynn W. Turner, *William Plumer of New Hampshire 1759–1850* (Chapel Hill, 1962), 32.

13 Albert J. Beveridge, *The Life of John Marshall* (Boston, 1916–19), IV, 14–15.

14 Anderson, *Giles*, 77.

15 *Federalist* 52, 363.

16 Eugene Perry Link, *Democratic-Republican Societies, 1790–1800* (New York, 1942), 161.

17 Leonard W. Levy, *Freedom of Speech and Press in Early American History* (New York, 1963 [1960]), 211.

18 Roane to James Barbour, Dec. 29, 1819, "Missouri Compromise," 7.

19 Marshall to Story, July 13, 1819, June 15, Sept. 18, 1821, "Letters of John Marshall," 326, 327, 330, 331.

20 Faulkner, *Marshall*, 99–100n.

21 Thomas Ritchie to James Barbour, undated, "Missouri Compromise," 15.

22 Marshall to Timothy Pickering, Mar. 20, 1826, "Letters of John Marshall," 321.

23 Harriet Martineau, *Retrospect of Western Travel* (London, 1838), I, 193.

24 Donald L. Robinson, *Slavery in the Structure of American Politics 1765–1820* (New York, 1971), 336.

25 Martineau, *Society in America*, I, xii.

26 Charles I. Foster, *An Errand of Mercy: The Evangelical United Front 1790–1837* (Chapel Hill, 1960), 223.

27 Chevalier, *Society*, 284.

28 *Proceedings of the First Ten Years of the American Tract Society* ([Boston] 1824), 44.

29 Nathaniel Bouton, *History of the Origin and Organization of the American Home Missionary Society* (New York, 1860), 6.

30 Don Harrison Doyle, *The Social Order of a Frontier Community: Jacksonville, Illinois 1825–70* (Urbana, 1978), 26.

31 Marshall to Story, Sept. 22, 1832, "Letters of John Marshall," 352.

Chapter 12:
The Jacksonian Resolution

1 Calhoun to Jackson, June 4, 1826, Hemphill, X, 110.

2 James C. Curtis, *Andrew Jackson and the Search for Vindication* (Boston, 1976), 79.

3 Jackson to Andrew J. Donelson, Jan. 18, 1824, Bassett, III, 224.

4 Jackson to William B. Lewis, May 7, 1824, "Letters and Papers of Andrew Jack-

son. Part 2," *Bulletin of the New York Public Library*, IV (June 1900), 196.

5 Roane to James Barbour, Feb. 16, 1819, "Letters of Spencer Roane," 172.

6 Wiltse, I, 375–6.

7 Jackson to George W. Martin, Jan. 2, 1824, Bassett, III, 222; Jackson to Donelson, Sept. 13, 1832, ibid., IV, 475.

8 Jackson to William B. Lewis, "Letters and Papers," 193.

9 Jackson to Van Buren, May 4, 1830, American Historical Association *Annual Report* (1918), II: *The Autobiography of Martin Van Buren*, ed. John C. Fitzpatrick, 321.

10 "Veto Message," July 10, 1832, *Messages and Papers of the Presidents*, comp. James D. Richardson (New York, 1897–1916), III, 1153, 1144.

11 Biddle to Clay, Aug. 1, 1832, *Correspondence*, 196.

12 Jackson to John Branch, Aug. 14, 1830, Bassett, IV, 172.

13 Jackson to John Coffee, Feb. 19, 1832, ibid., 407.

14 *Messages and Papers*, III, 1145.

15 Patrick Noble quoted in Alfred Glaze Smith, Jr., *Economic Readjustment of an Old Cotton State: South Carolina, 1820–1860* (Columbia, 1958), 125.

16 Charles Ingersoll quoted in Louis Hartz, *Economic Policy and Democratic Thought: Pennsylvania, 1776–1860* (Cambridge, 1948), 45.

17 Elbert B. Smith, *Magnificent Missourian: The Life of Thomas Hart Benton* (Philadelphia, 1958), 123.

18 *Messages and Papers*, III, 1153.

19 Draft, South Carolina Exposition, Nov. 1828, Hemphill, X, 496.

20 Calhoun to John McLean, Oct. 4, 1828, ibid., 428.

21 Madison to Edward Everett, April 1830, Hunt, IX, 385n, 388n, 387n.

22 Marshall to Story, Oct. 15, 1830, "Letters of John Marshall," 342.

23 Madison to Everett, April 1830, Hunt, IX, 390n.

24 Paulding to Van Buren, July 10, 1837, *The Letters of James Kirke Paulding*,

ed. Ralph M. Aderman (Madison, 1962), 198.

25 James Renwick quoted in Brown, *Republic in Peril*, 182.

26 Chevalier, *Society*, 50; Tocqueville, *Democracy*, I, 402.

Part Three:
DEMOCRATIC SOCIETY

Chapter 13:
Economy

1 Aug. 4, 1850, *The Diary of Orville Hickman Browning: Volume I, 1850–1864*, eds. Theodore Calvin Pease and James G. Randall (Springfield, Ill., 1925), 14.

Chapter 14:
Democratic Culture

1 *Plumer's Memorandum*, 18.

2 Clarina Howard Nichols in *History of Woman Suffrage*, eds. Elizabeth Cady Stanton et al. (New York, 1881–1922), I, 522.

3 Lydia Sigourney, *Letters to Mothers* (Hartford, 1838), 10.

4 Ibid., 88.

5 Hawes, *Lectures*, 82; T. S. Arthur quoted in Bernard Wishy, *The Child and the Republic* (Philadelphia, 1968), 31.

6 Burnap, *Spheres*, 116–17.

7 *America of the Fifties: Letters of Fredrika Bremer*, ed. Adolph B. Benson (New York, 1924), 72.

8 Jacob Gross to family members (translation), Dec. 28, 1856, Chicago Historical Society.

9 Thomas Grattan quoted in Arthur W. Calhoun, *A Social History of the American Family* (Cleveland, 1917–19), II, 56.

10 Hawes, *Lectures*, 69.

11 Chevalier, *Society*, 205.

12 Frederick Marryat, *Diary in America*, ed. Jules Zenger (Bloomington, 1960), 43.

13 George W. Burnap, *Lectures to Young Men* (Baltimore, 1848 [1840]), 70, 173–4.

14 Hawes, *Lectures*, 98; Noah Brooks, *Washington in Lincoln's Time*, ed. Herbert Mitgang (New York, 1958 [1895]), 33.

15 Horace Mann, *Lectures on Education* (Boston, 1848), 125.

16 Hawes, *Lectures*, 34–5.

17 Jacob Waterbury quoted in Joseph F. Kett, *Rites of Passage: Adolescence in America 1790 to the Present* (New York, 1977), 104.

18 Henry Ward Beecher, *Lectures to Young Men* (New York, 1850 [1844]), 224.

19 Francis Wayland, *The Elements of Moral Science*, ed. Joseph L. Blau (Cambridge, 1963 [1835]), 24.

20 Burnap, *Lectures*, 129; Stephen Nissenbaum, *Sex, Diet, and Debility in Jacksonian America* (Westport, 1980), 113.

21 Finney, *Lectures*, 459–60.

22 Burnap, *Lectures*, 153.

23 Beecher, *Lectures*, 142.

24 Horace Mann, *A Few Thoughts for a Young Man* (Boston, 1850), 45–6.

25 Beecher, *Lectures*, 406.

26 Burnap, *Spheres*, 117.

27 *Autobiography of Rev. James B. Finley*, ed. W. P. Strickland (Cincinnati, 1854), 172.

28 Mann, *Thoughts*, 21.

29 Edward Beecher, *Narrative of Riots at Alton* (New York, 1965 [1838]), 56.

30 Hawes, *Lectures*, 56.

31 Colton, *History*, 134.

32 Anne C. Loveland, *Southern Evangelicals and the Social Order 1800–1860* (Baton Rouge, 1980), 11.

33 Finney, *Lectures*, 380.

34 Colton, *History*, 212.

35 Finney, *Lectures*, 135, 440–1.

36 Ibid., 129.

37 I am indebted to Henry Binford for this quotation of Mar. 15, 1851.

38 "Sixth Report [1833]," *Permanent Temperance Documents*, 39.

39 Arthur Alphonse Ekirch, Jr., *The Idea of Progress in America, 1815–1860* (New York, 1944), 83.

40 Tocqueville, *Democracy*, I, 67.

41 "American Literature," *Western Monthly Magazine*, III (Jan. 1835), 22.

42 Charles Sumner, *Orations and Speeches* (Boston, 1851), I, 385.

43 Colton, *History*, 150.

44 Carl Siracusa, *A Mechanical People: Perceptions of the Industrial Order in Massachusetts, 1815–1880* (Middletown, 1979), 63.

45 Ekirch, *Idea*, 200.

46 Timothy Flint, *Recollections of the Last Ten Years in the Valley of the Mississippi*, ed. George R. Brooks (Carbondale, 1968 [1826]), 285.

47 Siracusa, *Mechanical People*, 73–4.

48 Robert J. Parks, *Democracy's Railroads: Public Enterprise in Jacksonian Michigan* (Port Washington, 1972), 76.

49 Sumner, *Orations*, 365.

50 Mann, *Lectures*, 117.

51 John Ware, *An Address Delivered Before the Massachusetts Society for the Suppression of Intemperance* (Boston, 1826), 13.

52 William G. McLoughlin, *The Meaning of Henry Ward Beecher* (New York, 1970), 139.

53 Finney, *Lectures*, 466.

54 David E. Schob, *Hired Hands and Plowboys: Farm Labor in the Midwest, 1815–60* (Urbana, 1975), 89.

55 Burnap, *Spheres*, 293.

56 Chevalier, *Society*, 288, 224.

57 Jesse D. Bright to R. M. T. Hunter, July 29, 1855, American Historical Association *Annual Report* (1916), II: *Correspondence of Robert M. T. Hunter*, ed. Charles Henry Ambler, 168.

58 Marryat, *Diary*, 44; Mar. 29, 1851, *Diary and Letters of Rutherford Birchard Hayes*, ed. Charles Richard Williams (Columbus, 1922–26), I, 352. I am indebted to William Alan White for the quotation on Milwaukee.

59 Finney, *Lectures*, 273.

60 Channing to James Freeman Clarke, April 22, 1837, Clarke, *Autobiography*, 119.

61 Dickson D. Bruce, Jr., *And They All Sang Hallelujah* (Knoxville, 1974), 78.

Chapter 15:
The Institutional Web

1 Thomas H. O'Connor, *Lords of the Loom: The Cotton Whigs and the Coming of the Civil War* (New York, 1968), 63.

2 Daniel Webster to George Herbert, Jan. 7, 1801, Wiltse, I, 31.

3 Joseph Howard Parks, *Felix Grundy* (Baton Rouge, 1940), 176.

4 Nov. 3, 1852, *Diary of Orville Browning*, 80.

5 Remini, *Van Buren*, 191.

6 Mary P. Ryan, *Cradle of the Middle Class: The Family in Oneida County, New York, 1790–1865* (Cambridge, Eng., 1981), 125.

7 Buley, *Old Northwest*, II, 269.

8 Chevalier, *Society*, 40–1; Amasa Walker, *The Nature and Use of Money and Mixed Currency* (Boston, 1857), 53.

9 Jackson to William Duane, June 26, 1833, Bassett, V, 126; to Andrew J. Donelson, Feb. 8, 1823, ibid., III, 186. Catron to Polk, July 10, 1837, *Correspondence of James K. Polk*, eds. Herbert Weaver et al. (Nashville, 1969–   ), IV, 229–30.

10 John Quincy Adams to George Bancroft, Mar. 31, 1838, "Letters of John Adams and John Quincy Adams," 250.

11 Marryat, *Diary*, 277.

12 *Autobiography of Peter Cartwright*, 138.

13 [Jacob Young], *Autobiography of a Pioneer* (Cincinnati, 1857), 232.

14 Martineau, *Society in America*, III, 227–8.

15 Ronald G. Walters, *The Antislavery Appeal* (Baltimore, 1976), 47.

16 *Western Monthly Review*, III (May 1830), 597.

17 Francis Hilliard, *The Elements of Law* (Boston, 1835), v.

18 Timothy Walker, *Introduction to American Law* (Boston, 1882 [1837]), vii–viii.

19 Hilliard, *Elements*, vi.

20 Maxwell Bloomfield, *American Lawyers in a Changing Society, 1776–1876* (Cambridge, 1976), 154.

21 David Grimsted, "Rioting in Its Jacksonian Setting," *American Historical Review*, LXXVII (April 1972), 371.

22 [Horace Mann], *The Massachusetts System of Common Schools* (Boston, 1849), 17.

23 *Memoirs Speeches and Writings of Robert Rantoul, Jr.*, ed. Luther Hamilton (Boston, 1854), 82.

24 A combination of two quotations in Lloyd P. Jorgenson, *The Founding of Public Education in Wisconsin* (Madison, 1956), 119.

25 John C. Spooner quoted in Vincent P. Lannie, *Public Money and Parochial Education* (Cleveland, 1968), 134.

26 *Autobiography of Peter Cartwright*, 155.

27 Peter Tolis, *Elihu Burritt* (Hamden, 1968), 126.

28 *History of Woman Suffrage*, I, 70.

29 Michael Fellman, *The Unbounded Frame: Freedom and Community in Nineteenth Century American Utopianism* (Westport, 1973), 154.

30 Thomas Dublin, *Women at Work: The Transformation of Work and Community in Lowell, Massachusetts, 1826–1860* (New York, 1979), 126.

31 *History of Woman Suffrage*, I, 316.

32 Burnap, *Spheres*, 45–6.

33 Estelle B. Freedman, *Their Sisters' Keepers: Women's Prison Reform in America, 1830–1930* (Ann Arbor, 1981), 32–3.

34 *History of Woman Suffrage*, I, 482.

35 Finney, *Lectures*, 287.

36 Wendell Phillips, *Speeches, Lectures, and Letters* (Boston, 1891), 109.

Chapter 16:
A Society in Halves

1 Chevalier, *Society*, 188.

2 I am indebted to Craig Buettinger for this quotation and information.

3 Henry Barnard, *Report on the Condition and Improvement of the Public Schools of Rhode Island* (Providence, 1846), 73.

4 *Working Man's Advocate* in Commons, VII, 294.

5 Finney, *Lectures*, 153.

6 Beecher, *Lectures*, 49.

7 Ronald G. Walters, *American Reformers 1815–1860* (New York, 1978), 161.

8 Buley, *Old Northwest*, I, 363.

9 Eugene H. Berwanger, *The Frontier Against Slavery* (Urbana, 1967), 124.

10 Anthony F. C. Wallace, *Rockdale: The Growth of an American Village in the Early Industrial Revolution* (New York, 1978), 331.

11 "Annual Message to the Legislature. January 4, 1842," *The Works of William H. Seward*, ed. George E. Baker (New York, 1853), II, 309; Barnard, *Report on Rhode Island*, 34.

12 Commons, VIII, 94.

13 John R. Howe, *From the Revolution Through the Age of Jackson* (Englewood Cliffs, 1973), 138.

14 "Circular of the Fall River Mechanics," June 29, 1844, Commons, VIII, 86.

15 "Eighth Report," *Permanent Temperance Documents*, 23.

16 Harry N. Scheiber, *Ohio Canal Era* (Athens, 1969), 74.

17 Bruce Laurie, *Working People of Philadelphia 1800–1850* (Philadelphia, 1980), 144.

18 Thomas Rodney Diary, Aug. 14, 1801.

19 Arthur B. Darling, *Political Changes in Massachusetts 1824–1848* (New Haven, 1925), 67.

20 "Annual Message to the Legislature. January 5, 1841," *Works of William H. Seward*, II, 280.

21 Frederick Law Olmsted, *Journey in the Seaboard Slave States* (New York, 1856), 492.

22 Dickson D. Bruce, Jr., *Violence and Culture in the Antebellum South* (Austin, 1979), 122–3.

23 Olmsted, *Journey*, 573.

24 *History of Woman Suffrage*, I, 527.

25 "Report of H. Knox, Secretary of War, to the President of the United States," June 15, 1789, *American State Papers* (Washington, 1832), IV, 13.

26 "Fourth Annual Message," Hunt, VIII, 222.

27 Jefferson to George Rogers Clark, Jan. 1, 1780, Boyd, III, 259.

28 Nicholas Biddle, *Eulogium on Thomas Jefferson* (Philadelphia, 1827), 35.

29 Reginald Horsman, *The Origins of Indian Removal 1815–1824* (East Lansing, 1970), 16.

30 Ware, *Address*, 15.

31 William J. Cooper, Jr., *The South and the Politics of Slavery 1828–1856* (Baton Rouge, 1978), 31.

32 "Critical Notes," *Western Monthly Magazine*, III (April 1835), 248.

33 Mann, *Lectures*, 136.

34 Burnap, *Lectures*, 109.

35 Horace Bushnell, *The Northern Iron* (Hartford, 1854), 26.

36 Mann, *Lectures*, 55–6.

37 Burton J. Bledstein, *The Culture of Professionalism* (New York, 1976), 263.

38 Link, *Democratic-Republican Societies*, 7.

Chapter 17:
A Crisis in Parallelism

1 Mrs. Rufus Lenoir quoted in Gordon B. McKinney, *Southern Mountain Republicans 1865–1900* (Chapel Hill, 1978), 19.

2 Olmsted, *Journey*, 421.

3 Philip Shriver Klein, *President James Buchanan* (University Park, 1962), 402.

4 Martineau, *Society in America*, II, 30–1.

5 William Greenough quoted in Ekrich, *Idea*, 56–7.

6 Toombs to George W. Crawford, Feb. 6, 1846, American Historical Association *Annual Report* (1911), II: *The Correspondence of Robert Toombs, Alexander H. Stephens, and Howell Cobb*, ed. Ulrich Bonnell Phillips, 74; *The Letters of William Cullen Bryant*, eds. William Cullen Bryant II and Thomas G. Voss (New York, 1975–81), II, 518n.

7 Cooper, *South*, 206.

8 Joseph Holt Ingraham quoted in Harold D. Woodman, *King Cotton & His Retainers* (Lexington, 1968), 135.

9 Cushing quoted in Weinberg, *Manifest Destiny*, 203; Slidell quoted in Robert E. May, *The Southern Dream of Caribbean Empire 1854–1861* (Baton Rouge, 1973), 172.

10 J. E. Cairnes quoted in Gavin Wright, *The Political Economy of the Cotton South* (New York, 1978), 132.

11 Taylor to Jefferson Davis, April 20, 1848, *Letters of Jefferson Davis*, III, 307.

12 Remarks, Mar. 14, 1850, ibid., IV, 90.

13 David M. Potter, *The Impending Crisis 1848–1861*, completed and edited by Don E. Fehrenbacher (New York, 1976), 67–8; Bushnell, *Northern Iron*, 21.

14 John McCardell, *The Idea of a Southern Nation* (New York, 1979), 98.

15 Jack P. Maddex, *The Virginia Conservatives, 1867–1879* (Chapel Hill, 1970), 21.

16 Douglas to Howell Cobb, April 2, 1854, *The Letters of Stephen A. Douglas*, ed. Robert W. Johannsen (Urbana, 1961), 300.

17 Atchison to R. M. T. Hunter, [April] 4, 1855, *Correspondence of Robert M. T. Hunter*, 161.

18 Thomas W. Thomas to Alexander H. Stephens, Jan. 12, 1857, *Correspondence of Toombs, Stephens, and Cobb*, 390.

19 J. Hamilton Cowper to John Murray Forbes, Nov. 6, 1856, *Letters and Recollections of John Murray Forbes*, ed. Sarah Forbes Hughes (Boston, 1900), I, 150–1.

20 Albert D. Kirwan, *John J. Crittenden* (Lexington, 1962), 305.

21 "Speech at Chicago, Illinois," July 10, 1858, *The Collected Works of Abraham Lincoln*, ed. Roy P. Basler (New Brunswick, 1953), II, 493.

22 Frederick Grimké quoted in Bloomfield, *American Lawyers*, 266.

23 *The Lincoln-Douglas Debates of 1858*, ed. Robert W. Johannsen (New York, 1965), 315.

24 Toombs to Alexander H. Stephens, Feb. 10, 1860, *Correspondence of Toombs, Stephens, and Cobb*, 462.

25 "Introduction," *Lincoln-Douglas Debates*, 9.

26 Bernard Crick, *In Defence of Politics* (London, 1962), 105.

27 Leonard P. Curry, *Blueprint for Modern America: Nonmilitary Legislation of the First Civil War Congress* (Nashville, 1968), 210.

28 Harold Schwartz, *Samuel Gridley Howe* (Cambridge, 1956), 252.

29 Reginald Horsman, *Race and Manifest Destiny* (Cambridge, 1981), 167.

Epilogue

1 Corporal Jackson Cherry quoted in Leon F. Litwack, *Been in the Storm So Long* (New York, 1979), 336.

2 "Racial Consequences of Immigration," *The Century Magazine*, LXXXVII (Feb. 1914), 615–16.

3 Henry George, *Progress and Poverty*, Modern Library ed. (New York, n.d. [1879]), 527.

4 "Progress of Culture," *The Complete Works of Ralph Waldo Emerson*, ed. Edward Waldo Emerson (Boston, 1904), VIII, 210. I am indebted to Larry Miller for this citation.

Selected Bibliography

I include here those works that I know have had some formative influence on my interpretations. As the specialist will recognize, the influence has often emerged from sharp disagreement, but my debt is certainly none the less for that. The peculiar pattern of my interests, the particular sequence in my reading, and no doubt some lapses in my memory of how an interpretation developed explain the absence of many other excellent works that I have used with profit.

Abernethy, Thomas P. *The South in the New Nation 1789–1819.* Baton Rouge: Louisiana State University Press, 1961.

Alexander, Thomas B. *Sectional Stress and Party Strength: A Study of Roll-Call Voting Patterns in the United States House of Representatives.* Nashville: Vanderbilt University Press, 1967.

Ammon, Harry. "The Richmond Junto, 1800–1824," *Virginia Magazine of History and Biography,* LXI (October 1953), 395–418.

Appleby, Joyce. "The Social Origins of American Revolutionary Ideology," *Journal of American History,* LXIV (March 1978), 935–58.

Aronson, Sidney H. *Status and Kinship in the Higher Civil Service: Standards of Selection in the Administrations of John Adams, Thomas Jefferson, and Andrew Jackson.* Cambridge: Harvard University Press, 1964.

Atherton, Lewis E. *The Southern Country Store 1800–1860.* Baton Rouge: Louisiana State University Press, 1949.

Bailyn, Bernard. *The Ideological Origins of the American Revolution.* Cambridge: Harvard University Press, 1967.

Banner, James M., Jr. *To the Hartford Convention: The Federalists and the Origins of Party Politics in Massachusetts, 1789–1815.* New York: Alfred A. Knopf, 1970.

Barney, William. *The Road to Secession: A New Perspective on the Old South.* New York: Praeger, 1972.

Beeman, Richard R. *The Old Dominion and the New Nation, 1788–1801.* Lexington: University Press of Kentucky, 1972.

Benson, Lee. *The Concept of Jacksonian Democracy: New York as a Test Case.* Princeton: Princeton University Press, 1961.

Berg, Barbara J. *The Remembered Gate: Origins of American Feminism: The Woman and the City, 1800–1860.* New York: Oxford University Press, 1978.

Berkhofer, Robert F., Jr. *Salvation and the Savage: An Analysis of Protestant Missions and American Indian Responses, 1787–1862.* Lexington: University of Kentucky Press, 1965.

Berlin, Ira. *Slaves Without Masters: The Free Negro in the Antebellum South.* New York: Pantheon Books, 1974.

Berthoff, Rowland. *An Unsettled People: Social Order and Disorder in American History.* New York: Harper & Row, 1971.

Berwanger, Eugene H. *The Frontier Against Slavery: Western Anti-Negro Prejudice and the Slavery Extension Controversy.* Urbana: University of Illinois Press, 1967.

Bestor, Arthur E., Jr. "Patent-Office Models of the Good Society: Some Relationships Between Social Reform and Westward Expansion," *American Historical Review,* LVIII (April 1953), 505–26.

Billias, George Athan. *Elbridge Gerry: Founding Father and Republican Statesman.* New York: McGraw-Hill, 1976.

Bloomfield, Maxwell. *American Lawyers in a Changing Society, 1776–1876.* Cambridge: Harvard University Press, 1976.

Boorstin, Daniel J. *The Americans: The National Experience.* New York: Random House, 1965.

———. *The Lost World of Thomas Jefferson.* New York: Henry Holt, 1948.

Boyd, Julian P. *Number 7: Alexander Hamilton's Secret Attempts to Control American Foreign Policy with Supporting Documents.* Princeton: Princeton University Press, 1964.

Brodie, Fawn M. *Thomas Jefferson: An Intimate History.* New York: W. W. Norton, 1974.

Brown, Richard H. "The Missouri Crisis, Slavery, and the Politics of Jacksonianism," *South Atlantic Quarterly,* LXV (Winter 1966), 55–72.

Brown, Roger H. *The Republic in Peril: 1812.* New York: Columbia University Press, 1964.

Browne, Gary Lawson. *Baltimore in the Nation, 1789–1861.* Chapel Hill: University of North Carolina Press, 1980.

Bruce, Dickson D., Jr. *And They All Sang Hallelujah: Plain-Folk Camp-Meeting Religion, 1800–1845.* Knoxville: University of Tennessee Press, 1974.

Bruchey, Stuart Weems. *Robert Oliver, Merchant of Baltimore 1783–1819.* Baltimore: Johns Hopkins University Press, 1956.

Buel, Richard, Jr. "Democracy and the American Revolution: A Frame of Reference," *William and Mary Quarterly,* XXI (April 1964), 165–90.

Calhoun, Daniel. *The Intelligence of a People.* Princeton: Princeton University Press, 1973.

Chambers, William Nisbet, and Walter Dean Burnham, eds. *The American Party Systems.* New York: Oxford University Press, 1975.

Charles, Joseph. *The Origins of the American Party System.* Chapel Hill: University of North Carolina Press, 1956.

Coleman, Peter J. *Debtors and Creditors in America: Insolvency, Imprisonment for Debt, and Bankruptcy, 1607–1900.* Madison: State Historical Society of Wisconsin, 1974.

Combs, Jerald A. *The Jay Treaty: Political Battleground of the Founding Fathers.* Berkeley and Los Angeles: University of California Press, 1970.

Cooke, Jacob E. "The Compromise of 1790," *William and Mary Quarterly,* XXVII (October 1970), 523–45.

———. *Tench Coxe and the Early Republic.* Chapel Hill: University of North Carolina Press, 1978.

Cooper, William J., Jr. *The South and the Politics of Slavery 1828–1856.* Baton Rouge: Louisiana State University Press, 1978.

Cott, Nancy F. *The Bonds of Womanhood: "Woman's Sphere" in New England, 1780–1835.* New Haven: Yale University Press, 1977.

———. "Passionlessness: An Interpretation of Victorian Sexual Ideology, 1790–1850," *Signs,* IV (1978), 219–36.

Countryman, Edward. *A People in Revolution: The American Revolution and Political Society in New York, 1760–1790.* Baltimore: Johns Hopkins University Press, 1981.

Craven, Avery Odelle. *Soil Exhaustion as a Factor in the Agricultural History of Virginia and Maryland, 1606–1860.* Urbana: University of Illinois Press, 1926.

Crenson, Matthew A. *The Federal Machine: Beginnings of Bureaucracy in Jacksonian America.* Baltimore: Johns Hopkins University Press, 1975.

Cross, Whitney R. *The Burnt-over District: The Social and Intellectual History of Enthusiastic Religion in Western New York, 1800–1850.* Ithaca: Cornell University Press, 1950.

Cunningham, Noble E., Jr. *The Jeffersonian Republicans: The Formation of Party Organization, 1789–1801.* Chapel Hill: University of North Carolina Press, 1957.

Curtis, James C. *Andrew Jackson and the Search for Vindication.* Boston: Little, Brown, 1976.

Dangerfield, George. *Chancellor Robert R. Livingston of New York 1746–1813.* New York: Harcourt, Brace, 1960.

Danhof, Clarence H. *Changes in Agriculture: The Northern United States, 1820–1870.* Cambridge: Harvard University Press, 1969.

David, Paul A. "New Light on a Statistical Dark Age: U. S. Real Product Growth before 1840," *American Economic Review,* LVII (May 1967), 294–306.

Davis, David Brion. *The Problem of Slavery in the Age of Revolution, 1770–1823.* Ithaca: Cornell University Press, 1975.

————. "Some Themes of Counter-Subversion: An Analysis of Anti-Masonic, Anti-Catholic, and Anti-Mormon Literature," *Mississippi Valley Historical Review,* XLVII (September 1960), 205–24.

Dawley, Alan. *Class and Community: The Industrial Revolution in Lynn.* Cambridge: Harvard University Press, 1976.

De Conde, Alexander. "Washington's Farewell, the French Alliance, and the Election of 1796," *Mississippi Valley Historical Review,* XLIII (March 1957), 641–58.

Degler, Carl N. *At Odds: Women and the Family from the Revolution to the Present.* New York: Oxford University Press, 1980.

————. *Neither Black Nor White: Slavery and Race Relations in Brazil and the United States.* New York: Macmillan, 1971.

De Pillis, Mario S. "The Social Sources of Mormonism," *Church History,* XXXVII (March 1968), 50–79.

Doherty, Robert. "Social Bases for the Presbyterian Schism of 1837–1838: The Philadelphia Case," *Journal of Social History,* II (Fall 1968), 69–79.

————. *Society and Power: Five New England Towns 1800–1860.* Amherst: University of Massachusetts Press, 1977.

Donald, David. *Lincoln Reconsidered: Essays on the Civil War Era.* New York: Alfred A. Knopf, 1956.

Douglas, Ann. *The Feminization of American Culture.* New York: Alfred A. Knopf, 1977.

Doyle, Don Harrison. *The Social Order of a Frontier Community: Jacksonville, Illinois, 1825–70.* Urbana: University of Illinois Press, 1978.

Dublin, Thomas. *Women at Work: The Transformation of Work and Community in Lowell, Massachusetts, 1826–1860.* New York: Columbia University Press, 1979.

DuBois, Ellen Carol. *Feminism and Suffrage: The Emergence of an Independent Women's Movement in America 1848–1869.* Ithaca: Cornell University Press, 1978.

Ekirch, Arthur Alphonse, Jr. *The Idea of Progress in America, 1815–1860.* New York: Columbia University Press, 1944.

Elkins, Stanley M. *Slavery: A Problem in American Institutional and Intellectual Life.* Chicago: University of Chicago Press, 1959.

————, and Eric McKitrick. "The Founding Fathers: Young Men of the Revolution," *Political Science Quarterly,* LXXVI (June 1961), 181–216.

Ellis, David Maldwyn. *Landlords and Farmers in the Hudson-Mohawk Region 1790–1850.* Ithaca: Cornell University Press, 1946.

Ellis, Richard E. *The Jeffersonian Crisis: Courts and Politics in the Young Republic.* New York: Oxford University Press, 1971.

Faragher, John Mack. *Women and Men on the Overland Trail.* New Haven: Yale University Press, 1979.

Faulkner, Robert Kenneth. *The Jurisprudence of John Marshall.* Princeton: Princeton University Press, 1968.

Fehrenbacher, Don E. *The Dred Scott Case: Its Significance in American Law and Politics.* New York: Oxford University Press, 1978.

Fellman, Michael. *The Unbounded Frame: Freedom and Community in Nineteenth Century American Utopianism.* Westport: Greenwood Press, 1973.

Fischer, David Hackett. *Growing Old in America.* New York: Oxford University Press, 1977.

————. *The Revolution of American Conservatism: The Federalist Party in the Era* of *Jeffersonian Democracy.* New York: Harper & Row, 1965.

Fishlow, Albert. *American Railroads and the Transformation of the Ante-Bellum Economy.* Cambridge: Harvard University Press, 1965.

————. "The Common School Revival: Fact or Fancy?" in *Industrialization in Two Systems: Essays in Honor of Alexander Gerschenkron,* ed. Henry Rosovsky, 40–67. New York: John Wiley, 1966.

Foner, Eric. *Free Soil, Free Labor, Free Men: The Ideology of the Republican Party before the Civil War.* New York: Oxford University Press, 1970.

Formisano, Ronald P. *The Birth of Mass Political Parties: Michigan, 1827–1861.* Princeton: Princeton University Press, 1971.

————. "Deferential-Participant Politics: The Early Republic's Political Culture, 1789–1840," *American Political Science Review,* LXVIII (June 1974), 473–87.

Foster, Charles I. *An Errand of Mercy: The Evangelical United Front 1790–1837.* Chapel Hill: University of North Carolina Press, 1960.

Fredrickson, George M. *The Black Image in the White Mind: The Debate on Afro-American Character and Destiny, 1817–1914.* New York: Harper & Row, 1971.

Freehling, William W. *Prelude to Civil War: The Nullification Controversy in South Carolina, 1816–1836.* New York: Harper & Row, 1966.

Gallman, Robert E. "Professor Pessen on the 'Egalitarian Myth,'" *Social Science History,* II (Winter 1978), 194–207.

Gara, Larry. *The Liberty Line: The Legend of the Underground Railroad.* Lexington: University of Kentucky Press, 1961.

Garraty, John Arthur. *Silas Wright.* New York: Columbia University Press, 1949.

Gatell, Frank Otto. "Money and Party in Jacksonian America: A Quantitative Look at New York City's Men of Quality," *Political Science Quarterly,* LXXXII (June 1967), 235–52.

Gates, Paul Wallace. *The Farmer's Age: Agriculture, 1815–1860.* New York: Holt, Rinehart and Winston, 1960.

Genovese, Eugene D. *The Political Economy of Slavery: Studies in the Economy & Society of the Slave South.* New York: Pantheon Books, 1965.

————. *Roll, Jordan, Roll: The World the Slaves Made.* New York: Pantheon Books, 1974.

Gilbert, Felix. *To the Farewell Address: Ideas of Early American Foreign Policy.* Princeton: Princeton University Press, 1961.

Goldfield, David R. *Urban Growth in the Age of Sectionalism: Virginia, 1846–1861.* Baton Rouge: Louisiana State University Press, 1977.

Goodman, Paul. *The Democratic-Republicans of Massachusetts: Politics in a Young Republic.* Cambridge: Harvard University Press, 1964.

Green, George D. *Finance and Economic Development in the Old South: Louisiana Banking, 1804–1861.* Stanford: Stanford University Press, 1972.

Greenberg, Dolores. "Reassessing the Power Patterns of the Industrial Revolution: An Anglo-American Comparison," *American Historical Review,* LXXXVII (December 1982), 1237–61.

Greene, Evarts B. "The Code of Honor in Colonial and Revolutionary Times, with Special Reference to New England," *Publications of the Colonial Society of Massachusetts,* XXVI (1927), 367–88.

Griffin, Clifford S. *Their Brothers' Keeper.* New Brunswick: Rutgers University Press, 1960.

Grimsted, David. "Rioting in Its Jacksonian Setting," *American Historical Review,* LXXVII (April 1972), 361–97.

Grob, Gerald N. *The State and the Mentally Ill: A History of Worcester State Hospital in Massachusetts, 1830–1920.* Chapel Hill: University of North Carolina Press, 1966.

Gutman, Herbert G. "Work, Culture, and Society in Industrializing America, 1815–1919," *American Historical Review,* LXXVIII (June 1973), 531–88.

Halttunen, Karen. *Confidence Men and Painted Women: A Study of Middle-class Culture in America, 1830–1870.* New Haven: Yale University Press, 1982.

Handlin, Oscar, and Mary Flug Handlin. *Commonwealth: A Study of the Role of Government in the American Economy: Massachusetts, 1774–1861.* Cambridge: Harvard University Press, 1947.

Haraszti, Zoltán. *John Adams & the Prophets of Progress.* Cambridge: Harvard University Press, 1952.

Hareven, Tamara K., ed. *Anonymous Americans: Explorations in Nineteenth-Century Social History.* Englewood Cliffs: Prentice-Hall, 1971.

Harrison, J. F. C. *The Second Coming: Popular Millenarianism 1780–1850.* New Brunswick: Rutgers University Press, 1979.

Harrison, Joseph H., Jr. "Oligarchs and Democrats: The Richmond Junto," *Virginia Magazine of History and Biography,* LXXVIII (April 1970), 184–98.

Hartz, Louis. *The Liberal Tradition in America: An Interpretation of American Political Thought Since the Revolution.* New York: Harcourt, Brace & World, 1955.

Hatch, Nathan O. "The Christian Movement and the Demand for a Theology of the People," *Journal of American History,* LXVII (December 1980), 545–67.

Henderson, H. James. *Party Politics in the Continental Congress.* New York: McGraw-Hill, 1974.

Higham, John. *From Boundlessness to Consolidation: The Transformation of American Culture, 1848–1860.* Ann Arbor: William L. Clements Library, 1969.

Hirsch, Susan E. *Roots of the American Working Class: The Industrialization of Crafts in Newark, 1800–1860.* Philadelphia: University of Pennsylvania Press, 1978.

Hofstadter, Richard. *The Idea of a Party System: The Rise of Legitimate Opposition in the United States, 1780–1840.* Berkeley and Los Angeles: University of California Press, 1969.

Holt, Michael F. *The Political Crisis of the 1850s.* New York: John Wiley, 1978.

Horlick, Allan Stanley. *Country Boys and Merchant Princes: The Social Control of Young Men in New York.* Lewisburg: Bucknell University Press, 1975.

Horwitz, Morton J. *The Transformation of American Law, 1780–1860.* Cambridge: Harvard University Press, 1977.

Hovenkamp, Herbert. *Science and Religion in America 1800–1860.* Philadelphia: University of Pennsylvania Press, 1978.

Howe, Daniel Walker. *The Unitarian Conscience: Harvard Moral Philosophy, 1805–1861.* Cambridge: Harvard University Press, 1970.

Howe, John R., Jr. "Republican Thought and the Political Violence of the 1790's," *American Quarterly,* XIX (Summer 1967), 147–65.

Hughes, J. R. T., and Nathan Rosenberg. "The United States Business Cycle Before 1860: Some Problems of Interpretation," *Economic History Review,* XV (April 1963), 476–93.

Hurst, J. Willard. *Law and the Conditions of Freedom in the Nineteenth-Century United States.* Madison: University of Wisconsin Press, 1956.

Jenks, Leland Hamilton. *The Migration of British Capital to 1875.* New York: Alfred A. Knopf, 1938.

Jensen, Merrill. *The New Nation: A History of the United States During the Confederation, 1781–1789.* New York: Alfred A. Knopf, 1950.

Johnson, Paul E. *A Shopkeeper's Millennium: Society and Revivals in Rochester, New York 1815–1837.* New York: Hill and Wang, 1978.

Jordan, Winthrop D. *White over Black: American Attitudes Toward the Negro, 1550–1812.* Chapel Hill: University of North Carolina Press, 1968.

Kaestle, Carl F. *The Evolution of an Urban School System: New York City, 1750–1850.* Cambridge: Harvard University Press, 1973.

Kaplan, Lawrence S. *Jefferson and France: An Essay on Politics and Political Ideas.* New Haven: Yale University Press, 1967.

Katz, Michael B. *The Irony of Early School Reform: Educational Innovation in Mid-Nineteenth Century Massachusetts.* Cambridge: Harvard University Press, 1968.

———. "Social Class in North American History," *Journal of Interdisciplinary History*, XI (Spring 1981), 579–605.

Kelly, Alfred H. "Constitutional Liberty and the Law of Libel: A Historian's View," *American Historical Review*, LXXIV (December 1968), 429–52.

Kerber, Linda K. *Women of the Republic: Intellect and Ideology in Revolutionary America*. Chapel Hill: University of North Carolina Press, 1980.

Kett, Joseph F. *The Formation of the American Medical Profession: The Role of Institutions, 1780–1860*. New Haven: Yale University Press, 1968.

———. *Rites of Passage: Adolescence in America 1790 to the Present*. New York: Basic Books, 1977.

Klingaman, David C., and Richard K. Vedder, eds. *Essays in Nineteenth Century Economic History: The Old Northwest*. Athens: Ohio University Press, 1975.

Koebner, Richard. *Empire*. London: Cambridge University Press, 1961.

Kohn, Richard H. *Eagle and Sword: The Federalists and the Creation of the Military Establishment in America, 1783–1802*. New York: The Free Press, 1975.

Kraditor, Aileen S. *Means and Ends in American Abolitionism: Garrison and His Critics on Strategy and Tactics, 1834–1850*. New York: Pantheon Books, 1969.

Landes, David S. *The Unbound Prometheus: Technological Change and Industrial Development in Western Europe from 1750 to the Present*. Cambridge: Cambridge University Press, 1969.

Latner, Richard B. *The Presidency of Andrew Jackson: White House Politics 1829–1837*. Athens: University of Georgia Press, 1979.

Levine, Peter D. *The Behavior of State Legislative Parties in the Jacksonian Era: New Jersey, 1829–1844*. Cranbury: Associated University Presses, 1977.

Levy, Leonard W. *Freedom of Speech and Press in Early American History: Legacy of Suppression*. New York: Harper Torchbooks, 1963 [1960].

———. *Jefferson & Civil Liberties: The Darker Side*. Cambridge: Harvard University Press, 1963.

Lewis, R. W. B. *The American Adam: Innocence Tragedy and Tradition in the Nineteenth Century*. Chicago: University of Chicago Press, 1955.

Lifton, Robert Jay. *Revolutionary Immortality: Mao Tse-tung and the Chinese Cultural Revolution*. New York: Random House, 1968.

Lindstrom, Diane. *Economic Development in the Philadelphia Region, 1810–1850*. New York: Columbia University Press, 1978.

Litwack, Leon F. *North of Slavery: The Negro in the Free States, 1790–1860*. Chicago: University of Chicago Press, 1961.

Lockridge, Kenneth. "Land, Population, and the Evolution of New England Society, 1630–1790," *Past and Present*, XXXIX (1968), 62–80.

McColley, Robert. *Slavery and Jeffersonian Virginia*, 2nd ed. Urbana: University of Illinois Press, 1973.

McCormick, Richard P. *The Second American Party System: Party Formation in the Jacksonian Era*. Chapel Hill: University of North Carolina Press, 1966.

McCoy, Drew R. *The Elusive Republic: Political Economy in Jeffersonian America*. Chapel Hill: University of North Carolina Press, 1980.

McDonald, Forrest. *Alexander Hamilton: A Biography*. New York: W. W. Norton, 1979.

———. *The Presidency of Thomas Jefferson*. Lawrence: University Press of Kansas, 1976.

MacLeod, Anne Scott. *A Moral Tale: Children's Fiction and American Culture 1820–1860*. Hamden: Archon, 1975.

McLoughlin, William G., Jr. *Modern Revivalism: Charles Grandison Finney to Billy Graham*. New York: Ronald Press, 1959.

Marshall, Lynn L. "The Genesis of Grassroots Democracy in Kentucky," *Mid-America*, XLVII (October 1965), 269–87.

———. "The Strange Stillbirth of the Whig Party," *American Historical Review*, LXXII (January 1967), 445–68.

Mathews, Donald G. *Religion in the Old South*. Chicago: University of Chicago Press, 1977.

————. "The Second Great Awakening as an Organizing Process, 1780–1830: An Hypothesis," *American Quarterly*, XXI (Spring 1969), 23–43.

Mays, David John. *Edmund Pendleton 1721–1803: A Biography*. 2 vols. Cambridge: Harvard University Press, 1952.

Mead, Sidney E. *The Lively Experiment: The Shaping of Christianity in America*. New York: Harper & Row, 1963.

Meyers, Marvin. *The Jacksonian Persuasion: Politics & Belief*. Stanford: Stanford University Press, 1957.

Miles, Edwin Arthur. *Jacksonian Democracy in Mississippi*. Chapel Hill: University of North Carolina Press, 1960.

Miller, Douglas T. *Jacksonian Aristocracy: Class and Democracy in New York 1830–1860*. New York: Oxford University Press, 1967.

Mitchell, Robert D. *Commercialism and Frontier Perspectives on the Early Shenandoah Valley*. Charlottesville: University Press of Virginia, 1977.

Miyakawa, T. Scott. *Protestants and Pioneers: Individualism and Conformity on the American Frontier*. Chicago: University of Chicago Press, 1964.

Mohr, James C. *Abortion in America: The Origins and Evolution of National Policy, 1800–1900*. New York: Oxford University Press, 1978.

Mokyr, Joel. *Industrialization in the Low Countries, 1795–1850*. New Haven: Yale University Press, 1976.

Montgomery, David. *Beyond Equality: Labor and the Radical Republicans 1862–1872*. New York: Alfred A. Knopf, 1967.

————. "The Shuttle and the Cross: Weavers and Artisans in the Kensington Riots of 1844," *Journal of Social History*, V (Summer 1972), 411–46.

Moore, Glover. *The Missouri Controversy 1819–1821*. Lexington: University of Kentucky Press, 1953.

Nagel, Paul C. *One Nation Indivisible: The Union in American Thought, 1776–1861*. New York: Oxford University Press, 1964.

Nash, Gary B. "The American Clergy and the French Revolution," *William and Mary Quarterly*, XXII (July 1965), 392–412.

Nathans, Sydney. *Daniel Webster and Jacksonian Democracy*. Baltimore: Johns Hopkins University Press, 1973.

Neu, Irene D. *Erastus Corning: Merchant and Financier 1794–1872*. Ithaca: Cornell University Press, 1960.

Nevins, Allan. *The Emergence of Lincoln*. 2 vols. New York: Charles Scribner, 1950.

Nichols, Roy Franklin. *The Disruption of American Democracy*. New York: Macmillan, 1948.

Niemi, Albert W., Jr. "A Further Look at Interregional Canals and Economic Specialization: 1820–1840," *Explorations in Economic History*, VII (Summer 1970), 499–520.

Nissenbaum, Stephen. *Sex, Diet, and Debility in Jacksonian America: Sylvester Graham and Health Reform*. Westport: Greenwood Press, 1980.

North, Douglass C. *The Economic Growth of the United States 1790–1860*. Englewood Cliffs: Prentice-Hall, 1961.

Pearce, Roy Harvey. *Savagism and Civilization: A Study of the Indian and the American Mind*. Baltimore: Johns Hopkins University Press, 1965.

Perkins, Bradford. *Prologue to War: England and the United States 1805–1812*. Berkeley and Los Angeles: University of California Press, 1963.

Perkins, Edwin J. *Financing Anglo-American Trade: The House of Brown, 1800–1880*. Cambridge: Harvard University Press, 1975.

Pessen, Edward. *Jacksonian America: Society, Personality, and Politics*. Homewood: Dorsey Press, 1969.

————. *Most Uncommon Jacksonians: The Radical Leaders of the Early Labor Movement*. Albany: State University of New York Press, 1967.

Peterson, Merrill D. *The Jefferson Image in the American Mind*. New York: Oxford University Press, 1960.

Pole, J. R. *Political Representation in England and the Origins of the American Republic*. London: Macmillan, 1966.

Pollard, Sidney. *The Genesis of Modern Management: A Study of the Industrial Revolution in Great Britain.* Cambridge: Harvard University Press, 1965.

Porter, Glenn, and Harold C. Livesay. *Merchants and Manufacturers: Studies in the Changing Structure of Nineteenth-Century Marketing.* Baltimore: Johns Hopkins University Press, 1971.

Potter, David M. *The Impending Crisis 1848–1861,* completed and edited by Don E. Fehrenbacher. New York: Harper & Row, 1976.

———. *People of Plenty: Economic Abundance and the American Character.* Chicago: University of Chicago Press, 1954.

———. *The South and the Sectional Conflict.* Baton Rouge: Louisiana State University Press, 1968.

Pred, Allan R. *Urban Growth and the Circulation of Information: The United States System of Cities, 1790–1840.* Cambridge: Harvard University Press, 1973.

Prince, Carl E. *New Jersey's Jeffersonian Republicans: The Genesis of an Early Party Machine 1789–1817.* Chapel Hill: University of North Carolina Press, 1967.

Rakove, Jack N. *The Beginnings of National Politics: An Interpretive History of the Continental Congress.* New York: Alfred A. Knopf, 1979.

Remini, Robert V. *Martin Van Buren and the Making of the Democratic Party.* New York: Columbia University Press, 1959.

Richards, Leonard L. *"Gentlemen of Property and Standing": Anti-Abolition Mobs in Jacksonian America.* New York: Oxford University Press, 1970.

Richardson, James F. *The New York Police: Colonial Times to 1901.* New York: Oxford University Press, 1970.

Ridgway, Whitman H. *Community Leadership in Maryland, 1790–1840: A Comparative Analysis of Power in Society.* Chapel Hill: University of North Carolina Press, 1979.

Riesman, David, et al. *The Lonely Crowd: A Study of the Changing American Character.* New Haven: Yale University Press, 1950.

Riley, James C. "Foreign Credit and Fiscal Stability: Dutch Investment in the United States, 1781–1794," *Journal of American History,* LXV (December 1978), 654–78.

Risjord, Norman K. "1812: Conservatives, War Hawks, and the Nation's Honor," *William and Mary Quarterly,* XVIII (April 1961), 196–210.

Rock, Howard B. *Artisans of the New Republic: The Tradesmen of New York City in the Age of Jefferson.* New York: New York University Press, 1979.

Rogers, Charles C., Jr. *Evolution of a Federalist: William Loughton Smith of Charleston (1758–1812).* Columbia: University of South Carolina Press, 1962.

Rogin, Michael Paul. *Fathers and Children: Andrew Jackson and the Subjugation of the American Indian.* New York: Alfred A. Knopf, 1975.

Rohrbough, Malcolm J. *The Land Office Business: The Settlement and Administration of American Public Lands, 1787–1837.* New York: Oxford University Press, 1968.

Rorabaugh, W. J. *The Alcoholic Republic: An American Tradition.* New York: Oxford University Press, 1979.

Rosenberg, Carroll Smith. *Religion and the Rise of the American City: The New York City Mission Movement, 1812–1870.* Ithaca: Cornell University Press, 1971.

Rothman, David J. *The Discovery of the Asylum: Social Order and Disorder in the New Republic.* Boston: Little, Brown, 1971.

Royster, Charles. *A Revolutionary People at War: The Continental Army and the American Character, 1775–1783.* Chapel Hill: University of North Carolina Press, 1979.

Rubin, Julius. *Canal or Railroad? Imitation and Innovation in the Response to the Erie Canal in Philadelphia, Baltimore, and Boston.* Philadelphia: American Philosophical Society, 1961.

Ryan, Mary P. *Cradle of the Middle Class: The Family in Oneida County, New York, 1790–1865.* Cambridge: Cambridge University Press, 1981.

Scheiber, Harry N. "Federalism and the American Economic Order, 1789–1910,"

Law and Society Review, X (Fall 1975), 57–118.

———. *Ohio Canal Era: A Case Study of Government and the Economy, 1820–1861.* Athens: Ohio University Press, 1969.

Scott, Donald M. *From Office to Profession: The New England Ministry 1750–1850.* Philadelphia: University of Pennsylvania Press, 1978.

Seaburg, Carl, and Stanley Paterson. *Merchant Prince of Boston: Colonel T. H. Perkins, 1764–1854.* Cambridge: Harvard University Press, 1971.

Sellers, Charles Grier, Jr. *James K. Polk: Jacksonian 1795–1843.* Princeton: Princeton University Press, 1957.

———. "Who Were the Southern Whigs?" *American Historical Review,* LIX (January 1954), 335–46.

Shade, William Gerald. *Banks or No Banks: The Money Issue in Western Politics 1832–1865.* Detroit: Wayne State University Press, 1972.

Sharp, James Roger. *The Jacksonians versus the Banks: Politics in the States After the Panic of 1837.* New York: Columbia University Press, 1970.

Silbey, Joel H. *The Shrine of Party: Congressional Voting Behavior 1841–1852.* Pittsburgh: University of Pittsburgh Press, 1967.

Simpson, Albert F. "The Political Significance of Slave Representation, 1787–1821," *Journal of Southern History,* VII (August 1941), 313–42.

Siracusa, Carl. *A Mechanical People: Perceptions of the Industrial Order in Massachusetts 1815–1880.* Middletown: Wesleyan University Press, 1979.

Sisson, Daniel. *The American Revolution of 1800.* New York: Alfred A. Knopf, 1974.

Sklar, Kathryn Kish. *Catherine Beecher: A Study in American Domesticity.* New Haven: Yale University Press, 1973.

Smelser, Marshall, "The Federalist Period as an Age of Passion," *American Quarterly,* X (Winter 1958), 391–419.

Smith, Daniel Scott. "Family Limitation, Sexual Control, and Domestic Feminism in Victorian America," in *A Heritage of Her Own,* eds. Nancy F. Cott and Elizabeth H. Pleck, 222–45. New York: Simon and Schuster, 1979.

Smith, Henry Nash. *Virgin Land: The American West as Symbol and Myth.* Cambridge: Harvard University Press, 1950.

Smith, Wilson. *Professors & Public Ethics: Studies of Northern Moral Philosophers Before the Civil War.* Ithaca: Cornell University Press, 1956.

Smith-Rosenberg, Carroll. "The Female World of Love and Ritual: Relations Between Women in Nineteenth-Century America," *Signs,* I (Autumn 1975), 1–29.

Soltow, Lee. *Men and Wealth in the United States 1850–1870.* New Haven: Yale University Press, 1975.

———, and Edward Stevens. *The Rise of Literacy and the Common School in the United States: A Socioeconomic Analysis to 1870.* Chicago: University of Chicago Press, 1981.

Somkin, Fred. *Unquiet Eagle: Memory and Desire in the Idea of American Freedom, 1815–1860.* Ithaca: Cornell University Press, 1967.

Spivak, Burton. *Jefferson's English Crisis: Commerce, Embargo, and the Republican Revolution.* Charlottesville: University Press of Virginia, 1979.

Stagg, J. C. A. "James Madison and the 'Malcontents': The Political Origins of the War of 1812," *William and Mary Quarterly,* XXXIII (October 1976), 557–85.

Stampp, Kenneth M. *The Peculiar Institution: Slavery in the Ante-Bellum South.* New York: Alfred A. Knopf, 1956.

Stewart, James Brewer. *Holy Warriors: The Abolitionists and American Slavery.* New York: Hill and Wang, 1976.

Taylor, George Rogers. *The Transportation Revolution 1815–1860.* New York: Rinehart, 1951.

Taylor, Robert J. *Western Massachusetts in the Revolution.* Providence: Brown University Press, 1954.

Taylor, William R. *Cavalier and Yankee: The Old South and American National Character.* New York: George Braziller, 1961.

Teaford, Jon C. _The Municipal Revolution in America: Origins of Modern Urban Government 1650–1825._ Chicago: University of Chicago Press, 1975.

Temin, Peter. _The Jacksonian Economy._ New York: W. W. Norton, 1969.

Thernstrom, Stephan. _Poverty and Progress: Social Mobility in a Nineteenth Century City._ Cambridge: Harvard University Press, 1964.

Thomas, John L. _The Liberator: William Lloyd Garrison, a Biography._ Boston: Little, Brown, 1963.

———. "Romantic Reform in America, 1815–1865," _American Quarterly_, XVII (Winter 1965), 656–81.

Thornton, J. Mills III. _Politics and Power in a Slave Society: Alabama, 1800–1860._ Baton Rouge: Louisiana State University Press, 1978.

Turner, Victor W. _The Ritual Process: Structure and Anti-Structure._ Chicago: Aldine, 1969.

Tushnet, Mark V. _The American Law of Slavery 1810–1860: Considerations of Humanity and Interest._ Princeton: Princeton University Press, 1981.

Tyack, David B. _The One Best System: A History of American Urban Education._ Cambridge: Harvard University Press, 1974.

Tyrrell, Ian R. _Sobering Up: From Temperance to Prohibition in Antebellum America, 1800–1860._ Westport: Greenwood Press, 1979.

Vinovskis, Maris A. _Fertility in Massachusetts from the Revolution to the Civil War._ New York: Academic Press, 1981.

Wade, Richard C. _Slavery in the Cities: The South, 1820–1860._ New York: Oxford University Press, 1964.

Wallace, Anthony F. C. _Rockdale: The Growth of an American Village in the Early Industrial Revolution._ New York: Alfred A. Knopf, 1978.

Wallace, Michael. "Changing Concepts of Party in the United States: New York, 1815–1828," _American Historical Review_, LXXIV (December 1968), 453–91.

Walters, Raymond, Jr. _Alexander James Dallas: Lawyer—Politician—Financier 1759–1817._ Philadelphia: University of Pennsylvania Press, 1943.

Ward, John William. _Andrew Jackson: Symbol of an Age._ New York: Oxford University Press, 1955.

Warner, Sam Bass, Jr. _The Private City: Philadelphia in Three Periods of Its Growth._ Philadelphia: University of Pennsylvania Press, 1968.

Watson, Harry L. _Jacksonian Politics and Community Conflict: The Emergence of the Second American Party System in Cumberland County, North Carolina._ Baton Rouge: Louisiana State University Press, 1981.

Wells, Robert V. "Family History and Demographic Transition," _Journal of Social History_, IX (Fall 1975), 1–19.

Welter, Barbara. "The Cult of True Womanhood: 1820–1860," _American Quarterly_, XVII (Summer 1966), 151–74.

Wiecek, William M. _The Sources of Antislavery Constitutionalism in America, 1760–1848._ Ithaca: Cornell University Press, 1977.

Wills, Garry. _Inventing America: Jefferson's Declaration of Independence._ Garden City: Doubleday, 1978.

Wood, Gordon S. _The Creation of the American Republic 1776–1787._ Chapel Hill: University of North Carolina Press, 1969.

Woodman, Harold D. _King Cotton & His Retainers: Financing & Marketing the Cotton Crop of the South, 1800–1925._ Lexington: University of Kentucky Press, 1968.

Wooster, Ralph A. _The People in Power: Courthouse and Statehouse in the Lower South 1850–1860._ Knoxville: University of Tennessee Press, 1969.

Wright, Conrad. _The Beginnings of Unitarianism in America._ Hamden: Archon, 1976 [1955].

Wright, Gavin. _The Political Economy of the Cotton South: Households, Markets, and Wealth in the Nineteenth Century._ New York: W. W. Norton, 1978.

Wyatt-Brown, Bertram. _Lewis Tappan and the Evangelical War Against Slavery._ Cleveland: Press of Case Western Reserve University, 1969.

———. "Prelude to Abolitionism: Sabbatarian Politics and the Rise of the Second Party System," *Journal of American History*, LVIII (September 1971), 316–41.

Young, Alfred F. *The Democratic Republicans of New York: The Origins 1763–1797*. Chapel Hill: University of North Carolina Press, 1967.

Young, James Sterling. *The Washington Community 1800–1828*. New York: Columbia University Press, 1966.

Index

Abbott, Jacob, 269
abolition movement, 244, 272, 285, 306, 313, 318, 319, 320, 331, 343, 355, 369, 370
abortions, 164
Adams, Abigail, 43, 50
Adams, John, 4, 11, 13, 14, 16, 42, 43, 50, 66, 72, 80, 184, 187, 355, 373; envoy to Britain, 17; and Hamilton, 106–8; and Jefferson, 88, 110; as president, 50, 91–4, 99, 103–9, 112, 121, 123; reputation of, 15, 102, 104, 107, 170; as vice-president, 51, 52, 75
Adams, John Quincy, 85, 137, 138, 180, 199, 302, 355; as congressman, 239; as president, 216, 217, 233, 235; reputation of, 235; as secretary of state, 192, 193
Adams, Samuel, 26
Addison, Alexander, 93
agriculture, see farming
Alabama, 132
Albany Regency, 204, 205, 211, 250
alcohol consumption, 164, 274, 275, 292, 316–18, 329, 334
Alcott, William, 163
Alien and Alien Enemies Act, 93
Alien and Sedition Acts, 91, 93, 95, 96, 97, 100, 106, 119, 120, 223
Amendments to the Constitution, see Constitutional Amendments
American Anti-Slavery Society, 244
American Bible Society, 231
American Colonization Society, 339, 340
American Federation of Labor, 382
American Home Mission Society, 166, 231
American Legal Association, 308
American party, 365, 366
American Social Science Association, 379
American Society for the Promotion of Temperance, 317
American Sunday School Union, 231
American System, 216–17, 218, 232, 235, 237, 240, 241, 242, 252
American Temperance Society, 164, 231, 232, 317
American Tract Society, 231

Ames, Fisher, 40, 70, 79, 101, 104, 112, 113, 116, 118, 136, 178, 192
Amish community, 284
Annapolis Convention, 4
anti-Catholicism, 335–7, 339, 365, 368
antifederalists, 10, 36, 39, 40, 41, 46, 55, 56, 65, 72, 82, 84; and Constitution, 26–32
Anti-Masonic party, 156
antimonopoly leagues, 382
antimony, 162
Appalachian Mountains, 132, 146, 215
Appleton, Nathan, 146, 149
apprenticeships, 266, 267, 270
architecture, 292–3
aristocracy, 5, 10, 22, 23, 25, 27, 36, 54, 60, 63
Arkansas, 132
Arminianism, 144, 160
army, national, 9, 25, 32, 48, 62, 63, 69, 81, 91, 94, 97, 116, 124
Arnold, Benedict, 328
Articles of Confederation, 3, 4, 23, 26, 27, 54, 133
arts, 168, 283, 354
Asbury, Francis, 158–9, 165–6
Association of Medical Superintendents, 311
asylums, 323, 336
Atchison, David, 364
Atlantic and Michigan Railroad, 141
Auburn Prison, 311
Aurora (newspaper), 178

Bache, Benjamin, 102
Baldwin, Roger, 364
Baltic Sea, 148
Baltimore, Maryland, 141, 148, 166
Baltimore and Ohio Railroad, 204
Bank of Baltimore, 153
Bank of Maryland, 153
Bank of Pennsylvania, 153
Bank of Philadelphia, 153
Bank of the United States: First, 198; Second, 218–21, 226, 229, 232, 233, 238–41, 252, 302, 317 n.

bankruptcy, 139, 226, 227, 301, 348
banks and banking, 150–4, 195, 196, 203, 204, 211, 238–40, 258, 263, 300–2, 324, 325, 351, 381; charters, 152–4; and depression, 154; national, 47, 57, 59, 62, 95; state, 153, 240, 245
Bank Wars, 241, 251
Baptists, 157, 158, 159, 167, 280, 281, 303–6, 343
bar associations, 307
Barbour, James, 203
Barker-Benfield, G. J., 317 n.
Barnard, Henry, 272, 309, 311, 323, 332
Barnum, P. T., 277
Bayard, James, 13, 76, 104, 169–70, 180, 183, 186
Becker, Carl, 89
Beckley, John, 83
Beecher, Henry Ward, 274, 276, 286, 289, 328
Beecher, Lyman, 129, 160, 230, 232, 367
behavior, social, 328–30
Bell, John, 372
Bellamy, Edward, 382
Benevolent Empire, 231–2, 243, 244, 245, 304, 305, 313, 317, 319
Benton, Thomas Hart, 205, 207, 246, 363, 367
Bible readings, 278
Biddle, Nicholas, 129, 179, 227, 229; and U.S. Bank, 218–21, 232, 233, 238–41, 317 n.
Bill of Rights, 29, 32, 33, 40, 54, 119
Binney, Horace, 331
birth control, 163
birth rate, 164
blacks: churches, 341; after Civil War, 376, 377, 380; and courts, 342; education, 341; free, 37, 339, 341, 342, 347, 369; rights, 339; violence against, 339, 366; and the vote, 167; see also slavery
Blackstone, Sir William, 11, 307
Blair, Francis P., 298
Blair, John, 114
Blithedale Romance, The (Hawthorne), 278
Bloomfield, Joseph, 195
body, 277, 307; see also health; medicine
Bonaparte, Napoleon, 105, 113, 171, 172, 173, 177, 178, 183, 191, 237
Boston, growth of, 148
Boston associates, 263
Boudinot, Elias, 212
Braintree, Massachusetts, 13
Breckenridge, John C., 372
Bremer, Fredrika, 270

bribery, 69
bridges, 139, 153
Brown, Alexander, 150
Brown, John, 370
Brown Brothers, 150
Browning, Orville, 261, 298
Bryan, Samuel, 36
Buchanan, James, 207, 246, 363; as president, 369, 370, 371
Buffon, Comte George Louis de, 18
Burgh, James, 41
Burke, Aedanus, 40
Burnap, George, 163, 271–2, 349
Burr, Aaron, 12–13, 49, 52, 373; charge of treason, 124, 175; duel with Hamilton, 99–100; as vice-president, 110
Burritt, Elihu, 313
Bushnell, Horace, 268, 277, 283, 323, 349, 361
business, 154, 257–64; competition in, 262; and laborers, 326, 327; small, 327, 332, 334, 335; see also commerce; credit; labor
Butler, Pierce, 117

Cabot, George, 49, 91
Calhoun, John C., 137, 138, 190, 296, 297, 298, 343; background, 210, 211, 216; and Monroe, 209, 212; and Second U.S. Bank, 218; and slavery, 360–3, 367; as vice-president, 238–40, 246–8
California, 358, 360, 363
Callander, James, 103
Calvinism, 84, 145, 157, 159, 160, 288, 304, 335
Campbell, Alexander, 158, 305, 381
Campbell, George, 186
canals, 137, 139, 140, 141, 142, 150, 151, 153, 156, 192, 203, 204, 217, 228, 262, 285; see also Erie Canal; transportation
Cane Ridge camp meeting, 157
Canning, George, 182, 192
capitalism, 193, 243, 258, 263, 334
capital, national, 50, 59
Carey, Henry C., 282
Carrington, Edward, 102
Carter, James, 309
cartography, 141
Cartwright, Peter, 159, 161, 289, 296, 305, 312
Catholics, 37, 255, 331, 347, 351; Protestant prejudice against, 335–7, 339, 365, 368
Catron, John, 302
caucuses, 155, 204–5, 211

census (1820), 148
centralizers, 72, 78, 86, 123, 131; and
    Constitution, 24–33 *passim; see also*
    Federalist party
Channing, William Ellery, 289
character, 12–16, 20, 41, 236, 269, 271, 277,
    329
Charles River Bridge v. *Warren Bridge*,
    242
Chase, Samuel, 223, 224
Cherokee Indians, 242, 345, 346
Chesapeake incident, 171, 173, 175, 177,
    178, 187
Chesapeake and Ohio Canal, 204
Chevalier, Michel, 230, 251, 271, 286, 289,
    302, 322
Cheves, Langdon, 218, 226
Chickasaw Indians, 345
Child, Lydia Maria, 166
children and child-rearing, 163, 230, 265–
    72, 275–81, 288, 289, 323, 383, 384
Chillicothe Junto, 204
China, 148, 150
Chippewa Indians, 346
Choctaw Indians, 345
Christ, second coming of, 284, 313, 318,
    320
Christianity, 145, 280, 283, 307, 329; *see
    also individual denominations*
civil rights, 383
Civil War, 256, 264, 374–6
classes, social, 321–2, 335, 346–51, 381–4
Clay, Henry: background, 129, 137, 138,
    171, 184, 187, 188, 190, 191, 210, 211,
    217, 218, 229, 232, 233, 351, 354; and
    compromise of 1833, 241; as
    congressman, 194, 200, 202, 207, 238;
    and Missouri Compromise, 214–16;
    presidential candidacy, 239, 240, 296,
    298; as senator, 250; and slavery, 360,
    361
Clayton, John M., 370
Clinton, DeWitt, 140, 155, 185, 195–9
Clinton, George, 134, 180; and
    Constitution, 26, 101; as governor of
    New York, 43, 196
Cobbett, William, 102
Cohens v. *Virginia*, 227
coins, 61
Coles, Edward, 340
Coltin, Calvin, 283
Commentaries (Story), 227
commerce, 24, 140–51 *passim*, 170, 172,
    174, 257–64; British maritime rules on,
    17, 74–5, 79, 112, 138–9; French rules
on, 17; interior, 164, 200, 298, 300, 303;
    international, 138, 148, 150, 242; and
    Panic of 1837, 261, 263; urban, 259; and
    Walker Tariff, 263; western, 149, 150,
    260; *see also* business; trade
common law, 223, 224, 308
communism, 383
communitarian experiments, 314, 330, 331,
    382
community, role of individual in, 280–3
comprehensive programs, 209–33 *passim*,
    244, 247, 255
Compromise of 1850, 296, 360, 361
Concord Regency, 204
Confederacy, 373, 376, 377
Congregationalists, 160, 229, 244, 280, 281,
    304, 305
Congress, 3, 4, 33, 49, 59, 61, 64, 83, 94, 95,
    169, 295; first, 32; personnel changes, 82;
    and Pre-emption Act, 152; and public
    land, 147; and Sedition Act, 106, 117;
    and War of 1812, 186, 187
Connecticut, 199
conspiracies, fear of, 367, 369, 370, 372
Constitution, 4, 5, 10, 20, 22, 36, 37, 39, 42,
    121, 374; amendments proposed, 31–2;
    attitudes and opinions on, 40, 41, 54, 55,
    63, 64, 68, 74, 78, 85, 93–6, 369;
    commerce clause, 228, 243; drafting of,
    21–34 *passim*; ratification of, 31, 32, 33,
    40, 87; signers of, 25, 31; and slavery, 24;
    and states' rights, 134, 247–8; Supreme
    Court interpretation, 224–8; three-fifths
    clause, 24, 202
Constitutional Amendments, 31–3; Tenth,
    33, 95; Eleventh, 94; Twelfth, 119;
    Thirteenth, 376; Fourteenth, 377;
    Fifteenth, 377
Constitutional Convention, 4, 12, 15, 21,
    24–34, 35–44, 49, 55, 58, 63, 69, 101
Constitutional Union party, 372
Continental Army, 44
Continental Congress, 15, 69; First, 3;
    Second, 3
Continental Navy, 44
Convention of 1800, 108
Conway, Martin, 374
Cooper, James Fenimore, 344
Corning, Erastus, 150, 263
corruption, 41, 62, 65, 368
cotton industry, 148, 191, 258, 259, 260,
    325, 343, 357
courage, 98
courts, and treatment of the poor, 347–8
Coxe, Tench, 197

Crawford, William, 206, 207
credit, 150–1, 153, 154, 211, 219–21, 238, 239, 259–63, 294, 299, 300–2, 324, 327, 357, 364, 381; international, 191, 220, 259, 298–303, 325; ratings, 301
Creek Nation, 9, 345
Crick, Bernard, 373
criminals, 310, 311, 323
Crittenden, John J., 297, 366
Croswell, Edwin, 298
Crowninshield, Jacob, 170
culture, 265–90 passim
currency, 18, 61, 219–20, 260; hard, 240, 241, 302; paper, 53–4, 151, 153, 154, 243; paper v. hard, 151
Cushing, Caleb, 359
Cushing's Manual, 292

Dallas, Alexander, 8, 212
Dallas, George M., 302
Dana, Francis, 224
Dana, Richard Henry, 342
Dana, Samuel, 186
Dane, Nathan, 133, 312
Dartmouth College v. Woodward, 225, 226
Davis, Jefferson, 162, 361
Dayton, Jonathan, 185
Dearborn, Henry, 170
DeBow, J. D. B., 293
debt, 154, 165, 333; national, funding and programs, 50, 57, 58, 59, 62, 63, 64, 75, 168, 170, 191
Declaration of Independence, 8, 51, 74
Deism, 84, 144, 160
Delaware, 136
democracy, 10, 12, 22, 23, 28, 79, 129, 155, 167, 207, 211, 255
Democracy in America (Tocqueville), 285
Democratic party, 250, 251, 252, 294, 297, 298, 351, 358, 372; created, 249
democratic-republican societies, 73–4, 80, 82
Democratic Society of Pennsylvania, 118
depressions: 1820s, 147, 148, 154, 192, 201, 203; 1837–1840s, 192, 244, 245, 251, 300, 324, 325, 334, 360; 1850s, 371; 1870s, 377; 1890s, 382
despotism, 27, 28, 40, 72, 133
development policies, 152–4, 169, 180, 188–9, 194–8, 203–6
devil, the, 160, 161, 372
Dickerson, Mahlon, 197, 199, 205, 206, 207
Dickerson, Silas, 197
Dickinson, John, 31, 91, 119, 136
diet, 277

diseases, 161
Disciples of Christ, 305
doctors, 145, 161–4; see also health; medicine
Donelson, Andrew Jackson, 237
Douglas, Stephen A., 297, 330, 354, 362–4, 367, 370, 373
Douglass, Frederick, 343
Dow, Lorenzo, 306
Downing, Andrew Jackson, 292
dowries, 266
Dred Scott case, 370, 371
drinking, see alcohol comsumption
Duane, William, 102, 117, 169, 183, 198
dueling code, 99–100, 185–6, 187, 328–9
dueling war, 187, 188
Dwight, Theodore, 212
Dwight, Timothy, 230, 231

Eaton, Peggy, 237–8
economy, 59, 63; commercial 1820s–40s, 257–64; growth rate during 1840s–50s, 322; post–Civil War, 380–3; and social classes, 351; see also credit
education, 166, 168, 272, 308–13, 331–5, 355–6, 362
Edwards, Justin, 165, 317
Egypt, 105
elections, 14, 23, 24, 25, 36, 119, 145, 155, 294–6; national, 81, 83–4; state, 83, 84, 154; see also presidential elections
Elements of Law, The (Hilliard), 307
Ellicott, Joseph, 197
Ellsworth, Oliver, 31, 73
emancipation, 338, 343
Embargo Act, 174–83 passim
Emerson, Ralph Waldo, 282, 283, 286, 323, 349, 379
empires, 133, 134
energy sources, 262
England, see Great Britain
Episcopalianism, 84
Erie Canal, 132, 140, 141, 143, 165, 192, 198, 203, 205, 258, 260, 288
Erikson, Erik, 50 n.
Erskine, David, 182, 185
Essex decision, 171, 174
estates, 13
etiquette, 292
Europe: society and attitudes, 16–19; and wars in (1793–1814), 19, 67–78, 80, 82, 86, 90–3, 104, 105, 107, 112, 143, 148, 150, 169–80
Eustis, William, 180

Evans, George, 332
executive: form of government, 22–5;
   power, 48, 54–5, 57, 61, 69, 78–9, 86, 94,
   96, 115
exercise, 277
exports, 174, 191, 192

factories, 264, 331
family: life, 255, 265–9; patriarchal, 266,
   267, 274; *see also* men; women
farmers' alliances, 382
Farmers and Mechanics Bank, 153
farming, 147, 152, 260, 263, 281, 287, 324–
   7, 347, 348, 355–7, 364; and credit, 324,
   325; income, 147; machinery, 326
Farwell, John V., 278
"Federal Farmer," 26, 27, 28, 33, 38, 41
federal government, and states' rights, *see*
   states' rights
federalism, "dual," 248
Federalist, the, 48, 69, 122; #10, 30, 31, 84;
   #22, 70; #37, 48; #39, 31;#45, 31; #46,
   31; #51, 31; #67, 101
Federalist party, 80–98 *passim,* 106–24
   passim, 169, 174, 177–87, 192, 224, 350;
   and Constitutional debate, 26–33; and
   debating style, 98–104; demise of, 194,
   195, 200, 206; emergence of, 15, 35–9,
   48, 49, 55, 61, 72; formed, 80; and
   westward expansion, 136; *see also*
   antifederalists
Female Reform Society, 316
Fenno, John, 102
Finney, Charles Grandison, 159, 160, 161,
   232, 275, 276, 280, 281, 286, 288, 289,
   306, 328
firearms industry, 261
fire-fighting, 331
Fitzhugh, George, 300, 343
flag, U.S., 354
Fletcher v. *Peck,* 225
Flint, Timothy, 307, 309
Florida, 172, 236
food production, 325, 326
forms, 60 and *n.*
Forstall Act, 324
Fowler, Lorenzo, 328
Fowler, Orson, 328
Fox Indians, 345
France, 10, 16, 18; and American
   commerce, 17; American-French
   Alliance, 18–19, 69–71, 101; Directory,
   68, 90, 105; and Louisiana Purchase, 112;
   revolutionary, relations with U.S., 19, 69–
   78, 80, 82, 86, 90–3, 105, 107, 112, 182,

187; territory, 132; at war with Britain,
   68, 70, 80; at war with Spain, 70
Franklin, Benjamin, 42, 165
French Revolution, 5, 49, 67–8, 72, 73, 74,
   76, 80, 81, 83, 117–18, 143
Fries, John, 147
Fugitive Slave Act, 362, 369, 370
Fuller, Margaret, 315

Gallatin, Albert, 92, 141, 197, 212, 236; as
   secretary of treasury, 111, 114, 170, 175,
   177, 181, 182, 188, 190
gambling, 230, 274, 276, 316, 318
Gardenier, Barent, 186
Garrison, William Lloyd, 313, 314, 319,
   320, 367, 374
Gazette of the United States, 59, 60
General Land Office, 353
Genet, Edmond, 71, 72, 80, 101
gentry, 7–20, 22, 23, 37, 40, 43; and
   upholding honor through debate and
   duel, 98–104
geography, 117
George, Henry, 378
George III, King of England, 74
Germans: immigrants, 337; Pennsylvania,
   350–1
Gerry, Elbridge, 15, 21, 43, 44, 68, 119; and
   Constitutional Convention, 25, 26, 27,
   31; as governor of Massachusetts, 198;
   and XYZ mission to France, 90, 91, 105
Gibbons v. *Ogden,* 228
Giles, William Branch, 65, 82, 88, 122, 223;
   as senator, 169
Goodrich, Chauncey, 117, 202
Gore, Christopher, 103, 199
Gouge, William, 302
Graham, James, 348
Graham, Sylvester, 162, 166, 275
Granger, Gideon, 84, 170
Great Britain: alliance with Spain, 70;
   credit, 191, 220, 259, 298–303, 325;
   defeat in American Revolution, 16;
   economy of, 191, 220, 259; impressment
   of American seamen, 182, 185, 338;
   industry, 257, 258, 261, 263; maritime
   rules, 17, 74–5, 79, 138–9, 188; raid on
   Washington, 189; relations with U.S.
   during European wars, 70, 74–80, 82, 91,
   95, 107, 112, 191; trade, 148, 149; and
   War of 1812, 148, 184–7, 191; war with
   France, 68, 70, 80
Great Revival, 157, 158, 159, 165
Greece, 192
Greenough, William, 358

Gresham's Law, 307
Grimké, Frederick, 248
Gross National Product, 383
Grove, William Barry, 72
Grundy, Felix, 184, 297
guilt, 277, 279, 280, 281
Gulf of Mexico, 132, 136

habit, 271–2
Haddock, Charles B., 312
Hall, James, 282, 349
Hamilton, Alexander, 4–5, 9, 13, 16, 17, 18, 36, 38, 41, 78, 81, 82, 92–4, 99; and Adams, 106–8; and Burr, 49, 99–100; and Constitutional Convention, 29, 30, 31, 58, 70, 101; domestic programs, 85, 86; reputation, 13, 102, 104; as secretary of treasury, 45–64, 67, 70–7, 106; and western expansion, 134, 136; and Whiskey Rebellion, 72–3
Hancock, John, 39, 43
Harper, Robert Goodloe, 197
Harpers Ferry, Brown's raid on, 370, 371
Harrison, William Henry, 250
Hartford Convention, 201, 202, 212, 235
Hartley, Robert, 311
Hawes, Joel, 271, 278
Hawthorne, Nathaniel, 278
Hayes, Rutherford B., 288
Hayne, Robert Young, 210
health, 145, 161–5, 277, 307, 331, 379
hell, 269–70
Helper, Hinton Rowan, 366
Hemmings, Sally, 13
Henry, Patrick, 12, 15, 26, 43, 65, 355
Henshaw, David, 207
hierarchy, social, 11, 12, 21, 36, 40, 44, 83, 144, 145, 152, 165, 166, 248, 249; *see also* social classes
Hiester, Joseph, 199
Hill, Isaac, 296
Hilliard, Francis, 307, 308
historical associations, 286
Holland, 191
Holland Land Company, 197
Holmes, Oliver Wendell, 328
honor, 16, 39, 46, 98–104, 198, 236, 355
households, 13, 265–6, 276
House of Representatives, 25, 27–8, 31, 49, 56, 64, 65, 95, 250; and democratic-republican clubs, 74; and Jay Treaty, 79, 80; Ways and Means Committee, 94; *see also* Congress; Senate
Houston, Sam, 363

Howe, Samuel Gridley, 314, 374
Howells, William Dean, 382
Hull, William, 189
Hume, David, 35
Hunter, David, 329
Hutchinson, Thomas, 367
hydropathy, 162
hygiene, 277

"Idea of a Perfect Commonwealth" (Hume), 35
Illinois, 132, 147
immigrants, 255, 326, 335–7, 339, 365, 366, 368, 378, 383
impeachment, 25, 36
imports, 174, 191, 192, 259, 262, 263
independence, 17, 169, 184, 196, 197
Indiana, 203; statehood, 132, 147
Indians, American, *see* Native Americans
Industrial Revolution, 256
industry, 153, 168, 191, 257–64, 331, 376
infants, 268, 269; damnation, 280; mortality, 163
Ingersoll, Charles J., 184
insanity, 310, 311, 323, 336
inventors, 286
Iowa, 132
Iredell, James, 97
Ireland, 93
Irish immigrants, 326, 335–7, 339, 347, 365, 368
iron industry, 256, 259, 261, 262, 263
Irving, Washington, 179
Izard, Ralph, 49

Jackson, Andrew, 91, 130, 273, 296, 354, 355, 362, 367; background, 235, 236; and Biddle's Bank, 238–42; candidacies, 206, 207, 234–6; as congressman, 235; and Native Americans, 346; as president, 237–50; reputation, 235, 236, 237; and Revolution, 235, 236; and War of 1812, 190
Jackson, James, 136
Jackson, Rachel, 237
Jacobin Terror, 68, 72, 80, 84, 97
Jarvis, Edward, 336
Jay, John, 3, 9, 14, 16, 19, 22, 23, 35, 39, 49, 61, 92, 93, 97; and Constitutional Convention, 23, 29, 68–9; and Jay Treaty, 19, 75–7, 81, 85; and Missouri Compromise, 213; negotiations with Gardoqui, 202; as Supreme Court justice, 223; and western expansion, 133
Jay, Sarah Livingston, 266

Jay Treaty, 16, 45, 46, 75–81, 85, 88, 90, 91, 105, 185
Jefferson, Thomas, 4, 5, 9, 11, 12, 17, 18, 35, 40, 41, 42, 43, 70–89 *passim*, 184, 188, 192, 213, 215, 219, 223, 236; characterization and reputation of, 13, 15, 51, 98, 99, 100, 102, 108, 135, 162; and Constitution, 30, 33, 68, 115; and Declaration of Independence, 8, 51, 74; domestic policy of, 119, 120, 124, 171, 175; embargo policy of, 113, 124; and executive power, 69; foreign policy of, 120, 171, 175; and French Alliance, 101; as governor of Virginia, 14, 99; and Kentucky, 134–5; and Kentucky Resolutions, 95, 96; and Louisiana Purchase, 112; as minister to France, 8, 10, 14, 17, 22, 51, 53, 54, 58, 70, 72, 112, 113, 136; and Monticello, 13, 236; and Native Americans, 345, 346; as president, 14, 20, 48, 51, 110–24, 131, 134–6, 168–84 *passim*; and religion, 144; retirement of, 67, 176; and Revolution, 52, 53; and revolution of 1800, 110, 112, 122, 123, 225; as secretary of state, 44–66, 106, and slavery, 213, 340; as vice-president, 92–5; and western expansion, 134, 141
Johnson, Tom, 379
judiciary, 22, 24, 25

Kansas: statehood, 373; Territory, 363–4, 370
Kent, James, 312
Kentucky, 132, 134
Kentucky Resolutions, 95, 96, 111, 121, 135, 202
Kierkegaard, Sören, 200
King, Edward, 137, 138
King, Rufus, 15, 21, 44, 70, 173, 183, 185, 189, 200, 202, 211, 212, 215, 216, 226, 236, 266–7; and Constitution, 24, 38, 39; death of, 232; as minister to Britain, 17, 78, 92, 108; and slavery, 214, 339; and westward expansion, 136–7
King, William, 199–200
Knights of Labor, 382
Know-Nothing (American) party, 365–6
Knox, Henry, 44; as secretary of war, 44, 106, 345

labor, 347; farm, 347; reform, 332–4, 347; skilled, 332, 335; transient, 326, 327, 330, 334, 335, 347, 348; unions, 156; urban, 347

Ladd, William, 313
Lafayette, Marquis de, 42
Lancaster Turnpike, 139
land: bonanzas, 144; development, 242, 252, 322; distribution, 164; government, 147, 152; public, 147, 216, 217, 332, 333; speculation, 138, 139, 140, 147, 150, 153, 170, 197, 252; squatters, 147, 152
Lane, Harriet, 356
Latin America, 192, 360
Latter-Day Saints, 284
Law, Thomas, 197
law, 222–9, 232–3, 308, 379; lawyers, 223, 224; practice, 307–8, 312
Lawrence, Abbott, 295
Lawrence, James, 190
Lee, Richard Henry, 3, 16, 19, 22, 23, 54; and Constitutional Convention, 26, 27, 33; and western expansion, 133, 134
Leggett, William, 156
legislature, 22; bicameral, 24; caucuses, 155
Leib, Michael, 198
Lewis, Morgan, 195
libel suits, 100
Lincoln, Abraham, 296, 300, 367, 370, 371; as president, 354, 356, 369, 372, 373, 374
Lincoln, Levi, 170
Lincoln, Mary Todd, 356
literacy, 166, 309
literature, 354, 382
livestock, 357
Livingston, Robert R., 19
Lloyd, James, 93
Loco-Focoism, 349
Louis XVI, King of France, 68, 72
Louisiana Purchase, 112, 115, 122, 124, 131, 135, 136, 191, 213, 358
Lovejoy, Elijah, 320
Lowell community, 331
Lyon, Matthew, 135

McCulloch v. Maryland, 225, 226, 229
McGuffey, William Holmes, 289
McHenry, James, 44, 106, 108
machinery, 262
McKean, Thomas, 37, 85, 99, 122, 195
Maclay, William, 102
Macon, Nathaniel, 137, 171, 179
Macune, Charles, 382
Madison, Dolly Payne Todd, 13
Madison, James, 5, 8, 9, 10, 12, 14, 16, 36–71 *passim*, 78–89, 101, 155, 223, 236; and Bill of Rights, 32, 33, 40;

Madison, James (*cont.*)
  characterization of, 13, 15, 98, 104; and
    Constitution, 55, 56, 180, 247–8; and
    Constitutional Convention, 22–34, 35;
    and *Federalist*, 124; as president, 176,
    180–90, 198, 200, 201, 202, 212; as
    secretary of state, 112, 114, 115, 120, 121,
    122, 170, 175; and slavery, 213; and
    Virginia Plan, 133; and Virginia
    Resolutions, 94–6, 134–5
Maine, 199, 215
Manhattan Company Bank, 153
Manifest Destiny, 358
Mann, Horace, 163, 165, 269–77, 285, 309,
  349
manufacturing, *see* industry
Marbury v. *Madison*, 225, 226
maritime: opportunity, 144–9; policy, 16,
  174–83
marriage, 270, 271, 316, 338; arranged, 266;
  interracial, 342, 344, 347
Marshall, John, 42, 70, 74, 99, 119, 161,
  162, 221–2; minister to France, 90, 91; as
  Supreme Court justice, 222–9, 236, 242,
  243
Martineau, Harriet, 142, 211, 228, 269, 271,
  307, 329, 358
Maryland, 36, 199, 204
Mason, George, 44, 46; and Constitution,
  27, 28, 31, 63; on executive power, 69;
  and western expansion, 134
Masons, 368
Massachusetts: and Constitution, 26, 30,
  32, 33, 87; politics, 196, 198, 199
Massachusetts Hospital Life Insurance
  Company, 263
Mechanics' Bank, 153, 154
Mechanics Society, 165
mechanization, 326, 332
medical associations, 307
medicine, 145, 161–5, 307, 379
Mediterranean Sea, 148
Meigs, Return Jonathan, 154
men: brawls and fights, 328; role of, in
  family, 265–70, 275, 278, 384; young
  adulthood of, 270–5, 278
mental illness, 323, 336
Mercantile Agency, 301
Merchants Bank, 153, 195
mercury, 161, 162
metals, 251, 259, 263
Methodists, 157, 158, 159, 166, 280, 281,
  288, 303–6, 341, 343
metric system, 217
Mexican Americans, 347

Mexican War, 358, 359, 360
Mexico, 142, 357
Miami Indians, 345
Michigan, 132
migration, 147, 324–7, 330; *see also*
  westward expansion and migration
military titles, 99
Millerite movement, 284, 313, 318, 320
Mississippi, 132
Mississippi River, 75; navigation rights to,
  133, 134
Mississippi Valley, 132
Missouri, 202; statehood, 132, 147, 201,
  202
Missouri Compromise, 203, 212, 213, 215,
  216; line, 360, 363
monarchy, fears of, 5, 10, 11, 12, 18, 22, 23,
  25, 27, 54, 60, 74, 78, 96, 115
money market, 256
monocrats, 121, 122
monopolies, 156, 206, 207, 229, 239, 243,
  290, 378, 381, 382
Monroe, James, 12, 14, 99, 104, 136, 218;
  and Constitution, 26, 181; as minister to
  Britain, 172, 185, 190; as minister to
  France, 19, 44, 76, 77, 90; and Monroe
  Doctrine, 192; and Northwest
  Ordinance, 133; as president, 52, 63, 192,
  193, 198, 200–1, 206, 215, 228;
  retirement of, 232; as secretary of state,
  181
Monroe Doctrine, 192
Montesquieu, Baron Charles de Secondat
  de, 26, 30, 135, 136
Monticello, 13, 236
Moody, Dwight, 379
morality, 229–32, 269–88, 309, 316
Morgan, Charles, 221
Morgan, J. Pierpont, 380
Mormons, 167, 305, 347
Morris, Gouverneur, 9, 19, 66, 198; and
  Constitution, 31; as minister to France,
  44
Morris, Robert, 114, 138, 139; as secretary
  of treasury, 44, 47
Morse, Samuel F. B., 336
mortgages, 324
Mount Vernon, 13
Murray, William Vans, 87

Nashoba community, 355
Nashville Junto, 204
National Banking Act, 380
National Gazette, 59, 102
nationalism, 34, 38, 39

National Road, 140, 217, 242
Native Americans, 167, 242, 250, 255, 344–6
natural sciences, 311
navy, 9, 91
Negroes, *see* blacks
neocolonialism, 18, 20, 68, 71, 76, 77, 78, 80, 88, 104, 112, 122, 172, 178, 192
Nettleton, Asahel, 160
Neutrality Proclamation, 70, 71, 80
New England, 117–19, 178
New Guide to Health (Thomson), 162
New Hampshire, 195, 199
New Harmony community, 314, 331
New Jersey, 195–9
New Orleans, 172, 174, 178, 259; battle of, 190
newspapers, 102, 103, 116, 121, 178, 201, 205, 294, 313
New York: and Constitution, 26, 30, 32, 33, 40, 49, 58; government of, 43, 195–9; growth of, 140, 148
New York Central Railroad, 150
New York City: port of, 141, 259; as religious headquarters, 231, 232
New York *Evening Post*, 156
Nicholas, Wilson Cary, 38, 111
Nicholson, John, 138, 139
north (U.S.), 355–66, 374, 375
North Carolina, 195, 200
Northwest Ordinance, 133
Northwest Territory, 135–9, 230; *see also* westward expansion
Noyes, John Humphrey, 314, 355
Nullification Proclamation, 246, 356
nunneries, 274, 336

Ohio: canals, 141; politics, 197–9; statehood, 132; transportation development, 203
O'Kelly, James, 158
Oneida community, 314, 355
Oneida Manufacturing Company, 195
oratory, 166, 293
Oregon Territory, 357
Ottawa Indians, 346
Owen, Robert, 314, 331

packets, transatlantic, 191
Paine, Thomas, 9, 18, 84, 102, 103, 145
painting, 354
pamphleteers, 102
panics: of 1819, 192, 201; of 1837, 192, 241, 300

"Paper System, the," 53–4
parallelism, 287–90, 314, 320, 362, 363, 368, 371, 374, 381
parties, political, 177–9, 180, 184, 294–8, 303; campaigns, 207, 295, 298; caucuses, 155; after Civil War, 377, 378; competition between, 118, 119, 120, 123, 124; conventions, 295, 298; first formed, 80; loyalty, 296; national, 82–3; nomination methods, 155; and sectionalism, 371–2; slogans, 295–6; and social classes, 349, 350; state, 82–3; after War of 1812, 199; worker's, 156; *see also* Constitutional Union party; Democratic party; Federalist party; Know-Nothing (American) party; Republican party; Whig party
patriotism, 20
Paulding, James K., 249
pediatrics, 163
Pendleton, Edmund, 36, 37, 52, 85, 114, 115; and Constitution, 30
Pennsylvania: and events leading to Whiskey Rebellion, 63, 64, 72–3; government of, 22, 43; growth and population, 140; politics, 195–9; transportation development, 203
Pennsylvania Constitution, 11
Pennsylvania Germans, 37, 195
Perkins, Thomas, 149, 150
Perry, Oliver Hazard, 190
Peters, Richard, 308
Phelps, Dodge and Co., 259, 263
Philadelphia, 141, 148
Philadelphia Convention of 1787, *see* Constitutional Convention
philanthropy, 330, 331
Phillips, Wendell, 272, 319
phrenology, 328
Pickens, Francis W., 359
Pickering, Timothy, 46, 99, 136, 222; as secretary of state, 106, 107, 108; and slavery, 339
Pinckney, Charles Cotesworth, 17, 84, 106, 107, 136, 180, 213; as minister to France, 90
Pinkney, William, 173, 212
plantations, 356, 364
Plumer, William, 9, 118, 169, 171–2, 185, 199, 224
poetry, 283
Poland, 68
police, 331
police state action, 33
politicians, debating style, 98–104

politics: of development, 152–4, 169, 180, 188–9, 194–8, 203–6; division between electoral and legislative, 349–50; of social class, race, and religion, 349–51, 364, 365, 366, 367
Polk, James K., 241; as president, 241, 250, 358, 359
poor whites, 255, 310, 322, 323, 332, 333, 336, 347–8, 366, 367
popular sovereignty, 155, 156
population: black, 340; from 1824 to 1840, 249; total, 132, 249, 325; of Virginia, 146
populism, 349
Porter, Peter B., 197
ports, 141, 148, 149, 151, 258, 259
Potawatomi Indians, 346
predestination, 157, 158, 160, 167
Pre-emption Act, 152
pregnancy, 276
premillennialism, 284, 313, 318, 320
Presbygationists, 229, 230
Presbyterians, 157, 159, 160, 229, 280, 281, 304–6, 341; split in 1837, 244
presidency, 27, 36, 61; and impeachment, 25, 36; term of, 25, 52
presidential elections, 234, 249, 294, 295, 298, 348
press, 102, 103, 116, 121, 178, 201, 205, 294, 313
prisons, 310, 311, 323
Progress and Poverty (Johnson), 379
prohibition, 318; *see also* temperance movement
promiscuity, 274
property rights, 225, 226, 228, 242, 324
Prosser, Gabriel, 341
prostitution, 163, 316
Protestantism, 145, 164, 166, 229–31, 244, 274, 280, 289, 303–9, 314, 329, 331, 334, 335, 336; prejudice against Irish Catholics, 335–7
public works, 331

quiddism, 196–9, 210, 216, 224, 229, 237, 239, 243
Quincy, Josiah, 184, 186

race, 337–40, 360
railroads, 141, 142, 150, 156, 256, 258, 262, 285, 288, 323, 380, 381; transcontinental, 377
Randolph, Edmund, 15, 32; as attorney general, 44, 46, 64, 77
Randolph, John, 12, 37, 137, 162, 172, 179, 186, 196 n., 217, 228

Rantoul, Robert, 282, 312
rationalism, 144, 161
Reconstruction, 376, 377
re-export trade, 174
reformers, 312–20; *see also* religion; revivals
religion, 83, 84, 121, 143–5, 157–67, 229–32, 276–83, 288, 289, 303–7, 362, 379; conversion, 279, 280, 281; and health, 161, 162, 164; personal choice in, 158–60; and predestination, 157, 158, 160, 167; revivals, 157, 159, 166, 279–81, 304–6; *see also individual denominations*
reproductive system, 163, 164
Republican party (Jeffersonian), 80–98 *passim*, 109–24 *passim*, 135, 168–70, 177–80, 183, 184, 187, 194, 195, 200, 224, 225; emergence of, 18, 20, 38, 48, 52, 53, 62, 72; *see also* Democratic party
Republican party (modern), 366, 369, 372
republics, 10
revivals, 157, 159, 166, 279, 280, 281, 304–6
Revolution, American, 43, 99, 144, 145; French subsidy of, 18–19, 69
revolution of 1800 (and Jefferson), 110, 112, 122, 123, 225
Reynolds, Maria, 13
Richmond Junto, 204, 205
Riesman, David, 383
rights, individual, 143–6, 164–7
Ritchie, Thomas, 205, 206, 207, 215
Rittenhouse, David, 9
roads, 137, 139, 140, 141, 203; interior, 258; paving of, 33; plank, 287–8, 318
Roane, Spencer, 40, 213, 214, 215, 225, 226
Rockefeller, John D., 381
Rodney, Caesar A., 13, 14, 170, 171
Rodney, Thomas, 14, 111, 120
Rogin, Michael Paul, 317 n.
Rose, George, 177
Ross, Edward Alsworth, 378
Ross, James, 197
royalism, 19
Ruggles, Timothy, 99
Rush, Benjamin, 43, 46, 99, 111, 162, 183, 308
Rush, Richard, 218
Rutledge, Edward, 9, 133
Rutledge, John, Jr., 178

sabbath, 230, 275, 277, 330, 365
Saint-Domingue, 341
St. Clair, Arthur, 135
Sanborn, Franklin B., 311

Saux Indians, 345

School and the Schoolmaster, The, 309

schools: enrollment, 166; religious instruction in, 309; *see also* education

science, 144, 217, 257, 283, 311, 379

Scotch-Irish immigrants, 37, 83, 335

secession, 118–19

sectionalism, 355–73 *passim*

Sedgwick, Theodore, 70

Sedition Act, 91, 93, 95, 96, 97, 100, 106, 116, 119, 120, 223

Seminole Indians, 345

Seminole Wars, 347

Senate, 25, 27, 36, 123; and Constitution, 78; and Jay Treaty, 79, 80; and seniority system, 273; *see also* Congress

Seneca Indians, 345

Seward, William Henry, 297, 331, 337, 371

sex, 162, 274, 275

Shakers, 347

Shaw, Lemuel, 308

Shays, Daniel, 147

Shays' Rebellion, 22, 38, 55, 147

Sherman, Roger, 30

Sherman Act, 381

shipping, and Embargo Act, 174–83 *passim*

Short, William, 71

Sigourney, Lydia, 268

Simms, William Gilmore, 374

Skidmore, Thomas, 285

skin color, 337–44 *passim*

slaveholders, 83

slavery, 24, 37, 137, 170, 212–20, 227, 228, 236, 243, 338–47, 355–75 *passim*; abolished, 376; and dramatic decrease in, 364–5; enforcement of, 341, 355; and Missouri controversy and Compromise, 202, 260–4; and slave trade, 365; *see also* abolition movement; blacks

Slidell, John, 359

Smith, Adam, 135

Smith, Elias, 158

Smith, Gerrit, 343

Smith, Joseph, 367

Smith, Melancton, 10, 39; and Constitution, 26, 29

Smith, Robert: as secretary of the navy, 170; as secretary of state, 181

Smith, Samuel, 99, 101, 153, 181

Smith, William Loughton, 49–50, 76, 180

Snyder, Simon, 195, 198, 199

social classes, 321–2, 335, 346–51, 381–4

Social Darwinism, 379

Society of the Cincinnati, 44, 68, 74

Society of Washington, 317, 334

Sons of Temperance, 317

south (U.S.), 355–75 *passim*; secession conventions, 372, 373; *see also* slavery

South Asia, 148

South Carolina, 195, 203; and nullification, 227, 246–7, 356

Spain, 134, 148, 174, 177; alliance with Britain, 70; territory in North America, 108, 132, 136, 236; treaty with U.S., 131

Specie Circular, 241, 242

speech, freedom of, 120

squatters, 147, 152

standard of living, 383

Standard Oil, 380

Stanton, Elizabeth Cady, 315, 316, 317

state: bank, 153, 240, 245; constitutions, 3, 246; debts, 48, 192, 245; government, 25, 224, 235, 244–51; politics, 154, 155, 168–9, 179; politics of development, 152–4, 169, 180, 188–9, 194–8, 203–6; role of, in federal government, 24, 25, 28, 29, 36, 37, 95, 96; sovereignty, 23

states' rights: and federal government, 23–34 *passim*, 48, 55, 56, 63, 64, 120, 201–3, 247–9; and Marshall, 224–8; and Taney, 243

steamboats, 140, 147, 151, 228, 259, 260, 288

steam power, 262

stereotyping, 328, 335–7, 356

stockbreeding, 325

Stone, Barton, 158

Stone, Huldah, 315

Story, Joseph, 129, 190; as Supreme Court justice, 226–9, 232, 233, 239, 243, 303, 312

stoves, 262

Stowe, Harriet Beecher, 272

Strong, Caleb, 195; and Constitution, 31

Sturges v. *Crowninshield,* 225

suffrage: laws, 315; white male, 155, 348; women's, 167

Sullivan, James, 195

Sumner, Charles, 272, 282, 285, 297

Sunday schools, 230, 303, 304, 306, 309

supernaturalism, 164

Supreme Court, 36, 94–6, 203; and Marshall, 222–9, 236, 242, 243; and Taney, 242, 243, 370, 371; *see also* individual decisions

Swift v. *Tyson,* 243, 303

Talleyrand-Périgord, Charles Maurice de, 50, 74

Tallmadge, James, 202, 215
Taney, Roger, 199; as Supreme Court
  justice, 242, 243, 370, 371
Tappan, Arthur, 243–4, 319
Tappan, Lewis, 272, 300, 301
tariffs, 47, 206, 216, 217, 241–7, 377;
  Walker Tariff, 242, 263
tax(es), 24, 25, 32, 53, 63, 64, 72–3, 94, 122,
  123, 124; evaders, 48, 74; excise, 47, 53,
  57, 63; national, 188
Taylor, John, 77, 94–5, 118, 179, 213, 225,
  226
Taylor, John W., 215
Taylor, Zachary, 361
technology, 262, 263, 271, 286
temperance movement, 317, 318, 319, 334
Tennessee, 132
territory, *see* Northwest Territory;
  westward expansion
Texas, 138, 298; annexed, 357, 358;
  independence of, 132
textile industry, 259, 261, 262, 263, 325,
  326, 347
Thomas, Jesse, 215
Thomson, Samuel, 162
Thomsonians, 162–5
Thoreau, Henry David, 283
Tiffin, Edward, 154
Tilden, Samuel, 374
time, 261
titles: of nobility, 18, 99; military, 99
Tocqueville, Alexis de, 165, 205, 251, 282,
  283, 285, 294, 312, 322, 349
Tompkins, Daniel, 194
Toombs, Robert, 358, 371
topography, 141
Tories, 18, 111, 144, 350
Tracy, Uriah, 37, 169–70
trade, 70, 143, 148–51, 191; *see also*
  commerce
transients, 326, 327, 330, 334, 335, 347,
  348
transportation, 139–42, 147, 150, 151, 153,
  156, 168, 192, 203, 216, 217, 241, 258,
  260, 285, 351, 381; *see also* canals;
  railroads; roads; steamboats; turnpikes
Treaty of Ghent, 190, 191, 193, 200, 202
Treaty of Paris, 3
Trollope, Frances, 289
Turner, Frederick Jackson, 382
Turner, Nat, 341
turnpikes, 139, 140, 141, 142, 152, 153,
  154, 156, 203, 204
Two Years Before the Mast (Dana), 342
Tyler, John, 203, 357

Uncle Tom's Cabin (Stowe), 272, 343
Union, 246–8, 374; Plan of, 229
Union Bank, 153
Union College, 282
unions, labor, 156
Unitarianism, 160, 284, 289
United States: alliance with France, 18–19,
  69–71, 101; commercial economy of,
  1820s–1840s, 257–64; criticism of
  government, and penalties, 91; and
  maritime restrictions during European
  wars, 174–8; and Native Americans, 345,
  346; relations with Britain during
  European wars, 70, 74–80, 82, 91, 95,
  107, 112; relations with revolutionary
  France, 19, 69–78, 80, 82, 86, 90–3, 105,
  107, 112, 182, 187; treaty with Spain, 131
universities, 217, 379
urban migration, 259, 264, 273–4, 330, 331
utopias, 382

Valley Forge, 12
values, early 19th-century, 265–90 *passim*,
  293, 294
Van Buren, Martin, 202, 205–12, 216, 238,
  296, 297, 298, 351; as president, 241; as
  presidential candidate, 240, 249–50; as
  vice-president, 240, 249
Vatican, 336, 337
Vermont, 49
Vesey, Denmark, 341
vice-presidency, 119
Virginia: and Constitution, 26, 32; and
  democratic-republican clubs, 74;
  government and politics, 11, 14, 15, 43,
  58, 64, 65, 70, 79, 86, 114, 117, 196;
  population of, 146; and transportation
  development, 203–4
Virginia Assembly, 12
Virginia Dynasty, 115, 131, 198, 217
Virginia Plan, 24, 133
Virginia Report, 95, 112, 120, 211, 224, 226
Virginia Resolutions, 64, 95, 96–7, 107,
  115, 121, 202
virtue, 274, 275, 276, 289
voting, 167; patterns and shifts of, 179; and
  social classes, 349, 351; statistics, 348,
  352, 383; *see also* suffrage

Walker, Amasa, 284
Walker, Timothy, 308
Walker Tariff, 242, 263
war debt, *see* debt, national
War Department, U.S., 345
War Hawks, 184, 187, 209

War of 1812, 130, 137, 147, 148, 178–93 *passim*, 200, 201, 209
Warren, James, 74
Warren, Mercy, 43, 183
Washington, Booker T., 380
Washington, George, 4, 9, 13, 22, 35, 38, 39, 108; character and reputation of, 11, 15, 41–3, 45, 46, 61, 104, 105, 111–12, 295; and Constitutional Convention, 32, 44, 69, 75; death of, 85; as president, 14, 15, 42–66 *passim*, 90, 106; and Revolution, 12, 41–2, 52, 75; and slavery, 213; and western expansion, 134, 139
waterways, *see* canals; steamboats
Wayland, Francis, 275
wealth, 13, 322, 337, 356, 381
Webster, Daniel, 129, 138, 186, 209–12, 216, 227, 229, 354; as congressman, 210, 238, 239, 296; and slavery, 360, 361
Webster, Noah, 354
Weed, Thurlow, 298
Weld, Theodore Dwight, 272, 307, 319
Wentworth, John, 329
Wesley, John, 304
West Indies, 9, 74, 75, 191
westward expansion and migration, 70, 91, 97, 131–9, 146, 149, 150, 213, 215, 230, 244, 260, 271, 279, 357, 358, 362, 367; *see also* commerce; transportation
Whig party, 250–2, 294, 297, 298, 351, 358, 365, 366; created, 249; fracture after 1852, 365
Whiskey Rebellion, 8, 46, 72–3, 90, 93, 116, 119
White House, 168
Whitney, Eli, 135
Williamson, Isaac H., 199

Wilmot, David, 358
Wilmot Proviso, 359, 361
Wilson, James, 10, 21; and Constitutional Convention, 24, 25, 29, 30; as Supreme Court justice, 223
Winthrop, James, 10, 37, 39; and Constitution, 26, 27, 69–70, 133
Winthrop, Robert, 283
Wisconsin, 132
witches, 145
Wolcott, Oliver, Jr., 40, 46, 49, 72, 76, 92, 118; as secretary of treasury, 106, 108, 189, 199
Wolcott, Oliver, Sr., 76
women, 13, 37, 43; abuse of, 316, 317 *n.*; and body, 163; community role, 280, 281; family role, 265–78 *passim*, 289, 290, 384; groups, 163; and medicine, 163; reform groups, 315–18; rights, 144, 166, 167, 314–15, 343; suffrage, 167; virtue of, 274–6, 289; as wage earners, 333–4; young adulthood of, 270, 271, 274, 278
Women's Prison Association, 316
Woodward, Samuel B., 314
worker's parties, 156
World War I, 318
Worthington, Thomas, 154, 199
Wright, Fanny, 355
Wright, Silas, 204, 206, 250
Wythe, George, 114

XYZ affair, 69, 93, 97, 105, 112, 113, 121, 172, 225

Yates, Abraham, 27
Yorktown, battle of, 3
Young, Jacob, 289

ROBERT H. WIEBE, a graduate of Carleton College and the University of Rochester, is Professor of American History at Northwestern
University. He is the author of several books,
including *The Search for Order, 1877–1920*,
and *The Segmented Society*.

A NOTE ON THE TYPE

The text of this book was composed in a digi-
tized version of Trump Mediæval. Designed
by Professor Georg Trump in the mid-1950s,
Trump Mediæval was cut and cast by the
C. E. Weber Type Foundry of Stuttgart, West
Germany. The roman letter forms are based on
classical prototypes, but Professor Trump has
imbued them with his own unmistakable
style. The italic letter forms, unlike those of so
many other type faces, are closely related to
their roman counterparts. The result is a truly
contemporary type, notable for both its legibil-
ity and its versatility.

Composed by Dix Type, Inc.,
Syracuse, New York

Printed and bound by Maple Press,
York, Pennsylvania

Designed by Iris Weinstein